WITHDRAWN

Y0-BFY-194

HN
16
,R4

The Ideology of
SOCIAL PROBLEMS

CHARLES E. REASONS
University of Calgary, Canada

WILLIAM D. PERDUE
Eastern Washington University

Distributed by:

Mayfield Publishing Co.
285 Hamilton Ave., Palo Alto, CA 94301

HIEBERT LIBRARY
Fresno Pacific College - M. B. Seminary
Fresno, Calif. 93702

111309

PHOTO CREDITS

Wide World Photos	xvi
United Press International	28
United Press International	94
Andy Sacks/Editorial Photocolor Archives	158
Peter Karas Photography	234
Brown Brothers Stock Photos	308
Peter Karas Photography	376
Steve Hansen/Stock, Boston	434
Peter Southwiok/Stock, Boston	488
Daniel S. Brody/Stock, Boston Lois L. Ross, Photo Journalist	542
Owen Franklin/Stock, Boston	604
Peter Menzel/Stock, Boston	668

Copyright © 1981 by Alfred Publishing Co. Inc.
Printed in the United States of America
All rights reserved. No part of this book shall be reproduced
or transmitted in any form or by any means, electronic or
mechanical, including photocopying, recording, or by any
information or retrieval system without written permission
of the Publisher:

Alfred Publishing Co., Inc.
15335 Morrison Street
Sherman Oaks, California 91403

Current printing last digit: 10 9 8 7 6 5 4 3 2 1

Library of Congress Cataloging in Publication Data

Reasons, Charles E 1945–
   The ideology of social problems.

   Bibliography: p.
   Includes index.
   1. Social problems.   I. Perdue, William D., 1943–
joint author.   II. Title
HN16.R4   362'.042   81-305
ISBN 0-88284-110-6   AACR1

DEDICATION

To the movement for Economic Democracy and all who understand that political and economic freedom are inseparable.

ACKNOWLEDGMENTS

A number of people have made significant contributions to this project. Those serving formally as reviewers took their responsibilities seriously, providing the authors with the diversity of criticism necessary to refine our thinking and tighten our arguments. These include Stan L. Albrecht (Brigham Young University), John Farley (Southern Illinois University at Edwardsville), Cary Kart (University of Toledo), Malcolm Spector (McGill University), Steven Spitzer (Harvard Law School), Eleanor Vanderhagin (Keene State College), and John Wildeman (Hofstra University).

Other colleagues have served as informal reviewers and critics, or provided administrative support and research aid. These include David Bunting, Jeffers Chertok, Ralph Coates, Douglas Gwynn, Bilal Hashmi, Bill Hoekendorf, Gene Lupri, Rick Ponting, Alfred Prince, Bob Stebbins, Bruce Throckmorton, Herbert Roll, Gladys Symons, Nicholas Versluys, Maureen Wilson, and Bill Zwerman.

While academic content is vital, a text remains a means of communication. Two members of the Alfred staff worked hard to keep the project on track in this respect. Copy editor Bernice Lifton aided the authors in the development of clearer writing and more lucid arguments. Editorial assistant Lori Fowler coordinated the maze of input throughout the production phase of the project.

Literally scores of students at the University of Nebraska, the University of Calgary, and Eastern Washington University have critiqued earlier drafts of this manuscript. Others have served as library search aides and contributed to the initial preparation of graphics. Several of these students distinguished themselves through their efforts. They include Patricia Jones, Jennie Oesterreicher, Milena Oesterreicher, John Seem, Trudy Smith, and Audrey Swaffield.

Typists who offered skill, patience, and frequent grammatical assistance were Lori Buob, Monique Canas, Rani Dhaliwal, Patti Fredericksen, Gloria Hall, Janice Hillmo, Dee Hilt, Myrtle Murray, Merlette Schnell, and Donna Story-Kimball.

And finally, to Steven Manus of Alfred Publishing, whose insightful criticism, patience, and humanism forced the authors to abandon a dreary textbook style, we express our deep appreciation.

CONTENTS

PREFACE   xiii

1 THE PARADIGMS OF SOCIAL PROBLEMS 1

What Is a Social Problem?   2

"Objective" and "Ideological" Approaches to
Social Problems   3

Sociological Paradigms   4

Society as Order   8   Society as Conflict   10

Structural Sociology: The Conflict Style   15

The Institutional Focus   15   Political-Economy   16
Class and Elites   16   Ideology   18

Ideology of Capitalism   18

Challenges to Prevailing Ideologies   19

The Ideologies of Sociologists   19

2 THE IDEOLOGY OF SOCIAL PROBLEMS:
A THEORY OF CONFLICT   29

Defining Social Problems   30

Symbolic Interactionist Sociology:
A Critical Review   33

Class, Power and Ideology   34

The Ideology of Social Problems   35

The Corporate Elite   38

Corporate Giantism   39

Ownership of Land   39

V

Contents

General Corporate Ideology 44

Specific Ideologies for Social Problems 46

Transmission of Ideologies 50

The Means of Influence: The Media Industry 53

The Corporate Networks 56

NBC 56   CBS 58   ABC 59

The Structure of the Broadcasting Networks 60

The Best News Money Can Buy 63

Ideological Hegemony 69

The Making and Shaping of Social Problems 70

Emergence 71   Institutionalization 74

Maintenance 79

Conclusion 80

3 INEQUALITY 95

Viewpoint:
"Who Owns America? The Same Old Gang" 97

The Prevailing Ideologies 101

The Myth of the Middle Class 102

The Disappearing Poor 106   The Functionalist
Theory of Stratification: The Ideology of Sociology 109

The Advantages of Poverty 110

Corporation Dominance: Survival of the Fittest? 113

Defending Inequality: The Military "Solution" 116

Emergence 117

Free to Lose 17   Rise to the Merger 119

The State as Corporate Ally 120

Poor People's Movements 121

The Great Depression 122   The Rise and Fall of the
National Welfare Rights Organization 125

Institutionalization 126

The Wealthfare State 127   The Warfare State 130

The Poorhouse State 131   The War on Poverty: A Casualty
of the 1960s 132   The Public Welfare Panacea 133

Maintenance 135

Keeping the Rich Rich 135   Some Are More Equal than
Others 138   Keeping the Warfare State 141

Keeping the Poor Poor   146

Alternative   147

4   WORK: ALIENATION AND FREEDOM   159

You Are What You Do   160

Viewpoint   161

Alienation   163

On the Alienation of Alienation   165

The Prevailing Ideologies   167

Survival of the Fittest   168   The Happy Worker   171
The Affluent Worker   176   We Are Just One Big Family:
Humanizing the Workplace   182

Emergence   185

The Trade Union Movement   186   Pure and Simple
Unionism   190   White Collar Unionism   198

Institutionalization   201

Dying for a Living   205

Maintenance   212

Political History of OSHA   213
Worker Protection under the Corporate State   214

Alternative   219

5   ENVIRONMENTAL CONTRADICTION: THE POLITICS OF ECOLOGY   235

Viewpoint: "The Politics of Energy"   236

The Prevailing Ideologies   242

Environmental Progress   243   It Is Only an Accident   244
Give a Little, Get a Little   251   The Energy Trade-off:
Petro-Power   253   The OPEC Scapegoat   255
The Coal Trade-off   258
The Subtle Tyranny of Noise: Another Trade-off   259
People, Christians, and Engineers: Environmental Devils   264

Emergence   271

Can Business Save Us?   274   Atoms for Peace   275
Three Mile Island: Children Playing in the Woods   277

Contents

Institutionalization 281
Ideology Revealed in Legislation and Enforcement 284
Sue the Turkeys? 287

Maintenance 288
The Pollution Solution: Corporation Style 290

An Alternative Vision 295
Something to Believe In 296

6 WHOSE LAW? WHAT ORDER?   309

Viewpoint: "The Law School" 310

The Prevailing Ideologies 312
Street Crime 312   Suite Crime 314   Public Image of
Crime 316   The Politics of Crime Statistics 319
Not Really Crimes 321   Crime and Moral Depravity 325

Emergence 372
When Wasn't There a Crime Wave? 327   Whose Law? 328

Institutionalization 331
From Feudal to State Law 332   Theft 336
Rape and Witchcraft 336   Victimless Crime 338
Juvenile Delinquency 339   Competition and
Legislation 341   Political Crime and Criminal
Politics 342

Maintenance 343
The Maintenance of Racism 344   The Maintenance of
Sexism 347   The Maintenance of Poverty 347
The Maintenance of Government and Corporate Crime 348

Criminal Law: An Alternative View 350
A Jurisprudence of Insurgency 350   From Rotten Apples
to Rotten Barrels 352   Human Rights Crimes 356
Violent Personal Injury Crimes 358

7 EXPLAINING CRIMINAL BEHAVIOR   377

Viewpoint: "Crime and Criminals" 378

The Prevailing Ideologies 385
The Villainous Family 385   The Criminal Type 389

Emergence 394
Classical School 395   Positive School 396

The Born Criminal 397   The Bad Environment 400
Power/Conflict 404

Institutionalization 407

Demonology 407   Pure Reason 408
Kinds of People 410   Kinds of Environment 413
Power/Conflict 415

Maintenance 417

Biological Determinism 417   The Return of Free Will 419
The Role of Social Control Agents 420

Alternative 422

**8 THE CRIME CONTROL
ESTABLISHMENT   435**

Perspective 436

Dismantling the System 436

The Prevailing Ideologies 439

The Thin Blue Line 440   Blind Justice 446
The Ideology of Deterrence 447
A New Consciousness? 448

Emergence 450

From Constabulary to Police 450   Old Time Justice 451
Eye for an Eye 452

Institutionalization 453

Why Police? 454 The Basis of Justice 456   Let's Make
a Deal 457   Lock 'Em Up 458   Pennsylvania and
Auburn Systems 459   A Place for Everyone and Everyone
in Their Place 461

Maintenance 462

Crime Control and Due Process Models 466   Police
Violence 467   Maintaining Corporate Order: Symbolic
Enforcement and Incestuous Relationships 470   Ideology
as Reality: Law Enforcement and the Corporate World 472

Alternative 474

Policing the Police 474   The Underside of Justice 476
Correcting Corrections 479

9 THE DEMONOLOGY OF DRUGS   489

Contents

**Viewpoint:
"The Scapegoat as Drug and the Drug as
Scapegoat"** 490

The Prevailing Ideologies 493

Drug Abuse 493   The Puritan Ethic 497
The Dope Fiend Mythology 498   Prescription Dope 500

Emergence 502

Emergence of the "Opium Problem" 503
International Concern 504   Minority Oppression 506

Institutionalization 510

Criminalization of the Addict 513   Banning Booze 516
Reefer Madness 517

Maintenance 519

Bureau Under Attack 521   A New Challenge: Kids and
Dope 522   The Enlightenment 522   The Corporate
Connection 525   A Look at the Future 528
The Drug Treatment-Education-Industrial Complex 530

Alternative 532

The British Approach 532

10   RACE AND RACISM   543

A Shorter, Poorer Life 544

Viewpoint: "A Cause for Concern" 549

The Francophone Situation 553   Overt
Discrimination 555   "Nice Guy" Discrimination 555
Institutional Discrimination 556
Legislative Discrimination 557   Labor Role 558

The Prevailing Ideologies 559

A Confusion of Tongues 559   The Media is the Message:
Blaming the Victim 560   Roots 562   Individual
Racism 563   Eugenics: Re-creating the Master
Race 567   Cultural Imperialism 569

Emergence 570

Racism and Colonialism 571
The Slave Trade 573   The Foundation of Fascism 575

Institutionalization 578

Assimilation 579   Pluralism 579   Legal Protection 580
Population Transfer 582   Extermination 585

Holocaust   586   The Final Solution   587

Maintenance   588

Colonial Model   589

Alternative: Minority Liberation   590

Black Power   590   Red Power   592   Brown Power   593
French-Canadian Power   594   The Struggle Continues   594

11   SEX AND SEXISM   605

A Woman's Place Is . . .   606

Viewpoint: "Barbarous Rituals"   607

The Prevailing Ideologies   615

Fascinating Womanhood   617
Motherhood and Apple Pie   621   Sexism in Science   624
Male Chauvinism and Social Inequality   626
Sexist Socialization   629   A Piece of the Action   632

Emergence   636

Early Contractualism: Suffrage   637   Later Contractualism:
Civil Rights   640

Institutionalization   643

The Women's Movement and Civil Rights   644   The Equal
Rights Amendment   645   Our Bodies, Ourselves   646
The Restricted Vision: Equal Opportunity Is Not Equality   647

Maintenance   650

Professional and Managerial Women   651
Supporting the Bureaucracy   652
Women and the Corporate Economy   654

Alternative   659

Beyond Sisterhood   659

12   AGE AND AGEISM   669

**Viewpoint:
"Age, Class, and Social Inequality"   672**

The Prevailing Ideologies   673

A Family Affair   673   The Over-the-Hill Gang   677
The Asexual Elder   678   Stereotypes of Aging   679
Unemployment of the Elderly   680   The Best Years of Our
Lives   681   Disengagement and Free Will   684

Contents

Modernization and the Aging   685

Emergence   690

Can You Spare a Dime?   692

Institutionalization   698

Social Security Modeled on Private Insurance   698
A System of Inequalities   699   Institutionalization:
Medicare   701

Maintenance   703

Aging Benefits the Bureaucracy   704
Health Uninsurance: Schemes and Arrangements   706

Alternative   709

House Select Committee on Aging Public Hearing on
Fragmentation and Proliferation of Service   709
Critique of Training   710

PREFACE

Whether social scientist or student, critic or citizen, those who seek to understand a society and its problems hold certain *assumptions* about the existing social order. Such preconceptions can be best understood as answers to basic questions such as: "What makes society possible?" "What represents the most humanly desirable form of society?" "How does social change occur?" "Why do members of a society conform—or why do they resist the way things are?"

In 1958, the sociologist Ralf Dahrendorf cast these assumptions in the form of "models" of society. While often unstated, they have served historically to guide sociological inquiry. The *order model* portrays society as an organism or system based on consensus, or agreement, among its members. Sociologists of this view are concerned with the continuation of a supposedly well-integrated human community. Conversely, the *conflict model* directs attention to the use of power and coercion by ruling forces in the preservation of their private interests. This view necessarily attaches great importance to social change. Logically, while order sociologists see problems in terms of faulty socialization, their conflict counterparts focus on the way in which a society is organized and the human consequences of institutional failure.

Until recently, order sociology prevailed in North America. However, the turbulence of the 1960s and early 1970s presented a distinctive challenge to the assumption of a society based on the general good. Conflict sociologists argued that the portrait of consensus was false, a product of ideological distortion. Scholars in the area of stratification turned with renewed vigor to the examination of inequality and the concentration of wealth. Political sociologists focused on state power and the growth of bureaucratic empires. The "democratic" theory of society was found wanting. Predominantly male, the makers of social order appeared as inheritors of uncommon wealth, exclusively white, and all too frequently occupants of interlocked positions of corporation and governmental influence.

Over time, three distinct forms of conflict sociology have taken shape. Two of these have European roots while the third bears the stamp of North American philosophical pragmatism. The *structural* form is clearly tied to the class analysis of capitalist society first developed by Karl Marx in the mid-nineteenth century. The Marxist focus is on the power of a ruling class to control the State through the ownership of the major means of production (factories, land, natural resources). While the Marxist concern with political-economy continues as an important component of conflict sociology, the early twentieth-century work of Max Weber added another dimension. Weber saw power not only as a consequence of economic control by an owning class, but also as the result of influence exerted by organized interest groups (Weber termed these status and party) and large-scale bureaucracies. Weber's legacy is evident in much contemporary *interactionist* sociology. Finally, a much more recent development is the growing emphasis on *social policy.* For those of this persuasion, defects in laws and programs have perpetuated social problems. Therefore, policies are to be analyzed historically and critically while innovative alternatives are presented. This final component of the *conflict triad* is shaped by a cultural emphasis on "workable knowledge." The philosophical system of pragmatism developed primarily by John Dewey is an extension of this emphasis and is well reflected in the social policy tradition.

It would be naive to discount the enormous differences within the conflict triad. However, as is frequently the case in knowledge, the weakness of one position is the strength of another. The Marxist analysis of social structure remains the most effective way of understanding class and power. For example, one cannot ignore the massive influence of corporation owners and managers in North American society. Therefore, the architecture of the modern corporate world is a compelling study for all who are concerned with the distribution of rewards and influence. On the other hand, while Weber and his heirs often appear oblivious to the unique problems of capitalism, they are perhaps more precisely aware of the processes by which organized movements seek to press their interests into official and popular recognition.

Often overlooked by those interactionists who carry Weber's intellectual torch are the larger political-economic forces which shape organized movements. Prominent among these forces is a prevailing or dominant ideology, which in North America consists of ideas favorable to the maintenance of the existing corporate order. Disseminated by the "means of influence" (the media and education), these ideas influence the development of more specific ideologies about social problems. Thus, while an organized movement, interest group, or bureaucracy may crusade to gain support for its members' particular definition of and solution for a social problem, larger ideological interests are also served.

For example, during the past two decades a resurgent mainstream women's movement in the United States and Canada has sought the recognition of the problem of sexism. However, within this movement a specific ideology of "male chauvinism" has taken hold defining men and their behavior as the "problem." While the behavior of men often smacks of sexual superiority, chauvinism casts sexism simply in terms of gender. We find such views limited. In a structural sense, the exploitation of women may be a particular case of the more general exploitation of labor in corporate society. Women, while doing vital work, are underpaid, thus depressing the wage structure. Movement ideologies (such as male chauvinism) that divert attention from this possibility by promoting a battle of the sexes do service to the existing corporate order.

While sometimes painfully atheoretical, sociologists concerned with policy have undertaken the vital question of social technology. An examination of laws and programs is fundamental to understanding how problems are perpetuated and their recognition distorted. The question of what is to be done cannot be separated from an analysis of the forces behind policy. For example, an energy policy that favors solar power and conservation over nuclear power threatens both the bureaucratic interests of the United States Nuclear Regulatory Commission (an interactionist concern), and the profits of the corporate energy industry in a society committed to growth (a structural concern).

This text, written from the conflict vantage point, focuses on the ideology of social problems. An original theory has been developed and is presented in the second chapter. Throughout the chapters which follow, we seek to identify the general ideology of corporate society, the specific ideologies of movements and groups seeking recognition for social problems, and the connections between the two. We also seek to show the relationship between ideology, policy, law, and program. In such ways we will seek to synthesize the divergent strengths of the conflict triad.

Plan of Book

The authors share several convictions about the discipline of sociology, the field of social problems, and the nature of textbooks.

First we wanted to avoid confronting students with a wide range of disconnected facts and anecdotes about topical issues. Rather, we have attempted to set down in clear language some intellectual tools which will help the reader analyze and understand the problems of modern corporate society.

Accordingly, we present two contrasting ways of looking at social problems in the first chapter. Such is basic to the construction in chapter two of our theory entitled the Ideology of Social Problems. This theory serves to organize the text. Once the first two are mastered, any or all of the chapters which follow can be approached.

It should be noted that we have chosen to provide an intensive analysis of fewer problems rather than attempt a more superficial overview of the many popular topics which might be included. However, certain of the more crucial concerns are found in chapters bearing other titles. An examination of the Table of Contents will reveal that such issues as media concentration, power, militarism, and so forth play a central role in this text.

1

THE PARADIGMS OF SOCIAL PROBLEMS

Abstract

Those who study social problems are influenced by two contrasting "paradigms," or models. Each of these consists of logically interrelated assumptions concerning (1) the nature of human existence; (2) the nature of society; (3) the nature of sociological explanation. The order paradigm views human nature as selfish and aggressive; society as a form of necessary control; and social problems as the outcome of faulty socialization. The conflict paradigm sees human nature as cooperative and social; society ideally as a facilitator of equality; and social problems as the outcome of structural inequality.

. . . the only common characteristic of crimes is that they consist . . . in acts universally disapproved of by members of each society; . . . crime shocks sentiments which, for a given social system, are found in all healthy consciences. . . .

. . . an act is criminal when it offends strong and defined states of the collective conscience. . . .

. . . crime brings together upright consciences and concentrates them. —Emile Durkheim

The criminal justice system does not protect us against the gravest threats to life, limb, or possessions. Its definitions of crime are not

1

*simply a reflection of the objective dangers that threaten us. The
workplace, the medical profession, the air we breathe, and the
poverty we refuse to rectify lead to far more human suffering, far
more death and disability, and take far more dollars from our
pockets than the murders, aggravated assaults, and thefts reported
annually by the F.B.I. —Jeffrey H. Reiman*

The above definitions of crime provide quite different interpretations.
For Durkheim (1858–1917) crime is simply a serious offense against the
public conscience. For Reiman, crime is a frequently distorted official
definition that is a means of diverting attention from the real problems of
social life.

What then is the nature of crime? Whose definition of the crime problem is of greater value? More generally, how are social problems defined
and what definitions are the acceptable ones? To answer these questions
we need to understand that social problems are a product of human enterprise. In contemporary heterogeneous societies, individuals and groups
with different values and interests will advance various definitions of
social problems. It follows that the differences in power and influence
among those holding competing definitions play a significant role in
determining the *prevailing* definition of social problems. Today, the most
widely used sociological approaches emphasize the basic necessity (and
often the implicit *desirability*) of existing social institutions. For many,
therefore, a social problem will be defined simply as a threat to the way
things are. This text will critically assess existing institutions and the views
of problems that are dominant in North American society in the 1980s.

WHAT IS A SOCIAL PROBLEM?

Of central concern in the establishment of a theory of social problems is
the meaning of this troublesome concept. While its meaning may be self-
evident to the layperson, serious students should be aware of the tenuous
nature of such a designation. Many early writers took the societal ills they
were examining as a given—that is, as inherently problematic—and
failed to provide a general definition. Therefore, social problems were
simply those problems found in textbooks dealing with the subject.

Subsequent attempts at formally defining social problems contain
several common elements. Horton and Leslie's effort succinctly includes
the properties of these definitions:

> A social problem is a condition affecting a significant number of
> people in ways considered undesirable about which it is felt some-
> thing can be done through collective social action (1978, p. 4).

This definition has five distinctive elements: (1) a condition (2) affecting a significant number of people (3) in ways considered undesirable (4) about which it is felt something can be done (5) through collective action. These elements are a starting point but leave many questions unanswered. Is the condition real or imagined? Does it affect a significant *number* of people or a number of *significant* people? Considered undesirable by whom? What type of collective action? These and other questions arise, given the above definition.

"OBJECTIVE" AND "IDEOLOGICAL" APPROACHES TO SOCIAL PROBLEMS

Of essential importance in defining social problems and answering the above questions is the distinction between "objective" and "ideological" factors. The "objective" emphasis has predominated in social problems writing.[1] In this approach the focus is upon an identified condition with emphasis upon describing and explaining the occurrence of that condition. One typically asks why the problem arose and why it persists. For example, what are the causes for the existence, continuation, and growth of drug addiction and drug abuse?

The "ideological" emphasis poses a somewhat different question. How and why is a specific condition labeled a social problem while other conditions are ignored? For example, why are drug addiction and drug abuse generally considered problematic and other issues such as worker safety, neocolonialism, and economic inequality less often the focus of public concern? What are the ideological forces involved in such labeling? While this emphasis has been advocated for some time by a few students of social problems, it has largely remained of secondary importance to writers in the field. However, more recently much of the criticism of social problems analysis has been based upon the neglect of the subjective element (Mills, 1943; Horowitz, 1968; Neubeck, 1979). Merely to examine the condition identified as problematic at different times in the same society or at the same time in different societies confirms the shifting nature of definitions. More importantly, we find the same problem subject to *various* explanations. For example, there is greater emphasis on sexism as a problem today than twenty years ago. Does this mean that sex-based discrimination was *not* a problem then? And how shall we account for the

---

[1]The objective approach takes for granted what the "ideological" approach views as problematic. Definitions of social problems are shaped and formed by social forces and social history. Therefore, we cannot simply accept these ideas as "true." See Peter L. Berger and Thomas Luckman, *The Social Construction of Reality*. New York: Doubleday Anchor Books, 1967.

condition of the "second sex"? As a consequence of male chauvinism? Of nature? Or of powerful, if not always apparent, social forces typically ignored? Therefore, as Blumer (1971, p. 300) has noted, "It would seem logical that students of social problems ought to study the process by which a society comes to recognize its social problems."

SOCIOLOGICAL PARADIGMS

The designation of a certain aspect of social life as a problem is not the exclusive domain of sociologists. It would be uncommon indeed to find a member of the adult population who had no opinion as to the major difficulties faced in contemporary society. Sociologists are beginning to inquire seriously into the nature of "paradigms," or models of society. As we shall see, these models, or ways of looking at the world, shape not only scholarly explanations and definitions, but also the general views most of us hold about social problems. As the authors proceed, it may well be that the reader will see some strong similarities between what is in his or her head and the more formalized assumptions that together make up the constrasting paradigms for social problems.

In *The Structure of Scientific Revolutions* (1970), the philosopher of science Thomas Kuhn argued that there was a linkage between the events of history and particular breakthroughs in knowledge. He also proposed that the particular circumstances of a scientist's life may influence the course of scientific investigation and the knowledge that follows. Rather than viewing science as a process that uncovers unquestionable truth, he identifies it as a distinctly human enterprise. In speaking of the differences in scientific conclusions, Kuhn argues:

> What differentiated these various schools was not one or another failure of method—they were all "scientific"—but what we shall come to call their incommensurable [different] ways of seeing the world and of practicing science in it. Observation and experience can and must drastically restrict the range of admissible scientific belief, else there would be no science. But they cannot alone determine a particular body of such belief. An apparently arbitrary element, compounded in personal and historical accident, is always a formative ingredient of the beliefs espoused by a given scientific community at a given time (1970, p. 4).

"Different ways of seeing the world"? "Arbitrary elements"? "Personal and historical accidents"? Hardly the stuff we expect scientific knowledge to be made of! However, what Kuhn demonstrates for the physical sciences, others have shown for sociology (Eckberg and Hill, 1979). The scientific enterprise does not begin formally with the development of theoretical explanations. There exists, in effect, a *pretheoretical* base or a model of social order; a perspective or point of view that strongly influences every step in the study of social phenomena in general or social problems in particular. A paradigm is not to be confused with a theory. The former is a general "mind-set" consisting of assumptions or "givens." The latter refers to a set of logically interrelated propositions developed in answer to the question "why?" Theoretical propositions, in turn, guide the research process.

A paradigm specifies the issues and questions that represent the subject matter of social inquiry. As will become clear, this selective process is vital because the nature and scope of the solutions one develops are dependent upon the questions one initially poses. For example, two criminologists may be studying the same general phenomenon. However, one focuses on the explanation of criminal behavior, developing questions and conducting research on why the incidence of crime varies from time to time and what the social characteristics of "criminals" are. Another criminologist studies law and the legal system to determine the specific interests behind the "majesty" of law. One who understands the nature of paradigms would be sensitive to the possibility that these criminologists may hold quite different views on the nature of a society.

Numerous scholars have sought to identify and systematize the often unstated assumptions that together comprise the two major paradigms for sociology (Dahrendorf 1958; Horton 1966; Chambliss 1973). In developing our own discussion, we shall find that each paradigm contains assumptions about the nature of: (1) human existence; (2) society; and (3) sociological explanation.

It should be clearly understood at the outset that a paradigm represents an "ideal" type. That is, the essential elements of each approach are exaggerated, proving a standard against which sociological work can be measured. As is true in the larger society, one will be hard pressed to find a sociologist who entirely "fits" one paradigm. Most analyses of social problems, like most sociologists, will combine characteristics of both approaches. Nonetheless, social thought can be characterized as being predominantly *order* or *conflict*.

> As a generalization, groups or individuals committed to the maintenance of the social status quo employ order models of society and equate deviation with nonconformity to institutionalized norms. Dissident groups, striving to institutionalize new claims, favor a conflict analysis of society and an alienation theory of their own discontent (Horton, 1966, p. 703).[2]

[2]This distinction between those who largely defend the status quo and those bent on social change parallels Mannheim's "ideology" and "utopia."

Society as Order

Until recently, the dominant model in sociology has emphasized equilibrium, balance, continuity, and social control. Commonly termed the order, or functionalist, paradigm, this viewpoint sets forth the following logically interrelated and essential assumptions:

1. The nature of human existence is competitive, contentious, private, and self-absorbed. (See Thomas Hobbes, in Sennett 1977; also John Horton 1964.)

2. Given the natural human disposition toward disorder, any society can exist and continue only through the establishment of enduring institutions that systematically regulate the most important of human interactions. (Political, economic, educational, religious, familial.) The preservation of existing institutions thus becomes a social imperative.

3. The nature of society is one of interdependent and integrated institutions and a supportive ideological base (values, norms, beliefs). Thus a society can be properly conceived as an *organism* if one prefers a biological analogy (Durkheim 1947), or as a system if a mechanical similarity is sought (Parsons 1937). Given the nature of an organism or a system, each part contributes to the maintenance of the whole and is naturally adaptive.

4. The institutions and ideological supports of a society prevail in their specific form because of essential agreement, or consensus, among the members of that society. Examples of "form" for the economic institution are capitalism and socialism; supportive ideologies would be individualism and collectivism, respectively.

5. Given the necessity of order and the reality of consensus, all members of a society are expected to conform, adapt, or adjust to these legitimate social arrangements.

6. It is expected that the process of socialization whereby members of a society learn to revere its institutions and respect its rules will on occasion fail, thus giving rise to problematic behavior. Such behavior, when widespread, can be properly termed a social problem.

7. To resolve those tensions that threaten the integrity of social order, behavior must be modified through resocialization (rehabilitation, psychotherapy, and so forth) or neutralized through formal systems

of control supported by state power (establishment and expansion of criminal law, police power, prison systems, asylums, and the like).

8. Social change therefore can only involve essentially minor adjustments that are consistent with the existing nature of the social system.

9. It logically follows that explanation, analysis, and description of social problems will be centered at a "low level of abstraction" (Mills 1943, p. 165).

Paradoxically, though the order paradigm is based on such societal concerns as systems, institutions, and values, these are simply taken for granted. Thus, the existing order is "legitimated." After all, it is assumed that the contentious nature of human beings must be controlled. Further, it is supposed that the institutions and values essential to "bonding" human beings in social relationships are based on popular agreement among the members of a society. Thus, explanations advanced by those influenced by the order paradigm tend to focus at a low level of abstraction. By *abstraction* we mean that much thought exists apart from material or concrete objects. The human ability to manipulate symbols makes such possible. For example, we can think in terms of "society," "system," and "attitudes," though these abstractions have no physical being. By *level* of abstraction we mean that those describing, analyzing, or explaining social problems do not necessarily think on the same plateau. The levels of abstraction that follow from the internal logic of the order paradigm are represented by the concentric circles in Figure 1-1.

Figure 1-1. Order Levels of Abstractions

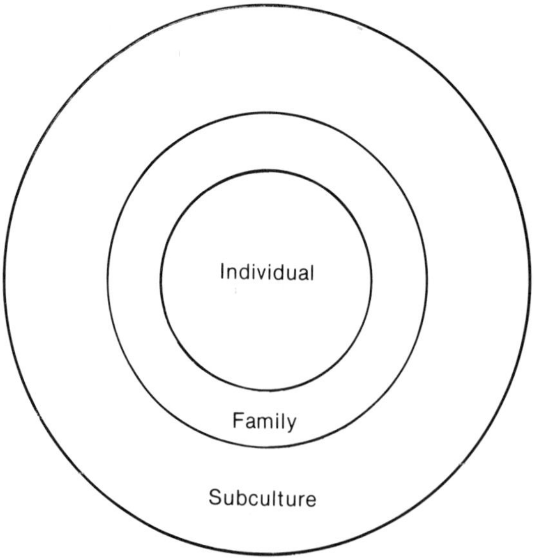

Individual

Family

Subculture

The innermost circle, representing the lowest level of abstract thought of relevance for social problems, is termed "individual." To be clear, this level represents "kinds of people" thinking and emphasizes the characteristics and qualities of individuals. Specific aspects of people are carefully scrutinized and elaborately analyzed to explain the social problem.

Examples of this "level" would include such work as Cesare Lombroso's attempts to explain crime through the identification of a criminal "type," or atavism. Lombroso held that criminals were physically distinct from noncriminals. (Vold 1958.) Other examples of thinking on this plane include Sigmund Freud's psychoanalytic theory, which is strongly rooted in biological/instinctual explanations for behavior, and the recent development of "sociobiology." Freud's vision of human personality encompasses life (Eros) and death (Thanatos), instincts (unlearned behavior), unconscious motivation, and conflicts that are primarily sexual (Hall and Lindzey 1966). A more contemporary development is sociobiological theory which holds that genetic information determines social behavior (Wilson 1975). Other contemporary examples include attempts on the part of Arthur Jensen (1969), and Richard Herrnstein (1973) to explain racial differences in social position by means of intelligence tests; believed by these authors to measure learning capacity.[3]

Thus, at the level of the individual, one personalizes a social problem. The focus is on the troublesome, the out-of-step, the different. The "problem" consists of the supposed defects of the mentally ill, the drug addict, the criminal, the poor, the minorities. And in all cases, the approach is the same. What emerges is a biographical portrait that separates the individual from society.

Most thinkers seeking to deal theoretically with social problems are not content with the individual level of abstraction. Contemporary textbooks often include a "social disorganization" (kinds of environment) category. Whether "kinds of people" with its biographical focus, or disorganization with its environmental emphasis, both types of social thought represent the order paradigm. The difference between these categories is the level of abstraction employed. For order sociologists, the types of environmental influences most frequently studied are the family and subculture, captured symbolically by the remaining concentric circles.

The family as an important social unit has received enormous attention from sociologists and others. Family "disorganization" has been cited as an explanation for juvenile delinquency (Nye 1958), mental illness (Mischler and Waxler 1968), poverty (Matza and Miller 1976, p. 656), alcoholism (Strauss 1976, p. 203), crime (Johnson 1968, pp. 81–82), and other problems. Work in the subcultural tradition holds that there are subterranean communities, smaller islands within the larger cultural sea. Various categories of people, distinctive by reason of such features as ethnicity, race, and class are seen to have *distinctive subcultural values*

[3]Sociobiology is in some important ways a rebirth of "social Darwinism" (see Chapter Four). For a critique of unintelligent intelligence tests, see Chapter Four.

that put them at a disadvantage or into conflict with the representatives of the larger culture (Sellin 1938). Thus, Edward Banfield (1974) identifies a "subculture of poverty," Walter Miller (1958) a "lower class subculture" that "generates" delinquency, Albert Cohen (1957) a "delinquent subculture," and Harold Finestone (1957) a "drug subculture."

It would be an unnecessary and encyclopedic undertaking to identify even a small number of the inquiries that might serve as appropriate examples for levels of abstraction in the order model. However, theory and research in the order tradition are identifiable by means of a common connecting thread. The institutions that prevail are taken as necessary and legitimate, with attention directed toward the more immediate, intimate, and restricted social and psychological experiences. Though the order paradigm has given rise to important work on the nature of societal endurance and continuity, the implicit and often explicit concern with controlling, moderating, and/or removing threats to equilibrium leaves important questions neither asked nor answered. Work in the order tradition is heavily geared to the study of individual behavior in an always limited social context. Though some attention may be given to the discrepancy between the general success goals set forth by the culture and the lack of "fair access" for all members of a society (Merton 1938), the success goals per se are not challenged. Equal opportunity, for example, is not equality. Further more, a concern with faulty socialization does not lead to critical questioning of the *content* of the conventional norms and values of conformists.

Finally, the order approach to social problems focuses attention on the underclass, the powerless, and the outsider. When it becomes evident that problems originate with the higher classes, particular and specific explanations are advanced. In order sociology, the *existence* of higher classes (and necessarily lower ones) is less a "problem" than the periodic abuse of power by an individual member of a dominant class. For example, when the former President of the United States, Richard Nixon, became embroiled in political scandal, the larger question of the exercise of state power gave way to "idiosyncratic explanation."

> The idiosyncratic explanation is that the problem [of Watergate] lies with Richard Nixon the man. Here was a unique individual who was never able to control his own rage and insatiable ambition. He was elected President of the United States through political accident and sheer diligence. His feelings of insecurity, combined with his unscrupulousness, caused him to take steps which were illegal. Confronted by evidence of his misdeeds, he could only dig himself in deeper and deeper like an ignoble version of a tragic hero. The idiosyncratic theory holds that Nixon has jeopardized what is basically a good system through his evasiveness and contempt for the democratic process, and thus his removal from the presidency should restore the system to correct working order (Wolfe 1976).

**THE
IDEOLOGY
OF
SOCIAL
PROBLEMS**

Society as Conflict

In opposition to the view of harmony and consensus is an alternative paradigm for the study of society and social problems. Most frequently called the "conflict model," this viewpoint holds that the only historical constant is *change*. Social problems are seen to be rooted in the very fabric of the existing order. Thus, the problems at hand continue due to *resistance* to change. The assumptions that together comprise the conflict paradigm can be summarized as follows:

1. The nature of human existence is cooperative, collective, and social (Horton 1964).

2. Given the natural disposition toward a social existence, any society can be considered human only to the extent that institutions facilitate cooperation, sharing, and the common interest. Institutions have no sacred standing, no life of their own, and their nature is dynamic rather than static.

3. In a society of structured inequality, marked by vast differences in wealth, status, and power, the social nature of human existence is denied. Existing institutions primarily serve private rather than public interest.

4. The institutions and ideological supports of a class-divided society prevail due to constraint, coercion, and influence.

5. Given the necessity of change and the reality of constraint, the legitimacy of social order is in question. Conformity, adaptation, and adjustment become problematic.

6. Faulty socialization becomes a matter of defective norms rather than defective control. Thus, the rules themselves become problematic.

7. To resolve the threats to the social nature of human beings, institutions and ideologies must be significantly changed.

8. Behavioral change can therefore only involve essentially minor adjustments that are consistent with the cooperative and collective nature of social existence. Massive commitment to behavioral change is a form of "blaming the victim." Further, such a focus diverts attention from the problematics of the broader society.

9. It therefore follows that explanation, analysis, and description of

10

social problems will be centered at a "high level of abstraction" (C. Wright Mills 1943).

Rather than taking the existing order for granted, the conflict paradigm requires a serious questioning of modern industrial society. The widespread differences in rewards and influence raise the possibility that "some are more equal than others." For example, an economic system based on private ownership is of greater service to the Rockefeller, DuPont, and Weyerhaeuser families than to those working in coal mines or on assembly lines. Likewise, advantages for whites and males are not in the interests of blacks and women.

Given the skepticism toward a social order marked by differences of race, class, sex, age, and other attributes, it follows that conflict sociology must employ a high level of abstraction. As revealed in the following return to our concentric circles, this paradigm directs explanation, analysis, and description of social problems along *structural* lines. (See Figure 1-2.)

A structural level of abstraction is most properly conceived as the *societal plane of thought*. The conflict paradigm shares with its order counterpart the view that the structure of society includes social institu-

Figure 1–2. Conflict Levels of Abstraction

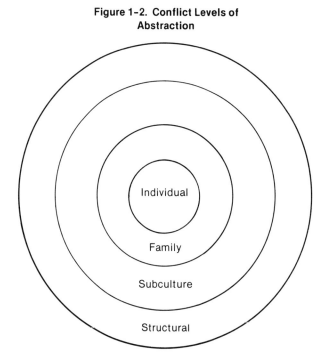

Individual

Family

Subculture

Structural

tions and supportive ideology. However, to understand is not necessarily to embrace. *Nor does the existence of institutions or ideologies in a particular form confirm their necessity.* After more preliminary discussion, we shall examine the properties of that type of structural sociology that is consistent with the conflict paradigm. For now, it is enough to say that those influenced by the conflict paradigm are *unconvinced* that social problems originate *outside* the "existing order of things." A structural interpretation of social problems is evident in the following definition.

> A social problem is a condition that involves the social injury of people on a broad scale. The injury may be physical in manifestation (as with disease stemming from a health service system geared to income), social-psychological (as with alienation), economic (as with poverty), political (as with the oppression of dissident groups), or intellectual (as with nonexistent or inadequate education). Social problems ensue from institutional defects and are not to be best interpreted or understood through individuals, families, or subcultures. Thus, the social problem as such is not an aberration but rather a normal consequence of the way in which a society is organized.

Our discussion and the above "definition" should not be taken to mean that sociology in the conflict style does not call for a study of such things as behavior, families, and subcultures. To the contrary, such topics are often explored. The point of difference is that these are always *connected* to the institutional order of the broader society. Sociology in the conflict tradition will therefore stress *structural penetration* into the intimate and the personal. In short, though social difficulties may appear to be mere matters of antisocial conduct, family breakdown, and subcultural disadvantage, this text will emphasize the less-apparent structural forces and contradictions that represent the roots of such "problems." In so doing, we necessarily share the view of C. Wright Mills, who noted the relationship between public issues and private troubles.

> The facts of contemporary history are also facts about the success and the failure of individual men and women. When a society is industrialized, a peasant becomes a worker; a feudal lord is liquidated or becomes a businessman. When classes rise or fall, a man is employed or unemployed; when the rate of investment goes up or down, a man takes heart or goes broke. When wars happen, an insurance salesman becomes a rocket launcher; a store clerk, a radar man; a wife lives alone; a child grows up without a father. Neither the life of an individual nor the history of a society can be understood without understanding both (1959, p. 3).

At this point, the reader should be cautioned to avoid the erroneous conclusion that every time he or she encounters the term "conflict" in sociology, the author or speaker in question is prepared to analyze existing institutions critically. The terms "culture-conflict," "value-conflict," and "conflict of interests" are frequently to be found (Fuller and Myers 1941). However, there is an important difference between these terms and the properties of structrual sociology we shall identify shortly. This is because culture and/or status "conflict" indicate the assumption of a *pluralist* model of society. The pluralist model is a contemporary variation of the order paradigm. Pluralists are somewhat wary of the accuracy of a view of social order as based purely on consensus, given the heterogeneity of modern industrial societies. Indeed, within these societies many languages, customs, and statuses—together with such drives as the women's movement and the various crusades for the civil rights of racial, age, and sexual preference minorities—indicate an absence of tranquility. However, for the pluralists *order prevails because the competing groups accept the legitimacy of master social institutions seeking only to improve their relative standing.* Thus, as a later chapter reveals, the union movement in the United States has been confined historically to the issues of wages, hours, and working conditions and has not addressed the questions of ownership and managerial control. Research in this tradition is vital, however. It reveals, perhaps inadvertently, that when the definitions of social "problems" are constructed by movements shaped by a pluralist ideology, few questions will be raised about structural origins.

Nevertheless, more recent analyses *have* set forth the concerns of class, wealth, and power. One author writing in the conflict mode argues that sociologists as well as other members of society have failed to examine critically "large-scale systemic" problems.

> Because macro problems are rooted in societal organization, their reduction and elimination may well require an eventual transformation of the prevailing order. Macro problems will not yield to minor technical or administrative reforms. They can be dealt with only if the majority of men and women in this society work consciously and collectively to bring about change. To do so, Americans must analyze, plan, and seek to reorganize society with a vision in mind. The kind of transformation our own vision suggests cannot come about by wishful thinking. Nor is it likely to happen if we simply back away and trustingly leave our future in the hands of societal elites and their appointed "experts" (Neubeck 1979, p. 14).

Thus, major postulates of sociological theories based on the conflict paradigm logically follow:

1. Society is the setting within which various struggles take place.

2. The state is an important agent participating in the struggle on the part of one side or another.

3. Social inequality is a consequence of coercive institutions that legitimate force, fraud, and inheritance as the chief avenues for obtaining rights and privileges.

4. Social inequality is a chief source of social conflict.

5. The state and law are instruments of oppression employed by the dominant classes for their own benefit.

6. Classes are social groups with distinctive interests that inevitably bring them into conflict with other groups with opposed interests.

7. Finally, conflict theories ask *who benefits* from the consequences that particular social events have for the society, and *for whom it is functional* when assessing the function of social phenomena (Chambliss 1973).

For example, in analyzing differential crime rates in North America between Native Americans and whites, a conflict approach would emphasize inequality in resources as a major cause of such differences. Since Native Americans are not possessors of state power, definitions of crime and the administration of justice will not represent their interests. The law and criminal justice system may be viewed, at least in part, as functioning to keep this group in a subordinate position within society (Reasons 1972 and 1978; Dandurand 1974).

While the conflict paradigm provides an approach to analysis, it still fails to define specifically and exhaustively what should be identified as social problems and what should not. As Skolnick and Currie state:

> All writers on social problems take a particular position on what does constitute a problem and what does not; this is a moral and political choice, and there is nothing objective about it. Nor can there be (1973, pp. 14–16).

In summary, the major advantages of the conflict paradigm seem to be (1) its intellectual orientation, in that the model generates critical thought whereas order assumptions fit too well the conventional wisdom; (2) its holistic nature, in that a critical view of structure often discloses connections between public issues and private troubles (Mills 1959), as well as connections among nation-states and economic systems at a global level; and (3) its focus on societal properties (institutions and ideologies) rather than the properties of people in society (behavior). However, the sociology based on the conflict paradigm has frequently been lacking in factual, objective data (Navarro 1977, VIX). It is the intention of this text to bring together important statistical and empirical data as well as detailed historical cases in support of specific arguments.

14

STRUCTURAL SOCIOLOGY: THE CONFLICT STYLE

To this point, we have seen that the order and conflict paradigms share a concern with the nature of sociological institutions and the problem of social order. However, order assumptions in the aggregate emphasize equilibrium, continuity, and consensus. Such a focus must necessarily fail to recognize the difference between a social problem and social change. The two become synonymous. What must follow for order sociologists is an emphasis on defective socialization. Conflict assumptions, on the other hand, stress that the institutions prevailing in a society of structured inequality may represent the "haves" more than the "have nots." For the conflict sociologist, significant social change is more a matter of societal *reorganization* rather than *disorganization* (Mills 1943). Therefore, the existing institutional order is a crucible for social problems. With this in mind, it is possible to summarize the four essential properties of "structural sociology" that provide a basis for conflict analysis. Such constructs are complex, interdependent, and overlapping. They are separated and simplified here to provide a point of departure.

The Institutional Focus

It is apparent that the major thrust of sociology written in the conflict style requires the understanding of social institutions. By institutions we mean established and organized practices centering around fundamental human activity. The *economic institution* refers to the organized production and distribution of wealth. The central purpose of the economic institution is the satisfaction of the material needs of people. The *political institution* has to do with the established nature of rule and government. The fundamental question of politics is "Who decides?" Thus, political purpose is cast in terms of power. The institution that centers on human learning may be formally termed *education* in modern industrial societies. Its purpose is the construction and transmission of formal knowledge. The organization of practices having to do with theological beliefs and rituals is termed *religion*; and its manifest function is worship. Finally, the *family/kinship* institution centers on marriage, lineage, and procreation. The major purpose of the family in modern societies appears to be companionship.

The necessity of dealing intellectually with such established and organized human practices cannot be overstated. For "by delineating these institutional orders, which form the skeletal structure of the total society, we may conveniently analyze and compare different social structures. Any social structure according to our conception, is made up of a certain combination or pattern of such institutional orders" (Gerth and Mills 1964, p. 26).

Political-Economy

A great debate has raged historically in sociology on the relative significance of different institutions. Order theories by and large do not assert the priority of one or the other. However, there is a tendency among conflict theorists to emphasize the importance of power and wealth. Not all conflict sociologists employ the term "political-economy"; still, it is frequently the case that their description, analysis, and explanation show a distinct preference for these "master" institutions (Forcese and Richer 1975, pp. 92–101).

Those who examine the political economy of social problems hold that the state is not organized, nor does it function, as a neutral agent of "the people."

> It follows that repression will similarly not be a neutral phenomenon but will have a class basis. We can predict, with good accuracy, that when the state intervenes to repress an organization or an ideology, it will be a dissenting group, representing relatively powerless people, that will be repressed and the interests upheld will be those of the powerful (Wolfe 1978, p. 51).

Class and Elites

Given an emphasis on structural inequality, the concerns of class and elites necessarily follow. The concept of class always centers on the distribution of economic resources. For some, including Karl Marx (1818–1883), class as the "relationship to the means of production" was sufficient to explain power. For others, including Max Weber (1864–1920), political and economic power were to be separated.

To be clear, Marx argued that in most societies two classes of people can be identified. One of these possesses the "major means of economic production" (for example, the land, factories, natural resources). The other is a "subject" or working class acted on by an owning or dominant class, which through economic power heavily influences the state, its laws, its agencies of force (police and military), and its "intellectual production," or ideas. Given the nature of capitalist society in particular, with its drive toward increasing concentration of wealth and power, an ongoing conflict of classes is inevitable (Bottomore 1965a and 1965b).

For Max Weber, the nature of inequality involved three dimensions of social life. He agreed with Marx that the fundamental determinant of *class* is property. However, Weber was not content to deal with class determinants of power. To the contrary, he argued that political power is often independent of economic power and that the differential distribution of such influence creates *parties*. Also arising in history are *status groups* that represent different standings in society due to life-style, occupation, family background, or other indicators of social prestige. For Weber, the possibility of political inequality remained even when major property distinctions disappeared. Thus, he was concerned with the bureaucratization of influence in the modern industrial state. Whatever the form of the economic institution in a society, the necessary emergence of a system of rule by specialized governmental and administrative units would threaten the quest for a flourishing human life. However, while not rejecting capitalism per se, Weber held that *bureaucratic power* would be most entrenched in the modern capitalist form of economic order because of its growth, complexity, and technological gigantism (Weber 1947; Anderson 1974, pp. 116–121; Forcese and Richer 1975, pp. 98–100).

Weber's thought represents the foundation for later work done by sociologists who shared Weber's multifaceted conception of power. The American sociologist C. Wright Mills was to embrace Weber's conception of power through explicitly denying a necessary economic base. In his modern classic entitled *The Power Elite* (1956), Mills identified a tripartite structure of influence. What he termed "the higher circles" consisted of an interlocking corporate, military, and political elite. Often with similar biographies, attending the same schools, members of the same exclusive clubs, moving in the same circles, members of the elite direct affairs of state, organize the agencies of force, and administer the systematic production and distribution of wealth. The elite become a self-replenishing force, populating the controlling positions in the social order from within a relatively small and homogeneous group. According to Mills, those who lead frequently cross the dividing lines of social power. By a continuous process of interchange, military warlords, political leaders, and corporate directors move from one position of power to another. Thus, presidential cabinets are dominated by those with long records of corporation service (Mintz 1975), while many generals upon retirement from military service find their way onto the boards of directors of defense contractors (Eitzen 1978, pp. 258–259).

Ideology

The significance of ideology in the labeling of phenomena as social problems has not generally been recognized and acknowledged among either lay people or professional students of social problems. A dominant ideology may be so pervasive that it is not perceived by observers and analysts of society. Ideology includes one's beliefs and perceptions on (1) how the present social, economic, and political order operates; (2) why this is so, and whether it is good or bad; and (3) what should be done about it. We gain our ideological perspective from the many sources of socialization in our society: the family, school, peers, religion, among others. An ideology helps us describe and interpret our daily world.

IDEOLOGY OF CAPITALISM

Today, the dominant economic ideology in the North American societies of Canada and the United States is capitalism with its emphasis upon individualism, the profit motive, and expansion. Ideological purists are prone to cast capitalism as a free enterprise marketplace regulated by the interplay of supply and demand. Politically, ours is presented as a system of laws that supposedly protects all citizens. Accordingly, each individual is seen as having an equal voice or vote in the political arena and the marketplace. In the latter sphere, one "votes" for the allocation of resources and production and distribution of goods and services when purchasing products. By buying some and not others, the consumer is supposedly casting a ballot. All of this presumably works best with a minimum of governmental coercion and interference. Further, in the "game of society," everyone is responsible for "number one" and has equal opportunity in pursuit of a livelihood. Social betterment comes automatically through the natural process of individual self-fulfillment.

This basic capitalistic ideology has a number of variations. While "conservatives" stress the virtues of *laissez-faire* (noninterference), "liberals" often point to the necessity of enlightened political regulation of business and industry. The 1980 presidential campaign is a case in point. While the Republican candidate, Ronald Reagan, frequently identified governmental interference as the "devil" behind inflation, unemployment, and various other ills, Jimmy Carter, the standard bearer of the Democratic party, emphasized the need for state controls and governmental services. Of course, Mr. Reagan did not object to "governmental interference" as long as it took the form of federal capital for defense contracts.[4] On the other hand, Mr. Carter seemed to be assuring the

[4]For a discussion of the "military-industrial complex," see Kaufman, 1970; Melman, 1974; Anderson, 1976; and Chapter Three on Inequality.

electorate that the political tail could wag the economic dog. Critics of capitalism argue that state regulation historically has proven to be no stumbling block to the consolidation of corporate power (Wolfe 1978; Miliband 1969). Rhetoric aside, conservatives and liberals may disagree on technique. However, the question is whether their positions come together on using state power and revenues to maintain and expand the existing economic order.

Challenges to Prevailing Ideologies

Within recent times there have been major challenges to the mainstream ideologies. The upheavals in the 1960s and 1970s concerning the Vietnam War, simultaneous inflation and unemployment, the energy crisis, environmental ruin, French-Canadian decolonization, poverty, racism, sexism, and the abuse of state power alerted North Americans that there was no end to ideological dissent, as some had foreseen (Bell 1961; Lipset 1960). New terms have entered our common vocabularies: "stagflation," "the China Syndrome," "separatism," and the "myth of the middle class." The old virtues of competition, material success, and military preparedness may not be quite as comforting in the 1980s.

During times of upheaval and crisis, there will usually emerge challenges to dominant ideologies. Karl Mannheim, German intellectual, suggested in his classic work, *Ideology and Utopia* (1936), that democracies would and, in fact, should experience the most ideological conflict. Therefore, democratization of a society will bring increasing challenges from the lower strata and the emergence of competing belief systems calling for alternatives to the existing order. Mannheim reserved the term ideology for those idea systems (such as capitalism in Contemporary North America) which support the status quo. Emerging competing belief systems (such as economic democracy, worker control, and socialism) represent utopia.

THE IDEOLOGIES OF SOCIOLOGISTS

Given the effect of ideologies on individual and group perceptions of social problems, what about the scholars who work in the field? Are social scientists immune to such external influences, or does their work reflect a basic underlying ideology? Do sociologists tend to be unwitting or conscious supporters of the status quo, or do they represent utopia (Erikson 1970; Horowitz 1968)?

Sociologists, like their subjects of study, are influenced by the various agencies of socialization and by values and norms arising from their shared class, age, sex, and racial and ethnic backgrounds. Also at play are "professional reflexes," that is, their way of studying society. This is gained during graduate training and reinforced by colleagues through journals, professional associations, elaborate reward structures, among other things. Through both normal social processes and professional training, therefore, the sociologist tends to view the world and society in a certain way. It was once thought that the sociologist could approach his or her subject matter free of value judgments and with complete detachment and objectivity and that this should be the model for sociological analysis. However, few today maintain that the value choices are not made in their work, although the extent of such influence will continue to be debated (Gouldner 1962; Seely 1968). This has led some to suggest that the sociologist make explicit his or her ideological perspective and reasons for choosing specific topics for study.

> Some sociologists who emphasize an "objective" approach to social inquiry are not motivated by the canons of scientific method, but by an orientation which regards action research as value-loaded, and implies a commitment to social change. But this orientation toward research is no longer valid, and the sociologist increasingly is called upon for research which contributes to the solution of social problems (Weinberg 1970, p. 44).

A classic study of the influence of ideology upon students of social problems was done by C. Wright Mills. In "The Professional Ideology of Social Pathologists" (1943), he pointed out how the values and norms of the white Anglo-Saxon Protestant, living out middle-class ideals in small communities, were taken without question as the basis for defining "pathological" behavior and social problems in the first four decades of this century. The background of most "pathologists" gave them a singular view of social problems, largely focusing upon the individual as the problem and calling for adjustment and adaptation as the answer. Bend and Vogelfanger (1971) have more recently found some of the same bias in social problems writing that Mills noted: (1) the analysis of social problems as personal pathologies and (2) the nonrandom selection of social problems. Certain phenomena are not identified as social problems while the uniformity of topics addressed and the way they are analyzed suggests an ideological sameness. For example, problems such as alcoholism, drug abuse, suicide, and mental illness are more "popular" than the problems of the concentration of wealth, the growth of corporate power, and the world of work. Of crucial importance, whatever the problem, a structural critique is commonly absent.

The issue becomes not one of trying to eliminate the ideological basis of sociological analysis but of recognizing and acknowledging this ideological factor and taking it into account in the treatment of social phenomena.

In discussing the role of the intellectual in defining social problems, Henshel and Henshel note the influence of personal and professional ideology upon professional students of social problems.

> In short, their expertise may be greater than anyone else's, but their common experiences will tend to provoke a common world view, which may or may not be in the best interest of the rest of society. Correspondence of background can apply not only to the professional lives of intellectuals but also to their social origins (1973, p. 75).

In short, academicians, like other professionals requiring lengthy educational apprenticeships, come disproportionately from middle- and upper-class backgrounds that produce similarities in experience and perspectives. Professional socialization within lengthy graduate programs tends to produce further similarities. Therefore, we should concern ourselves with the extent to which such experiences are translated into sociological explanations of social problems. This necessitates the cultivation of a sociological imagination that enables us to grasp history and biography and their relationships within society (Mills 1959).

As the reader by now has probably concluded, this text is about the making and shaping of social problems within a context of wealth and power. Through personal involvement in and identification with a number of social movements for structural change, the authors have come to share the assumptions of the conflict paradigm. We view society as a contested struggle between groups with opposed aims and interests, with the human being as an active creator of self and society. Though institutions are resistant to change, they are not immutable, nor are they immune to criticism. It follows that the definitions of social problems provided by those with institutional power must be critically assessed.

BIBLIOGRAPHY

Anderson, Charles
    1974   The Political Economy of Social Class. Englewood
                            Cliffs, N.J.: Prentice-Hall.

Anderson, Jack
    1976   "Weapons Makers and Pentagon Brass Are Happy
                            Family." Rocky Mountain News, February 1,
                            p. 56.

Banfield, Edward C.
    1974   The Unheavenly City Revisited. Boston: Little,
                            Brown.

Becker, Howard S.
1966

Social Problems: A Modern Approach. New York:
John Wiley.

Bell, Daniel
1961

The End of Ideology: On the Exhaustion of Political
Ideas in the Fifties. New York: The Free Press.

Bend, E., and
Vogelfanger, M.
1971

"A New Look at Mills' Critique." In Mass Society
in Crisis. Bernard Rosenberg, Israel Gerver, and
F. William Howton, eds. New York: Macmillan,
pp. 271–78.

Blumer, H.
1971

"Social Problems as Collective Behavior." Social
Problems 18 (Winter):298–306.

Bottomore, T. B.
1965a

Elites and Society. New York: Basic Books.

1965b

Classes in Modern Society. London: George Allen
and Unwin.

Chambliss, William J.
1973

Sociological Readings in the Conflict Perspective.
Reading, Mass.: Addison-Wesley.

Clement, Wallace
1975

The Canadian Corporate Elite: An Analysis of
Economic Power. Toronto: McClelland and
Stewart.

1977

Continental Corporate Power, Economic Elite
Linkages between Canada and the United States.
Toronto: McClelland and Stewart.

Cohen, Albert
1955

Delinquent Boys: The Culture of the Gang. New
York: The Free Press.

Dahrendorf, Ralf
1958

"Toward a Theory of Social Conflict." Journal of
Peace and Conflict Resolution II: 170–183.

Dandurand, Yvon
1974

"Ethnic Group Members and the Correctional
System: A Question of Human Rights." Canadian
Journal of Criminology and Corrections 16
(January): 35–52.

Dolbeare, Kenneth M.,
and Patricia
1973

American Ideologies: Competing Beliefs of the
1970s. 2d ed. Chicago: Markham.

Durkheim, Emile
1947

The Division of Labor in Society. New York: The
Free Press.

1966

The Rules of the Sociological Method (translated
by Sarah Solovay and John Mueller; edited by
George E. G. Catlin). New York: The Free Press.

Eckberg, Douglas Lee,
and Hill, Lester, Jr.
1979

"The Paradigm Concept and Sociology: A Critical
Review." American Sociological Review 44
(December): 925–37.

Eitzen, D. Stanley
1978

In Conflict and Order: Understanding Society.
Boston: Allyn and Bacon.

Erickson, Kai T.
1970

"Sociology and the Historical Perspective." The
American Sociologist 5 (November):331–38.

Finestone, Harold
1957

"Cats, Kicks, and Color." Social Problems, vol. 5,
no. 1 (July):3–13.

Forcese, Dennis, and
Richer, Stephen
1975

Issues in Canadian Society. Scarborough, Ontario:
Prentice-Hall of Canada.

Friedrichs, Robert W.
1970

A Sociology of Sociology. New York: The Free Press.

Fuller, Robert C.
1938

"The Problem of Teaching Social Problems." American Journal of Sociology 44 (November): 415–35.

Gerth, Hans, and
Mills, C. Wright
1964

Character and Social Structure. New York:
Harcourt Brace Jovanovich.

Gouldner, Alvin W.
1962

"Anti-minotaur: The Myth of a Value-Free
Sociology." Social Problems 9 (Winter): 199–213.

Hall, Calvin, and
Lindzey, Gardner
1966   Theories of Personality. New York: John Wiley.

Henshel, Richard L., and
Anne-Marie
1973   Perspectives on Social Problems. Don Mills,
                              Ontario: Longman Canada, p. 75.

Herrnstein, Richard
1973   I.Q. in the Meritocracy. Boston: Little, Brown.

Hobbes, Thomas
1977   "Leviathan." In The Psychology of Society, Richard
                              Sennett, ed. New York: Random House, pp. 20–26.

Horowitz, Irving Louis
1968   Professing Sociology: Studies in the Life Cycle of
                              Social Science. Chicago: Aldine.

Horton, John
1964   "The Dehumanization of Anomie and Alienation:
                              Problems in the Ideology of Sociology." British
                              Journal of Sociology 15: 283–300.

1966   "Order and Conflict Theories of Social Problems."
                              American Journal of Sociology 72 (May):701–13.

Horton, Paul B., and
Leslie, Gerald R.
1970   The Sociology of Social Problems. 3d ed. New York:
                              Appleton-Century-Crofts.

Israel, Joachim
1971   Alienation: From Marx to Modern Sociology.
                              Boston: Allyn and Bacon.

Jensen, Arthur R.
1969   "How Much Can We Boost I.Q. and Scholastic
                              Achievement?" Harvard Educational Review,
                              Winter, 1–123.

Johnson, Elmer H.
1968   Crime, Corrections, and Society. Homewood, Ill.:
                              The Dorsey Press.

1973   Social Problems of Urban Man. Homewood, Ill.:
                              The Dorsey Press.

Julian, Joseph
1972   Social Problems. New York: Appleton-Century-
                              Crofts.

Kaufman, Richard
1970

"The Military Industrial Complex." In American Institutions. Jerome H. Skolnick and Elliot Currie, eds. Boston: Little, Brown, pp. 178–92.

Kuhn, Thomas
1970

The Structure of Scientific Revolutions. 2d ed. Chicago: The University of Chicago Press.

Lipset, Seymour
1960

Political Man. Garden City, N.Y.: Doubleday.

Mannheim, Karl
1936

Ideology and Utopia. New York: Harcourt Brace Jovanovich.

Matza, David, and
Miller, Henry
1976

"Poverty and Proletariat." In Contemporary Social Problems. Robert K. Merton and Robert Nisbet, eds. New York: Harcourt Brace Jovanovich, pp. 641–73.

Marchak, Patricia M.
1974

Ideological Perspectives on Canada. Toronto: McGraw-Hill-Ryerson.

Melman, Seymour
1974

"The Best Bang Money Will Buy." Rocky Mountain News, December 15, p. 4.

Merton, Robert K., and
Nisbet, Robert A., eds.
1971

Contemporary Social Problems. 3d ed. New York: Harcourt Brace Jovanovich.

Merton, Robert K.
1938

"Social Structure and Anomie." American Sociological Review 3 (October):672–82.

Miliband, Ralph
1969

The State in Capitalist Society. New York, New York: Basic Books.

Miller, Walter
1958

"Lower Class Culture as a Generating Milieu of Gang Delinquency." Journal of Social Issues, vol. 14 no. 3:5–19.

Mills, C. Wright
1943

"The Professional Ideology of Social Pathologists." American Journal of Sociology (September) 165–80.

1956   The Power Elite. New York: Oxford University Press.

1959   The Sociological Imagination. New York: Oxford University Press.

Mintz, Beth
1975   "The President's Cabinet, 1897–1972: A Contribution to the Power Structure Debate." The Insurgent Sociologist, vol. 5 no. 3 (Spring):131–48.

Mischler, Elliot, and Waxler, Nancy, eds.
1968   Family Processes and Schizophrenia. New York: Science House.

Navarro, Vincent E.
1977   Medicine under Capitalism. New York: Neale Watson Academic Publications.

Neubeck, Kenneth S.
1979   Social Problems: A Critical Approach. Glenview, Ill.: Scott, Foresman.

Nye, Francis Ivan
1958   Family Relationships and Delinquent Behavior. New York: John Wiley.

Parsons, Talcott
1937   The Structure of Social Action. New York: The Free Press.

Popper, Karl
1961   The Logic of Scientific Discovery. New York: John Wiley.

Reasons, Charles E.
1972   Race, Crime, and Justice. Pacific Palisades, Calif.: Goodyear.

1978   "Two Models of Race Relations and Prison Racism: A Cross-Cultural Perspective." In The Sociology of Law: A Conflict Perspective. Charles E. Reasons and Robert M. Rich, eds. Toronto: Butterworths, pp. 367–89.

Reiman, Jeffrey H.
1979   The Rich Get Richer and the Poor Get Prison: Ideology, Class and Criminal Justice. New York: John Wiley.

Reynolds, Larry T., and
Janice M.
1970   The Sociology of Sociology. New York: David
McKay.

Seeley, John R.
1968   "Social Science? Some Probative Problems." In
Radical Perspectives on Social Problems. Frank
Lindenfeld, ed. New York: MacMillan, pp. 4–13.

Sellin, Thorsten
1938   Culture, Conflict and Crime. New York: Social
Science Research Council.

Skolnick, Jerome, and
Currie, Elliot
1973   Crisis in American Institutions. 2d ed. Boston:
Little, Brown.

Strauss, Robert
1976   "Alcoholism and Problem Drinking." In Contemporary Social Problems. Robert K. Merton and
Robert Nisbet, eds. New York: Harcourt Brace
Jovanovich, pp. 183–217.

Tuchman, Gaye
1974   The TV Establishment: Programming for Power
and Profit. Englewood Cliffs, N.J.: Prentice-Hall.

Vold, George
1958   Theoretical Criminology. New York: Oxford
University Press.

Weber, Max
1947   The Theory of Social and Economic Organization.
New York: Oxford University Press.

Wilson, Edward O.
1975   Sociobiology: The New Synthesis. Cambridge,
Mass.: Belknap.

Wolfe, Alan
1976   "Extralegality and American Power." Society,
March–April: 44–47.

1978   The Seamy Side of Democracy: Repression in
America. New York: Longman.

1
THE PARADIGMS OF SOCIAL PROBLEMS

2

THE IDEOLOGY OF SOCIAL PROBLEMS: A THEORY OF CONFLICT

Abstract

This chapter presents a theory on the origin of ideas, both academic and "common sense," about social problems. Those idea-systems (ideologies) that are in the interests of power and wealth are thought to prevail in contemporary North American society. They are widely distributed by the media and the schools. These dominant ideologies affect us all, particularly those involved in movements to define and resolve social problems. The theory on the *Ideology of Social Problems* consists of the following propositions:

Proposition 1: For every society, a set of structural imperatives can be identified that make possible the existing form of political and economic order.

Definitions: (1) By *set*, we mean a number of things that are logically connected.

(2) By *structural imperatives*, we mean arrangements and properties that are central to the continuation of the existing form of master (that is, political and economic) institutions.

29

Proposition 2: The structural imperatives for a given political-economic order are directly legitimated, rationalized, and supported by a set of ideas that together constitute a general ideology.

Proposition 3: The structural imperatives for a given political-economic order are indirectly legitimated, rationalized, and supported by different subsets of ideas, each of which constitutes a specific ideology, and each of which is consistent with the general ideology.

Corollary: The specific ideologies for social problems that prevail in corporate society will tend to be those that are consistent with the general ideology of "corporatism."

Proposition 4: Both general and specific ideologies are transmitted by organized means of influence.

Proposition 5: The emergence, institutionalization, and maintenance of social problems occur in an ideologial context that is both general and specific.

> . . . *we have come increasingly to see the social definition of social problems as a matter of great importance in itself and a highly problematic matter. Indeed, we have come to recognize that the social definition of social problems is crucial to determining whether anything will be done politically to deal with things we may personally consider to be problems. And we have come to recognize that these social definitions of what are and are not social problems are the outcomes of political processes that may be largely independent of the social conditions, the "things out there."—Jack Douglas*

The opening chapter of this text centers on the ideological dilemmas inherent in approaching matters of social controversy. As the above comment makes clear, the definition of a particular phenomenon as a "problem" is neither objective nor clear-cut.

DEFINING SOCIAL PROBLEMS

Social problems are a product of human enterprise. Individually and collectively we are all variously involved in their making and shaping. By defining certain situations as bad and/or supporting other definitions and actions that concern them, we are participants in the creation of a social problem. Furthermore, by supporting dominant definitions we are helping to maintain the popularity of such definitions and subsequently of the problem itself. On the other hand, we are responsible in different ways for the disappearance (at least from public awareness) of social problems by declaring them remedied, no longer of significance, or by redefining them in positive terms.

An important element in the "creation" of a social problem is making the general public and/or significant specific publics aware of the existence of competing definitions. As Fuller and Myers stated:

> Social problems do not arise full-blown, commanding community attention and evoking adequate policies and machinery for their solution. On the contrary, we believe that social problems exhibit a temporal course of development in which different phases or stages may be distinguished. Each stage anticipates its successor in time and each succeeding stage contains new elements which mark it off from its predecessor. A social problem thus conceived as always being in a dynamic state of "becoming" passes through the natural history stages of awareness, policy determination, and reform. . . . (1941)

The argument of these sociologists is provocative. They claim that any problem that seizes the public imagination does not do so because it is clearly a matter of "evil." (Witness, for example, the changing historical definitions associated with alcohol use and abortion.) Rather, specific problems seem to come and go . . . they appear to be born, peak, and vanish. Perhaps they disappear forever or maybe they are reborn at a later period in history. Fuller and Myers were convinced that such problems had a "natural history" that depended in large part on public *opinion*. Thus, it is not so much the objective dimensions of a problem that change. Instead, changing cultural values together with access to the means to shape public opinion account for the rise and fall of social issues.

For example, though alcohol abuse remains a clear problem in the eyes of many, the "solution" of Prohibition does not appear a popular one today. Times have changed and the Prohibition forces are not as prominent politically as they once were. To cite another case, abortion retains the same objective properties today as in the past: interruption of the development of the embryo or the fetus in the mother's womb. However, the legal definition of abortion has undergone considerable change. (See Chapter 11 on Sex and Sexism.) For some, abortion is a social problem. Others believe that despite the serious nature of the issue, women in the last analysis have the right to control their own bodies. Thus, *restriction* on abortion becomes the problem.

This chain of argument binds together a number of other important works in the field of social problems. Howard Becker (1966) holds that interest groups seek general support for their particular problems through gaining access to the power and authority of the state. In a similar fashion, Ross and Staines (1972) point to the "constellations of power, influence and authority" that accompany the rise and fall of social issues.

In a purely subjective emphasis, Herbert Blumer has further politicized sociological analysis. He urges that we view the recognition of problems as a consequence of movements that are successful in capturing *center stage*. Access to political and economic influence, particularly the mass media, represents the power to shape norms, policies, and laws to reflect particular interests. As Blumer states:

> We have scarcely any studies, and pitifully limited knowledge, of such relevant matters as the following: the role of agitation in getting recognition for a problem; the role of violence in gaining such recognition; the play of interest groups who seek to shut off recognition of a problem; the role of other interest groups who foresee material gains by elevating a given condition to a problem (as in the case of police with the current problems of crime and drugs); the role of political figures in fomenting concern with certain problems and putting the damper on concern with other conditions; the role of powerful organizations and corporations doing the same things; the impotency of powerless groups to gain attention for what they believe to be problems; the role of the mass media in selecting social problems; and the influence of adventitious happenings that shock public sensitivities (1971, p. 302).

In introducing a political component to the definitions of social problems, a legitimate concern with the status and influence of relatively powerless groups may emerge. It is often the case that *we tend to see things not as they are but as we are.* And what we are—our attitudes, beliefs, and world view—is often a consequence of *where we are.* In other words, those who view welfare mothers as living comfortably at taxpayers' expense are probably not welfare mothers. Those who believe there are plenty of jobs for people who want them have probably not spent much time standing in unemployment lines. As we shall see at a later point, Karl Marx, who along with Emile Durkheim and Max Weber strongly influenced the development of sociology, argued that social *being* determines social *consciousness*. In other words, what we think about social problems may well reflect our standing or position in the social order. Since standing carries with it different degrees of influence, it follows that what is officially recognized as a social problem may reflect the interests of owners and managers more than workers; the wealthy more than the lesser classes; men more than women; whites more than blacks; Hispanics, and Native Americans, and English-Canadians more than French-Canadians.

SYMBOLIC INTERACTIONIST SOCIOLOGY: A CRITICAL REVIEW

The contemporary sociologists mentioned above, together with legions of others, work in what is called the "symbolic interactionist" tradition in sociology. Influenced heavily by the writings of George Herbert Mead (1934) and Charles Horton Cooley (1909), interactionists have sought to understand the human being as a creator and manipulator of a symbolic universe. The richness and diversity of human language represent a major vehicle for interaction between and among individuals and groups. This focus on Homo sapiens as a *symbol bearer* and a *creature of culture* has quite logically led to a concern with the development and meanings of symbolic systems. Prominent among such symbolic systems are the normative standards, rules, and principles by which conformity and deviance, adaptation and maladaptation, successes and problems are judged.

Another aspect of the interactionist tradition has been a humanistic emphasis. This is evident in attempts to understand the world of meaning from the differing points of view of different social groups including the outcasts and the under classes. Influenced by an emphasis on meanings and definitions together with an intention to see the world as others see it, interactionists have shown that norms, standards, policies, and laws are not the simple product of a fixed and unchanging societal consensus. Such subjective dimensions of social life always reflect a dynamic process of becoming, and intensely involved in this process are organized interest movements (Thio 1978).

In our introductory chapter we noted Max Weber's conception of power. Weber (1947) held that power and class could be separated. He argued that there were such social entities as parties and status groups. In other words, human beings differ in their relative power or relative honor and such attributes are not necessarily related to property. Wittingly or unwittingly, many North American interactionists have assigned great importance to the Weberian concerns of status and power. Such a focus does make clearer the heterogeneous nature of the modern industrial state. Interactionist research of the historical variety has sought to identify the particular shifts in power and the rise and fall of normative standards that serve to identify social problems. For example, Anthony Platt (1969) traces the formation of the juvenile court in the United States to a "child-saving movement," whereby native-born white Anglo-Saxon Protestant rural and small-town forces, sought to "rescue" the sons and daughters of the poor Catholic immigrant urban dwellers from their "wicked" customs. A similar analysis by Joseph Gusfield (1963) accounts for the historical development of the Prohibition period.

The concern with interests may shift from a more general cultural movement to a specific political focus. To illustrate, Howard Becker

(1963) accounts for the criminalization of marijuana use as a consequence of the vigorous activities of the Federal Bureau of Narcotics. Faced with a declining budget and possible bureaucratic extinction, the FBN alerted the Congress of the United States to the "problem" of marijuana use. Congress responded with the passage of the Marijuana Tax Act of 1937, and the "war on dope" was officially on.

At the social-psychological level, where group and institutional forces intersect personality, interactionists have explored what it means to be labeled, stigmatized, and typed. Modern classics include Goffman's *Asylums* (1961), which demonstrates that the norms of "mental illness" in "hospitals" have little to do with health and a great deal to do with whether or not one conforms to institutionalized expectations. Thomas Scheff (1967) argues that the development of "mental illness" is partially a consequence of the social exclusion directed toward those labeled as "queer," "strange," or "different." Edwin Lemert (1967) holds that an official label attached by authorities or significant others following the primary or initial unconventional behavior may confirm a deviant "identity." Such a reaction is thought to increase the probability of additional or *secondary* deviance. Thus, the label operates as a *self-fulfilling prophecy*.

CLASS, POWER AND IDEOLOGY

Missing from most work in the traditional interactionist style is a structural analysis of the role of a *dominant class* in the formation of normative systems and in the shaping and molding of the recognition accorded social problems. However, those working in interactionist sociology have raised important questions that in turn generate broader ponderables. First of all, is it possible to identify a historical process that details the rise and fall of particular social problems? Further, what is the nature of those forces behind the definition of a particular social problem? In other words, what is the societal context in which definitions about social problems are formed? Is it *merely* one of differential status (that is, honorific standing) and party (power)?

The latter question is the beginning point for our construction of a theory for social problems. For if a definition of social problems can be determined at least in part by the power of interest groups (namely, status and party), it follows that such a definition can also be affected by the power of classes. If the identification of a social problem can be influenced by ideology and paradigms, it follows that the level of abstraction at which the "problem" is studied can also be influenced. (If necessary, review levels of abstraction in Chapter One.) In short, we believe there is much more to power than the coming and going of historically specific movements. We believe there is much more to ideology than different cultural values, or specific occupational beliefs.

In Chapter One, the authors presented the assumptions for both the order and conflict paradigms in sociology. We therefore have a foundation on which to construct a formal explanation or theory for social problems. In this chapter, we shall construct a theory entitled "The Ideology of Social Problems." This theory is in the conflict tradition because it holds that social problems are often *wrongly* defined and understood due to powerful ideologies that are structural in origin. Thus, the conflict emphasis on structure (institutions, political-economy, class/elites, and ideology) is clearly evident throughout our theory.

In short, we believe that influential ideas may keep people from thinking clearly and openly about the problems of society. We believe such idea systems frequently lead to erroneous opinions and faulty knowledge within both sociology and the broader society. As "perceptual filters" they help to ensure that we close our minds to alternative, perhaps more accurate, understanding.

THE IDEOLOGY OF SOCIAL PROBLEMS

Proposition 1: *For every society, a set of structural imperatives can be identified that make possible the existing form of political and economic order.*

Definitions: (1) By *set*, we mean a number of things that are logically connected.

(2) By *structural imperatives*, we mean arrangements and properties that are central to the continuation of the existing form of master (namely, political and economic) institutions.

The institutions that center on the production and distribution of wealth together with the organization of power and influence represent the essence of social structure or master institutions. This axiom is consistent with conflict assumptions concerning the nature of society and social problems. In the North American societies of Canada and the United States, the form of the prevailing economic order is a corporate system in which the means of production (factories, land, natural resources) are privately owned and operated for profit. As political democracies, the governments of these societies rule by means of the elected representatives of the people. However, as Wolfe has demonstrated (1978), historically when democracy exists within a private property system, the problem of disproportionate influence follows. Thus, state power frequently serves the interests of dominant owning classes and in such societies, "Freedom is a function of possession" (MacPherson 1962).

To understand the corporate form as the economic master institution, it is necessary to remember several things. First of all, only a small number of business firms are legally considered corporations. Also, most corporations are not very large in sales or assets. To illustrate statistically, in 1975 there were more than 2 million corporations in the United States, 1.1 million partnerships, and 10.8 million sole proprietorships.[1] However, when business firms are compared by receipts, the total for all proprietorships was $339.2 billion, for all partnerships $146.0 billion, and for all corporations, a staggering $2,961.7 billion. Further, the top 12 percent of all corporations received 90 percent of total corporate receipts (*Statistical Abstract of the United States*, 1979:555).

It would be a serious mistake to focus on the corporation to the exclusion of other social influences. However, the importance of this master institution, the relationship of that institution to state power, together with the growth in corporation revenues and assets cannot be ignored. We believe that the United States and Canada increasingly represent the "corporate society." In fact, one author has recently pointed out the corporate connections *between* Canada and the United States (Clement 1977).

By corporation we mean to identify both a legal and social structure. In the sense of law, a corporation is a body authorized by law to act as a single-person. Further, it is an organizational form that allows for continuation beyond the death of owners. This latter property is known as the capacity of succession.

In the sense of social relationships, the corporation represents a marked departure from the small-scale entrepreneurial "free enterprise" that prevailed in numerous Western societies before the coming of the Industrial Revolution. Early capitalism was an economic order marked by traders and merchants, craftsworkers and apprentices, laborers and landowners. Though manufacturing and commercial interests of significant size could be identified, large-scale technology was not the order of the day. The economic order was competitive, not concentrated. Late Nineteenth Century North America saw the development of an expanded factory system, trusts in crucial economic sectors, the rise of industrial barons, and a clearly defined working class that carried the seeds of well-organized trade and industrial unionism (Dowd 1977).

The modern corporate order gave birth to a new set of social relationships. Shareholders came to represent an often remote form of ownership advancing their interests through increasingly influential corporate

---

[1]A *sole proprietorship* means that a business is owned by a single person who receives all profits and is responsible for all liabilities; a *partnership* means that two or more owners divide profits and are jointly responsible for liabilities; a *corporation* means that ownership is divided into equal shares with profit and liabilities dependent on the number of shares owned.

managers. The traditional blue collar work force changed to include the new white collar legions (Mills 1956). The economic order now reveals growing concentration in the nature of oligopolistic and monopolistic tendencies and realities (Baran and Sweezy 1966; Clement 1975 and 1977). State resources (that is, tax revenues) have become an ever important form of capital investment (Anderson 1976, p. 83).

The structural imperatives of this master institution can be identified succinctly:

1. *Corporate Ownership*: The major means of production and distribution are largely privately owned. However, the organization of economic control is increasingly corporate in nature. Although individual holders of great wealth do exist, the corporation represents the *consolidation* of individual wealth and power.

2. *Profit*: The cornerstone of the corporate order is financial gain, the realization of a surplus beyond the cost of operations.

3. *Growth*: Economic expansion in the form of higher productivity, increasing sales, bigger profits, new markets, technological change, and the like, is not only the measure of health but also the basis of survival. Today the impetus for growth is evident in the development of the multinational corporation and the corresponding global nature of corporate economy.

4. *Concentration*: Larger firms come to dominate an economic order to the continuing exclusion of smaller interests.

5. *Technocracy*: Large-scale technology calls for an important occupational category of technicians functioning to apply science to achieve corporate ends.

6. *Control Networks*: The consolidation of different corporate interests is achieved through *interlocking directorates* and the *translocation of elites*. The former refers to the linking of corporate boards of directors by means of common membership. The latter describes the movement of corporate executives into important circles of influence outside the corporation. Such spheres might include governmental service, philanthropic foundations, and advisory committees exercising important influence in national and international affairs.

7. *Contractual Relationships*: Custom, loyalty, and personal bonds are replaced by law, policies, collective bargaining agreements, and other contractual forms.

37

8. *Managerial Model*: An occupational category of control specialists comes to direct the economic and political order.[2]

THE CORPORATE ELITE

Sociological theory that centers on the domination of societies by a group of "elites" is not original with this historical period. Although the writings of C. Wright Mills (1956), William Domhoff (1970), and others are more contemporary, they constitute a part of a larger historical flow of social thought. One of the earlier writers in the elite tradition was Vilfredo Pareto (1848–1923), who divided the social order into masses and elite. The latter was successful in reaching positions of prominence within the political structure (governing elite) or outside it. According to Pareto (1970), the elite retain power only through coercion and deception and through bringing into positions of authority the more talented members of the masses. A failure to co-opt the potential leaders of the nonelite sets the stage for a decline in power.

For Gaetano Mosca (1859–1941), the emphasis was also (as with Mills and Pareto) on political stratification. In his view (1970), common people are incapable of self-rule, are not well organized, and have an inherent need to be ruled. According to Mosca, members of the ruling group tend to be intelligent and ambitious because they are socially conditioned to believe they are born to rule. One group of elites supposedly holds primacy in the economic sector, another represents religious authority, still another controls secular authority, and a final coterie dominates the organized means of military power.

It is critical to note a point made earlier with regard to the concept "conflict." The use of the term "elite" in a work does not ensure that an author will deal critically with the question of power. Nor are elite theorists necessarily bound to the conflict paradigm. For Mosca, there existed a pluralism at the elite level. He argued that each faction checked the domination by others through exerting a "countervailing power" (Forcese and Richer 1975, pp. 101–102).

The elite tradition has historically raised questions of theoretical importance. However, only within the past decade have such questions generated increasingly sophisticated research. The resurgence of interest in elite theory, together with the quest for empirical evidence, no doubt reflects the increasing influence of the conflict paradigm, given the

---

[2]A wealth of empirical data bearing on these and other properties of the corporate order is presented throughout this text. Of special importance are materials to be found in the remainder of this chapter and the following chapters on Inequality and Work. (Important general references are Anderson 1976; Dowd 1977; Wolfe 1978; Edwards, Reich, and Weisskopf 1972; Neubeck 1979; Clement 1975 and 1977.)

historic events of the Sixties and Seventies. Further impetus in this area can also be traced to the extent to which computer capability has become a tool in social research. Whatever the tool, research on elites has revolved around two important concerns. First, to what extent is institutional leadership open to membership outside an inner elite circle? Secondly, does a specific social category, such as the class that owns and controls the means of production and distribution, tend to control the power positions in a corporate society?[3]

The Executive Branch of the government of the United States has received recent attention from those elite theorists in the critical tradition. Freitag (1975) and Mintz (1975) found that nearly 90 percent of the members of the presidential cabinets from 1897 to 1973 were of elite business and/or upper-class origin. In other words, such persons met one or more of the following criteria of business elite standing: (1) had served as director or officer of a major corporation, (2) was a present or past member of a leading corporation law firm, or (3) represented a major corporation as an attorney. Indicators of upper-class membership included being listed in a "blue book" for the socially prominent, attending a "prep" school noted for its social standing, or having membership in an elite social club.

Similar research by Dye confirms the existence of the translocation of the elite (1976). For this researcher, the corporate elite numbered 3,572 and included the directors and presidents of those industrial corporations, banks, utilities, insurers, communications firms, and transportation companies which control half the corporate assets in the United States. The governmental elite numbered 286 and included not only the president and vice-president, cabinet secretaries, presidential advisors, supreme court justices, and ambassadors at large; but also under-secretaries and assistant secretaries of all executive departments, the chairpersons of congressional committees and the ranking minority committee members, congressional majority and minority party leaders and whips, members of the Federal Reserve Board and the Council of Economic Advisors. Also included in the governmental elite were top ranking military officers.

Focusing on the connections between the upper echelons of political and corporate power, Dye found that 26.7 percent of the members of the governmental elite held prior positions as members of a corporate elite, and 83.5 percent of the government elite were previously in another elite government position. Further, nearly 40 percent of those in the higher corporate echelons were previously members of the top governing circles, while over 56 percent of the latter group had been associated with prominent law firms.

Dye's indicators of elite standing are somewhat different from those of Mintz and Freitag. His governing elites include a lower range of political

---

[3]An excellent overview of the "empirical side of the power elite debate" can be found in Kerbo and Della Fave (1978).

positions. Interchange of top management from corporate to governmental institutions is more striking when one deals with a more *restrictive* definition of governing elites than Dye employs. In other words, those at the very top may "wear a different hat" for a season, but they remain on top.

When a methodological decision is made to reduce substantially by definition elite membership, an "inner group" can be identified. Useem reserves the term "business elite" for those who are "primary owners or top managers of several major corporations" (1979, p. 553). Such executives were distinguished from others who were in the upper level of *only one* corporation. Useem found that an "inner group" of corporate directors could be identified by the number of memberships they held on the boards of directors of leading United States corporations.

> The largest firms were those identified by the standard and generally accepted annual ranking conducted by *Fortune* magazine. The firms were ranked into groups including the following: 500 largest industrial corporations, 50 largest retail corporations, and 50 largest commercial banks; 50 largest life insurance companies; and 50 largest utilities (ranked by assets); 50 largest transportation companies (ranked by operating revenues); and 47 other large firms not readily classed within the previous groups (Useem 1979, p. 558).

This study found a pattern of interlocking directorships among the directors of these 797 corporations. A total of 1,570 individuals were multiple directors, that is, having two or more memberships on the boards of the expanded *Fortune* list. Beyond this, however, other connections can be identified.

Multiple directors tend to be found in positions of control in nongovernmental, nonprofit institutions (Useem 1979, p. 561). These individuals are also distinctively more apt to serve on advisory bodies for government agencies and to hold membership in major business policy associations. Also of importance is the finding that those directors sitting on the boards of the largest corporations are more extensively involved in other forms of institutional governance (serving as a federal advisor, a board member of a research or scientific organization, a top official of an economic development organization, and so on) than are the directors of corporations with fewer resources.

Other studies bear on the issue of elite interlock. Only a few can be mentioned here. Evidently, the elite remain quite busy. Dye (1976) found a lifetime average of 11.1 elite positions held by members of the higher circles of corporate power. Allen (1974) found that larger corporations, as expected, have more interlocks, though they do not necessarily have more directors. More precisely, as the size of the corporation increases, the number of interlocks also increases (Dooly 1969).

What of differences between the elite who gain power through owner-ship and those whose influence is tied basically to corporate position? Soref (1976) found that the owners were more likely to represent upper-class origins. Further, they were more heavily involved in major policy-making and more apt to be influential in the affairs of other corporations.

Those studying interlocks must be aware of the statutory prohibitions that address this issue. In an examination of the legislative record, Bunting (1976) reports that scholarly studies and congressional inquiries since the end of World War II have detailed the shortcomings of law in the area of interlocks. What emerges is a crazy quilt of conflicting defini-tions that seek to address the issue in certain economic sectors and ignore it elsewhere. The problem extends beyond the language of prohibitive statutes.

> While the prohibitions might be defective, enforcement has been ludicrous. Federal regulatory agencies or administrative units charged with enforcing interlocking statutes but empowered to grant exemptions have routinely granted them. For example, of 10,937 applications for exemptions filed with the Interstate Com-merce Commission between 1921 and 1964, [(only)] 46 were denied, 190 withdrawn, and 245 apparently remained pending. On the other hand, the Justice Department and the Federal Trade Commission . . . enforce prohibition in a lax, haphazard manner. The FTC filed 13 complaints from 1914 to 1965; the Justice Depart-ment did not systematically investigate interlocking until 1947; it began its first formal litigation in 1952. Since statistics are not published, *recent enforcement activities are unknown* (Bunting 1976, p. 46).

The nature of corporate order cannot be understood if confined to the nation-state. Of increasing importance to power structure research is a focus on transnational interlocking. In one hallmark study, Clement demonstrates that interlocking is indeed an international affair. As this author observes, "Lines of interest ran with lines of capital, not with lines drawn by politicians on maps" (1977, p. 73). Accordingly, interlocking is common among dominant United States and Canadian corporations.

> Canada is an independent nation-state enveloped by spillover from the most powerful capitalist society in the world, which includes some of the costs and benefits of that society's wealth. While Canada's economy is largely controlled and shaped by U.S. capi-talists, these capitalists do not operate in a complete power vacuum in Canada. What has been forged over the past century is an alliance between the leading elements of Canadian and U.S. capital that reinforces mutually the power and advantage of each (Clement 1977, p. 6).

CORPORATE GIANTISM

Interest in interlocks as a mechanism of corporate power should not divert attention from an examination of corporation assets. Power is not simply a function of membership on governing boards. As noted earlier, interlocking is more prevalent for directors and officers of *larger* corporations. The increasing concentration of corporate assets in recent history is staggering. In 1950, there were a total of 629,300 incorporated businesses in the United States. By 1976, that number had grown to 2.1 million. However, most of this growth in *numbers* involved those with relatively low assets. For example, in 1976 there were 1.2 million corporations with assets of under $100,000. *Thus some 58 percent of the total number of such bodies controlled less than 1 percent of the total assets ($38 billion of a total $4,723 billion).* In that same year, corporations with assets of $250 million and over—representing only one tenth of one percent of the total number of corporations—had $3,124 billion in assets, *or some 65.9 percent of the total. In comparison, in 1960 the top one tenth of one percent held only 45.8 percent of total assets* (Statistical Abstract of the United States 1979, p. 563).

The trend in the direction of corporate giantism parallels another relevant development. In 1950, there existed in the United States some 2.7 million commercial and industrial businesses engaged in the vital economic sectors of mining and manufacturing, wholesale trade, retail trade, construction, and commercial service. By 1974, that number had *declined* slightly to 2.6 million. In the same period, the population of the United States had *increased* from 152 million persons to 212 million, a rise of 39.4 percent (*Statistical Abstract of the United States* 1977, pp. 525 and 526, respectively). The reality is more business for fewer firms.

Ownership of Land

In the agricultural sector, still another parallel is evident. In 1930 there were 6.5 million farms in the United States. By 1978, that number had declined to 2.4 million. In 1930, the average farm consisted of 151 acres of land. By 1978, that average was 444. *Stated another way, while the number of farms declined 64 percent, the average acres per farm increased 194 percent.* In every year since 1930, the average number of farms has declined from the previous year. In every year the average size of each farm has increased over the previous year. Even more disturbing is the picture of vanishing farmland. In 1953 and 1954, farmland totaled

1.2 billion acres. By 1978, the corresponding figure had fallen to 1.052 billion acres; a total loss of 148 million acres primarily to urban development in just over two decades (*Statistical Abstract of the United States* 1979, p. 682). In Canada there were 430,522 farms in 1966 compared to 338,578 in 1976. While both the total acreage in farming and the number of farms decreased during this period, the average size of the farms increased (Bosran 1979).

At the present time, some owners of smaller family farms are choosing to incorporate for tax purposes. However, such "corporate" farming should not be confused with the increasing movement by large corporations into the agricultural sector. While farming remains largely a family affair, in 1974 the average farm owned by a parent corporation consisted of over 9,000 acres (*Statistical Abstract of the United States* 1979, p. 685).

Land is central to the exercise of economic power. It goes without saying that many of the largest corporations on the continent are dependent on land-based resources for their profits. Such resources include, but are not limited to, oil, gas, coal, food, minerals, and timber. As would be expected, given the distribution of wealth in general, land wealth in particular is concentrated in the hands of a few. In the United States at the time of this writing, it is estimated that some "3 percent of the popula-

Figure 2-1. U.S. Landholdings of Select Corporations (Acres)

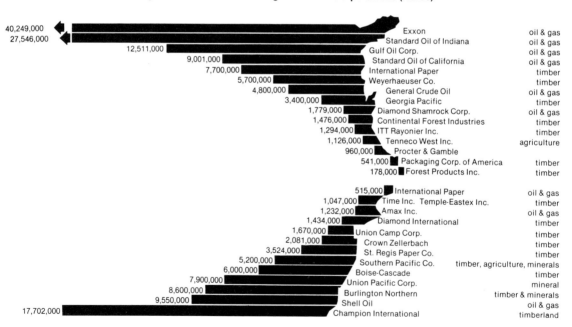

40,249,000	Exxon	oil & gas
27,546,000	Standard Oil of Indiana	oil & gas
12,511,000	Gulf Oil Corp.	oil & gas
9,001,000	Standard Oil of California	oil & gas
7,700,000	International Paper	timber
5,700,000	Weyerhaeuser Co.	timber
4,800,000	General Crude Oil	oil & gas
3,400,000	Georgia Pacific	timber
1,779,000	Diamond Shamrock Corp.	oil & gas
1,476,000	Continental Forest Industries	timber
1,294,000	ITT Rayonier Inc.	timber
1,126,000	Tenneco West Inc.	agriculture
960,000	Procter & Gamble	
541,000	Packaging Corp. of America	timber
178,000	Forest Products Inc.	timber
515,000	International Paper	oil & gas
1,047,000	Time Inc. Temple-Eastex Inc.	timber
1,232,000	Amax Inc.	oil & gas
1,434,000	Diamond International	timber
1,670,000	Union Camp Corp.	timber
2,081,000	Crown Zellerbach	timber
3,524,000	St. Regis Paper Co.	timber
5,200,000	Southern Pacific Co.	timber, agriculture, minerals
6,000,000	Boise-Cascade	timber
7,900,000	Union Pacific Corp.	mineral
8,600,000	Burlington Northern	timber & minerals
9,550,000	Shell Oil	oil & gas
17,702,000	Champion International	timberland

Source: Peter Meyer, "Land Rush: A Survey of America's Land," *Harper's* January, 1979.

tion own 55 percent of all American land and 95 percent of the private land" (Meyer 1979, p. 49).

The total land area of the United States amounts to just under 2.3 billion acres. Of this, the federal government owns 761 million, state and local government 136 million, while Indian trust land amounts to 50 million acres. The remaining 1.3 billion acres is in private hands. According to the Economic Research Service, only 568 companies control (by means of ownership, lease, mineral, or surface rights) over 300 million acres, which is some 23 percent of all private United States landholdings. These same companies own some 2 billion acres worldwide—an area that if contiguous would swallow the whole of Europe. To be more specific, in 1973 a Ralph Nader study team found that over 60 percent of California's private land was owned by only 25 landholders. These included Standard Oil, Southern Pacific, the Times Mirror Corporation, Penn Central, Boise-Cascade, and others. Another Nader report found that seven "absentee corporations" owned one-third of the state of Maine's total land area of 20 million acres. Further, the 1974 Census of Agriculture revealed that almost 40 percent of all private farmland was owned by nonfarmers (Meyer 1979).

The bar graph in Figure 2-1 depicts the landholdings in the United States of some of the larger corporations.

GENERAL CORPORATE IDEOLOGY

Proposition 2:   *The structural imperatives for a given political-economic order are directly legitimated, rationalized, and supported by a set of ideas that together constitute a general ideology.*

This proposition argues that the world of ideas contains a "mirror image" of the essential properties or arrangements of the prevailing economic and political order. The general ideology represents a constellation of sacred beliefs that permeate the society in what Mannheim describes as a *total* fashion (Mannheim 1936). The general ideology of corporate society may be termed "corporatism." Its major symbols include:

1. *Privatism*: Perhaps the hallmark of corporate order is an emphasis on personal and private as opposed to public and social interests. Expressed commonly in such phrases as "looking out for number one," the "me generation," and "how to be your own best friend," this symbol becomes a stimulus to various industries. For example, insurers commonly remind viewers of television commercials that the welfare of "survivors" is still largely a personal (not community) responsibility.

2. *Progress*: The basic ideology of corporate order will present the idea of moving forward in the commodity sense of growth. For example, progress in health care will be described in terms of costly (and profitable) technology rather than effective preventive public care.

3. *Triumph of the Will*: According to this common belief, individual determination can remove all obstacles. All social barriers will fall if one "believes," "works," and "never says die." In corporate society, tales of heroes overcoming impossible odds become stereotyped media fare. For example, Wonder Woman is able to master the roles of career woman, housewife, and mistress simultaneously (provided she wears the appropriate perfume), while the *handicapped hero* is handsome, personable, married, and always gainfully employed (despite being paralyzed from the neck down). An obvious corollary of this belief is "It's your own fault if you do not succeed."

4. *Commodification of Human Qualities*: Goods and services available in the marketplace are offered as substitutes for human qualities. Banks become friendly, automobiles something to believe in, while soft drinks bring people together.

5. *Trickle Down*: According to this ideological component, what benefits (through greater profit) the private (increasingly large corporate) sector creates benefits for those below. For example, reducing corporate taxes is supposed to provide more jobs. However, in an increasingly capital-intensive economy, large-scale technology is valued over labor. Thus, corporate investment in advanced technology is intended frequently to reduce labor costs rather than create a need for more workers. For example, Exxon Corporation, which competed throughout the late 1970s with General Motors for the position of leading industrial corporation, had total revenues of $28.5 billion in 1973 and $64.9 billion in 1978. Its work force over the same period decreased from 137,000 to 130,000. Previously in 1970, Exxon employed 143,000 persons (*Moody's Industrial Manual* 1974 and 1979).

6. *Conspicuous Consumption*: You are where you live, what you wear, drive, and eat. This prime symbol was advanced by means of a $43.7 billion advertising industry in 1978 (*Statistical Abstract of the United States* 1979, p. 595).

7. *Nuclear Familism*: In the corporate order, the fragmented, usually small, nuclear family is advanced as the ultimate reason for being. Primarily a consumptive unit, the family when "good" enables its individuals to achieve. When "bad," this social unit is the "cause" of serious social problems.

8. *Equal Opportunity*: Although the title of much antidiscrimination legislation, this prime symbol is the corporate interpretation of fair play. In general, the call is for a place at the starting line for all who wish to race. It is in lieu of questioning why there must be winners and losers or why it is not possible to improve the conditions of the whole people.

9. *Chattel Relationships*: A sense of property ownership dominates social relationships. Possessive demands intensify as the circle of intimates grows increasingly smaller.

10. *Expertise*: Corporatism includes the belief that important political, economic, and other social decisions should be left to those in power who are in a position to "know." Thus, decisions revolving around human values are declared to be matters for scientists, technicians, managers, and specialists.

11. *Economy of Scale*: This idea is best described as "big is best." Economic problems are seen as too large and complex to be solved without massive capital investment by those giants who can afford it. For example, oil profits are defended by the industry as necessary to spur the discovery of new domestic sources of petroleum. Petroleum profits may go toward other ventures however. For example, Mobil Corporation acquired Montgomery Ward in 1974, a year after the first energy crisis produced record profits for Big Oil (*Moody's Industrial Manual* 1979, p. 2664).

12. *Careerism*: The corporate order is no haven for the Renaissance person. Careerism involves the components of antiintellectualism, and antitheoreticalism. The emphasis is on solving problems without first understanding them. This signals a time for the advance of the manager, technician, and vocational education. Studies in the liberal arts that occasionally raise questions about the sanctity of the existing order are widely branded as irrelevant to earning a living.

Specific Ideologies for Social Problems

Proposition 3: *The structural imperatives for a given political-economic order are indirectly legitimated, rationalized, and supported by different subsets of ideas, each of which constitutes a specific ideology, and each of which is consistent with the general ideology.*

Corollary: *The specific ideologies for social problems that prevail in corporate society will tend to be those that are consistent with the basic ideology of "corporatism."*

The theoretical argument here is clear. Whether one is dealing with formal sociological explanations of social problems or the conventional and ordinary reasons people give for their occurrence, one should expect to find the influential presence of general ideology ("corporatism"). In essence, the specific ideologies for social problems may be expected to "explain" or give "reasons" for the prevalence of disorders like poverty, racism, crime, and drug abuse. Given our understanding of corporatism, such specific ideologies should function to direct attention systematically from the structural source, that is, corporate order.

For example, social problems are often seen as "kinds of people" difficulties. In speaking to this ideological concern, William Ryan (1972) identified two basic tendencies. Both, however, represent ways of "blaming the victim." For some, problems arising from such things as race and class are clearly matters of individual fault. If those at the bottom, the argument goes, really wanted to, they could pull themselves up by their bootstraps. A second variety of "victim-blaming" is perhaps more important because it is quite subtle. It focuses on family or neighborhood, culture or subculture, forces of environment or nature. In these instances, the tendency is not to blame the victims personally, but to blame their immediate world of influence. Thus, *they never had a chance*.

It should be apparent that blaming the victim is a specific ideology logically consistent with the general set of beliefs described earlier. Students of society should be cautioned, however, not to take the elements of corporatism developed earlier as an exhaustive list. Nor should one attempt to relate specific ideologies to given components of general ideology in straight-line fashion. However, as should be evident from the above description of corporatism, blaming the victim reflects either "triumph of the will" (individual blame) or a more liberal "lack of equal opportunity" (family or subculture blame).

An examination of specific ideologies of social problems leads us to recognize the many "devils" commonly cited to explain troublesome events.

> If deviation and conformity are so alike, it is not surprising that deviant behavior should seem to appear in a community at exactly those points where it is most feared. Men who fear witches soon find themselves surrounded by them; men who become jealous of private property soon encounter eager thieves. And if it is not always easy to know whether fear creates the deviance or deviance the fear, the affinity of the two has been a continuing course of wonder in human affairs (Erickson 1966, p. 22).

**THE
IDEOLOGY
OF
SOCIAL
PROBLEMS**

In Kai Erickson's view the "crime wave" of witches and their imagined power was real for the inhabitants of the Massachusetts Bay Colony and for the witches in the seventeenth century, although the assumed power of the witches was difficult to verify. Nevertheless, the problems encountered by the puritans were "explained" by the convenient specific ideology of witches, which was in turn consistent with a more general theocratic ideology. Further, those who challenged the leadership of the colony did so at their peril. One might view a more recent counterpart of witches in the McCarthy hysteria of the 1950s, when communists were believed to permeate American government.

In contemporary society, specific ideologies for the energy crisis can be found. The emergence of oil and gas shortages in 1973 and again in 1978 were believed by many in the United States to be a consequence of increased consumption and unrealistic environmental safeguards. However, there is growing evidence to suggest such shortages were largely artificially created by oil companies for political and economic reasons (see Chapter Five). Given the power to influence definitions, existing conditions can be identified as social problems. Thus, puritanism may give birth to witches, Cold War ideology to McCarthyism, and the interests of petrocorporations to an energy panic.[4]

Because of prevailing ideologies there is a gap between existence and perception. An example of the void between the objective condition and its social reality is the image of the drug user and the drug problem in contemporary society. The "dope fiend" mythology discussed by Alfred Lindesmith in 1940 still exists in the public mind (Lindesmith 1940a, 1940b; Brecher 1972). Lindesmith identified a number of myths regarding the effects of drugs upon users, the nature of addicts, and the circumstances surrounding addiction. For example, many assume that drug peddlers are lurking about school yards and street corners attempting to seduce innocent youths into the dead-end road of addiction. However, a great amount of literature exists that points out that the sellers of illicit drugs are often users who give or sell drugs to friends and established clientele, rather than risk a sale to a stranger and/or potential narcotics agent. Nonetheless, the image of the pusher invokes the fear and horror of many citizens.

> Who is more malignant, more evil than the drug peddler? Can there be a criminal more loathed and feared than the pusher who is thought to seduce children into a life of slavery? He is the demon who spreads crime and corruption in the slums, who controls the minds and bodies of others by exploiting the cravings he has himself created. These are the images the drug peddler conjures up in the public mind (Blum 1971).

[4]The energy crisis has also proved to be a stimulus to the development of nuclear power, an energy source of dubious safety. The petrocorporations are heavily involved in the selling of nuclear power.

Therefore, we have to look beyond the prevailing specific ideology regarding the drug problem in order to gain understanding. As Blum notes in *Society and Drugs*:

> It is a discriminating demonology which posits more devil per drop in some preparations than in others. Aspirin, tobacco, barbiturates and tranquilizers are of little concern, alcohol occupies a middle ground, the amphetamines, which once were of little importance, are now growing worrisome, but it is heroin, cannabis, L.S.D., and other hallucinogens which are deemed most devilish—that is, awesome, seductive, and menacing. Such a discrimination is a bit awkward on strictly pharmacological grounds, but if the characteristics of users and settings are considered, we see that the attribution of menace is linked closely to the degree to which the committed user of each drug advertise their [sic] escape from the fold (Blum 1969).

While there is no significant place for so-called witches today, the same idea exists in illicit drugs. Demons in drugs serve as excuses for otherwise unacceptable actions and states of mind. The power attributed to certain illicit drugs is such that those identified as users are immediately reclassified socially as "heads," "users," or "dopers." The imagery, while largely fabricated, is important in directing attention from the legalized and advertised drugs of the corporate world. Thus, as Blumer states: "The societal definition, and not the objective makeup of a given social condition, determines whether the condition exists as a social problem" (1971).

The specific ideologies for social problems often consist of stereotypes of deviants. In an analysis of stereotypes among the general public, Simmons found:

> The marijuana smoker stereotype emerges as an insecure escapist, lacking self-control and looking for kicks; the beatnik is [a] sloppy, immature nonconformist; the adulterer is immoral, promiscuous, and insecure; the homosexual is perverted and mentally ill; the political radical is ambitious, aggressive, stubborn, and dangerous. The only characteristic imputed frequently to all five types was irresponsible—lacking self-control. All but the radicals were described as lonely and frustrated. Immaturity was encircled by at least some fraction of respondents for each of the types (1965).

It is obvious that such stereotypes are consistent with the general ideology of corporatism. The imagery of "lack of self-control" or "irresponsibility" presents the view of people lacking the willpower and individual qualities necessary to overcome obstacles. At this point it is appropriate to inquire how such images and others are diffused throughout a social order.

Transmission of Ideologies

Proposition 4:   *Both general and specific ideologies are transmitted by organized means of influence.*

Every society has formal or informal ideological organizations or institutions that transmit belief systems. Such are essential to what may be termed the socialization process. In tribal societies, the elders are often responsible for passing on the myths and wisdom that are central to the continuation of that form of social life. In a feudal order, the church or other forms of religious authority play a primary role. In modern industrial societies, the wisdom of the aged and the dogma of the church are no longer the centers of ideological influence (Chambliss and Ryther 1975). The development of formal education, particularly in the twentieth century, is connected historically with the needs of an ever-expanding and centralized corporate economy. The educational institution became a vehicle for transmitting dominant values and beliefs to waves of immigrants and their children. Such concerns, together with the advancing of a form of vocational training for those channeled into blue collar occupations, were and are educational priorities. Today the emphasis on the technical, the routine, and the "useful" is increasingly evident, not simply for the blue collar workers, but for the modern legions of the white collar working class as well (Cohen and Lazerson 1972).

The following critique of "vocationalism" applies well to education in the corporate society:

> After all, the growth system only wants technically competent manpower, not a corps of free-thinking liberal arts graduates. Given mainly technical training, the products should know their place in the system and not harbor any unrealistic aspirations about pursuing a challenging and rewarding career infused with autonomy and opportunity. Everyone can't be on top and most of the work to be done is highly routine; general scientific and social knowledge can only serve to instill unrealistic mobility aspirations and may lead to widespread rebellions against the priorities of the growth system (Anderson 1976, p. 99).

The rise and fall of ideas relating to social problems are of critical importance for this text. It is essential that we understand not simply the content of those belief systems that prevail, but also their origins in social history. In this sense, it is necessary to adopt a *sociology of knowledge* approach to the problem of ideology.

The shaping of ideas becomes crucial in the context of modern technological development. It was C. Wright Mills who argued that "among the means available to power which now prevail is the ability to manage and to manipulate the consent of men" (1963, p. 23). To expand on Mills, the *prevailing* ideas and definitions concerning social problems supposedly triumph in free competition with rival interpretations, analyses, and explanations. However, the importance of ideology is that commonly held beliefs about social problems may also appear so "obviously correct" to both professional sociologists and the general public that no one seriously questions them. In the words of the philosopher Alfred North Whitehead: "There will be some fundamental assumptions which adherents of all the variant systems unconsciously presuppose. Such assumptions appear so obvious that people do not know what they are assuming because no other way of putting things has ever occurred to them" (1949, p. 71). However, we should inquire into the social origins of such "obvious truths." The mass media play a crucial role in the making and shaping of social problems. Our perceptions of the corporate order, the legal system, poverty, minority groups, and illicit drugs are greatly shaped by the *means of influence.* Since many citizens do not have direct and/or continual experience with these phenomena, they rely upon images presented in the mass media. Through viewing police, attorney, and detective series on television, an individual gains an understanding, albeit erroneous, of the legal system, its actors, and the good and bad guys. Such presentations are generally distorted, using mythical characterizations of the nature of police and legal work and of the crime problem and criminals. However, they are significant in shaping and reinforcing definitions of the crime problem and necessary remedies (Henshel and Silverman 1975).

Access to the media and subsequent legitimation is disproportionately in the hands of officialdom. As Ross and Staines note:

> Missile gaps, the threat of communism and domestic subversion are all, as social issues, largely the creatures of the official pronouncement. They are official images of the social order. Officials who wish to control the arena of public discussion may thus follow the symbolic but nonetheless potent strategy of controlling the public agenda, that is, the set of legitimate public issues (1972).

Also important is the ability to marshall coercive forces to influence what is reported.

> The sanctions which the powerful exercise to control media routines may be direct and crude (e.g., threatening speeches, advertising boycotts, antitrust suits against broadcasters) or subtle (e.g., journalism awards, and the encouragement, through regularized interviews, leaks and press conferences of newsroom patterns which inhibit followup, experimentation and deviation (Molatch and Lester 1974).

Those in positions of influence in society have more success in presenting phenomena to audiences for their evaluation and reaction. Those having ready access to the media, for example, politicians, celebrities, business persons, writers, and media personnel have a great deal of influence in presenting potential "social problems" to the general public. By selecting certain phenomena to present and others to neglect, the gatekeepers of ideas manage and manipulate situations to "create" social problems and to "eliminate" other potential problems (Clement 1975).

For example, many citizens in North America appear to accept the following "conventional wisdom" regarding crime:

> Society is becoming more permissive and respect for traditional morals is declining. Evidence of this lies in the fact that the crime rate is increasing and that society deals progressively more leniently with lawbreakers. Sentences are getting lighter and shorter, with rehabilitative measures being substituted for the purely punitive. (Indeed this may be a direct cause of the rising crime rate.) The offender is dealt with progressively more fairly as well. Discrepancies in sentencing are diminishing, owing to a variety of measures, such as legal aid and better training of magistrates. The implications to be drawn from this are obvious. More police are needed to combat rising crime and more severe methods of determining and correcting offenders are needed. Since juvenile delinquency is often the beginning of a criminal career, and juvenile crime is rising especially sharply, particular efforts should be made to apprehend and correct young delinquents before they become established (MacDonald 1969, p. 212).

While such beliefs are widely presented in the mass media by politicians and agents of the legal system, among others, such assumptions may be mythical. McDonald tested the above "conventional wisdom" in Canada and found that between 1950 and 1966 the overall crime rate had not increased (except for trivial infractions), sentences had not become more lenient, nor had disparities in sentencing decreased (1969). Nonetheless, such beliefs persist and are used in the definition of the crime problem, in the allocation of economic and financial resources, and in developing policies and practices in the "war against crime."

The inequities in our society in income, assets, education, health care, social services, and legal protection provide another illustration of the significance of ideology in analyzing phenomena. Those who receive the better services and benefits from our current economic system view such differences as largely a consequence of personal ability, efforts, thrift, motivation, and moral character. While the increasingly accepted liberal view emphasizes "differential opportunity" structures for education and jobs, most of the remedial efforts are directed at changing the individual who is poor and correcting "individual deficiencies." This "poverty" perspective is found in many social problems texts, with the emphasis on describing the poor and their defects and subsequent remedial suggestions such as job training and education. The poverty perspective is also common media fare.

Those taking an inequality approach to the distribution of goods and services critically analyze social structure and the distribution of rewards and goods, with particular emphasis upon the rich and the super rich as part of the problem. Such an approach may indicate the stake the non-poor have in maintaining inequality and poverty. The emphasis in this social-structural perspective is upon all of the economy (Neubeck 1979; Dowd 1977). The inequality perspective is uncommon media fare.

Therefore, the student must critically assess the interests of those perceiving a phenomenon and attempting to make it a social problem and those vying interests that attempt to keep the phenomenon from being designated a social problem. One should look at the person or persons who identify a problem within a specific sociohistorical period and sociocultural context. We should ask which cherished ideological values are being threatened and which are being promoted. While we cannot transcend ideology, we can become aware of the ideological basis of our thinking. We can also become aware of the corporate nature of the modern media industry. For this industry is the molder and shaper of many ideas about social problems.

THE MEANS OF INFLUENCE:
THE MEDIA INDUSTRY

Modern communications technology has advanced to the point where the transmission of ideas is virtually instantaneous and global. But beyond such realities of technique are the questions of power and ideology. For the nature of communications is such that public dialogue, qualification, and alternative viewpoints have largely vanished. (Compare the spectacle of a recent American President holding periodic "town meetings" with the scope and breadth of a presidential news conference that preempts regular programming.)

A formal examination of the media industry must be undertaken with one thought firmly in mind. This industry that trades in the dissemination of ideas is part and parcel of the corporate order. What applies to the general must also hold for the particular. Thus, the structural imperatives identified earlier also apply to the "means of influence."

In an extension of the "reflection hypothesis" (Tuchman 1974), the authors will contend that the means of influence represent not only the structural imperatives, but also the general ideology of the larger corporate order (see Proposition Two). In other words, the mass media will reflect the same essential structural properties and drives as do the petroleum or automotive or other industries. However, what makes the media distinctive is the production of ideas. In an extension of the logic developed earlier, advertising and programming content should also reflect the general ideology of corporatism.

Most people living in Western democracies believe that when media are operated as state monopolies, an obvious threat to the free discourse of ideas exists. It is an intellectual necessity to examine how much we in North America are insulated from the unobstructed exchange of ideas.

> The predominance of private ownership in the broadcast industry does not mean that radio and television are either socially or politically independent of the corporate capitalism that dominates the American economy. Using the reflection hypothesis, one expects to find patterns of ownership within broadcasting that are similar to patterns in other industries. In fact, as in other industries, the ownership-pattern of television stations is one of local monopolies, regional concentrations, multiple ownerships, multi-media ownerships, and conglomerates. Similarly, one might expect to find shared social and political values. (This does not mean that all stations are either Republican or Democrat. Rather, they share elements of corporate philosophies, particularly the drive toward profit.) (Tuchman 1974, p. 3)

What applies to the television industry in particular may apply to the broader media industry in general. Ben H. Bagdikian, a professor of journalism at the University of California at Berkeley and a one-time national news editor for the *Washington Post* declared in a 1978 Federal Trade Commission symposium on media concentration that executives of 100 corporations in the media industry "constitute a private ministry of information and culture for the United States" (Broadcasting 1978). Clement (1975, pp. 287–324) has documented the concentration in the media in Canada, where the Canadian Broadcasting Corporation competes with private corporations. Similar arguments and studies on concentration of the means of influence are numerous (Bagdikian 1971 and 1972; *Editor and Publisher* 1977; Miliband 1969).

We have already examined the reality of "interlocks," the means by which common membership on important boards of directors and other positions of organizational influence serve to link the "higher circles." One such interlock graphically portrays the reflection hypothesis. It involves the Advertising Council (Hirsch 1975), a private nonprofit group responsible for the major share of "public service announcements" broadcast on television and radio, and appearing in the printed media. The Council operates on donations from the corporate sector, foundation grants, and reimbursements from other organizations that sponsor public service campaigns. Its Board of Directors consists of executives from advertising agencies and the broadcasting and publishing world as well as corporation marketing experts. The Advertising Council in 1970 used time and space worth some $460 million. Its ads enable most broadcasters to meet federal government regulations that some time be contributed by the industry in the "public good."

The reflection hypothesis logically leads to the following argument. If interlocks are common in corporate society, then specific interlocks should be evident for the membership of the Advertising Council. An analysis of the 139 members of the Council in 1970 seems to confirm the hypothesis. (As the reader examines the following, it is critical to note that one person may hold membership in the power structure of several different organizations simultaneously, thus representing several "interlocks.")

In summary, Hirsch used two widely available publications to develop a "network" of interlocks. Those members of the Advertising Council appearing in *Who's Who* and/or *Poor's Register of Corporations, Directors and Executives* were identified to determine their "connections" with the following: (1) the businesses listed in the *Fortune* magazine roster of leading corporations and financial institutions; (2) three policy organizations commonly known to play powerful roles in the shaping of domestic and international affairs (the Committee for Economic Development, the Council on Foreign Relations, and the Business Council); (3) major foundations such as the Ford and Rockefeller endowments.

> The results showed the Ad Council, which claims to represent all segments of American society, has two interlocks each with organized labor, education and social welfare groups, and 243 interlocks with the largest corporations and banks. ITT, U.S. Steel, Time-Life, Inc., and First National City Bank are names typical of the Council's connections to the corporate world. . . . The Council is also well tied to the rest of the corporate power structure with almost a third of its membership belonging to at least one of the major policy discussion groups: the CED, the CFR, and the Business Council. The Ford Foundation is represented with four interlocks and the Rockefeller and Carnegie foundations have one each . . . (Hirsch 1975, p. 66).

We shall go on to examine other matters of structure that bear on the question of ideology. However, public service announcements are specifically important because they are supposed to be in the "public interest." Accordingly, one might be well advised to examine such messages closely. The common ideological process converts what Mills refers to as a "public issue" into a "private trouble." In other words, problems of structure are reduced to more restricted levels of analysis. It follows then that individual's faults will be maximized and messages that might implicate or indict corporate order will be largely if not completely absent. Note the following examples: (1) The obsession with timber loss will center on forest fires due to human carelessness rather than clear-cutting practices (cutting all the trees in a stand) by the timber industry. (2) The energy crisis will be blamed on selfish consumers who decline to shiver in their homes or form car pools, rather than on such things as the industrial obsession with growth in energy consumption and the virtual absence of a public transportation system. (3) Environmental assault will be cast along the lines of "People start pollution; only people can stop pollution," in a manner reminiscent of Smokey the Bear's "Only *you* can prevent forest fires." (4) Economic problems will be presented as problems of individuals. Thus, the Ad Council sponsors such messages as "A healthy American economy depends on you." (5) Automobile death and injury will center on the driver or proposed changes to improve road conditions rather than on the safety hazard represented by the machine itself. (6) Accidents, disease, and death arising from the workplace will be blamed on poorly trained or careless workers rather than on unsafe working environments with poor standards and minimal policing.

THE CORPORATE NETWORKS

Turning to the major television networks, it is commonplace to note that CBS, NBC, and ABC are all corporations. However, the *extent* to which they are embedded in corporate America is often overlooked. The historical and financial profile that follows is constructed from *Moody's Industrial Manual* (1979, pp. 83, 334, 335, 868, 2869), Gaye Tuchman's *The Television Establishment* (1974, pp. 1–39), and Ben Bagdikian's *The Information Machines* (1971, pp. 175–181).

NBC

The National Broadcasting Company, Inc., is a wholly owned subsidiary of RCA Corporation. RCA was incorporated in Delaware in 1919 by General Electric Company as the Radio Corporation of America. NBC was established in 1926 to develop radio broadcasting as a vehicle for the sale of radios by its parent corporation.

RCA Corporation is highly diversified with respect to business and products. Though popularly known for radio and television manufacturing, the corporation is heavily engaged in the production of video cassette players, television tubes and parts, semiconductor devices, and closed-circuit video cameras. RCA manufactures electronic equipment for broadcasting and communications purposes, cable television and motion picture equipment, and aviation and navigation devices including radar systems. As a leading government contractor, RCA designs, engineers, and manufactures military and space electronics equipment and systems. Such products include but are not limited to satellite systems, early warning ballistic missile defense systems, and lasers. This type of equipment is also sold to foreign governments.

RCA also manages programs for both the Defense Department and the

National Aeronautics and Space Administration in the United States. Among these programs are the Missile Tracking System for the Air Force's Eastern Test Range; the Navy's Atlantic Underseas Test and Evaluation Center; the Atlantic Fleet Weapons Training Facility and telecommunications operations in Puerto Rico; the Army's White Sands Missile Range and others. An RCA subsidiary both operates and maintains the Ballistic Missile Early Warning System station in Great Britain.

RCA has one or more subsidiaries in Argentina, Australia, Belgium, Brazil, Canada, England, Italy, France, Germany, Spain, Malaysia, Mexico, Puerto Rico, and Taiwan. It therefore qualifies as an important multinational power.

The corporation deals in foods through Banquet Corporation in the United States and Canada and Oriel Foods, Ltd., and Morris and David Jones, Ltd., in Great Britain, all wholly owned subsidiaries. It deals in carpets in both the United States and Canada through Coronet Industries, and publishing through Random House (which publishes under other labels including Alfred A. Knopf, Ballantine Books, Pantheon, Vintage, and Modern Library among others). It rents cars through Hertz (We're Number One) and, last but not least, broadcasts through NBC.

The NBC network is a corporation that serves (as of 1978) 213 television affiliates and 268 radio affiliates in the United States. (A network leases air time from affiliates and then sells that air time to advertisers.) In addition, NBC owns television stations in Chicago, Cleveland, Los Angeles, New York, and Washington, D.C. It has four AM and four FM radio stations located in Chicago, New York, San Francisco, and Washington, D.C. The Federal Communications Commission restricts to five the number of stations that can be owned by a network. However, it is obvious that NBC's stations are in densely populated areas.

As Table 2-1 indicates, RCA's sales and revenue for 1978 totaled in excess of $6.6 billion. Only $1.2 billion of this came from its broadcasting operations.

TABLE 2-1
RCA Sales and Other Revenue (in millions)

Year:	1978	1977	1976
Electronics-consumer products & services	$1,725	$1,500	$1,376
Electronics-communications products & services	839	759	671
Broadcasting	1,215	1,098	955
Vehicle renting & related services	938	837	781
Communication	324	289	259
Government business	524	442	364
Other products and services	1,060	984	942
Other income	19	14	16
TOTAL	$6,644	$5,923	$5,364

Source: *Moody's Industrial Manual* 1979, p. 2869.

CBS

What is now CBS, began as United Independent Broadcasters, in 1927. Although not a subsidiary of a larger corporation, CBS has expanded well beyond broadcasting. It is divided into four groups: CBS/Broadcast, CBS/Records, CBS/Columbia, and CBS/Publishing. The broadcasting group has six divisions. These consist of the *CBS Television Network*, with 200 affiliates in the United States and agreements with the Canadian Broadcasting Corporation and the CTV network to broadcast CBS programming into Canada; the *CBS Entertainment Division*, which is responsible for entertainment programming; the *Sports Division*, which handles athletic events; the *Television Stations Division*, which operates the five CBS-owned television stations; the *Radio Division*, which is responsible for the seven AM and FM radio stations owned by the corporation together with the some 270 affiliated radio stations of the CBS Radio Network; and the *News Division*, which deals in news and public affairs productions.

The television and radio stations are concentrated in excellent broadcasting areas. The former are to be found in New York, Chicago, Philadelphia, St. Louis, and Los Angeles. The latter are found in the same cities plus Boston and San Francisco.

CBS Corporation also numbers among its ventures records (labels include Columbia, Columbia Masterworks, Epic, Odyssey, and Portrait) and music publishing. Through its international division, CBS manufactures and markets records and other products in over twenty countries. The last activity involves a joint venture with SONY Corporation to produce, manufacture, and distribute records and related products in Japan. Other business includes a mail order record and tape club, hobby and craft supplies,[5] musical instruments ranging from Steinway pianos to Fender guitars and amplifiers, specialty audio equipment sold through its 94 Pacific Stereo Stores, toys (Gabriel, Creative Playthings, Child Guidance, Wonder Horsies, Erector, Tinkertoy, and Gym-Dandy). CBS publishes books through Holt, Rinehart and Winston, and its magazines include *Road and Track*, *Cycle World*, *Woman's Day*, *Field and Stream*, and *Mechanix Illustrated*. The corporation is also involved in paperback publishing (Fawcett Crest, Fawcett Gold Medal, and Popular Library), college and university textbooks (W.B. Saunders), and the international distribution of published materials.

As Table 2-2 demonstrates, the revenues for CBS amounted to almost $3.3 billion in 1978, with only some $1.3 billion of this total coming from its broadcasting interests.

---

[5]The CBS involvement in leisure-time activities is revealed in its purchase of the New York Yankees in the mid-1960s. The team was sold in 1973 for $10 million in cash.

**TABLE 2-2
CBS Revenues**

Revenues	1978	1977
Broadcast Group	$1,327.5	$1,183.9
Records Group	946.5	787.7
Columbia Group	598.9	465.5
Publishing Group	442.3	401.6
Other	24.1	30.7
Deletion Of Intergroup Revenues	d49.2	d43.1
TOTAL	$3,290.1	$2,826.3

Source: *Moody's Industrial Manual* 1979, p. 335.

ABC

The broadcasting corporation now known as American Broadcasting Companies, Inc., was formed in 1949 as United Paramount Theatres, Inc. United Paramount Theatres came into existence because of a successful antitrust suit brought against Paramount Pictures by the Department of Justice. As a result of this suit, Paramount could not both produce motion pictures and own the theatres in which they might be viewed. The name of the corporation was changed in 1953 to American Broadcasting-Paramount Theatres, Inc. The present name of the corporation was approved in 1965.

The business activities of ABC center around broadcasting. However, the corporation is also engaged in publishing and leisure-time activities. In 1978, the ABC Network included a total of 200 television affiliates and 1,596 radio stations. It owns five television stations operating in the attractive market areas of New York, Chicago, San Francisco, Los Angeles, and Detroit. The company also has radio stations in the same cities plus Houston and Washington, D.C. In addition, ABC has interests in a number of foreign broadcasting companies.

In the field of publishing, ABC produces a number of agricultural publications for farmers, several specialized law service magazines, as well as leisure magazines such as *Modern Photography* and *High Fidelity*. Through its subsidiary, Word Inc., ABC publishes religious books and materials. Word also produces and distributes records, tapes, and music. Also through its subsidiaries ABC publishes magazines dealing with industrial/technical activities and woodworking, and puts out multiple listing/service books for realtors. In yet another area the corporation owns outdoor recreational concerns in Florida (Weeki Wachee Spring, Silver Springs, and Wild Waters), as well as the ABC Entertainment Center in Los Angeles.

Despite its diversification, ABC receives most of its revenues from broadcasting. In 1978, the corporation had sales of approximately $1.8 billion, with 87 percent of the total coming from this source. This is not to imply, however, that 13 percent of this (or any other) corporation's business is unimportant.

The Structure of the Broadcast Networks

The ventures of the broadcasting industry represented by the major networks show dramatically that NBC/RCA, CBS, and ABC are indeed of the corporate world. The nature of their holdings indicates that the networks have a clear and compelling interest in federal defense and space expenditures, the promotion of leisure-time activities and music (especially that requiring electrical instruments and amplification systems), and the support of the private automobile.

Beyond such apparent vested interests are far more important structural concerns. First of all, taken as a whole, the broadcasting giants examined here are more than electronic leviathans. RCA Corporation only does some 18 percent of its business through its broadcasting subsidiary, NBC. CBS receives only some 39 percent of its revenues from broadcasting. The exception, as mentioned, is the smallest network, ABC, which also has substantial holdings in other areas. *Such a reality raises grave doubts about the capacity of this industry of ideas to examine freely and critically the corporate order and its general ideology.*

Another structural concern has to do with the multinational nature of the broadcasting element of the "means of influence." Network news and public affairs programming represent a platform for the presentation of global views. International affairs frequently revolve around political and economic movements that represent ideologies clearly hostile to corporate interests. (For example, mass-based movements are often directed toward freeing a local economy from foreign domination.) Corporations by their nature must be concerned with profitability abroad. Can they be expected to sponsor programming that is neutral, much less sympathetic, toward anticorporate social change?

The list of holdings also confirms that the broadcasting industry is increasingly engaged in publishing. Together with the ownership of television and radio stations in major markets, this trend represents growing power in the shaping of ideas. Of greater importance of course is the dependence of their affiliates on the major networks. Unless a television station wishes to endure the expense of producing its own programming, it will sell time to the networks. Thus, the world view of network corporation executives will be the standard for programming in North America.

Network profits are naturally dependent on the selling of time leased from affiliates to advertisers. Advertising has always been defined as a means of selling a product. It is, of course, a massive industry (as noted earlier) and the competition among broadcasters, printed media, and direct mail concerns is intense. However, advertising represents more than a means of promoting products. Any criticism of this particular industry must go beyond artistic annoyance or even the observation that Madison Avenue urges conspicuous consumption in a day of increasing resource scarcity. The structural point to be made is that advertising is a means by which the very ideology of corporatism is advanced. Frequently, corporate advertisers are openly selling the corporate order. Major petrocorporations claim to be conscious of the environment, committed to conservation, and working to develop domestic oil supplies despite "governmental interference." Huge conglomerates (highly diversified corporations) sing the virtues of free competition, and a millionaire comedian proudly proclaims that the corporation that is working to keep our trust is really owned by "just us folks" (see "Viewpoint" for Chapter Three). These and similar claims will be examined in the following chapters. However, the reality of advertising dollars means that "programming [is] a tool with which to sell the audience to advertisers" (Tuchman 1974, p. 7). It follows that (1) programming in the corporate order will be a commodity like any other, with little or no attention given to the public interest; and (2) programming content that is offensive to advertisers, who in effect are paying for it, will seldom be tolerated.

The nature of broadcast content, according to defenders of the media establishment, is dependent on the wishes of the viewer. Like any other commodity, the success of programming is supposedly dependent on its popularity with the consumer in the marketplace. Media scholars, however, question this view.

> One of the myths about American television is that it operates as a cultural democracy, wholly responsible to the will of the viewing majority in terms of the programs that survive or fade. More aptly in the area of entertainment, mainly, it is a cultural oligarchy ruled by a consensus of the advertising community. . . . In truth, programs of great popularity go off the air, without regard for the viewers' bereavement, if the kinds of people it reaches are not attractive to advertisers (Brown 1974, p. 98).

As Brown points out, stockholders in the broadcasting industry are not prone to inquire as to the quality of the programming; rather they are concerned with larger profits. It follows that programming that has been around for a while (and thus is increasingly expensive) and directed toward lower-income members of the audience (such as the aging) tends to disappear despite popularity. Specific examples in the United States would include Red Skelton, Jackie Gleason, and Lawrence Welk (who when dropped by ABC, syndicated his own show and attracted such sponsors as Geritol for tired blood and Rose Milk for tired skin). By the same logic, golf and tennis receive television coverage far in excess of their mass appeal. Such sports, of course, appeal to the "right" segment of the market.

This is not to say that ratings do not exist. The primary company in the field is Nielsen, which attaches a mechanical device to a supposedly representative sample of 1,500 televisions, provides those in the selected households with viewing diaries, and by these methods determines how many are watching. Ratings have been attacked on the basis of sample bias in that paradoxically both black (Brown 1974) and better-educated viewers (Tuchman 1974) appear strongly underrepresented. Also, as demonstrated above, good ratings do not necessarily save a show, nor do poor ones inevitably put an end to one. However, the belief in consumer influence is deficient for more important reasons. For *the measure of power is not the choice from among limited alternatives, but the ability to fix the range of such alternatives*. If the choice of programming is only among shades of mediocrity, the choice appears meaningless. As Brown succinctly notes, "The viewer is not the customer but only the consumer of television" (1974, p. 96). The customer with the clout is corporate America, even though corporate advertising costs can be expected to be passed on to the consumers.

If one doubts the influence of the "phantom audience," what about federal regulation? Policing of the networks is the charge of the Federal Communications Commission. The structural relationship between this agency of the state and the broadcasting industry is open to question. Tuchman argues (1974) that the FCC has a "cozy" relationship with the networks and accordingly is a practitioner of "symbolic politics," meaning that regulation is more a matter of image than substance. To be specific, this bureaucracy has traditionally addressed issues raised by the industry. For example, VHF (very high frequency) stations were established before the coming of UHF (ultra high frequency) technology. The VHF stations were primarily network affiliates. The coming of UHF meant that more stations could broadcast in a community. However, the VHF stations complained that excessive competition would not allow the industry to pursue the public interest. Rather the emphasis would be on crass commercialism. The FCC put a halt to the licensing of the UHF competitors, an action that ensured that VHF network affiliates would control local markets. After the FCC moved to grant licenses to UHF stations, the position of such newcomers was one of extreme economic disadvantage (Krasnow and Longley 1973, pp. 19–20).

Another dimension of the structural argument has to do with the interchange between the broadcasting industry and the commissioners of the FCC. The broadcast industry, politics, the military, and prior staff service with the FCC are commonly represented in the backgrounds of those charged with the regulation of television and radio. Upon leaving government service, commissioners frequently find their way into the broadcast industry (Tuchman 1974, p. 10). Such an arrangement, common for regulatory agencies and the industries they are supposed to "watchdog," might well be characterized as a form of political incest.

A final point is in order concerning the interlocking directorates of the television industry. A subcommittee staff study of the Committee on Governmental Affairs, United States Senate, released in January 1978, addressed the question of interlocking among major United States corporations. This study made use of computer-based analysis of the directorates of the 130 companies that in 1976 were the largest firms in their fields. These included industrials, commercial banks, life insurance companies, diversified financial companies, retailers, transportation companies, utilities, and investment advisory companies. Together, their assets totaled over $1 trillion, an amount equal to some 25 percent of the total corporate assets of the United States (United States Senate, Committee on Governmental Affairs 1978, p. 28).

Focusing specifically on the three media giants RCA, CBS, and ABC, the staff report contains important data bearing on the structure of these corporations. RCA/NBC represents a total of 43 direct interlocks with other corporations and elite organizations. (See Figure 2-2.) The number of direct interlocks for CBS and ABC were thirty-nine and twenty-nine, respectively. Expanding the network analysis to indirect interlocks,[6] the numbers are 192, 146, and 112, respectively (United States Senate, Committee on Governmental Affairs 1978, pp. 297–99, 368–71, 749–53).

THE BEST NEWS MONEY CAN BUY[7]

Before turning from an examination of the means of influence, it is necessary to focus on the power of the press. At an earlier point in history, one would not expect to receive an argument when citing the abuse of the printed word. At the turn of the century, a form of "yellow journalism" prevailed. Sensationalism, innuendo, and frequent fabrication were abundant newspaper fare. One of the more captivating examples of this involved the publishing empire of William Randolph Hearst.

> For more than fifteen years after 1911, the elder Hearst used all his communications agencies to provoke a war between Mexico and the United States. His papers ran such headlines as: MEXICO PREPARES FOR WAR WITH THE U.S. He owned the International

---

[6]Direct interlocks mean that a director sits on another corporate board. Indirect interlocks mean that two corporations may not be directly interlocked, but each has a member on a third corporate board.

[7]"The Best News Money Can Buy" is Ben Bagdikian's term.

Figure 2-2. Graphic Prepared by Jennie Oesterreicher and Patti Jones, Eastern Washington University

DIRECT INTERLOCK$

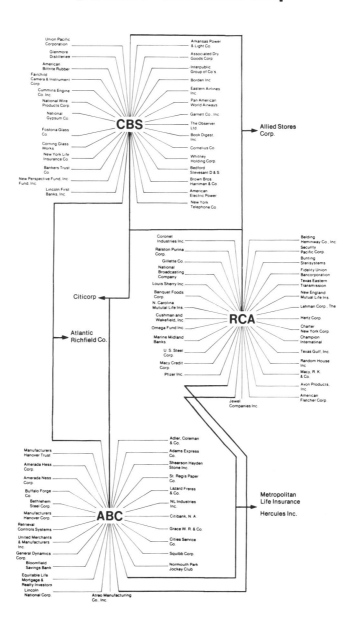

Film Service, which made films about the Mexican plots to overthrow the American government. In the 1920s he ran in all Hearst
papers a spectacular series based on documents showing that Mexico
had bribed four United States senators with $1,115,000.

Most Hearst readers had no way of knowing that the Hearst family
owned 2,500 square miles of Mexican mines, timber, chicle, and
ranches that were threatened with government seizure (Bagdikian
1972, p. 65).

The bribery charges were untrue, and Hearst was unsuccessful in culti-
vating a war with Mexico. However, this episode is cited here to make a
point. When examining the press, it is important not to focus on such
flagrant abuses as yellow journalism. More important are structural
issues: specifically, the nature of ownership and the more subtle transmission of general ideology.

The concentration of press ownership in the United States displays a
trend similar to that evident in the broadcasting industry. The prevailing
form is one of transcontinental "group"[8] ownership of newspapers. In
short, giant newspaper chains are being forged to create what *Editor and
Publisher* (July 9, 1977) refers to as a "nationwide federation of dailies."

The statistical evidence of group ownership in recent history confirms
increasing concentration. In 1970, a total of 157 groups owned 879
papers, an average of 5.6 per group. As of 1976, the average had risen to
6.3, with 167 groups owning some 1,047 daily newspapers. In other
words, the number of group-owned dailies grew from approximately 50
percent to almost 60 percent of the total in six years. Group-owned dailies
accounted for 71 percent of the nation's 61 million weekday circulation
and 78 percent of the 52 million Sunday and weekend sales in 1976. A
more striking picture of newspaper ownership is possible if one examines
only those groups with circulation in excess of 500,000. Typical of corporate society, wealth and potential influence are concentrated at the
top. As the following list makes clear, in 1976 the 22 groups representing
only 13 percent of all groups (167) had a circulation of almost 30 million,
approximately one-half the total circulation (61 million).

In 1976, the number of independents not affiliated with groups
amounted to 615 dailies. The most attractive of these continue to be pursued by groups. "Attractive" means that groups are not interested in acquiring newspapers in cities where there exists real competition for the
circulation and advertising markets. At the time of this overview of
newspaper ownership, there were only thirty-seven cities in the United
States which represented competitive markets (*Editor and Publisher*
1977, p. 11).

In the summer of 1979, *Gannett* acquired the Cincinnati *Enquirer* and

[8]Groups were at one time referred to as "chains." The latter term is superior in that it
graphically captures the connections of various dailies.

TABLE 2-3
Newspaper Groups Ranked According to Circulation
(aggregate weekday circulations of more than 500,000)

Knight-Ridder	3,681,301	Thomson	935,460
Newhouse	3,204,212	Pulliam	758,692
Tribune (Chicago)	3,099,120	News (Detroit)	665,542
Gannett	2,771,936	News America	645,570
Scripps Howard	1,894,962	Freedom	635,307
Times Mirror	1,879,870	Washington Post	602,818
Dow Jones	1,782,622	Copley	601,019
Hearst	1,435,527	McLean	586,294
Cox	1,179,370	Cowles	564,144
New York Times	975,255	Media General	545,142
Capital Cities	949,935	Harte Hanks	543,263

Note: In most cases the figures are net paid averages as of September 30, 1976.
Gannett Co. has reported that 1977 circulation is near 3 million. Other groups have
had gains also.
Source: *Editor and Publisher,* July 9, 1977.

the Oakland (California) *Tribune* with a combined circulation of some 355,000. These acquisitions, among others, propelled *Gannett* past *Knight-Ridder* into position as the largest newspaper chain in the United States (*Time* 1980, p. 93). The following list of Gannett's subsidiaries (exclusive of the *Enquirer* and *Tribune*) provides evidence of the scope of group ownership. Similar documentation can be had for the holdings of the other giants in Table 2-4.

The interests of printed media giants are not confined to newspaper ownership. *Knight-Ridder* owns and operates Commodity News Service, Inc., a commodity wire service that provides market news by teletype to analysts, brokers, and traders. In addition, this firm owns three television stations (*Moody's Industrial Manual* 1979, p. 2546). *Newhouse* owns both television and radio stations in St. Louis; Birmingham, Alabama; Harrisburg, Pennsylvania; and Syracuse and Elmira, New York. Mr. Newhouse also has an interest in Conde-Nast Publications, which publishes *Vogue, House & Garden, Glamour, Bride,* and *Mademoiselle* (*Broadcasting Yearbook* 1979, p. A-51).

In addition to newspaper and broadcasting interests, *Times Mirror* publishes law and medical books, telephone directories, audiovisual materials, and various magazines. The company also operates cable television systems in California and New York and owns lumber and plywood plants in Washington, Oregon, and California. Its subsidiaries own 265,000 acres of timberland (*Moody's* 1979, p. 4295).

Dow Jones is perhaps best known for its *Wall Street Journal.* It also publishes *Barron's National Business and Financial Weekly,* a well-regarded guide to the business and industrial world. The company also operates both the *Dow Jones News Service* in the United States and the *Canadian Dow Jones News Service.* It also markets *Dow Vue,* which

Table 2-4
Gannett Newspapers

Binghamton Press Co. (N.Y.)	News-Press Publishing Co. (Fla.)
Cape Publications (Fla.)	News Printing Co. (Pa.)
*Chillicothe Newspapers (Ohio)	Niagara Falls Gazette Publishing Corp. (N.Y.)
Citizen Publishing Co. (Ariz.)	Northwestern Publishing Co. (Ill.)
Courier-News Co. (N.J.)	Oklahoma Press Publishing Co. (Okla.)
Elmira Star-Gazette (N.Y.)	*Pacific Media (Del.)
El Paso Times (Tex.)	Palladium Publishing Corp. (Ind.)
Empire Newspaper Supply Corp. (Del.)	Pensacola News-Journal (Fla.)
*Fairpress (Conn.)	*Political Analysis (Del.)
Federated Publications (Del.)	*Press-Citizen Co. (Ia.)
*5KW (Ohio)	*Reno Newspapers (Nev.)
*Fort Collins Newspapers (Colo.)	Rockford Newspapers (Del.)
Fremont Messenger Co. (Ohio)	St. Cloud Newspapers (Minn.)
*Fremont Newspapers (Neb.)	Salinas Newspapers (Cal.)
Gannett Florida Corp. (Fla.)	The Saratogian (N.Y.)
Gannett Louisiana (La.)	*Sioux Falls Newspapers (S.D.)
Gannet Newspaper Advertising Sales (Del.)	Speidel Newspapers (Del.)
Gannett News Service (Del.)	Southern New Jersey Newspapers (N.J.)
Gannett Pacific Corp. (Del.)	Springfield Newspapers (Mo.)
*Guam Publications (Hawaii)	*Springair (Mo.)
*Hawaii Newspaper Agency (Hawaii) 55% owned	The Statesman-Journal Co. (Ore.)
Huntington Publishing Co. (W. Va.)	*Stockton Newspapers (Cal.)
Ithaca-Journal News (N.Y.)	*Suburban Newspaper Group (N.J.)
Louis Harris and Associates (Del.)	Sun Co. of San Bernardino, Cal. (Cal.)
*Louis Harris International (N.Y.)	The Times Company (Ohio)
McClure Newspapers (Del.)	Times Herald Co. (Mich.)
Nashville Banner Publishing Co. (Tenn.)	*Times Enterprises (Tex.)
*National Research Center for the Arts (Del.)	The Times Publishing Co. (La.)
New Mexican (N.M.)	Tucson Newspapers (Ariz.) (50% owned)
The News-Journal Co. (D.C.)	Utica Observer-Dispatch (N.Y.) (96.6% owned)
*Newspaper Printing Corp. (Tex.) (50% owned)	*Valley of the Sun (Ariz.)
*Newspaper Printing Corp. (Tenn.) (50% owned)	Visalia Newspapers (Cal.)
*Newspaper Production Corp. (L.A.) (75% owned)	Westchester Rockland Newspapers (N.Y.)
*Newspaper Reality Corp. (Tex.) (50% owned)	WHEC (N.Y.)

*Owned by subsidiary of Company.
Source: *Moody's Industrial Manual* 1979, p. 737.

displays Dow Jones news and stock quotations on a television-like screen. Through a joint venture with the Associated Press, Dow Jones operates international news services that serve clients in thirty-four countries. Other joint ventures put Dow Jones into the publication of English-language newspapers in Hong Kong; the most prominent of these being the *Asian Wall Street Journal* (*Moody's* 1979, p. 1615).

For many years earlier in the century, the publishing empire founded by William Randolph Hearst was the largest of the "chains," consisting of twenty-six weekday and seventeen Sunday papers (*Editor and Publisher* 1977, p. 10). Today, in addition to its newspaper holdings, the *Hearst Corporation* publishes and distributes magazines and books; owns and deals in antiques and objects of art; produces both news film and motion pictures; and owns three television and three radio stations. Hearst also does business in real estate, ranching, and timberlands, and distributes periodicals and books in Canada (*Directory of Corporate Affiliates* 1979, pp. 441–42).

Though the newspaper circulation of Cox Broadcasting Corporation does not belong in the same league with Gannett, the company is heavily involved in broadcasting and other communications enterprises. Cox owns five VHF television stations together with five AM and seven FM radio stations in prime markets. A subsidiary of this corporation operates cable television systems in seventeen states. Also through subsidiaries, the corporation publishes trade magazines, produces motion pictures, and operates car auctions on behalf of automobile dealers and car rental and leasing companies (*Broadcasting Yearbook* 1979, p. A-48).

The concentration of media ownership and control gives rise logically to an absence of ideological diversity. The "same old gang" may well present the "same old thing." Nor are such conditions confined to the United States. In Canada, the problem of increasing media power parallels developments described above. Clement (1975, pp. 287–325), in his examination of the structure and concentration of Canada's newspapers and broadcasting industry, cites the report of the Canadian Senate Committee on Mass Media. The Senate report confirmed a trend toward fewer and fewer owners. This is well exemplified in the finding that competition between or among rival newspapers was absent in all save *five* Canadian cities. At the turn of the century there were some thirty-five cities in Canada with two or more dailies. Seven decades later, that number had dropped to fifteen and in five of these the two papers had the same owner. The following table indicates the great control of newspapers in each province by newspaper groups.

Given the somewhat parallel political and economic histroy of the two countries, together with the development of a continental corporate order, it should come as no surprise to find such broad-scale development of group ownership in Canadian society. Thus, according to the report cited above, 66.4 percent of 116 daily newspapers were group owned as

TABLE 2–5
Percentage of Circulation Controlled by
Newspaper "Groups" in Canada, 1970

British Columbia	95%	Quebec (French)	50.6%
Alberta	95	(English)	97.5
Saskatchewan	100	New Brunswick	92.7
Manitoba	88.3	Prince Edward Island	72.6
Ontario	75.9	Nova Scotia	9.0
		Newfoundland	81.1

Source: *Senate Report on Mass Media,* cited in Wallace Clement, *The Canadian Corporate Elite,* The Carleton Library No. 89, Toronto: McClelland and Stewart, 1975.

were 48.5 percent of 97 private television stations and 47.4 percent of private radio stations. As in the United States, federal licensing policy is supposed to reduce or remove excessive competition, which allegedly frees the media industry to better pursue the public interest. However, it actually guarantees a monopoly.

> In the case of newspapers, the circulation wars of yesteryear have created monopoly or near-monopoly situations which now confer large benefits on the survivors. In other words, what the forces of accumulation and concentration did in publishing years ago, the forces of government "regulation" have been able to accomplish for broadcasting today (Clement 1975, p. 289).

As in the United States, the availability of capital is necessary for expansion and expansion involves buying out those segments of the media industry that are capital deficient. Consistent with other economic sectors, growth and large-scale technologies favor large, capital-sufficient organizations. What follows is the movement toward media concentration in corporate society. Other factors also benefit those at the top of the Canadian pinnacle. For example, circulation warfare among newspapers in Canada has historically favored those interests of sufficient size and resources to endure losses in the short run in order to eliminate the competition. Further, the media industry is no exception to the corporate law that the rich get richer. In 1970, 8.4 percent of a total 221 radio stations (separate from television interests) had 69 percent of the revenue. Of the twenty-nine television stations (separate from radio), 27.6 percent had 92 percent of the revenue. A mere 4 percent of the 545 printing and publication firms (those with revenues in excess of $25,000) had 63.7 percent of the total revenue for all firms (Clement 1975, pp. 289–90).

IDEOLOGICAL HEGEMONY

Antonio Gramsci (1971) argues that the potential power of ideology is such that one major concept of life, thought, and reality becomes the single basis for social institutions and relationships. Gramsci's work on *hegemony* (literally, dominance) was to some extent shaped by the work of Marx and Engels (1947, p. 39) on the *German Ideology*. The two nineteenth-century authors had developed the argument that those ideas that favored the interests of a *ruling class* would tend to dominate the world of ideas.

More recently, David Sallach (1974) has held that the primary ideological institutions of a society are heavily influenced by those who represent "privileged access." The "hegemonic process" results in the elimination of alternative views on social order. According to this author, the controlling interests in a society limit debate, primarily by means of early childhood education and the mass media.

While thought provoking, such conceptions of ideological control leave important questions unanswered. It might be argued that Gramsci's view of a single concept of life is overdrawn. It might also be accurate to suggest that Marx centered heavily on the nineteenth-century world of formal knowledge (philosophy and social criticism) and the role played by privileged intellectuals in maintaining the existing order. Sallach's work, like that of his predecessors, is theoretically promising and empirically disappointing.

While the term hegemony faces the constant danger of being made absolute and trivial, the argument of a dominant ideology cannot simply be dismissed. Before a general ideology can be identified as prevailing (heavily influential, if not dominant) because of the power of those at the top, a rigorous examination of the nature of the ideological institutions of class society must be undertaken. Our preliminary effort has shown that the corporate organization of the North American communications revolution provides a necessary structural condition for hegemony. *If the existence of concentration and the elimination of competitors is a threat to the marketplace, how much more is the concentration and elimination of ideas a clear and present danger to a democratic society?*

THE MAKING AND SHAPING OF SOCIAL PROBLEMS

Proposition 5:   *The emergence, institutionalization, and maintenance of social problems occur in an ideological context that is both general and specific.*

This final proposition is in part a summary of the previous four. All of the earlier propositions are necessary to our understanding of an ideological context. Before we examine the history of social problems, we must understand the nature of corporate structure, general ideology, specific ideology, and the means of influence. That understanding is fundamental to making use of ideology to comprehend why some problems are recognized and others ignored; why some explanations are readily accepted and others are not; and why certain "solutions" are embraced and others rejected.

Given our understanding of corporate structure, idea-systems, and the means of influence, it is now possible to identify a historical process that shows the ideological making and shaping of social problems. As with any "ideal type," not all phenomena identified as social problems will neatly "fit." Nor are the phases that constitute the process sequential in an absolute sense. By this we mean that our phases cannot be neatly superimposed on history. One "stage" will not be represented by a certain period of years, to be followed by another historically specific stage, and so forth. A processual viewpoint sees social problems in a constant stage of becoming. Thus, phases will be often interdependent and overlapping.

Our historical model has three fairly distinct phases. First, within an already existing world of ideas (ideological context), there will be groups and movements working to gain recognition for a problem that concerns them. Because of the influence of the general and specific ideologies discussed earlier, such movements and interest groups will tend to act in ways that are consistent with these prevailing ideas. This part of the process is termed *emergence*. Next, it is necessary to consider what happens after a problem is "born," or emerges. Those movements or interest groups that are successful will have their aims and objectives formally recognized in such things as laws, policies, and public programs. This phase of the natural history model is here termed *institutionalization*. Finally, after such official recognition, we should expect to see those who benefit from the "problem" working to continue its recognition. This final phase can be called *maintenance*.

Emergence

The birth of a "social problem" is not a spontaneous response to "evil." A problem emerges ideologically as its makers work to mobilize followers, garner public support, and above all gain access to the means of influence. Behind this coming of the problem are organized forces that assume one of two basic forms: the social movement and the interest group.

Social movements consist in the banding together of persons intent on changing or defending an existing aspect of the social order. Movements have a fully developed imagery that depicts what is "right" and what is "wrong" and display organization, leadership, planning, and continuity over time. With organization come goals, a hierarchy of membership, and some potential for formal institutionalization of the aims and purposes of the movement (Genevie 1978, pp. xvii, xx).

Oberschall addresses the mobilization of a social movement as follows:

> The minimum conditions of collective protest are shared targets and objects of hostility held responsible for grievances, hardship, and suffering, augmented in some cases by more deeply rooted sentiments of collective oppression, common interests and community of fate. These minimum conditions give rise, however, to only short-

term, localized, ephemeral outbursts and movements of protest such as riots. For sustained resistance or protest an organizational base and continuity of leadership are also necessary (1973, p. 119).

Thus a movement requires an organizational base, that is, a social foundation allowing for the systematic development of movement, aims, and ideology, and the direction of collective action toward movement objectives. To clarify, the organizational base might consist of those who share similar occupational, economic, religious, ethnic, tribal, or sexual standing in the social order. Given the organizational base, together with the sentiments of common oppression, suffering, and/or unrealized aspirations, the potential for mobilization is evident. However, the aims and objectives of organized movements are not forged in an ideological vacuum. Movements working to bring about recognition and action regarding a particular social problem are shaped by the general ideology or by the relevant specific ideologies that prevail. What is meant by "organization base" and "ideological influence" can be captured in a single example. As detailed in Chapter Four, the trade union movement in the United States and Canada had as its organizational base the various workers' unions that were organized around specific trade occupations. This movement was able to gain formal recognition from corporate and state leaders. However, success had its price. Those leading the particular form of the union movement that prevailed confined the objectives of organized labor to "pure and simple" issues, namely, wages, hours, and working conditions. They left to owners and their managers the day-by-day control of the workplace and the broader economic order. By this arrangement, those elements of the movement calling for control of the workplace by labor, or workplace democracy, were effectively neutralized.

The relative stability and formalization of social movements make them more effective in creating and maintaining a social problem than the more elementary forms of collective behavior, such as mobs, riots, and vocal crowds. Turner and Killian's definition seems appropriate: "A social movement is a collectivity acting with some continuity to promote a change or resist a change in the society or group of which it is a part" (1972). This definition allows for those movements attempting to *maintain* the status quo, a distinction not made explicit in other definitions (Long and Long 1961; Blumer 1969).

In a recent review of definitions of social movements, Killian notes that

> . . . these definitions have two features in common. Central to all is the effort of men to intervene in the process of social and cultural change. Most of them emphasize the goal of bringing into being new social and cultural forms. Turner and Killian also include efforts to resist changes which appear imminent. But in either case, men are viewed as actors, not as passive responders to the flow of culture or the homeostatic tendencies of the social system. Also

essential to those definitions is the notion that the men's acts are collective. They are not the discrete activities of so many scattered individuals, but of people acting together with a sense of engaging in a collective enterprise (1973, p. 15).

Some analyses of the importance of social movements in creating specific social problems have been attempted. Such phenomena as pornography, prostitution, juvenile delinquency, the befouled environment, drugs, and open housing have been tied to the emergence of "moral crusades."[9] However, these studies are seldom if ever structural in scope. Consequently, the importance of class, ideology, and conflict are overlooked.

An important aspect of many social movements is the leadership structure. Becker has suggested that "moral entrepreneurs" are significant in advancing certain phenomena as social problems. Such individuals, by virtue of their initiative, political power, access to decision makers, skillful use of publicity, and success in neutralizing any opposition, are able to translate their interests into public policy and programs. Becker points to the example of the Marijuana Tax Act as largely a product of "moral entrepreneurs," specifically, Harry Anslinger as head of the Federal Bureau of Narcotics (1966). Of course, an individual does not need to be the head of a government bureaucracy to be a moral entrepreneur. For example, in the first two decades of the twentieth century, Dr. Charles B. Towns was a major figure in bringing about legislation restricting drug use. As one biographical article notes: "Towns looked about him and saw a world sodden with alcohol, dazed with drugs, and befuddled with tobacco." As Towns himself observed, "It is a queer business I'm in—this straightening out of moral kinds" (Mervin 1912). Moral entrepreneurs have been a significant force in the making and shaping of the drug problem (Musto 1973; Geshen 1973; Sonders 1971; Reasons 1974).

The emergence of a social problem is not always directly related to a formal, organized social movement. Frequently, organized interest groups that have already attained legitimacy and recognition play key roles in the emergence phase. By organized interest group we mean those

[9]See Louis A. Zurcher, Jr., R. George Kirkpatrick, Robert G. Cushing, and Charles K. Bowman, "The Anti-Pornography Campaign: A Symbolic Crusade," *Social Problems* 19 (Fall) 1971:217–38; Joseph R. Gusfield, *Symbolic Crusade: Status Politics and American Temperance Movement*, Urbana, Ill.: University of Illinois Press, 1966; Louis Filler, *Crusades for American Liberalism*, Yellow Springs, Ohio: The Antioch Press, 1950; Anthony M. Platt, *The Child Savers: The Invention of Delinquency*, Chicago: The University of Chicago Press, 1969; R. Smith, "Status Politics and the Image of the Addict," *Issues in Criminology* 2(Fall) 1966:157–75; Arnold H. Taylor, *American Diplomacy and the Narcotics Traffic, 1900–1939: A Study in International Humanitarian Reform*, Durham, North Carolina: Duke University, 1960; Juliet Z. Saltman, *Open Housing as a Social Movement: Challenge, Conflict and Change*, Lexington, Mass.: P.C. Heath and Company, 1971; Armand L. Mauss, ed., *Social Problems as Social Movements*, Philadelphia: J. B. Lippincott Company, 1975.

sharing a common cause who seek to influence the representatives of political and economic power. According to David Riesman (1961), "veto groups" such as farm, labor, professional, racial, and ethnic organizations are able to mobilize public opinion and influence those in power to recognize what these groups perceive as a "problem." Riesman argues, we believe unconvincingly, that such groups have the power to veto, or block, definitions and courses of action that might do substantial harm to their interests. To the contrary, the preponderance of evidence assembled throughout this text should cause one to question seriously the belief that political power is widely dispersed among competing interest groups.

Interest groups do exist and they do contribute to the ideological making and shaping of social problems. However, the *extent* to which their definitions of problems *coincide* with the broader interests and general ideology of the corporate society determines their success. For example, the American Medical Association has played an important role historically in the blocking of national health care in the United States. However, the interests of the AMA are highly consistent with the specific interests of the medical and insurance industries in particular and the broader nature of corporate structure and ideology. To be explicit, the AMA considers medical service to be the "private property" of the physician, who should be free to determine his or her own fees in the marketplace. This position is not unlike that of Exxon Corporation on energy.

There are other obvious forces at work in the making and shaping of social problems. The emergence of a problem need not await the coming of a social movement or organized interest group. Those intimately tied to the corporate and political order, who command the center of the public stage, are in a position either to define a problem directly or heavily influence the reasons we give for those that cannot be denied. For example, no one could successfully deny the economic problem of inflation. People are daily reminded of the decreasing value of the dollar. However, corporate ideology can work directly through the mass media. Thus, we are led to account for inflation by blaming the undisciplined demands of the consumer or "wasteful" government spending on social programs, rather than addressing the increasing corporate power to manipulate supply, artificially create needs through advertising, and raise prices at will in a decreasingly competitive economy.

Institutionalization

In the second phase of the history of a social problem, institutionalization occurs. Institutionalization usually is evidenced by the passing of laws and/or the creation of specific bodies to deal with the disorder. Such actions confirm the success of the forces discussed above in the establishment of their definition of the social problem as *the* definition of the social problem. This official description legitimates a particular perspective on the phenomenon and shuts off opposing perspectives. Through such means as executive order, legislative decision, and city council action, certain definitions are legitimated.

For example, the matter of dealing with Native people has in many respects been quite similar in Canada and the United States (Mickenberg 1971). Historically, the cornerstone of the policies of both countries has been assimilation, that is the "Indian problem" would be solved by making them like whites (Smith 1975; Cohen and Mause 1968). The moral premise of such a policy has been noted by Smith:

> This moral premise takes a variety of forms, but in general terms it states that Indians who choose to live an Indian style of life are to be considered "uncivilized." They are therefore culturally and morally different from British subjects and therefore require special legislation, among other things, for (a) their protection from (particularly unscrupulous) others, (b) for the restraint of moral vices, and (c) to regulate their passage from an "uncivilized" to a "civilized state" (1975, xvii).

Since Native peoples have had little or no power in defining the nature of their relationship with whites, white interests are dominant in legislation and policies affecting them. Such relationships have been institutionalized as the "Indian problem" through various treaties and laws. For example, in Canada:

> The Indian Act regulates almost totally the life-styles, both as individuals and communities, of those 250,000 status Indians on reserves. The misguided policy behind this legislation is twofold: first, the Indian is viewed as incapable of managing his own affairs, and therefore benevolent paternalism is essential; and secondly, the values, culture and life-style of native persons are looked upon as inferior to those of non-native society. It is apparent, therefore, that the Indian Act serves as a mechanism to assimilate the native person into non-native society. The effect of the Indian Act upon four generations has been to virtually destroy Indian culture and identity. The colonial administration and legal framework on the reserve has rigorously imposed the non-native [culture] at every level of significant community and individual decision-making, such as in respect to local government and the use of monies or the use of lands. This has resulted in the virtual destruction of the Indian people (Cumming 1973, p. 243).

Such domination and control by whites over Indians is evident in the United States as well. Given the relative powerlessness of Indians historically and contemporarily, their interests were not incorporated into the institutionalization of white-Indian relationships. Increasingly, Indian people have challenged the ability and legitimacy of whites to define and run their affairs and are presenting an alternative view of Indian-white relations, that is, a native perspective. Their definition of the problem is not an "Indian problem" but a "white problem." Contemporary effects to institutionalize the native perspective of the problem are evidenced in legal and extralegal actions by Indian organizations. Thus, resistance runs the gamut from lawsuits by which Indian peoples seek to enforce their treaty rights to occasional armed encounters with state authority, such as the Federal Bureau of Investigation (FBI) and the Royal Canadian Mounted Police (RCMP).

The set of actors in the institutional stage of the ideological making and shaping of social problems may be quite different from those working in the emergence phase. Also, the influence of the prevailing ideology may strongly redirect a movement from its original idealistic aims toward those more "practical" and "realistic" (those that do not represent major change in the status quo). Therefore, the "institutionalized" definition may differ from that of those initially pressing the social issue. As Blumer stated regarding the official plan for action of a phenomenon identified as a social problem, it

> . . . is a defining and redefining process in a concentrated form—the forming, the re-working and the recasting of collective pictures of the social problem. . . . The official plan that is enacted constitutes, in itself, the official definition of the problem (1971).

Since most major persistent phenomena identified as social problems are dealt with by the formulation of statutes, the analysis of laws dealing with specific social problems will contribute to our understanding of the various interests, individuals, and organizations involved. Use of the law and legal institutions to solve major social problems has been an important aspect of twentieth-century North America. The belief in the amelioration of social ills through appropriate legislation arose with the emergence of the social sciences in the late nineteenth and early twentieth century. Accordingly, the law permeates contemporary society. The significance of sociological studies of the law for the student of social problems should be self-evident, for this type of institutionalization carries the legitimate, official sanction of the state. While some sociologists in the past have taken the law as given, recent analyses focus upon the law and legal institutions as part of the problem (Reasons 1973; Quinney 1972).

Arnold Rose (1968) has suggested that certain laws often produce social problems instead of ameliorating them. In a penetrating analysis he notes how "law-innovators and law-enforcers," in seeking to cope with one set of issues, create new areas of concern. Rose's observations are particularly applicable to the area of "victimless crimes" such as prostitution, gambling, drug use, homosexuality, drunkenness, pornography (Schur 1965; Geis 1972). An example of such analysis is provided by the dissenting view of three members of the President's Commission Task Force *Report on Narcotics and Drug Abuse:*

> Many persons concerned with the problem have for years been questioning whether the criminalization of narcotics and marijuana distribution has not served to defeat the objective of controlling and perhaps eliminating drug abuse and the crime associated with it. The gnawing question to which there has never been a satisfactory answer is whether the policy of criminalization does in fact make the drug user a proselytizer of others in order that he may obtain the funds to acquire his own drugs. . . . In this important area the Commission has been unable to face fundamental questions. Instead, for reasons that are quite understandable but in our view not justifiable, it assumes that the laws and the traditional methods of enforcement which have obtained for over fifty years, are the only proper way in which to meet the problem. . . . *The time will come when we will have to determine casual relationships and consider the possibility that traditional methods of law enforcement produce more rather than less crime, particularly of a collateral character.*

Therefore, we should look at the law and legal actors as not only a means of institutionalizing certain phenomena as social problems, but also as a means of generating secondary social problems. Thus, the very illegality of narcotics use sends the price of dope on the street skyrocketing. The user then must push, deal, or steal to support a habit. The value of narcotics is therefore increased by the willingness of the state to legislate in this area of private morality.

Another way to institutionalize a social problem is to create a committee, commission, or other formal group officially charged with investigating and reporting upon the phenomenon. Some examples are the Presidential Commissions on Civil Disorders, Campus Unrest, Crime, Violence, Obscenity and Pornography, and the Three Mile Island nuclear accident; and Canada's Commission Reports on corrections, drugs, poverty, and women.[10] The establishment of a commission to study a particular problem legitimizes the phenomenon as a social disorder and appeases

---

[10]See *The Challenge of Crime in a Free Society*, Washington, D.C.: U.S. Government Printing Office, 1967; *Report of the National Advisory Commission on Civil Disorders*, Washington, D.C.: U.S. Government Printing Office, 1968; *Report of the National Commission on the Causes and Prevention of Violence*, Washington, D.C.: U.S. Government Printing Office, 1970; *Report of the Canadian Committee on Corrections*, Ottawa: Information Canada, 1969; *Final Report of the Canadian Committee of the Commission of Inquiry Into the Non-Medical Use of Drugs*, Ottawa: Information Canada, 1973; *Report of the Royal Commission on the Status of Women in Canada*, Ottawa: Information Canada, 1970; *Report of the Special Senate Committee on Poverty in Canada*, Ottawa: Information Canada, 1971; *Report of the President's Commission on the Accident at Three Mile Island*, Washington, D.C.: U.S. Government Printing Office, 1979.

those agitating to have something done about it, while providing time for the issue to become diffuse and less threatening to those in power.

The outright rejection or the more prevalent evasion of the findings and recommendations of these commissions by those in political power suggests how such commissions are used. As Rist acutely observed:

> Commissions created for political reasons discover that their final reports regarding sensitive social problems will be accepted or rejected in such a manner as to maximize the political benefits of the recipient, especially if the recipient is the President (1973, p. 113).

A more structural critique would hold that commissions carefully avoid analysis or recommendations that call for changes in the political-economy of corporate order. The Report of the President's Commission on the Accident at Three Mile Island is a case in point. (One notes with interest that the term "nuclear" is omitted from the title even though the crisis which occurred in March of 1979 in the State of Pennsylvania originated in a nuclear power plant.) Staying dutifully within the framework of the presidential charge, the commissioners specified in the preface to the report what they *did not do*.

> We did not attempt to reach a conclusion as to whether, as a matter of public policy, the development of commercial power should be continued or should not be continued. That would require much broader investigation, involving economic, environmental, and political considerations.

However, in the next line, the preface takes an obvious turn.

> *We are aware there are 72 operating reactors in the United States with a capacity of 52,000 megawatts of electric energy. An additional 92 plants have received construction permits and will roughly triple the present nuclear capacity to generate electricity. This would be a significant fraction of the total U.S. electrical generating capacity of some 600,000 megawatts. . . .*

> Therefore, the improvement of the safety of existing and planned nuclear power plants is a crucial issue. It is this issue that our report addresses . . . (*Report of the President's Commission on the Accident at Three Mile Island* 1979, p. 4—italics added).

Despite statements of intent to the contrary, the Commission, in pointing to the growing contribution of nuclear energy to electrical generating capacity, legitimated an increasing role for the nuclear industry. Perhaps the ultimate safety question, that involving the phase-out of a high-risk, cost-ineffective energy production system, was not considered. (For an analysis of Three Mile Island and the Nuclear Industry, see Chapter Five.)

With the ideological institutionalization of the social problem achieved, its continuation is given to the "keepers of the social problem." For example, Bureaus of Indian Affairs in both the United States and Canada are given jurisdiction over the "Indian problem" and administer the Indian Acts and other federal policies (institutionalization). However, these agencies then actively participate in the *maintenance* of the problem, as described in statutes and other definitions of policy by those in positions of political power. As organizations, they have a vested interest in relationship to staffing, budget needs, and the like. Therefore, as the "keepers," Bureaus of Indian Affairs must continually give evidence of the magnitude of the problem, while noting that progress is being made. Simply put, their job is to see to it that the "danger" does *not* disappear. Otherwise these bureaucracies would lose their reason for being (Kitsuse and Spector 1973).

Both rule creators and the rule enforcers are tied to the problem, although their allegiance may vary in intensity. Maintenance seems to be heavily dependent on the ability of agencies, bureaucracies, or others to claim that a problem exists, and that action is being taken (or could be taken) to eventually eradicate the trouble. For example, law enforcement officials point to the rising crime rates and argue that given adequate personnel and facilities, and fewer legal restrictions, they could usher in a new millenium of peacefulness. As Ross and Staines note:

> The FBI and the Defense Department nevertheless remain the masters of the manipulation of problem-size. Crime waves and missile gaps are announced in fine accordance with the timing of basic budgetary and political needs (1973, p. 154).

Agents of social control and "keepers of social problems" obviously are dependent on the phenomenon they are mandated to oversee. Karl Marx observed this relationship between the "forces of peace" and the "criminal forces." While he noted that the state produced the criminal, the criminal is also "productive."

> The criminal produces not only the crime but also the criminal law, he produces the professor who delivers lectures on this criminal law, and even the inevitable textbook in which the professor presents his lectures as a commodity for sale in the market. . . . Furthermore, the criminal produces the whole apparatus of the police and criminal justice, detectives, judges, executioners, juries, etc. . . . The criminal therefore appears as one of those "equilibrating forces" which establish a just balance and open up a whole perspective of useful occupations. (In Bottomore [ed.], 1956, p. 229–30.)

79

Marx's tongue-in-cheek analysis is not intended to argue the necessity of crime. Rather, bureaucracies tend to acquire an inertia to continue on through the constant development of a reason for being. When keepers exist in a social order constantly plagued by unemployment, they may have an even stronger interest in maintaining a social problem.

An example of organizational analysis of "the keepers of a social problem" is Dickson's study in enacting and expanding narcotics legislation, especially in bringing about the Marijuana Tax Act, which greatly increased the agency's budget and jurisdiction.

> The utility of the organizational approach lies in that it can be extended to other similar moral crusades or to entire social movements, where the emphasis so far has been on the work of individual crusades rather than on the organizations and their environments. Further, to the extent these movements follow the general societal pattern and become increasingly complex, organized, and bureaucratic, organizational approach will become even more important in analysis and prediction (1975).

When the question of interests is posed, one is well-advised to entertain this concern at a *structural* level. *Thus, while it is important to identify the particular bureaucratic and other "keepers" who are maintained through the constant discovery and rediscovery of social problems, it is perhaps vital to lift our eyes just a bit higher.* Ultimately, maintenance means preservation of the established order. To be clear, the continuation of the environmental problem represents a reason for being for the Environmental Protection Agency. However, perhaps of greater value is the recognition that its enforcement of environmental regulations is weak and largely symbolic. Such is clearly in the interest of a corporate order committed to growth. Further, the environmental crisis has become a commodity as evidenced in the emergence of a pollution control industry. (See Chapter Five.) To cite another example, the definition of crime as a problem certainly "maintains" the criminal justice system: legislators, law enforcement officers, judges, lawyers, correction workers. But beyond this, that system's focus on street crime clearly diverts attention from corporate illegality. The question of who benefits from defining a social problem in a particular way is indeed provocative.

CONCLUSION

To this point, both a discussion of paradigms and the development of a theory entitled "the ideology of social problems" have been undertaken. It has been necessary to present certain evidence in order to clarify and illustrate the theoretical propositions contained in this chapter. However, the emphasis has been on providing conceptual tools with which to address the important issues in the field. Every topical chapter that follows is an examination by means of logic, historical research, and empirical evidence of the theory developed herein. At the conclusion of each chapter, an "alternative" viewpoint will be expressed. Such is not intended as a total solution. However, it should be of interest to those who might wish to consider new directions. *The reader is encouraged to review the abstract at the beginning of this chapter before reading each of the chapters that follows.*

BIBLIOGRAPHY

Allen, Michael
1974   "The Structure of Interorganizational Elite Corporations: Interlocking Corporate Directorates." American Sociological Review 39:393–406.

Anderson, Charles
1976   The Sociology of Survival: Social Problems of Growth. Homewood, Ill.: The Dorsey Press.

Bagdikian, Ben H.
1971   The Information Machines: Their Impact on Men and the Media. New York: Harper & Row.

1972   The Effete Conspiracy and Other Crimes by the Press. New York: Harper & Row.

1978   Quoted in Broadcasting, December 18.

Baran, Paul A., and
Sweezy, Paul M.
1966   Monopoly Capital. New York: Monthly Review Press.

Becker, Howard
1963   Outsiders: Studies in the Sociology of Deviance. London: Free Press.

1966   Social Problems: A Modern Approach. New York: John Wiley.

Berger, Peter L., and
Luckman, Thomas
1966   The Social Construction of Reality. Garden City,
New York: Doubleday.

Blum, Richard
1969   Society and Drugs. San Francisco: Jossey-Bass.

1971   "Drug Pushers: A Collective Portrait." Transaction
8 (July–August):18–21.

Blumer, Herbert
1969   "Social Movements." Studies in Social Movements:
A Social Psychological Perspective. Barry Mc-
Laughlin, ed. New York: The Free Press, pp. 8–29.

1971   "Social Problems as Collective Behavior." Social
Problems 18 (Winter):298–306.

Bogart, Leo
1969   "How the Mass Media Work in America." In
Violence and the Media. Vol. 9. Washington, D.C.:
U.S. Government Printing Office, pp. 165–216.

Bosram, Grurcharn S.
1979   "The Rural Depopulation of the Prairies." In John
Allen Fry, ed. Economy, Class and Social Reality.
Toronto: Butterworth.

Bottomore, T. B.
1964   Karl Marx: Selected Writings in Sociology and
Social Philosophy. New York: McGraw-Hill, pp.
229–30.

Brecher, Edward M.
1972   Licit and Illicit Drugs. Boston: Little, Brown.

Broadcasting Yearbook
1979   "Crossownership." Washington, D.C.: Broadcasting and Publications Inc.

Brown, Les
1974   "Television: The Business behind the Box." In The
Television Establishment: Programming for Power
and Profit. Gaye Tuchman, ed. Englewood Cliffs,
N.J.: Prentice-Hall.

Bunting, David
1976   "Corporate Interlocking, Part IV: A New Look at
Interlocks and Legislation." Directors and Boards
1:39–47.

Chambliss, William, and
Ryther, Thomas
    1975   Sociology: The Discipline and Its Direction. New
York: McGraw-Hill.

Cicourel, Aaron V.
    1968   The Social Organization of Juvenile Justice. New
York: John Wiley.

Clement, Wallace
    1975   The Canadian Corporate Elite: An Analysis of
Economic Power. Toronto: McClelland &
Stewart.

    1977   Continental Corporate Power: Economic Linkages
between Canada and the United States. Toronto:
McClelland & Stewart.

Cohen, David K., and
Lazerson, Mervin
    1972   "Education and the Corporate Order." Socialist
Revolution, March–April: 1–26.

Cohen, Warren H., and
Mause, Phillys I.
    1968   "The Indian: The Forgotten American." Harvard
Law Review 81 (June): 1818–58.

Cooley, Charles Horton
    1909   Social Organization. New York: Charles Scribner's
Sons.

Cressey, Donald R., ed.
    1961   The Prison: Studies in Institutional Organization
and Change. New York: Holt, Rinehart and
Winston.

Cumming, Peter A.
    1973   "Native Rights and Law in an Age of Protest."
Alberta Law Review, vol. 11: 238–59.

Dickson, Donald T.
    1968   "Bureaucracy and Morality: An Organization
Perspective on a Moral Crusade." Social Problems
16 (Fall): 143–56.

Directory of Corporate
Affiliates
    1979   Skokie, Illinois: National Register Publishing Co.

Domhoff, William
1970
The Higher Circles. New York: Random House.

Dooley, Peter
1969
"The Interlocking Directorate." American Economic Review 59:314–23.

Douglas, Jack D.
1974
Defining America's Social Problems. Englewood Cliffs, N.J.: Prentice-Hall, p. xi.

Dowd, Douglas F.
1977
The Twisted Dream: Capitalist Development in the United States since 1776. Cambridge, Mass.: Winthrop.

Dye, Thomas R.
1976
Who's Running America? Englewood Cliffs, N.J.: Prentice-Hall.

Editor and Publisher
1977
"167 Groups Own 1047 Dailies: 71% of total Circulation." July 9, pp. 10, 11, and 43.

Edwards, Richard C., Reich, Michael, and Weisskopf, Thomas E.
1972
The Capitalist System. Englewood Cliffs, N.J.: Prentice-Hall.

Erickson, Kai
1966
Wayward Puritans: A Study in the Sociology of Deviance. New York: John Wiley.

Forcese, Dennis, and Richer, Stephen
1975
Issues in Canadian Society. Scarborough, Ontario: Prentice-Hall of Canada.

Freitag, Peter
1975
"The Cabinet and Big Business: A Study of Interlocks." Social Problems 23:137–52.

Fuller, Richard C., and Myers, Richard R.
1941
"The Natural History of a Social Problem." American Sociological Review 6 (June):320–29.

Gans, Herbert J.
1972
"The Positive Functions of Poverty." American Journal of Sociology 78 (Fall): 275–89.

Geis, Gilbert
1972   Not the Law's Business? Chapter 1. Washington,
        D.C.: U.S. Government Printing Office.

Genevie, Louis E.
1978   Collective Behavior and Social Movements. Itasca,
        Ill.: F. E. Peacock.

Geshen, Charles E.
1973   Drinks, Drugs, and Do-Gooders. New York: The
        Free Press.

Goffman, Erving
1961   Asylums. Garden City, New York: Doubleday.

Gramsci, Antonio
1971   Prison Notebooks. New York: International.

Gusfield, Joseph R.
1963   Symbolic Crusade: Status Politics and the
        American Temperance Movement. Urbana, Ill.:
        University of Illinois Press.

Henshel, Richard L., and
Silverman, Robert A.
1975   Perceptions in Criminology. Toronto: Methuen.

Hirsch, Glenn
1975   "Only You Can Prevent Ideological Hegemony:
        The Advertising Council and Its Place in the
        American Power Structure." The Insurgent
        Sociologist 5, 3 (Spring): 64–82.

Julian, Joseph
1973   Social Problems. New York: Appleton-Century-
        Crofts, p. 7.

Kadish, Sanford
1967   "The Crisis of Overcriminalization." Annals
        (November): 157–70.

Kerbo, Harold R., and
Della Fave, L. Richard
1978   "The Empirical Side of the Power Elite Debate:
        An Assessment and Critique of Recent Research."
        Paper presented at the Annual Meeting of the
        American Sociological Association, San Francisco,
        September.

Killian, Lewis M.
1973

"Social Movements: A Review of the Field." In Social Movements: A Reader and Source Book. Robert R. Evans, ed. Chicago: Rand McNally (college).

Kitsuse, John I., and Spector, Malcolm
1973

"Toward a Sociology of Social Problems: Social Conditions, Value Judgments and Social Problems." Social Problems 20 (Spring):415.

Kolko, Gabriel
1962

Wealth and Power in America: An Analysis of Social Class and Income Distribution. New York: Praeger.

Krasnow, Erwin G., and Langley, Lawrence D.
1973

The Politics of Broadcasting Regulations. New York: St. Martin's.

Lemert, Edwin
1967

Human Deviance, Social Problems and Social Control. Englewood Cliffs, N.J.: Prentice-Hall, pp. 3–12.

Lindesmith, Alfred R.
1940a

"Dope Fiend Mythology." Journal of Criminal Law, Criminology and Political Science 31 (July–August):119–208.

1940b

"The Drug Addict as a Psychopath." American Sociological Review 5 (December):914–20.

Long, Gladys Engel, and Long, Kurt
1961

Collective Dynamics. New York: Thomas Y. Crowell.

Lowenthal, Max
1950

The Federal Bureau of Investigation, New York: Harcourt Brace Jovanovich.

Lowry, Ritchie P.
1972

"Toward a Sociology of Secrecy and Security Systems." Social Problems 19 (Spring):437–50.

Macpherson, C. B.
1962   The Political Theory of Possessive Individualism. London: Oxford University Press.

Mannheim, Karl
1936   Ideology and Utopia. New York: Harcourt Brace Jovanovich.

Mannis, Jerome G.
1974   "The Concept of Social Problems: Vox Populi and Sociological Analysis." Social Problems 21 (Summer):1–15.

Marx, Karl, and Engels, Friedrich
1947   The German Ideology. New York: International.

McDonald, Lynn
1969   "Crime and Punishment in Canada: A Statistical Test of the Conventional Wisdom." The Canadian Review of Sociology and Anthropology 6 (November):212–36.

Mead, George Herbert
1934   Mind, Self and Society. Chicago: The University of Chicago Press.

Merton, Robert, and Nisbet, Robert
1976   Contemporary Social Problems. New York: Harcourt Brace Jovanovich.

Mervin, S.
1912   "Fighting the Deadly Habits: The Story of Charles B. Towns." American Magazine 74 (October):710.

Meyer, Peter
1979   "Land Rush: A Survey of America's Land." Harper's January:45–60.

Mickenberg, Neil H.
1971   "Aboriginal Rights in Canada and the United States." Osgoode Hall Law Journal: 119–55.

Miliband, Ralph
1969   The State in Capitalist Society: Analysis of the
        Western System of Power. New York: Basic Books.

Mills, C. Wright
1956   White Collar. New York: Oxford University Press.

1959   The Sociological Imagination. London: Oxford
        University Press.

1963   "The Structure of Power in American Society." In
        Power, Politics, and People. Irving Horowitz, ed.
        New York: Ballantine, pp. 23–28.

Mintz, Beth
1975   "The President's Cabinet, 1897–1972: A Contribu-
        tion to the Power Structure Debate." Insurgent
        Sociologist 5:131–48.

Molatch, Harvey, and
Lester, Marilyn
1974   "News as Purposive Behavior: On the Strategic
        Use of Routine Events, Accidents, and Scandals."
        American Sociological Review 39 (February):103,
        105, 110.

Moody's Industrial
Manual
1974   Volumes I and II, New York: Moody's Investor
        Service, Inc.

1979   Volumes I and II, New York: Moody's Investor
        Service, Inc.

Morris, Norval, and
Hawkins, Gordon
1970   The Honest Politician's Guide to Crime Control.
        Chicago: University of Chicago Press.

Mosca, Gaetano
1970   "The Ruling Class." In Power in Societies. Marvin
        E. Olsen, ed. New York: Macmillan.

Musto, David F.
1973   The American Disease: Origins of Narcotic Control. New Haven: Yale University Press.

Neubeck, Kenneth J.
1979   Social Problems: A Critical Approach. Glenview, Ill.: Scott, Foresman.

New York Times
1971   The Pentagon Papers. New York: Bantam Books.

1973   The Watergate Hearings: Break-in and Cover-up. New York: Bantam Books.

Oberschall, Anthony
1973   Social Conflict and Social Movements. Englewood Cliffs, N.J.: Prentice-Hall.

Packer, Herbert L.
1968   The Limits of the Criminal Sanction. Stanford: Stanford University Press.

Pareto, Vilfredo
1970   "Elites and Force." In Power in Societies. Marvin E. Olsen, ed. New York: MacMillan.

Platt, Anthony
1969   "The Rise of the Child-Saving Movement: A Study in Social Policy and Correctional Reform." The Annals January: 21–38.

President's Commission on Law Enforcement and Administratoin of Justice Task Force Report
                 "Narcots and Drug Abuse." Washington, D.C.: U.S. Government Printing Office, pp. 302–303.

President's Commission on the Accident at Three Mile Island
                 "The Need for Change: The Legacy of T.M.I." Washington, D.C.: U.S. Government Printing Office.

Quinney, Richard
1970   The Social Reality of Crime. Boston: Little, Brown.

1972   "The Ideology of Law: Notes for a Radical Alternative to Legal Repression." Issues in Criminology 6 (Summer):41–54.

Reasons, Charles E.
1973   "The Politicizing of Crime, the Criminal, and the Criminologist." The Journal of Criminal Law and Criminology 64 (December):471–77.

1974   "The Politics of Drugs: An Inquiry into the Sociology of Social Problems." Sociological Quarterly 15 (Summer):381–404.

1975   "The Addict as a Criminal—Perpetuation of a Legend." Crime and Delinquency 21 (January): 19–27.

Riesman, David
1961   The Lonely Crowd. New Haven, Conn.: Yale University Press.

Rist, Ray C.
1973   "Policy, Politics, and Social Research: A Study in the Relationships of Federal Commissions and Social Science." Social Problems 21 (Summer): 113–28.

Rose, Arnold M.
1968   "Law and the Causation of Social Problems." Social Problems 16 (Summer):33–43.

Ross, Robert, and Staines, Graham L.
1971   "The Politics of Analyzing Social Problems." Social Problems 20 (Summer):18–40.

1973   "The Politics of Analyzing Social Problems." Social Problems 21 (Fall):154.

Ryan, William
1972   Blaming the Victim. New York: Random House.

Sallach, David L.
1974   "Class Domination and Ideological Hegemony."
The Sociological Quarterly Winter:38–50.

Scheff, Thomas
1967   Mental Illness and Social Processes. New York:
Harper & Row.

Schur, Edwin M.
1965   Crimes without Victims: Deviant Behavior and
Public Policy. Englewood Cliffs, N.J.: Prentice-
Hall.

Sellin, Thorsten
1938   Culture, Conflict and Crime. New York: Social
Science Research Council.

Silver, Isidore
1974   The Crime Control Establishment. Englewood
Cliffs, N.J.: Prentice Hall.

Simmons, J. L. with
Chambers, Hazel
1965   "Public Stereotypes of Deviants." Social Problems
13 (Fall):229.

Skolnick, Jerome H., and
Woodworth, J. Richard
1967   "Bureaucracy, Information and Social Control: A
Study of a Moral Detail." In The Police: Six
Sociological Essays. David I. Bordua, ed. New
York: John Wiley.

Smith, Derek G., ed.
1975   Canadian Indians and the Law: Selected
Documents 1663–1972. Toronto: McClelland and
Stewart.

Sonders, Mark
1971   "Addicts and Zealots." Harper's 240 (June):71–80.

Soref, Michael
1976

"Social Class and a Division of Labor within the Corporate Elite: A Note on Class, Interlocking, and Executive Committee Membership of Directors of U.S. Firms." Sociological Quarterly 17:360–68.

Spector, Malcolm, and Kitsuse, John I.
1973

"Social Problems: A Reformulation." Social Problems 21 (Fall):154–55.

Sykes, Gresham M.
1965

The Society of Captives: A Study of a Maximum Security Prison. New York: Atheneum.

Taishoff, Sol
1979

Broadcasting Yearbook, Washington, D.C.: Lawrence B. Taishoff.

Thio, Alex
1978

Deviant Behavior. Boston: Houghton Mifflin.

Time
1980

"Gannett Goes for the Gold." April:93.

Tuchman, Gaye
1974

The T.V. Establishment: Programming for Power and Profit. Englewood Cliffs, N.J.: Prentice-Hall.

Turner, Ralph H., and Killian, Lewis M.
1972

Collective Behavior. Englewood Cliffs, N.J.: Prentice-Hall.

United States Bureau of the Census
1977

Statistical Abstract of the United States. Washington, D.C.: U.S. Government Printing Office.

1979

Statistical Abstract of the United States. Washington, D.C.: U.S. Government Printing Office.

U.S. Senate
1978

"Interlocking Directorates Among the Major U.S. Corporations." A staff study prepared by the Subcommittee on Reports, Accounting and Management of the Committee on Government Affairs, Washington, D.C.: U.S. Government Printing Office.

Useem, Michael
    1979   "The Social Organization of the American Business
                        Elite." American Sociological Review, vol. 44,
                        no. 4 (August):553–71.

Weber, Max
    1947   The Theory of Social and Economic Organization.
                        New York: Oxford University Press.

Whitehead, Alfred N.
    1949   Science and the Modern World. New York:
                        Macmillan.

Wolfe, Alan
    1978   The Seamy Side of Democracy: Repression in
                        America. New York: Longman.

2
A THEORY OF CONFLICT

3

INEQUALITY

Abstract

In this chapter, the reality of *inequality* in corporate society is examined. While the term "poverty" is more frequently encountered, it draws attention only to the individual, family, and subcultural worlds of the poor. However, the problem in North American society is not one of an absence of wealth but rather its distribution. To understand the reasons for the coexistence of "haves and have-notes," it is necessary to focus on social structure.

Early in this chapter, the *prevailing ideologies* for inequality are presented, analyzed, and criticized. Taken together, they offer a series of justifications for the failure of the poor to succeed. Each serves to obscure the structural origins of class inequality. We then proceed to examine the historical *emergence* of inequality and movements designed to counter the problem. Subsequently, it will be shown that inequality has been *institutionalized* in the laws, programs, and policies of the wealthfare state, the warfare state, and the poorhouse state. Finally, in the section on *maintenance,* we shall demonstrate that keeping the poor poor is the other side of keeping the rich rich.

95

A socially just society is a society where equality is the accepted principle for the distribution of resources and where inequalities have to be justified. Inequalities would exist as a result of the application of need, merit and contribution to the common good as criteria for allocating resources. In other words, inequalities would be acceptable only on the grounds of equity, of the way they benefit the generality and the way they benefit the worst-off members of society.

Inequalities would be judged indefensible if they were simply the result of birth or inheritance; if they were simply the result of social circumstances; if they were simply the product of differences in natural abilities; if they were not to the benefit of all and if others were harmed by them. In a socially just society, prosperity and unsatisfied need would not coexist; the needs of all would be satisfied before resources were allocated for any other purposes.—Vic George and Paul Wilding

Democratic ideology places a great deal of emphasis upon individual equality. In constitutions, legislation, political speeches, textbooks, and the media, one is constantly reminded that his or her society is one in which the freedom and equality of every person is highly valued. As is frequently the case, however, the prevailing ideology does not fit well the reality of social order. It appears indeed that some are *more* equal than others.

While the political ideal of "all persons created equal" is laudable, it ignores social, political, and economic reality. The history of human societies has been one of various forms of *stratification*, or ordering of people according to certain socially significant factors such as wealth, power, age, sex, occupation, among others (Lenski and Lenski 1978; Bottomore 1965). While stratification has existed throughout human history, the nature and extent of it have varied a great deal.

In corporate society popular reference to such terms as class, poverty, and personal influence usually addresses the question of wealth. Thus, differences in the value of property become significant indicators of stratification. The argument here is that property inequality is a logical consequence of corporate society. Given the democratic ideal of shared power and the suspicion that those who do not share the wealth may be in a poor position to influence public policy, inequality becomes a problem requiring ideological legitimation. Of course, the ultimate ideological "solution" is to deny the problem altogether, as the following piece clearly demonstrates.

Viewpoint

Who owns America? The same old gang (Excerpts)

Do you remember those full-page newspaper ads that showed a little old lady stroking *her* locomotive, supposedly owned by millions of ordinary Americans just like her? Or Standard Oil's gushing claim, "Yes, the people own the tools of production. . . . How odd to find that it is here, in the capitalism [Karl Marx] reviled, that the promise of the tool has been fulfilled." Well, it's happening again.

A current Texaco television commercial has Bob Hope asking us to "take a look at the owners of America's oil companies." and then leads [sic] us on a tour of a typical community made up for just plain folk like you and me. A recent book, received with much fanfare in the press, repeats the refrain. Its author, long-time management consultant and publicist Peter Drucker, tells us that an "unseen revolution" has wrought "a more radical shift in ownership than Soviet communism." Even more amazing, "The socialism of Marxist theory has been realized for the first time on American soil."

Not only are the means of production now in everyone's hands, but the U.S. Chamber of Commerce confides that the United States has become a "postindustrial society." College textbooks inform us that a "dramatic shift from blue collar to white collar, from brawn to brain has occurred," and the best-seller *Future Shock* rhapsodizes that "for the first time in human history," a society—*our* society—has "managed within a few short decades to throw off the yoke of manual labor." A book on "power in America" celebrates the passing of classes and suggests that we organize popular visits to "Newport, and bus tours through Grosse Pointe, for purely educational purposes—like seeing Carlsbad Caverns once." It is time, the author advises us, to shout, "The Working Class is dead. Long live the memory of the Working Class." And, summing it all up, a popular book on how to be a politician announces that "the economic class system is disappearing. . . . Redistribution of wealth and income . . . has ended economic inequality's political significance."

So, what has happened to classes? Who does own America, and how has it all been changing? Has the capitalist class really been "lopped off" at the top, as Harvard's Talcott Parsons once pithily put it? Has the ownership of American corporations become so dispersed that control has shifted to "professional managers" who are merely the "trustees" for all of us—stockholders, employees, suppliers, consumers, and the public—as Donald S. McNaughton, the chairman of Prudential Life, announced in a recent speech? Has the yoke of manual labor really been lifted? Is the working class now a mere memory? Or are the claims that prompt these questions really pseudofacts that are as plausible and persuasive as they are deceptive? The answer, I think, is clear: Economic inequality weighs as heavily and cuts as deeply as ever, and neither capitalists nor workers have vanished from American life.

Let's look first at who owns what. It's certainly hard enough to find out, even if, like Government economists you have access to Internal Revenue Service (IRS) data. No law requires Americans to report their net worth, and besides, wealth is deliberately hidden, whether out of modesty or to avoid taxes. Still, an ingenious method of estimating wealth has been devised, to make the dead disclose what the living conceal. It is called the "estate multiplier technique," and it uses IRS data on estate tax returns. It treats those who die in any year as a "stratified sample" of the living on whose estates tax returns would have to be filed if they died during the year—that is, those with estates worth $60,000 or more. All told, only 4 percent of the adults in this country have estates as large as $60,000, counting *everything* they own, including cash in hand or under the mattress itself. But within that group, a minute number of Americans make up the real owners of America.

The Rose Bowl's 104,696 seats would still be half empty if only every adult American who owns $1 million or more in corporate stock came to cheer, and it would be even emptier if only those who have $100,000 in state and local bonds got a seat. If you counted all state, local and Federal bonds (except US Savings Bonds), and added Treasury bills, certificates, notes, and mortgages—even foreign bonds—held by Americans in amounts of at least $200,000, you would still find well over a quarter of the Rose Bowl seats not taken. Only 55,400 adults have $1 million or more in corporate stock. A mere 40,000 have $100,000 or more in state and local bonds (all

Federal tax exempt), and 73,500 adults have $200,000 or more if we count all bonds and debt holdings.

This tiny owning class at the tip of the top, barely more than one-twentieth of 1 percent of American adults, has a fifth of *all* the corporate stock, nearly two-thirds of the worth of *all* state and local bonds, and two-fifths of *all* bonds and notes. No wonder it took five years of trying by an outstanding economist, James D. Smith, to get the IRS to allow him to study its information—and by then some of the data had been destroyed.

Contrast what this propertied class owns to what the rest of us have. Nine out of ten adults in the United States could sell everything they own, pay off their debts, and have no more than $30,000 left. Worse, more than half of all Americans would have a total "net worth" of no more than $3,000. The bottom half of all American families combined have only three cents of every dollar's worth of all the wealth in the country.

Back at the top, if we count up what the richest 1 percent of the population own, we find that they have a seventh of all the real estate in the country, more than half the corporate stock, and almost all the trust assets. They even had a seventh of all the *cash* in every checking and savings account and pocket and purse in America.

Summed up, that is a quarter of the net worth of the entire population held by the top 1 percent. If we take a slice as large as the richest 4 percent—everyone whose total gross assets (not counting debts) are worth at least $60,000—their combined wealth is more than a trillion dollars—enough to buy the entire national product of the United States and have plenty left over to pick up the combined output of a few small European countries, including Switzerland, Norway, Denmark, and Sweden.

Maurice Zeitlin
Progressive Magazine
June 1978

If stratificationist Maurice Zeitlin is correct (and we believe he is), the problem of inequality cannot be swept away by euphoric definitions. In the discussion that follows, we will examine the prevailing ideologies that seek to deny, distort, or legitimate a society of classes. At the onset, however, it is necessary to introduce some important definitions.

To this point the terms "wealth," "income," and "class" have been used rather loosely. Most of us intuitively sense some connection among them, yet there are critical differences. In a general sense *income* refers to payment received. However, the source of one's income introduces an important sociological distinction. For most of us, payment is received primarily for labor or services; that is, income is a consequence of doing our jobs. Such is not the case for the "more fortunate," those representing the higher circles in North American society. For these few, income is derived primarily from property or investments.

For example, in the United States in 1976, taxpayers with adjusted gross incomes of less than $50,000 received between 85 and 90 percent of their income from salaries and wages. However, those in the $50,000 to $499,000 category received only 53.9 percent of their income from these sources. Finally, individuals in the superrich category ($500,000 and up) received only a paltry 16.9 percent of their income from salaries and wages (*Statistical Abstract of the United States* 1978, p. 271). Those in upper-income brackets depend heavily on such resources as stock dividends, interest, and the sales of capital assets described below. Therefore, it is not simply the amount of income but its source that separates people into economic categories.

Wealth on the other hand centers on the value of property. It has to do with a range of assets including stocks, bonds, real estate, utilities, cash, debt instruments, life insurance, trusts, and other miscellaneous holdings. Some of these forms of wealth yield income. For example, investors in shares of stock in a corporation receive a dividend, or a share of the profits. Those who own real estate may rent their property to tenants. However, both shares of stock and real property may (and usually do) increase in value, adding to the wealth of the owner. As we shall discover in the following pages, wealth for most of us consists of such things as household goods, ownership of a home, an automobile, and perhaps a small savings account. If we own stock or income property, these represent only a small part of the payments we depend on to live.

Even the fabled "home ownership" form of wealth is somewhat deceptive. Most "owners" are not really owners at all. The financial institution that holds the mortgage to the property is legally entitled to seize that property if the "owner" defaults on the mortgage payments. Most owners really own only "equity" in their home, automobiles, and, frequently, in their household goods. Equity refers to the balance that remains, assuming the sale of property, after all outstanding encumbrances are paid. For example, if one owns an $80,000 house with a $50,000 mortgage, one's equity will be $30,000. Further, if the owner secures the services of a real estate agent who receives a typical 8 percent commission, the equity will shrink by some $6,400. If the owner pays a state tax on the sale of say, 1.5 percent, then the real wealth diminishes by another $1,200. It is easy to see that the lending institution and its owners truly represent the "wealth" in this example. Not only does the owner of record pay substantial interest on the home loan, he or she has typically paid a substantial fee (loan costs) to the lender in order to get the loan in the first place.

We introduced the term *social class* in the introductory chapter because of its crucial importance to conflict sociology. Rather than representing simple differences in wealth and/or income, class is an intricate construct requiring a number of definitional criteria. These include: (1) a shared position in the economic order; (2) a distinct culture and world view; (3) interests that conflict with those of other classes; (4) membership in a "community of fate" with global, as opposed to simply local or national, standing. The satisfaction of such objective criteria means that those who qualify share the same class position. They thus constitute a "class-in-itself." Given the development of the subjective criterion of a consciousness or awareness of the foregoing objective criteria, together with subsequent political organization, a class-in-itself becomes a "class-for-itself" (Marx 1962, p. 334; Anderson 1974, pp. 50–51; Dahrendorf 1959, p. 17).

Before we continue, a word of caution is in order. A serious treatment of inequality compels one to make generous use of statistical information. Although "number anxiety" is a common problem, the tables and quantitative information that follow should be of vital interest to every member of society. After all, the concerns of class, wealth, income, and work affect each of us directly. It is important also that statistics are interpreted sociologically. By this we mean that numbers change rapidly over a span of time. Indeed, one of the problems of the North American economy is inflation; the shrinking value or purchasing power of the dollar. Therefore, figures on income and wealth may appear to change dramatically in a short period. However, if we interpret numbers as indicators of social reality, we will find a pattern emerging. For example, over the years almost everyone's income goes up, as does the total national income. The important thing is that the *share* of income held by different segments of the population over time may tell us a great deal about inequality. Extending our argument further, the reader may substitute more-current figures for the ones we use as they become available. *If our logic is correct, more-current data will reveal the same recurring social pattern.*

THE PREVAILING IDEOLOGIES

In Chapter Two an attempt was made to construct a theory for social problems. The logic of that theory is straightforward. If we understand how a society is put together (that is, its structural imperatives), then we should expect to see how that order is defended by means of idea-systems that affect how each of us thinks. Once we understand these ideologies, we shall be in a position to understand the historical emergence of inequality; to explore the institutionalization of the problem and its supposed "solutions"; and to determine just who benefits from a society of classes.

THE IDEOLOGY OF SOCIAL PROBLEMS

The Myth of the Middle Class

One's view of inequality is greatly shaped by his or her position in society. Persons in the lower classes tend to be more conscious of their position since they are constantly reminded of the commodity affluence in society through the mass media and daily observations. Advertisements in newspapers, on the radio, and television declare that most persons can afford this car, house, dishwasher, or other consumer good. Of course the position supposedly held by "most persons" is that of the middle-of-the-road, middle-income, average consumer known as the "middle class." Like the elusive "silent majority" or "common person" claimed by politicians seeking support, and the legal equivalent of the "reasonable man," the middle class is held out as virtually an all-inclusive group. In fact, corporate ideology emphasizes only one class, the middle, while the data on wealth and income suggest something else entirely.

As a specific ideology, the myth of the middle class obscures the reality of great inequities. According to one Canadian scholar (Marchak 1975, pp. 16–25), if the middle class is defined by life-style to include the ownership of a house, car, and possibly a boat or summer cottage, with the ability to have occasional holidays abroad or maintain a university student, then only the upper 20 percent or so of the Canadian population is "middle class."

Suppose we conceptualize class in a different fashion. If we center on the *source* of income, we will find that most members of North American society depend on wages, salaries, or self-employment, deriving less than 10 percent of their income from investment or state "welfare" payments. The owning class that derives substantial income and wields enormous economic and political power through its investment assets constitutes no more than the top 1 or 2 percent of the population. Those at the bottom, who are primarily dependent on cash assistance together with food, medical, and other "poverty programs," constitute less than 10 percent of the population. We believe that these differences in source of income should cause one to entertain the possibility that those between the investment rich and the welfare poor are more accurately termed a working rather than a middle class. For even if an increasing number of those in the middle wear a white collar, and even if some are reasonably well-off technicians and professionals, most still sell their labor for a wage (while a relative few are self-employed).

The "myth of the middle class" (Parker 1972) might be more accurately termed "white collar ideology." For as an increasing segment of the labor force in corporate society no longer wears the blue collar of the traditional working class, the conclusion is drawn that a new class has been born. It often appears that even those who represent these occupational categories draw dubious boundary lines. For example, a recent survey in the United States (Vanneman and Pampel 1977) found that blue collar respondents make a distinction between manual and nonmanual workers (as working and middle class, respectively). Also, political and social attitudes are greatly affected by such conceptions. With regard to this nonmanual (white collar) segment of the labor force, Braverman (1974) argues that it:

> . . . corresponds increasingly to the formal definition of working class. That is, like the working class it possesses no economic or occupational independence, is employed by capital and its off-shoots, possesses no access to the labor process or the means of production outside that of employment, and must renew its labor for capital incessantly in order to subsist. This portion of employment embraces the engineering, technical, and scientific cadre, the lower ranks of supervision and management, the considerable numbers of specialized and "professional" employees occupied in marketing, financial and organizational administration, and the like, as well as outside of capitalist industry proper, in hospitals, schools, government administration and so forth (1974, pp. 403–404).

Increasingly absent from the North American stratification system are those termed by C. Wright Mills, the "old middle class" (1951, pp. 3–12). These were the owners of small businesses and the holders of land during the eighteenth and nineteenth centuries. With the relentless historical growth of monopolistic corporations, those who owned the property on which or with which they worked were swallowed up. Thus, whatever the historical credibility of the term "middle class," it appears consigned to the past.

However, the consolidation of property and bureaucratization of society have done more than hasten the disappearance of a more or less independent middle class. The white collar legions of modern history also represent a repository for those whose work lives represent diminishing skills. For example, in 1978 in the United States, clerical workers numbered 16.6 million (36 percent) of a total 46.7 million white collar workers. Thus, this occupational group is the largest single category in corporate society (*Statistical Abstract of the United States* 1978, p. 418). The term "clerical worker" refers to such occupations as bookkeeper, secretary, stenographer, cashier, bank teller, file clerk, telephone operator, office machine operator, payroll clerk, receptionist, postal clerk, typist and stock clerk (Braverman 1974, pp. 295–6). In 1978, these workers had a median weekly paycheck of $175.00, trailing professional and technical workers ($294); managers and administrators ($323); sales-workers ($232); craft workers ($279); operatives ($191); nonfarm laborers ($193) and transport equipment operatives ($249) (*Statistical Abstract of the United States* 1979, p. 420). *However, the clerical occupations were not always so poorly compensated.*

As Braverman details (1974, pp. 294–7), in the eighteenth and early nineteenth centuries the term "clerk" in Great Britain usually indicated one who was a manager, a confidant of the employer, enjoying high standing and pay. "In the United States, in 1900, clerical employees of steam railroads and in manufacturing establishments had average annual earnings of $1,011; in the same year, the average annual earnings of workers in these industries was $435 for manufacturing and $548 for steam railroads." In both Great Britain and the United States in the mid-nineteenth century, clerks accounted for less than 1 percent of the labor force. By 1961, clerks accounted for *13 percent* of the gainfully employed in Britain. In 1979, this occupation accounted for over 18 percent of the employed in the United States (*Statistical Abstract of the United States* 1979, p. 415).

Thus, the myth of the "middle class" masks real differences in economic situation and life chances among identifiable groups in society (Parker 1972). In Western democracies, where all are said to be equal, such realities as class lines, class boundaries, and class consciousness are denied and/or ignored. White collar workers are glibly labeled middle class, a distinction that loses sight of the common source of income that ties them to the working class.

When economic differences are recognized in North America, they are frequently cast in terms of education, occupation, and income. Largely ignored are related questions of ownership of wealth and the marshalling of political power. While many in other democratic nation-states, such as Great Britain and the Scandinavian countries, have begun to examine the nature of class stratification, a striking feature of both the United States and Canada is the relative absence of the term "class" in the pronouncements of the media, government, industry, and the academy.

The lack of class awareness and analysis is understandable, given the general ideology of corporatism. The focus upon competition, equality of "opportunity" (not equality), and individual achievement through triumph of the will prevails. Such an emphasis upon the individual as a free-willed being who determines his or her own fate fails to acknowledge structural factors that render persons unequal. For example, poor people in the United States and Canada are disproportionately found among the aged, nonwhite, lesser educated, rural, female-headed households (Manzer 1974; World Almanac and Book of Facts 1977). What is it about these groups of people that finds them with lower incomes? According to corporate ideology, if people are "captains of their own destiny," then it follows that if they are poor, they suffer largely through their own fault, while if they are rich, they enjoy the fruits of their extraordinary efforts. In turn, this ideology means people are not apt to view economic position as an outcome of class oppression. Thus the paradox is that the ideal of a "classless society," often scorned as impractical and utopian, has been created by definition, if not in reality. For the "classless" society in North America has emerged as a *one-class* society—that of the mythical middle.

In corporate society one is taught that all have the opportunity to compete and achieve. This is part of our economic socialization. In a recent study, youngsters from grades 3, 6, 9, and 12 in a southwestern United

States city were surveyed regarding their views on economics (Cummings and Taebel 1978). The researchers asked questions about trade unions, private ownership of industry, and state intervention in economic affairs. They thought that since trade unions are more collective in outlook and counter the general ideology of privatism, youths would increasingly be antiunion as they became older. Also, as corporate ideology emphasized private ownership and minimal state intervention, the investigators believed that with age students would look more favorably on private ownership and less favorably on state intervention.

It is evident in Table 3-1 that as students move through the educational process, they become less nonevaluative and neutral and more negative toward unions. The researchers point out that high school seniors viewed unions as too big, too powerful, and a threat to social stability. The expectations regarding private ownership are confirmed in Table 3-2. Support for private ownership increased with grade level. By the twelfth grade, free enterprise was viewed as the only workable economic system, while

TABLE 3-1
Orientation toward Trade Unionism by Grade Level

Orientation to Trade Unionism	Grade Level			
	Third	Sixth	Ninth	Twelfth
Nonevaluative	34.6%	30.8%	22.2%	17.2%
Neutral	48.1%	40.4%	24.4%	23.4%
Negative	17.3%	28.8%	53.5%	59.4%
Total Number of Students	52	52	45	64

Source: Cummings and Taebel 1978, p. 203.

TABLE 3-2
Orientation toward Private Ownership of Major Industries by Grade Level

Orientation to Private Ownership	Grade Level			
	Third	Sixth	Ninth	Twelfth
Negative	18.0%	40.7%	24.5%	14.1%
Neutral	66.0%	33.9%	30.6%	22.5%
Positive	16.0%	25.4%	44.9%	63.4%
Total Number of Students	50	59	49	71

Source: Cummings and Taebel 1978, p. 204.

communism and socialism were seen as directly opposed to individual prosperity, fulfillment, and success.

Table 3-3 indicates that the majority of third and sixth graders saw the state as a benevolent institution. Moreover, the older the students, the more negative their views on intervention. When asked about the causes of inequality, third and sixth graders tended to view poverty as beyond the control of the individual, and supported state help. However, the older group reflected well the prevailing ideology of corporatism.

> More significantly, 12th graders have acquired explanations of inequality which explicitly identify individuals as the authors of their socioeconomic destinies. Character flaws and motivational deficiencies are often seen as the reasons for poverty and economic insecurity. Deficiencies in skill and training are also identified as being among the more important causes of income inequality; these latter arguments are the basis of what orthodox economists call *human capital* or *marginal productivity* analysis (Cummings and Taebel 1978, p. 207).

The Disappearing Poor

One of the specific ideologies of inequality that prevails in corporate society holds that the poor are rapidly disappearing. The problem with this assertion has to do with a reasonable definition of "poverty." Of course, the easiest way to dismiss the problem is by definition. For example, in the United States in 1977, only 3.6 percent of all families had an income under $3,000. Should the poverty lines be set at that point, a large number of the poor would be statistically eliminated. This "solu-

TABLE 3-3
**Orientation Toward State Intervention in
Economic Affairs by Grade Level**

Orientation Toward State Intervention	Grade Level			
	Third	**Sixth**	**Ninth**	**Twelfth**
Positive	67.0%	66.2%	32.0%	30.9%
Neutral	21.4%	19.7%	32.0%	27.9%
Negative	11.7%	14.1%	36.0%	41.2%
Total Number of Students	103	71	50	68

Source: Cummings and Taebel 1978, p. 206.

tion" however does not address the question of who could survive on this income. What then is meant by "poverty level"?

Most poverty statistics in the United States are based on a definition developed first by the Social Security Administration (1964) and later revised by a federal interagency committee (1969). This poverty index actually represents a range of poverty lines that reflect such factors as family size, sex of the family head, number of children under eighteen, and whether the residence is farm or nonfarm.

The 1964 definition of poverty was based on an "economy food plan" developed by the Department of Agriculture. This "diet" represented the least costly of four food plans found nutritionally adequate *for temporary use only* by the department. An earlier survey by this agency (1955) found that families spend one-third of their income for food. Therefore, the poverty line was established by multiplying the amount required to provide an "economy food plan" by three. In 1969, a federal interagency committee recommended that the original methodology be accepted in order to establish a base-year poverty line (1963), but that annual adjustments in the levels be based on changes in the Consumer Price Index (a measure of the rising cost of living) rather than changes in the cost of food included in the economy food plan (US Bureau of the Census 1979, p. 203). thus, due to the original Social Security Administration—Department of Agriculture definition, a miserly poverty level had been institutionalized. Therefore, subsequent adjustments for the percentage increase in the cost of consumer goods were to be computed on this base, effectively perpetuating the systematic understatement of poverty in America. The nature of this definitional distortion is evident in the following table.

TABLE 3–4
Weighted Average Thresholds at the Poverty Level in 1977
by Size of Family and Sex of Head (Farm–NonFarm Residence)

Size of family unit	Total	Nonfarm			Farm		
		Total	Male Head[1]	Female Head[1]	Total	Male Head[1]	Female Head[1]
1 Person (unrelated individual)	$3,067	$3,075	$3,214	$2,969	$2,588	$2,672	$2,498
14 to 64 years	3,147	3,152	3,267	3,023	2,709	2,776	2,569
65 years and over	2,895	2,906	2,936	2,898	2,476	2,495	2,463
2 Persons	3,928	3,951	3,961	3,907	3,318	3,325	3,176
Head 14 to 64 years	4,054	4,072	4,095	3,981	3,466	3,474	3,278
Head 65 years and over	3,637	3,666	3,670	3,646	3,128	3,131	3,079
3 Persons	4,806	4,833	4,860	4,708	4,093	4,110	3,893
4 Persons	6,157	6,191	6,195	6,162	5,273	5,274	5,213
5 Persons	7,279	7,320	7,329	7,238	6,247	6,247	6,237
6 Persons	8,208	8,261	8,268	8,197	7,026	7,026	7,040
7 Persons or more	10,137	10,216	10,249	9,995	8,708	8,706	8.738

[1]For one person (i.e., unrelated individual), sex of the individual.
Source: U.S. Bureau of the Census 1979, p. 206.

The interpretation of this table is forthright. For example, a two-person nonfarm family with the head age sixty-five or over making the princely sum of $3,667 in 1977 *would not be considered below the poverty line.* Yet, even by this and similar standards in 1977, a grim 24.7 million Americans lived below the poverty threshold (US Bureau of the Census 1979, p. 1).

What happens if one turns to a slightly more realistic definition of poverty status? In the autumn of 1976, the Department of Labor reported that a typical four-person urban family required an income of $10,041 to maintain a "lower-level" standard of living; $16,236 for an "intermediate" standard; and $23,759 for a "higher" level. All lower-level families were assumed to be renters spending a monthly total of $164 on housing (including utilities and furnishings, $64 on transportation, $67 on clothing, $75 on medical care, and $250 on food, in addition to taxes, and miscellaneous costs and consumption (US Bureau of Labor Statistics 1979, pp. 486–8).

How many American families had incomes of less than $10,000 in 1976? According to the Bureau of the Census, *30 percent of all families in the United States did not earn what the Department of Labor reported to be the "lower-level" standard of living* described above (*Statistical Abstract of the United States* 1978, p. 452). Such statistics are not strictly comparable as the average family size was 3.37 (not 4) and not all families are urban. However, the point is nonetheless clear.

What about the welfare recipients in the United States? For many people, a discussion of poverty focuses on this class of pariahs. Are their numbers diminishing? In 1970, those requiring welfare assistance in the form of cash payments numbered some 13.3 million persons, roughly 6.5 percent of the population. In 1977, the corresponding percent total was 15.6 million, or 7.1 percent of the total (*Statistical Abstract of the United States* 1978, p. 356). Irrespective of the standard, poverty in America is widespread.

If the poor and near-poor are not disappearing, perhaps it is because the national income is simply not enough to meet the needs of all. For example, each year the Bureau of the Census reports the median income for all families. In 1977, that figure was $16,009. Given such a modest income for the "typical" family, it might appear that there is something of a crisis in national compensation. However, this income level is deceptive and to understand this we must define our statistical terms.

For the statistician, "median" income is the midpoint of an array or range of numbers. It is the point at which 50 percent of the distribution falls below and 50 percent above. For example, in the distribution 2, 4, 6, 8, and 100, the median is 6. The median is not what most people think of as an "average" or, statistically, a "mean." The mean or "average" of the above distribution is 24 (120/5). However, as this distribution is skewed (in this case "top-heavy"), the number 24 is much greater than most of the numbers that constitute the array. Likewise, the distribution of national income is skewed. It is too top-heavy.

If we understand the above example, then we know that the median income does not result from taking the total family income in the country and dividing by the number of family units. Rather, it is simply a mid-point of a distribution. What if one wishes to examine "mean" or "average" income? In 1977, the per capita income in the United States was $7,019 (World Almanac 1979, p. 108). This is the figure that results if the national income is divided by the total population. In that same year, the average size of a family was 3.37 (*Statistical Abstract of the United States* 1978, p. 43). If the per capita income is multiplied by average family size, the resulting figure is $23,654. For a "typical" family of four, the income would be $28,076. *One might wish to compare the per capita income figures with the official poverty level for a family of four ($6,157); the Department of Labor's "lower-level" budget ($10,041 in late 1976); and the median income for all families ($16,009). Only the upper fifth of American families had an income in excess of $25,000 in 1977 (Statistical Abstract of the United States 1978, p. 452).*

Comparing median income with per capita income leads us to certain clear conclusions. First of all, the problem of poverty in America is essentially a matter of *distribution*. Some apparently have a great deal, while others have very little. Secondly, when agencies of the state establish and the means of influence commonly report the official poverty line and median family income, they do in fact establish false standards that have ideological consequences.

Unrealistically low poverty standards allow for the systematic understatement of the extent of poverty in a society. In similar fashion, an emphasis on median as opposed to per capita income or average family income systematically distorts the maldistribution of national income. The extent of structural inequality is accordingly obscured.

The Functionalist Theory of Stratification: The Ideology of Sociology

Inequality supposedly reflects individual differences in capabilities and motivation. This evaluation is based upon the ideological symbols of individualism, competition, free will, and equality of opportunity. Such ideology is not confined to the media or the world view of a political and economic elite. It is expressed in the social sciences as the *functionalist theory of stratification.*

Functionalist theory views stratification as inevitable and necessary for the continuation of society. The argument is that because more rewards are given to those who occupy more socially "important" positions, persons are motivated to achieve those positions. Supposedly, stratification ensures that the most qualified people fill the most important positions in society. As functionalism is based on the order paradigm, it assumes that most people agree on the social significance of various positions and their accompanying rewards (Davis and Moore 1945). The logic of functionalism compels one to hold that famous athletes, comedians, or movie personalities are more important to the smooth functioning of society than the politician, teacher, bus driver, mechanic, or garbage collector. But do people truly agree upon the significance of such positions? Do the salaries of leading executives as shown in Table 3-5 simply reflect a public consensus as to the importance of such "labor"?

How valuable are such executives to the functioning of society? By means of comparison, in 1976 miners earned an average $256 per week, or $13,312 a year (*Statistical Abstract of the United States* 1978, p. 761). Due to inflation, it is a bit inaccurate to compare 1976 miners' wages with the salaries chief executive officers earned in 1979. However, it is essentially correct to say that the average miner works a year to make what Frank Rosenfelt of MGM makes in a day. Further, what should we think of the fact that executive salary is generally unrelated to company performance (Broom and Cushing 1977)? Also, should politicians be from among the richest members of society or should they represent the whole people? (See Table 3-6).

What about those who are well-off because of their "nonmeritorious" inheritance of stocks, bonds, or other assets?

The point is that while corporate ideology seeks to justify differences in income and wealth on the basis of merit and efforts, it also largely ignores differences in inheritance, the winds of chance, and the access to political power. Also, it discourages us to consider the importance of various jobs to the continuation of society. One merely has to experience a strike of garbage collectors to appreciate the significance of this "low status" occupation.

The Advantages of Poverty

If one cannot ignore the poor in North American society, then perhaps one can join with Andrew Carnegie (1835–1919), Scottish immigrant, steel industrialist, builder of libraries, concert halls and other philanthropic works, to identify the "advantages of poverty." In his essay by that title, Carnegie praised the "honest poor" who labored as wage-receivers, "leading lives of virtuous privation," so that their sons could supposedly become "leaders."

> They appear upon the stage, athletes trained for the contest, with sinews braced, indomitable wills, resolved to do or die. Such boys

TABLE 3-5
Total Compensation for Leading U.S. Corporation Executives:1979*

Corporation	Name	Salary & Bonus†	Options, Rights† & Benefits†	Contingent Renumeration†	Total Compensation
Metro-Goldwyn-Mayer	Frank E. Rosenfelt	$ 343,700	$4,870,000	-	$5,213,700
Warner Communications	Steven J. Ross	1,210,184	2,695,521	$1,199,308	5,105,013
American Standard	William A. Marquard	629,583	18,382	3,183,488	3,831,453
Standard Oil (Ind.)	John E. Swearingen	613,862	25,054	3,011,059	3,649,975
Mobil	Rawleigh Warner, Jr.	1,187,055	2,406,385	46,750	3,640,190
Gulf United	E. Grant Fitts	450,000	2,212,717	497,775	3,160,492
Cabot	Robert A. Charpie	597,750	-	2,529,654	3,127,404
Superior Oil	Howard B. Keck	648,021	18,911	2,218,895	2,885,827
City Investing	George T. Scharffenberger	729,100	5,894	1,850,095	2,585,089
Colt Industries	George A. Strichman	631,040	1,432,895	375,000	2,438,935
Pennzoil	J. Hugh Liedtke	440,525	72,502	1,865,490	2,378,517
Revlon	Michel C. Bergerac	899,900	1,442,520	3,750	2,346,170

*In addition to the top twelve chief executive officers listed here, another 60 had total compensation of $1 million or above in 1979.

†Definitions: *Salary and bonus*: Cash Compensation. *Options, rights, and benefits*: "Fringes" such as club dues, life insurance, use of company car or plane, etc. Primarily derived from exercise of stock options and increased value of company stock. *Contingent Renumeration*: Primarily increased value of pension plan, deferred compensation agreements, and performance-based incentive plans.

Source: Compiled from data presented in *Forbes* Magazine, June 9, 1980, pp. 116–117.

TABLE 3-8
**The Distribution of Wealth among Members of
the United States Senate as Compared with
the American Population as a Whole**

Net Worth Category	Percentage of US Senate	Percentage of US Population
Less than $20,000	0	56.0%
$20,000–$49,999	5.0%	24.0
$50,000–$199,999	38.0	16.0
$200,000–$999,999	28.0	2.0
$1,000,000 or more	28.0	0.3
	99.0	98.0

Sources: Ralph Nader's Citizen Action Group report as summarized by Lloyd Shearer, "The Richest Men in the US Senate," *Parade*, May 23, 1976, p. 7. The percentages for the US Senate are based only on the seventy-eight for whom reliable data were available.

> always have marched, and always will march, straight to the front and lead the world; they are the epoch makers. . . . It will, I think, be seen that the possession of ease is almost fatal to greatness and goodness, and that the greatest and best of our race have necessarily been nurtured in the bracing school of poverty—the only school capable of producing the supremely great, the genius . . . (in Kirkland, pp. 53–64).

Does such an unabashed endorsement of "triumph of the will" correspond with the realities of the contemporary poor? We fear rather that the captains of industry and the leaders of state are essentially a self-replenishing and cohesive group, most frequently born to wealth and the associated trappings of power (Moore 1979). The condition of the most impoverished members of society is perhaps best reflected in a recent study relating income poverty to infant mortality. This demographical analysis has determined that within the white population of legitimate births, the risk of neonatal and postneonatal mortality is some 50 percent greater for infants born in poverty than for those born to the nonpoor. For in a society of structured inequality, nutritional resources and health care facilities continue to reflect the conditions of privilege (Gortmaker 1979).

The "advantages" of poverty may also be reflected in a close look at the welfare payments that supposedly free some of the poor from the ordeal of work. Table 3-7 reveals the average monthly benefits to the recipients for the five largest welfare programs in the United States for 1976. An examination of the benefits must begin with an understanding of what these programs are intended to do. Medicaid is a program designed to provide medical services for the poor. It is to be distinguished from Medicare (see Chapter Twelve), a medical insurance program for the elderly who need not be poor in order to be covered. Aid to Families with Dependent Children (AFDC) is the largest program, with approximately 10.8 million recipients in 1977 (*Statistical Abstract of the United States* 1978, p. 356). AFDC seeks to aid poor families with children under the age of eighteen. Supplemental Security Income (SSI), a part of the social security program, is designed for the poorest of the aged, blind, and disabled. General assistance is meant to reach impoverished persons who do not otherwise qualify for the above programs.

A brief look at welfare in the United States justifies the observation that it is a crazy quilt of overlapping piecemeal programs sustaining both federal and state bureaucracies. One thing is abundantly clear. The average beneficiary can do little more than subsist, and even that minimum is dependent on the region of the country in which one resides. This is true because federal support for welfare programs administered at the state level is dependent on state contributions. (For example, in 1976 in the state of Mississippi, the average AFDC recipient received a total cash grant of $14 per month.)

The total outlay for the above major poverty programs was nearly $36 billion in 1976. However, this large sum if divided equally among the nation's "official" poor would yield an average benefit of $1,389 for the entire year (*Statistical Abstract of the United States* 1978, p. 360). Thus, the "typical" welfare family of 4 would have received total assistance valued at $5,556. Such a sum represents a little over one-half the lower level standard of the B.L.S. for a typical 4-person urban family in 1976. Modern-day Carnegies may wish to believe that the poor are somehow advantaged. Those assets seem to include the physical deaths of infants and the economic mortality of being on "welfare."

Corporation Dominance: Survival of the Fittest?

According to the prevailing ideology, property inequality, reflected not simply in the holdings of individuals but also in the assets and revenues of businesses, is supposedly a matter of merit. At the personal level, if one individual is rich and another poor, the former's position supposedly reflects hard work, diligence, and a variety of socially valued traits, while the latter's indicates personal failings or faults. Extended to the corporate level, if a corporation has come to a position of dominance (or shared dominance with a few others), such success is supposedly due to efficiency, pioneering technology, managerial talent, and a host of other laudable reasons. Those squeezed out disappear not because they are small, not because they are the victims of monopoly and oligopoly, but because they did not win the "survival of the fittest" game.

Is it true that increasing economic dominance by giant corporations is a

TABLE 3-7
Outlays for the Five Largest Welfare Programs—Total, Federal, and Per Recipient: 1976

(Covers outlays by Federal, State, and local governments for, in most cases, year ending June 30. AFDC: Aid to families with dependent children; SSI: Supplemental security income)

Region and State	All outlays Total (mil. dol.)	All outlays Per poor resident (dol.)	Federal Total (mil. dol.)	Federal Percent of total outlays	Medicaid Total	Medicaid Federal	AFDC Total	AFDC Federal	SSI	Food stamps	General assistance
U.S.	35,937	1,389	22,261	61.9	134	73	73	40	116	24	103
Northeast	11,990	2,428	6,441	53.7	185	95	96	49	134	21	108
Maine	195	1,711	148	75.9	119	84	55	39	88	23	22
N.H.	83	1,317	56	67.5	141	85	74	44	111	23	35
Vt.	89	2,244	66	74.2	139	97	78	55	115	20	-
Mass.	1,430	2,924	735	51.4	114	57	95	48	139	20	115
R.I.	193	2,075	116	60.1	139	79	76	43	102	19	79
Conn.	431	1,850	238	55.2	155	77	83	42	135	22	70
N.Y.	6,314	2,859	3,234	51.2	224	112	111	56	114	17	117
N.J.	1,181	1,965	678	57.4	120	60	83	41	113	25	83
Pa.	2,073	1,886	1,172	56.5	234	130	85	47	128	20	122
Midwest	8,468	1,589	5,095	60.2	123	66	75	40	106	23	103
Ohio	1,396	1,474	927	66.4	130	71	65	35	102	26	74
Ind.	435	1,087	297	68.3	154	88	55	31	102	24	-
Ill.	2,185	1,970	1,254	57.4	85	43	79	39	118	26	114
Mich.	1,860	2,601	973	52.3	138	69	88	44	131	18	134
Wis.	765	1,947	456	59.6	176	106	98	59	111	18	82
Minn.	569	1,745	345	60.6	239	136	90	51	88	21	103
Iowa	284	1,131	183	64.4	153	87	86	49	84	21	34
Mo.	495	855	355	71.7	60	35	44	26	97	25	62
Kans.	244	953	143	58.6	132	71	75	41	83	19	94
Nebr.	121	738	79	65.3	150	84	65	37	95	21	-
S. Dak.	63	578	47	74.6	149	100	67	45	86	23	18
N. Dak.	50	625	34	68.0	201	116	79	46	88	22	25

South	8,750	784	6,985	79.8	105	66	42	28	95	26	71
Del.	62	1,088	39	62.9	92	46	63	31	99	25	33
Md.	552	1,643	339	61.4	123	61	58	29	111	26	102
D.C.	258	2,016	148	57.4	130	65	73	37	119	21	144
Va.	495	924	347	70.1	126	73	64	37	89	23	78
W. Va.	218	604	187	85.8	85	61	53	38	104	22	17
N.C.	654	855	532	81.3	118	80	55	37	99	25	20
S.C.	357	732	308	86.3	83	54	28	21	91	26	50
Ga.	725	962	594	81.9	108	67	32	24	93	25	30
Fla.	776	701	647	83.4	88	50	40	23	104	30	-
Ky.	545	840	454	83.3	76	55	56	40	105	25	-
Tenn.	552	779	465	84.2	94	61	34	24	92	27	-
Ala.	501	651	419	83.6	84	54	30	22	92	25	13
Miss.	400	530	353	88.3	62	41	14	11	94	26	12
La.	642	693	551	85.8	95	68	36	26	100	26	53
Ark.	334	705	291	87.1	79	59	39	30	86	26	1
Okla.	386	869	288	74.6	217	146	60	41	111	20	11
Tex.	1,293	681	1,023	79.1	135	81	32	23	85	24	-
West	6,729	1,512	3,740	55.6	115	60	82	42	152	23	101
Mont.	64	653	47	73.4	157	99	55	35	95	26	32
Idaho	72	673	55	76.4	134	91	83	56	103	22	-
Wyo.	17	370	13	76.5	(NA)	(NA)	63	39	87	24	37
Colo.	292	1,659	194	66.4	123	67	67	37	101	27	71
Utah	102	713	76	74.5	151	106	81	57	97	21	101
Nev.	51	962	32	62.7	190	95	55	27	107	29	-
Ariz.	122	419	101	82.8	-	-	41	22	102	25	84
N. Mex.	146	521	128	87.7	91	67	45	33	100	27	73
Calif.	4,852	1,925	2,460	50.7	112	56	85	43	167	22	103
Oreg.	299	1,068	203	67.9	111	66	85	50	102	23	83
Wash.	491	1,379	308	62.7	119	64	84	45	124	24	103
Alaska	37	974	22	59.5	397	198	103	52	158	38	55
Hawaii	185	3,033	103	55.7	100	50	104	52	128	28	119

Source: *Statistical Abstract of the United States 1978*, p. 360.

matter of simply doing the job better? Or do larger firms receive often unrecognized support that has little to do with merit?

> A report released last month by the House Small Business Committee's Subpanel on Antitrust, Consumers and Employment concluded that: "Instead of encouraging small-business innovation the Government has made it more difficult by giving most of the Federal funds for research and development to the largest firms, which are the least efficient vehicles for the development of new technology" (Reece 1978, p. 5).

It is not that the state necessarily intends to support inefficiency. As we shall see later, state welfare, whether directed to corporations or individuals, is predicated on the principle: "Them that has, gets." As far as technological innovation is concerned, large corporations do not appear very "deserving."

> Yet, according to a Commerce Department study cited in the same [above] report, "small business accounted for more than half of all scientific and technological developments since the beginning of this century." Another study cited in the report found that from 1953 to 1973, "small firms produced about four times as many innovations per research and development dollar as medium-sized firms, and about 24 times as many as the largest firms" (Reece 1978, p. 5).

Defending Inequality: The Military "Solution"

"Making the world safe for democracy" was cited by the administration of Woodrow Wilson as the prime reason for the United States' entering the First World War. This specific ideology addresses the question of "national defense," and is introduced here for two reasons.

First of all, the defense of corporate order is by definition a defense of inequality. On a global level the most casual observer would be forced to concede that American foreign policy has little to do with democracy and a great deal to do with the interests of multinational corporations (Chomsky 1973). The United States provides arms, loans, weapons systems, and other aids to a variety of nations in the Third World (primarily the developing countries of Asia, Africa, and South America) whose leaders have little interest in rule by the people. A few of such arms customers were prerevolutionary Iran, ruled by Shah Pahlavi before his exodus in 1978; prerevolutionary Cuba, under Batista before his ouster in 1958 by forces led by Castro; prerevolutionary Vietnam ruled first by the French colonialists and then by a succession of military and civilian leaders before the end of the American military involvement in 1975; and prerevolutionary Nicaragua, ruled by the Somoza family before the successful "Sandanista" movement in 1978. At this writing the United States continues to support military regimes in Chile and Pakistan, among others. All of these regimes represent examples of enormous economic and political inequality and most have been censured by international organizations (such as Amnesty International), commissions, and scholars.

Secondly, the defense of corporate order, as we shall demonstrate in a later section, is a means of *producing* inequality. The investment of staggering amounts of the nation's wealth brings return to these corporate contractors who do business with the Department of Defense. However, such expenditures trickle down only to those workers who are employed in the military and military-based industries, workers whose talents might better be used elsewhere. The trickle, of course, dries up before it reaches those truly in need.

If there is a pattern to the military "solution," domestic and international, it appears to include the support of regimes and policies that oppose mass-based movements. Loosely labeled "socialism," the rise of such forces constitutes a clear and present danger to corporate interests abroad as later data will confirm.

With the identification and critique of the prevailing ideologies for inequality in corporate society behind us, it is now possible to turn to the emergence, institutionalization, and maintenance of this problem. The reader is advised to review pages 70–80 in Chapter Two before continuing.

EMERGENCE

The roots of inequality in contemporary North American society must be found in the shifting historical currents termed mercantilism, the Industrial Revolution, and corporatism (Clement 1977, pp. 15–20). Once we understand this historical development of class society, it will be possible to identify more specific social movements and interest groups that have successfully struggled to institutionalize particular (ideologically compatible) definitions of the problems of inequality.

Free to Lose

Mercantilism held sway in the emerging states of Western Europe in the period ranging from the sixteenth through the eighteenth centuries. Thus, for three centuries, colonial expansion was at its zenith as the Crown sought to establish the yoke of control over trade. Whether the commodity involved was precious metal, coffee, spices, or slaves, rival powers competed often to the point of warfare to secure these riches and the sea lanes that made feasible their passage. Economic arrangements in Great Britain represent a case in point.

> More specifically, there was virtually no area of economic life untouched by State controls, subsidies, or regulations. Overseas trade was carried on through numerous Crown-chartered trading monopolies, only the most famous of which was the East India Company. Industries deemed critical by the State were similarly vested with monopolies of production . . . (Dowd 1977, p. 7).

Under mercantilism, the state regulated the supply of labor, its geographic movement, and its working conditions. Government controls also affected the sale of land and the state, by means of taxation, in effect regulated the finance industry. Through the nature of the charter issued by the Crown, the Bank of England had a virtual banking monopoly (Dowd 1977, pp. 6–7).

It was in this historical context that Adam Smith, historian, economist, moralist, wrote *The Wealth of Nations* (1776). In it, he essentially repudiated mercantilism because it rendered the economy subject to favors bestowed by the Crown. Instead of state regulation, Smith proposed a system he called *laissez-faire*, whereby the demands of the marketplace would determine "what should be produced, who should produce it, how it should be produced, and how the production should be distributed." It might come as a surprise to some of today's "free marketeers" that the foundation for their ideas is more than two centuries old. It would perhaps be an even greater surprise to know that the notions of "the law of supply and demand" and the gospel of free competition were played out historically. For with the coming of the Industrial Revolution and the emergence of a new land born in hostile reaction to the British Crown, the stage was set for a test of Adam Smith's ideas.

The nineteenth century was to be an epoch of massive industrial growth and technological gigantism, first in Great Britain and then in the United States (particularly in the post-Civil War period). The constraints of mercantilism slowly slipped away. The new powers were to be those of the private sector. By 1840 in Great Britain, the vision of Adam Smith had largely been realized. Free trade was the order of the day (Dowd 1977, pp. 11–15).

During this period the forces of industrialism were to grow slowly at first, and then with a gathering momentum surge forward in the last several decades of the century. It was fed through this period by cheap and abundant raw materials, exploited labor, and the emptiness of state regulation. In the pre-Civil War era, property ownership was reasonably diffuse (Mills 1951, pp. 6–8) and competition prevailed. However, the free-market economy carried within its own seeds of destruction. For success in the marketplace came not as a simple consequence of building a better product at a lower cost. Businesses were not to disappear simply because they could not meet the competition. With the coming of large-scale technologies, only those with access to significant amounts of capital could afford methods of production that provided obvious marketplace advantage. Smith's idea of the free market, regulated essentially by the "invisible hand" of competitive response to the forces of supply and demand, was based on an economic model that held only for the early stages of industrial capitalism. This was a time when competitors were numerous, operating in a context of expanding economic opportunity created by the decline of mercantilism, the rise of industrial innovation and, especially in North America, bountiful labor and resources. The "Achilles' heel" of the so-called free-market system proved to be the concentration of vital large-scale, technologically dependent industries. With economic sectors more and more dominated by this tendency toward monopolization, Adam Smith's invisible hand [of competition] became truly invisible.

As the informal regulation born of competition lessens, the inherent drive of the private economy toward profit maximization is unchecked. To dominate the marketplace, the marshalling of capital is necessary. In the last three decades of the nineteenth century in North America, the corporation form of economic organization became increasingly prominent. Ironically, from the mid-1870s through the mid-1890s, it appeared that Smith's vision might be realized in America. This was a period of low prices due to technological efficiency and foreign competition secured through "free trade." However, with the lowering of prices came the lowering of profits. It was competition, not state regulation that proved to be the arch-enemy of corporate power (Dowd 1977, pp. 68–71).

Rise of the Merger

The method employed by the leading corporations of the day to avoid the strange depression of decreased profits was known at the time as the combination movement, the contemporary term for which is the merger. Sometimes the decision to merge came as a consequence of agreement among the parties involved. On other occasions, a state of industrial warfare prevailed as "robber barons" resorted to a variety of tactics including armed violence, sabotage, and the destruction of the property of those who were "uncooperative." The establishment of the Rockefeller oil trust is perhaps the best-known example of making an offer the competitor couldn't refuse (Josephson 1934). By whatever means, between 1897 and 1905, the combination movement saw 318 corporations gain control of over 5300 industrial firms (Dowd 1977, p. 71). The same market system that had brought about corporate power had unavoidably bestowed upon its creation the means by which the market could be destroyed.

The tendencies toward corporate concentration, oligopoly, and monopoly have continued unabated since the waning years of the last century to the older pattern of the *horizontal merger*, by which one concern acquires those that directly compete with it, was added the *vertical merger*. This pattern, in which a single entity owns its suppliers and customers, is increasingly evident in the petroleum and other industries. For example, "Big Oil" today owns production technology, refineries, and transportation modes (supertankers, trucks, and so forth) with retailers totally dependent on product allocation by the corporation whose output they sell. In addition, the concentration of corporate power continues in the form of the *conglomerate*, by which essentially unrelated industries come under the control of a single firm (Dowd 1977, p. 73).

The State as Corporate Ally

The corporate consolidation evident in the modern North American economic order is not confined to the development detailed to this point. Another ally was to be recovered from the dust of history. Within the context of public outcry for regulation and control of robber barons run amuck, the corporate powers that prevailed began to fashion a tenuous alliance with the state. To be specific, state regulatory agencies came to provide the appearance of control while often securing a monopoly or favored market condition for the powerful and established concerns within the industry they were to regulate. For example, farmers protesting transportation monopoly demanded the regulation of the railroads that gave rise to the Interstate Commerce Commission in 1886. The railroads, however, managed to shape regulatory legislation and policy to their liking (Kolko 1965). Perhaps even more critically, the state through its powers of taxation became a source of new capital (see the later discussion on the military-industrial complex, pp. 130–131). The contemporary state system includes not only branches of government and the various levels of bureaucracy but also the means of social control: courts, police, and the military (Miliband 1969). As we shall demonstrate throughout this text, these have proven to be among the foremost of corporate assets. Under mercantilism, the Crown dispensed its favors to the privileged few. Under corporatism, the privileged few also carry the sceptre of state power.

POOR PEOPLE'S MOVEMENTS

With an understanding of the structure of inequality in hand, it is possible to examine a few of the specific movements designed to right inequality. A number of examples from North American history have sought to address some facet of the problem. For example, chapters that follow examine what have been termed the women's movement, the labor movement, and the civil rights movement. Here the focus is on those forces defined more or less explicitly as "poor."

Historically it appears that we have a "Columbus complex" regarding inequality, periodically rediscovering want and affluence. With the emergence of capitalism and industrialism, great differences in wealth became magnified in the growing urban areas. Extreme wealth justaposed with extreme want ultimately helped to bring about reform attempts: the human rights movements of the seventeeth and eighteeth centuries, the French Revolution, and others. However, these and other manifestations of inequality have often been confronted without consideration of the economic foundation of political powerlessness. Thus, various movements in Western societies (such as women's rights, civil rights, poor people's betterment, and labor) have sought to gain the vote, representation in government, or changes in the legal system without questioning the relationship between ownership of wealth and the control of the state.

The squalor and deprivation of the working class in England described by Karl Marx, Frederick Engels, and other nineteenth-century writers were real and largely the products of exploitation. Conditions of extreme inequality thus provided the stimulus for a variety of sociopolitical movements for reformation, including revolution. For example, the populist movement in turn-of-the-century North America identified large corporations and their wealth with corruption and exploitation (Wolfe 1978). Twentieth-century revolutions in Russia, Mexico, Cuba, Algiers, China, Southeast Asia, and Nicaragua among others, have largely been based upon class inequalities and class oppression. At this writing, the ongoing conflict in Northern Ireland, though often interpreted in religious terms, runs along class lines. Protestants who dominate the economy and the state, favor continued British rule; while the Catholic minority, economically and politically disadvantaged, is more sympathetic to uniting with the Republic of Ireland.

Of course, the reaction to inequality will be based upon understanding its causes. If, for example, poor people are viewed as having deficiencies in character, skills, or training that causes their impoverishment, then those in power will emphasize correcting such defects. They will launch job training, motivational training, and other similar programs to alleviate the problem. However, if poverty is viewed as a logical consequence of the way corporate societies are organized, then the stress will be on changing the patterns of ownership.

Matza (1966) has pointed out that historically society has categorized the poor as deserving and undeserving. The aged, the physically or mentally handicapped, and children are generally viewed as deserving social assistance. On the other hand, the able-bodied poor are generally viewed as disreputable because it is assumed they have largely chosen this fate. Actually, the majority of the employable poor in Canada are working at degrading, low-paying jobs (National Council of Welfare 1977). Furthermore, only about 1 percent of those on welfare in the U.S. are unemployed males (Julian 1977). Although unemployment is a continuing crisis in North American societies, the onus for one's work status continues to rest on the individual.

The Great Depression

That specific era of American history known as the Great Depression began roughly with the stock market crash of October 1929 and continued through the next decade until the economic stimulus of the Second World War ended the nightmare. It was during this period that serious questions were posed concerning the viability of corporate society. It was also then that the state proved to be an invaluable ally in the struggle to preserve a tottering economic order.

Faced with growing legions of paupers, the American system of relief proved incapable of effective response. Before, the destitute had been dependent on the handouts of the private sector and minimally funded local public programs. Such meager resources were hardly adequate in the wake of such an economic cataclysm. America, despite its abundance of resources, was to witness widespread starvation (Shannon 1960, pp. 36–54).

In a society of classes, the workers' movements often capture center stage. However, during the Great Depression the factories were to empty out; and those who were displaced were to unite in opposition to the bankruptcy and inadequacy of an unplanned relief system (Piven and Cloward 1977, pp. 41–76).

At the onset of the decade, few arrangements existed to provide systematically for the needs of the poor. Before the corporate order embraced the "equal opportunity" ideology, "a social darwinist" variation of "privitism" prevailed. "Charity" was left to private sources and those served by them were stigmatized.

> Work and self-reliance meant grueling toil at low wages for many people. So long as that was so, the dole could not be dispensed permissively for fear some would choose it over work. Thus, most of the poor were simply excluded from aid, ensuring that they had no

alternative but to search for whatever work they could find at whatever wage was offered. And if they found no work, then they would have to survive by whatever means they could (Piven and Cloward 1977, p. 42).

Shackled by a rigid commitment to what he perceived to be the ultimate virtues of "home rule," President Hoover determined that relief was still a concern for state and local governments. In the summer of 1932, facing a presidential campaign in the fall, Hoover finally consented to a form of federal relief action. The Emergency Relief Act of 1932 authorized that the relief system be bolstered through government loans of up to $300 million from the Reconstruction Finance Corporation. However, this same RFC that lent $90 million to the Central Republic Bank and Trust of Chicago in 1932 lent only $30 million to the states for the purpose of relief in that same year. Apparently, federal help for the hungry was considered a greater intrusion on the principles of free enterprise than federal help for banks (Perdue 1974, pp. 53–54).

Set against the grim material realities was the continuing admonition on the part of the political and industrial elite to respond with "courage." Few were impressed by such sermons. More skeptical observers were fearing the very survival of the profit system. The Dean of the Harvard Business School declared that "capitalism is on trial and on the issue of this trial may depend the whole future of Western Civilization" (Leighton 1932).

An overview of the social reality of the early Depression suggests that fear of revolution was not to be easily assuaged. Food riots plagued metropolitan areas and more than 3,000 "hunger marchers" descended on Washington in 1932. The most serious display of class violence was to come from the farmers of the Upper Midwest rather than the suffering workers dismissed from industry, however. The National Farm Holiday Association, in the summer of 1932, attempted to force farm prices up by stopping the flow of food into urban areas. This was a "stay on the land" movement rather than a "back to the land" migration, for farmers were being evicted in increasing numbers from their homes. Omaha, Council Bluffs, Des Moines, and Sioux City were blockaded by hordes of picketing farmers. The participants likened their "illegal" action to the Boston Tea Party. Though the farmers often used the term "revolution," history appears to bear out the interpretation that such talk referred basically to an urgent rejoining of the urban-rural battle. They pictured themselves as engaged in an agricultural holy war against the "Eastern Establishment" or vaguely defined "international bankers" (Vorse 1932).

It was within this setting of uncertainty and despair that the loosely knit movement of the unemployed came into being. Those involved were simply seeking to cope with the day-to-day problems of securing food or halting or delaying eviction processes. However, in 1934 a Socialist leader by the name of David Lasser argued that an organization of national scope was required. Such a vision was reflected in a growing number of attempts to unite the local movements. Finally, in 1935 the Worker's Alliance of America was formed which claimed a membership of 600,000 in forty-three states. Its leadership as well as its guiding ideology, however, were not consistent with the ideological orientation of corporate society. To the contrary, the Worker's Alliance defined the Great Depression as further evidence of the exploitative nature of the economic order (Piven and Cloward 1977, pp. 72–76).

In a manner analogous to the opposing currents in the labor movement (described in the next chapter), a race was being run between such organizations as the Worker's Alliance and the emerging federal relief programs. For in 1933, a new administration espousing a "new deal" for the American people had taken office. During the Roosevelt years, these programs formed the foundation for what we will shortly describe as the modern "poorhouse" state. The result was the disappearance locally and nationally of the largest poor people's movement ever to oppose corporate power. The Roosevelt landslide of 1936 buried the gaudy and unrestricted capitalism of the Twenties and signaled the formal institutionalization of a "relief" role for state power. The desperation measures of the Thirties were destined to survive, as state responsibility toward the poor had been redefined. The Republican Party platform of 1940 underscores this reality. Based on the dual realization that the people now expected something more substantial than the chance to become millionaires, and that Roosevelt's policies were directed toward the salvation of the capitalist system, the Republican philosophy drifted away from the *laissez-faire* of bygone years. The candidate of the party, Wendell Wilkie, was the former president of a Southern utility company (Commonwealth and Southern) who had actively opposed the TVA as a form of state socialism.[1] This same Wilkie in 1940 declared the TVA a *fait accompli* and proposed it be given a fair chance. Here was the Wall Street lawyer from Indiana proclaiming that the system of 1929 could not be allowed to stand and that an extension of federal control over the economy was necessary, even though the Democrats had gone too far. Though this attempt to meet Roosevelt on his own ground was doomed to failure, the Republican campaign of 1940 signaled the understanding that capitalism had undergone some refurbishment due to the ordeal of the Depression decade. New Deal programs, "socialistic" by the standards of the Twenties, had paradoxically managed to give hope to the American corporate order at its darkest hour (Perdue 1974, pp. 70–71).

Interested scholars can only speculate about the destiny of American society had this nation not found the economic "salvation" of armed conflict. The United States had by no means recovered from the Depression prior to the stimulation of the economy through defense spending.

[1]The Tennessee Valley Authority is a federally owned system of dams that generates hydroelectric power and provides flood control to a vast area.

Roosevelt's third presidential landslide came at a time when 7.5 million workers were unemployed, approximately 14 percent of the civilian work force. Though the war years lie beyond the scope of this inquiry, it is important to note that the rise of the economy in response to the stimulation of military expenditures was not lost on industrial leaders. Charles Wilson, President of General Motors, elated over the war boom, advocated a "permanent war economy" (Barnet, in Chomsky 1973). He did not, needless to say, propose a permanent state of shooting war to implement his program. Continuous preparation, a readiness for armed conflict would suffice.

The Rise and Fall of the
National Welfare Rights Organization

During the Great Depression, the state developed a variety of programs that were administered to, and purportedly for, poor people. While the Worker's Alliance was no doubt a stimulus to the welfare efforts of the Roosevelt Administration, it passed away quietly. However, in the 1960s poor people again organized to have a voice in policies and programs that affected them. Such programs featured the rhetoric of "maximum feasible participation," which instilled fear into local and federal politicians and bureaucrats and brought about repression. However, it also produced many professionals and poor people dedicated to establishing a power base among the poor. This effort was particularly evident in the National Welfare Rights Organization (NWRO).

Formed in 1967, NWRO encompassed various local welfare rights organizations in the United States that had emerged in the 1960s (Jackson and Johnson 1974; Steiner 1971; Piven and Cloward 1977). Membership grew from 5,000 in 1967 to over 30,000 in 1969. One had to be a recipient, a former recipient, or member of a poor family to join. The major goals of the organization were decent jobs for those who could work and adequate income for those who could not. These goals were pursued by organizing around local issues and lobbying for changes in national policy. Due to welfare cutbacks within a context of stagflation,[2] the National Welfare Rights Organization was bankrupt by 1975. While other causes for its failure are being debated, the NWRO undoubtedly provided for increased attention to inequality in society and efforts to eradicate it. Like other movements in North America (trade unions, civil rights, suffragette), the NWRO attempted to address political solutions in

[2]By the mid-Seventies, many of the movements of the 1960s had largely disappeared, victims of an end to the catalyst that was Vietnam, the assassination of symbolic leaders, and an economic order in which unemployment and inflation climbed together.

isolation from their economic base. Nonetheless, efforts by poor persons collectively to change their plight will continue to be pursued. As one observer of poverty in Canada remarks:

> To fully overcome poverty the poor have to shed their fatalism, well-grounded apathy and despair. To do this they have to have power to make themselves seen, heard, and felt in Canada (Knight 1973, p. 2).

For the poor to be more effective, coalitions with other groups appear necessary. By focusing more upon the corporate structure of inequality in society rather than simply on poverty, advocates of economic equality may form a larger base for sociopolitical change. Roach and Roach (1978, p. 167) believe that the "basic task of activists who are concerned about poverty is the promotion of socialist consciousness among the rank and file in the trade unions." While the appeal to a class consciousness and workers' struggle is not new, it does create a "community of fate" for working people and the poor. By looking beyond official definitions of the poor and poverty and looking at the distribution of income, one may gain some understanding of how a nation's political and economic institutions are related.

INSTITUTIONALIZATION

The structural imperatives of corporate society—profit, growth, and concentration—cannot be separated from inequality. The predictable consequences of this form of social order have been largely responsible for the rise of what is loosely termed the welfare state. Stated ideally, the welfare state organizes its power to modify the play of market forces in at least the following three ways: (1) guaranteeing qualified individuals and families some income irrespective of the market value of their work or property; (2) narrowing somewhat the extent of insecurity by enabling individuals and families to meet certain contingencies such as sickness, old age, and unemployment; and (3) ensuring that all citizens, without distinction of status or class, are offered the best standards available in certain social services (Briggs 1965). As we shall shortly demonstrate, the state in corporate society has been far more efficient in seeing to the welfare of the rich, the corporations, and the military than to the welfare of the poor.

Before we examine the institutionalization in law and policy of the problem of inequality, it is necessary to be clear on one vital point. *Inequality* has not really been defined by many as a problem in North America. Because classes are a part of the corporate order of things, the domination of the economic order by giant businesses and the preserving of the wealth of the owning class are simply a natural consequence of the way in which American and Canadian societies are organized. Curiously, the problem of inequality is more frequently termed the problem of *poverty*. Our contention is quite simple. One cannot understand the sociology of poverty unless one also understands the sociology of wealth.

Welfare generally refers to a state of health, prosperity, and well-being. The most casual examination of a society of classes shows that the poor are relatively unhealthy, and frequently degraded. On the other hand, there are those persons and organizations whose welfare seems remarkably in order. To understand this, it is necessary to redefine the term "welfare." In so doing, we may find that there exists a state-sponsored "dual-welfare" system that, quite by design, favors the haves over the have-nots (Tussing 1974).

When the subject of state support for the poor comes up, there are those who view this as "socialism," a denial of the individual right to triumph by strength of will. If state support represents "socialism" and its absence "free enterprise," then it is clear that corporate society has institutionalized socialism for big business, the wealthy, and the military while preserving the virtues of rugged individualism for the poor.

The Wealthfare State[3]

If one examines the laws, policies, and programs of the state that supposedly have to do with the public welfare, it becomes clear that the most obvious welfare system is the one that serves the poor (Tussing 1974). On the other hand, the least visible welfare system and, we might add, one that is much more efficient and effective is that for the nonpoor. For example, a huge welfare apparatus is set up to process the needy. When they receive medical benefits, if any, they are clearly marked as "welfare" recipients. If they use food stamps to purchase groceries, they are also set apart. Of course, many people have their favorite story of the poor person using the taxpayers' money to make Cadillac payments, buy filet mignon, and get free medical care. As previously proven, such myths are without serious basis in fact. (Table 3–7 substantiates this.) However, there are those "more fortunate" who seem to do quite well. How do they do it?

A hidden system of state supports serves the nonpoor. For purposes of analysis, we shall employ the term "wealthfare" to describe this far less visible set of government handouts. Throughout this section, our analysis is guided by a simple logic. If those with wealth and power are in a posi-

---

[3]The term "wealthfare" is used by Jonathan Turner to describe state support of the nonpoor.

tion to influence the state, then the state is likely to do a better job of meeting their needs than those of the poor and powerless. This rather obvious argument seems to have escaped the net of general critics of "welfare."

At the onset, we are compelled to mention that welfare for the poor does prove beneficial to the nonpoor. The federal food stamp program in the United States, for example, was developed under the auspices of the Department of Agriculture, an agency interested foremost in the prosperity of agribusiness. Poor people must eat and those involved in the production, processing, distribution, and sale of foods benefit. A similar argument can be made with regard to other expenses.

The above consideration notwithstanding, there are other much clearer and more compelling examples of state support for the nonpoor. For obvious reasons, such supports are not generally referred to as welfare. The less visible government "wealthfare" assumes the form of civilian and defense contracts, price supports, export-import subsidies, and the notorious "tax loopholes" (Turner 1977, pp. 204–8).

The United States government spent an estimated $24 billion on research and development in 1978 (*Statistical Abstract of the United States* 1978, p. 625). Such monies produce knowledge and useful materials, devices, systems, methods, or processes that *frequently directly benefit industry*. Of course, some of this money trickles down to unionized workers who are not among the poor. However, it seldom reaches those industries that Michael Harrington (1968) characterizes as the "sweatshops of cockroach capitalism." Thus, the "working poor" in addition to the welfare poor, are not beneficiaries. For example, government R & D money is used to pay industrial polluters to develop the means to control pollution. (See Chapter Five).

Government price supports are designed to control the value of many commodities in the marketplace. To illustrate, the "target price" of an agricultural product is set by the U.S. Dept. of Agriculture at a cerain level. If the farmer cannot sell the product on the open market for this price, then the government will pay a cash subsidy in the amount of the difference. Such a policy is obviously of greater value to large, increasingly corporate-owned farms than to smaller operators.

Export-import policies are also intended to regulate the marketplace. Through quotas and taxes, the importing of foreign goods is restricted and high prices (and profits) are maintained. The basic industries of important sectors of the economy are most clearly affected (such as textiles, steel, automobiles, and chemicals).

The most important form of "wealthfare" is the hidden subsidy generally referred to as "tax loopholes." Actually the term "loophole" is misleading. It implies that those who write the tax laws inadvertently allow some to reduce their taxes. To the contrary, what Philip Stern (1973) referred to as the "rape of the taxpayer" is still applicable—and intentional. In short, tax laws are intended to stimulate the economy. They also allow the preservation of capital and the accumulation and transmission via inheritance of huge personal fortunes. While the intricacies of tax law are beyond the scope of this effort, it will suffice to examine the general costs of what has recently been termed "tax expenditures."

> Tax expenditure data are intended to show the cost to the Federal Government, in terms of revenue it has foregone, from tax provisions that have been enacted as incentives for the private sector of the economy or have that effect even though initially having a different objective. The tax incentives usually are designed to encourage certain kinds of economic behavior as an alternative to employing direct expenditures or loan programs to achieve the same or similar objectives. The provisions take the form of exclusions, deductions, credits, preferential tax rates or deferrals of tax liability (U.S. Congress, Joint Committee on Taxation 1977, p. 1).

Translation: Tax expenditures (more clearly, tax losses) mean that the federal government has "forgiven" taxes that it would have otherwise collected in order to provide the private sector with a stimulus (incentive) to behave in a certain way. This is done in lieu of a direct expenditure or loan program. However, whether the state is making a direct payment (as with welfare for the poor) or forgiving taxes (welfare for the nonpoor), the consequence is precisely the same. Both represent expenditures.

The Joint Committee on Taxation regularly prepares a little-known report showing in detail the specific areas in which tax losses occur. It is important to realize that "tax expenditures" (lost tax revenue) do *not* include the ordinary deductions related to the process of earning income. To be clear, such directly related deductions are considered simply the cost of doing business. For example, businesses are allowed to depreciate capital assets such as machinery over a period of years and to deduct these sums from earnings to reduce tax liability. This is obviously a tax advantage, but the Joint Committee on Taxation *does not* consider this a tax expenditure. However, tax law also permits *accelerated* depreciation, which simply means that rather than depreciating a capital asset over the item's expected life, it can be depreciated over a shorter time frame. A purely hypothetical example makes this point clear. Suppose a business invests $100,000 in a small computer with an expected life of ten years. The normal depreciation would be $100,000/10 or $10,000 per year. This would be deducted from total revenues as a cost of doing business. However, if through accelerated depreciation, the investment was depreciated out in five years, the claimed deduction would be $20,000 per year. The *tax expenditure* would be the tax revenue lost as a consequence of the *accelerated* portion of the depreciation only, namely the tax due on an additional $10,000 per year.

Other major examples of tax expenditures for corporations include investment credits (this, as with all tax *credits*, means that a percentage of the cost of capital assets is *deducted directly from the tax owed* rather than from total sales), the exclusion of interest on state and local debt, and the deferral of tax on income of foreign corporations owned by domestic concerns.

Significant examples of "forgiven taxes" for individuals include deductions for property tax and mortgage interest, capital gains tax reductions that limit tax liability for the investor and help preserve the estate for heirs at the time of death,[4] and the exclusion of pension contributions. Having identified the nature of wealthfare, we shall pose specific answers to the question "Who benefits" in the section on maintenance.

The Warfare State

For reasons having to do with the global and domestic welfare of corporate society, an alliance has been formed between the armed forces establishment and those corporations providing the weaponry, hardware, and other equipment required to support this organization. Termed the "military-industrial complex" by President Dwight David Eisenhower in his 1961 farewell address, the massive development of "Pentagon capitalism" (Melman 1970) has been institutionalized. This aspect of the corporate economy represents the ultimate form of conspicuous consumption, with weapons systems continually declared obsolete, thus justifying the letting of other contracts so that newer weapons may be built. However, beyond the economic costs, which critics believe would be better invested in human needs, an examination of the "warfare state" is required for other reasons.

> In the spring of 1975, the American military officially withdrew from South Vietnam, a small peasant society located eight thousand miles away in Southeast Asia. Vietnam was reunited under a revolutionary government that the United States had failed to defeat in a decade of military action that left fifty-six thousand Americans dead and hundreds of thousands more maimed and disabled. The war in Vietnam caused unprecedented domestic political unrest. It cost American taxpayers an estimated $150 billion and created a cycle of inflation and recession in our overall economy. The devastating impact of the war on the Vietnamese will probably never be calculated in full (Neubeck 1979, p. 190).

The institutionalization of the military-industrial complex is a recent development. Prior to the Second World War, the United States had little

[4]A capital gain means that a capital asset (such as land) may be worth more when one sells it than when one buys it. The profit or "gain" is taxed only at 40 percent of the rate of tax on income from other sources, such as one's labor.

in the way of a standing army. However, as the earlier statement of Charles Wilson of General Motors (later Secretary of Defense) attests, while the American military opposed the international foe represented by the fascist powers of Germany, Japan, and Italy, *military spending* did battle with the domestic plague known as the Great Depression. When the war ended, the former had been defeated and the latter at least temporarily contained.

In addition to the economic "salvation" of war spending, other factors can be identified. The world conflict had for example given rise to what C. Wright Mills (1956) was to term the "military elite." Such an officer class held a new legitimacy in the postwar era. Also during this era the Soviet Union was to emerge as a power in Eastern Europe. With the successful conclusion of the Chinese Revolution in 1949, a society representing 25 percent of the world's population and heretofore a vassal of colonial powers was to become a symbolic leader of the Third World. The threat to an increasingly multinational corporate order could not be denied.

The Poorhouse State[5]

Having examined the institutionalization of welfare for the wealthy and powerful, it is possible to examine the system that exists to process the poor. An important historical parallel to the modern poorhouse state can be found in the English nineteenth-century Poor Laws. Fundamental to such laws was the historical exploitation of labor during the Industrial Revolution. One was supposed to work and if one did not, one was socially and morally disvalued. This notion of work morality did not apply of course to property owners, only to the underbelly of the working class. Those who did not work were put in poorhouses or workhouses, where the possibility for discussion and organization existed. One author suggests that this "community of fate" helped bring about the beginnings of the working class movements for change (Matza 1966, p. 659).

The Great Depression of the 1930s saw the establishment of a national welfare program for the first time in United States history. Prior to this period, "relief" was a joint private and public affair. However, for the latter type, local financing prevailed. With the massive demands for relief of the unemployed, such resources were quickly exhausted. After a number of "emergency" acts and agencies had been established and burdened to extinction or futility, it became evident that temporary measures would not suffice. In January 1935 some 21 million persons were on relief rolls, a number accounting for about one-sixth of the total population

[5]"The Poorhouse State" is Richard Elman's (1966) term for the welfare system for the poor.

(McIntyre 1964, pp. 14–15). Later that year Congress passed the Social Security Act, designed to provide some benefits for retired workers as well as support for their survivors.

The public assistance sections of the Social Security Act provided grants to cooperating states designed to cover from one third to one half of the costs. Those covered included the elderly (Old Age Assistance), the blind (Aid to the Blind), and mothers with dependent children (Aid to Dependent Children) (McIntyre 1964, pp. 18–19). In 1950, Congress added Aid to the Permanently and Totally Disabled, and in 1960, Medical Assistance for the Aged. Although subject over the years to legislative amendment and reorganization, these programs have remained the foundation of the poorhouse state.

The War on Poverty: A Casualty of the 1960s

In response to increasing attention being given to poverty in the media, the civil rights movement, and the emergence of a poor people's movement, the United States government launched a War on Poverty in 1964 (Pilisuk and Pilisuk 1973). The Economic Opportunity Act of 1964 established eleven major programs for the poor. Included among these programs were the Neighborhood Youth Corps (which gave part-time work to dropout teeenagers who needed money to stay in school), a College Work Study Program (intended to help college students from poor families), an Adult Basic Education Program, a Small Business Loan Program, a Rural Loan Program, and a Work Experience Program (providing on-the-job training). These lines of action were low keyed and oriented to directly assisting the poor; however, they were not greatly effective in bringing about change.

The Job Corps program was more visible and subject to media attention and controversy. It provided for the establishment of residential training centers for school dropouts ages fourteen to twenty-two. Headstart was one of the most ambitious projects, establishing a preschool program for "culturally disadvantaged" children to help in their future education. It was followed by Upward Bound which offered precollege tutoring for minority students. The Community Action Program was to provide financial support for various local projects such as child development, legal aid, child care. Its requirement of "maximum feasible participation" by the poor, alienated local and national politicians as well as the welfare bureaucracy (Wofford 1969). Volunteers in Service to America (VISTA) recruited volunteers to work with migrant laborers, on Indian reservations, in poor urban and rural areas, hospitals, schools and institutions for the mentally ill and retarded. The orientation was that of a volunteer going in and helping these "unfortunates" help themselves. Since most of the problems of poverty stem from the structural inequality of corporate order, attempts to change, train, and organize the poor proved ineffective. On one level, the approach represented a misguided cultural elitism. On another, training, organization, and participation mean little without the "pay-off" of more and better jobs and improved services (Pilisuk and Pilisuk 1973).

The "War" on Poverty became a casualty of a greater conflict: the war on Vietnam. Retrospectively, the former could hardly be called a war, given the relatively small amount of money and personnel assigned to it compared with the "limited action" in Vietnam and Indochina. During the 1960s, antiwar protestors suggested that if victory was so important in Vietnam, then why not simply declare the war "won," thus saving money and lives. While such a strategy was not adopted in that war, it appears to have been successful in bringing to a close the War on Poverty.

The Public Welfare Panacea

Also institutionalized in North America is a "poverty establishment" that employs hundreds of thousands and costs billions to operate (Roby 1974; Armitage 1975). From the standpoint of professional ideals, social welfare is supposedly based upon the following shared values: (1) concern for the individual; (2) faith in human nature; (3) equality and equity; (4) faith in democracy; and (5) community (Armitage 1975, pp. 7–15). However, these values often conflict with the prevailing ideologies in Western corporate societies such as competition and survival of the fittest. "Looking out for number one" is based on the order paradigm, which views human nature as egoistic and in need of control. Further, unplanned industrial development, urbanization, and commercialism pursued under the direction of private interests often conflict with the notion of community. The processes of inheritance, corporate ownership, and individual competition for scarce goods also counter a sense of community and concern for others. The manner in which people are alienated and made to fit modern technology further compounds the problem of inequality. (Refer to Chapter Four for a discussion of alienation.)

These contradictions reflect the problems inherent in viewing poverty and inequality as individual problems when they are largely consequences of structural relationships. While various income supplements such as old age assistance, pension plans, and unemployment insurance help persons survive, these programs largely fail to address the basic issues involved. For example, why are people unemployed or employed in low-paying marginal jobs? Corporate ideology holds that poverty is due to individual characteristics and thus the person who is unemployed or underemployed deserves that fate. However, an individual's wage depends on many factors, most of which are largely beyond one's control. Such factors include: (1) individual characteristics like age, race, sex, family class status, and where one was raised; (2) individual characteristics (over which one has only a degree of control) such as education, skill level, health, personal motivation, and region of employment; (3) industry characteristics such as profit rates, product market concentration, technology, unionization, and industry relationship to government; and (4) local labor market characteristics such as unemployment rates, rate of growth, and structure of labor demand (Wachtel 1971). In looking at these four factors it becomes evident that "willpower" is a largely irrelevant (as well as a poorly defined) solution. Even those characteristics that one can influence somewhat (such as education) are largely dependent upon family and social class.

> In sum, the individual has very little control over his or her labor force status. If you are black, female, have parents with low socio-economic status, and dependent upon labor income, there is a high probability that you will have relatively low levels of human capital which will slot you into low paying jobs, in low wage industries, in low wage labor markets. With this initial placement, the individual is placed in a high risk category, destined to end up poor sometime during her working and nonworking years. She may earn her poverty by working fulltime. Or she may suffer either sporadic or long periods of unemployment. Or she may become disabled, thereby reducing her earning power even further. Or when she retires, social security payments will place her in poverty even if she escaped this fact throughout her working years. With little savings, wealth, or private pension income, the retiree will be poor (Wachtel 1971, p. 5).

The impact of social welfare and government taxing upon inequality is minimal. Regarding taxation Kolko (1977, p. 348) states:

> The conclusion is inescapable: Taxation has not mitigated the fundamentally unequal distribution of income. If anything it has perpetuated inequality by heavily taxing the low and middle-income groups—those least able to bear its burden.

Thus, public welfare programs have not really affected the overall structure of inequality in North America (Adams et al. 1971; Barth, Carcagno, and Palmer 1977). To say that the welfare system for the poor has no great effect upon inequality does not mean it has no social effects. As noted earlier, poverty serves the nonpoor in several ways. Also, a large welfare bureaucracy benefits by the regulation of the poor. In addition, relief is a potent means of social control. Piven and Cloward (1971) argue that relief programs regulate labor in two ways. First, when there is mass unemployment and subsequent outbreaks of turmoil, such as during the depression of the 1930s or riots of the 1960s, relief programs are initiated or expanded (for example, the War on Poverty) to absorb or control enough of the unemployed to restore order. Secondly, those who are "useless" to the labor market, such as the aged and the disabled, are put on relief, which is so degrading and punitive that those working are fearful of such a fate. A specific example of the social regulation function of relief is the way it has been used to control ghettos in the United States' urban areas (Leman 1971).

MAINTENANCE

Keeping the poor poor is the other side of keeping the rich rich. With this thought in mind, we turn to an examination of the benefits for the various sectors of the "welfare state."

Keeping the Rich Rich

Whereas functionalist theory holds that inequality is necessary, theories of inequality based on the conflict paradigm (Marx 1962; Braverman 1974; Anderson 1974) pose the question, Necessary for whom? Conflict theorists of stratification view the perpetuation of inequality as a consequence of opposing class interests. The argument is that some classes have power and are able to establish and maintain the unjust distribution of goods and rewards. Further, the class one is born into is more significant in determining one's place in life than ability and motivation. Thus, state power principally serves the interests of an owning class, which in turn is supported by a corporate, political, and military elite. (Some of those who represent an elite of power are holders of great wealth; others boast more modest assets.)

Data supporting the conflict theorists include the unequal distribution of income over time among population fifths. (See Table 3–12). Also, we find that certain groups such as the working class, and nonwhites have lower incomes, less-skilled occupations, lower education attainment, poorer physical and mental health, and a shorter life expectancy. Such figures justify the emphasis of the conflict perspective upon the significance of class status and power in maintaining inequality (Manzer 1974; Ritzer, Kammeyer, and Yetman 1979, pp. 239–48). Moreover, as we have seen, little attention is given to the state's "wealthfare" program for the nonpoor. One way in which such inequality is institutionalized in law is through the income tax system. Purportedly a progressive taxing system weighing most severely upon the well-to-do, it in fact is largely regressive, placing a disproportionate burden on the poor and salaried in society.

Table 3–8 shows that as family income increases in the United States there is greater savings in tax benefits. In 1976, it was reported by the Internal Revenue Service of the United States that many rich people paid little or no tax. Nearly 250 individuals with over $200,000 annual incomes paid no taxes at all! This is all quite legal, given the class bias in the tax laws (*U.S. News and World Report* 1974). The welfare reaped though such laws can be viewed as a giveaway by the government.

Canada also has a tax system favoring the rich (Table 3-9). In 1976 $7.1 million was allowed in tax breaks, with 36 percent of this going to the top 10 percent of tax filers. This bounty comes from just twenty exemptions, deductions, and credits allowed in the law (National Council of Welfare 1979).

What are the specific sources of these legal and intended "tax savings" that represent in effect the grace of the federal government? Looking at such tax "expenditures" in some detail is an exhaustive procedure. However, what we do find is that not only individuals but corporations as well (whose profits primarily benefit *some* individuals) are the beneficiaries. The United States Congress estimates that in 1980 United States corporations saved $4.3 billion in the deduction of interest on state and local debt, and $1.9 billion through the deferral of earned income by domestic corporations with international sales and foreign corporations controlled by American firms. Individuals saved $7.4 billion on the deduction of mortgage payment interest, $6.2 billion through the deduction of property taxes, and $3.1 billion on the deduction of interest paid for consumer credit. Further, individuals saved $13 billion through the exclusion of pension and retirement funds from taxable income, and a whopping $18.2 billion on capital gains taxes (United States Congress, Joint Committee on Taxation 1977, pp. 7–11).

It should be emphasized that all of these tax savings to individuals are more in the interests of corporate economy and those who own and con-

TABLE 3–8
Portion of Family Income Paid in Income Taxes in United States

Annual Family Income	Payment Required by Tax Law	Average Paid after Loopholes	Average Amount Saved via Loopholes
$2,500	1.9%	0.5%	$35
5,000	7.5	2.8	235
10,000	12.4	7.6	480
20,000	20.8	12.1	1,740
75,000	46.0	26.8	14,400
250,000	58.0	29.6	71,000
1,000,000	60.5	30.4	301,000

Source: Based on data from Philip M. Stern, *The Rape of the Taxpayer* (New York: Random House, 1973), p. 11.

**TABLE 3-9
Share of Tax Benefits to Canadian Taxpayers
by Income Decile, 1976**

Decile	Average Tax Saving for 1976	Percentage of 1976 Tax Expenditure
1st	0	0
2nd	$59.57	1.0%
3rd	179.23	3.1
4th	312.29	5.4
5th	372.09	6.5
6th	445.93	7.8
7th	570.15	10.0
8th	735.57	12.8
9th	992.04	17.3
10th	2,068.40	36.1

Source: National Council of Welfare, *The Hidden Welfare System Revisited*, Ottawa, 1979.

trol it than of those in the working and impoverished classes. The deductions for mortgage interest, property taxes, and consumer credit interest payments are all intended to encourage people to borrow and buy. They represent an invaluable aid to lending institutions, landowners, housing developers, and those who manufacture, distribute, and retail all manner of consumer goods. Pension and retirement funds may be excluded from taxation (or at least deferred); however, they represent an enormous source of capital. Such funds are frequently invested in corporate stock. Lest one be tempted to believe that such "investment" of pension funds has in fact converted the working class into an owning class, it should be recalled that a huge aggregate sum when divided by all who are in a specific category may yield a minimal average. For example, in 1975 some 30.3 million workers were members of private pension funds which represented total reserves of *$212.6 billion*. This amounted to *less than $7,000 per person* (*Statistical Abstract of the United States* 1978, p. 343). Members are fortunate if they do not lose their pensions, for example, by losing their jobs before they qualify. Moreover, individual members of a pension fund do not truly *control* that fund.

Table 3-10 depicts the cost of the tax expenditure aspects of the "Wealthfare" state.

By way of comparison, in 1977 tax expenditures (losses) cost the government $114.5 billion. Such losses as already demonstrated benefit the rich and the affluent more than the working class and the poor. *The total outlays for the five largest United States "poorhouse" programs in 1976 amounted to $36 billion, some 31 percent of the wealthfare expenditures for 1977* (*Statistical Abstract of the United States* 1978, p. 360).

TABLE 3-10
Sum of the Tax Expenditure Items by
Type of Taxpayer and Fiscal Year*
(in millions of dollars)

Fiscal Year	Corporations and Individuals	Corporations	Individuals
1977	$114,470	$27,050	$87,465
1978	124,395	28,740	95,710
1979	133,865	30,370	103,545
1980	146,285	32,425	113,935
1981	157,460	32,240	125,280
1982	168,465	31,425	137,100

*These totals represent the mathematical sum of the estimated fiscal year effect of each of the 85 tax expenditure items included in the report. Years 1978–1982 are projections.
Source: United States Congress, Joint Committee on Taxation, "Estimate of Federal Tax Expenditures" 1977, p. 10.

Some Are More Equal than Others

The idea of "democracy" if at all serious should address the question, To what extent do we approach income equality? A society perfectly equal in personal income is presented in Table 3-11. Tables 3-12 and 3-13 provide income data for both the United States and Canada.

The top 20 percent of the families in the United States consistently receive approximately eight times the income of the bottom 20 percent and more than the income received by the entire bottom 60 percent of the population. This has changed little over the twenty-nine year period examined. In fact, there has been little change among the various fifths during this period. Furthermore, the top 5 percent receive typically about three times the income of the bottom 20 percent and about the same as the entire bottom 40 percent of the families of the United States.

Canada has slightly more inequality in its income distribution. During the twenty-two year period from 1946 to 1974, the top 20 percent earned approximately ten to fifteen times the income of the bottom 20 percent and more than the lower three fifths combined. A more recent analysis states that in 1977 the income distribution was basically the same as in 1951 (Calgary Herald 1979).

While there are minor differences between the two countries, the United States and Canada are strikingly similar in extent of inequality. In both countries the top 20 percent earn far more than even the closest fifth, accounting for about 40 percent of individual income. In Canada, the

TABLE 3-11
Income Distribution in a Society of Perfect Equality

Population Ranked by Quintile	Percentage of Income Received
First fifth	20%
Second fifth	20
Third fifth	20
Fourth fifth	20
Last fifth	20
	100%

position of the top 20 percent has made slight gains in recent years while the percentage of income going to the bottom 40 percent of families has been slowly decreasing. In the United States, the income distribution remains remarkably constant.

While the foregoing data shed light on income distribution, we must keep in mind the distinction made early in this chapter between income and wealth. For example, a building may produce rent income, but it also is an asset that typically grows in value each year. In the United States in 1972, there were an estimated 12.8 million individuals alive who owned gross estates in excess of $60,000. This 6.1 percent of the population had total net assets of $1.9 trillion (IRS 1976, pp. 1–2). However, let us narrow our scope somewhat to look at the richest of the rich.

As Table 3-14 clearly shows, the distribution of wealth represents an even greater concentration at the top than does the distribution of income. Thus in 1972, the top 1 percent of the total population in the United States held over $1 trillion in assets. However, if we focus on the means of economic control in corporate society, we find that the top ½ of 1 percent held almost half of all corporate stock, over half of all bonds, 39 percent of all debt instruments (such as mortgages and notes) and over 80 percent of all trusts. Despite protests to the contrary, it is becoming quite clear that the estate and taxation laws of the state continue to facilitate the development of large personal fortunes at the top while spawning extensive impoverishment at the bottom.

Wealth may be cast in terms of individual or corporate assets. As indicated in Chapter Two, the concentration of corporation assets mirrors the concentration of personal fortunes. Tables 3-15, 3-16, and 3-17 list dominant people and dominant corporations in North America. The extent of foreign control of Canadian corporations in Table 3-16 is further testimony that the corporate order does not recognize national boundaries. Concerning profits, the raison d'être of corporations, *Forbes* (1980, p. 223) states in its report on profits "The good news! Total profits of the top 500 US companies rose sharply in 1979. The bad news? It went mainly to a favored few."

TABLE 3-12
Income Distribution by Fifths and by Top Five Percent for United States Families, Selected Years between 1947 and 1975 (Percentage)

Families	Year								
	1947	1950	1955	1960	1964	1969	1972	1974	1975
Lowest Fifth	5.1%	4.5%	4.8%	4.9%	5.2%	5.6%	5.4%	5.4%	5.4%
Second Fifth	11.8	12.0	12.2	12.0	12.0	12.3	11.9	12.0	11.8
Middle Fifth	16.7	17.4	17.7	17.6	17.7	17.7	17.5	17.6	17.6
Fourth Fifth	23.2	23.5	23.4	23.6	24.0	23.7	23.9	24.1	24.1
Highest Fifth	43.3	42.6	41.8	42.0	41.1	40.6	41.4	41.0	41.1
Top 5 Percent	17.5	17.0	16.8	16.8	15.7	15.6	15.9	15.3	15.5

Sources: *Statistical Abstract of the United States*, 1974, Bureau of the Census, United States Department of Commerce, Washington, D.C.: United States Government Printing Office, 1974, No. 619, p. 384; "Money Income and Poverty Status of Families and Persons in the United States: 1974," Current Population Reports Series P-60, No. 99, Bureau of the Census, United States Department of Commerce, Washington, D.C.: United States Government Printing Office, 1974, Table 4, p. 8; *The World Almanac and Book of Facts*, 1978, New York: Newspaper Enterprise Association, Inc., 1977, p. 198.

TABLE 3-13
Income Distribution by Fifths for Canadian Family Units, Selected Years between 1946 and 1974 (Percentage)

Families	Year								
	1946	1951	1954	1957	1961	1965	1967	1971	1974
Lowest Fifth	5.3%	4.4%	4.4%	4.2%	4.2%	4.6%	4.1%	3.7%	3.1%
Second Fifth	11.8	11.2	12.0	11.9	11.9	11.9	11.5	10.6	9.0
Third Fifth	16.7	18.3	17.8	18.0	18.3	18.0	17.8	17.7	16.0
Fourth Fifth	22.2	23.3	24.0	24.5	24.5	24.4	24.6	24.8	24.8
Highest Fifth	44.0	42.8	41.8	41.4	41.1	41.4	41.9	43.2	47.1

Sources: Leo A. Johnson, "Income Disparity and the Structure of Earnings In Canada, 1946–74," in *Social Stratification: Canada*, 2d ed. James E. Curtis and William G. Scott, eds., Scarborough, Ontario: Prentice-Hall of Canada, 1979, p. 149; Leo A. Johnson, "Illusions or Realities: Hamilton and Penaid's Approach to Poverty," *The Canadian Review of Sociology and Anthropology*, 14 (August) 1977, p. 345.

TABLE 3-14
The Concentration of Wealth—1972

	1972				
	Value of gross personal assets held by—			Percent held by—	
	All persons	Top ½ percent of all	Top 1 percent of all	Top ½ percent of all	Top 1 percent of all
Total Assets	**4,344.4**	**822.4**	**1,046.9**	**18.9**	**24.1**
Real estate	1,492.6	150.9	225.0	10.1	15.1
Corporate stock	870.9	429.3	491.7	49.3	56.5
Bonds	158.0	82.5	94.8	52.2	60.0
Cash	748.8	63.6	101.2	8.5	13.5
Debt instruments	77.5	30.3	40.8	39.1	52.7
Life insurance	143.0	6.2	10.0	4.3	7.0
Trusts	99.4	80.3	89.4	80.8	89.9
Miscellaneous	853.6	59.5	83.3	6.8	9.8
Liabilities	808.5	100.7	131.0	12.5	16.2
Net worth	3,535.9	721.7	915.9	20.4	25.9
Number of persons mil	(x)	1.04	2.09	(x)	(x)

Source: *Statistical Abstract of the United States* 1978, p. 476.

Keeping the Warfare State

It appears that the state does well in the maintenance of the wealthy (both individuals and corporations). Many of these individuals and corporations additionally benefit from that government wealthfare program identified earlier as "national defense." Because of the unparalleled prominence of the concerns of war and peace during the nuclear age, evidence bearing on the extensiveness of the warfare state is presented here.

At this writing, President Carter, who in his 1976 campaign promised cuts in defense spending, has proposed a $161.7 billion military budget for 1981 (*Spokesman-Review* 1980). This sum is almost double the $85.5 billion outlay for "national defense" in 1975. As incredible as these sums are, they do not tell the whole story. In 1979, for example, the estimated $114.5 billion (plus supplementary allocations spent for this purpose) supposedly represented 23.2 percent of the total federal outlay (*Statistical Abstract of the United States* 1979, p. 257). However, a careful examination of the budget reveals a number of hidden expenses. For example, veterans' benefits, interest on the national debt (basically incurred due to defense spending), and much of the space program are primarily military items. They do not appear, however, as defense expenditures. Further,

TABLE 3-15
America's Richest People

Estimated worth. Family or individual (birth date). Source of wealth. Founder.

$3 Billion to $5 Billion
du Ponts, Wilmington, Del. Chemicals. Eleuthere Irenee (1771–1834), fndr.
Mellons, Pittsburgh, Pa. Mellon National Bank. Thomas (1813–1908), fndr.

$2 Billion to $3 Billion
Gettys, Los Angeles, Cal. Getty Oil. J. Paul (1892–1976), fndr.
Daniel K. Ludwig (b. 6/24/1897), N.Y., N.Y. Shipping, real estate.

$1 Billion to $2 Billion
Rockefellers, N.Y., N.Y. Standard Oil. John D. (1839–1937), fndr.

$600 Million to $1 Billion
Fords, Detroit, Mich. Ford Motor Co. Henry (1863–1947), fndr.
Hunts, Dallas, Tx. Oil. H. L. (1889–1974), fndr.
Pews, Philadelphia, Pa. Sun Oil. Joseph N. (1848–1912), fndr.
Pritzkers, Chicago, Ill. Hyatt Hotels, real estate. A.N. (B. 1897), Jack (b. 1/6/1904), fndrs.

$400 Million to $600 Million
Bechtels, San Francisco, Cal. Engineering and construction mgmt. Stephen D. Sr. (b. 9/24/1900), Stephen D. Jr. (b. 1925), fndrs.
Henry Crown (b. 6/13/1896), Chicago, Ill. General Dynamics.
Marvin Davis (b. 1926), Colorado, Col. Oil.
Michel Fribourg (b. 5/20/1913), Palo Alto, Cal. Hewlett-Packard.
Klebergs, Kingsville, Tx. King Ranch, real estate. Richard King (1824–1885), fndr.
Charles Koch (b. 11/1/1935), Witchita, Kan. Oil marketing.
Ray Kroc (b. 10/5/1902), Chicago, Ill. McDonald's.
MacMillans, Wayzata, Minn. Grain exporting. William Cargill (1844–1909), fndr.
Samuel I. Newhouse (b. 1895), N.Y., N.Y. Newspapers.
David Packard (b. 1913), Palo Alto, Cal. Hewlett-Packard.
Phipps, N.Y., N.Y. Carnegie Steel. Henry (1839–1930), fndr.
Leonard Stern (b. 3/28/38), N.Y., N.Y. Hartz Mountain pet foods, real estate.

$300 Million to $400 Million
Walter Annenberg (b. 1908), Philadelphia, Pa. and Palm Springs, Cal. Publishing TV Guide, others.
John T. Dorrance, Jr. (b. 2/7/1919), Philadelphia, Pa. Campbell Soup.
Ernest Gallo (b. 1909) and Julio Gallo (b. 1910), Modesto, Cal. Wine.
J. Seward Johnson (b. 1895), Princeton, N.J. Johnson & Johnson.
Kennedys, Hyannis, Mass. Real estate and investments. Joseph P. (1888–1969), fndr.
Forrest E. Mars (b. 1904), Washington, D.C. Candy.
Milton J. Petrie (b. 1906), N.Y., N.Y. Petri Stores, women's clothing.
Pitcairns, Philadelphia, Pa. Pittsburgh Plate Glass. John (1841–1916), fndr.
Rosenwalds, Philadelphia, Pa., N.Y., N.Y., New Orleans, La. Sears, Roebuck. Julius (1866–1932), fndr.
DeWitt Wallace (b. 11/12/1889), Chappaqua, N.Y. Reader's Digest.

Source: *The World Almanac and Book of Facts* 1979, p. 108.

TABLE 3-16
Canada's Largest Corporations

Company	Sales or operating revenue C$000	Foreign owner-ship %	Foreign owner(s)
General Motors of Canada Ltd. (Oshawa, Ont.)	6,115,434[1]	100	General Motors Corp, Detroit
Ford Motor Company of Canada (Oakville, Ont.)	5,725,000[1]	88	Ford Motor Co., Dearborn, Mich.
Imperial Oil Ltd. (Toronto)	4,970,000[2]	69.6	Exxon Corp., New York
Canadian Pacific Ltd. (Montreal)	4,700,136[3]	29.2	U.S. 14%; Britain 7.4%; other 7.8%
George Weston Ltd. (Toronto) M	4,590,090	—	
Bell Canada (Montreal)	3,559,887	6.1	Wide distribution, U.S. and Europe
Alcan Aluminum Ltd. (Montreal)	3,220,704[4]	52.9	U.S. 39.3%; other 13.6%
Chrysler Canada Ltd. (Windsor, Ont.)	3,119,063[1]	100	Chrysler Corp., Detroit
Massey-Ferguson Ltd. (Toronto)	2,935,987[4]	40	Wide distribution, mostly U.S.
Canada Safeway Ltd. (Winnipeg) M	2,581,893	100	Safeway Stores Inc., Oakland, Cal.
Shell Canada Ltd. (Toronto)	2,349,295[2]	71	Royal Dutch/Shell Group
Gulf Canada Ltd. (Toronto)	2,322,100[2]	68.3	Gulf Oil Corp., Pittsburgh
Dominion Stores Ltd. (Toronto) M	2,215,836	—	
Simpson-Sears Ltd. (Toronto) M	2,093,378	50	Sears, Roebuck & Co., Chicago
Inco Ltd. (Toronto)	2,077,364[4]	35	U.S. 33%; other 2%
Canada Packers Ltd. (Toronto)	1,878,408	—	
TransCanada Pipelines Ltd. (Toronto)	1,870,325	—	
MacMillan Bloedel Ltd. (Vancouver)	1,707,260	—	
Steinberg Inc. (Montreal) M	1,767,687	—	
Brascan Ltd. (Toronto)	1,576,958[4]	34	Wide distribution, U.S. and Europe

(1) Figures include sales to parent and affiliated companies: General Motors $2,753 million; Chrysler unstated; Ford $2,339 million. (Ford also consolidates $1,257 million sales of overseas subsidiaries.) (2) Excise taxes deducted. (3) After eliminating inter-company transactions. (4) In U.S. dollars.

*Industrials, except M = merchandiser.

Source: *The World Almanac and Book of Facts* 1979, p. 510.

the percentage (23.2) is deceptively low because of the way in which the federal budget is calculated.

In the United States, all federal monies are included in one comprehensive budget. The nature of such monies is twofold. *Federal* funds are derived primarily from taxation and borrowing. They are *not restricted* by law to specific governmental functions. *Trust* funds, on the other hand, are taxes and other receipts which are designated to be spent in specific ways (*Statistical Abstract of the United States* 1979, p. 251). The primary source of unrestricted federal funds is the individual income tax. While there are approximately ten reported federal trust funds, the two largest, accounting for over 77 percent of the total trust fund outlays, are O.A.S.D.I. (Old Age, Survivors, and Disability Insurance) and the health insurance trust funds. These "social insurance" trust funds provide retirement, health, survivors, and disability benefits for the general public. They are financed primarily through a payroll tax (matched by employers' contributions) commonly referred to as "social security." These

TABLE 3-17
The 50 Largest Industrial Corporations (Ranked by Sales)

Rank '79	'78	Company	Sales ($000)
1	2	Exxon (New York)	79,106,471*
2	1	General Motors (Detroit)	66,311,200
3	4	Mobil (New York)	44,720,908
4	3	Ford Motor (Dearborn, Mich.)	43,513,700
5	5	Texaco (Harrison, N.Y.)	38,350,370
6	6	Standard Oil of California (San Francisco)	29,947,554
7	9	Gulf Oil (Pittsburgh)	23,910,000*
8	7	International Business Machines (Armonk, N.Y.)	22,862,776
9	8	General Electric (Fairfield, Conn.)	22,460,600
10	12	Standard Oil (Ind.) (Chicago)	18,610,347*
11	11	International Telephone & Telegraph (New York)	17,197,423
12	13	Atlantic Richfield (Los Angeles)	16,233,959
13	14	Shell Oil (Houston)	14,431,211*
14	15	U.S. Steel (Pittsburgh)	12,929,100
15	18	Conoco (Stamford, Conn.)[1]	12,647,998
16	16	E.I. du Pont de Nemours (Wilmington, Del.)	12,571,800
17	10	Chrysler (Highland Park, Mich.)	12,001,900
18	19	Tenneco (Houston)	11,209,000
19	17	Western Electric (New York)[2]	10,964,075
20	23	Sun (Radnor, Pa.)	10,666,000
21	33	Occidental Petroleum (Los Angeles)	9,554,795
22	26	Phillips Petroleum (Bartlesville, Okla.)	9,502,775
23	20	Procter & Gamble (Cincinnati)[3]	9,329,306
24	27	Dow Chemical (Midland, Mich.)	9,255,387
25	21	Union Carbide (New York)	9,176,500
26	32	United Technologies (Hartford)[4]	9,053,358
27	28	International Harvester (Chicago)[5]	8,392,042
28	22	Goodyear Tire & Rubber (Akron, Ohio)	8,238,676
29	40	Boeing (Seattle)	8,131,000
30	25	Eastman Kodak (Rochester, N.Y.)	8,028,231
31	42	LTV (Dallas)[6]	7,996,809
32	43	Standard Oil (Ohio) (Cleveland)	7,916,023
33	24	Caterpillar Tractor (Peoria, Ill.)	7,613,200
34	35	Union Oil of California (Los Angeles)	7.567,698*
35	31	Beatrice Foods (Chicago)[7]	7,468,373
36	30	RCA (New York)	7,454,600
37	29	Westinghouse Electric (Pittsburgh)	7,332,000
38	34	Bethlehem Steel (Bethlehem, Pa.)	7,137,200
39	47	R.J. Reynolds Industries (Winston-Salem, N.C.)[8]	7,133,100*
40	36	Xerox (Stamford, Conn.)	7,027,000
41	49	Amerada Hess (New York)	6,769,941
42	38	Esmark (Chicago)[5]	6,743,167
43	52	Marathon Oil (Findlay, Ohio)	6,680,597*
44	44	Ashland Oil (Russell, Ky.)[9]	6,473,867*
45	37	Rockwell International (Pittsburgh)[9]	6,466,100
46	39	Kraft (Glenview, Ill.)	6,432,900
47	51	Cities Service (Tulsa)	6,276,500
48	45	Monsanto (St. Louis)	6,192,600
49	46	Philip Morris (New York)	6,144,091*
50	41	General Foods (White Plains, N.Y.)[10]	5,472,456

Source: *Fortune* Magazine, May 5, 1980, p. 276.

and other trust funds, are *restricted*. What happens if we examine all military spending as a percentage of the unrestricted (by law) federal monies? (Remember approximately two-thirds of the unrestricted monies come from individual income taxes.)

The state support of the military organization is further evidenced by the breakdown of property owned by the federal government. In 1972, the total value of such holdings was $454.5 billion. The value of the specific property that had as its major function "national defense" was $248 billion. Thus, military property amounted to 55 percent of the total. (This is a conservative estimate as it excludes such primarily military facilities as veterans' hospitals and space exploration installations.) (*Statistical Abstract of the United States* 1978, p. 264)

The Department of Defense remains a prime investor in corporate America. In 1977, the value of military procurement contracts amounted to $55.6 billion (*Statistical Abstract of the United States*, p. 376). Of greater concern perhaps is the global trade in armaments. Recent data (1968 through 1977) confirms that the United States ranks as the number one supplier of arms. For example in 1977, the United States exported over $6.5 billion worth of arms. (This figure exceeded that of the Soviet Union by some $1.6 billion.) A major customer before his downfall was Shah Mohammed Pahlavi of Iran, who purchased arms valued at $2.3 billion in 1977 alone (*Statistical Abstract of the United States* 1979, p. 367).

The warfare state is a drain on the national economy. However, though wasteful, it is a source of profits and jobs domestically and a defender of corporate America abroad. Given the imperatives of growth and profit, the corporate system has assumed a multinational form. *In 1966, sales by foreign affiliates of United States based multinational companies amounted to $97.8 billion. One decade later (1976), the total sales by these affiliates amounted to $514.7 billion, an increase of over 400 percent*

TABLE 3–18
Adjusted Military Expenditures by the United States, 1979
(In Billions of Dollars—Estimated)

Total budget outlays	$493.4
Less Total Trust Funds Outlays	−171.7
Unrestricted Funds: Outlays	321.7
National Defense	114.5
Other Primarily Military-Related Expenditures	
Interest on National Debt	43.0
General Science, Space	5.2
Veterans' Benefits	20.3
Total military outlays	183.0
Military Spending as a Percentage of Unrestricted Funds	56.9%

Source: *Statistical Abstract of the United States* 1979, pp. 257 and 259.

(*Statistical Abstract of the United States* 1078, p. 575). Increasingly, the military establishment is a means of protecting foreign-based operations where labor and vital raw materials are cheaper and new markets are available for American manufactured goods (Neubeck 1979, pp. 202–3).

The rationale for the interplay among multinational corporate interests, foreign policy, the military, and the superspy apparatus known as the Central Intelligence Agency is captured in the following statement:

> The overriding goal of American policy has been to construct a system of societies that are open to free economic intervention by private enterprise (which in many ways is publicly subsidized). The goal was formulated clearly by George Ball (a state department official) who "urged a greater unification of the world economy to give full play to the benefits of multinational corporations," which are "a distinctly American development. Through such corporations," he observed, "it has become possible for the first time to use the world's resources with maximum efficiency"—for the benefit of whom he does not reveal (Chomsky, in Chambliss 1973, p. 95).

Keeping the Poor Poor

While it is part of the corporate ideology to be for equal opportunity, Gains (1972) has pointed out that the nonpoor have a stake in keeping the poor. He identifies the following "benefits" of poverty: (1) Poverty assures the "dirty" work is done through maintaining a class of people to fill the menial, temporary, dead-end jobs. (2) Both directly and indirectly the poor subsidize activities benefiting the more affluent such as providing cheap domestic help or paying a higher proportion of their income in taxes. (3) Poverty creates jobs for such persons as welfare workers, criminal justice personnel, pawnshop owners, among others. (4) the poor buy inferior quality goods and provide incomes for less-competent (often because of heavy workloads) doctors, lawyers, teachers. (5) They can be identified and used as a scapegoat for alleged or actual deviance to define and uphold dominant norms. (6) The needy, particularly those disabled or otherwise incapacitated, allow us to evidence pity, compassion, and charity toward the "less fortunate." (7) They provide vicarious participation for the nonpoor in their supposed excesses, such as uninhibited sex and drug use. (8) The poverty of others helps the self-image of the affluent because they know they are better off than others. (9) Those in want help the well-off achieve since the poor are systematically excluded from competition educationally and occupationally. (10) The poor provide a purpose for philanthropic organizations and the aristocracy inclined to "help" them. (11) The poor have helped build civilization through slave labor. (12) Their poetry and music such as jazz, blues, spirituals, and "country" have enriched the lives of the more affluent. (13) The poor serve as symbolic constituencies and opponents for several political groups; thus it is safe to speak for or against them. (14) The costs of "progress," such as urban renewal, and the costs of warfare in casualties are often absorbed by the poor. (15) The poor are significant politically in that they can be ignored; thus state power can be vested in the well-to-do.

All of the above consequences of poverty demonstrate the place of the poor in history. Of course, this argument does not mean that they are inevitable or necessary, excepting in socioeconomic system for which inequality is a structural imperative.

Alternative

In February 1980, *Le Monde,* the most influential of French newspapers, held an election in which the editorial staff chose their new director. Such a step was a logical extension of a reality that appears beyond belief for the North American press in particular and for corporate society in general. For *Le Monde* is owned mostly by its employees and operated entirely by them (*New York Times* 1980).

In searching for an alternative to structural inequality, it is necessary to begin to think beyond the limitations of traditional North American ideology. For such ideology tends to reflect the imperatives of the corporate form of private ownership, growth, concentratoin, and the attendant problems of impoverishment and militarism. Thus, several options are presented here that are not in the interests of the powers that be.

In addition to the notion of worker control exemplified in *Le Monde* and explored in detail in the following chapter, the concept of public ownership, or nationalization, requires attention.

Public ownership or nationalization would call for the systematic movement of vital economic sectors from private hands. As a beginning point, these would include the media, defense, energy, communications, transportation, and health-care industries. What is often unrealized is that virtually all utilities are government operated in every major country in the world except the Federal Republic of Germany, Spain, and the United States. With the exception of Swissair, most foreign railroads and major airlines are publicly owned. So are the steel industry in Austria and the Swiss firm that manufactures watch movements. The French government produces Renault automobiles and the Italian government owns the Alfa Romeo company. The latter also sells most of the gasoline in the country (Galbraith 1974).

The Soviet Union and its Eastern European satellites systematically provide such things as day care centers, medical care, and housing. Many social services are also made available in the social democracies such as Sweden and Norway. These are considered a right of citizenship and thus are provided by the State. In Western corporate societies, one is "free" to provide for such services on one's own—of course, some people are freer than others. The availability of social services varies among corporate states. For example, Canada has a national health plan while, at this writing, the United States does not.

Still, critics of corporate society also point out that there is a continuing problem of power inequality in the Soviet bloc countries along with an increasing number of jobs requiring less in the way of skills. In such societies with a strong centralized government, "worker ownership" is more a slogan than a reality. It has not proven to mean either work satisfaction or worker control (Braverman 1974, pp. 14–16).

In the Soviet and Eastern European societies, where equality is defined in essentially economic terms, those who dominate the political system are the most powerful, while in corporate societies power is concentrated among those controlling property. However, a recent study has shown that for those societies without state ownership of the major means of production (some of which continue to evidence powerful corporation influence), a strong socialist party serves to reduce inequality. (While political labels often shed more heat than light, a definition of socialism centers on the belief of societal, communal, or public ownership and operation of major industries. All members of a society are to share in the work and the benefits.)

For example, while federal tax policies in the United States continue to support the wealthy and the warfare state, the government budget in social democratic nations serves to redistribute the wealth in a much more egalitarian manner (Hewitt 1977). (For the strength of socialist parties in democratic societies, see Table 3–19). The question before us, therefore, is how to move toward a society dominated by neither corporate or state power, an owning class or a self-perpetuating elite. This issue, in a variety of forms, will dominate the coming years.

TABLE 3–19
Average Postwar Legislative Strength of
Socialist Parties, 1945–1965*

Norway	52.0
Israel	50.8
Sweden	48.5
United Kingdom	48.5
Australia	45.0
New Zealand	44.9
Austria	44.7
Denmark	41.8
Belgium	37.4
Luxembourg	32.6
Netherlands	30.8
Venezuela	28.7
Japan	27.5
Germany	27.1
Switzerland	25.1
France	25.1
Finland	24.9
Trinidad	18.8
Italy	17.0
Ireland	10.5
Canada	7.1
Argentina	2.3
South Africa	1.8
Puerto Rico	0
United States	0

*Figures are expressed as a percentage of Socialist Party strength in postwar legislatures, each separate legislature weighted by its duration.

Source: Christopher Hewitt, "The Effect of Political Democracy and Social Democracy on Equality in Industrial Societies," *American Sociological Review*, 42 (June):450–64.

BIBLIOGRAPHY

Adams, Ian William
Cameron, Hill, Brian, and
Penz, Peter
1971   The Real Poverty Report. Edmonton, Alberta: M.G. Hurtig.

Anderson, Charles H.
1974   The Political Economy of Social Class. Englewood Cliffs, N.J.: Prentice-Hall.

Armitage, Andrew
1975   Social Welfare in Canada: Ideals and Realities. Toronto: McClelland and Stewart.

Barth, Michael D.,
Carcagno, George J.,
and Palmer, John L.
1977   "The Coverage of the Transfer System." In Problems in Political Economy: An Urban Perspective. 2d ed. David M. Gordon, ed. Lexington, Mass.: D.C. Heath and Company, pp. 321–25.

Bottomore, T. B.
1965   Class in Modern Society. London: George Allen and Unwin.

Braverman, Harry
1974   Labor and Monopoly Capital: The Degradation of Work in the Twentieth Century. New York: Monthly Review Press.

Briggs, Asa
1965   "The Welfare State in Historical Perspective." In Social Welfare Institutions. M. Zaid, ed.

Broom, Leonard, and
Cushing, Robert G.
1977   "A Modest Test of an Immodest Theory: The Functional Theory of Stratification." American Sociological Review 42 (February):157–69.

Business Week
1931   October 7.

Calgary Herald
1979   "Income Equality Far Off." May 19:E5.

Carnegie, Andrew
    1962   "The Advantages of Poverty." In The Gospel of
                            Wealth. Edward C. Kirkland, ed. Cambridge,
                            Mass.: Harvard University Press, pp. 53–64.

Chomsky, Noam
    1973   "At War with Asia." In Problems of Industrial
                            Society. William Chambliss, ed., Reading, Mass.:
                            Addison-Wesley, pp. 95–111.

Clement, Wallace
    1977   Continental Corporate Power: Economic Elite
                            Linkages between Canada and the United States.
                            Toronto: McClelland and Stewart.

Cummings, Scott, and
Taebel, Del
    1978   "The Economic Socialization of Children: A Neo-
                            Marxist Analysis." Social Problems 26 (December):
                            198–210.

Dahrendorf, Ralf
    1959   Class and Class Conflict in Industrial Society.
                            Stanford, Calif.: Stanford University Press.

Davis, Kingsley, and
Moore, Wilbert E.
    1945   "Some Principles of Stratification." The
                            American Sociological Review 10, 2:242–49.

Dowd, Douglas
    1977   The Twisted Dream: Capitalist Development in
                            the United States Since 1776. Cambridge, Mass.:
                            Winthrop.

Edwards, Richard
    1972   "Who Fares Well in the Welfare State?" In
                            Richard C. Edwards, Michael Reich, and Thomas
                            E. Weisskopf, eds., Cambridge, Mass.: Harvard
                            University Press, pp. 44–51.

Elman, Richard
    1966   The Poorhouse State. New York: Dell.

Forbes
    1980   "The Forbes Profits 500." (May 12):223–34.

Galbraith, John K.
    1974   "What Comes after General Motors?" The New
                            Republic (November 2): 13–14.

Gans, Herbert J.
1972   More Equality. New York: Pantheon Books.

George, Vic, and Wilding,
Paul
1976   Ideology and Social Welfare. London: Routledge
                                       and Kegan Paul.

Gortmaker, Steven L.
1979   "Poverty and Infant Mortality in the United States."
                                       American Sociological Review 44 (April):280–97.

Gouldner, Alvin W.
1970   The Coming Crisis in Western Sociology. New
                                       York: Basic Books.

Goyden, John C., and
Curtis, James C.
1977   "Occupational Mobility in Canada over Four
                                       Generations." The Canadian Review of Sociology
                                       and Anthropology 14 (August):303–19.

Harrington, Michael
1968   Toward a Democratic Left. New York: Macmillan.

Hewitt, Christopher
1977   "The Effect of Political Democracy and Social
                                       Democracy on Equality in Industrial Societies: A
                                       Cross-National Comparison." American
                                       Sociological Review 42 (June):450–64.

Howe, Florence, and
Lauter, Paul
1977   "How the School System Is Rigged for Failure." In
                                       The Capitalist System. Richard E. Edwards,
                                       Michael Reich, Thomas E. Weisskopf, eds.
                                       Englewood Cliffs, N.J.: Prentice-Hall, pp. 230–35.

Jackson, Larry R., and
Johnson, William A.
1974   Protest by the Poor. Lexington, Mass.: D.C. Heath.

Janowitz, Morris
1976   Social Control of the Welfare State. New York:
                                       Elsevier.

Jasso, Gullermia, and
Rossi, Peter H.
1977   "Distributive Justice and Earned Income."
                                       American Sociological Review 42 (August):634–51.

Josephson, Matthew
1934

The Robber Baron, The Great American
Capitalists. New York: Harcourt Brace Jovanovich.

Julian, Joseph
1977

Social Problems. 2d ed. Englewood Cliffs, N.J.:
Prentice-Hall.

Knight, Brian M.
1973

"Poverty in Canada." In Canada and Radical Social
Change. Dimitrias I. Roussopoulous, ed. Montreal:
Black Rose Books, pp. 12–26.

Kolko, Gabriel
1965

Railroads and Regulations, 1877–1916. Princeton,
N.J.: Princeton University Press.

1977

"Taxation and Inequality." In Problems in Political
Economy: An Urban Perspective. David M.
Gordon, ed., 2d ed. Lexington, Mass.: D.C. Heath,
pp. 343–48.

Leighton, George R.
1932

"And If the Revolution Comes . . . ?" Harper's
(March):466–74.

Leman, Beverly
1971

"Social Control of the American Ghetto." In The
Triple Revolution. Robert Perrucci and Marc
Pilisuk, eds. Boston: Little, Brown, pp. 550–60.

Lenski, Gerhard and Jean
1978

Human Societies. New York: McGraw-Hill.

Levin, Henry M.
1976

"Educational Opportunity and Social Inequality in
Western Europe." Social Problems 24 (December):
148–72.

Mandell, Bette, ed.
1975

Welfare in America: Controlling the "Dangerous
Classes." Englewood Cliffs, N.J.: Prentice-Hall.

Manzer, R.
1974

Canada: A Socio-Political Report. Toronto:
McGraw-Hill Ryerson.

Marchak, M. Patricia
1975

Ideological Perspectives on Canada. Toronto:
McGraw-Hill Ryerson.

Marx, Karl
1962   "The Eighteenth Brumaire of Louis Bonaparte."
In Selected Works, Vol. 1. Lawponce and
Wishart, eds.

Matza, David
1966   "Poverty and Disrepute." In Contemporary Social
Problems. Robert K. Merton and Robert A. Nisbet,
eds. New York: Harcourt Brace Jovanovich. pp.
619–69.

McIntyre, Duncan
1964   Public Assistance: Too Much or Too Little. Ithaca,
N.Y.: Cornell University Press.

Melman, Seymour
1970   Pentagon Capitalism: The Political Economy of
War. New York: McGraw-Hill.

Miliband, Ralph
1969   The State in Capitalist Society. New York: Basic
Books.

Mills, C. Wright
1951   White Collar. New York: Oxford University Press.

1956   The Power Elite. New York: Oxford University
Press.

Mitchell, Broadus
1947   The Economic History of the United States. Volume
IX. New York: H. Wolff.

Moore, Gwen
1979   "The Structure of a National Elite Network."
American Sociological Review 44:673–92.

National Council of
Welfare
1977   The Working Poor. Ottawa: National Council of
Welfare.

1979   The Hidden Welfare System Revisited. Ottawa:
National Council of Welfare.

Neubeck, Kenneth J.
1979   Social Problems: A Critical Approach. Glenview,
Ill.: Scott, Foresman.

New York Times
1980   "Le Monde Selecting New Editor." February 23.

Parker, Richard
1972   The Myth of the Middle Class. New York: Harper
                             & Row.

Perdue, William D.
1974   The Great Depression and the Interpretation of
                             Social Phenomena: An Inquiry into the Ideology of
                             Sociology. Unpublished Ph.D. dissertation.
                             Washington State University.

Pilisuk, Marc and
Phyllis, eds.
1973   How We Lost the War on Poverty. New Brunswick,
                             N.J.: Transaction Books.

Piven, Frances Fox, and
Cloward, Richard A.
1971   Regulating the Poor. New York: Pantheon Books.

1977   Poor People's Movements. New York: Pantheon
                             Books.

Reece, Ray
1978   "That Lucky Old Sun Got Nothin' to Do but Roll
                             Around Heaven All Day." The Texas Observer.
                             December:2–8.

Ritzer, George, Kammeyer,
Kenneth, C. W., and
Yetman, Norman R.
1979   Sociology: Experiencing a Changing Society.
                             Boston: Allyn and Bacon.

Roach, Jack and Janet K.
1978   "Mobilizing the Poor: Road to the Dead End."
                             Social Problems 26 (December):160–71.

Roby, Pamela
1974   The Poverty Establishment. Englewood Cliffs, N.J.:
                             Prentice-Hall.

Rocher, Guy
1975   "Formal Education: The Issue of Opportunity." In
                             Issues in Canadian Society: An Introduction to
                             Sociology. Dennis Forcese and Stephen Richer, eds.,
                             Scarborough: Prentice-Hall of Canada, pp. 437–61.

Rubinson, Richard, and
Quiton, Dan
1977   "Democracy and Social Inequality: A Reanalysis."
                             American Sociological Review 42 (August):611–23.

Shannon, David A.
1060

The Great Depression. Englewood Cliffs, N.J.:
Prentice-Hall.

Spokesman Review
1980

"New U.S. Defense Budget Hits $161.7 Billion
Total." March 2:A5.

Squires, Gregory P.
1977

"Education, Jobs, and Inequality: Functional and
Conflict Models of Social Stratification in the
United States." Social Problems 24 (April):436–50.

Steiner, Gilbert Y.
1971

The State of Welfare. Washington, D.C.: The
Brookings Institution.

Stern, Philip
1973

The Rape of the Taxpayer. New York: Random House.

Turner, Jonathan
1977

Social Problems in America. New York: Harper & Row.

Tussing, A. Dale
1974

"The Dual Welfare System." Society 2(2)
January–February.

United States Bureau
of Census
1978

Statistical Abstract of the United States: (99th edition).
Washington, D.C.: U.S. Government Printing Office.

1979

Statistical Abstract of the United States: (100th
edition). Washington, D.C.: U.S. Government
Printing Office.

1979

Characteristics of the Population below the Poverty
Level: 1977. Washington, D.C.: U.S. Government
Printing Office.

United States Bureau of
Labor Statistics
1979

Handbook of Labor Statistics: 1978. Washington,
D.C.: U.S. Government Printing Office.

United States Congress
Joint Committee on
Taxation
1977

"Estimates of Federal Tax Expenditures." Prepared
for the Committee on Ways and Means and the
Committee on Finance. Washington, D.C.: U.S.
Government Printing Office.

United States Internal
Revenue Service
1976   "Statistics of Income—1972. Personal Wealth."
Washington, D.C.: U.S. Government Printing
Office.

U.S. News and World
Report
1974   June 3, p. 49.

Vanneman, Reeve, and
Pampel, Fred C.
1977   "The American Perception of Class and Status."
American Sociological Review 42 (June):422–37.

Vorse, Mary H.
1932   "Rebellion in the Cornbelt: American Farmers Beat
their Plowshares into Swords." Harpers 166
(December):3–7.

Wachtel, Howard M.
1971   "Looking at Poverty from a Radical Perspective."
The Review of Radical Political Economics 3
(Summer):1–8.

Webbink, Paul
1941   "Unemployment in the United States, 1930–1940."
Papers and Proceedings of the American Economic
Association, 30 (February):250–51.

Wofford, John G.
1969   "The Politics of Local Responsibility: Administration of the Community Action Program: 1964–
1966." In James L. Sundquist, ed., On Fighting
Poverty. New York: Basic Books.

Wolfe, Alan
1978   The Seamy Side of Democracy: Repression in
America. New York: Longman.

World Almanac
1977   World Almanac and Book of Facts. New York:
Newspaper Enterprise Association.

1979   World Almanac and Book of Facts. New York:
Newspaper Enterprise Association.

Zeitlin, Maurice
1978   "Who Owns America? The Same Old Gang." The
Progressive. June:14–19.

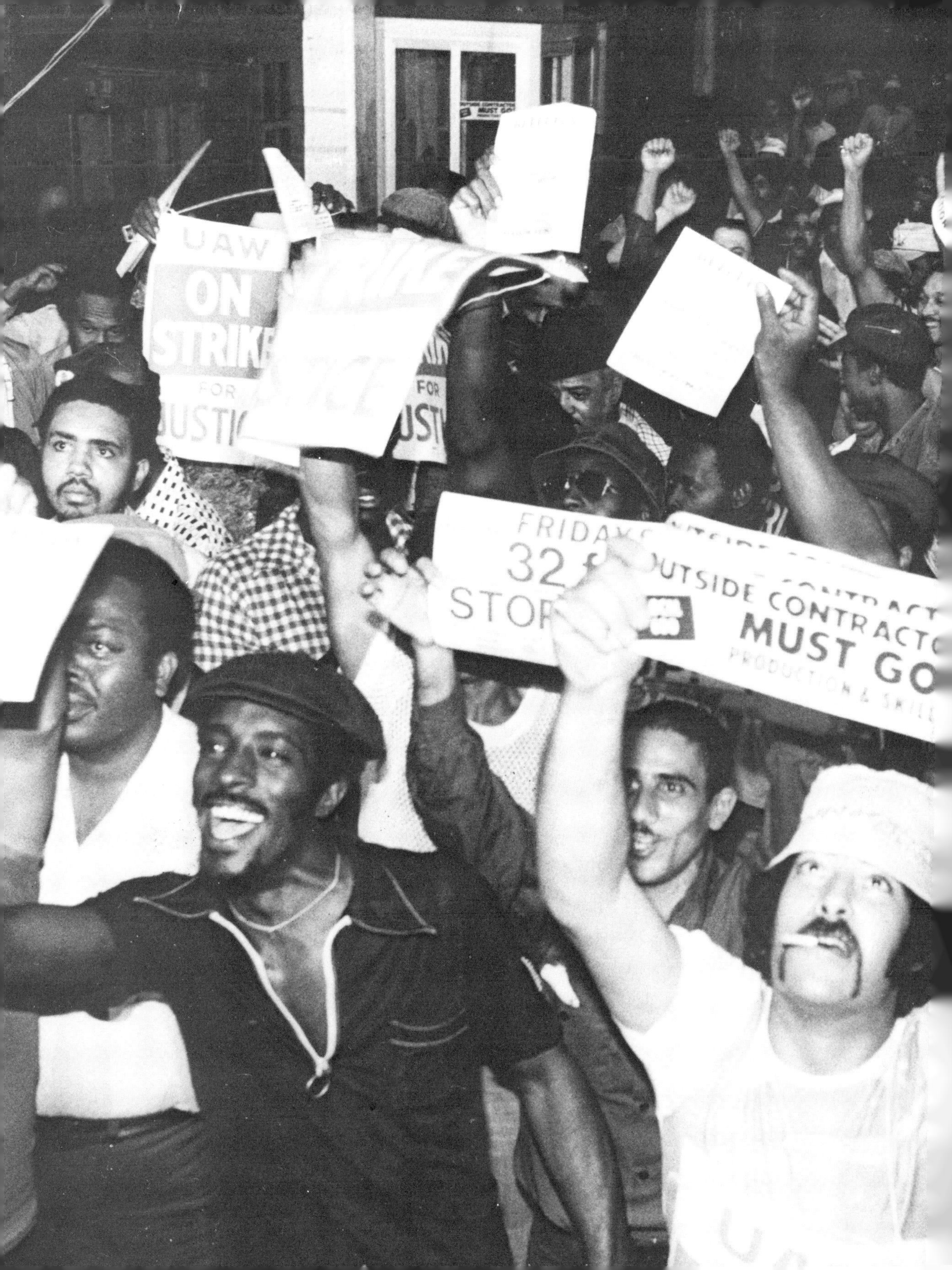
UAW
ON
FOR
MUST GO

4

WORK: ALIENATION AND FREEDOM

Abstract

While it might seem somewhat curious to include a chapter on work in a text on social problems, further reflection provides a different view. One's occupation is related to such obvious things as income and life satisfaction. However, more than these, work is a master political symbol. It serves to define social classes and, in turn, where power resides.

After a critical examination of the *prevailing ideologies* that deny or distort the nature of work in corporate society, we turn to the *emergence* of the problem. A central historical role was played by competing labor unions. Those who did not strongly challenge the interests of owners survived, while those seeking worker involvement in directing the economic order did not. The *institutionalization* of the "work problem" was subsequently realized through laws and policies that promise much (and deliver little) in the way of collective bargaining and occupational safety and health. With regard to *maintenance,* the development of work regulations has given *governmental* regulatory agencies a reason for being. Overall, the problem of "dying for a living" reflects a corporate order in which workers have little influence.

159

Facing the situations of pain and conflict to which the alienated (person) is exposed, we shall see our sufferings as due to unfortunate mishaps. Instead of coming to grips with the inherent forces of alienation we shall merely react with feelings of nostalgia and sadness, or with complaints and empty protests. —Fritz Pappenheim

Perhaps the clearest understanding of the corporate society can be had if we comprehend what it means to work in it. Working in North American society entails the assignment of a position in the hierarchy of production. Thus, many find themselves stripped of power and personal influence, shorn of self-direction, and clearly without the sense of mastery provided by creative labor. Though such description brings to mind the factory worker in industry, it is not intended to portray the traditional working class alone. To the monotonous and mechanistic world of the blue collar must be added new legions of sales and clerical workers, technocrats and bureaucrats, and the organization manager who "dresses for success."

It would be folly to equate the various echelons in the industrial order. As later evidence will show, occupations vary widely in the material senses of safety and income production. On the subjective dimension of "prestige," various members of society ascribe different worth to different jobs. However, no matter what one does "for a living," work in the corporate order is both fragmented and external. For the blue collar world, the job is an endless repetition of some small segment of the productive process. For those making decisions, the managerial world is detached from the role that human labor plays in converting the raw into the finished and the part into the whole. Management has been assigned the mental component of the work role while workers are compelled to contribute sweat and blood. The one is safer, less prone to occupational disease, and not so clearly acted upon while the other is simultaneously invaluable and disvalued. Neither is complete.

YOU ARE WHAT YOU DO?

It is useful to pause for a moment to consider the importance of work. When one is asked what he or she *does*, the response is inevitably work-centered. When we say that people *succeed*, that judgment is usually made within the context of their work. And many have found that to be unemployed, retired, or "only" a housewife carries important social disadvantage. Work then becomes a master symbol of identification. It represents a means of defining self to others and is a vital source of esteem.

Beyond the function of identification, we suggest that work holds the key to much of human *actualization*. Work potentially involves the accomplishment of a definite result, a wellspring of creative self-expression, and an end unto itself. It is an extension of our inner being into the sustaining environment. Thus, work becomes more than an activity that affords a livelihood. It goes beyond wages, hours, working conditions or stock options, attaché cases, and the key to the executive washroom.

However, when a comparison is made between the portrait of work potential painted above and the stifling, fragmented, empty, and sometimes dangerous reality that many people experience in their jobs, an obvious paradox emerges. A convenient solution to the paradox is provided by those who maintain that the potential of work has been *romanticized*. Such critics might borrow Thomas Hobbes's description of human nature to argue that work by its nature is "solitary, brutish, nasty, short." Another possibility, offered by others, is that work in North American society is unjustly criticized and that *worker satisfaction* is really quite high. Other logical resolutions concede the deficiencies of the work situation but suggest they are part of the common *technological* nature of all industrial societies. Finally, it is possible to connect work problems to the specific structure of the corporate society.

The properties of the corporate system have been detailed clearly in the first two chapters. The imperatives of growth, expansion, profit, and private ownership have important implications for the particular division of labor that follows these imperatives. By *particular* division of labor, we mean that it is possible to extend our thought beyond simple task division. An assignment of differential tasks to groups is a common feature of all social orders. *What distinguishes North American societies is a process of task specialization that increases worker productivity, minimizes the cost of human labor, and increases the return on investment for stockholders. Beyond these concerns, however, is the extension of a yoke of control through the separation of mental and manual labor and the development of techniques of legitimation that ensure obedience and dependency.* The viewpoint that follows deals with what it is like to be acted upon.

Viewpoint

Class, in the sense writers like Marx, Saint-Simon, and Proudhon used the term in the nineteenth century, was a matter of power. Different classes of men existed in society because some men had control of other men's labor, and most men were not masters of what they did or made. In his

Sociological Tradition, Robert Nisbet observes that at the end of the last century, a change occurred In the concept of the relationship between class and power: writers like Max Weber added a new dimension, embodied in the concept of "authority." A worker can know his foreman has power over him, and yet if only a matter of brute coercion is involved, why doesn't the worker rise up against the foreman when the latter takes unfair advantage of him? Why is it so hard for the oppressed to revolt against injustice? To answer such questions, men like Weber and Gramsci sought to describe the transformation of power into legitimate rule. They asked what values society spawns to legitimize the right of some to control the lives of many, convincing the worker that he *ought* to submit his labor to the will of others.

This idea of legitimacy is rather more complex than it first appears. If a man feels he obeys someone he ought to obey, what happens to his own self-image? The foreman tells a worker he will have to work extra hours if he wants to keep his job during depression times; the worker's freedom is thus diminished, of course, but if the worker feels the foreman has the right to take away his freedom, how can the man feel he has *any* rights, how can he respect himself? The rule might follow, tentatively, that when power becomes legitimate, whatever dignity a man accords to his ruler he must necessarily deny himself.

Now a badge of ability seems the perfect tool to legitimatize power. This concept of human potential says that the few are more richly endowed than the many and that only the few can know themselves—i.e., recognize themselves as distinctive individuals. Having gained "more" dignity by virtue of greater personal power, it is logical that they ought to rule the many. Apply to that simple meritocratic argument the tentative rule proposed above about legitimized power: the more inclined are the many, the masses, to a belief that dignity exists in these terms, and the more they surrender their own freedom to the few, the less chance they have of respecting themselves as people with any countervailing rights (excerpted from Sennett and Cobb, *The Hidden Injuries of Class* 1973, pp. 76–78).

Simply put, corporate structure creates a division of labor where work, with its potential for creative self-expression, is transformed into labor sold for wage or salary. The conversion of work to labor signals the loss of mastery and dignity. In the process, one submits to ruling forces such as far-removed members of an owning class whose personal fortunes consist of investment assets. The more immediate impersonal powers of routine, fragmented duties, and production schedules are also beyond personal control. Labor becomes the means of toil toward an end. One describes work as "just a job," keeping the wolf away from the door, putting bread on the table, or making payments. Sweat and energy are sold in the same sense as any other commodity. In the words of Shakespeare, "Money is the universal whore," and we all become pimps selling our alienated labor to acquire various goods and services. Thus occurs the transformation of the freedom of work into the alienation of labor.

ALIENATION

The term *alienation* has been of fascination to many. It has been explored

> . . . (by) theologians and philosophers who warn that advances in scientific knowledge do not enable us to penetrate the mystery of Being, and do not bridge but often widen the gulf between the knower and the reality he tries to understand; by psychiatrists who try to help their patients return from the world of illusion to reality; by critics of the increasing mechanization of life who challenge the optimistic expectation that technological progress will automatically lead to the enrichment of human lives; by political scientists who note that even democratic institutions have failed to bring about genuine participation by the masses in the great issues of our period (Pappenheim 1968, p. 14).

However, it was Karl Marx who, in 1844, described the dimensions of alienation and in so doing placed the phenomenon in the broader context of economic organization. Describing the condition in general terms, Marx argued that alienation was an emptying process for the worker who toiled under the conditions of nineteenth-century industrial capitalism. The more one produced for others, the more impoverished became one's own life. The more one gave of personal energy, the less human he or she was. The consequence of alienated labor was that the very *products* that owed their existence to the worker came to assume the form of *fetishized commodities*. Thus, the objects of one's creation were no longer an extension of self, but rather came to dominate the maker.

> It is the same in religion. The more man puts into God, the less he retains in himself. The worker puts his life into the object, but now his life no longer belongs to him but to the object. . . . Whatever

the product of his labor, he is not. . . . The *alienation* of the worker in his product means not only that his labor becomes an object, an *external* existence, but that it exists *outside him*, independently, as something alien to him, and that it becomes a power on its own confronting him . . . (Marx 1961a, p. 69).

Elsewhere, Marx was to identify four dimensions of alienation. First, as we have already seen, the very work of one's hands comes to assume an independent status of power. In a corresponding fashion, work as a *process* or *activity* becomes external and detached, devoid of fulfillment, belonging to another. The third dimension follows logically from the first two. In this aspect, the worker is alienated from self. Since *work as life* has become only a means of *making a living, it must be that the essences of life—one's physical body, mental nature, human standing—are no longer under self-control. Therefore, the alienated person perceives what is most intimate and personal as estranged, and social relationships* are shattered. Men and women become objectified "others" sharing social space but not social identity.

C. B. Macpherson (1962) argued that where labor becomes a commodity, bought and sold at the marketplace, alienated market relationships will come to "permeate all social relationships."

> Whatever the degree of state action, the possessive market model permits individuals who want more delights than they have to seek to convert the natural powers of other men to their use. They do so through the market, in which everyone is necessarily involved. Since the market is continually competitive, those who would be content with the level of satisfactions they have are compelled to fresh exertions by every attempt of the others to increase theirs. Those who would be content with the level they have cannot keep it without seeking to transfer more powers of others to themselves, to compensate for the increasing amount that the competitive efforts of others are transferring from them (1962, p. 59).

Such a society prompts not merely the exploitation of labor but the conversion of personality into a commodity. The individual presents the proper self, business includes a public relations component, and political candidates sell a public image. All of this is in the name of getting ahead.

The study of "job satisfaction" and "morale" in industry also tends to view the worker as a commodity (Gruneberg 1976). The "human side of enterprise" is translated as the identification of "motivated workers," the promotion of "organizational effectiveness," and "management development" (Hampton 1969). The study of organizational behavior includes the relationship of morale and satisfaction to other variables. These include group pressures to conform, group competition and cooperation, and supervision styles (Applewhite 1965). Other inquiry scrutinizes the application of behavior modification techniques (the changing of behavior through altering the external contingencies of reinforcement) to the problem of productivity (Luthans 1975). This type of focus conjures up the vision of the worker as a pigeon in a Skinner box, being fed (reinforced) when the right key is pecked.

ON THE ALIENATION OF ALIENATION

In corporate society today, when alienation is converted into boredom, power changed into the suggestion box, and job satisfaction reduced to a response on a questionnaire, something is lost in the translation. The reason for this should be clear. If alienation is defined sociologically, it is a powerful tool for understanding the structural sources of work as a social problem. On the other hand, when it is converted conceptually and reduced to "boredom," any serious questioning of the class-based nature of work and the economic order will be stillborn. In this sense, the idea of alienation becomes conceptually impoverished, a shadow of its penetrating and clarifying potential.

We have seen that the emphasis on problems at work have fostered inquiry into those human properties thought to affect productivity. Frequently those properties are collapsed into a paste pot called alienation. A popular intellectual treatment of alienation in the corporate society has been to define its components in ways that have absolutely nothing to do with the imperatives of that system. And, as always, the kinds of solutions developed follow the way in which the problem is defined. In *Alienation and Freedom* (1964), Robert Blauner gives his readers essential lessons on how to grasp the alienation of alienation. Because we believe this author misses the point, in the same way many others do, it is necessary to understand and criticize his views.

First, Blauner "divides" alienation into four components. Though he engages in some discussion of each, he moves to a concrete method of recognizing them. The first, *powerlessness*, is defined as one's ability to control the *pace of one's work*. *Meaninglessness* seems to refer to whether or not one can fathom or appreciate the nature and consequences of one's work and the products created therefrom. *Isolation* means that the worker is not really a member of the community of the specific workplace. Finally, *self-estrangement* signifies that work is not central to the person's identity, that it does not rank with other central social commitments. Self-estrangement means that work is without *intrinsic* value.

Secondly, Blauner "accounts" for such conditions by venturing outside the workplace. The origin of the problem, he argues, is with the nature of *technology*. Technology for Blauner is "the complex of physical objects and technical operations (both manual and machine) regularly employed in turning out the goods and services produced by an industry" (1964,

p. 6). Thus it appears that the domination of the worker by the machine is more or less the inevitable consequence of the increasing sophistication of such machines.

Blauner's argument is similar to many heard both in and out of academic circles. Its popularity is evident in the types of alternatives that logically flow from its central premises. First of all, Blauner dismisses "worker control" over the policies of management. The worker could reduce alienation simply by having some say in the production schedule. It therefore follows that the institutionalization in industry of the "flex-time" system would resolve this weighty problem. Workers under such an arrangement can report to work somewhat early or late, put in their eight hours and leave. Isolation for Blauner could be somewhat resolved through union membership, and meaninglessness through plant tours designed to promote understanding of the total work operation. It further appears that the cure for self-estrangement awaits the rebirth of the lost "work ethic."

Blauner's obsession with the machine generalizes the problem of alienation to all industrial societies. In so doing, he implicitly dismisses as inconsequential the social, political, and economic forces that shape and direct technology. To the contrary, we believe that a technology may be advanced that maximizes the potential for human growth.

> Outside the logic of the growth [that is, corporate] society, automation could be pursued strictly as a means of eliminating drudgery and dangerous and undesirable labor. Automation could play a major role in enlarging the amount of free time available for the pursuit of social and self-development. Advanced technology in all of its forms could be harnessed for the goals of liberation. Then work could begin to take on voluntary and creative aspects, and become integrated with the rest of the human personality and community (Anderson 1976, p. 116).

A number of examples may make this clear. Despite a clear and compelling case for action, the giant transnational petrocorporations direct investment and influence political action away from solar energy and other renewable power sources (Commoner 1976). "Mineral rights" are a form of private property to which corporate claim is attached; no such scheme for claiming ownership of the rays of the sun yet exists. While a solar technology might not be in the interests of Exxon, it appears clearly in the interests of ecological survival. And the quality of the environment is a precondition for the quality of *human* growth. Similar arguments could be advanced in the fields of work and medical care. It is certainly possible to harness production technology in the interest of worker safety. However, as we shall soon see, occupational carnage continues (Scott 1974). Further, despite spiraling increases in the cost of medical service in the United States, the poor (especially the minorities and aged) get sick more frequently and die sooner than the more affluent (Navarro 1977). Such a contradiction can be understood only in the context of a class society. Medical technology in the corporate order reflects a greater concern with increasingly expensive hardware (and the profit margin thereof) while public health care focused on prevention languishes.

So long as alienation remains a superficial synonym for the problems of the workplace, so long as the emphasis is on the reduction of monotony and routine, so long as the "problem" is defined in terms of improving the public image of the worker, then little in the way of critical thought will be forthcoming. Instead, the emphasis will be on the substitution of the apparent for the real, the symbolic for the substantive and the "new image" for control.

If the conditions of alienation (powerlessness, meaninglessness, and self-absorption) are to be tied to social structure, it is logical to argue that strong ideological currents must be overcome. Those who control the corporate order, and through it heavily influence affairs of state, are in a position, as C. Wright Mills argued, to "control consent." One's very existence or being must be seen within the framework of the *possessive marketplace*. Private ownership, individualism, competition, Sennett's "badges of ability"—all these prevail as grand symbols of the corporate social order. As such, they dominate the common course of socialization. Accordingly, in corporate society problems with work will not be defined in the sense of what we have termed *labor* (that is, a human commodity bought and sold as any other). To do so would require a break with the legitimations that preserve the existing order. If within that order work and the worker are perceived as problems at all, subsequent inquiry will be in the direction of restricted reform. Attention will be given to modifying the physical conditions of the workplace without addressing the social relationships of workers. One might expect grudging concessions in the number and locations of on-the-job toilets but no voice in managerial decisions. Further, it will be legitimate to probe the psyche of the worker, especially as this might improve morale and boost output. Such efforts at endowing production with a human face will fall well short of challenging the boundary lines of class.

THE PREVAILING IDEOLOGIES

In the late nineteenth and early twentieth centuries, increasing numbers left the farms to seek work in the urban factories of North America. The forces of industrialization and urbanization coexisted with massive movements of immigrants to the "new country." As corporation capitalism became rooted more and more in the factory system, human labor was required. The sons and daughters of craftworkers came to experience in a real sense impoverishment and the death of dignity. Those trapped in the tenements of the urban ghettos, caught in a system where the entire family toiled in misery to scratch out a bare subsistence, frequently branded by alien language and custom, were in little position to speak out. The voices that were heard then did not bother to deny the misery of the workplace. Rather, they held out the promise of escape for the talented few.

Survival of the Fittest

George Santayana held that those who do not remember the past are condemned to relive it. Perhaps it is true that yesterday contains the seeds of today. And in the yesterday that was turn-of-the-century United States and Canada, *survival of the fittest* became a cardinal symbol that shaped the perception of work as a social problem.

When Charles Darwin wrote on the evolution of the species, he presented his view of natural selection. Put simply, those life forms that were able to adapt to a changing environment survived. Those unable to do so perished. A social version of this view was developed formally by the British sociologist Herbert Spencer, and quickly became popular in some academic circles in North America. However, the essential points of social Darwinism would not be confined to the academic servants of power.

> Industrial society is hard, hard as animals in nature who find the struggle to survive—a life-and-death battle. The justice of industrial capitalism in America, said Andrew Carnegie, is that society here will not fail to reward a man of talent. If a man is worthy of escaping poverty's terrors, he can do so.

If he doesn't have the ability to "make it," by what right does he complain? (Sennett and Cobb 1973, p. 72)

Andrew Carnegie, who later sold Carnegie Steel to J. Pierpont Morgan, was true to his convictions. He bitterly opposed unions while simultaneously endowing libraries. His intention, no doubt, was to be certain that the conditions of work were harsh enough to test the mettle of worker character.

As previously suggested, it is likely that the seeds of social Darwinism continue to bear fruit. Stripped of its biological baggage, this specific ideology is little more than a rationalization for inequality. What sets it apart are its genetic pretensions. Poor workers who remained poor were labeled innately inferior; they supposedly got off the evolutionary tree at a lower (not quite human) limb. However, it is not necessary to return to 1900 to find examples of the "survival of the fittest" ideology. More recent attempts at biological determinism of social position can be found.

Is Intelligence Inherited? In 1969, Arthur Jensen, a professor of educational psychology at the University of California, argued that intelligence is primarily inherited. Jensen even provided a precise statement of genetic determination. He found that some 80 percent of one's IQ (Intelligence Quotient) is inherited, while 20 percent of it is due to environmental factors. Given the fact that the tests that supposedly measure *innate intelligence* show blacks scoring below whites, Jensen found it plausible to argue that blacks are genetically deficient (Jensen 1969).

Following the same trail, Harvard psychologist Richard Herrnstein proposes that not only is intelligence inherited but the existing system of social stratification (inequality) is also due to genetic advantage or disadvantage. According to Herrnstein, those who are successful (in other words, those who do the "important" jobs in a society and earn the most money) have the simple advantage of greater inherited mental ability. Social classes are based on merit, and the secret of merit is not the social position of one's parents but rather their innate intelligence. Those who occupy the front offices in the factories are intellectually advantaged. Those who meet the production schedule are genetically determined inferiors.

Both Jensen and Herrnstein used the data of the British psychologist Sir Cyril Burt to reach their conclusions on the importance of nature (genetics) over nurture (environment) in the determination of intelligence. Burt's work, conducted in the Forties and Fifties, claimed that different environments did not significantly affect the intelligence of identical twins. Some five years after his death in 1971, Burt's research was caught up in a storm of controversy (Gillie 1977). He has been widely accused of fraud. Specifically, it appears that Burt reported tests that were not performed, manufactured results, and attached the names of fictitious coauthors to his research to substantiate its credibility.

Beyond the problem with the data base is the somewhat simplistic view of "intelligence" tests. If intelligence tests are geared to social advantage, if they are in fact culture-bound, then no claim of measurement of *innate* intelligence can be made. In point of fact, differences in background (environment) mean differences in language, vocabulary, and experiences (Chomsky 1972). It is perhaps more to the point to argue that *IQ is less a measure of intelligence, and more a measure of income.* The disturbing implication, however, is that such supposedly objective measures are fully institutionalized. For example, they have become a basis for program determination in the public schools. Once a quantitative figure is assigned, expectations and attention will follow. In the classic sense of the "self-fulfilling prophecy," those who score high are expected to do well and are encouraged to do so. Those who score low encounter minimum standards "tailored" to their "individual" needs. The probability of success or failure varies accordingly.

Variations of social Darwinism that legitimate a structure of inequality are certainly not confined to quasi-biological grounds. The Horatio Alger saga of rags to riches, Carnegie's vision of the deserving poor, Emerson and Thoreau on self-sufficiency—all of these come together at the locus of individualism. All of these explanations are ways of blaming the victim (Ryan 1971). On the bottom line, when the virtues of heroic individualism, hard work, ambition, and achievement motivation are recited, the end result is to glorify the mythical hero who, like the Phoenix, rises from the ashes to condemn in backhanded fashion those who comprise the underbelly of social order. Stripped bare, stories about individual triumph are *rationalizations* for ascribed class position. The claim is that those on the bottom *deserve* to be there.

The Worker's Place in a Stratified Society The place of the worker must be seen in the broader context of a stratified social order. In 1945, sociologists Kingsley Davis and Willard Moore offered a functionalist (order) view on social inequality. Simply put, they argued that differentials in prestige and income appear in societies because some work is more important than other work and requires a more extensive period of training with a corresponding delay of gratification. (The image of the struggling medical school student comes to mind). Social inequality, therefore, is not simply a factual description of a society that accords vast differences in power and wealth to its members. It is, rather, necessary to ensure the equilibrium of the social order.

One cannot deny that any movement to upset the unequal distribution of wealth and power in North American and other class societies would disturb the equilibrium. By the same logic, the abolitionist movement, underground railroads, and slave revolts must have proved unsettling to the plantation owners in the Southern United States prior to the Civil War. However, the ideological implications of Davis and Moore's view clearly coincide with the common legitimations for differences in social position referred to in the Viewpoint for this chapter. The problem with functionalist theory is that it is based on the order paradigm (see Chapter One). Therefore, the focus is on what is best for "society." The issue might better revolve around the interests of *people* in society. The functionalist emphasis is on the preservation of existing *institutions*, while the latter is on changing or replacing those institutions when necessary to meet the needs of more people. Functionalists argue that the forms of inequality (such as owners, managers, workers) are necessary and beneficial. The question is: necessary and beneficial for whom?

The differences in the worth attached to various kinds of work can be faulted on other grounds. For example, in North America some are paid enormous sums to hit a ball into a hole in the ground with a stick, others to hit a puck into a net with a big stick while on ice, others to hit a larger ball over a fence with a bigger stick. It is doubtful that the social order would collapse without such occupations. The same argument could be made for many entertainers. Are such tasks really more necessary and beneficial than those executed by coal miners and agricultural workers?

The functional importance of underpaid nurses is evident to anyone who has been hospitalized. Further, we do not warm our homes with golf balls.

To appreciate the vital nature of frequently disvalued work in society, we must understand the interdependence of work roles. The neurosurgeon would be helpless without surgical instruments, hospitals, and an enormous range of services that depend on the so-called ordinary or common worker. Even if we are to grant the differences in training between the physician and the steelworker, could one exist without the other?

Material presented in Chapter Three demonstrates an enormous concentration of wealth in North America. The logic of functional necessity claims simply that those who have this wealth have engaged in socially beneficial work. According to biological determinists, such persons were no doubt aided in their rise to the top through their genetic advantage. The evidence, however, is clear. The superrich in corporate society have been aided less by genes than by the inheritance of large family fortunes (Lundberg 1968). If those who believe in earned success and hereditary advantage are entirely convinced by their arguments, they should advocate a system of sharply graduated inheritance taxes. This would give those with a hereditary edge the incentive to realize their innate potential. What we are led to conclude in our examination of individualistic ideology is that those born to wealth must not need the incentive of wealth to work hard. That incentive remains for the poor.

The Happy Worker

Another specific ideology that affects our perception of the problem of work is what Harvey Swados (1970) referred to as the "myth of the happy worker." This myth assumes many forms. In 1898, Frederick W. Taylor, the father of "scientific management," became a consultant for Bethlehem Steel. A discussion of Taylor's thought will be taken up later. Here it is important to understand that explanations about work are typically based on an *image* of the worker. Taylor defined his worker as essentially a dumb brute. Accordingly, through bonus incentives, factory workers would be transformed into "greedy robots." Like draft horses, however, they were *content* to perform the repetitive and mechanical routines while allowing others to do their thinking for them (Rose 1975, pp. 31–53).

The image of the happy worker dealt with critically by Swados is more contemporary. No longer do we encounter the vision of the contented ox. Rather, those who sell their labor for a wage are now portrayed as members of the great middle classes. Swados takes issue with the contention that blue collar and middle class are increasingly indistinguishable.

But there is one thing the worker doesn't do like the middle class: he works like a worker. The steel mill puddler does not yet sort memos, the coal miner does not yet sit in conferences, the cotton millhand does not yet sip martinis from his lunchbox. The worker's attitude toward his work is generally compounded of hatred, shame and resignation (Swados, in Josephson and Josephson 1970, p. 107).

Swados almost inadvertently places the myth of the happy worker in the context of a larger myth, that of the expanding middle class. Table 4-1 provides occupational statistics that bear on this issue.

Upward Mobility   For many observers, the concept of an expanding middle class implies upward mobility. If this is true, members of the traditional working class are moving upward in ever-expanding numbers. The data demonstrate clearly that white collar workers are comprising a steadily increasing percentage of the employed work force (43.4 percent in 1960 to 50.8 percent in 1978). In a corresponding fashion blue collar composition declined from 36.6 to 32.8 percent over the same time span. However, one is prone to error if the terms "white collar" and "middle class" are treated as synonymous. This is because the former includes categories other than the professional/technical and managerial/administrative occupations that are basic to any claim of upward mobility. In point of fact, in 1960 these occupational categories constituted 51 percent of the white collar work force. In 1978 the corresponding figure was 52 percent. Conversely, for the clerical and sales categories, also white collar occupations, the figures are 49 percent and 48 percent, respectively. Between 1960 and 1978 the demand for clerical workers had increased by some 6.8 million jobs. This white collar category was slightly ahead of the increase in demand for professional/technical personnel and more than double the job increase at the managerial/administrative level. In Canada the service sector of the work force (defined differently than the service sector in the U.S.) is the most rapidly expanding group. The service sector, including a large number of "white collar" retail clerks and other salespersons, increased by 39 percent between 1961 to 1971, while the industrial sector decreased by 20 percent (Canada Year Book 1978–79, p. 352). Thus in both societies the greatest growth is seen in jobs that tend to be minimum wage, and largely nonunionized. Furthermore, it is vital to remember that even the advantaged professional/managerial jobholders are also *wage and salary employees*. They, too, sell their labor or services and encounter increasing work-related problems, as later data will show.

There are additional points that must be raised concerning the premise of upward mobility. First of all, we are confident that most people think of moving up as bringing freedom, dignity, meaningful work, and increases in real income. Such is not achieved through merely changing the color of the work collar. Further, as Braverman (1974) argues, perhaps many of the fabled middle class today are in actuality a new working

TABLE 4-1
Employed Persons, by Major Occupation Group: 1960 to 1978
(In thousands of persons 16 years old and over)

OCCUPATION GROUP	1960	1965	1970	1973	1974	1975	1976	1977	1978 Jan-Apr
Total	65,778	71,088	78,627	84,409	85,936	84,783	87,485	90,546	91,846
White Collar workers	28,522	31,852	37,997	40,386	41,738	42,227	43,700	45,187	46,673
Percent of total	43.4	44.8	48.3	47.8	48.6	49.8	50.0	49.9	50.8
Professional & technical	7,469	8,872	11,140	11,777	12,338	12,748	13,329	13,692	14,252
Managers & administrators	7,067	7,340	8,289	8,644	8,941	8,891	9,315	9,662	10,026
Sales workers	4,224	4,499	4,854	5,415	5,417	5,460	5,497	5,828	5,795
Clerica workers	9,762	11,141	13,714	14,548	15,043	15,128	15,558	16,106	16,600
Blue Collar workers	24,057	26,247	27,791	29,869	29,776	27,962	28,958	30,211	30,095
Craft and kindred workers	8,554	9,216	10,158	11,288	11,477	10,972	11,278	11,881	11,853
Operatives, excluding transport {	11,950	13,345	13,909	{10,972	10,627	9,637	10,085	10,354	10,539
Transport equipment operatives {				{ 3,297	3,292	3,219	3,271	3,476	3,487
Nonfarm laborers	3,553	3,686	3,724	4,312	4,380	4,134	4,325	4,500	4,217
Service Workers	8,923	8,936	9,712	11,128	11,373	11,657	12,005	12,392	12,608
Farm Workers	5,176	4,053	3,126	3,027	3,048	2,936	2,822	2,756	2,469

Source: *Statistical Abstract of the United States 1978*, p. 418.

class. Their view of their work is probably not so different from the description Swados gives of the blue collar worker's contempt for what he or she does. However, those in the lower echelon white collar positions are convinced of their advantages and the *relative* desirability of what they do. As such, they are oblivious to the possibility that real social position in the workplace is ultimately a question of control and freedom, not the nature of the costume worn.

Measuring Worker Satisfaction   Another variant of the happy worker symbol can be found in the widely reported surveys on job satisfaction. As Table 4-2 demonstrates, workers generally report they are "satisfied." However, before we rush to dismiss the arguments on worker alienation, serious reservations about the meaning of such surveys must be raised.

First, those in the human sciences understand well that measures of job satisfaction may also be termed measures of job *resignation*. There is a fundamental difference in meaning between fulfillment and pleasure on the one side and the knowledge that one is not going to escape one's place on the other. Secondly, as demonstrated in the heading to Table 4-2, satisfaction involves the combination of a range of responses on a Likert scale.[1] Those who are *fairly* satisfied (or frequently partly satisfied and

TABLE 4-2
Satisfied Workers as a Percentage of Total Workers: 1962 to 1977

[Survey questions asked were variants of "How satisfied are you with your job (or your work)?" Figures for "satisfied" combined responses such as "very satisfied," "somewhat satisfied," and "fairly satisfied."]

Worker Characteristic	1962	1964	1972	1973	1974	1975	1976	1977
Sex:								
Male	84	92	86	86	87	90	87	87
Female	81	(NA)	86	89	89	87	87	90
Ethnicity:								
White	84	92	87	87	89	89	88	88
Black & other	[1]76	[1]88	78	85	83	85	79	85
Age:								
21–29 years	74	[2]87	76	80	81	82	84	83
30–39 years	82	[3]93	88	87	84	88	91	88
40–49 years	84	92	89	88	91	92	89	86
50 years and over	88	94	92	93	94	93	93	95
Education:								
Grade school	83	94	86	86	86	87	83	88
High school	81	90	86	85	90	91	88	88
Some college	86	89	83	86	87	90	88	86
College degree	90	94	85	93	86	85	87	88
Graduate work	84	93	95	98	93	87	92	92

NA: Not available.   [1] Black only.   [2] 21–30 years.   [3] 31–40 years.

Source: *Statistical Abstract of the United States*, 1978, p. 402.

[1]A Likert scale refers to a set of responses to questions usually spread over increments such as: highly agree, agree, uncertain, disagree, and highly disagree.

partly dissatisfied) are grouped with the *somewhat or moderately* satisfied and the *very* satisfied. Though such a procedure is commonplace in scale analysis, the results can be misleading.

With the problems of such measurement of satisfaction in mind, let us turn to other evidence. Quinn and Shepard (1974) in a landmark survey of work in America found that almost half of their representative sample expressed a preference *not to be in their present job.* Cooper (1979) found increasing dissatisfaction among employees and greater interest in "intrinsic" rewards (having to do with the quality of their work life) other than the traditional matters of wages, hours, and working conditions. Spray et al. (in Negandhi and Wilpert 1978, pp. 154–172) conducted a survey of steelworkers to determine job satisfaction. They found that 30 percent of their respondents were dissatisfied with their work, 55 percent were moderately satisfied, and 15 percent were very satisfied. Given the typical breakdown of scales, some 70 percent could be identified as satisfied. However, when satisfaction was measured separately for each of the six mills in this study, the generalization of "satisfaction" did not hold. The variation ranged from almost total satisfaction for some mills to almost 50 percent dissatisfaction with one. The authors conclude that "the differences in satisfaction scores are highly visible and organizationally specific." Further, "they render general satisfaction surveys highly suspect, at least in the steel industry."

We believe that the issue of work fulfillment transcends survey questions on job satisfaction. In 1952, Walker and Guest, in an article in the *Harvard Business Review*, found that "the average worker appeared to be oppressed by [a] sense of anonymity *in spite of the fact that he declared himself well satisfied with his rate of pay and the security of his job.*" Little has changed in the past quarter-century. Reports of job satisfaction as determined by survey questionnaires continue to coexist with accounts by workers themselves that they feel like "nothing" or like an easily replaced piece of machinery. Moreover, issues relating to the "happy worker" continue to dominate the literature, not only in the sociology of work and alienation, but also in studies and books intended basically for consumption by university students in management as well as by active managers. As this writing occurs, the list of reference materials is revealing. A few of the titles are: *Alienation and Freedom; The Quality of Working Life, Volumes I and II; Job Satisfaction; Work and the Quality of Life; The Motivation Crisis; A Matter of Dignity; False Promises; People, Progress and Employee Relations; The Doomsday Job;* and *Humanizing the Workplace.* This text does not contain the space to list all such titles. It is doubtful that such interest would be shown if job satisfaction surveys were taken seriously.

Methodology and Measuring Worker Satisfaction   A final point is most critical. It represents an issue of *methodology*, or simply *how* we go about answering questions in sociological research. Asking people about job satisfaction or "happiness," assumes that alienation (or its absence) is a matter of attitude toward work. If workers report they *feel* satisfaction, or that they do not *feel* what some have portrayed as the attitudinal components of alienation (powerlessness, meaninglessness, isolation, and self-estrangement), they are not alienated (see Seeman 1961; and Blauner 1964). Our argument is that alienation is more than a state of mind; it is a state of being. Therefore, asking people what is on their mind is not sufficient to understand the sociological nature of alienation (Horton 1964). We must rather ask questions bearing on *objective* conditions of freedom. Simply put, to what extent do workers have power over their lives in the workplace? Such a fundamental question has to do with who does the firing and hiring, who shares in the fruits of labor, and to what extent the benefits go to absentee owners or stockholders and their managerial representatives (see "Workplace Democracy" at the end of the chapter).

The Affluent Worker

Another specific ideology that shapes how we perceive work is that of the "affluent worker." Workers may not be free at the workplace, and they may not be going anywhere, but at least they are well paid. According to many, workers in the United States are affluent, hence complacent. It is therefore doubtful that they will be an important force for change. Assessing the validity of the claims of affluence for the worker must begin with the unemployment statistics. It is difficult to term affluent someone who is out of a job unless, of course, the person is wealthy and chooses not to work. As shown in Table 4-3, unemployment rates in Canada and the United States exceed those of several other industrial capitalist countries. Further, as evidenced in Table 4-4, while all workers are endangered, those most poorly paid are most vulnerable to job loss.

Since 1970 in the United States, the rate of unemployment has risen for all occupational groups. The growth in the rate has been uneven, but the disconcerting fact is that the specter of joblessness has made inroads into even the upper-echelon "white collar" occupations. As always, the impact of unemployment varies widely, ranging in 1977 from a low of 2.8 percent for managers/administrators to 12.0 percent for nonfarm laborers. The rate for operatives, a category that includes most factory workers standing on production lines, was 9.5 percent. Translated into real numbers, an official unemployment rate of 7 percent for 1977 means that 6.8 million workers were without jobs. However, that figure, which is roughly equivalent to the population of Los Angeles, represents a serious distortion of the extent and nature of unemployment in the United States.

TABLE 4-3
Unemployment Rates for Seven Industrial
Capitalist Countries, 1959-1976

	U.S.	Canada	Great Britain	France	West Germany	Japan	Sweden
1959	5.5	6.0	3.1	2.4	1.8	2.3	N.A.
1960	5.5	7.0	2.0	2.5	0.8	1.7	N.A.
1961	6.7	7.1	1.9	1.9	0.5	1.5	1.5
1962	5.5	5.9	2.8	1.8	0.4	1.3	1.5
1963	5.7	5.5	3.5	2.1	0.5	1.3	1.7
1964	5.2	4.7	2.5	1.6	0.3	1.2	1.5
1965	4.5	3.9	2.2	2.0	0.3	1.2	1.2
1966	3.8	3.6	2.4	2.1	0.3	1.4	1.6
1967	3.8	4.1	3.8	2.7	1.0	1.3	2.1
1968	3.6	4.8	3.7	3.2	1.2	1.2	2.2
1969	3.5	4.7	3.7	2.8	0.7	1.1	1.9
1970	4.9	5.7	3.1	2.8	0.8	1.2	1.5
1971	5.9	6.2	3.9	3.0	0.8	1.3	2.6
1972	5.6	6.2	4.2	3.0	0.8	1.4	2.7
1973	4.9	5.6	3.2	2.9	0.8	1.3	2.5
1974	5.6	5.4	3.2	3.1	1.7	1.4	2.0
1975	8.5	6.9	4.7	4.3	3.8	1.9	1.6
1976	7.7	7.1	6.4	4.6	3.8	2.1	1.6

Source: Stirling and Kouri, 1979.

TABLE 4-4
Unemployment Rate* by Occupations: 1970-1977

* Annual averages of monthly figures. Persons 16 years old and over.

Occupation of Last Job	UNEMPLOYMENT RATE (Percent)							
	1970	1971	1972	1973	1974	1975	1976	1977
All Unemployed	4.9	5.9	5.6	4.9	5.6	8.5	7.7	7.0
OCCUPATION GROUP								
Professional & technical	2.0	2.9	2.4	2.2	2.3	3.2	3.2	3.0
Managers & administrators except farm	1.3	1.6	1.8	1.4	1.8	3.0	3.1	2.8
Sales workers	3.9	4.3	4.3	3.7	4.2	5.8	5.4	5.3
Clerical workers	4.1	4.8	4.7	4.2	4.6	6.6	6.4	5.9
Craft & kindred workers	3.8	4.7	4.3	3.7	4.4	8.3	6.9	5.6
Operatives, except transport	(NA)	(NA)	7.6	6.1	8.2	14.7	10.8	9.5
Transport equipment operatives	(NA)	(NA)	4.7	4.1	5.1	8.5	7.7	6.6
Nonfarm laborers	9.5	10.8	10.3	8.4	10.1	15.6	13.7	12.0
Service workers	5.3	6.3	6.3	5.7	6.3	8.6	8.7	8.2
Farm workers	2.6	2.6	2.6	2.5	2.5	3.5	4.5	4.6

NA: Not available.

Source: *Statistical Abstract of the United States* 1978, p. 411.

Definitions of Unemployment In a seminal article, Leggett and Cervinka (1073) demonstrate what Mark Twain meant when he argued that there are three kinds of liars: liars, damn liars, and statisticians. In this case we hasten to add that the numbers are neutral. However, they are incapable of self-defense. The issue of unemployment has ultimately to do with how one *defines* unemployment. The Bureau of Labor Statistics (BLS), which is responsible for the unemployment figures religiously and regularly intoned by network personnel, has defined unemployment so that it is much easier to be considered employed than not. If we update the Leggett–Cervinka article, we find that the key to understanding unemployment statistics is to understand the definition of *civilian labor force*, *employed persons*, and *unemployed persons*.

The civilian force consists simply of all persons who are considered either employed or unemployed. If you concluded, however, that this must be nearly all adults, you would be in serious error. First of all, the BLS relies on monthly data drawn from the *Current Population Survey* conducted by the Bureau of the Census. During the week that includes the twelfth of the month, the Bureau of the Census "polls" a scientific sample of households. This survey provides current and comprehensive data on the labor force. The BLS publishes the data monthly in *Employment and Earnings* and *Monthly Labor Review*. Now that we know where the data come from, we can proceed to make a methodological and political point.

The Bureau of Labor Statistics simply reports the employment numbers defined in the *Current Population Survey* as follows:

> Employed persons comprise (a) all civilians who, during the survey week, *did any work for pay or profit (minimum of an hour's work)* or worked 15 hours or more as unpaid workers in a family enterprise, and (b) all persons who were not working but had jobs or businesses from which they were temporarily absent for noneconomic reasons (illness, bad weather, vacation, labor-management dispute, etc.) (*Statistical Abstract of the United States* 1978, p. 396). (Italics added.)

Translation:

1. You are considered employed if you worked only one hour during the survey week. Thus, all part-time workers, including those who want full-time jobs, are considered employed. The commonly reported employment statistics make full-time and part-time work synonymous.

2. If you work fifteen hours or more on a family farm or in the family store, or other family enterprise, even if you are not paid, you are considered employed.

3. If you are not working because you are sick, or the weather's bad, or you are on vacation, or *strike*, you are employed. Notice that people

on strike are not receiving wages or salary and that a large number of workers do not receive sick pay, paid vacation, or "bad weather" compensation from their employers.

Turning to the definition of unemployment,

> Unemployed persons comprise all civilians who had no employment during the survey week, who made specific efforts to find a job within the previous 4 weeks (such as applying directly to an employer, or to a public employment service, or checking with friends) and who were available for work during the survey week. Persons on layoff from a job or waiting to report to a new job within 30 days are also classified as unemployed. All other persons 16 years and over are "not in the labor force" (*Statistical Abstract of the United States* 1978, p. 396).

Translation:

1. If you want a job, but have become discouraged and stopped looking, you are not unemployed. You are simply not in the labor force. Thus, as far as the unemployment statistic commonly reported by the media and political leaders is concerned, you do not exist.

2. If you want a job, have searched for one, couldn't find it, and have decided to go to school instead, then you are not unemployed because you are not available for work during the survey week.

3. If you want a job, have been looking for one, but are under 16, you are not unemployed. You, too, do not exist as far as the labor force is concerned.

4. If you are a housewife, old, or a victim of forced retirement and would rather be working but know that there is little if any place for you in the economy, you will not likely be looking for work and will therefore not be in the labor force.

Now, if we put what we know together, we can understand how the employment statistics represent an apparent (as opposed to real) reduction in the extent of this economic problem in the United States. By placing people who are working part-time in the "employed persons" category, the Bureau of Labor Statistics added 14.5 million "jobs" for the average month in 1977. Granted, some people want to work part-time; others, however, are awaiting a full-time opportunity. Further, if growth in number of jobs is considered a measure of the health of the economy, it must be remembered that in 1977 approximately one job in seven (14.8 percent of the total) was part-time (*Statistical Abstract of the United States* 1978, p. 402).

The contention that part-time workers as well as other "day workers" are satisfied with their lot is addressed in the following:

> Temporary and casual workers suffer many injustices in addition to the dissatisfactions the normal work force experiences. They are nonunion, so they lack protection; they are victims of dual discrimination, from temporary agencies and industry; their wages are not comparable to those of regular employees, and they have no fringe benefits.

> In actuality, though it satisfies the needs of industry and those who do not want a steady job, the casual-labor industry is an inefficient system that impedes permanent employment, lessens equal-employment opportunity, and virtually reduces some individuals to servitude. It may also discourage unionization and foster fly-by-night business "operators" (Russell, in Fairfield 1974, p. 154).

Finally, it must be noted that the "not in the labor force" category includes many persons who would otherwise be considered unemployed. In 1977 there were 7.7 million persons in school, 9 million retired (or otherwise "too old") and 31.5 million with "home responsibilities." Of course, not all of these desire to work, but it is more than plausible to argue that many would select a work option if they had their preference. The total number of persons sixteen and over *not in the labor force* for 1977 was 59 million (*Statistical Abstract of the United States* 1978, p. 403). One time-series analysis of annual unemployment rates in the United States concluded that the Bureau of Labor Statistics rate tends to be at least one-third too low (DuBoff 1977). A labor force survey in New Brunswick, New Jersey, concluded that the actual unemployment rate for the city in 1975 was 43 percent due to changes in definition (Leggett et al. 1977). Finally, in 1978, over 5.3 million adults in the United States who were *outside* the labor force indicated that they "wanted a job now" (US Department of Labor 1978). If these were counted, the rate of unemployment would quite obviously skyrocket.

A Saskatchewan Labor Force Survey done in 1973 in Canada found that the unemployment rate increased from the official rate of 1.9 percent to 7.2 percent when people were asked if they wanted a job. The figure increased to 20 percent when people were asked "Would you be interested in working (either full-time or part-time) if there were changes in the job market or in your household or personal situation?" Such changes included better health, child care or help with housework, completion of school, approval of spouse, satisfactory pay and working conditions, or meaningful work. Eighty-seven percent of these "hidden" unemployed were women (Stirling and Kouri 1979).

Graphic illustration of the conservative nature of government unemployment rates is presented in Fig. 4-1. Rate 1 is the conventional unemployment rate while the other three indices use other criteria (which

**Figure 4–1. Conventional and Alternate Monthly
Unemployment Rates, Canada, 1977**

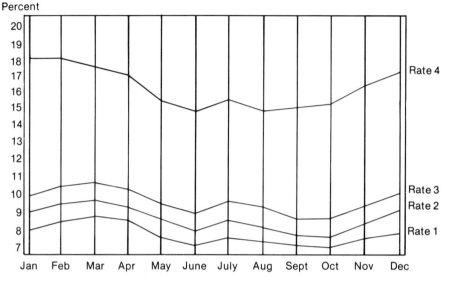

ªFor a description of each unemployment rate see text.

Source: *Statistics Canada*, Cat. 71–001. Monthly.

Source: Stirling and Kouri, 1979.

are as valid as the government figures). Rate 2 counts part-time labor force participation in full-time equivalents and counts the time "unemployed" (in full-time equivalents) of part-time workers wanting full-time employment. In Rate 3, one-half of those with personal reasons for not looking for work are included on the assumption that they want work since they looked for it in the past six months. Finally, Rate 4 reflects inclusion within the unemployed of those not in the labor force who want work and are available, even though they are not searching for work. For ideological and practical purposes, the government in Canada and the United States selects the most conservative estimate (Stirling and Kouri 1979).

One final point is in order. In January of 1967, the lower age limit for official United States statistics on the labor force was raised from 14 to 16 years. The youthful unemployed have traditionally represented the highest percentage of the jobless. This redefinition slashed a total of 102,000 individuals from the "unemployed persons" category, placing them "not in the labor force" (*Statistical Abstract of the United States* 1967, p. 223; 1968, p. 217). Though it is sometimes difficult for the more affluent members of a class society to realize, for the poor at ages 14 and 15, many of whom are school dropouts, work is often a matter of economic survival. However, as far as the government of the United States is concerned, fourteen- and fifteen-year-olds do not simply drop out of school. In 1967, they also dropped out of the labor force.

Wages and Salaries   A final test of the "affluent worker" imagery can be made through an examination of the median weekly earnings for full-time wage and salary workers in the United States. Although at first glance it appears that incomes are up when 1977 is compared with 1973, Table 4-5 demonstrates that when an index figure is employed, earnings for all (save two) occupational groups actually declined between 1973 and 1977. The index figure adjusts wages and salaries for inflation by using constant, that is, 1967 dollars.

The index shows a mild increase for private household workers whose median weekly salary in 1973 was $39 and in 1977, $59. The "improvement" in such pitiably low wages is no doubt due to the increased demand for domestic help, which in turn is a consequence of the greater number of women going to work to help their families cope with the ravages of inflation. The index for sales workers also demonstrates an increase in constant 1967 dollars. However, that improvement was less than one index point.

A final word might be said concerning the professional/technical and managerial/administrative occupations. People holding such jobs have traditionally been considered the mainstays of middle-class affluence and respectability. The significant decline in real earnings for these groups is particularly striking. As will be demonstrated later, this loss, in addition to the decline in other, nonmonetary, privileges, is basic to understanding the growth in union affiliation among the lower ranks of professional and technical workers. Thus, what some refer to as the "new working class" may be gathering members from heretofore unexpected sources.

Work will not be defined as a problem if the worker is perceived as happy, affluent, or content in his or her place. *If* the law of society and the workplace is "survival of the fittest" (or some more contemporary phrase that implies the same thing), then the "talented" will advance to their "deserved" status. Conversely, those intended to be passed over will be spared the sense of failure that comes from responsibilities and demands that exceed their "limitations." However, should one be prepared to challenge seriously these assertions, then something different in the way of an account or interpretation of the problem will follow. As always, the prevailing evaluations will tend to correspond with the dominant ideology of the corporate society.

We are Just One Big Family: Humanizing the Workplace

Those who identify work as a social problem frequently remark on the dehumanizing and authoritarian nature of the workplace. Bluestone notes (1974, p. 51) that "the workplace is probably the most authoritarian environment in which the adult finds himself in a free society." Notice that the problem of work is here perceived as "antidemocratic." Bluestone

TABLE 4-5
Full-Time Wage and Salary Workers—Weekly Earnings and Index of Earnings: 1973 to 1977

OCCUPATION	MEDIAN EARNINGS—Current dollars					INDEX—Constant 1967 dollars = 100				
	1973	1974	1975	1976	1977	1973	1974	1975	1976	1977
All Workers	$159	$169	$185	$197	$212	110.1	105.5	105.5	106.4	107.3
Professional & technical	212	228	246	256	277	110.3	107.6	105.5	103.4	104.8
Managers, administrators[1]	238	250	274	289	302	109.8	104.3	104.3	103.7	101.2
Sales workers	163	172	189	198	225	108.8	103.5	104.4	102.7	109.7
Clerical workers	130	140	150	158	167	107.7	105.5	103.3	102.2	101.1
Craft and kindred workers	195	211	223	239	259	112.2	109.9	106.1	106.9	109.2
Operatives, except transport[2]	132	141	157	162	171	105.3	101.1	103.2	100.0	98.9
Transport equipment operatives	169	180	198	214	231	105.8	101.7	102.5	104.1	105.0
Nonfarm laborers	138	149	154	161	181	111.8	109.7	103.2	102.2	107.5
Private household workers	39	50	54	60	59	90.6	106.3	106.3	109.4	100.0
Other service workers	111	117	123	134	142	112.0	106.7	102.7	105.3	104.0
Farm workers	96	107	111	120	127	125.9	125.9	119.0	122.4	120.7

[1] Excludes farm.   [2] For index, May 1972 = 100.

Source: *Statistical Abstract of the United States 1978*, p. 423.

follows a common course when he attempts to contrast the rules of yester-year with those of today. In so doing, a vision of increasing democratization is fashioned.

In 1872, Mr. Zachary U. Geiger, owner of the Mt. Cory Carriage and Wagon Works, published the following rules and regulations for his employees:

1. Employees will daily sweep the floors, dust the furniture, shelves and showcases.

2. Each day fill lamps, clean chimneys and trim wicks; wash the windows once a week.

3. Each clerk will bring in a bucket of water and scuttle of coal for the day's business.

4. Make your own pens carefully. You may whittle nibs to your individual taste.

5. This office will open at 7 a.m. and close at 8 p.m. daily except on the Sabbath, on which day it will remain closed.

6. Men employees will be given an evening off each week for courting purposes, or two evenings if they go regularly to church.

7. Every employee should lay aside from each pay a goodly sum of his earnings for his benefits during his declining years so that he will not become a burden upon the charity of his betters.

8. Any employee who smokes Spanish cigars, uses liquors in any forms, gets shaved at a barber shop, or frequents public halls will give good reason to suspect his worth, intentions, integrity and honesty.

9. The employee who has performed his labors faithfully and without fault for a period of five years in my service and who has been thrifty and attentive to his religious duties and is looked upon by his fellow-men as a substantial and law-abiding citizen will be given an increase of 5 cents per day in his pay, providing that the just returns in profits from the business permit it (Bluestone 1974, p. 50).

When these rules are taken in concert with the views and practices of Henry Ford, a pattern of "profits before people" emerges. Henry Ford made industry history when he announced the five-dollar day. (He only announced it, he didn't pay it.) However, in concert with the "worker as brute" imagery put forth by Frederick W. Taylor, Ford declared that "the assembly line is a haven for those who haven't got the brains to do anything else." Ford hired no women, for he believed their "place" to be in the home. He also denied employment to divorced men, those who smoked, and those who drank. He hired people to "inspect" the homes of his workers and to report on their private lives.

Against this background of "tyranny," the 1972 remarks of Richard Gerstenberg, chairman of the board of directors of General Motors, appear most enlightened. Gerstenberg declared an intention to humanize the workplace. He was opposed to boredom and making employees work harder or longer in the name of productivity. He was for job satisfaction, pride in workmanship, and, *when feasible* (italics added), involving "the employee personally in decisions that relate directly to his job" (Bluestone 1974).

The problem with "then and now" contrasts is they often yield a vision of substantial change. True, today's workers no longer suffer some forms of the invasion of personal privacy evident above. However, the societal context within which industry exists has changed. For example, despite the union faults that shall be detailed later, these organizations have provided a collective means of minimizing attempts by owners to control workers completely. Further, rules stressing the sanctity of the family and the avoidance of vice simply correspond with the broader values of American culture during the period in question. Today a more "secular" society has emerged. One should be cautious, therefore, in attributing to an enlightened management and a humanized workplace changes that reflect other social and cultural forces.

A concern with humanizing the workplace exists within the ideological constraints of class-divided society. Accordingly, when an interpretation of the problem of work is attempted, the particular evaluations that prevail may well be consistent with the major properties of the corporate society. It therefore follows that however the problems of work are evaluated, the imperatives of profit, growth, and private property will not appear among the "devils" identified. The overriding intention will not be humanizing or democratizing work for the worker. Rather, the objective will be the development of new "techniques" that further the efficiency and productivity of the labor system. Declarations to the contrary notwithstanding, people *remain* incidental to profit.

EMERGENCE

Emphasis on twentieth-century evaluations of the work "problem" should not blind one to the common ideological ground that ties such interpretations to the past. The trade union movement, beginning in the nineteenth century, represented a basic repudiation of the ideology of survival of the fittest. Those who organized the labor movement realized that the ideology of individual merit was little more than a mechanism for controlling the many. In truth, there was little hope for escape from the factory system, the sweatshop, the mills, or the mines. However, those goals that were to prevail for the trade union movement proved *compatible* with the imperatives of corporate order. Then as now, the concrete issues of wages, hours, and working conditions were largely divorced from the broader questions of inequality and control.

The Trade Union Movement

In the prerevolutionary United States, labor did not confront the rapidly increasing might of concentrated industry. Workers were yet to learn that the collective action of the trade union might shorten the working day, secure higher wages, and improve working conditions. Further, the master craftworker or skilled artisan was a small-scale operator who usually toiled along with his skilled employees and apprentices. Skilled workers frequently became masters and the unskilled had the hope of land on the frontier. This is not to suggest that small shopkeepers, artisans, and skilled and common laborers enjoyed untrammeled freedom. To the contrary, colonial legislatures were dominated by members of the landowning and merchant classes. In the eighteenth century, property requirements restricted suffrage to a tiny minority of the population. Colonial America was a land of large estates, debtor's prisons, and impoverished immigrants. The political and economic losers in a "planter's aristocracy" were to unite in a protracted struggle with the British Crown. The intention was not simply to break the back of the mercantile policy that made the colonies economic vassals of the Empire. Rather, the intention of the masses was to secure the promise of democracy for themselves (Foner 1947, Chapters 1–3). However, once this struggle was concluded, such dreams were to give way to the traditional workings of the alliance between those who held economic resources and the State. As Beard (1961) notes, the framers of the Constitution of the United States were those who made freedom a consequence of possession.

> The movement for the Constitution of the United States was originated and carried through principally by four groups . . . : money, public securities, manufacturers and trade and shipping.

> The members of the Philadelphia Convention which drafted the Constitution were, with a few exceptions, immediately, directly, and personally interested in, and derived economic advantages from the establishment of the new system.

> No popular vote was taken directly or indirectly on the proposition to call the Convention which drafted the Constitution.

A large propertyless mass was, under the prevailing suffrage qualification, excluded at the outset from participation (through representatives) in the work of framing the Constitution.

The Constitution was ratified by a vote of probably not more than one-sixth of the adult males (of the population).

The Constitution was essentially an economic document based upon the concept that the fundamental private rights of property are anterior to government and morally beyond the reach of popular majorities.

The Constitution was not created by "the whole people"; . . . neither was it created by "the states"; . . . it was the work of a consolidated group whose interests knew no state boundaries and were truly national in their scope (Beard 1961, pp. 324–25).

In the last decade of the eighteenth century, the first American trade unions appeared. They were organized around a particular craft [such as the New York Typographical Society (1794) and the Journeyman Cabinet and Chair Makers (1796)] and were isolated from other unions and other urban centers. However, the impetus for a more unified movement during the first third of the nineteenth century was to come from the political symbolism of the "ten-hour workday." The high point of this struggle came with the founding of the Mechanics Union of Trade Associations of Philadelphia in 1827. This is the first recorded instance of *class* solidarity transcending craft boundary lines in the United States to form a federation of all trades throughout the City of Brotherly Love. Similar developments followed in New York and New England. By the 1840s, these early unions had been buried by politicians and the press, as well as by the permeable nature of class lines at this historical period. State leaders and the newspapers heaped scorn on the "radicals and levellers" while the colonial economy provided the skilled worker the opportunity to establish his or her own shop. The most critical factor in the decline, however, was an economic depression in 1837 that devastated production and left a third of the working class unemployed. Within this context of vulnerability, employers cut wages from 30 to 50 percent and began the rapid introduction of machine technology, a process that was to hasten the replacement of master craftworkers with the immigrants, women, and children of the factory system (Foner 1947, pp. 121–72).

The locus of worker resistance was to shift after 1840 to the factories. Factory "magazines" were the first products of a labor press organized by women workers to combat owner propaganda. These underground publications repudiated the claims of a "Factory Garden of Eden" printed in the "legitimate" press. Throughout New England the saga of dangerous working conditions and starvation wages was told. Working women played a leading role in strikes in the cotton mills of Pittsburgh and Allegheny City in 1845 as part of a movement for a ten-hour day. By 1860, the average working day in the United States was eleven hours, a one-and-one-half hour reduction from 1830 (Foner 1947, p. 218). However, it is imperative to note that machine technology was at the base of increased productivity. This was not only to make a shortening of the workday possible, given agitation, but was later to prove instrumental in the passage of child labor legislation.

During the Civil War, working people from the industrialized Northeast were to oppose the Southern feudal order in great numbers. However, they also opposed the class-based Conscription Act of 1863, which enabled the affluent to escape military service through the payment of $300 or the provision of a (usually paid) substitute. Draft riots notwithstanding, industrial workers were historically destined to oppose an order based on plantation slavery. To workers, slavery meant cheap labor.

> Free society, the slave owners argued, was not only a delusion but a danger. In a free society "greasy mechanics" and "filthy operatives" . . . organized trade unions, engaged in strikes and other subversive activities. Abolitionism was only one of the many isms in the North. From the antislavery movement flowed "inexorably common schools, socialism and all other isms." . . . Slavery . . . protected the South "from the demands for Land Limitation . . . antirent troubles, strikes of workmen . . . diseased philanthropy, radical democracy and the progress of socialistic ideas in general" (Foner 1947, p. 280).

Post-Civil War Labor Movement   After the Civil War, other short-lived organizations were to take the lead in reestablishing something of a union movement. In 1866, the National Labor Union (NLU) was formed when representatives of the various fragmented labor organizations came together. Although the NLU collapsed in 1872, its objectives were to become planks in labor's later platform: strikes were denounced in favor of arbitration, apprenticeship was to be regulated, Oriental immigrants were to be denied entrance, a federal Department of Labor and a National Bureau of Labor Statistics were to be established, and the contract system of prison labor opposed. The most crucial parts of the program were the establishment of the eight-hour day, support for cooperative stores, and filling the need for cheap credit.

The demise of the NLU coincided with a severe postwar depression during the remainder of the 1870s. The typical nightmare of far-reaching unemployment broke the back of most national unions. "Of the thirty national unions in existence when the crisis broke in 1873, there were only eight or nine by 1877" (Foner 1947, p. 439). It was within this bleak context that two different ideologies competed for recognition. Unions representing skilled workers were interested in the establishment of mutual aid in the case of strikes, a boycott of nonunion products, and the realization of federal labor legislation. Other unions were to entertain a broader vision: workers could not hope fundamentally to change their conditions short of economic revolution.

In 1864, the International Workingmen's Association, commonly referred to as the First International, was founded. Karl Marx and Friedrich Engels were clearly identified with this organization, the former authoring its inaugural address. In 1869, the Socialist Party of New York became Section I of the International Workingmen's Association in the United States. Friedrich Sorge, a longtime socialist, was a delegate from this union to the founding meeting of the National Labor Union. He predicted the decline of the NLU because of its "reactionary romanticism," which called for the implementation of Abraham Lincoln's solution to the concentration of capital: the conversion of laborer to capitalist (Chambliss and Ryther 1975; Foner and Chamberlin 1977).

In 1873, Sorge wrote:

> The principal duty of the members and sections of the IWA shall be:
>
> (1) To organize the working people of the industrial centers as well as of the agricultural districts into trade unions, not only on the narrow basis of obtaining higher wages but on the broad basis of the complete *emancipation of labor*, the demand of a normal working day being the first step to it.
>
> (2) To combine those trade unions into central bodies who, jointly with the Federal Councils of the respective countries, shall represent the trade unions and sections and conduct the political movement of the workingmen of their country, whenever such movements shall be deemed opportune. (In Foner and Chamberlin 1977, p. 22; italics added.)

Beginning with the great railroad strikes of 1877, continuing through the ironworkers' strike in Homestead, Pennsylvania, and the miners' strikes in Coeur d'Alene, Idaho, in 1892 and on to 1903, when the Western Federation of Miners struck at Cripple Creek, Colorado, workers encountered massive violence. Those who opposed the unions often hired their own strikebreakers and private police forces. Pinkerton agents were frequently called upon to protect the factories, mills, and mines. However, with the founding of the Industrial Workers of the World (IWW), popularly called "The Wobblies," the owning class came to depend even more on the State with its formal monopoly on legitimized force.

Before we consider the nature and fate of the "Wobblies," it is crucial to make clear that a competing union ideology was to emerge from the ashes of the National Labor Union and its counterpart among nontrade workers, the Knights of Labor. What was to become the American Federation of Labor (AFL) began in 1881, when delegates to the Federation of Organized Trades and Labor Unions of the United States and Canada met in Philadelphia. This organization was to carve out narrow ground and stand in stark isolation from other labor alternatives. The Federation rejected the flirtation with the past that characterized the then-defunct NLU. Also repudiated were the Knights of Labor, whose aims embraced a zeal for organizing unskilled workers, an antipathy to strike, a support of "small business," and the "diversionary" objective of temperance. The following declaration of principles adopted by the Federation makes clear that this type of union movement would not seriously endanger the standing of owners:

> (1) Legal incorporation of trade and labor unions; (2) compulsory school attendance; (3) the banning of child labor for those under fourteen; (4) apprenticeship laws; (5) the national eight-hour legislation; (6) against the competition of prison labor; (7) against the truck system; (8) the legal right of the workers to the fruit of their labor *through wage demands*; (9) repeal of the conspiracy laws; (10) creation of a national labor bureau; (11) *a protective tariff for American industry*; (12) a ban on importation of contract labor; and (13) the use of the right to vote to send representatives from the trade associations to legislative bodies (Foner and Chamberlin 1977, pp. 263–64; italics added).

At its sixth annual conference in Columbus, Ohio, in 1886, the old Federation of Organized Trades and Labor Unions became the American Federation of Labor. It is vital to note that the American Federation of Labor at the onset was organized around "trades" or "crafts," thus splitting the "elite" of the working class from the growing masses of the semiskilled factory operatives. Further, the AFL was to opt for nonviolent and legal methods designed to ensure their "piece of the action." The record is clear. Those involved in the formulation of this organization were to call not only for the protection of industry by the State (tariffs), but also for the full enforcement of immigration laws designed to discriminate against Chinese labor.

Pure and Simple Unionism

What is seldom understood about the modern American labor movement is that a battle of immense proportions took place during the final decade of the nineteenth century, followed by major skirmishes throughout the first quarter of the twentieth. The resolution of that conflict was to determine the direction of the workers' struggle. This in turn led to the institutionalization of a *particular* definition of the work "problem," one holding that the grievances of labor could be resolved without endangering the emerging corporate society.

A tireless and dedicated leader of the Cigarmakers' Union came to prominence during the early years of the American Federation of Labor. Samuel Gompers was to be singled out by historians as the architect of a distinctive brand of trade unionism that found accommodation with the existing order. Gompers came to personify a number of strategies that collectively were described as "pure and simple unionism." Perhaps primary among these was an aversion to strikes. This was particularly appealing to those who owned and controlled the factories, mills, and mines, especially during the 1890s, which saw the development of still another American depression. In 1894, employees of the Pullman Company struck in response to wage cuts ordered by George Pullman. The American Railway Union joined the strike, the Knights of Labor endorsed it, and the Farmers' Alliance offered to feed the strikers. The ripple of class solidarity spread to other workers, including Federation members, and found positive public support. Gompers, however, convinced representatives of the Federation to accept a declaration that the railway strike *not be endorsed or supported*. As President Cleveland had sent troops into Chicago to suppress the work stoppage, the AFL leadership had stationed itself squarely in the camp of the State. So died the movement for a general strike.

This component of "pure and simple" was to be evident at a later phase of the AFL movement. Gompers and another prominent Federation leader by the name of John Mitchell refused to support the strike called by the Amalgamated Association of Iron and Steel Workers in 1901. Rather, they associated with the National Civic Federation, an organization committed to the avoidance of strikes and lockouts, the principle of collective contracts, and mediation of disputes. Despite its objectives, the National Civic Federation extended membership and support to *nonunion employers*, who were not obliged to adhere to its goals. The ensuing mediation failed to resolve the ironworkers' grievances and, without broader union support, the strike was eventually lost (Lorwin 1972, pp. 35–37, 62–65).

The final decade of the nineteenth century seemed to represent a crucible for radical action. Agricultural leaders of the People's Party formed in Nebraska in 1892 won the support of the Knights of Labor in a political movement directed toward monopolies and corporations. The party, which polled over a million votes in the elections of 1892, called among other things for the movement of the railroads and telegraphs from private to public ownership. In 1893 the annual convention of the AFL received a proposal from Thomas J. Morgan of the Machinists Union that identified an eleven-point program for political action. One of these "planks" specified the *collective ownership of the means of production and distribution*. By a vote of 2,244 to 67, delegates agreed to bring the resolution to their locals to receive instructions on how it should be handled in the 1894 convention. Samuel Gompers, at this point not clearly dissociated with the socialists in the movement, turned to socialist support to win the office of the presidency by a narrow margin. Gompers and his supporters in leadership then determined to break the back of the socialist forces in the Federation.

When the 1894 convention of the Federation met in Denver and took up the main issue before it . . . both socialists and anti-socialists were in a fighting mood. The debate lasted five days. The program was taken up plank by plank, and the first nine were passed in modified form. When plank ten advocating the collective ownership of the means of production was reached, the anti-socialists began ridiculing it by proposing various substitutes. In the confusion created by parliamentary maneuvers the plank was defeated and as a climax the convention voted down the preamble in favor of political action as well as the resolution to adopt the program as a whole. *Many delegates voted against the resolution though instructed otherwise by their unions* (Lorwin 1972, pp. 38–39; italics added).

Gompers and his followers paid a price for their victory, described by Gompers as keeping the union out of "politics." He was defeated for the presidency at the convention in 1894. However, in 1895 Gompers was again elected, by eighteen votes, to the union's highest office. Within the official circles of the American Federation of Labor, the problems of workers were no longer to be defined as a struggle of classes. The solution to exploitation was no longer seen as requiring an end to the concentration of wealth and power. The AFL was to be "nonpolitical" through exercising the vote and learning to lobby. Samuel Gompers and other leaders of the movement were to dine with Harvard President Charles W. Eliot and prominent bankers at the fashionable Exchange Club. It was Eliot who characterized the scab[2] as a "modern hero" (Lorwin 1972, pp. 47, 73, 78, 88–90).

The Industrial Workers of the World   Those whose vision went beyond a "piece of the action" did not simply fade away. Some referred to Gompers's aims as "pure and simpledom." In response to the failure of the AFL to support the strike by the Leadville miners in 1896, the Western Federation of Miners withdrew to organize the Western Labor Union. From this beginning emerged the Industrial Workers of the World (IWW).

The IWW was the inheritor of the view of those who had argued earlier that the ultimate origin of worker exploitation was the structure of the economic order. Despite the negative portrayal of this movement by the press, the "Wobblies" were for the major part nonviolent activists who between the organization's formal founding in 1905 and the outbreak of the First World War bore the brunt of state power. For example, a state police force in Pennsylvania opposed striking Wobblies. Further, a Committee on Public Safety in Minnesota, a Commission on Immigration and

[2]"Scab" refers to workers who threaten union strength through taking the place of a striking worker, refusing to strike, or working for less than union scale.

Housing in California, and a Council of Defense in Washington State sought official solutions to the problem of Wobbly "agitators." There was one slight problem. Few Wobblies had broken the law. Such a technicality was solved at the highest levels. First, the Congress passed a new naturalization law in 1917 that granted the Secretary of Labor the power to issue warrants to deport "undesirable aliens." Foreign-born Wobbly leaders thus disposed of, a second strategy was devised to handle those who were native born. In a pattern presaging political trials of the 1960s, over 100 Wobbly defendants were convicted in Chicago of "conspiracy" against industrial production and against the draft. A jury, it was found, could be persuaded to convict defendants on the basis of political beliefs. The twelve "peers" of the Wobblies deliberated less than an hour (Wolfe 1978, pp. 22–25).

Perhaps the greatest irony is that the decline and fall of the IWW was to achieve for the "pure and simple" a triumph denied over three decades. The "nonpolitical" Gompers leadership had secured from State and owners only grudging concessions. In an account of the convention proceedings of the AFL in 1899, one speaker proudly proclaimed that mayors and governors were hosting banquets in honor of the movement. In a similar vein, the State responded through the establishment of a National Bureau of Labor Statistics in 1887, the extension of the eight-hour day law to letter carriers in 1888 and to those employed on government contracts in 1892. Further, the Chinese Exclusion Act of 1882 had been strengthened, as was the Alien Contract Labor Law of 1885.[3] As of 1893, federal convict labor could no longer compete with free workers. In 1898, President McKinley met with the Executive Council of the Federation and later that year included proposed labor legislation in an address to Congress. In 1914, a "Magna Carta" for labor was passed by Congress. The *Clayton Act* was to modify existing antitrust legislation by stating that labor is not a commodity or article of commerce. (The irony was that antitrust legislation had been directed more *against unions* than against the centers of finance capitalism—see section on Institutionalization in this chapter.) The truth of the matter was that the Clayton Act *did not except labor* from antitrust legislation despite the act's enshrinement by the Gompers leadership (Lorwin 1972, pp. 41–42, 44, 120–21).

Such modest victories were little when compared with the stimulus provided by the IWW to the establishment of the AFL. Indeed, there had been some powerful owners who understood that the right kind of union represented no threat to the concentration of wealth and power. In 1901, Samuel Gompers reported that J. Pierpont Morgan of the United States Steel Corporation "affirmed that he was not hostile to organized labor" (Lorwin 1972, p. 64). However, the recognition by the State of that wisdom was to await the development of a final program to eliminate the Wobblies as a labor force.

[3]Such examples of institutionalized racism confirmed that the AFL leadership focused on the problem of cheap "alien" labor rather than a system of labor exploitation.

. . . and that something was provided by liberals such as Felix Frankfurter, conservative unionists such as *Samuel Gompers*, and so called enlightened businessmen such as Ralph Easley of the *National Civic Federation*. They suggested that, along with other forms of repression, the government should convince employers to recognize "legitimate" union activity. Lieutenant Colonel Brice P. Disque convinced lumber manufacturers that ". . . granting workers the shadow of *industrial democracy* without the substance kept them contented and productive." So instrumental was Frankfurter, then a young Harvard law professor, in urging such an approach on the Wilson Administration that he, as much as anyone, can be credited with the final destruction of the IWW as a meaningful force in American life. The carrot and the stick had been combined, and never again would the IWW threaten the security of any dominant interest in the United States (Wolfe 1978, p. 25; italics added).

Thus, we have come full circle. And the "shadow of industrial democracy" has been revealed as an ideological weapon in the arsenal of state power.

The Congress of Industrial Organizations   To this point, we have considered the emerging dominance of the AFL in the *trade* union movement. One more important event in the process of defining the "problem" of work can be selected for closer study. In 1935, following the adjournment of the AFL convention held in Atlantic City, a small band of prominent labor leaders, among them John L. Lewis of the United Mine Workers, met to organize a program for industrial unionism. Their target was to be the nonunion workers in mass production. Once again it was within the context of a depression, this one the most serious in American history, that critical labor events were to occur.

The AFL was still firmly committed to the elitist concept of "trade," a position that clearly fragments the common interests of workers. Thus, in 1938 Lewis and his associates convened the first meeting of the Congress of Industrial Organizations (CIO) in Pittsburgh. The CIO claimed a total membership of nearly 4 million workers, many of them miners, steelworkers, and factory operatives. The CIO was to enter the political mainstream in full force through massive support for President Franklin Delano Roosevelt and his "New Deal" programs designed to stabilize the tottering economy of the United States. More importantly, the torch of the now-defunct IWW had been passed to hands within the CIO.

Many industrial unions (and a few in the staid AFL) entertained a vision beyond the "pure and simpledom" doctrine of the now-deceased Samuel Gompers. Toward the end of the 1920s, a number of leaders of the industrial unions, particularly the needle trades workers, were clearly critics of the existing economic order. "Anticapitalists" held key positions in the unions of the mills, mines, and smelters and the automotive, electrical, radio, and shipping industries. Thus, the CIO was ripe for a "red purge." This was to come with fury at the hands of a coalition representing the AFL, the owners, and the State.

> The red purge of the CIO that is ordinarily located in the postwar McCarthy period actually began in 1938. It was merely interrupted by the war years, and then resumed vigorously in the late 1940s. The beginning of the campaign was signaled in 1938 by widely publicized hearings of the House UnAmerican Activities under Chairman Martin Dies. John Frey testified and the *New York Times* headlined his message the next day: "Communists Rule the CIO, Frey of the AFL Testifies: He Names 248 Reds." Meanwhile, the CIO was assaulted by unfavorable press and radio commentary depicting the unions as violent and communistic . . . while the National Association of Manufacturers financed the printing of two million copies of a pamphlet which depicted John L. Lewis holding a picket sign aloft that read "Join the CIO and Build a Soviet America" (Piven and Cloward 1977, pp. 164–65).

The assault was directed toward a random and somewhat amorphous group of progressives. During this time, the National Labor Relations Board, designed to oversee the rights assured labor by the Wagner Act of 1935, was purged of prolabor members. State legislators responded to the perceived threat with antistrike and antiboycott legislation as well as with other laws that attacked picketing, union shops, and union dues. Unions were required to register and jail terms for violations were severe (Piven and Cloward 1977, p. 166).

The attack on the "radical" element of the CIO was interrupted by the Second World War. After the Japanese devastated Pearl Harbor, Roosevelt received a pledge from the AFL and the CIO not to engage in strike actions. The unions by and large were faithful to that pledge, even though the stimulus of defense spending was to result in skyrocketing corporate profits and controlled wages.[4] After the war, the familiar problems of the postwar corporate society appeared: inflation and unemployment. The result was widespread strikes among workers seeking a living wage. The State responded when President Harry Truman used *wartime powers* to seize various industries. In 1947, Congress passed the Taft-Hartley Act, which represented a legislative repudiation of the labor movement. Taft-Hartley includes, among other provisions, presidential power to halt for a period of eighty days strikes that threatened public health and safety, a requirement that certain union officers take a loyalty oath affirming they

---

[4]While the early war years saw an increase in weekly earnings, wage-price controls and a no-strike pledge by the union brought an end to the upswing. Weekly pay for manufacturing workers amounted to $36.65 in 1942, $43.14 in 1943, $46.08 in 1944, and $44.41 in 1945 (*Statistical Abstract of the United States* 1946, p. 21). In the meantime, the consumer's price index which is a measure of the cost of living rose from 105.2 in 1941 to 129.9 in 1945 (*Statistical Abstract of the United States* 1946, p. 290).

were not members of the Communist Party as a precondition for access to the National Labor Relations Board, and the end to union shops (which require nonmember workers to join a union) in states that passed "right to work" laws.

The above specific developments occurred within a global context of an emerging "cold war" relationship between the United States and the Soviet Union. Given the beginnings of the transnational development of corporation power, together with the postwar expansion by the Soviet Union into Eastern Europe, the time was ripe for the identification of a political scapegoat. Again, it was the progressive leadership of the union movement (clearly a target of Taft-Hartley) that came to bear the albatross of labor reversals. During the hysteria of the McCarthy era, when the junior senator from Wisconsin was ferreting out "communists" in high places, an ex-member of the Socialist Party by the name of Walter Reuther signed a no-strike, five-year contract with the automakers. It was the same Reuther who had led the movement to purge "Reds" from the United Auto Workers in 1947. In 1949–1950, CIO President Philip Murray and his leadership also began a purge that culminated in the exclusion or withdrawal of eleven "pro-Communist" unions. After the witchhunt, the old-guard AFL and the newly purified CIO merged on December 5, 1955 (Aronowitz 1973, pp. 214–51; Piven and Cloward 1977 pp. 155–75). Walter Reuther, then president of the CIO, was later to voice a fitting epitaph for those elements of the union movement that were seeking major social change: "We make collective bargaining contracts, not revolutions."

Canadian Labor Union Movement   The union movement in Canada was particularly strong in the West, where it developed into a socialist movement in the early part of this century. The American Federation of Labor moved into western Canada in the late nineteenth century. Based on Samuel Gompers's basic tenets of acceptance of capitalism and rejection of partisan political action, it was firmly established by 1914. However, the workers in western Canada not only shared the ideas of union strength to win struggles in their daily lives; many also believed in the broader objectives of socialism. After an unsuccessful attempt in 1918 to change the Canadian Trades and Labor Congress from Gomperism to a philosophy requiring fundamental social and political changes, they split and formed the One Big Union (Bercuson 1978).

The idea of One Big Union was to cut across trade lines and become a national and international union for workers to bring about major social and economic changes. The Winnipeg General Strike of 1919 greatly aided the rise of the One Big Union because it highlighted major class conflict. As one writer observes:

> . . . the Winnipeg strike was a most significant occurrence in Canadian history, if for no other reason than that it was the first

and only time in Canadian history that a majority was split clearly into two opposing classes (McNaught 1959, p. 99).

Essentially, employers refused to negotiate with the Metal Trades Council and subsequently some 30,000 workers (12,000 of them non union) walked off the job. The city council then fired their civic employees and all but sixteen members of the police force who refused to sign an anti-strike agreement. A special police force was formed by leading business-men and professionals and violence ensued. In a parade supporting strikers and prohibited by civic authorities, one person was killed and thirty were injured with the Riot Act being read. On the forty-second day the union capitulated and workers returned to their jobs. It was a critical chapter in Canadian labor history because it pitted workers (including clerks and postal workers; transportation, telephone, electrical, railroad, and telegraph employees; firemen and even policemen) against business-people, professionals, and the Royal Canadian Mounted Police. Canadian newspapers and many officials saw the strike as Communist inspired, while the workers argued that refusal to recognize the union was the major issue (Marchak 1975). The first interpretation was widely pro-moted and led to increased repression of unionism.

Like the United States government, the Canadian leaders of the State greatly feared the labor movement during this time of war and the Russian Revolution. Given the socialist principles of some members and the increasing unionization of workers, various illegal and repressive tac-tics followed.

As one Canadian historian observes:

> Throughout Canada, the militia, the Mounties, provincial and municipal police, and other government agencies spied on unions, socialist parties, ethnic clubs and schools, and probably each other. Canadians were placed under intense secret observation. Despite all this activity, all the manpower and money expended on spying, not a shred of evidence of real revolutionary preparation, arms stock-piling, secret drilling, illegal fundraising was ever uncovered (Bercuson 1978, p. 103).

The One Big Union took great pride in the "class struggle" evident in Winnipeg, yet it rapidly lost support afterwards as the government and other union officials saw it as a threat to the Canadian way of life. Undoubtedly, with its socialist goals it was a threat to the status quo. A. G. Broatch, a Calgary, Alberta, machinist and alderman representing the Calgary Labor Council, spoke of the aims of the One Big Union at the Western Labor Conference, May 13, 1919.

> We have declared we are out for the destruction of production by profit and the competitive system. If we elect representatives on that platform and send them to the House of Parliament it will be their aim to destroy that system. Without doing it you are only

doing half the job. I don't believe, and I am yet to be convinced, that the action you propose to take, striking alone, will ever give you that end (Caragata 1979, pp. 71–72).

Due largely to the government repression and interunion competition, the 1920s saw the One Big Union lose support, and other unions that were compatible with the tenets of corporatism gain strength. During the depression of the 1930s, the Co-operative Commonwealth Federation (CCF) arose in the Canadian prairies, presenting a class analysis of society and striving for the elimination of class distinctions in its *Regina Manifesto* of 1933. However, labor unions largely rejected the CCF, while the unionists were regarded as "right-wing" conservatives by the CCF. The Trades and Labour Congress of Canada was busy fighting about the status of the Canadian Committee for Industrial Organization (CIO) within the American Federation of Labor (AFL) and had little concern with a radical organization made up largely of teachers, church and social workers, and farmers. Nonetheless, the CCF softened its anticapitalism to an antielite position and made an alliance with the trade unions in 1961 forming the New Democratic Party, which remains the only socialist-oriented political party of any size in Canada (Marchak 1975, pp. 77–82).

In 1955, the Canadian Labour Congress (CLC) was formed by a merging of the Trades Congress and the Canadian Congress of Labour in Canada to make the largest union in Canada. This followed the lead of the AFL-CIO merger in the United States that same year. Given the influence of United States union movement in Canada, this is not surprising (Smucker 1980).[5]

White Collar Unionism

The record of trade and industrial unionism makes clear the development of a symbiotic relationship between the unions on the one side and the owners and their managerial agents on the other. Historically, the left wing of the labor movement was repressed and those bearing in their program a firm recognition of the legitimacy of the existing economic order prevailed. Unionism was thus transformed into a conservative force seeking only accommodation with corporate power, not its reduction or elimination. The forms of accommodation were to represent the "legitimate" channels for redress of grievance: the vote, lobbying, campaign support, and labor legislation. Labor insisted only on the right to bargain

[5]In 1976, nearly 1.6 million Canadian workers were affiliated with United States unions (see Table 4-6).

for its membership, securing contracts that deal with "pure and simple" wages, hours, and working conditions and implicitly recognizing control as a managerial prerogative. The mediation and arbitration of differences were introduced, thus lessening the probability of the occasional strike. To understand the history of blue collar unionism is crucial if one is to grasp the meaning of a more recent development: white collar unionism. For the model of accommodation, with its conventional political strategies and reliance on law and other forms of contractual solution, is now guiding those members of the white collar legions who, as we have demonstrated earlier, have not been able to escape the erosion of salaries and the specter of unemployment.

Table 4-6 demonstrates the extent of labor union membership in the United States from 1955 to 1976. The statistical record is clear. While total union membership as a percentage of the work force has declined somewhat (from 24.4 percent in 1955 to 20.1 percent in 1976), white collar membership as a percentage of total union membership has increased (from 13.6 percent in 1955 to 18.4 percent in 1976).

In a related point, we see that government workers comprise 11.2 percent of union membership in 1970 and 13.5 percent in 1974 (*Statistical Abstract of the United States* 1978, p. 431). Taken together, these statistics indicate shifting occupational trends in the United States.

In Canada, as of January 1, 1977, there were 3.1 million union members, representing 38 percent of nonagricultural paid workers and 31 percent of the total civilian labor force. Eighteen unions reporting 50,000 members or more accounted for 52 percent of the total membership. The largest are presented in Table 4-7. The Canadian Union of Public Employees (CUPE) and many others in the top ten, such as government employees and teachers, represent largely white collar workers. The service sector of the labor force in Canada grew about 39 percent from 1961 to 1971 while the industrial sector shrank by 20 percent, reflecting an increase in the number of white collar workers. Canadian Labour Congress affiliates accounted for 68 percent of total union membership in 1977, with over half of them affiliated with the AFL-CIO in the United States. In fact, 49 percent of union membership in 1977 was in international unions with headquarters in the United States (*Canada Year Book* 1978–79).

Although it remains theoretically possible for the new working class to relate their emerging dilemma to the broader picture of economic and political crisis, its members will have to transcend the "pure and simple" model fashioned historically by the power of the State and the economic interests of the owning class. At this point, the organizations of the poorly paid professions (nurses, teachers, and social workers) seem to adhere to objectives and philosophies that in no way challenge the imperatives of the corporate order. Such groups, along with other public-employee unions in both the United States and Canada, conceive of conflict not in the social sense of class but in the narrow sense of collective bargaining (Etzioni 1969; Arthurs 1971; Chickering 1976).

TABLE 4-6
Labor Union Membership: 1955 to 1976
(thousands)

ITEM	1955	1960	1965	1970	1972	1974	1976
Union Membership, total (thousands)	17,749	18,117	18,519	20,752	20,893	21,643	21,006
AFL-CIO (thousands)	16,062	15,072	15,604	15,978	16,507	16,938	16,526
Independent or unaffiliated unions (thousands)	1,688	3,045	2,915	4,773	4,386	4,705	4,480
Male (thousands)	(NA)	14,733	(NA)	16,408	16,315	16,985	16,805
Female (thousands)	(NA)	3,304	(NA)	4,282	4,524	4,600	4,201
White collar membership (thousands)	2,463	2,192	(NA)	3,353	3,434	3,762	3,857
Percent of total membership	13.6%	12.2%	(NA)	16.2%	16.5%	17.4%	18.4%
US members, excluding Canadians (thousands)	16,802	17,049	17,299	19,381	19,435	20,199	19,432
Percent of total labor force	24.4%	23.6%	22.4%	22.6%	21.8%	21.7%	20.1%
Percent of nonagricultural employment	33.2%	31.4%	28.4%	27.5%	26.4%	25.8%	24.5%
Canadian members of US unions (thousands)	947	1,068	1,220	1,371	1,458	1,444	1,573
Number of unions, total	199	184	191	185	177	165	176
Unions affiliated with AFL-CIO	139	134	129	120	113	111	112

NA: Not available.

Source: *Statistical Abstract of the United States* 1978, p. 430.

TABLE 4-7
Ten Largest Canadian Unions, 1979

1. Canadian Union of Public Employees (CLC)[1]	228,687
2. United Steelworkers of America (AFL-CIO/CLC)[2]	193,340
3. Public Service Alliance of Canada (CLC)	159,499
4. International Union, United Automobile, Aerospace, and Agricultural Implement Workers of America (CLC)	130,000
5. National Union of Provincial Government Employees (CLC)	101,131
6. United Brotherhood of Carpenters and Joiners of America (AFL-CIO/CLC)	89,010
7. International Brotherhood of Teamsters, Chauffeurs, Warehousemen and Helpers of America (Ind.)[3]	86,603
8. Quebec Teachers' Congress (Ind.)	85,000
9. International Brotherhood of Electrical Workers (AFL-CIO/CLC)	63,914
10. Ontario Public Service Employees' Union (Ind.)	63,340

Source: *Canada Year Book, 1978–1979*

[1] Canadian Labour Congress.

[2] American Federation of Labor, Congress Industrial Organizations/Canadian Labour Congress.

[3] Independent.

INSTITUTIONALIZATION

The scope for the institutionalization of the work "problem" is broad indeed. We will maintain our position that formal recognition in law is perhaps the primary form of institutional legitimation. Accordingly, we shall single out two important components of labor law. The first area includes that legislation bearing clear historical importance to the right of labor to *organize*. The second involves the recognition in law of the *health and safety* of workers.

What might be called national labor policy in the United States is contained in a relatively few landmark statutes. The history of labor policy is, of course, ever changing. Earlier, such policy was set forth in court findings and was reflective of the ideological bent of the presiding judge. Today's major statutes are the detailed legislative products of congressional deliberation. As labor law (with other law) is a social product, an examination of its social context will clarify just which particular aspects of the problem of work have been institutionalized.

The first congressional act that addressed the labor movement was the Sherman Antitrust Act of 1890. It was a political response to "populist" forces, including small businesses, small farmers, and workers who were feeling the full fury of monopoly industry. However, as is frequently the case, symbolic political victory is hollow. The law held that every combination, in the form of a trust or otherwise, that restrained interstate or foreign trade or commerce was illegal; the act contained further "anti-monopoly" language. However, those "persons" guilty of monopoly might be not only corporations but also "associations." The claim of victory for the common person turned sour quickly.

> In actual fact, concentration increased rather drastically after the passage of the Sherman Act. The greatest wave of industrial consolidation was between 1897 and 1904. During those years new corporate assets increased by a factor of over 600 percent when compared to the previous six years. Furthermore, 57 percent of industrial output came to be controlled by 4 percent of American firms (Wolfe 1978, p. 28).

Although Sherman Antitrust did nothing to halt continuing concentration in the economy, it did provide an *antilabor* weapon. As Wolfe reports, the United States Supreme Court in a number of cases applied the act to "monopolistic unions," while failing to apply it to trusts.

Earlier, the Clayton Act of 1914, referred to by the AFL leadership as a Magna Carta for labor, was discussed. The Clayton Act supposedly excluded labor organizations from trust and monopolistic standing. However, the courts relied increasingly on the use of the injunction to halt strikes and boycotts.

> On January 3, 1921, the United States Supreme Court handed down a decision against the unions in Duplex v. Deering. It held that, *notwithstanding the Clayton Act*, the boycott conducted by the International Association of Machinists against the nonunion Duplex Company, a manufacturer of printing presses, to force unionization of its plant was illegal under the Sherman Act. . . . The majority opinion held that Congress had not intended to "confer a general immunity for conduct violative of the anti-trust laws or otherwise unlawful, because it had emphatically used the words "lawful" and "lawfully," "peaceful" and "peacefully" in speaking of labor activities." In the same year, in American Steel Foundries v. Tri-City Trades and Labor Council, picketing was limited to "peaceful" picketing, and to the stationing of a single picket at each entrance of a factory (Lorwin 1972, pp. 221–12; italics added).

Labor policy continued to be fashioned in the courts until 1926, when the Railway Labor Act passed. Later extended to the airlines industry, the act acknowledged the right of workers to organize among themselves without employer interference, together with the promotion of collective bargaining. This legislation was followed by the Norris-LaGuardia Act of 1932, which sought to restrict the use of the injunction by the courts (Commerce Clearing House Editorial Staff 1976, pp. 16–17). However, the provisions of the Railway Labor Act proved unenforceable, when the railroads simply refused to cooperate (Piven and Cloward 1977, p. 112). The Norris–LaGuardia Act, like the later Wagner Act of 1935, was enacted within the context of the most severe of American depressions. Together these acts represented the full implementation of the earlier strategy that had helped to crush the Wobblies: the recognition by the state of "safe unionism."

The National Industrial Recovery Act of 1933 recognized collective bargaining. However, no provisions were made for the enforcement of the law. In 1935, the National Labor Relations Act (the Wagner Act) extended the language of the Railway Labor Act to all interstate business. It became an unfair labor practice for an employer to refuse to bargain collectively with the legitimate representatives of his or her employees. It is critical to note that this legislation occurred within the context of widespread unemployment, starvation, and growth in union membership. Intellectual circles were buzzing with the prospects of the decline and fall of the capitalist system. Accordingly, the major objective of the Wagner Act was "industrial peace," largely through self-organization and collective bargaining.

During World War II, defense spending became a cornerstone of state support for the corporate order. Afterwards, cold war hysteria culminating in witch-hunts directed toward left wing unions, war-inspired definitions of "patriotism" and "sacrifice," and the substitution of postwar recession for the greatest of American depressions, set the stage for declining labor influence. The National Labor Relations Act was amended by the Taft-Hartley Act of 1947, discussed earlier. Taft-Hartley affirmed that industrial strife was at times due to unfair labor practices on the part of unions as well as employers. A final amendment to the NLRA was the Labor-Management and Disclosure Act of 1959, which called for an end to unethical standards on the part of employers and unions. The express intent of this amendment (also termed the Landrum-Griffin Act) is to *maintain a free flow of commerce* (Commerce Clearing House Editorial Staff 1979, pp. 16–17).

Both provincial and federal labor law in Canada has been largely aimed at preventing strikes and lockouts.

> What has been particularly notable about Canadian labour legislation, in comparison with the British and even in comparison with the American, is the extent to which the rights of unionization and free collective bargaining have been hedged around by, even embedded in, a massive legal and penal structure. This places such tremendous statutory restriction on labour and gives such a large role for the law and courts to play, that the legitimation aspect of labour legislation in Canada's case seems at least balanced, if not actually overshadowed, by the coercive aspect (Panitch 1977, p. 19).

Two laws that epitomize the Canadian approach are the Industrial

Disputes Investigation Act of 1907 and the Industrial Relations and Disputes Investigation Act of 1948. While labor law prior to World War II largely followed the British approach, the Industrial Disputes Investigation Act had a unique Canadian feature. Specifically, it introduced compulsory conciliation with special provision for the mandatory postponement of any strike or lockout under federal jurisdiction while a board of inquiry conducted an investigation. Thus, the State could postpone indefinitely a strike or lockout while investigating it. Similar provincial legislation was passed in the 1930s covering essentially all workers, not just federal employees (Huxley 1979).

Following the Wagner Act in the United States, the Industrial Relations and Disputes Investigation Act of 1948 was a federal law soon copied by the provinces. While providing certain features of the Wagner Act such as the right of recognition, it retained aspects of the Industrial Disputes Investigation Act of 1907. Specifically, these were compulsory conciliation and postponement of strikes together with stipulations affecting the content of agreements. For example, a collective agreement must contain a clause prohibiting strikes or lockouts during the term of an agreement (Huxley 1979). Thus, the right to strike is only available for "agreements in the making" and the mechanisms of free collective bargaining are greatly reduced.

Federal labor legislation in the United States further restrains unions from requiring activities that are considered "uneconomic." Also represented in the statutes of many states, uneconomic practices refer to an "artificial" increase in the cost of labor. Such practices, generally called "featherbedding," include the spreading of work, the establishment of unnecessary or redundant jobs, or seeking to preserve work practices that impede "technological progress" (Commerce Clearing House Editorial Staff 1979, pp. 64–67). While a concern with the artificial inflation of labor costs appears legitimate at first glance, a closer look brings into clear view a hidden injury. Taken together, "featherbedding" regulations speak to a larger contradiction. In a social order where production and profit are valued over any human right to work in dignity, technological change or production "efficiency" often results in widespread job loss. When machine technology is introduced, an industry becomes more *capital* intensive and less *labor* intensive. *The problem is not that technology makes some jobs obsolete. The problem in corporate society is that technology frequently makes workers themselves obsolete.* The industry that introduces machine technology often does so to reduce the cost of labor. Further, no requirements exist that compel the retraining of the displaced worker. Workers who seek to protect themselves from such "planned obsolescence of labor," or in a similar vein seek to protect themselves from production "speedups," are subject to charges of featherbedding. In a society that values the worker above profit, systematic and planned retraining of those displaced by technology would become a priority.

Dying for a Living

In the United States, the might of Industrial America is represented in a group called the National Association of Manufacturers (NAM). This body opposed significant labor legislation in the past such as child-labor laws, legislation establishing a minimum wage for women, and a reduction in the length of the workday. When an occupational health and safety bill was introduced in the House of Representatives in 1968, the National Association of Manufacturers also opposed it. Their reasoning is based on that specific ideology in the corporate society called "blaming the victim."

In a manner reminiscent of the official accounts of the near nuclear disaster at the Three Mile Island Nuclear Station Unit 2 in the state of Pennsylvania in March and April of 1979 (see Chapter Five), officials for the NAM opposed federal safety legislation, citing the "human factor" as the crux of the safety problem.

> Each employee must be motivated through training, education and supervision to understand and to want to perform work safely. This desire must come from within—it cannot be imposed through the threat of civil or criminal sanctions against the employer. . . . NAM had been educating its workers, the spokesman pointed out, as far back as 1912 when it produced an education film entitled *The Crime of Carelessness* (Scott 1974, p. 278).

The Chamber of Commerce, representing the business community, also opposed such legislation, citing statistics to show that workers are "safer at the workplace than at home, on the highway or at play."

National Safety Council figures for 1976 do show that more employees are killed in motor vehicle accidents than on the job. To be precise, 21,400 workers died in automobile accidents off the job, compared with 12,500 who lost their lives in industrial accidents. Such figures (rounded) compare with a loss of 8,700 deaths off the job and away from home (non-motor vehicle) and 8,100 fatalities at home. Before the NAM and members of the Chamber of Commerce begin to celebrate the fact that they appear to be number two in carnage, a few modest criticisms are in order. First of all, sociological inquiry suggests we look at the connections among seemingly separate events and incidents. The imperatives of growth and profit in the corporate system have resulted in a number of consequences, among which is the monopolization of transportation by what we term elsewhere the "automotive-petroleum" alliance. Slaughter on the highway arising from the absence of a planned and efficient system of public transportation, together with deaths suffered by workers on the job, can be traced to the same structural source. A second criticism is clearly in order. If one wishes to cite deaths to workers in motor vehicle accidents, it seems reasonable to remind all concerned that many such accidents occur on the way to and from work. One should recall this easily the next time he or she is caught in "rush hour" traffic.

The decline in on-the-job deaths due to injury (from 16,500 in 1945 to 12,500 in 1976) has occurred as the work force has expanded. However, such an improvement can be explained by two major factors. First of all, as an increasing percentage of the work force becomes "white collar," accidental deaths will necessarily decline. Secondly, improvements in occupational safety have been traditionally resisted by owners and managers, who cite costs while faulting human error. Historically, it has been these same "careless workers" who have struck, often launching the "wildcat" or unofficial form of work stoppage in response to unsafe working conditions. A notable example of this was the rejection of a proposed contract by the membership of the United Mine Workers in the coal strike of 1977. Mine workers refused to ratify a contract with inadequate safety provisions that would have ended the "wildcat" strike. Our point is that declines in death rates have not easily come to the worker.

Blaming the victom is evident in the approach of business and industry to "accident prevention." But beyond this focus is the reality of statistical distortion. For when the safety numbers game is played, it matters not that one is injured. What is counted in official statistics is whether or not there is *lost work time* due to injuries.

> A casual visitor to a plant can't help but notice the lost-time scoreboard, the signs plastered everywhere, the safety trophies on the wall. And having devised the incentives—the awards, the newspaper announcements, the banquet presentations—for the best safety programs, corporations find ever more ingenious ways to protect their record, i.e., to suppress the true number of lost-time accidents. Who can be surprised if no one counted the injured worker crying in pain on a stretcher in a dark corner of the Mobil Oil refinery? After all, he remained on the premises. Or the woman folding towels from a wheelchair in the women's restroom at Chrysler, or the construction worker directing traffic with a bandage-swathed hand, or the many more like them (Scott 1974, p. 279)?

This is not to suggest that the official lost-time picture is bright. The number of workdays lost due to occupational injury and illness in 1977 was over six days per employee per year in the United States for the private sector. However, such rates vary widely, depending upon the industry. For mining, the number of lost days was 12.9; for construction, 11.2; for transportation and public utilities, 9.6; and for manufacturing, 8.2. As a point of contrast, the lost workday figure per employee for 1977 in the finance, insurance, and real estate industries was only 1.04. All of these figures represent an increase over comparable statistics for 1974. *Given the fact that the original source of most statistics on occupational health is industry*, it is safe to conclude that these numbers do not exaggerate the problem (*Statistical Abstract of the United States* 1979, p. 432).

> Official statistics barely represent the tip of the iceberg as far as the magnitude of the US occupational health and safety problem is concerned. In a report done for the BLS (Bureau of Labor Statistics) to assess the adequacy of the pre-OSHA occupational injury statistics, it was found that, among an intensively studied sample of California firms, the *ratio of serious injuries to reported disabling injuries was ten to one. This finding suggests that the true national level of "serious" but not "disabling" occupational injury is nearer to 25 million than 2.5 million per year.* Such chronic underreporting was found to be attributable in part to the widespread practice of shifting injured workers to "less demanding" jobs and similar abuses, methods of avoidance, and lax reporting practices. Sometimes a "less demanding job" meant lying in bed in the plant dispensary all day (Ashford 1977, p. 2; italics added).

In Canada, a worker dies on the job every six hours and one worker in ten is injured annually (Katz 1978). Of those work-related injuries, 46 percent were disabling in 1977. Goods-producing industries account for one-third the work force but two-thirds of the fatalities, with fishing, forestry, and mining being the most hazardous. Since these statistics are based on workers' compensation data, it is underestimated by about 25 to 30 percent of the work force not covered by this plan (Health and Safety 1978). The minimum figure for 1977 based on workers' compensation data is that 14,000 workers are hospitalized on any given day, with 800 million in direct costs and nearly $3.5 billion in indirect costs. While comparable data are difficult to find, Table 4-8 suggests that Canada ranks poorly in its fatality rate compared with other Western industrialized countries. Disease takes even a larger toll in North America. The combined effects of both injuries and diseases in the workplace amount to a massive assault on the worker (Reasons et al. 1981).

In 1972, the President's Report on Occupational Safety and Health added an additional chapter to the long-standing concern of work-related injury in the United States. This report officially recognized that there is more to safety than the prevention of accidents that do immediate and apparent harm. It acknowledged that there may be as many as 100,000 deaths a year in the United States from occupationally caused *disease*, in addition to 390,000 new cases of disabling occupational disease each year (Scott 1974, p. 3). For example, over 90 percent of the cancer cases in the United States are "induced, maintained or promoted by specific environmental factors" (quoted in Ashford 1977, p. 94). The cancer death rate for certain occupational groups is substantially higher than that for the general population. As Table 4-9 demonstrates, cancer inducing agents are commonly found in the workplace for many who sell their labor for a wage.

TABLE 4-8
Fatality Rates by Industry in Ten Industrial Nations, 1972–1976
(per 100,000 employees)

Incidence of rates of fatal accidents in manufacturing industry for selected countries, 1972–76

Country	Code*	1972	1973	1974	1975	1976
Great Britain	I/c	4	4	5	4	3
France	II/c	12	10	10	. .	. .
Federal Republic of Germany	II/a	18	17	16	16	. .
Irish Republic	I/b	7	10	8	9	5
Italy	II/a	8	8	8	. .	. .
Netherlands	I/a	4	4	4	4	. .
Sweden	II/d	4	3	3	. .	. .
Canada	I/c	14	15	21	15	10
United States of America	I/d	4	3	3	3	. .
Japan	I/d	3	3	2	2	1

*See Note 1.
  Including mining and quarrying.
  Provisional.

Based on sample surveys.
Establishments employing 100
or more workers.

Sources:
Health and Safety Executive,
International Labour Office.

Incidence rates of fatal accidents in the construction industry for selected countries, 1972–76

Country	Code*	1972	1973	1974	1975	1976
Great Britain	I/c	19	22	16	18	15
France	II/c	47	45	46	. .	. .
Federal Republic of Germany	II/a	39	37	33	35	. .
Irish Republic	I/b	14	15	15	8	9
Italy	II/a	55	51	62	. .	. .
Netherlands	I/a	13	12	8	10	. .
Sweden	II/d	8	6	8	. .	. .
Canada	I/c	90	96	121	96	75
United States of America	I/d	23	13	16	16	. .
Japan	I/d	19	21	16	13	6

*See Note 1.
  Based on sample surveys

Establishments employing 100
or more workers.
Provisional.

Sources:
Health and Safety Executive,
International Labour Office.

TABLE 4-8 (Cont.)

Incidence rates of fatal accidents on the railways for selected countries, 1972–76

Country	Code*	1972	1973	1974	1975	1976
Great Britain	I/b	20	18	15	19	21
Federal Republic of Germany	II/a	38	26	26	26	..
Irish Republic	I/c		19		40	21
Italy	II/c	10	18	14	12	15
Netherlands	I/a		15	7	22	..
Sweden	II/d	14	7	18	..	..
Canada	I/c	30	33	49	25	25
United States of America	I/d	12	14	11	10	..
Japan	I/d	8	7	6	4	3

*See Note 1.
  Including railway workshops and accidents
  involving road vehicles operated by federal railways.
  Regular staff only; including railway workshops.

Including railway workshops.
Including railway workshops and construction of
  railway lines.
Provisional.
Establishments employing 100 or more workers.

Note:
Figures are no longer published for France. The
latest year for which a figure is available is 1969, when
when there were 13 fatalities per 100,000 employees.

Sources:
Department of Transport,
International Labour Office.

Incidence rates of fatal accidents in the mining and quarrying industries for selected countries, 1972–76

Country	Code*	1972	1973	1974	1975	1976
Great Britain:						
Mining and quarrying	I/a	..	45	33	37	35
Coal mining only	I/a	39	47	29	35	29
France	I/a	51	69	105	39	
Federal Republic of Germany	II/a	62	69	56	46	..
Irish Republic	I/b	65	85	43	45	65
Italy	II/a	35	26	41	..	..
Netherlands	I/a	29		10		..
Sweden	II/d	28	28	20	..	..
Canada	I/b	182	208	279	198	172
United States of America	I/d	53	42	38	33	31
Japan	I/d	69	51	62	61	33

*See Note 1.
  Excluding quarrying.
  Provisional.
  Establishments employing 100 or more workers.

Sources:
Health and Safety Executive,
International Labour Office.

Note 1 The codes given in the first column of each table, referring to the basis on which the accident incidence or frequency rates were calculated, are defined as follows:

Method of notification
 I Reported accidents.
 II Compensated accidents.

Exposure to risk
(a) Rates per 100,000
  man-years of 300 days each.
(b) Rates per 100,000 wage earners (average numbers).
(c) Rates per 100,000 persons employed (average
  numbers).
(d) Rates per 100 million man-hours worked.

TABLE 4-9
Common Occupational Carcinogens

Agent	Organ Affected	Occupation
Wood	Nasal cavity and sinuses	Woodworkers
Leather	Nasal cavity and sinuses; bladder	Leather and shoe workers
Iron oxide	Lungs; larynx	Iron ore miners; metal grinders and polishers; silver finishers; iron foundry workers
Nickel	Nasal sinuses; lungs	Nickel smelters; mixers and roasters; electrolysis workers
Arsenic	Skin; lungs; liver	Miners; smelters; insecticide makers and sprayers; tanners; chemical workers; oil refiners; vintners
Chromium	Nasal cavity and sinuses; lungs and larynx	Chromium producers, processors, and users; acetylene and aniline workers; bleachers; glass, pottery, and linoleum workers; battery makers
Asbestos	Lungs (pleural and peritoneal mesothelioma)	Miners; millers; textile, insulation, and shipyard workers
Petroleum, petroleum coke, wax, creosote, anthracene paraffin, shale and mineral oils	Nasal cavity; larynx; lung; skin; scrotum	Contact with lubricating, cooling, paraffin, or wax fuel oils or coke; rubber fillers; retort workers; textile weavers; diesel jet testers
Mustard gas	Larynx; lungs; trachea; bronchi	Mustard gas workers
Vinyl Chloride	Liver; brain	Plastics workers
Bis-chloromethyl ether, chloromethyl ether	Lungs	Chemical workers
Isopropyl oil	Nasal cavity	Isopropyl oil producers
Coal soot, coal tar, other products of coal combustion	Lungs; larynx; skin; scrotum; bladder	Gashouse workers, stokers and producers; asphalt, coal tar and pitch workers; coke oven workers; miners; still cleaners
Benzene	Bone marrow	Explosives, benzene or rubber cement workers; distillers; dye users; painters; shoemakers
Auramine, benzidine, alpha-Naphthylamine, beta-Naphthylamine, magenta, 4-Aminodiphenyl, 4-Nitrodiphenyl	Bladder	Dyestuffs manufacturers and users; rubber workers (pressmen, filtermen, laborers); textile dyers

Source: National Cancer Institute.

Though not perceived with the dread associated with malignancy, other diseases are also deadly. Respiratory disorders are escalating in epidemic proportion throughout the population. The National Lung and Heart Institute Task Force *Report on Respiratory Diseases* reports that even when cancer and certain other diseases are excluded, some 150,000 deaths occur annually from respiratory illness. Much of the dying is job-related. For example, despite the higher-than-average rate of injuries to coal miners, four miners die from black lung disease for every one who dies in an accident. When the toll of occupational disease is further expanded to include what is most likely a good percentage of the deaths due to heart disease (2 million annually), the resulting total renders the estimate of 100,000 yearly deaths conservative indeed (Ashford 1977, pp. 93–96).

It has only been in recent years that a few diseases are recognized as compensable in Canada by the provincial workers' compensation schemes. Less than 10 percent of compensation awards are disease related, while the previously presented estimates suggest diseases are more frequent than on-the-job accidents (Katz 1978). Since occupational safety and health are almost solely provincial matters, relatively little national data exist. Quebec, which is the world's largest asbestos producer, had no asbestos-dust standard until 1978, although scores of workers die annually from such exposure (Tataryn 1979, p. 96). Yellowknife, the capital of the Northwest Territories, has one of the highest levels of arsenic pollution in the world as a consequence of its goldmining operations. However, the federal government and companies involved have consistently denied its harmfulness and deceived the Yellowknife citizenry (Tataryn 1979, pp. 106–53). Finally, respiratory diseases, particularly silicosis, are prevelant among uranium miners in Eliot Lake, Ontario, although again workers had to fight for such acknowledgment (Tataryn 1979, pp. 61–105).

In *Dying for a Living*, Tataryn (1979) notes several elements he believes are present in occupational and environmental disputes.

1. The principal victims of unsafe environments created by industries generally come from the ranks of the working class and the poorest segments of society. Consequently, the victims frequently do not have the resources to mount the concerted scientific and political campaigns necessary to alter their environmental circumstances.

2. Industries, health professionals, and government officials have not conscientiously informed people exposed to industrial contaminants about the risks associated with that exposure.

3. Governments frequently fail to act as independent third parties in environmental and occupational health quarrels. They have consistently operated as if they and industry have a common interest.

4. Scientific data and medical opinions can be bought.

5. There is little reason to believe there are "safe" levels of exposure to cancer-causing agents.

6. In occupational and environmental health controversies, "shifting the blame" is a favorite technique used by industry and government to deflect criticism of their activities.

7. Environmental health controversies are usually ignited by independent investigations conducted by persons outside the managerial group in industry and government—the group who should logically be most concerned about how their actions affect the public health.

8. The government's response to an environmental health crisis can usually be measured by how much media attention is lavished on the problem.

MAINTENANCE

Whose interests are served by work-related legislation and policies in North America? As passed, the Occupational Safety and Health Act of 1970, imposes on virtually every employer in the private sector in the United States an unprecedented general duty to "furnish to each of his employees employment and a place of employment which are free from recognized hazards that are causing or likely to cause death or serious physical harm to his employees" (quoted in Ashford 1977, p. 12). The act also called for the establishment of standards to be enforced by the Occupational Safety and Health Administration (OSHA) in the Department of Labor. Further, this legislation established a review commission to rule upon the enforcement of standards by OSHA, together with a research body in the old Department of Health, Education and Welfare termed the National Institute for Occupational Safety and Health (NIOSH). NIOSH recommends safety and health standards to OSHA as well as publishing a list of all known toxic substances.

In addition to the establishment of these three agencies, the act called into being a National Advisory Committee on Occupational Safety and Health, whose membership was to include representatives of management, labor, safety and health professionals, and the public. This committee was charged with making recommendations to the Secretaries of Labor and H.E.W. (Occupational Safety and Health is now the province of the Department of Health and Human Resources.)

In sum, federal legislation has obviously proven to be a stimulus to bureaucratic maintenance. What is conspicuously absent is any semblance of worker control in the area of industrial death and dying. The Occupational Safety and Health Act of 1970 provides employees the right to request an OSHA inspection and to tour the workplace with an OSHA inspector (Ashford 1977, pp. 12–13). However, the issue of health and safety is clearly vested in agencies of the State rather than the worker.

The first law of the corporate society remains the Golden Rule: those who have the gold make the rules (see Chapters One and Two). If this is true, the definition of the work "problem" that prevails will be one that does not "rock the boat." It therefore follows that the political economy of occupational health and safety will reveal a clear commitment to industrial and, to a lesser extent, bureaucratic survival. Workers themselves may not fare so well (Doern 1977).

Political History of OSHA

We have given detailed attention to health and safety because we assume that the extension of life is a desirable social value. Accordingly, the political history of the Occupational Health and Safety Administration should be traced. This agency is charged with the creation of standards and their enforcement. One concrete example of the creation of standards concerns the identification of toxic chemical compounds. A total of 17,000 of these agents were designated as "toxic substances" in 1976. However, OSHA had developed standards regulating exposure for only 400 of this total. Some 1,500 of such substances are suspected to be human carcinogens, but only fifteen were subject to OSHA standards in 1976 (Northrup 1978, p. 183). The last of the fifteen to be included was vinyl chloride.

Vinyl chloride is a colorless gas used in the production of polyvinyl chloride (PVC). In turn, polyvinyl chloride is used to manufacture some 50 percent of all plastic products. Estimates of the number of workers in these industries range from 350,000 to 700,000. Originally described as a miracle material, polyvinyl chloride is inexpensive and malleable (Northrup 1978, pp. 310, 315). Uncontrolled, it is also an industrial agent of death.

In 1971, an employee at the B.F. Goodrich polyvinyl chloride plant in Louisville, Kentucky, died of angiosarcoma, a rare form of cancer of the liver. Between December 1973 and February 1974, an additional four workers died of the same disease. On January 22, 1974, the deaths (three, soon to be five) due to angiosarcoma were reported to the National Institute for Occupational Safety and Health. Prior to the Goodrich notification, federal officials had not considered vinyl chloride a dangerous substance. Their position was echoed by Manufacturing Chemists Association (MCA), the trade group for the chemical industry. Research conducted at the Elean Institute for Cancer Research in Rome in 1970 had demonstrated a link between vinyl chloride and cancer in laboratory animals. In early 1973, Bonn University researchers found evidence of liver damage in nineteen of twenty (95 percent) of the workers in a single PVC plant. However, until the deaths reported at B.F. Goodrich, neither the responsible agencies of the State nor the MCA considered vinyl chloride dangerous. In fact, MCA Data Sheet SD-56 stated *vinyl chloride was not suspected of causing cancer. The fact sheet was withdrawn only after a cluster of worker deaths in one facility occurred* (Northrup 1978, pp. 328–33).

According to two statisticians employed by the Office of Occupational Safety and Health Statistics, better data are required to provide information on "problem" areas (Root and McCaffrey 1978, p. 16). This office is a part of the Bureau of Labor Statistics (BLS), which is charged under the Occupational Health and Safety Act of 1970 with providing reliable information on occupational injury and disease. In 1978, the BLS introduced the Supplementary Data System which uses as its main data source workers' compensation first reports. As the following criticism reveals, the formal usage of such data simply ensures the continued understatement of the extent of occupational injury and disease. A study conducted at the University of Washington indicated that:

> . . . 31% of over 1,100 medical conditions found in 908 participants were of probable occupational origin, with an additional 10% indicating "suggestive history." The probable incidence of occupational disease was 28.4 per 100 workers. Only 2% of this occupational disease had been reported on the employer's log (required by OSHA), *and only 3% was found in workmen's compensation records* (Ashford 1976, p. 96; italics added).

Worker Protection Under the Corporate State

On October 5, 1978, the US Court of Appeals for the Fifth Circuit struck down OSHA's benzene standard. The court held that OSHA had not adequately presented the expected benefits of the standard (which reduced the permissible exposure limit from ten parts per million to one part per million). Benzene is a clear, colorless liquid used in a variety of workplaces, including rubber-fabricating facilities, printing plants, and chemical factories. It is also a known carcinogen that causes leukemia and other blood disorders. The message of the judiciary in this case was clear. In the preparation of its standards, OSHA must develop a record that will withstand a hostile judicial analysis. (Industry attempts to challenge OSHA standards in the Fifth Circuit because the court's record is favorable to industry.) (Beck 1978, pp. 6–8).

The decision of the Fifth Circuit cited the language of the Occupational Safety and Health Act of 1970, which requires standards to be "reasonably necessary." This example of studied ambiguity leaves enormous range for interpretation. As is frequently the case in the corporate society, deciding what is reasonable is a matter of "cost-benefit analysis." The economic costs of developing tough standards on worker safety are weighed in the balance and found wanting. Corporations are seldom convinced that "safety pays" (Ashford 1977, pp. 325–26). There are three sides involved in every hazard: (1) those who create it, (2) those who experience it, and (3) those who regulate it. In the political economy of risk, those with the least power (workers) are subject to the most risk (Ravetz 1977).

As is uniformly the case with agencies of the State, a "friendly relationship" exists between OSHA and industry. Accordingly, people working for OSHA use the term "voluntary compliance" to describe the Department of Labor's approach to health and safety regulation. Compliance with standards occurs "voluntarily" to the degree that it occurs at all. This is because OSHA does not have the prerequisites to ensure industry compliance. Its standards and regulations are a model of bureaucratic tedium and detail; its inspection force is too small to restrain the employer by means of a significant chance of inspection; and the penalties it imposes are deterrents only to small operators. A further (largely nonexistent) prerequisite for compliance would be that workers be informed of their protection under the law (Ashford 1976, pp. 246–69).

The simple power of inspection is a specific case of the failure of the adversary logic of the pluralist model of power. According to this view, held by consumer groups and others, government can "watchdog" the private sector. However, "if OSHA were to conduct 100,000 inspections per year with no repeat inspections, it would require forty-five years to inspect just once each of the estimated 4.5 million workplaces covered by the act. The current rate of inspections (1976) is about 6,600 per month, 79,000 per year" (Northrup 1978, pp. 215–16). In short, if a disdain for worker health and safety logically follows from the structure of the corporate society, such a pattern will be *pervasive. If, in defiance of all logic, government agencies were to have the will to enforce, they would not have the resources to do so.*

As previously noted, occupational safety and health standards and enforcement are largely a provincial matter in Canada, with no federal OSHA-type law. In the only national study of safety enforcement, the Department of Labour conducted a mailed questionnaire survey of laws and enforcement practices (Economics and Research Branch 1975). As is readily apparent in Table 4-10, most jurisdictions had few prosecutions, while Prince Edward Island, Manitoba, and Alberta had none! Furthermore, fines were the norm, although imprisonment is provided for in most jurisdictions. These data do not suggest that there were few violations; rather, they indicate the lack of rigorous enforcement. For example,

TABLE 4-10
Results of Prosecutions Undertaken in the Provincial and Federal Jurisdictions[1]
Under the Survey Safety Enforcement Legislation, 1972–1973

	Newfoundland		Prince Edward Island		Nova Scotia		New Brunswick		Quebec		Ontario		Manitoba		Saskatchewan		Alberta		British Columbia		Federal Jurisdiction	
	1972	1973	1972	1973	1972	1973	1972	1973	1972	1973	1972	1973	1972	1973	1972	1973	1972	1973	1972	1973	1972	1973
Conviction but sentence suspended	—	—	—	—	—	—	—	—	—	—	18	—	—	—	—	—	—	—	—	—	—	—
Fine only	4	4	—	—	5	3	9	5	250	150	232	159	—	—	—	1	—	—	4	2	—	1
Charges dismissed	—	—	—	—	—	—	3	4	79	15	34	31	—	—	—	1	—	—	1	—	—	—
Charges withdrawn	—	—	—	—	—	—	—	—	4	—	167	104	—	—	—	—	—	—	—	—	—	—
Prosecutions in process	—	—	—	—	—	—	—	—	67	365	— *	—	0	0	0	2	0	0	—	3	—	—
TOTAL	4	4	0	0	5	3	12	9	400	530	451	294	0	0	0	2	0	0	5	5	0	1

[1] The administering authority in Saskatchewan was not empowered to prosecute under the Workmen's Compensation Accident Fund Act, but it is empowered to prosecute under the Occupational Health Act, 1972. Prosecutions are carried out in Manitoba by the Attorney-General. No sentences of "imprisonment only" or of "fine and imprisonment" were passed in any of the provinces.

Source: Economics & Research Branch, *Safety Enforcement Policies & Practices in Canada*. Ottawa: Canada Dept. of Labour, 1975.

in Alberta, the fastest-growing province in Canada, annual construction accidents rose from 15,076 in 1970 to 27,920 in 1977, with more than 280,568 working days lost in 1977 due to accidents. Over $29 million was paid in compensation. There are 48 Occupational Health inspection officers in the province, and an estimated 10,000 construction sites at any given time. To visit each site biweekly, each officer would have to make 20 visits a day. In 1977, of 16,761 sites inspected 9,883 were found in violation. None were prosecuted. Of 48 charges leveled against all industries for 1977 violations of the Occupational Health and Safety Regulations of Alberta, eight brought conviction. Only fines were levied, ranging from $300 to $3,500, with five being less than $800 (Ross 1979).

It is important to understand that there are structural limitations that affect the contractual solution. Union power, by and large, has resulted in increased labor costs. Given the necessary contradiction between wages and profits, even a union movement that embraces corporate ideology must be contained. As we have seen, federal legislation since the Wagner Act of 1935 has been negative, ineffectual, or nonexistent. Antiunion ideology remains strong, especially in the southern region of the United States and some Canadian provinces such as Alberta. Further, the increasing white collar composition of the labor force means a larger number of workers have an historical antipathy to "blue collar" organizations. These and other factors serve to restrain union membership and thus hold down the cost of labor. Accordingly, the range of union membership as a percentage of the labor force has been remarkably small in recent history. In 1933, union members comprised 5.2 percent of the labor force in the United States. That percentage increased fourfold in a single decade to 20.5 percent of the work force in 1943. More than three decades later, the comparable statistic was 20.1 percent (1976). The highwater mark was reached in 1953 when union members constituted some 25.2 percent of the work force (*Statistical Abstract of the United States* 1958, p. 236; and 1978, p. 430). Thus the range of membership over a thirty-three-year period is only slightly over 5 percent. Further, the statistics of the last two decades have revealed a series of small but steady declines.

A final note on maintenance must be presented. The structural imperatives of corporate society compel growth and the concentration of wealth and power. It therefore follows that smaller firms will be the losers in the competitive struggle for survival. If the State serves the interests of corporate power, one must argue that legislation, regulation, and policies bearing on work will not do damage to the iron law of corporate society: the survival of the giants.

One intensive study details the cost of compliance with OSHA standards for the aerospace and chemical industries (Northrup 1978). Although OSHA has the power to fine, it rarely exercises that prerogative. For the twenty aerospace firms participating in the study, OSHA fines over a period of four and one-half years amounted to a total of $35,193, or something less than three cents per worker per year. With regard to capital outlay for health and safety, OSHA standards have not as yet presented aerospace with costs that will likely have an adverse impact on product or profitability. Further, there is little evidence that such regulations have substantially affected either technology or costs in the chemical industry. One exception is the vinyl chloride industry, which faced a stiff OSHA standard for worker exposure (1 part per million) after deaths detailed earlier. Despite claims by industry spokespersons that the industry would not survive such a regulation, the only plants actually to shut down were those representing a marginal financial standing. In the years immediately following the standard, there was a *program of vigorous expansion in the vinyl chloride and polyvinyl chloride industry.* This expansion involved such well-known names as B.F. Goodrich, Dow Chemical, Tenneco, and Firestone (Northrup 1978, pp. 91, 164, 278, 372–73, 408–09).

However, the economic potential of regulation may be expected to grow if clear and compelling cases similar to the vinyl chloride episode emerge. "The incremental capital and operating costs associated with compliance . . . were significant in their own right. . . . The ability of the industry to absorb these costs is not seriously in question, *although the burden on small firms may be overwhelming*" (Northrup 1978, p. 297; italics added). In other words, if the costs of compliance with OSHA standards should grow significantly (and this is not the record of recent history), the victims will hardly be B.F. Goodrich and Dow Chemical.

One major form of bureaucratic maintenance is the generating of volumes of paperwork bearing on the definition of the "problem." OSHA's standards quickly grew into a mountain of regulations, many of which bore little discernible connection to health and safety. A maze of regulations proved to be a massive burden for small businesses (Scott 1974). Such firms, whether through fear of the cost of compliance or through inability to discern the regulations, created a storm of protest. In response, OSHA embarked upon a standards-deletion project that trimmed 928 "turkeys" from its regulations. This deletion of 10 percent of the total volume of OSHA's code books required an eighteen-month period to complete (Bell 1978). OSHA has revealed a remarkable ability to generate and eliminate standards. Enforcement of such standards has proven to be quite another matter.

Alternative

"Workplace Democracy" (Excerpts)   **by Daniel Zwerdling**

When Karl Marx predicted that workers in the United States would seize control of their offices and factories, he never imagined the struggle would begin just ten blocks from the White House in the financial heart of Washington, D.C.—in an insurance corporation. But when I walked into Consumers United Group, Inc., a $60 million insurance company, one afternoon last year, I found the 340 secretaries, accountants, salespeople, file clerks, and other employees carrying out the revolution in full force.

While workers across the nation were being laid off in massive numbers and forced into unemployment lines and welfare rolls—industry laid off thirteen million people last year—the worker-elected congress at Consumers United Group was voting simply to *forbid* layoffs.

While clerical workers at other white-collar factories in the nation's capital were struggling to survive on annual wages starting at about $6,000, the worker congress and worker-elected board of directors at Consumers United were voting to boost the minimum wage of mailroom clerks to $10,600, plus the same share of the profits as is allocated to the company president. . . . "All the people voted in a special referendum a few years ago that our wages should keep pace with what the Government says is necessary for a 'moderate standard of living,'" one clerk explained.

The events at Consumers United Group, Inc.—usually called International Group Plans, or IGP—went practically unnoticed in the national press. But in just six years this insurance company has developed the most advanced and important experiment in workplace democracy—workers' control—in North America.

Workers' control is the concept that citizens should have the same democratic power over their lives in the workplace that the Constitution guarantees them in their communities and homes. Curiously, workers' control has always been considered an outrageously radical concept in this country, where people are raised on the rhetoric of democracy and self-determination and then spend most of their working lives submitting to a corporate dictatorship.

The accepted and favored concept of worker self-determination "power" in this country is collective bargaining, a sophisticated form of begging in which workers join together to plead with management to grant certain limited concessions; in the event management refuses to grant them, workers may attempt to force the corporation to come to terms by striking. Sometimes the strategy works; sometimes it doesn't. Coal miners struck earlier this year at grueling costs to themselves, their families, and their communities, in an effort to win better health benefits from the mining corporations, and they lost. At IGP, worker-elected representatives voted themselves one of the most generous health insurance plans in Washington, including three months' sick leave and maternity leave, fully paid.

The remarkable system of workers' power inside IGP, which sells insurance packages to such corporations as *McCall* and *Redbook,* offers dramatic proof that life for American workers could be dramatically different. Until recently, the notion that workers should have the power to shape their own destinies in the workplace was so alien that labor leaders did not oppose the idea so much as simply scoff at it. "The concept of workers' control is an exciting one," Jerry Wurf, president of the American Federation of State, County and Municipal Employees, said sardonically, "for soapbox oratory in the streets and rap sessions in the faculty lounge."

In Herkimer, New York, workers and community forces bought a library furniture plant which was being abandoned by the Sperry Rand conglomerate, and in South Bend, Indiana, 500 workers have bought, with Federal assistance, one of the nation's largest machine tooling plants. In Youngstown, Ohio, a coalition of city officials, union leaders, unemployed workers and government officials is trying to engineer a worker-community takeover of a sprawling steel mill shut down last January by an ailing conglomerate.

To recognize the implications of workers' control in this country, we must be clear about what workers' control is not. Workers' control is not, despite many media reports to the contrary, such "humanized" factories as Motorola, where corporate executives yank out the time clocks to "treat our employees like adults." Nor is it workers' control when Ford executives grant workers "control" over assembling an entire Thunderbird dashboard instead of screwing on only one part.

When General Foods unveiled its "humanized" Gravy Train factory on the outskirts of Topeka seven years ago, the media hailed it as a revolutionary development. "Workers Share the Helm" *The Topeka Capital-Journal* proclaimed. In this new, specially designed factory, teams of workers made recommendations on hiring and firing, disciplining and promoting workers; workers could decide among themselves to pack dog food into bags one day, and then rotate to hoisting bales of dog food on pallets the next.

The strategy is to give employees the illusion of power by yielding control over usually menial decisions—"Should I bag dog food today or hoist the bags on pallets"—without giving them power over the key decisions that shape their lives—how much they are paid and what benefits they get, who can work and who shall be laid off, what they produce and how fast they must produce it, and what to do with the profits of their work.

As union leaders have watched corporate managements "humanize" the workplace—and noticed worker satisfaction and productivity increase as a result—they have begun to initiate their own humanization-of-work experiments to boost worker freedoms and powers on the shop floor. Walk into Nabisco's cookie and snack factory in Houston: worker-elected representatives are chatting with management about the results of a plant-wide survey exploring changes the workers would like to make on the shop floor. Stroll through the mirror polishing department at Narman International Industries in Bolivar, Tennessee, which makes most of the auto rearview mirrors in the United States: workers and foremen are holding a meeting to discuss ways their production line could be reorganized. And at *The Minneapolis Star and Tribune,* representatives elected by reporters, copy editors and secretaries are chatting with the publisher and top executives about ways they think the corporate budget should be reallocated—and whom they would like to see hired as the new editor-in-chief.

Like the humanization-of-work projects, these labor-management committees—or quality-of-work-life projects, as they are frequently called—have brought a limited degree of participation to workers. Unlike the humanization-of-work schemes, they are not imposed by management: union leaders and workers play an equal part in designing their new areas of freedom and responsibility.

So far, most of these labor-management projects have produced only trivial results. At Nabisco's cookie plant, one union representative told me, the principal achievements of the project are more clocks on the production floor, new and attractive uniforms for women employees, and hotter and fresher food in the factory cafeteria. "We asked for curtains and carpeting in the cafeteria," one union representative said. "We got the curtains."

Today, workers and community residents who depend on the Vermont asbestos mine and Herkimer library furniture factory—now called the Mohawk Valley Community Corporation—own their own plants. Pushed to the wall by absentee conglomerates, they formed extraordinary coalitions—bankers, Rotary Club members, union officials, managers, shop floor workers, and their relatives and friends sold shares of stock to raise money to buy the corporations as if they were selling raffle tickets. In Herkimer, local groceries sold shares of stock to shoppers, and in Lowell, Vermont, even the high school student council chipped in. "Each of us got a territory and we went house to house like traveling salesmen," recalls Vermont Asbestos Group electrician Merle Lanpher.

Most Americans assume that companies closing their doors across the nation are losers, marginal firms ready for the trash heap; after all, a major conglomerate such as GAF or Sperry Rand would never shut down a subsidiary if it were capable of making a profit. The assumption is wrong. While some of the firms closing down probably cannot be saved, virtually all worker-community takeovers shatter the corporate myth: since workers and communities bought the plants, they are doing better than ever.

Sperry Rand didn't shut down its Herkimer library furniture factory because it wasn't making a profit, but because the factory wasn't earning the 22 percent profit on invested capital that Sperry Rand executives demand.

Workers and community residents in Saratoga Springs, New York, faced a crisis when the Cluett, Peabody Corp. announced it was closing its Saratoga Knitting Mill, a manufacturer of high-quality women's lingerie, because the plant had lost $11 million in six years. But when the conglomerate had gobbled up the firm in a merger it had dismembered the factory's sales force to save money—and so the company's line of fabrics just wasn't selling. After a coalition of employees and community interests bought the factory and restored its sales team, profits surged, the plant bought new equipment, and today the work force, which had been cut in half, is back to normal size.

Workers and communities can acquire control of a company and save themselves from economic extinction. But the worker-community purchases of these corporations alone have nothing to do with workers' control of the corporation—at least not yet. At most of the worker-community-owned firms—including Vermont Asbestos Group, Herkimer, Saratoga Knitting Mill and South Bend Lathe—ownership changed hands on paper only; the managers who managed the plants under conglomerate ownership still control the plants.

But something curious is happening in some of the worker and worker-community-owned plants: workers are becoming increasingly frustrated by the fact that nothing has changed since they became part-owners of their own factory. And they are starting to talk about exercising greater power in the workplace. "People are asking, 'What do we have different now than what we had before?'" says Gerald Vogel, an officer of the United Steelworkers local at South Bend Lathe. "When you get down to the real meat of it, there really isn't much difference." While workers don't expect or want power over day-to-day decision-making, Vogel contends they do expect that major corporate policies would "at least be discussed with us." Disgruntled workers recently submitted petitions to the company president asking for an equal share of power on the board of directors.

Humanization of work, labor-management quality-of-work-life communities, and worker-community-owned corporations are all workplace *reforms* which do not alter the fundamental relationship between management and workers. Real workers' control stands the traditional corporate power structure on its head: management does not grant the workers a few expanded powers on the shop floor, and the workers do not simply put some certificates of stock ownership in their bureau drawers. In worker-controlled firms, workers and their elected representatives control the corporation, period. At IGP, as one insurance clerk explains, "The mechanisms are all here, the freedom and power are all here for us to really take control and run this company the way we want."

The workers' control system at IGP is far from perfect. Many workers don't want to assume such great responsibility over their work lives—they have never attended a school or worked in a job that taught them how. "At Bell Telephone we had to raise our hands just to ask permission to go to the bathroom," says a former telephone operator who processes insurance claims. "But at IGP we're supposed to do everything on our own. No one tells us anything."

And many employees complain that in a high-pressure business, with thousands of clients and millions of dollars depending on swift and decisive action, the IGP policy of democratic decision-making in committees takes too long. They point to occasional work backlogs to prove it. "Our committee would take three weeks trying to solve a problem *I* could have solved like that," says one former manager with a snap of his fingers.

But despite the flaws in the democratic structure, IGP is doing something right: the company is earning a $1 million annual profit, and has achieved freedoms and benefits unobtainable at any other corporation in the nation. "IGP is the best thing that ever happened to me," one researcher said, echoing what many workers at IGP told me. "I'm trapped," she said, "because I couldn't ever go back to a normal job again."

If IGP were an isolated example of workers' control, you could write it off as a fluke—but it isn't. In the Northwest, sixteen worker-owned and controlled plywood factories are competing with such conglomerate plywood producers as Weyerhaeuser and Crown-Zellerbach—and are coming out ahead. Most of these cooperative mills were formed twenty or thirty years ago, when millworkers joined together—like the miners in Vermont—to buy out companies that were closing down.

At the $25 million Puget Sound Plywood, Inc., as at most of the co-op mills, workers elect a nine-person board of directors from among fellow workers in the plant. The board, in turn, hires a general manager, who is not a shareholder in the co-op, to run the business from day to day. But mill workers make it clear that they, not the general manager, make the vital decisions that most directly affect their lives. While workers in most plywood firms accept layoffs as a fact of life in this volatile industry, workers at most co-ops have made layoffs a thing of the past. "If things get bad, we'll take a pay cut," says Earl Altes, a member of Puget Sound, where the worker-owners pay themselves an average wage of up to 20 percent higher than unionized workers at conventional mills are paid.

Studies suggest that the worker-controlled plywood firms are from 25 to 60 percent more productive than conventional mills—and workers in the co-ops attribute their edge to the emotional commitment they bring to their jobs.

Perhaps the most dramatic example of how working people can use workplace democracy to overcome economic hardships and build a secure economic base can be found in the fields of the Salinas Valley, at the foot of the Gabilan Mountains. Five years ago, most of the seventy-five Mexican-American farmworkers and their families picking strawberries at the Cooperative Central Ranch were migrants and sharecroppers who followed the cotton, lettuce, peach, and plum crops north from Texas. Each year, they picked strawberries for a meager wage and watched the profits of their work drive by in the owner's gun-grey Jaguar. But then some federally funded community organizers bought the ranch with a Bank of America loan and transformed it into a co-op. Today, the ranch is a thriving model of worker democracy.

No boss tells the workers how to plant or how much they will be paid; the farmworkers elect a board of directors from among the membership. But most of the really important decisions are made by all the members of the co-op at their monthly meetings. The farmworkers recently voted to plow their profits into buying 700 acres of land and diversifying into vegetables so that their livelihood will not depend on a single, fragile crop. Co-op members have also voted to build low-cost housing on their new land for the members who need it most.

Since joining the co-op, many farmworkers have quadrupled their income, partly because members work harder, and partly because each earns a share of the profits. "The average farmworker here earned $25,000 in 1976," says Javier Ruiz, a member. After years of struggles in the courts and in the fields, the United Farm Workers have won the power to bargain with private corporate owners, and have won some valuable concessions. But at the Cooperative, the farmworkers own and run their own ranch.

Worker and worker-community control is not a panacea for the nation's economic ills. Inflation will not recede simply because workers, not corporate executives, own and control their own firms. Nor is there any guarantee that when workers and communities control enterprises they will produce only products that are socially useful and environmentally sound, any more than corporate executives do—though it seems unlikely that workers and communities would deliberately pollute the local environment as thoughtlessly as do corporate executives who live a thousand miles away.

But while worker and community control of enterprises will not provide a cure-all, it becomes increasingly clear that without worker and community control of industry the nation cannot hope to begin solving its economic ills. More and more Americans—union leaders, workers, government officials—are coming to recognize that workplace democracy is no longer merely a rhetorical flourish invoked by radical activists. It has become a practical strategy for survival in the 1980s.

(*The Progressive,* August 1978, pp. 16–24)

BIBLIOGRAPHY

Anderson, Charles
1976

The Sociology of Survival. Homewood, Ill.: Dorsey Press.

Applewhite, Philip
1965

Organizational Behavior. Englewood Cliffs, N.J.: Prentice-Hall.

Aronowitz, Stanley
1973

False Promises: The Shaping of American Working Class Consciousness. New York: McGraw-Hill.

Arthurs, A. W., ed.
1971

Collective Bargaining by Public Employers in Canada. Ann Arbor, Mich.: Institute of Labor & Industrial Relations.

Ashford, Nicholas
1977

Crisis in the Workplace: Occupational Disease and Injury. Cambridge, Mass.: MIT Press.

Beard, Charles
1961

An Economic Interpretation of the Constitution of the United States. New York: Macmillan.

Beck, Phil
1978   "OSHA and the Courts." Job Safety and Health 6
                        (8):6–8.

Bell, John
1978   "Unnecessary, Irrelevant, and Deleted." Job Safety
                        and Health 6(8):6–8.

Bercuson, David J.
1978   Fools and Wise Men: The Rise and Fall of the One
                        Big Union. Toronto: McGraw-Hill Ryerson.

Blauner, Robert
1964   Alienation and Freedom. Chicago: University of
                        Chicago Press.

Bluestone, Irving
1974   "Worker Participation in Decision Making." In
                        Humanizing the Work Place. Roy Fairfield, ed.
                        Buffalo, N.Y.: Prometheus, pp. 49–61.

Braverman, Harry
1974   Labor and Monopoly Capital: The Degradation of
                        Work in the Twentieth Century. New York:
                        Monthly Review Press.

Caragata, Warren
1979   Alberta Labour: A Heritage Untold. Toronto:
                        James Lorimer.

Chambliss, William, and
Ryther, Thomas
1975   Sociology: The Discipline and Its Direction. New
                        York: McGraw-Hill.

Chickering, A. Lawrence,
ed.
1976   Public Employee Unions. San Francisco: Institute
                        for Contemporary Studies.

Chomsky, Noam
1972   "The Fallacy of Richard Herrnstein's I.Q." Social
                        Policy 3 (May/June): 19–25.

Commerce Clearing House
Editorial Staff
1979   Labor Law Reports: Guidebook to Labor Relations.
                        Chicago: Commerce Clearing House.

Commoner, Barry
1976   The Poverty of Progress. New York: Alfred A. Knopf.

Cooper, M. R.
1979

"Changing Employee Values: Deepening Discontent?" Harvard Business Review (Jan.–Feb.): 117–25.

Davis, Kingsley, and
Moore, Willard
1945

"Some Principles of Stratification." American Sociological Review 10(2):242–49.

Doern, G. Bruce
1977

"The Political Economy of Regulating Occupational Health: The Ham and Beaudry Reports." Canadian Public Administration 30:1–35.

DuBoff, Richard
1977

"Unemployment in the United States: A Historical Summary." Monthly Review 29, November.

Economics and
Research Branch
1975

Safety Enforcement Policies and Practices in Canada. Ottawa: Canada Department of Labour.

Etzioni, Amitai
1969

The Semi-Professions and Their Organizations. New York: Free Press.

Foner, Phillip
1947

History of the Labor Movement in the United States. New York: International Publishers.

Foner, Phillip, and
Chamberlin, Brewster
1977

Friedrich A. Sorge's Labor Movement in the United States. London: Greenwood Press.

Gillie, Oliver
1977

"Did Sir Cyril Burt Fake His Research on Heritability of Intelligence?" Phi Delta Kappa, February:469–71.

Gruneberg, Michael M.
1976

Job Satisfaction. New York: Macmillan.

Hampton, David R.
1969

Behavioral Concepts in Management. Belmont, Calif.: Dickenson Publishing.

Health and Safety
1978

Labor Gazette 78 November/December:491–92.

Herrnstein, Richard
1973   I.Q. in the Meritocracy. Boston: Little, Brown.

Hinrichs, John
1974   The Motivation Crisis. New York: American
Management Association.

Horton, John
1964   "The Dehumanization of Anomie and Alienation:
A Problem in the Ideology of Sociology." British
Journal of Sociology 15:283–300.

Huxley, Christopher
1979   "The State, Collective Bargaining and the Shape
of Strikes in Canada." Canadian Journal of
Sociology 4(3):223–39.

Jensen, Arthur
1969   "How Much Can We Boost I.Q. and Scholastic
Achievement?" Harvard Educational Review,
Winter:1–123.

Katz, Larry
1978   "It's More Dangerous for Public Employees." The
Public Employee 1(1) Spring:7–9.

Leggett, John, and
Cervinka, Claudette
1973   "Countdown." In Taking State Power. John C.
Leggett, ed. New York: Harper & Row.

Leggett, John, Groglio, J.,
Scanlon, M., and Toth, P.
1977   Break Out the Double Digit: Mass Unemployment
in the City of New Brunswick. New Brunswick,
N.J.: John C. Leggett.

Lorwin, Lewis L.
1972   The American Federation of Labor. Clifton, N.J.:
Augustus M. Kelly.

Lundberg, Ferdinand
1968   The Rich and the Super-rich: A Study in the Power
of Money Today. New York: Bantam.

Luthans, Fred, and
Kreitner, Robert
1975   Organized Behavior Modification. Dallas, Tex.:
Scott, Foresman.

MacPherson, C. B.
1962   The Political Theory of Possessive Individualism. London: Oxford University Press.

Marchak, M. Patricia
1975   Ideological Perspectives on Canada. Toronto: McGraw-Hill Ryerson.

Marx, Karl
1961   Economic and Philosophic Manuscripts of 1844. Moscow: Foreign Languages Publishing House.

1966   "Economic and Philosophic Manuscripts." Tr. by T. B. Bottomore. In Marx's Concept of Man. Erich Fromm, ed. New York: Frederick Ungar.

McNaught, Kenneth
1959   A Prophet in Politics. Toronto: University of Toronto Press.

Michels, Roberto
1959   Political Parties: A Sociological Study of the Oligarchial Tendencies of Modern Democracy. New York: Dover.

National Safety Council Statistics Department
1977   Accident Facts. Chicago: National Safety Council.

Navarro, Vincente
1977   Medicine under Capitalism. New York: Neale Watson.

Northrup, Herbert Root, Rowan, Richard L., and Perry, Charles
1978   The Impact of OSHA. Philadelphia: Industrial Research Unit, Wharton School, University of Pennsylvania.

Pappenheim, Fritz
1968   The Alienation of Modern Man. New York: Monthly Review Press.

Peskin, Dean B.
1973   The Doomsday Job. New York: American Management Association.

Piven, Frances Fox, and Cloward, Richard A.
1977   Poor People's Movements. New York: Random House.

Panitch, Leo
  1977   "The Role and Nature of the Canadian State." In The Canadian State. L. Ponitch, ed., Toronto: University of Toronto Press, pp. 3–27.

Quinn, Robert P., and
Shepart, Linda J.
  1974   Quality of Environment Survey. Ann Arbor: University of Michigan Institute for Social Research.

Ravetz, Jerry
  1977   "The Political Economy of Risk." New Scientist 8 September:597–98.

Reasons, Charles E.,
Paterson, Craig, and
Ross, Lois
  1981   Assault on the Worker: Occupational Safety and Health in Canada. Toronto: Butterworths.

Root, Norman, and
McCaffrey, David
  1978   "Providing More Information on Work Injury and Illness." Monthly Labor Review 101 November 4:16–21.

Rose, Michael
  1975   Industrial Behavior. London: Penguin Books.

Ross, Lois L.
  1979   "Those Daring Young Men on the Skyscraper Beams." Saint John's Calgary Report 2(48) February: 14–15.

Russell, Jack
  1974   "Part-Time Employment: Ideal Work Life." In Humanizing the Work Place. Roy Fairfield, ed. Buffalo, N.Y.: Prometheus, pp. 151–55.

Ryan, William L.
  1971   Blaming the Victim. New York: Vintage Books.

Scott, Rachael
  1974   Muscle and Blood. New York: E. P. Dutton.

Seeman, Melvin
  1961   "On the Meaning of Alienation." American Sociological Review 26:753–58.

Selden, Frank
1919

"Have We a Just Standard of Industrial Intelligence?" American Journal of Sociology 24(6) May: 643–51.

Sennett, Richard
1976

The Fall of Public Man. New York: Alfred A. Knopf.

Sennett, Richard, and
Cobb, Jonathan
1973

The Hidden Injuries of Class. New York: Random House.

Smucker, Joseph
1980

Industrialization in Canada. Scarborough, Ont.: Prentice-Hall of Canada.

Spray, S. Lee, Adamek,
Raymond J., and
Negandhi, Anant R.
1978

"Cognitive Styles and Job Satisfaction of Steelworkers." In Work Organization Research. Anant R. Negandhi and Bernhard Wilpert, eds. Kent, Ohio: Kent State University Press.

Stirling, Robert, and
Kouri, Denise
1979

"Unemployment Indexes—the Canadian Context." In Economy, Class and Social Reality. John Allen Fry, ed. Toronto: Butterworths, pp. 169–205.

Swados, Harvey
1970

"The Myth of the Happy Worker." In Man Alone. Eric and Mary Josephson, eds. New York: Dell.

Tataryn, Lloyd
1979

Dying for a Living: The Politics of Industrial Disease. Toronto: Daneau and Greenberg.

Terkel, Studs
1974

Working. New York: Pantheon Books.

United States Bureau
of the Census
1946
1958
1978
1979

Statistical Abstract of the United States. Washington, D.C.: U.S. Government Printing Office.

United States Department
of Labor
1978   "Employment and Unemployment during 1978: An
        Analysis." Washington, D.C.: U.S. Government
        Printing Office.

Walker, Charles R., and
Guest, Robert A.
1952   "The Man on the Assembly Line." Harvard
        Business Review May/June 1952:71–83.

Warner, W. L.,
and Lowe, J. O.
1947   The Social System of the Modern Factory. New
        Haven, Conn.: Yale University Press.

Weber, Max
1958   The Protestant Ethic and the Spirit of Capitalism.
        Talcott Parsons. New York: Scribner.

Whyte, William Foote
1955   Money and Motivation: An Analysis of Incentives
        in Industry. New York: Harper & Row.

Wolfe, Alan
1978   The Seamy Side of Democracy. New York:
        Longman.

Yarros, Victor
1919   "The Coming Industrial Democracy." American
        Journal of Sociology 24(6) May:672–80.

5

ENVIRONMENTAL CONTRADICTIONS: THE POLITICS OF ECOLOGY

Abstract

In corporate society, the *ideologies* that prevail for environmental problems present us with a wide variety of rationalizations for ecological harm. All in all, the message is that progress in the sense of commodity growth is essential and that certain ecological damage must be expected. Thus, the symbols of "trade off" and "accidents" are widely disseminated by officialdom through the media and the press.

As always, the *emergence, institutionalization,* and *maintenance* of social problems (including the assault on the environment) are heavily influenced by the ideological and material forces of the powers that be. In this chapter we trace the development in recent history of the environmental movement: its institutionalization in laws, policies, and programs; and its maintenance by the "pollution-industrial complex" and the supportive environmental bureaucracy of the State.

But what now is Babylon? A shrine of sirens, a home of lizards and ostriches, a den of serpents. —Otto of Freising in Chronicon

Environmentalists have never been a joyous lot. The above voice from the Middle Ages still echoes in our midst, but the words are sometimes ignored. It if tempting to dismiss those who criticize a world of steel-belted radials, polyester fabrics, and recreational vehicles. They sometimes appear as modern-day prophets who weep over seas blackened by oil slicks, air contaminated by sulfur smog, and an earth stripped of coal and left barren and sterile. Yet, for those who are interested, a careful examination of the evidence gathered from the natural, social, and behavioral sciences can only evoke a somber reflection. As the human community begins the 1980's, the resolution of global environmental disruption emerges as an imperative for survival.

Viewpoint

THE POLITICS OF ENERGY   **by Barry Commoner**

Where do the interests of the *energy producing* industries lie in the choice between the two optional routes toward a national system of renewable energy? Among these industries there are three that together encompass all the sector's activities: electric utilities, on which all of the nuclear power industry and most of coal production depends; the gas utilities, on which the production and distribution of natural gas depends; the oil industry, which produces and sells crude oil, natural gas, and refinery products such as fuel oil and gasoline.

The electric utilities operate highly centralized power plants, and since this is precisely the design required by a (nuclear) breeder system, there is a nice fit between the two. But building breeders would also aggravate the utilities' two main problems—difficulties in raising capital and in meeting environmental standards. Neither of these problems could be solved by the utilities without government help. Before breeders were introduced, the government would need to shore up the faltering nuclear power industry, which, even before the accident at Harrisburg, was on the verge of collapse because it lacked sufficient orders. One possibility—already suggested by the Westinghouse Corporation—is that the government should itself buy the nuclear power plants, for later resale to utilities. Another likely maneuver, which has already been proposed by the adminstration, is to shorten the time required for nuclear plant construction by limiting environmental challenges. If breeders were built, these economic and environmental problems would become worse rather than better. Thus the transition to a breeder-based renewable energy system would serve the interests of the electric utilities, but only if they had a great deal of help from the government.

Even with government help, it is difficult to see how the electric utilities could survive a solar transition as viable private enterprises. To begin with, the expanded use of the solar bridging fuel, natural gas, would favor the electric utilities' only present competitors—the gas utilities (although some utilities sell both gas and electric power). New housing developments and industries would tend to install gas-driven cogenerators rather than link up to the electric utilities. (In New York, the electric utility, Consolidated Edison, is bitterly opposed to a plan to install diesel-driven cogenerators in a large office building.) Then, as solar devices are introduced, the competition would increase. And because of their particular financial structure, new competition is fatal for electric utilities. Suppose, for example, production of photovoltaic cells is expanded and their price falls enough to make them competitive with utility power. Some of the utility's customers would begin to switch to photovoltaic systems, and the demand for utility power would decline. However, as a franchised public utility, the power company is allowed a certain fixed rate of return on its capital investment, so that as the demand for power falls, the utility can compensate by *raising its rates.* (This has already happened in a number of instances where conservation measures have reduced demand. One reason electric rates are rising so rapidly is that demand has not increased as fast as was assumed. On the average, utilities are now using only 70 percent of their capacity, but the consumers pay for the capital cost of the total capacity.) But as the utility's rates go up, the photovoltaic option will become more attractive to its customers and more of them will switch to photovoltaics. Demand will fall even more; the utility will again raise its rates; more customers will go solar. And so on. Thus, in the solar transition, the utilities' effort to maintain their rate of return in the face of growing competition will set up a feedback process that can only end with absurdly high rates— and no customers. Unless they acquired some other source of income, a national commitment to the solar transition would guarantee the demise of electric utilities as viable private investments.

However, the utilities' power lines and some of their power plants would have an important—if not financially rewarding —role to play in the solar transition. Both energy and capital can be conserved by tying a solar installation into the utilities' power grid. In a mixed solar/conventional system, the high cost of a storage system can be reduced if utility power is available as backup. Energy can be saved if a solar source can feed electricity into the power grid when it is not needed locally. However, electric utilities would hardly need to be expanded to provide such services, and unless they can grow, they are unlikely to attract sufficient private capital to remain viable. In the solar transition, some other means would need to be found to maintain these services.

The interests of the utilities that distribute natural gas are self-evident. In a transition to a (nuclear) breeder-based system, the (presumably) stable price of the system's renewable electricity would compete more and more successfully with natural gas, which would become exponentially more expensive. The gas utilities would be phased out gradually in such a transition. In contrast, in a solar transition the gas utilities would be the purveyors of the essential bridging fuel, natural gas, and they would flourish. Their crucial role would continue into the solar system itself, since the methane gradually added to gas pipelines from new, solar sources would be distributed through their pipelines.

Where do the interests of the oil companies lie in a possible transition to a system of renewable energy? In either a solar or a (nuclear) breeder transition, oil and natural gas would be needed until the renewable source was large enough to take over. But in the long run, when the solar transition is complete, only stand-by natural gas production would be needed—not much of a prospect for the huge oil companies. However, in a transition to the breeder system, their prospects would be much better. The major oil companies own a considerable part of the nation's reserves of both coal (the bridging fuel in the transition) and uranium (a breeder fuel). (According to

Alfred F. Dougherty, Jr., of the Federal Trade Commission, eleven oil and gas corporations now control 51 percent of the known uranium reserves, and fourteen of the twenty major corporations now holding coal reserves are oil companies.) Thus, in a breeder transition, the major oil companies would be in an excellent position to continue to serve, as they do now, as the main suppliers of essential fuels. Morever, since the oil companies are among the largest, wealthiest corporations in the US, they might invest directly in the construction of breeders, which will call for very large amounts of capital.

In a transition to a solar system, oil companies would seem to have no advantages over any other holders of investment capital, but in certain ways they would find the transition inimical to their own special interests. First, the emphasis on natural gas as the bridging fuel and the early elimination of nuclear power would tend to reduce the value of the companies' large uranium holdings. On the other hand, insofar as they hold natural gas reserves, the oil companies could play an important role in the solar transition. However, natural gas production has often been a sideline for the major oil companies, developed only as an adjunct to oil production; many of the US gas producers are relatively small "independents," especially in the areas of "unconventional" gas reserves. The large oil companies therefore would have a good deal of competition in the production of natural gas, and they are more likely to invest in areas where their enormous wealth gives them a strong competitive advantage. If the oil companies were to engage in the production of solar energy devices, their huge capital resources would not be particularly advantageous, because the investments would tend to be diverse and relatively small-scaled. Thus the major oil companies are not likely to find a role in the solar transition that is suitable to their distinctive capabilities, in particular their ability to make very large investments.

In fact, the major oil companies are most likely to prefer neither of the renewable energy options. In recent years, as the price of energy has increased and oil company profits have risen, they have shown a growing interest in investing outside the field of energy. In November 1978, a survey of current trends in the oil industry by the trade magazine, *The Oil and Gas Journal,* reported "With (oil) prices increases, companies like Exxon Corp. and Phillips Petroleum Co. are generating such massive cash flows that traditional invest-ment areas can't absorb the capital" The report continued:

> What's in store ten years from now? The latter question is perhaps more critical in the oil industry than in other busi-nesses because it looms against a backdrop of shrinking US oil and gas reserves. And there are critical decisions to be made, such as what to do with cash flows from present investments as opportunities in traditional investment areas decline.

The oil companies' cash is already beginning to flow out of oil and natural gas production. In the last few years, inflated oil company profits have been used by Mobil to acquire Mont-gomery Ward and Container Corp; by Atlantic Richfield to buy Anaconda Copper and the London *Observer;* by Sun Oil to acquire a manufacturer of medical equipment; by Exxon to invest heavily in electronics; while Gulf Oil tried but failed to buy the Barnum and Bailey circus. At the same time, most of the major oil companies are increasing their already appre-ciable investments in chemical production. Such purchases diversify the oil company holdings, and according to a vice president of Standard Oil of California, "The thrust for diversi-fication comes from the depletion of oil and gas resources." *The Oil and Gas Journal* report also emphasizes the oil com-panies' view that investment in oil and gas production has become increasingly risky ". . . as we try to produce more difficult wells." Finally, although the industry has been drill-ing more domestic oil wells in the last few years because of the sharp rise in the price of oil, this will go on only if prices continue to rise fast enough. As one major oil company points out,

> These investments [in new US oil production] are being made in anticipation of prices rising over time to what we consider to be more rational levels. If these price increases do not come about, our economics on current projects will be seriously affected, and our ability and willingness to make future investments will be greatly decreased.

The chief executive officer of one of the country's largest oil companies—John E. Sweringen of Standard Oil Company (Indiana)—has been very explicit about the reason why oil companies diversify into other areas. In an interview with the Chicago *Tribune* he said: "We're not in the energy business.

We're in the business of trying to use the assets entrusted to us by our shareholders to give them the best return on the money they've invested in the company." Motivated by this philosophy, Mr. Sweringen has pushed his company into the chemical business, especially to produce raw materials for synthetic fibers, which, according to the *Tribune* interview is "... an investment which Wall Street analysts expect to pay off handsomely in the 1980s."

Thus, although the rising price of oil has generated unprecedented profits for the oil companies, they are increasingly reluctant to use them for "traditional investments"—that is, for the production of more oil and gas. This is the natural, inevitable outcome of the nonrenewability of these energy sources. As the deposits become progressively more costly to produce, unless the companies can be *certain* that the price of oil and gas will keep pace, they run the risk that their profits will fall. As the 1972 report of the National Petroleum Council pointed out, if the price of domestic oil had not begun to rise exponentially after that date, the oil companies' rate of return on their investment would have dropped to 2 percent by 1985.

The oil companies' uncertainty about their future profits is not surprising. They know from past experience that because oil and gas are so crucial to the economy, there is always the possibility—depending on the political outlook in Washington—that prices will be controlled. Because of this uncertainty, and the certainty that production costs will rise exponentially as oil and gas deposits are depleted, future investments in these resources are bound to become increasingly risky. The oil companies fought hard (and successfully) to deregulate natural gas, and are now agitating against the renewal of the oil price control legislation that expires in 1979 so that they can be more confident of higher future prices. For the same reason, they are heavily engaged in advertising campaigns to persuade the public that resolving the energy crisis depends on increased production, which can occur only—they say—if government regulations, especially on prices and environmental controls, are lifted.

It may seem paradoxical that while they stridently demand unrestrained control over the economics of oil and gas production as though their survival depended on it, the oil companies are quietly buying their way into other industries. But the two campaigns are in fact quite complementary: the faster energy prices rise, the more ready cash the oil companies will have to buy up other industries. This strategy would benefit from a national decision to take the breeder route, for it would give the oil companies an additional twenty-five years or more in which to collect high prices for oil and gas, and to invest the growing profits elsewhere, meanwhile profiting as well as from their extensive holdings of coal and uranium. (Excerpted from *The Politics of Energy,* 1979, pp. 70–73.)

The "energy crisis" is only one of a larger number of environmental issues that threaten Lifeboat Earth. Though a biologist, Barry Commoner understands that environmental concerns transcend the boundary lines of academic specialization. The above piece clearly demonstrates that the debate over energy sources is not primarily a matter of technological feasibility or simple economic cost. To the contrary, the opposition to solar energy is rooted in the very structure of corporate order.

To understand the specific question of energy, together with the more general problems of ecology, requires comprehension of the interdependence of the environment and society. Thus, the *ecosystem* is more than a community of animals, plants, and bacteria interrelated with its physical and chemical environment. In a larger sense, the physical quality of life reflects the competing interests of *social gains and commodity growth* (Anderson 1976). The society of the future may flourish with the shared resources, increased leisure, expanded education, and enhanced environmental quality of the former. Or it may founder in the nuclear, chemical, and social waste of the latter. This is the overriding issue of environmental sociology. To address it requires an understanding that human beings are but one of many species living in a finite world. As an ecosystem, this world cannot absorb unchecked commodity growth. Nor, can the pollution of the part be separated from the welfare of the whole (Catton and Riley 1978).

THE PREVAILING IDEOLOGIES

We have argued in previous chapters that the structural realities of the North American Societies of Canada and the United States include class division, the concentration of wealth and power in the hands of a relative few, and a corporate economic order that holds progress and growth as synonymous. In our examination of social structure, it has been our intent to draw the reader's attention to the political economy of ideological control. We have seen that ownership of the means of production (factories, mines, land) coexists with ownership or control of the means of influence (such as media, educational institutions). Consequently, the definitional model that traces the history of a social problem (emergence, institutionalization, maintenance) will reveal the essentials of corporate ideology. In short, most official, popular, and academic accounts of the environmental crisis may well serve to direct attention away from the contradictions of the corporate order.

We now turn to the systematic analysis of the ecological crisis. As with other social problems, it will be apparent that both understanding and solution are contingent upon the sort of questions we pose. These follow in part from the ideological assumptions we hold on the nature of social order. If socialization is "successful," people will not question the legitimacy of the existing political and economic order. In North American society, it is widely believed that power is shared; that government depends upon the just consent of the governed; that master institutions gain legitimacy through popular agreement; and that social problems can be resolved through pragmatic policy, political trade-offs, and the occasional rehabilitation or removal of "deviants." Most important is the conviction that more goods and services, measured by a growing Gross National Product, are socially desirable.

If ideological control exists, then the history of the environmental problem will reveal a selective perception during the emergence of the issue. Such an approach ensures that the environmental "problem" will be institutionalized so as to represent no significant threat to the existing order. It therefore follows that the ecological crisis will be maintained or "kept" in such a way that two major consequences can be identified. First, the problem will provide a stimulus to the pollution control industry. And secondly, it will provide a reason for being for a bureaucracy charged with controlling pollution while effectively stripped of power.

Consistent with the above argument is the position that *Corporate Society will deal with* the ecological crisis on the level of individual attitudes and choices. Should certain businesses or industries be identified as polluters, it will be made clear that *specific and isolated* firms are the offenders. The corporate order as a political-economic entity will remain essentially unchallenged.

Environmental Progress

A problem may be real, it may only be perceived as real, or a very real problem may be distorted. Few would deny the social costs of crime. However, the ideological constraints that serve to support a structure of inequality will lead observers to define crime by "street" offenses as opposed to "suite" transgressions. One should expect similar processes to affect the *accounts* of the ecological crisis.

To provide an *account* is to create through simple code words and metaphors an organizing and synthesizing mental picture (Scott and Lyman 1968). Such perceptual blinders may point up a problem while simultaneously diverting attention from its more threatening features. The ideological issue is forthright. If a society is beset with obvious environmental hazards that cannot be ignored, the danger is that a perceptual message will be prepared that confirms the obvious facts while denying the problem's structural origin.

Repression need not be conscious or openly coercive. Ideological control is part and parcel of the process of socialization. Most members of North American societies, as well as others, develop a series of "domain assumptions" (Gouldner 1970) that effectively direct debate. Consequently, it is easy for most of us to be aware of ideological forces in other societies. It is somewhat more difficult to apply the same skepticism to our own. For example, Canada is the second largest country in the world, with only one-tenth the population of the United States. Because of their land's expanse and undeveloped resources, many Canadians see the environmental problem as foreign, as down south in the United States. The ideologies of inevitable growth and infinite resources belie the reality of an increasingly concentrated population rapidly selling its dwindling nonrenewable resources abroad. In fact, the title of a major book on environmental issues in Canada reflects this view, *Much Is Taken, Much Remains* (Bryan 1973).

A recent Gallup Poll shows that while a majority of Canadians view pollution as serious, they perceive it as less of a problem in 1980 than in 1970. Table 5–1 presents the result of this survey.

It Is Only an Accident

Any dictionary definition of "accident" refers to the unavoidable and chance occurrence of an event. The emphasis is on episodes beyond human direction and control. Synonyms include "acts of God" or "acts of nature." When the term "accident" is employed, irrespective of the scope or magnitude of the tragedy, those who hear the message are left to believe that nothing could have been done to prevent it.

To recognize the impact of the accidental account, it is only necessary to consider the alternative. If an ecological problem is not viewed as an "accident," then it emerges as a matter of error or fault. The vision of a chance breakdown in the natural order of things is converted into an event that should have been prevented through social, political, and intellectual means. A simple example makes the point. Suppose a fire that results in numerous deaths is reported as an "accident." The clear message is that nothing could have prevented the tragedy. However, suppose that the victims were the aged, the poor, or transients living in one form or

**TABLE 5-1
Canadian Perceptions of Pollution**

"Have you heard or read anything about the dangers of pollution—that is, contamination of our air, rivers, and lakes?"

			Yes	No
NATIONAL	–	1980	92%	9%
	–	1977	93	7
	–	1975	93	7
	–	1970	91	9

"How serious do you yourself think the dangers of pollution are—very serious, or not at all serious?"

			Very Serious	Fairly Serious	Not At All	Can't Say
NATIONAL	–	1980*	52%	35%	4%	1%
	–	1977	57	35	5	3
	–	1975	56	37	5	2
	–	1970	69	27	3	1

"On the whole, would you say that pollution is a problem in your area?"

			Yes	No	Can't Say
NATIONAL	–	1980*	46%	42%	4%
	–	1977	53	42	6
	–	1975	57	40	3
	–	1970	61	35	4

Concern about the dangers of pollution has fallen over the past decade.

In 1970, 69 percent felt the dangers of pollution were very serious. This fell to 56 percent in 1975 and, today, 52 percent express a very serious concern about pollution.

Awareness of the problem has remained at about the same level—92 percent—throughout the decade. Fewer today, however, than in 1970 think that their area is affected.

Concern about pollution has dropped significantly in the western and Atlantic provinces since the question was last asked in 1977. In Ontario and Quebec concern is slightly above that found elsewhere.

Results are based on 1,038 person, in-home interviews with adult Canadians, eighteen years and over, during early February. A sample of this size is accurate within a four percentage point margin of error, 19 in 20 times.

*Note: Responses are based on the 92% answering question 1 in the affirmative.

Source: The *Calgary Herald,* March 26, 1980, p. A8.

another of substandard housing. In this case, the term "accident" covers up neglect of these populations. The following analysis intends to question the "normal" version of "environmental accidents."

It goes without saying that the environmental crisis is worldwide. In Italy, the rapid industrialization in the 1950s and 1960s buried ecological concern under the tide of "progress." One alarming aspect of the Italian experience revolves around two "environmental accidents," a phrase becoming all too commonplace in today's world (Renzoni 1977).

Late in 1974, the Yugoslavian freighter *Cavtat* sank in the southern outlet of the Adriatic Sea after a collision with another ship. The *Cavtat's* cargo was lead tetraethyl and tetramethyl, extremely toxic agents, which immediately sank in shallow waters some three-and-a-half miles from the town of Otrango on the Italian coast. Officials of the factory producing these chemicals sought to play down the dangers of lead contamination. However, at this writing, the distinct possibility remains that the fishing grounds of the region are vulnerable and, consequently, local food chains are endangered.

In the summer of 1976, a malfunction of a reactor in a chemical plant in Seveso in northern Italy resulted in the contamination of soil as far as four kilometers away. In this case, the chemical toxin "dioxin" killed numerous wild and domestic animals and produced skin lesions (chloracne) among humans, especially children. The governmental response has been to remove vegetation and at least ten centimeters of topsoil from the area of greatest contamination. (Dioxin contained in waste oil contaminated the soil in Missouri in 1970 and animals continued to die, although soil to a level of some fifteen to twenty centimeters was removed.). The total amount of earth to be removed in Seveso ranges from 200,000 to 400,000 cubic meters. The disposal and treatment of such materials leave unanswered the question of what is ultimately to be done with contaminated waste.

Southeast Asians are no strangers to the dioxin that contaminated the soil in Seveso. The agent, among others, was used for defoliation purposes during the Vietnam War. Scientific studies from Southeast Asia report that this substance induces pathological tissue change for the unborn fetus. The grim possibility of birth defects led some forty women around Seveso to choose legal abortion in local hospitals, while others went to private Swiss clinics.

The hazards of dioxin are not confined to European and Asian societies. One of the most toxic agents in existence, this chemical has been used in the manufacture of herbicides spread on gardens throughout the United States. Traces have been found in mothers' milk, shellfish, and dogs' flea collars (Peracchio 1979). Of greater significance, in a tragic case of "bringing the war home," Vietnam veterans exposed to the dioxin-contaminated defoliant *Agent Orange* continue today as victims of that conflict. In early 1980, some 3,000 of these veterans filed as plaintiffs in a suit against the five manufacturers of Agent Orange (Dow Chemical, Monsanto, Thompson-Hayward Chemical Co., Hercules, Inc., and Diamond Shamrock Corporation). Defense attorney Victor Yannacone, Jr., contended that the companies knew the risk but failed to warn the Pentagon or the soldiers. (The Agent Organge plaintiffs are suffering chloracne, liver damage, and cancer; their children exhibit serious and diverse birth defects.) The defendants claim that they were only following government specifications in the manufacture of the defoliant. The government in turn denied responsibility, leaving those exposed to Agent Orange without the disability payments or free hospital care reserved for war veterans suffering service-connected disability. At this writing, the case is expected to drag on for years (*Time* 1980).

The chemical industry is chief among the corporate polluters creating a wasteland in North American society. Some 30,000 to 50,000 dump sites in the United States contain hazardous wastes, many of them in densely populated urban areas (Nelson 1979). The Environmental Protection Agency warns that waste will eventually threaten the water supply of over 100 million citizens (*Spokane Chronicle* 1980).

The potential health crisis of chemical waste became a matter of public alarm in 1978 when people living near the Love Canal in Niagara Falls, New York, began to suffer severe health complaints including cancer. In May 1980, researchers provided evidence of damage to the residents' chromosomes. Subsequently, President Carter declared a state of emergency for the area. The Love Canal dump site was operated by Hooker Chemical Company (a subsidiary of Occidental Petroleum Corporation). During the 1940s and 1950s, Hooker dumped over 20,000 tons of chemical waste in the canal. Hooker filled in the site and contributed it to the Niagara Falls Board of Education which, not informed of the hazard, constructed a school and playground on it (Brown 1980). Documents revealed by the United States House of Representative Subcommittee on Crime in its *Report on Corporate Crime* show that Hooker Chemical knew as early as 1958 the hazards of the chemicals. An interoffice memo told of children being burned at the Love Canal site (US House of Representatives 1980, p. 17).

Such environmental "accidents" abound. Oil spills, derailments of chemical-carrying trains and resulting large-scale evacuations, thermal inversions—these have become a part of our everyday experience. Today, their frequency is such that the assumption that they are random and unavoidable is questionable. As we shall soon see, life in modern industrial societies is played out in a culture of material progress. North Americans are taught to view technological and scientific advance as desirable. To master the earth, to exercise dominion over every living thing, to expand and prosper—these are the concomitants of growth. In pursuing this course, humankind exercises the power to alter ecosystems in such subtle fashion that it is impossible to predict the full consequences. For environmentalists, one thing is certain. This fragile planet holds the key to human survival and it is being systematically violated. Historians of the future who write of the present age may choose to avoid the accidental account and describe environmental crisis as a normal and natural consequence of the corporate society.

Methylmercury is no accident; it is a dangerous by-product of industrial pollution and the application of fungicides. Shellfish and grain contaminated by this substance have been ingested by humans, resulting in cerebellar and visual pathway damage (Matsumoto et al. 1965; Pierce 1972). In a similar vein, the industrial dangers associated with the handling of manganese ores and compounds in mining, steelmaking, and battery manufacturing are well documented. Manganese toxicity produces damage to the central nervous system in both humans and experimental animals (Chandra and Shukla 1978).

In seeking domination and growth, the inventive human mind has produced the artificial herbicides, pesticides, and insecticides used abundantly to produce a higher yield of badly needed crops. Ironically, these synthetic agents remain in the food chains, working their way into living tissue. Despite some limited government action, the words of Rachael Carson still capture our time:

> These sprays, dusts and aerosols are now applied almost universally to farms, gardens, forests and homes—nonselective chemicals that have the power to kill every insect, the "good" and the "bad," to still the song of birds and the leaping of fish in the streams, to coat the leaves with a deadly film, and to linger on in soil—all this though the intended target may be only a few weeds or insects. Can anyone believe it is possible to lay down such a barrage of poisons on the surface of the earth without making it unfit for all life? They should not be called "insecticides," but "biocides" (Carson 1962, pp. 7–8).

How much has changed since the publication in 1962 of the ecology classic *Silent Spring*?

> While the pesticide industry has been going through boom times, the federal government has largely failed to protect the public and the environment. As a 1976 report by the National Academy of Sciences concluded, "The pest control enterprise places a billion pounds of toxic materials into the environment each year, but it is normal for us to have only the vaguest idea of how much of each compound was used and where, and even then only after half a decade's lag" (Environmental Defense Fund and Robert H. Boyle 1979, p. 117).

In the eastern part of North America, acid rain is becoming a major killer of nature. In Canada alone, nearly 140 Ontario lakes are dead, and 50,000 may be endangered by the year 2000. Rain with excessive acid content is caused by industrial emissions of sulfur dioxide and nitrogen oxides. Half of the acid contamination imperiling Canada comes from the United States. The Environmental Minister of Ontario argues that shutting down all Ontario sources of pollution "would have virtually no impact on the continuous damage of lakes" because of United States pollution crossing the border (Dolto 1980).

The litany is virtually endless. Lead poisons the blood of those who are economically trapped in areas contaminated by smelters. And as always, the children are especially vulnerable. Blue collar workers suffer not only from the alienation common to other workers in modern societies but exist under the cloud of pollutants. As we shall see, certain diseases are work related. This social fact denies the accuracy of the accident account.

The Cancer Plague Today a modern plague is loose in North America. It is not yet on the level of the Black Death that decimated the population of Europe in the fourteenth century. It does not strike so suddenly, or spread so rapidly, or leave the living outnumbered by the dead. But it is an epidemic, nonetheless. For many, this condition is so terrifying that people dread to speak its name, much less seek out the diagnostic examination that might confirm that fear.

> For every twenty-five Americans who died in 1900, only one died of cancer. In 1975, nearly one of every five Americans who died was a victim of cancer. Unless we begin to make rapid headway in initiating preventive policies—in eliminating the known environmental cause of cancer—we can expect that of all Americans alive today at least one out of four, perhaps even one out of three, will die of cancer (Agran 1977, pp. XI–XVI).

When cancer strikes, the victim is unaware of an epidemic. The common interpretation is that one has been singled out by fate, by some type of chance.

As is frequently the case when people are trapped by an unquestioned ideology, they seek a solution from the very processes that are at the root of the problem. So it is with the legacy of cancer. The technology of growth, which has added to the dilemma, is turned to for an answer. The belief is that one day in the near future the diligent efforts of dedicated researchers will pay off, and the "penicillin" will be discovered. The sobering fact is that there are over 100 forms of cancer. The numerous forms of the disease make a universal cure more a hope for a miracle than a trust in science.

Agran (1977) notes that in the past quarter-century, the struggle against cancer has produced some grudging victories, but the survival rates continue to paint a grim picture. In the mid-1950s, the survival rate for those suffering breast cancer was approximately 60 percent. By the mid-1970s, that rate had improved by only four percent. For the decade of the fifties, 8 percent of those contracting lung cancer survived five years past diagnosis. Two decades later, the five-year survival rate was only 9 percent. For the most common cancer of all, that involving the colon, the five-year survival rate remained unchanged from the 1950s to the 1970s: 44 percent.

Perhaps it is time to examine the origins of this epidemic. The identification of carcinogenic agents is apt to encounter some resistance because to search for the causes of cancer is to enter the sacred ground of the corporate industrial/chemical society and the structure of growth that underlies it. Further, it is to deny the "accident" explanation. However, an obsession with a cure for cancer results in misplaced emphasis. Cancer, perhaps 80 percent of it according to the World Health Organization (Environmental Defense Fund and Robert H. Boyle 1979, p. 5), is largely due to carcinogenic agents to be found in the environment. In creating the "silent spring" of chemical poison, our technology has contributed in large measure to the plague we encounter.

Consistent with the hidden injuries of a class-divided society, cancer appears first among blue collar workers because their jobs more frequently bring them into contact with carcinogens. Agran (1977) cites numerous epidemiological studies on occupational cancer. For example, some 2 million workers, including those who work in the rubber and petroleum industries, as well as painters, printers, and dry cleaners, work with benzene, a solvent known to produce leukemia. Rubber workers, whose work environment is a virtual storehouse of carcinogens, die of cancer of the stomach, the prostate gland, the blood and lymph-forming tissues at rates ranging from 50 to 300 percent higher than the general population.

Steelworkers, whose popular image is one of strength and health, are stalked by kidney and lung cancer. Of those whose jobs require working on top of the coke ovens, breathing coal tar emissions, some 20 percent die from lung cancer. The rate for the general population ranges from 3 to 4 percent.

Those miners of iron ore, chromium, nickel and uranium—metals that are used to increase the gross national product—also suffer job-related cancer. The lung cancer rate for uranium miners is staggering, accounting for some 50 percent of all deaths in this group.

Dye workers, specifically those who use benzidine and other related chemicals, are highly susceptible to bladder cancer. The sobering evidence is that urinary cancer for dye workers has become an occupational certainty on the level of black lung disease for coal miners.

The occupational connection for the cancer plague has also been well documented for asbestos workers. Those who work with this substance remain vulnerable whether they are involved in its manufacture or work with the finished product. They die of lung cancer at a rate some seven times that of control groups.

Few of us pause to consider the extent to which asbestos with its many applications surrounds us. It is a fibrous silicate mineral that is fire resistant and an excellent insulator. Accordingly, it finds its way into numerous products.

> A partial list includes floor tiles, shingles, roofing, wallboard, pipes, potholders, ironing board covers, electrical insulation tape, filters in gas masks, filters for processing fruit, wine and pharmaceuticals, plastics, brake linings, clutch facings, carpets, plaster, stucco, cement, and automobile undercoatings (Agran 1977, p. 30).

This ubiquitous commodity of industrial-chemical society is to be found in every automobile, airplane, train, ship, missile, and engine. It is used by some 5 million workers whose health is threatened daily by fine lethal fibers almost unconsciously swallowed and inhaled. Asbestos fibers do not disappear. They take up permanent residence in body tissue. Some of those workers exposed escape while others develop lung disease within months. Recently, we have learned that numerous shipyard workers exposed to asbestos fibers during the Second World War developed lung cancer decades later.

While industry claims that less than 5 percent of the cancer rate is occupationally related, a 1978 study by the National Cancer Institute and the National Institute of Environmental Health Sciences found that at least 20 percent (perhaps more) of all cancer in the United States may be related to one's job (Environmental Defense Fund and Robert H. Boyle 1979, p. 8). Looking specifically at the chemical industry one geographical analysis of cancer mortality examined the 139 counties where this industry is most concentrated. The study found abnormally high rates for cancer of the bladder, lung, liver, and certain other organs. The particular type of cancer was further associated with the particular type of chemical manufacturing (Environmental Defense Fund and Robert H. Boyle 1979, p. 15–18).

When the epidemiology branch of the National Cancer Institute published its *Atlas of Cancer Mortality for U.S. Counties: 1950–69*, in 1976, it produced

> . . . a furor in New Jersey, which has the highest cancer rate of all fifty states. Long proud to be known as the Garden State, New Jersey found itself with the unwelcome nickname of Cancer Alley. The state is highly industrialized, with approximately 1,200 chemical and allied plants, employing 130,000 persons and generating annual sales of $10 billion (Environmental Defense Fund and Robert H. Boyle 1979, p. 18).

As the following figure shows, the cancer mortality rate is rising along with the production of known carcinogens. Given a lag twenty to twenty-five years between exposure and the development of cancer, the legacy of the tremendous recent growth in the plastics industry, for example, is yet to be realized.

Give a Little, Get a Little

Most of us are familiar with the term "trade-off." It means that, to gain a desirable return, it is necessary to give up something. When coal companies are castigated for the strip mining that leaves the earth disrupted

**Figure 5-1. Cancer Mortality Rates and Chemical Production
as a Function of Time**

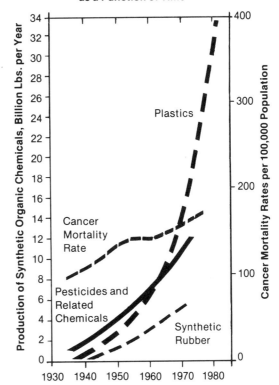

Source: The Environmental Defense Fund and Robert H. Boyle, 1979, P. 21.

and spoiled, when petrocorporations come under fire for oil spills or refinery pollution, when the operators of smelters are confronted with evidence on lead poisoning, they respond with some variation of the trade-off argument. Such environmental pollution is portrayed as the necessary price to be paid for growth, profit, jobs, and tax relief. Within the context of economic crisis (including but not limited to unemployment), the long-term considerations of environmental health are not taken seriously. Unemployment and inflation are with us today. Environmental catastrophe is tomorrow's child. The implicit message of this form of trade-off is clear: your money or your life. Thus, people are dying for a living (Tataryn 1979).

When economic well-being and environmental quality are presented in trade-off terms, a major contradiction has been uncovered. The question that concerns us is whether or not the contradiction is unavoidable. If so, then we must indeed choose between jobs on the one hand and clean air, pure water, and productive soil on the other. If not, it may be because the trade-off is a characteristic of a specific political-economy of growth.

Therefore, to change the structure of the corporate society, which is "hooked on growth" (Anderson 1976), would lessen the trade-off. Certainly, technological development presents problems for all industrial societies. For example, Soviet dam construction on the Volga River has produced land loss, flooding, and damage to fisheries (Micklin 1977). However, it appears logical to argue that the structural imperatives of corporate society are uniquely problematic.

The Energy Trade-off: Petro-Power

In 1850, the price of tallow candles in the United States reached some 15 cents a pound. The cost of sperm oil was also in an upward spiral, reaching $1.80 a gallon by 1855. A new energy source was clearly required. It was to be found in the form of petroleum, literally "rock oil," a discovery destined to loom large in history as the foundation for an industrial and technological revolution that was to transform the face of the globe (Mangone 1976).

At first, the refined rock oil was used only as a source of light to replace the oil from sperm whales in the lanterns of eastern cities of the United States. Then it was burned to provide the energy necessary to drive the machines that signal "progress" and a higher standard of living. It was a wonder substance, a black, sticky, oozing manna drawn from seemingly bottomless pits beneath the earth. Sweeping changes in transportation came to be fueled by oil. Ships were no longer at the mercy of idle winds, grain and cattle ceased being slave to local market conditions, human wanderlust could be satisfied with the turn of the ignition key. Even modern warfare was revolutionized. Napoleon was wrong. An army no longer marched on its stomach. It marched on oil.

Sperm oil, tallow, wood, and coal succumbed to black gold. When the supply of oil for industrialized nations began to dwindle, the nations of the Third World awaited the technological coming of the world's great petrocorporations. Iran, Saudi Arabia, Kuwait, Iraq, Indonesia, Mexico, Venezuela, and others offered corporate society limitless, inexpensive energy. The prime mover was growth, and conservation remained an unnecessary nuisance. As always, the "trade-off" came at the expense of environmental quality.

Ironically, the petroleum dependency of industrialized nations increased their economic dependency upon Third World countries. Petroleum development meant that oil wealth was to support both the elite of the industrialized societies and the indigenous elite of developing countries. However, the absence of production and refining technology for the emerging petro-states ensured their continuing dependency. Today, a petroleum-supported local elite coexists with the masses of the poor in oil-rich lands. This pattern is symptomatic of neocolonial economies, in which true political and economic control for many Latin American, Asian, and African countries is vested outside the particular nation that provides the natural and human resources (Pomeroy 1970). Increasingly, large multinational petrocorporations have converted the nonsocialist world into a market system. Petrodollars are flowing along with the oil reserves of the world's *nouveau riche*. The industrialized West imports a river of oil, signaling the advent of the supertanker with its attendant oil spills. The "trade-off" was a ready-made reply to blackened beaches and marine contamination.

When rock oil was no longer in cheap and plentiful supply and the industrial thirst for oil could not be quenched on dry land, attention was directed to the ocean floor. The Gulf of Mexico, the Persian Gulf, and the North Sea in turn became watery foundations for drilling platforms. Within a century, the Industrial Revolution that had been fueled by cheap oil had, in Frankenstein fashion, turned to threaten its creator. The search beneath the seas, accompanied by the necessity of drilling deeper wells, produced a capital-intensive industry favoring the giant producer and relegating the wildcatter to a footnote in history (yet another trade-off). In the Third World, oil-rich nations came to be guided by governments determined to gain some measure of control over that vital substance so indispensable to industrialized nations. Though losing nominal control through joint ventures and nationalization, Western petrocorporations retained the technology necessary for production and refinery operations. The energy crisis was to become a valuable commodity for the stockholders of petrocorporations as well as for the indigenous elite of Venezuela, Iran, the Arab states of the Persian Gulf, and others.

Today, North American energy politics are dictated by the specter of petroleum scarcity. Canada, more fortunate than her neighbor to the south, with greater accessible oil reserves, has been reevaluating national policy on petroleum exportation. The energy crisis, identified with the embargoes and restrictions on production introduced by OPEC[1] countries in 1973 and intensified by production slowdowns on the part of private petrocorporations, had fewer consequences for Canada than for other major industrial nations.

Canada's unique problem centers around transportation of oil. The immense reserves of western Canada do not reach the densely populated east. Consequently, Canada exports some 50 percent of her crude oil production while importing some 45 percent of her petroleum for domestic use. Lawson A. W. Hunter (1976) argues that if exports to the United States continue at current levels, then Canada's proven petroleum reserves will be exhausted by 1990. Should such a pattern of export be maintained, new energy sources will have to be developed and these are more than

[1]OPEC (Organization of Petroleum Exporting Nations) consists of a number of developing nations who, as members of a consortium, set a common price range for their crude oil.

likely to endanger the delicate Artic ecosystem, thus the specter of another trade-off. Such a development would be ironic for a nation that has been a major force in the formulation of international environmental law. As we have seen, the Canadian energy problems are compounded by a blatant form of neocolonialism: foreign ownership. For example, almost 70 percent of Imperial Oil is owned by Exxon Corporation (see Table 3–16 in Chapter Three).

Barry Commoner (1976) points out that this vanishing energy source remains as the fulcrum of the economy of the United States, Canada, and most of the world.

> Oil is the basis of the two industries—automotive and petro-chemical—which, together with the petroleum industry itself, make up nearly one fifth of the total US economy. And apart from their economic effects, the oil-based industries have powerfully molded the pattern of national life. Oil powers the horde of cars, the vehicles of the urban diaspora that has scattered people's homes and the places where they work and shop over wide, once-rural areas. The intensive use of petroleum-based fertilizers and pesticides has nearly transformed the farm from an outpost of nature into a branch of the chemical industry (1976, p. 33).

When the 1973 OPEC oil embargo rippled throughout the industrialized world, the immediate consequences were seen at the gasoline stations. As the price of gasoline climbed and its availability became questionable in many areas, the giant automotive industry experienced shock waves. At the zenith of the crisis, over 100,000 workers were laid off and plant capacity declined to 80 percent of potential. Utility bills rose, while farmers were required to pay the inflated costs of fuels and fertilizers, resulting in higher food prices. As Commoner succinctly notes, inflation and unemployment were now inextricably bound with energy in the context of an overall economic crisis.

The OPEC Scapegoat

The Organization of Petroleum Exporting Countries' declaration of an oil embargo in 1973 signaled the beginning of an upward spiral in the price of gasoline and other petroleum products. Constant media reference to "oil shieks" appeared to confirm that certain elements of the populations of countries far from North America were harvesting the riches of their invaluable resource. However, placing the blame elsewhere may obscure the fact that soaring OPEC prices have brought sharply escalating profits for "Big Oil."

Multinational petrocorporations have been primary beneficiaries of the conversion of the energy crisis into a commodity. According to the National Bureau of Research, "Big Oil" realized record profit margins at all three stages: production, refining, and marketing. Reported annual gains in net income for twenty-nine United States oil corporations did not exceed 10 percent for the 1967–1972 period. However, in 1973, net income after taxes rose 70 percent, and in 1974, it climbed 40 percent. To put it simply, in a two-year period 1973–1974, the oil giants more than doubled their profits (Silk 1980).

The dizzying spiral of profits has continued unabated since 1973. First-quarter profits for 1979 (compared with the first quarter of 1978) revealed the following increases:

Company	Percent Profit Increase
Conoco	343%
Standard Oil of Ohio	303
Amerada	279
Marathon	108
Kerr-McGee	89
Mobil	82
Texaco	81
Gulf	61
Standard Oil of California	43
Sun	43
Cities Service	42
Exxon	37
Standard Oil of Indiana	28
Shell Oil	16
Phillips Petroleum	4[2]

(Reported in the *Wall Street Journal*, April 24, 25, 26, 27 of 1979.)

While climbing oil prices mean escalating inflation, rising unemployment, and bad news for those seeking to heat their homes, a profit gusher has been struck by certain giants of the corporate world. An examination of the historical record, however, demonstrates that Big Oil has customarily benefited from a series of "energy crises" (Sherrill 1979). To be specific, in 1920 the United States was in a precarious position with regard to its oil supply. The culprit was Great Britain, which had refused Standard Oil entry into the oil fields of Iraq. Declaring that America's oil reserves were virtually depleted, Big Oil raised the price of gasoline

[2]A somewhat embarrassed Phillips Petroleum spokesperson explained that revenues were down primarily due to unexpected early encroachment of water into its Indonesian wells.

and imposed limits on its purchase in some areas of the country. Great Britain, responding to pressures from the State Department and Congress, relented and the "crisis" was averted.

In 1929, the Federal Oil Conservation Board warned of the exhaustion of oil resources and advised bringing in foreign oil to save national reserves. The primary beneficiaries of this policy proved to be Standard and Gulf, who operated in Venezuela, the most important source of foreign crude at the time. At this point, Gulf was controlled by the family of Andrew Mellon, Secretary of the Treasury during the Hoover Administration.

In 1947, Standard Oil of California, Texaco, Mobil, and Standard Oil of New Jersey formed the Arabian American Oil Company (ARAMCO). Such a consolidation of corporate power was justified by ARAMCO members as a consequence of another crisis in domestic oil supply. Both the Departments of State and Interior joined the crusade, proclaiming that the national oil supply was virtually depleted. Prices climbed, shortages were declared, yet at the time when public concern was the greatest (early 1947), some 220 million barrels of crude were in storage and not delivered to refineries.

In 1959, the petrocorporations were forced by world oil market conditions to do an about-face. Now there was so much cheap foreign oil that the abundance of supply threatened petro-profits. Big Oil argued that such a dependence on foreign oil represented a threat to national security. To make it economically feasible (profitable) to search for more domestic supply, mandatory controls over imported oil were declared a matter of patriotism. Congress responded with the 1959 Trade Agreement Act and cheaper foreign oil was imported at a level no higher than 12 percent of domestic production.

Finally, in 1973, with industry shortages already announced, the price of gasoline began to rise. When Egypt and Syria went to war with Israel in October of that year, the historical stage was set. OPEC met with the representatives of major oil companies two days after the war began to discuss a new world oil price structure. Formed in 1960, OPEC had heretofore taken absolutely nothing resembling a militant stand, even though Israel had been at war with Arab states during the 1960s. Nonetheless, OPEC raised the world price of crude 70 percent and cut off the United States completely. (Iran, Iraq, and Libya did not halt their oil exports). Industry profits soared and Big Oil came to dominate *Fortune* magazine's list of leading industrials. (Refer to Table 5–6 at the end of this Chapter). Today, the American Petroleum Institute, an organ of the oil corporations, is the primary source of information on oil supply and reserves. When the government wants such information, it must ask the industry. Despite the record of Big Oil intrigue, the manipulations of the past do not render conservation unimportant today. Increasingly, the corporate growth imperative is fueled by imported oil. This in turn is produced in areas of the Third World undergoing massive social change. Such dependence presents the constant threat of military intervention by U.S. Armed Forces. Conservation and a shift to renewable energy sources should be placed in the context of war and peace.

The Coal Trade-off

Any description of energy and its relationship to environmental trade-off must include a discussion of the "other" fossil fuel. As already noted, the nineteenth century's use of coal has largely been eclipsed by this century's enormous production of oil. Today it is coal in its abundance that is waiting to be used. Fully 33 percent of the world's coal supplies, some 437 billion tons, are in the United States, found from Alaska to Pennsylvania. If these reserves were used, enough energy would be produced to last this country some 300 years (*Time*, 1976, pp. 45–47).

Coal is somewhat similar to oil in that it is a high-carbon fuel and can be burned at high temperatures. Roughly 25 percent of the total energy produced in the United States comes from coal, which is used to generate electricity and provide heat and steam for industry. It is a virtual certainty that the energy demands of industrialized North America will cause the extensive exploitation of this once-scorned source of power; the burning of which will release dangerous pollutants into the atmosphere.

Seizing the coal from the earth requires one of two commonly known mining technologies. When the coal is buried beneath the surface, the underground mine is developed. More than two thirds of all coal miners in the United States work underground, producing some 50 percent of the nation's total coal output. From 10 to 20 percent of underground production comes from what is referred to as "low coal."

In a damp and mud-filled world, in areas often no more than three feet high and twenty feet wide, men work weary and stooped, breathing the icy air of low coal. They share their world with loud and angry machines that cut at the coal vein and sometimes human flesh. In the underground mine death is a constant companion, whether from the quick and terrifying cave-in or methane explosion, or the slow and more certain agony of black lung. The chilled workplace ensures the onset of arthritis and chronic back ailments. All these are endured by workers who often have no realistic economic alternative. Appalachia, for example, remains a rich land, a poor people, tied to the single industry of coal.

Underground mining carries evident environmental risks. Acid seepage, for example, presents the clear and present danger of ground water pollution. However, the more recent method of coal mining, in which huge power shovels strip away mountains, hills, and topsoil, carries other serious hazards. When the coal is removed, the strip mine is abandoned with the terrain all too frequently left a vast ecological wasteland. Despite recently enacted federal legislation requiring that land subject to strip mining be returned to its original *contours*, environmental damage is hardly undone. With the estimated costs of true reclamation ranging from $1,000 to $8,000 per acre, the economic incentive to leave the land wasted is immense (Commoner 1976). Also, returning land to its original contours does not ensure that it will sustain plant life or remotely resemble its prestrip condition. The land is the loser in another environmental trade-off.

The payoff in strip mining is easily understood. This technology recovers some 80 to 100 percent of the coal in a vein, compared with 40 to 60 percent for the underground alternative. From the vantage point of labor exploitation, the strip mine worker can extract three times as much coal as the underground miner. The enthusiasm of coal producers over expanding profits has not, as we have noted, created a great stampede toward land reclamation. Any impetus in this direction has been left to the federal government. However, the State's efforts have stopped short of requiring the mining industry to restore the earth. Other services have been forthcoming.

> In more recent years the federal government has assisted the mining industry by funding research for more efficient mining techniques, uses of coal, and gasification technology; by funding surveys to find strippable coal and low-sulphur coal; by restoring strip-mined lands and leasing federal coal lands to mining companies; by conducting economic studies on how to expand US coal exports; by taking over the unprofitable passenger part of the railroad business; and by passing legislation to ease miners' discontent (Ridgeway and Conner 1975, p. 46).

One should not conclude that the interest in coal is counter to the interests of the major oil corporations. To the contrary, Big Oil is in a position to become "Big Coal." The majors own almost one third of the proven coal reserves of the United States. Along these lines, Gulf Oil acquired Pittsburg and Midway Coal in 1963; Continental Oil bought Consolidated Coal (the world's largest) in 1965; and Occidental Petroleum bought Island Creek Coal in 1968. Exxon's coal holdings amount to 9 billion tons. By 1970, oil companies owned seven of the fifteen largest coal producers (Schneider 1978).

The Subtle Tyranny of Noise: Another Trade-off

In recent years, the environmental costs of an industrial-based, growth society have come to include destructive sound. Lately we have learned that the trade-off includes more than peace and quiet. When an older person demonstrates difficulty in hearing, it is not only a simple consequence of aging. Rather, he or she has lost hearing acuity partly due to the subtle, frequently ignored assault of noise.

The human ear is designed to detect the weak energy of sound vibrations and transform those vibrations into electrical signals that are then transmitted to the brain (Berland 1970). It is sensitive to the point that in an otherwise quiet setting the vibrations of a falling leaf can be detected. Today, modern industrial societies are more apt to generate the roar of aircraft, jackhammers, and traffic jams than the rustle of autumn leaves. The consequences of such din are not confined to hearing loss.

> Sound evokes much more than the sensation of hearing. The sound signal is transmitted, via the brain, to almost every nerve center and organ of the body. Therefore, sound influences not only the hearing center of the brain, but the entire physical, physiological, emotional and psychological makeup of the human being. The received sound wave evokes a combination of responses—auditory, intuitive, emotional, biological, associative. Sound's impact is a profound one (Baron 1970, p. 45).

What all this means is that when sound becomes noice, when the pleasant sounds of gentle breezes or flowing rivers or ocean surf become the jolting racket of sirens, diesel engines, and compressors, there will be undesirable psychological, physiological, and social consequences. Noise consists of both an objective and subjective dimension. Sound is noise when it damages the hearing mechanism. Sound is also noise when it disrupts communication, disturbs our sleep, interrupts our reading, intrudes on our sense of tranquility, and sends us diving beneath the pillows or to the aspirin bottle for relief.

The extent of noise pollution is difficult to determine. One disturbing factor is that people become noise habituated. In other words, the threshold for annoyance from sound can be raised. However, an increasing tolerance for noise does not mean that we avoid the consequences of destructive sound.

Solomon (1970) notes that peak noise levels in urban *residential* areas increased some 16 decibels between 1954 and 1967. (Decibel refers to a logarithmic unit of measure of sound pressure.) Experimental attempts to assess the impact of noise pollution suggest that this spiraling urban problem cannot be ignored. High-intensity noise produces autonomic stress reactions (such as increased blood pressure, respiration, glandular secretion), interferes with the execution of complex tasks, and is perceived as more annoying and disrupting than low-intensity noise. Noise that is unpredictable and difficult to control produces more stress than that which is predictable and subject to modulation. Such tensions tend to remain as residual aftereffects when the noise is muted. Thus, it seems that certain scientific evidence confirms what personal experience suggests: unpredictable and uncontrollable noise may be connected with aggression and irritability (Glass and Singer 1972).

Noise has been associated with a tendency to evaluate strangers negatively, the willingness to deliver more shocks to human subjects, and a decline in the frequency of helping others. Further, noise in urban environments is one of many contradictory inputs that overload the human capacity to respond fully and creatively. Stimulus overload produces dehumanizing adaptive responses causing its victims to disvalue the needs of others in order to concentrate on their own survival (Page 1977).

Destructive sound must be considered within a public health context. Certainly, there is more to health than freedom from disease. The World Health Organization employs a holistic conception of health, choosing to emphasize a state of well-being with obvious social-psychological dimensions. However, we need not focus exclusively on the relationship between noise and the less-tangible area of "life-quality." Noise stress increases the secretion of adrenalin, which in turn increases the amount of cholesterol in the bloodstream. Furthermore, exposure to noise results in increases in blood pressure. Blood vessels that undergo vasoconstriction (tightening) remain affected well after the noise is muted. It is not necessary to be conscious of noise. Noise stimuli will constrict blood vessels, change heart rate, and affect muscle tone without even awakening a sleeper (Baron 1970).

Noise pollution is as obvious factor in sleeping disturbance and deprivation. Sleep deprivation symptoms include itching, aches and pain, headaches, fatigue, visual irregularities, lack of concentration, lethargy and further disturbed sleep. In extreme cases, such deprivation produces the disturbance of the dream state (a condition associated with psychic abnormalities), memory lapses, hallucinations, and psychosis. The increasing market for tranquilizers, prescription sleeping pills, and "sleep aids" indicates that noise annoyance has become a commodity.

In short, noise is now recognized as an important cause of stress in our urbanized growth society. We know, for example, that there are complex-physiochemical reactions to stress. These include a hypersecretion of adrenalin, increased respiration, and a wide spectrum of cardiovascular changes designed to increase the probability of mastering or escaping the stress-inducing situation. However, this defensive stress reaction, when maintained on a constant or intensive level, can become a harmful condition. Adrenal glands can become enlarged, the lymph tissues tend to shrink, and the stomach and intestines may develop bleeding ulcers (Baron 1970).

The pernicious impact of destructive sound is not new to the experimental world.

> Years ago, investigators were looking for a standardized stressing agent, something that would consistently cause abnormalities in animals. By accident they discovered that noise could produce the

abnormalities they wanted; lesions in the urinary and cardiovascular systems, changes in the uteri and ovaries of female animals, alterations in the testicular structure of male animals. They also discovered that the acoustic stimulus could cause changes in the body's chemistry: an increased production of adrenal hormones, a decreased production of ovarian hormones, and other complex hormonal changes that influence fertility, growth, and other essential bodily functions (Baron 1970, p. 62).

Noise is a subtle tyranny, evidenced in adverse effects on health, tranquility, and social relationships. In a way, however, it is the not-so-obvious nature of noise pollution that renders it seductive and insidious. The Office of Noise Abatement of the Environmental Protection Agency has commissioned "noise surveys" to determine the attitudinal dimensions of this problem. In such surveys, the respondents commonly state that nothing can be done about the problem of destructive sound (Perdue 1979). The clear inference is that we must live with excessive noise. Supposedly, noise is the price that must be paid for progress in the corporate society. Such is another clear example of the specific ideology of the "trade-off."

As we have seen, ideology directs the way we view the environment crisis. Although the reader is encouraged to discover other accounts, we have identified those of "accident" and "trade-off." These "explanations" shape our point of view and may ultimately lead to a dismissal of the problem.

Where we are in society (in terms of class, sex, race) will shape the depth and breadth of our vision, our ability to establish connections between what appear to be separate events, and what we ultimately define as "good," "bad," or "ugly." The evaluation of plantation life can be expected to vary, depending on whether we view the world through the eyes of the master or the slave.

Our evaluations, however, are not conceived and developed in empty historical space. They do not follow automatically our position in the social order. Today, the communications revolution has accompanied the concentration of wealth and power. This historic connection has been described succinctly by an important modern sociologist.

> I cannot here describe the several great forces within American society as well as elsewhere which have been at work in the debilitation of the public. I want only to remind you that publics, like free associations, can be deliberately and suddenly smashed, or they can more slowly wither away. But whether smashed in a week or withered in a generation, the demise of the public must be seen in connection with the rise of centralized organizations, with all their new means of power, including those of the mass media of distraction (Mills 1963, p. 37).

All of this is to say that how we evaluate things embraces the most human of processes, the attachment of worth to events. Though our different positions in social structure *predispose* us toward different evaluations of the same reality, it does not follow that all members of a particular class will share the same views. In a similar fashion, different classes are exposed to the same powerful ideological institutions. For example, workers as well as the more affluent may blame environmental regulations for unemployment. In the fall of 1980, Anaconda Copper announced the closure of its operations in Anaconda, Montana, citing the cost of compliance with the Environmental Protection Agency's air quality regulations (Independent Record 1980). The corporation's smelting operation had already devastated the forests, vegetation, and pasture in the surrounding area, and the plant closure represented an economic disaster for the town of 10,000. Those among the affected workers who blamed "environmentalists" for their ills did not pose other questions which the reader might wish to entertain:

1. To what extent would Atlantic Richfield (ARCO), one of the world's largest petroleum corporations, benefit in the form of tax write-offs from the closure by their subsidiary, Anaconda Copper? [ARCO acquired Anaconda in 1977 (Moody's Industrial Manual 1980, p. 63)]. As in the case for the steel industry in particular, tax incentives reward corporations for closing down operations which are frequently profitable, yet not profitable enough (Brill 1980).

2. Should corporate ownership confer the right to severely damage the surrounding environment?

3. Should corporate ownership confer the right to threaten a local economy with collapse?

4. If Anaconda workers were in positions of shared control of the industry, would the environment be the same? Would the local economy be expendable?

Today, it is easy to complain about the absence of an informed public carrying on free debate on matters of great importance. The belief that such a public has ever existed may be an example of historical romanticism. But one thing is clear. To the extent that inequality exists in a society, to that extent political debate will reflect in microcosm that inequality.

People, Christians, and Engineers: Environmental Devils

Daily, human consciousness is influenced by a series of objective events that point silently yet eloquently to environmental hazards. Those in urban areas who breathe the searing combination of exhaust fumes and industrial combustion ash do not necessarily accept media campaigns or governmental pronouncements of "accidents" or "trade-offs." When the citizens of New Orleans are left to suffer the consequences of agricultural chemical runoff and the dumping of sewage into the Mississippi at northern points, the results for many are apparent and unacceptable. However, the vague sense that something is wrong is not an end unto itself. Our evaluation of environmental problems is shaped by the official view. The official view in turn reflects the general ideology of corporatism.

The consequence of such shaping will be the fragmentation of the "problem," which will thus be isolated, cut off from its structural roots. In large measure, this may be achieved through the creation of images that distort and simplify the environmental dilemma. The assault on the earth will not be explained as a logical consequence of commodity growth policies and practices. Rather, explanations will emphasize individual, not institutional, change. In the United States, to cite a recent example, a Native American has been transformed by television into a public relations commodity. In Indian dress and costume, the figure passes from surroundings of peace and beauty into a grim world of streams and land polluted by solid waste and air blackened by pollutants. As the Native American sheds a symbolic tear, the viewer is solemnly accused: "People start pollution. People can stop pollution."[3]

People Are The Culprits   One study reports the following responses to the question, "In your opinion, which one of the following statements best describes the basic cause of environmental degradation?"

	Percent
(a) Our society is preoccupied with economic growth and pays too little attention to environmental quality.	24.4
(b) The public is more concerned with convenience and comfort than with preservation of resources and prevention of pollution.	49.7
(c) As a socioeconomic system capitalism inevitably leads to exploitation and degradation of the environments.	7.2

[3] This "public service message" is produced by the Advertising Council, the members of which are solidly connected with the corporate world. (See Chapter Two.)

(d) Any society of 200 million with a high standard of living will face severe problems of avoiding environmental degradation.

18.8
_____
100%

(Bowman 1977, pp. 393–394)

These responses were not open-ended. Those answering the questions were required to select that item that most nearly represented their opinion. However, nearly one half of the respondents chose the imagery of a wasteful, prodigal public, and another 18.8 percent opted for the dual concerns of population size and life-style. Thus, nearly 70 percent of the sample selected the master symbols of "people" and "population"; 24.4 percent identified a "preoccupation" with growth. Only 7.2 percent saw a connection between ecological spoilage and capitalism. When one remembers that these respondents were university students, a population that is supposed to raise questions, the power of corporate ideology is obvious.

People are implored in media campaigns to "pitch in and clean up" North America, and the symbol of the citizen tossing waste into a receptacle appears on countless trash cans in urban areas. Stickers bearing messages to save energy and save jobs are placed on wall switches. Stores and industrial plants, quick to see the potential savings in utility bills, post highly visible notices that they are turning down thermostats to save energy. (One is compelled to observe that such public-spirited behavior is not evident when the issue of a progressive rate structure surfaces. At present, throughout most of North America, the largest commercial and industrial users of energy generally pay at a cheaper rate.) In today's environmentally conscious context, a popular commercial giveaway is the litter bag, complete, of course, with advertising.

It is hoped that a growing sensitivity to the use of such symbols may lead to the posing of larger questions: What is intended? What is implied? What is ignored? Who or what is to blame? It should be remembered that the symbols that shape our awareness are often "official" and bear the indelible stamp of wealth and power. In this sense, the making of social problems may involve distortion. The ecological crisis is a matter of "us," "them," "people." In a rare exercise of democracy, those who do not share the wealth or influence are left to share the blame.

The contention here is that the anonymous "people" will be subjected to much propaganda on environmental issues. While the purported intention of this is to inform and educate, the ideological consequence is to provide alternative "devils" that divert attention from the political economy of growth and find the "causes" of the environmental crisis in the habits, attitudes, and choices of the individual actor. The Department of the Interior (1968) and other agencies continually remind us that there are too many people living in crowded, noisy, and dirty conditions. The ugliness of life, the great waste, the decline of resources, the population explosion, a technology run amok are all systematically listed and deplored. It remains for citizens to then exercise "free choice" and refrain from polluting. This is supposed to spare us the fate of "dinosaurs" and "dodo birds."

C. Wright Mills (1943) reminded us that the early sociologists who wrote of the "pathologies" of a changing society had little understanding of the structure of social institutions. They were confined to a narrow recitation of facts representing a vast array of personal troubles. It is this same narrow bias that now characterizes the official statements on North American ecological problems.

In the official view, environmental enemy number one is portrayed as a "dirty animal." Though cunning and resourceful, the human group stands on the brink of too-rapid change. The unbridled forces of technology have produced more than the shock of blinding and rapid psychological adjustment.

> We cannot alter the past. At current speeds, the present becomes the past even as we set hand to it. At such speeds, our options for today are drastically narrowed. Only tomorrow can be dealt with.
>
> The technology to shape tomorrow is in our hands. What is still needed, and urgently, are the social and political means of giving intelligent direction to the awesome tools we have fashioned.
>
> The speed of change has introduced a new danger—the increasing role that chance plays in our human society and its interactions with the natural environment (US Department of Interior 1968, p. 9).

An analysis of the content of this and countless similar statements made frequently in North America reveals clearly the concerns. The danger is simply one of "change": too much and too soon. Our technology has outstripped the control of our social and political institutions. A disturbing by-product of such change is that it now moves exponentially, introducing the danger of "chance" catastrophe (Nuclear reactor accidents?). However, "we" can still seize control. "We" can still demonstrate the ingenuity and capabilities that have brought us through other perilous eras of history. It is "our" hand that is clearly on the throttle. "We" can halt the spoilage of water, land, and soil. According to Kenneth Boulding, our society can survive the perils of technology if it does not lose its "nerve." In the corporate society, individual will is expected to control environmental problems.

Perhaps no popular book on the emerging environmental problem affected the public consciousness in North America as did Rachel Carson's *Silent Spring* (1962). Carson conceptualized and worked on her book during the "quiet" decade of the fifties. Her work is graphically concerned with the often-ignored realities of the day: strontium 90, insecticides, pesticides, and the muted horrors of DDT. The book identifies synthetic chemical agents that stalk human life through the food chain, taking up permanent residence in the body tissue, leaving internal and external environments contaminated.

Carson called attention to practices that upset the balance of nature. She also pointed to contradictory state policies such as the Department of Agriculture's stimulation of chemical use in agriculture through paying farmers to remove acreage from planting. (Farmers simply used more chemicals to raise more crops on fewer acres.) But her work gives no systematic explanation of the social origins of this dilemma. It is as if reason alone will prevail, when reason is subordinate to power.

Also of popular and scholarly importance have been the works of Paul and Anne Ehrlich. During the Sixties and Seventies, these ecologists, blending the concerns of human population growth and biology, sounded the Malthusian alarm.[4] They argued that the "population bomb" threatened to explode as contaminated oceans and chemical-saturated land converted abundance to poison. It was to be only a matter of time before the haves turned against the have-nots in a bloody battle for survival (Ehrlich 1970).

The Ehrlichs employed a prophetic style in announcing a coming ecological doomsday. In so doing, they drew attention to the waste of industrial societies, coupled with the politics of chemical-induced abundance. In turn, these together generate more waste. In a world where the growing populations of the underdeveloped nations are often singled out as a threat to the human species, these authors lead their readers to the conclusion that population growth must be seen as strain on environmental resources. Undeniably, the greatest strain comes from the *developed* nations.

> In ecological terms, 22 million Canadians probably represent a drain on world resources equivalent through their high level of consumption to that of 400 million Indians; and this 22 million at our standard of living generate as much pollution as would 1 billion Indians. So, indeed, Canada and India are unequal (in ecological damage), but not in the reassuring manner many of us might imagine (Freeman 1974, p. 6; parentheses added).

When one chooses to emphasize population bombs, explosions, or some variations such as urban crowding, one may be led to the conclusion that the solution to a ravaged planet is the systematic distribution of contraceptives. However, the issue is not simply how many people but how much waste.

[4]Thomas Malthus (1766–1834) was an English writer who predicted that population left unchecked would clearly outdistance world food supplies.

The Army Corps of Engineers: A Devil Out of Context   If we are to believe government public service advertising, the enemy is us. For Rachel Carson, the devil was DDT and the chemical death rain it represented. For advocates of population control, people are in danger of reproducing themselves off the face of the earth. For former Justice of the United States Supreme Court William O. Douglas and the Sierra Club, the "devil" is embodied in the Army Corps of Engineers.

> But the Corps has no conservation, no ecological standards. It operates as an engineer, digging, filling, damming the waterways. And when it finishes, America the beautiful is doomed (Douglas 1969, p. 185).

The Army Corps of Engineers was created by an Act of Congress in 1802. It is the chief engineering consultant for the Congress of the United States. Further, it is entrusted with national navigation and flood control projects. In other words, the Corps builds dams, reservoirs, levees, and flood walls and dredges the sludge created by sewage and industrial waste from rivers and harbors to facilitate the movement of water traffic. Headed by an elite group of 200 military engineers, the Corps and its some 32,000 civilian workers are the chief beneficiaries of federal monies allocated for "water resource development."

> To their critics, the Engineers are mercenary pork-barrel soldiers, a simplification that nonetheless recognizes that the Corps is one popular conduit for the heavy flow of pork-barrel appropriations that annually emerge from Congress. . . . Pork-barrel projects infuse new federal money into constituencies, creating construction and service jobs, often producing large, continuing employment and payrolls . . . (Rosenbaum 1974, p. 173).

It is not the purpose here to exonerate the Army Corps of Engineers. However, *ideology makers frequently deal in the concrete, the apparent, and the immediate.* Despite the favorite standing of this ecological devil with many conservationist groups, it is vital to remember that the hallmark of sociological inquiry is *holistic* thought.

The Corps, like any bureaucratic organization, will be concerned with its own survival. In the language of this text, it is maintained through the construction of dams. But there are too many connections with other aspects of society to permit us to criticize the Corps in compartmentalized fashion. The sludge it dredges from rivers and harbors represents the industrial waste and sewage of a society choking on its own effluent. The dams it builds are advertised as a stimulus to the local economy, a source of jobs and tax revenues. The permits it gives to fill estuaries represent not only a boon to the National Sand and Gravel Association but to developers looking for new land on which to erect homes and shopping centers.

(Over one third of San Francisco Bay, more than 257 square miles, has been diked or filled for this purpose.) (Douglas, 1969) The Army Corps of Engineers cannot be understood in isolation.

Technological Change   Today, the Western world is caught up in the blinding reality of technological change. Humankind has entered an epoch of test tube babies, laser surgery, and communication satellites. Alvin Toffler's future shock scenario is played out on the front page and over the six o'clock news. The world is portrayed as slave to the gods of automation and cybernetics. In the words of Lewis Mumford, the power, the honor, and the glory belong to the machine.

> Just what are the changes that are reshaping the world, and what are their causes? In a somewhat restricted sense, the answer to the latter question is short and simple: science and technology . . . The motorcar has transformed living patterns, enabling the rise of the suburb and the decline of the city as it was thought of for centuries; the airplane has shrunk the globe and has transformed war; nuclear weapons and missiles have lifted general war from the category of rational policy; chemistry and genetics are transforming agriculture; modern medicine and public health are decreasing death rates and are increasing world populations; automation is transforming the job spectrum from production to service; television has added a new dimension to politics, and to entertainment, if that is the right word (Gomer 1968, p. 257).

It takes little imagination to find the technological "devil" in this presentation. The automobile, as we shall document later, *has* become an instrument for death and injury, energy depletion, and economic loss. The private transportation system, which makes it possible for suburbanites to escape the congestion of city life, leaves the urban core decaying, with a declining tax base and impoverished inhabitants. Atomic power raises not only the possibility of holocaust but the grim specter of accident as well. Better living through chemistry means polluted air and water. Fewer deaths mean a population increase as Planet Earth struggles to support over 4 billion hungry mouths. Automation becomes a means for increasing the unemployment rate. The mass media can be used to "sell" political leaders when not playing its customary role of a vast wasteland.

All of these things are true. What is ignored, however, is the simple truth that technology is context bound. According to Webster's *Third New International Dictionary*, technology is simply the science of the application of knowledge to practical problems. The *specific* knowledge we develop, and the *particular* problems we choose to identify and attempt to solve, have little to do with technology per se. The problem of the *uses* and *abuses* of applied knowledge is structural in origin. It is part of the fabric of master social institutions, and appears as a logical consequence of the way a society is organized.

In North America, the technological devil emerges as a distorted shadow of the corporate system. Otherwise, the technology misused by General Motors could be used to address the problems of public mass transportation. The technological capability that makes possible urban flight could become central to the planned reconstruction of our cities, a process that would leave workers near their work, consumers near the marketplace, and students close to learning centers. The technological genius that introduced the awesome power of atomic weapons could be used to develop renewable energy sources (solar, geothermal, wind). The agricultural know-how that overfeeds some and starves many could be used to meet the basic nutritional requirements of the global population. The technology that ensures unemployment for some could reduce the degree of disagreeable but necessary work for many. The technology that sells the candidate could create an electronic town hall and make the career politician extinct. In short, technology is more an instrument than a cause unto itself.

The Religious Factor   Our identification of ideologically created devils that shape our image of the ecological crisis would not be complete without some reference to a "supreme" symbol. In this case, the evaluational devil turns out to be Judaism and Christianity (Anderson 1976, pp. 119–120).

Much of the popular, official, and academic work on environmental problems looks at the cultural roots of the dilemma. A concern with the religious factor, as a cornerstone of culture, leads some to emphasize the coexistence of Western technology and Western religion. Given the assumption that cultural development determines the material course of a society, what follows is the posing of a causal relationship between the religious factor and the abusive use of technology (White 1967).

As an example of this line of reasoning, we note that the Book of Genesis sets forth an omnipotent God creating darkness and light, the earth and stars, plant and animal, man and woman (the latter as a kind of afterthought to provide "help" for the former). In a break from what are read today as environmental canons, God directed the man to dominate and master the earth.

> And God blessed them, and God said unto them, Be fruitful, and multiply, and replenish the earth, and subdue it, and have dominion over the fish of the sea, and over the fowl of the air, and over every living thing that moveth upon the earth (Genesis 1:28, King James version).

It appears that we have not only discovered the basis for environmental pillage, but also for the sexual exploitation of women. This observation leads to an important point. There is enough latitude in biblical and other accounts of the Judaic-Christian heritage to enable the reader to "discover" a blueprint for ecological crisis. One can also find in similar records an entirely different mandate. We need only recall the life and teachings of Saint Francis of Assisi, who sought communion with nature and all living things, to gain an alternative view of the "devil" at hand. Historically, however, we find that the religious tradition was far more central to certain tribal and feudal societies than to the modern industrial state. Abuses of technology appear pronounced in the most secular of societies. It is doubtful if those directing North American technological application today receive their direction from Genesis, St. Francis, or St. Matthew. Rather, they respond to the first law of the corporate order: grow or die.

EMERGENCE

While this text will emphasize the more recent history of the environmental movement, the concerns of "preservation and conservation" are of course more traditional (Albrecht 1976). In the closing decades of the nineteenth century in the United States, conservationists such as John Muir, who founded the Sierra Club in 1892, worked to publicize a "wilderness ethic." Certain interests of the preservationists were institutionalized in law.

> Numerous bills important to the conservationists were passed dur-
> this period. . . . The Yosemite National Park was set apart as a
> "forest reservation" in 1891. This was followed by several other
> national parks and wildlife refuges, the first of which was estab-
> lished on Pelican Island, Florida, in 1903. In 1907, the "forest
> reserves" became "national forests" with the name change indicat-
> ing, more than anything else, that these large tracts of land were
> now viewed as the continuing heritage of all the American people
> (Albrecht 1976, p. 153).

We wish to duly credit environmentalists past and present whose efforts have undoubtedly aided preservation. However, the environmental movement has been and continues to be context-bound. As the discussion which follows will show, neither the definitions of or solutions for the ecological problem are independent of corporate power and ideology.

It is vital to remember that the emergence phase represents a social problem in the process of becoming. The environmental movement emerged full-blown in the 1970s.

> After 40 years of private and public organizations' efforts to create
> continued interest and concern for improving the environment, a

national educational teach-in in April 1970 (Earth Day) renewed public awareness. As a result, schools gave released time for numerous student activities related to environmental conservation; the public media gave extensive news coverage to special environmental programs; politicians began to stake their careers on the issue, i.e., Senators Nelson and Muskie; scores of scholarly and journalistic books and articles appeared; textbooks were rewritten with emphasis on the problems of natural environment; hundreds of local groups formed to protect the local environment; even Saturday morning cartoon serials made efforts to support the cause . . . (Horsley 1977, p. 349).

The official launching of this reaction in the United States occurred in 1970, when President Nixon joined in to call for air and water purity and the reclamation of the living environment.

Critics noted the unfortunate timing of the resurgence of the environmental movement in the United States. It quickly threatened to capture center stage from a still-escalating war in Southeast Asia. The ecological movement was described far too harshly as a haven for the nondemonstrating, nonprotesting student membership of the "silent majority."[5] For example, Barry Weisberg argued in 1970 that the ecological movement was captive to the ideology of the corporate society. The original leadership was supposedly conventional, conformist, and confined to a fragmented view of eco-destruction. "They have virtually no critical understanding of the governments of oil, agri-business, public utilities, or chemicals."

The young conservationists who headed the government were often isolated from those advocating peace and women's and civil rights. Instead, they tended to reduce the ecological crisis to the level of individual action and private morality. Picking up litter replaced an assault on the twin pillars of the corporate system: planned obsolescence and conspicuous consumption promoted through a $43.7 billion (1978) a year advertising industry (*Statistical Abstract of the United States* 1979, p. 595). The movement stressed bicycles and a contempt for horsepower instead of analyzing the interdependencies of Exxon, General Motors, and the federal government.

> These tendencies were demonstrated too well by a recent selection of "youth" hand-picked by the Department of State to participate in the US Commission for UNESCO Conference on Man and His Environment in San Francisco last month. Virtually all "program" suggested by these participants lent credence to the status quo by advocating "better" candidates, new ecology colleges, yet additional "research," and more jobs for conservation-minded college kids (Weisberg 1970, p. 24).

[5] The "silent majority" was a term used by Richard Nixon to describe the supposed nondemonstrating masses who supported his policies. The term was also used by Homer. He referred to the dead.

We concur with Weisburg in that the State is most apt to favor those in a movement who do not rock the boat. The irony is that the ecological problem has outlived Vietnam as a public concern. However, concern is one thing. Structural analysis is quite another.

Before we understand the forces of history, we must ask whose interests are served by the movements seeking legitimacy. For any specific problem, there exists a range of alternate responses. The singling out of certain movements for media and official support is no different from the shaping of official ideology. In other words, one should expect to find *certain* environmental movements and efforts chosen for *legitimacy* by officialdom. The "chosen" will not be prone to emphasize the structural roots of ecological crisis and thus the need for structural change.

Although enjoying the limelight for the first time in the 1970s, the environmental movement is not so recent in origin (Barkley and Weissman 1970). Nor do we find the forces behind the movement to be only naturalist groups, the Sierra Club, or Weisberg's naive new conservationists. In the early part of the 1950s, the Ford Foundation established an organization known as Resources for the Future (RFF). In 1953, RFF arranged a major conservation conclave called the Mid-Century Conference. The conference was to embrace the policy on conservation developed by the Materials Policy Commission under the Truman Administration.

The joint policy of the Materials Policy Commission and the Mid-Century Conference called for *conservation through the extraction of raw materials from nations of the Third World.* Thus, in the 1950s, the notion of resources for future use meant how to go about ensuring that the wealth of the underdeveloped world would continue to aid the expansion of the corporate society. The "concern" for resource availability was expressed under the Eisenhower Administration in terms of access to the tin and tungsten of Southeast Asia. Conservation for some had come to mean entitlement to other people's resources (Barkley and Weissman 1970).

While the conservation movement of the Fifties was obsessed with resource scarcity, the succeeding decade found debate shifting to the unavoidable reality of pollution. It was argued that before the resources ran out, their conversion and refining would bury society in waste. Therefore, contrary to the doctrine of veto groups or countervailing power (which holds that government plays a watchdog role vis-à-vis big business), planners in organizations like Resources for the Future turned to the federal government. This action was not without historical precedent. Resource planners, at least of the established variety, chose as a blueprint the conservation movement that had flourished under the administration of Theodore Roosevelt. The hallmark of that movement had been the formulation of a cooperative alliance between the political and *monopoly* "trust" elite.

"The elite of business leadership," reports *Fortune*, "strongly desire the federal government to step in, set the standards, regulate all activities pertaining to the environment, and help finance the job with tax incentives." The congressional background paper for the 1968 hearings on National Policy on Environmental Quality, prepared with the help of Rockefeller's Conservation Foundation, spells out the logic in greater detail: "Lack of national policy for the environment has now become as expensive to the business community as to the Nation at large. In most enterprises a social cost can be carried without undue burden if all competitors carry it alike. For example, industrial waste disposal costs can, like other costs of production, be reflected in prices to consumers. But this becomes feasible only when public law and administration put all comparable forms of waste-producing enterprises under the same requirements" (Barkley and Weissman 1970).

Before "Earth Day" in the United States, before the establishment of the Environmental Protection Agency, before the discovery and enshrinement of Jacques Cousteau and the countless other symbols of environmental concern, the elite and their planners were busy in the fledgling movement. Flexible government regulations with soft deadlines were necessary to ensure that all competitors cleaned up their act, passing on the costs to consumers. The impact of such regulations could be expected to strangle only those smaller operations unable to afford the capital outlay for pollution control. Thus, the impact of environmental regulation was clearly to be a force in furthering corporate concentration.

Can Business Save Us?

One important impetus for the environmental movement in the Fifties and Sixties came not from those opposed to the corporate system; rather, it came from the planners, architects, designers, and controllers of that system. The head of the Materials Policy Commission under the Truman Administration was William S. Paley, Chairman of the Board of the Columbia Broadcasting System and a member of the first board of directors for Resources for the Future. Founder and major donor to the Conservation Foundation and a director of RFF was none other than Laurance Rockefeller. Rockefeller was also the chairperson of both the Citizens' Advisory Committee on Recreation and Natural Beauty and the White House Conference on Natural Beauty. President of the Conservation Foundation and director of the Task Force on Resources and Environment under the Nixon Administration was Russell Train, who became Undersecretary of the Interior (Barkley and Weissman 1970).

The interlocking directorates of the corporate world and the environmental movement set the stage for public involvement.

> Finally, the grass roots were given the word. RFF, Ford and
> Rockefeller (Foundations) had long worked with and financed the
> old-time conservation groups, from Massachusetts Audubon to the
> Sierra Club. . . . When . . . David Brower broke with the Sierra
> Club, it was Robert O. Anderson of Atlantic Richfield (now ARCO)
> and RFF who gave him $200,000 to set up Friends of the Earth
> (prudently channeling the donation through the organization's tax-
> exempt affiliate, the John Muir Institute) . . . When Senator Gay-
> lord Nelson and Congressman Pete McCloskey got around to pushing
> the National Teach-In, it was the Conservation Foundation, the
> Audubon Society and the American Conservation Association
> which doled out the money while Friends of the Earth was putting
> together the *Environmental Handbook*, meant to be the Bible of
> the new movement (Barkley and Weissman 1970, p. 21).

The environmental movement did not simply happen. Rather, it was at
least partially created and heavily financed by individuals and organizations having a strong interest in the preservation of the existing order.
What was to emerge as "the" movement of the Seventies, complete with
private and public backing, worked to legitimate corporate interests in
state policy. The foe was pollution, or the isolated polluter, or even the
Army Corps of Engineers. Unchallenged was the corporate economy and
its imperative of growth.

Atoms for Peace

As we have seen, the energy crisis is part and parcel of the ecological
problem. Perhaps a true test of the environmental concern of giant energy
corporations and the State can be made if we examine atomic power.

Until recently, the dominant imagery associated with the splitting of
the atom was captured in a terrifying mushroom cloud. After Hiroshima
was visited by the crew of the *Enola Gay* in August 1945, the Atomic
Energy Commission devoted its budget and efforts to research in and
development of atomic weaponry. This thrust was to remain intact until
1953, when the Eisenhower Administration redefined the atom's use as
"peaceful," a possible solution for energy needs.

Although nuclear power plants today account for little more than 4
percent of the nation's total energy supply, the Federal Energy Administration has glowingly described its potential as 15 percent of demand by
1985, and over 30 percent by the turn of the century (Commoner 1976).
The giant petrocorporations are fond of reminding us that they are energy
companies. Indeed, this is true, as Exxon's diversification embraces
ownership of gas, oil shale, coal, tar sands, and uranium, a pattern

repeated throughout the petroleum industry. What is clear is a corporate and state commitment to nuclear power.

Supported by the federal policy described above, the Atomic Energy Commission began to share nuclear technology and materials with power companies over the years. In the late 1970s, despite symbolic opposition from the Carter Administration, the United States Department of Energy sponsored a $641 million breeder reactor project[6] at the Hanford nuclear reservation in Washington State (Blumenthal 1980). While this reactor is technically not a plutonium-breeder, the breeder program is designed to bring on line exceptionally expensive commercial breeder reactors that produce plutonium. A piece of plutonium the size of a grain of pollen can produce cancer. It is also essential to the production of an atom bomb. Thus the increasing possibility of plutonium threat introduces still another nuclear hazard.

As Commoner (1976) argues, the "nuclear power system" is a far-flung operation spread widely throughout the United States. The uranium mines and refineries necessary to process the ore are located in the West. The conversion of uranium into the gaseous form, uranium hexafluoride, occurs in plants located in Illinois and Oklahoma. This form is used in the enrichment process carried on at Oak Ridge, Tennessee; Paducah, Kentucky; and Portsmouth, Ohio. (Enrichment means that reactor fuel is made from material in which the concentration of U-235 is increased from less than 1 percent to about 3 percent.) After enrichment, the uranium travels to approximately a dozen fuel-rod fabrication plants. (The fuel rods are capable of setting off a fission chain reaction in the nuclear reactor.) The fuel then travels to over seventy reactors spread throughout the United States. The transportation of such materials is done by truck and railroad car.

When the nuclear fuel is spent, fuel rods must be replaced in the reactor. The process of producing nuclear energy concludes with the attempt to recover the remaining uranium-235 and plutonium-239. After reprocessing, highly radioactive waste remains to be stored. Adequate facilities for the permanent and safe storage of materials that remain lethal for some 200,000 years simply do not exist (Commoner 1979, p. 53). Thus, today's storage of nuclear waste will be a legacy haunting future generations.

A final point with regard to nuclear energy should be made. Various statistical estimates of the probability of a cataclysmic nuclear accident have been produced. Even the more pessimistic ones seem reassuring, at least to people who have learned to consider a holocaust in terms of their personal chances of survival. Rather than reciting the enormous range in estimates for the probability of a massive nuclear reactor accident, it seems pertinent to draw from the record of history that the probability of avoiding death from atomic attack has been extremely good.

[6]A breeder reactor is so named because it "breeds" or produces more fuel than it uses.

To this point in time, only some 110,000 people out of an estimated total "all-time" world population of perhaps 100 billion have lost their lives to nuclear weapons. Such are good "odds," approximately a million to one.

The point is that probability estimates have a way of denying, or at least distorting, horrors that perhaps should remain indelibly etched into the human conscience. The historical odds against atomic death are of little comfort to the survivors of Hiroshima and Nagasaki and their children, to whom statistically improbable leukemia has been passed.

Despite a posture of assurance, the federal government's action speaks louder than its words. The Nuclear Regulatory Commission has an established policy banishing nuclear reactors from densely populated regions. Further,

> The Congress has acknowledged that the risk of huge losses from a reactor accident is so great as to require insurance backed by the wealth of the US Treasury. When the first reactors were built, no private insurance company—or combination of them—was willing to provide the amount of insurance that the power companies wanted. As a result, Congress passed the Price-Anderson Act, which enables the government to insure against the costs of a reactor accident up to the sum of $560,000,000 (Commoner 1976, p. 97).

Critics charge that 560 million dollars would be woefully inadequate to cover the cost of nuclear disaster.

Three Mile Island: Children Playing in the Woods

On Wednesday, March 28, 1979, at 3:54 A.M. what was to become a nuclear nightmare began to unfold. At the Three Mile Island nuclear facility in Pennsylvania, TMI Unit 2 suffered an "accident." A valve failure blocked a cooling system necessary to prevent the uranium core from overheating. The emergency pumps designed to cut in and bypass the defective valve did not work because weeks earlier, in direct violation of safety regulations, someone had closed their flow vents. The failure of a second valve resulted in the escape of thousands of gallons of water necessary to cool the reactor. As the temperature began to build and the water level dropped, parts of the reactor's fuel rods were exposed. The exposure represented the beginning of what is known as the "China syndrome" a core meltdown.[7] However, in the TMI control room faulty gauges indicated that the water level was returning to normal and that the problem was being solved by back-up safety systems. Five minutes after the "incident" began, the fuel rods began to crack.

[7] In theory, the reactor core could melt through the walls of the reactor vessel, through the floor of the containment vessel, and into soil and water.

Control operators discovered the defective valve that allowed the escape of highly radioactive water. It was shut but the escaped water later gave rise to radioactive gases that were pumped into the atmosphere by the plant's air-conditioning system. At 7:00 A.M., Metropolitan Edison, the owners and operators of the Three Mile Island plant, informed the federal Nuclear Regulatory Commission (NRC), civil defense authorities, and the Governor of Pennsylvania. Metropolitan Edison officials used the term "incident" and a vice-president indicated that the accident was not serious. At the same time, an investigator for the Nuclear Regulatory Commission dutifully repeated the utility corporation's assurances. He described the reactor as stable and safe (*New York Times* 1979).

As events of the next few days unfolded, their grim reality contradicted the early assurances from both Metropolitan Edison and the NRC. Simply put, the damaged reactor did not cool down as predicted. Experts warned of cancer, genetic defects, and other "lag" effects of exposure to the radioactive gases being periodically released into the atmosphere. More ominous was the continuing threat of a reactor gone amok, erupting radioactive waste into the surrounding area (*Newsweek* 1979).

By the middle of the afternoon on Friday, March 30, the damaged core was only one of the major problems. A hydrogen bubble in the top of the reactor began to form in response to the intense heat. With the bubble came the distinct possibility of an explosion. Before the end of the day, over 100,000 people had left the area of the reactor. Through it all, Metropolitan Edison denied the seriousness of the problem, declaring on March 31 that the crisis was over (*New York Times* 1979). Massachusetts Institute of Technology professor Henry Kendall commented on the assembled public and private troubleshooters called in to solve a problem for which there was no precedent: "They are way out in an unknown land with a reactor whose instruments and controls were never designed to cope with this situation. They are like children playing in the woods" (*Newsweek* 1979, p. 24).

Perhaps the most telling commentary on the dimensions of the TMI episode come from the transcripts of the "continuous session" called by the Nuclear Regulatory Commission on March 30 (*Nuclear Regulatory Commission Transcripts of Three Mile Island* 1979). Some of the dialogue is reproduced below. We will offer no comment except to note that the Nuclear Regulatory Agency is the federal agency chartered with the establishment and enforcement of safety regulations for nuclear power plants.

March 30, 1979

". . . I just had a call from my guy in the Governor's office and he says the Governor says the information he is getting from the plant is ambiguous, that he needs some recommendations from the NRC.

(Response) It is really difficult to get the data. We seem to get it after the fact. They opened up the valves this morning, or the let-down, and were releasing at a six curie per second rate before anyone knew about it" (p. 5).

"But the people at the site are obviously much better to direct and run emergency plans than we are. . . . It just seems like we are always second, third hand; second guessing them. We almost ought to consider the Chairman talking to the owner of the shop up there and get somebody from the company who is going to inform us about these things in advance if he can and then what he is doing about it if he can't. We seem not to have that contact" (p. 9).

"But you still think it is not necessary or reasonable to order a precautionary evacuation, just on the event that we have more bursts?" (p. 28, question from Governor Thornburgh by phone)

"I think it would be just as well to wait until we know that they are going to have to make some kind of a water transfer, that there may be a release . . ." (Response, p. 28).

"I talked to the Governor just a few minutes ago, and recommended to him that since it is uncertain about the continuing release, possible bursts and so on, that a precautionary evacuation of preschool kids and pregnant women and so could usefully go on . . ." (p. 39).

"All right, there was an uncontrolled release of radioactive material earlier today, we are not certain of the duration. It appears to us that it has stopped."

"Don't we know that it has been stopped?"

"Vice-President Herbein of the Company reports it has been stopped" (p. 46).

(Later, discussion turned to the subject of the hydrogen bubble that threatened an immediate disaster.)

"First of all, an explosion is not a guaranteed (inaudible) and it may or may not be enough hydrogen to get you to a flammable mixture in the containment unless it is trapped in a small volume" (p. 73).

"So the horse race you got, at this point, the hydrogen would be all that would be going out the two-inch power operated relief valve on the pressurizer and a two-inch wide isn't very big. It would take a lot of time to pass a lot of gas through a two-inch line" (p. 76).

"If you would rather go with one of these maneuvers right now, I would want you to move people as far as you felt comfortable moving them. . . . I must say to you, I have been recommending moving people since about four hours ago" (Dr. Mattson, pp. 28–83).

"Well, my principal concern is that we have got an accident that we have never been designed to accommodate, and it's in the best estimate deteriorating slowly, and the most pessimistic estimate it is on the threshold of turning bad. And I don't have a reason for not moving people. I don't know what you are protecting by not moving people" (Dr. Mattson, p. 84).

"The Chairman is going to be back here pretty soon and we are going to figure out what we are going to do" (p. 84).

"John, what is the status of evacuation plans in this area? I presume these are state plans. Suppose one did say right now that we ought to execute evacuation. Are there plans that would be put into effect or what would happen?"

"The evacuation is, as we understand it, under the control of the state."

"Sure, but do you know what plans they might be exercising or is it sort of everyone on his own, jumping into his car, and clogging the highways?" (p. 86).

"Let's see, Harrisburg is in which county? Yes, there are a lot of little towns around there. . . . I would say they ought to be able to get all the small towns in the counties and the local folks out within an hour, and probably certainly have the city cleared by two. . . . I'm estimating, since I don't live there, I really don't know. You know. It's a difficult question, Commissioner" (p. 96).

"Are they thinking just about a limited, a sort of sector evacuation, or can they handle something a little larger?"

"Well, you know, if the balloon went up, they would do the whole thing . . ." (p. 98).

". . . the core damage is considerably more extensive than we had thought yesterday . . ." (p. 122).

"It is a predicament where the Governor does not know what he is saying" (p. 138).

"We've got Harold Denton on the site down there talking to the press right now. We have been coordinating through Jody Powell (President's Carter's Press Secretary) and the agreement at the moment is that we are trying to avoid a two-headed press conference where people are down there taping Harold and then rush up here and prepare tapes of what I say or somebody would say up here" (NRC Chairman Hendrie, p. 146).

"Well, Dick, we've been sitting here for the longest time telling them everything's fine. It's a real struggle, with what to do. There's none of that flavor here. . . ."

"Well, I understand what you're saying; I'm worried about the effect that you're going to get; it's going to be hyped by a factor of a hundred. The question is how to phrase it. . . . You could put a little sentence in right there after expand to say . . . in the unlikely event that this occurred, increased temperatures would result and possibly further fuel damage" (pp. 177–78).

The transcripts reveal a series of other telling deliberations. On Saturday, March 31, the possibility of a core meltdown continued under discussion with the observation that though "not a very large possibility," a hydrogen explosion might occur that would breach the structure housing the reactor. Dr. Mattson's remarks are again significant.

> Let me say, as frankly as I know how, bringing this plant down is risky. . . . No plant has ever been in this condition, no plant has ever been tested in this condition, no plant has ever been analyzed in this condition in the history of the program (Burnham 1979).

Space does not permit a detailed analysis of the "accident" at TMI. On Sunday, April 1, 1979, the hydrogen bubble began to shrink. No action taken by the assembled experts had any proven effect on that occurrence. The TMI episode had resulted from mechanical and human failure and provides evidence of an obviously less than safe nuclear technology. Its end was due only to the vicissitudes of nature. According to official sources, no one died at Three Mile Island. However, the health consequences (especially fetal and infant damage) will not be apparent in the near future. We do have increasing knowledge that low-level radiation, one source of which is nuclear power plants, is dangerous; perhaps more damaging over time than large doses delivered at one time (Pawlick 1980).

More than 2,300 "incidents," including mechanical failure and operational errors, at American nuclear power plants were reported to the Nuclear Regulatory Commission in 1979, according to *Critical Mass*, a Ralph Nader affiliate (*Spokesman-Review* 1980). An Associated Press task force counted 2,835 such occurrences in 1978 (*Spokesman-Review*, 1979). The locations of American nuclear power reactors are listed in Table 5–2. The overwhelming majority came on line in the 1970s. The massive level of corporate and state investment seems to indicate that the commitment to nuclear energy will not suffer as a consequence of the near catastrophe at Three Mile Island.

INSTITUTIONALIZATION

In this phase, formal political processes work to identify in policy and in law problematic concerns. Legislation will be passed, regulatory or control agencies will be created, and an official definition will be formally adopted. Once a particular version of the problem is thus legitimated, those with opposing views appear "out of it." Thus, debate is seriously restricted. Further, and most important, institutionalization may reveal that a social problem has been defined in a "safe" way. If so, then it can no longer represent a threat to the existing order. In a logical continuance of our earlier argument, we will examine the possibility that the interests of those who control the corporate system are indeed mirrored in law and program action.

In the United States, President Richard M. Nixon took a definitive

TABLE 5-2

ENERGY

Nuclear Power Reactors in the United States

State	Site	Plant name	Capacity (kilowatts)	Utility	Commercial operation
Alabama	Decatur	Browns Ferry Unit 1	1,065,000	Tennessee Valley Authority	1974
	Decatur	Browns Ferry Unit 2	1,065,000	Tennessee Valley Authority	1975
	Decatur	Browns Ferry Unit 3	1,065,000	Tennessee Valley Authority	1977
	Dothan	Joseph M. Farley Unit 1	829,000	Alabama Power Co.	1977
	Dothan	Joseph M. Farley Unit 2	829,000	Alabama Power Co.	1979
Arkansas	Russellville	Arkansas Unit 1	850,000	Arkansas Power & Light Co.	1974
	Russellville	Arkansas Unit 2	912,000	Arkansas Power & Light Co.	1978
California	Eureka	Humboldt Bay Unit 3	63,000	Pacific Gas & Electric Co.	1963
	San Clemente	San Onofre Unit 1	430,000	So. Calif. Ed. & San Diego Gas & El. Co.	1968
	Diablo Canyon	Diablo Canyon Unit 1	1,084,000	Pacific Gas & Electric Co.	1977
	Diablo Canyon	Diablo Canyon Unit 2	1,106,000	Pacific Gas & Electric Co.	1978
	Clay Station	Rancho Seco Station	918,000	Sacramento Munic. Utility District	1975
Colorado	Platteville	Ft. St. Vrain Station	330,000	Public Service Co. of Colorado	1977
Connecticut	Haddam Neck	Haddam Neck	575,000	Conn. Yankee Atomic Power Co.	1968
	Waterford	Millstone Unit 1	652,000	Northeast Nuclear Energy Co.	1971
	Waterford	Millstone Unit 2	828,000	Northeast Nuclear Energy Co.	1975
Florida	Florida City	Turkey Point Unit 3	693,000	Florida Power & Light Co.	1972
	Florida City	Turkey Point Unit 4	693,000	Florida Power & Light Co.	1973
	Red Level	Crystal River Unit 3	825,000	Florida Power Corp.	1977
	Ft. Pierce	St. Lucie Unit 1	810,000	Florida Power & Light Co.	1976
Georgia	Baxley	Edwin I. Hatch Unit 1	786,000	Georgia Power Co.	1975
Illinois	Morris	Dresden Unit 1	200,000	Commonwealth Edison Co.	1960
	Morris	Dresden Unit 2	794,000	Commonwealth Edison Co.	1970
	Morris	Dresden Unit 3	794,000	Commonwealth Edison Co.	1971
	Zion	Zion Unit 1	1,040,000	Commonwealth Edison Co.	1973
	Zion	Zion Unit 2	1,040,000	Commonwealth Edison Co.	1974
	Cordova	Quad-Cities Unit 1	789,000	Comm. Ed. Co.-Ia.-Ill. Gas & Elec. Co.	1972
	Cordova	Quad-Cities Unit 2	789,000	Comm. Ed. Co.-Ia.-Ill. Gas & Elec. Co.	1972
	Seneca	LaSalle County Unit 1	1,078,000	Commonwealth Edison Co.	1979
Iowa	Palo	Duane Arnold Unit 1	538,000	Iowa Electric Light and Power Co.	1975
Maine	Wiscasset	Maine Yankee	790,000	Maine Yankee Atomic Power Co.	1972
Maryland	Lusby	Calvert Cliffs Unit 1	845,000	Baltimore Gas & Electric Co.	1975
	Lusby	Calvert Cliffs Unit 2	845,000	Baltimore Gas & Electric Co.	1977
Massachusetts	Rowe	Yankee Station	175,000	Yankee Atomic Electric Co.	1961
	Plymouth	Pilgrim Unit 1	655,000	Boston Edison Co.	1972
Michigan	Big Rock Point	Big Rock Point	72,000	Consumers Power Co.	1965
	South Haven	Palisades Station	668,000	Consumers Power Co.	1971
	Bridgman	Donald C. Cook Unit 1	1,054,000	Indiana & Michigan Electric Co.	1975
	Bridgman	Donald C. Cook Unit 2	1,060,000	Indiana & Michigan Electric Co.	1978
Minnesota	Monticello	Monticello	545,000	Northern States Power Co.	1971
	Red Wing	Prairie Island Unit 1	530,000	Northern States Power Co.	1973
	Red Wing	Prairie Island Unit 2	530,000	Northern States Power Co.	1974
Nebraska	Fort Calhoun	Ft. Calhoun Unit 1	457,000	Omaha Public Power District	1973
	Brownville	Cooper Station	778,000	Nebraska Pub. Power Dist.-IA. Power & Light Co.	1974
New Jersey	Toms River	Oyster Creek Unit 1	650,000	Jersey Central Power & Light Co.	1969
	Salem	Salem Unit 1	1,090,000	Public Service Electric & Gas, N.J.	1977
	Salem	Salem Unit 2	1,115,000	Public Service Electric & Gas, N.J.	1979
New York	Indian Point	Indian Point Unit 1	265,000	Consolidated Edison Co.	1962
	Indian Point	Indian Point Unit 2	873,000	Consolidated Edison Co.	1973
	Indian Point	Indian Point Unit 3	873,000	Power Authority of State of N.Y.	1976
	Scriba	Nine Mile Point Unit 1	610,000	Niagara Mohawk Power Co.	1969
	Ontario	R.E. Ginna Unit 1	490,000	Rochester Gas & Electric Co.	1970
	Brookhaven	Shoreham Station	819,000	Long Island Lighting Co.	1979
	Scriba	James A. Fitzpatrick	821,000	Power Authority of State of N.Y.	1975
North Carolina	Southport	Brunswick Steam Unit 1	821,000	Carolina Power & Light Co.	1977
	Southport	Brunswick Steam Unit 2	821,000	Carolina Power & Light Co.	1975
	Cowans Ford Dam	Wm. B. McGuire Unit 1	1,180,000	Duke Power Co.	1979
Ohio	Oak Harbor	Davis-Besse Unit 1	906,000	Toledo Edison-Cleveland El. Illum. Co.	1977
	Moscow	Wm. H. Zimmer Unit 1	810,000	Cincinnati Gas & Electric Co.	1979
Oregon	Prescott	Trojan Unit 1	1,130,000	Portland Gen. Electric Co.	1975
Pennsylvania	Peach Bottom	Peach Bottom Unit 2	1,065,000	Philadelphia Electric Co.	1974
	Peach Bottom	Peach Bottom Unit 3	1,065,000	Philadelphia Electric Co.	1974
	Shippingport	Shippingport Station	90,000	U.S. Energy Research & Devel. Admin.	1975
	Shippingport	Beaver Valley Unit 1	852,000	Duquesne Light Co.-Ohio Edison Co.	1977
	Middletown	Three Mile Island Unit 1	819,000	Metropolitan Edison Co.	1974
	Middletown	Three Mile Island Unit 2	906,000	Jersey Central Power & Light Co.	1978
South Carolina	Hartsville	H.B. Robinson Unit 2	712,000	Carolina Power & Light Co.	1971
	Seneca	Oconee Unit 1	887,000	Duke Power Co.	1973
	Seneca	Oconee Unit 2	887,000	Duke Power Co.	1974
	Seneca	Oconee Unit 3	887,000	Duke Power Co.	1974
Tennessee	Daisy	Sequoyah Unit 1	1,148,000	Tennessee Valley Authority	1978
	Daisy	Sequoyah Unit 2	1,148,000	Tennessee Valley Authority	1979
	Spring City	Watts Bar Unit 1	1,177,000	Tennessee Valley Authority	1979
Vermont	Vernon	Vermont Yankee Station	514,000	Vt. Yankee Nuclear Power Corp.	1972
Virginia	Gravel Neck	Surry Unit 1	822,000	Virginia Electric & Power Co.	1972
	Gravel Neck	Surry Unit 2	822,000	Virginia Electric & Power Co.	1973
	Mineral	North Anna Unit 1	907,000	Virginia Electric & Power Co.	1977
	Mineral	North Anna Unit 2	907,000	Virginia Electric & Power Co.	1977
Washington	Richland	N-Reactor/WPPSS Steam	850,000	U.S. Energy Research & Devel. Admin.	1966
Wisconsin	La Crosse	Genoa Unit 1	50,000	Dairyland Power Cooperative	1969
	Two Creeks	Point Beach Unit 1	497,000	Wisconsin-Michigan Power Co.	1970
	Two Creeks	Point Beach Unit 2	497,000	Wisconsin-Michigan Power Co.	1973
	Carlton	Kewaunee Unit 1	535,000	Wisconsin Public Service Corp.	1974

Nuclear plant capacity (kilowatts): operable 47,606,000; being built 95,308,500; planned 87,914,000; Total 230,828,500.

Source: *World Almanac and Book of Facts*, Newspaper Enterprise Association, 1979, p. 112.

move toward the institutionalization of the "environmental problem" when he established a Cabinet-level Environmental Quality Council in May 1969. Such a political creation was greeted with some skepticism by those who wanted an independent body on environmental matters. Congressional enactment of the National Environmental Policy Act of 1969 resulted in the abolition of the Cabinet-level Council and the establishment of a Domestic Council in the Executive Office of the President.

The National Environmental Policy Act also laid the groundwork for national policy on the environment. Federal agencies were charged to consider the environmental consequences of executing law and implementing decisions. Further, the Council on Environmental Quality was empowered to make recommendations to the President, conduct environmental investigations, monitor environmental protection standards, and oversee the trends of technological development.

Also in 1970, the Nixon Administration established the Environmental Protection Agency (EPA). Charged with the control of pollution, EPA represented the consolidation of the management of some fifteen federal agencies concerned with environmental control. This particular agency became responsible for pollution control standards, and was equipped with enforcement powers. Further, it was chartered to coordinate protective standards at the state and local level through grants and technical assistance.

While the war in Southeast Asia continued to build, and while student leaders were planning their own spring peace offensive, the political decision makers in the United States had decided to wage a quieter battle. In a way, the environmentalists who warned that the ecological battle would prove far more troublesome than any shooting war were right. The ecological crisis produced a vigorous official response. However, the nature of that response was and continues to be a reflection of the structural realities of North American society.

One aspect of the environmental problem concerns the production and distribution of energy. As a consequence of both the long-term waste associated with the exponential growth in energy use in the corporate economy, together with the short-run Arab oil embargo, a gigantic energy establishment has emerged. As of 1974 in the United States, some 300 federal bureaus, 35 congressional committees, and 450 agencies of state government were involved. Also included were the hundreds of professional, trade, and citizen associations, along with the energy coordinators of the oil and gas companies, electric utilities, coal companies, and 385 of the *Fortune* 500 leading corporations (*Energy Directory* 1975). While one institutional agency operated under the political mandate of environmental protection, a parallel development saw the coming together of a powerful alliance dedicated to the politics of the existing order (in other words, energy "abundance").

Ideology Revealed in Legislation and Enforcement

An examination of environmental legislation should reveal the ideological constraints on the institutionalization of the ecological crisis. For example, the 1970 Clean Air Act established two major deadlines for the control of pollutants. By July 1975, the amount of air pollution was to be reduced so that health was no longer damaged. By July 1977, air pollution was no longer to threaten vegetation, property, or aesthetic qualities (Klein and Leung 1976).

Observers noted that these dates passed to the sounds of silence. Congress amended the Clean Air Act in August 1977, giving the auto manufacturers until 1981 to reach the auto exhaust standards set for 1976. If that date is not amended further, it will be in the 1990s before present polluters are off the road.[8] The same amendments delayed industry compliance until 1980, state compliance until 1982, and compliance for some cities until 1987. At this writing, only Honolulu has met air quality standards in the United States (Rowse 1978, pp. 503–504).

Water standards received federal attention with the passage of the Federal Water Pollution Control Act of 1972, amended by the Clean Water Act passed in December 1977. The 1977 law was advertised as a means of improving the enforcement standards of the EPA (the limit on civil penalties is $5 million, with mandatory cleanup costs of up to $50 million). However, the reluctance of the agency to move against polluters in the past, due to budgetary limitations and a policy of "cooperation," suggests that the Clean Water Act is more ceremonial than substantive. Hundreds of chemical "accidents" occur annually, such as the massive spill of carbon tetrachloride into the Ohio River in February 1978, threatening the water supply of millions.

The Clean Water Act of 1977, like its Clean Air counterpart, represents the politics of delay.

> For industries, the 1977 Clean Water Act extends to July 1984, the deadline for applying the "best available technology (BAT) economically achievable" to reduce pollution of substances controlled by EPA. . . . But for all other pollutants—the vast majority . . . BAT must be applied no earlier than 1984 and no later than 1987.
>
> Industries can escape controls for these pollutants altogether or apply weaker controls if they can demonstrate to the EPA that their pollution will not prevent recreational activities, decimate fish populations or cause "unacceptable" health risk (Rowse 1978, p. 500).

[8]In response to a massive recession in the automotive industry, President Carter promised to ease environmental regulations in the summer of 1980. The recession was in part a consequence of the rapid rise in the cost of gasoline in concert with the failure of the U.S. automotive industry to convert early to the production of fuel efficient cars. Thus a slackening demand was primarily met by foreign producers.

Also threatening coastal and inland waters is the increasing incidence of oil spills from tankers. In 1977, some 4,000 ships transported 11 billion gallons of crude oil. The tanker crisis is a direct consequence of the market decisions of multinational corporations that freely secure construction materials in one country, labor in another, and register the ship in a nation where inspection is slack. These decisions are made on a purely economic basis. Thus, a number of tanker spills and accidents have involved ships registered in Liberia, where inspection and safety regulations are lax. In spite of this obvious negligence, the United States government and private business are, at the time of this writing, proposing the construction of the largest United States onshore oil port in the virgin waters of Port Angeles, Washington, Equipped with the carrot of jobs and business dollars, the sellers of this project play down the risks. An environmental report by Northern Tier Pipeline Co., the United States approved industry consortium, estimates a major tanker spill of some 48,000 barrels of crude on the average of every 3.6 years. This would pour about 2 million gallons of oil into the ocean and onto the beaches. However, representatives of the consortium argue this fails adequately to consider better safety precautions they will employ, a claim that has a familiar ring to it (Tofler 1980).

Table 5–3 provides the name and registry of some supertankers. Many Liberian tankers bear the name "Esso," better known in the United States as "Exxon."

Congress passed the Noise Control Act in 1972. Despite the fact that some 16 million citizens of the United States have impaired hearing, with some 98 million more in noisy cities facing the same fate, federal funds spent on noise abatement research declined to $28 million in 1977, only about 50 percent of the total expended four years earlier.

The responsibility for enforcing the Noise Control Act of 1972 has fallen to the Office of Noise Abatement and Control of the Environmental Protection Agency. EPA is charged with the systematic reduction of destructive sound in the United States. Notwithstanding, this objective has proven remote, given the interplay between agencies of government control and the industry to be regulated. For example, EPA's standards call for a significant reduction in aircraft noise. However, the airlines claim that such standards are not economically feasible. The Federal Aviation Administration agrees with the airlines. The Environmental Protection Agency to date has not pressed the airlines. Consequently, the "friendly skies" are filled with shock waves (Rowse 1978, pp. 508–509).

Another example of the institutionalization of the environmental problem is to be found in Public Law 95–87, an act entitled Surface Mining Control and Reclamation Act of 1977. This long-awaited piece of environmental legislation provides a lesson in the politics of pollution. In the "statement of findings and policy," Public Law 95–87 (Section 101) declares that "surface coal mining constitutes one method of extracting" coal, but that most of this source of energy "can only be extracted by

TABLE 5-3
Oil Tankers

Name	Registry
Pierre Guillaumat	France
Bellamya	France
Batillus	France
Esso Atlantic	Liberia
Esso Pacific	Liberia
Nissei Maru	Japan
Globtik London	Britain
Globtik Tokyo	Britain
Esso Mediterranean	Liberia
Berge Empress	Norway
Hilda Knudsen	Norway
Esso Deutschland	W. Germany
Al Rekkah	Kuwait
Berge Emperor	Norway
Jinko Maru	Japan
Chevron So. America	Liberia
Aiko Maru	Japan
Chevron No. America	Liberia
Golar Patricia	Liberia
Coraggio	Italy
Esso Japan	Liberia
David Packard	Liberia
Esso Tokyo	Liberia
Bonn	W. Germany
Shat-Al Arab	Iraq
Wahran	Algeria
Esso Madrid	Liberia
Esso Caribbean	Liberia
Berlin	Liberia
Brazilian Hope	Liberia
Bremen	Liberia
Jamada	Norway
Esso Le Havre	Panama
Titus	Norway
Brazilian Pride	Liberia
Brazilian Splendour	Liberia
Nisseki Maru	Liberia
Nisseki Maru	Liberia
Al Andalus	Kuwait
La Santa Maria	Spain

Source: *Lloyd's Register of Shipping* as of August 25, 1978.

underground mining methods." Furthermore, it is "essential to the national interest to insure the existence of an *expanding and economically healthy underground coal* mining industry" (italics added).

The language is clear. In an act supposedly designed to protect the environment from the ravages of *surface* mining, we find a mandate to ensure the economic health and well-being of the underground mining industry. Such a concern with the welfare of the industry is evidenced in Section 516 (b) (11), which requires the underground operator "to the *extent possible* using the best technology *currently available, [to] minimize* disturbances and adverse impacts of the operation on fish, wildlife and related environmental values, and achieve enhancement of such resources *where practicable*" (italics added).

In other words, if it is possible with existing technology to "minimize" environmental damage, one must do so. If it is not possible, or if the technology is not developed or adequate, then the operator cannot be found out of compliance. The "catch," however, is in the term "minimize." The literal meaning is to make smaller. How much "minimizing" shall the underground operator be required to do? That is the unanswered question.

Sections 502(f), (k), and (l) of this legislation represent the curious unification of environmental protection and energy expansion. The first declares that a balance must be struck "between protection of the environment and agricultural productivity" on the one hand, and "the nation's need for coal as an essential source of energy" on the other. Section 502(k) calls for the "full utilization of coal resources through the development and application of underground extraction technologies." Finally, 502(l) calls for additional programs and research to facilitate the "exploration, extraction, processing, development and production of minerals and the training of mineral engineers and scientists." The Surface Mining Control and Reclamation Act has thus emerged as a *mandate for energy expansion.*

It appears that in the corporate society the call for environmental preservation will be sounded politically within the context of expansion and development. What emerges is the full "integration" of ecological and growth objectives. The environmental crisis has been institutionally defined as compatible with the major purposes and dynamics of the coal industry.

Sue the Turkeys?

A common part of North American socialization involves the development of a faith in the remedies of law. In the case of environmental protection, many assume that polluters or government officials who fail to discharge their environmental responsibilities can be fought in court. What this argument lacks is an understanding of the symbolism of law. Often legal remedies are simply ceremonial exercises, without teeth, or encumbered by procedures weighted against environmentalists. The following examples make this point clear.

First of all, those looking to environmental litigation may be surprised to find they have no "standing" in court. As government supposedly represents the public interest, federal courts seldom consent to hear suits against public officials brought by private citizens. In a similar vein, no court has jurisdiction to hear cases brought against the United States government. Other legal weapons are also suspect. *Injunctions* (orders to execute certain actions or to refrain from harmful action) represent a seldom granted court remedy for environmental complaints. The determination to grant an injunction is most frequently made by the courts on economic, not environmental, grounds. The *class action* suit is also compromised. Environmental class actions against private defendants are denied unless the financial damage suffered by an *individual* victim of pollution exceeds $10,000. Finally, those seeking to sue to improve environmental quality are *plaintiffs* and thus have the *burden of proof* with regard to the issues of contention (Sloan 1971).

To conclude, the institutionalization of the environmental problem reveals a record of symbolic recognition, not legislative redress; delay, not action; and the politics of compromise, not confrontation. It follows that regulatory agencies seldom regulate, a failing ensured through bureaucratic policies of "peaceful coexistence" together with real budgetary deficiencies. It may well be that what has been institutionalized is the corporate system's version of capital punishment: "Those who have the capital need not fear the punishment."

MAINTENANCE

As indicated before, once the environmental or other social problem is institutionalized, certain interest will "keep" or maintain it. Consequently, an often-ignored aspect of social disorders is that some individuals or groups actually benefit from the way in which a particular problem is defined in law, policy, and regulation, as well as in the conventional wisdom.

Maintenance further is tied formally to the question of solution. Those charged with "doing something" about the environmental threat are dependent on that threat for their livelihood. For example, there would be few police without crime, few social workers without poverty, and no Environmental Protection Agency in the United States without the continuing assault on the earth. The ecological crisis has thus generated numerous economic spinoffs, not simply in the form of jobs for those in the protection "industry," but also in countless books, articles, media pieces, and the very words you are reading.

The reader should understand that the issue of maintenance centers around the continuation of a *particular* definition of the ecological crisis. There is more to maintenance than keeping a social problem "alive." It is the qualitative difference in definitions that is of importance. For example, police functions would differ drastically if crime were redefined as corporate or suite malfeasance rather than street lawlessness; social work functions would be altered if welfare were defined as a means of controlling the dangerous classes; and the protection of the environment would acquire a new direction if General Motors replaced the "litterbug" as a symbol of ecological degradation.

Beyond the concerns of bureaucratic and occupational survival, however, is the larger question of maintenance: the preservation and keeping of the corporate economy. As we have argued throughout, it is important to examine each phase of the historical model within the broader context of ideology. (See Proposition Five in Chapter Two.) We have already seen that the logical contradiction between growth and the slowdown requirements of ecological balance has been redefined through both the language of the law and the policies of enforcement agencies. Thus, an act calling for the control and reclamation of surface mining becomes a mandate for energy growth through the expansion of the coal industry. In the area of maintenance, we must be sensitized to the possibility that the environmental crisis can become a commodity. As examples, ecological and environmental concerns are used by advertisers to sell products while pollution control assumes the standing of an industry. Such would be only a logical extension of the prevailing ideology of the corporate order.

At first glance, it appears foolhardy to suggest that the control of pollution is compatible with the thrust and purpose of societies based on growth.

> It is generally accepted that the pollution abatement expenditure represents a commitment of funds for an asset which is basically unproductive by nature. Given the unproductive nature of this asset, it will generate negligible, if any, cash inflows while at the same time necessitating significant cash outflows. While the significant point is that the expenditure of such funds will typically depress the profitability of the firm, the extent of this depressing effect will depend upon the type of incentive utilized by government to bring about the expenditure and ability of the firm to shift the costs through higher prices (Ray 1974, p. 23).

To translate: business will lose money on pollution control unless government incentives and higher prices come to the rescue. As always, government incentives mean tax money, and higher prices mean the consumer pays more. The taxpayer and the consumer are, of course, one and the same.

However, if we are to show that pollution abatement is part and parcel of the corporate system, we must go beyond the observation that industry and business expect to recover such expenditures through political action and raising prices. These appear to be small incentive.

If we examine recent history, we find that the foremost business executives in this country are *favorably disposed* to ("reasonable") pollution control. *Fortune* magazine surveyed 500 such people in 1970 and found a willingness to "restrain" production increases, product diversification, and profit increase if this were ecologically beneficial (Diamond 1970). Along the same line, a later survey of top executives of major corporations conducted by the *Wall Street Journal* revealed that environmental protection programs had already been introduced for the majority, with more to follow. This survey demonstrated support for "ecology groups" and, curiously, for governmental pollution controls (*Wall Street Journal* 1972).

Earlier in our discussion of the emergence phase of the ecological problem, we noted that the nation's economic elite played a significant role in shaping the official reaction to the environmental issue. The position was advanced that environmental controls might predictably damage the smaller operation more than major corporations. But the issue of maintenance goes beyond the support of movements geared to raise "consciousness" and set the stage for formal law and policy. It also goes beyond the conviction that the great and powerful can survive government regulation. Maintenance means a corporate "solution" to pollution. The corporate economy is not dismissed as the problem's source but rather advanced as the "answer."

The Pollution Solution: Corporation Style

The following is part of a statement by Russell W. Peterson, speaking as the Chairman of the Council of Environmental Quality:

> The demand of our people for clean air is now established—not as a fad, but as a permanent requirement of our way of life. And our free enterprise system is responding: our laboratories and factories are now producing the ideas, the processes and the products necessary to satisfy that demand. In so doing, they are creating hundreds of thousands of jobs and numerous new investment opportunities. In fact, the fledgling environmental industry is one of the few growth sectors bucking the tide of the recession.
>
> In spite of the fact that this industry is another expression of free enterprise at work, we repeatedly encounter the argument that investments in environmental protection are nonproductive; that they are pure cost; that they drain funds badly needed for productive investment in other parts of the economy . . .
>
> This argument has a surface persuasiveness; yet one can dig a little deeper in our economic data and argue quite the reverse (Peterson, in Klein and Leung 1976, pp. v, vi).

It is indeed possible to argue the reverse. In 1970, Martin Gellin described the beginnings of a "pollutional-industrial complex." This was his term for the alliance between government (for example, tax money in the form of research and development funds) and the then-fledgling pollution control industry. When we combine government "incentives" with the data presented below, the message is clear.

In the United States, the environmental control industry is expanding rapidly.

> The industry as defined herein is represented by at least 600 participating firms (not counting the 10,000 waste collection companies), including over a dozen companies visibly identified as pollution control-related, several divisions of much larger corporations, and numerous small firms. . . . Based upon total pollution abatement spending as forecast by the Council on Environmental Quality, the pollution control industry could be called upon to provide equipment valued at $33.957 billion between 1974 and 1983 (in 1974 dollars). Related pollution abatement activities could total another $10.519 billion (in 1974 dollars) during this period (Klein and Leung 1976, pp. 1–2).

Pollution control has emerged not as an adversary of big business. Pollution control is big business.

Defenders of the corporate order would hasten to question any criticism of the profit motive as fundamental to environmental protection. If it works, why be concerned with profitability? The point to be made is that the system by definition is committed to growth. It follows that the pollution control industry advanced by that system will be based on the assumption of continued growth. For example, increasing energy use is necessary for growth and many forms of energy use damage the environment. Accordingly, those who advocate the maintenance of a pollution control industry speak of it in terms of energy *cost*.

> If all our power plants were using 3.5 percent sulphur-content fuels, they would need 62 trillion Btu's annually to meet environmental standards through the operation of limestone scrubbers— about the same amount of energy we used in 1969 to run our electric frying pans. Providing tertiary wastewater treatment to the entire population would require 182 trillion Btu's of electrical energy— about twice the amount we used in 1969 to operate electrical irons (Peterson, in Klein and Leung 1976, p. ix).

The point is not that the energy cost of environmental protection is small. The point is that environmental protection might best be achieved with a different set of imperatives from those of corporate structure (see Proposition Two in Chapter Two). For example, rather than consider the energy *costs* of environmental protection, why not consider the energy *conservation* and subsequent reduction of pollutants that would be achieved through a movement from existing massive reliance on the automobile to a public transportation system? Of course, such an alternative would hardly contribute to the maintenance of the existing political-economic order.

We earlier alluded to the role played by governmental agencies not simply in bureaucratic maintenance but also in the larger preservation of the corporate economy. For example, we noted that the Environmental Protection Agency of the United States has been reluctant to press the nation's airlines to comply with noise abatement standards. In what has become a standard response, government is looked to for assistance.

> In Congress, the battle switches in 1978 to whether airline passengers should be taxed up to $4 billion to provide a fund for airlines to buy new airplanes and noise reduction equipment. One bill (HR 8729), which was approved by the House Ways and Means Committee, was called a "subterfuge" by Ralph Nader. "It is designed," he said, "to raise capital for new airplanes with the consumer and the U.S. Treasury providing the down payment" (Rowse 1978, p. 508).

Nader understands that noise abatement standards stand to become a source of capital for the airlines. What should also be mentioned is that some of the proposed $4 billion should be expected to find its way into the noise control industry.

Political maintenance of the corporate economy is evidenced in other areas. In 1974, the Workshop on Alternative Energy Strategies (WAES) convened to consider the topic "Energy Supply to the Year 2,000." Workshop participants from various oil producing nations met over a two-and-a-half year period to consider a number of "scenarios" dealing with the kinds and amount of energy that industrial countries might expect to be developed in coming decades. In the area of coal production, for example, both the governments of Canada and the United States were provided with a "shopping list" called "vigorous response." "Restrained response" means any political action that would hinder energy development. (See Tables 5–4 and 5–5.)

Although workshop participants were described as neutral, they included the following: from the United States, Thornton Bradshaw, President, Atlantic Richfield Company; Walker Cisler, Chairman of the Board, Detroit Edison Company; John Conner, Chairman of the Board, Allied Chemical Corporation; Richard Gerstenberg, Director, General Motors Corporation; and Guyford Stever, Director, National Science Foundation. From Canada, Marshall Crowe, Chairman, National Energy Board; and Maurice Strong, Chairman, Petro-Canada.

The United States government's energy policy is most certainly not hostile to coal interests. As we have already seen, policy area 1, which calls for positive (for whom?) action in the area of surface mining laws, is quite consistent with Public Law 95–87, which is a mandate to the coal industry. Coal lands leasing, policy area 2, is also proceeding nicely. The New York-based Council of Economic Priorities, which is a non--profit, public-interest organization, reported that "federal and state coal leasing on public lands in the West is still a 'giveaway' of public resources." Historically, under a 1920 law, surface coal land was leased to large corporations, which held them for speculation. What the WAES participants called for in effect was a continuation of the same policies. It is doubtful they will be disappointed (Hill 1978).

A final example makes clear the nature of maintenance. The United States government holds some 33 percent of the nation's land, some 761 million acres in trust, ostensibly for the people. The government-owned forest land is intended for "multiple use." This concept was developed by Theodore Roosevelt and his conservation consultant, Gifford Pinchot. Federal land was to be used for commercial purposes, but also for public

TABLE 5–4
National Policy Responses for Coal: Canada

Policy Area	Vigorous Response	Restrained Response
1. Surface mining laws	Strip mining regulations are favorable for development on the eastern slopes of the Rocky Mountains.	Stringent land use regulations prevent development on the eastern slopes of the Rocky Mountains.
2. Coal lands leasing program	Favorable land reclamation policies stimulate production.	States of Uncertainty in land reclamation policies.
3. Provincial royalty rates	Fair and equitable provincial royalty rates.	Escalating royalty rates.
4. Air quality standards	Air quality standards permit the burning of coal without pollution control devices.	Air quality standards do not permit the burning of coal without pollution control devices.
5. Tax incentives	Tax incentives created to stimulate development.	No tax incentives for the producers.
6. Government action to attract labor	Government creates environment to attract labor to coal industry through wage rates and health and safety legislation.	Little or no government action to attract labor to coal industry.
7. Research and development programs	Government conducts and supports research and development programs in mining techniques.	No government-conducted or -supported research and development programs.
8. Government assistance with transportation	Government assists with transportation facilities, i.e., railways and slurry pipelines.	Government does not assist with transportation facilities.

Source: William F. Martin, *Energy Supply in the Year 2000*, Cambridge, Mass.: MIT Press, 1977, p. 109.

TABLE 5–5
National Policy Responses for Coal: United States

Policy Area	Vigorous Response	Restrained Response
1. Surface mining laws	Debate over surface mining laws is resolved to eliminate the uncertainties about reclamation standards.	Reclamation uncertainties are not resolved soon.
2. Coal lands leasing program	An effective coal lands leasing program is initiated by 1977.	Delays continue in the establishment of an effective program to lease federal coal lands.
3. Environmental impact statements	Government shortens the processing time of environmental impact statements to hasten the expansion stimulated by other government policies.	Processing time of environmental impact statements does not improve.
4. Air quality standards	Ambient air quality standards permit the burning of western coal without stack scrubbers.	Stack scrubbers required for western coal.
5. Miner/work force training programs	Government supports a miner training program to meet industry's work force requirements.	Government does not support miner/work force training programs.
6. Labor productivity	Government assists in increasing miner productivity.	Government does not assist in increasing labor productivity.
7. Equipment productivity	Tax incentives are immediately created to induce industry to purchase more productive mining equipment.	Tax incentives for increased equipment productivity are not instituted.
8. Research and development programs	Government supports R & D programs to improve mining techniques.	No government-supported R & D programs for mining techniques established.
9. Slurry pipelines	Government grants rights of eminent domain to coal slurry pipelines to support coal transportation needs.	Coal slurry pipelines continue to have right-of-way problems.
10. Railroad transportation	Government provides assistance to railroads for their expansion and maintenance of capacity to ensure increased coal-transportation capabilities.	Government does not assist expansion of railroad's coal-transportation capacity.
11. Federal siting laws	Government streamlines authorization procedures for new plants and facilities.	Present siting authorization procedures and delays continue.

Source: William F. Martin, *Energy Supply in the Year 2000,* Cambridge, Mass: MIT Press, 1977, p. 351.

enjoyment and conservation. However, since the inception of "multiple use," timber interests have cut ever-increasing quantities of trees.

In 1960, the Multiple Use–Sustained Yield Act was passed by the Congress of the United States. It called upon the United States Forest Service to decide the extent to which commercial logging should be allowed on public land. However, there was another little-known provision. Congress tied the level of appropriations for the Forest Service to the income from commercial timbering. To keep their appropriations at a high level, the Service must maximize timber production. This amounts to a political mandate for a practice known as clear-cutting, the primary form of timber production used by logging interests since the mid-1960s. This means that huge gaps, some as long as three miles and as wide as one mile, are carved into public forests. The resulting landscape can be easily compared to the desolation inflected in Southeast Asia during the Vietnam War (Rosenbaum 1974). Maintenance in this case is a symbiotic relationship between a federal bureaucracy and the industry it is charged to regulate.

An Alternative Vision

Treaty language between the government of the United States and vanquished Indian tribes often included the phrases, "for as long as the sky is blue, and the water flows and the grass grows." This promise of perpetuity, largely circumvented for the Native American, has come to represent a second contradiction in our lifetime. The air is often yellow, the water foul and stagnant, and the grass does not grow.

We have seen that the matter of defining a social problem is dependent upon the ideological context. At the conclusion of this chapter, it appears logical to argue that the environmental movement is the handmaiden of the corporate economy. It follows that an ecological alternative must necessarily question privatization, growth, and corporate ownership. We must also ask if there is any connection between setting one human against the other in a competitive struggle and setting the whole of society and its technology against nature.

In Chapter One, we suggested that any alternative to the existing order would involve the restructuring of a society that embraces domination and hierarchy. A system of acquisition that pits the greedy against the needy may, as an expected consequence, ravage the land and pillage resources. Necessarily, an alternative definition of the environmental crisis should look for movement from the private to the common, from the individual to the public.

In sociological style, it is possible to seek a new symbol of ecological decline. The new symbol would be at the heart, not the periphery, of the corporate economy. Also, new imagery should do more than rally opposition and help fashion group solidarity. It should represent the clearest connection to social structure. As such, it would push us beyond mere appearance and the symbolic politics of emotional reaction.

Many such symbols might prove basic to an alternative definition of the environmental problem. Our examination of solar energy has shown us the connections between the petrocorporations, nuclear energy, and what Barry Commoner terms the "poverty of progress." In an increasingly urban society seeking to cope with destructive sound, the concept of a "quiet community" becomes almost revolutionary. In a similar vein, the selection of occupational disease as an ecological symbol would fashion not only connections with the more concrete concerns of worker exploitation, but also with those involving alienation. However, for reasons that shall become apparent, we should like instead to draw the reader's attention to the nature of transportation in North America.

Something to Believe In

In the recent past, the maker of a luxury automobile proclaimed that it was "something to believe in." In 1976, citizens of the United States drove private automobiles nearly 1.1 trillion miles (*Statistical Abstract of the United States* 1979, p. 643). The volume of domestic intercity passenger traffic carried by the private automobile has remained at the same level (85 to 90 percent of total passenger traffic) for the past quarter-century. Between 1950 and 1977, bus passenger traffic declined from 5.2 percent to 1.8 percent of the total volume, and railroad traffic shrank from 6.4 percent to 0.7 percent. Airway traffic increased from 2.0 percent of the total volume in 1950 to 12.1 percent in 1973. The direction is clearly toward energy-inefficient transportation. (*Statistical Abstract of the United States* 1979, p. 635).

The private automobile is both an economic and ecological problem. It travels along ribbons of concrete and steel that claim increasing amounts of the national wealth. By 1977, municipal and rural highways measured some 3.87 million miles (*Statistical Abstract of the United States* 1979, p. 639). Each year, the urban metropolis is expanded by highway construction prefacing the conversion of agricultural land into roadbeds, parking lots, skyscrapers, tract homes, and shopping centers. Of prime concern for the energy issue, motor vehicles used 120 billion gallons of gasoline in 1977. Passenger vehicles used almost 81 billion gallons and trucks over 38 billion gallons (*Statistical Abstract of the United States* 1979, p. 650). While the railroads die a slow and predictable death in the United States, nearly 150 million autos, trucks, and buses compete for a place in the fast lane, the garages, and the parking lots (*Statistical Abstract of the United States* 1979, p. 646).

Transportation "progress" has come with costs other than energy waste. In 1977, there were some 24 million U.S. motor vehicle accidents, with a total of almost 5.6 million injuries and 50,000 deaths. The traffic death rate in 1978 was 23.0 per hundred thousand members of the resident population. The economic loss due to accidents for the same year was calculated at some $53 billion (*Statistical Abstract of the United States* 1979, p. 643). Tragedy aside, this sum pales when set alongside the estimated cost of operating automobiles. The 1976 estimate, based on a four-door sedan costing $4,900, with an assumed life of ten years or 100,000 miles, was 17.9 cents per mile. (For 1979, the cost rose to 19.6 cents per mile.) Using the 1976 rate (17.9 cents per mile), the total cost of the 1.1 trillion driven in 1976 was a staggering $197 billion. This sum far exceeds the 1976 gross national product for Canada ($191 billion) (*Statistical Abstract of the United States* 1979, pp. 651, 895). Given the preeminence of private transportation in the United States, it follows that the automotive-petroleum complex will dominate the economic order.

It is not possible to examine automotive hegemony in isolation. According to *Fortune* magazine, in 1979 nineteen of the top fifty United States industrials were oil companies (see Table 5–6).

When the total sales of these corporate giants for 1979 are compared with their sales for 1972,[9] the growth is staggering. All show a massive surge in sales for the seven-year period, with the increase for particular corporations ranging from more than 200 percent to over 400 percent. In every instance ranking by sales demonstrates an improved position relative to industry in general (For example, Exxon moved from number 2 to number 1, Mobil from number 7 to number 3, Texaco from number 8 to number 5, Gulf from number 11 to number 8, and on by analogy). In case you were wondering which corporation was number 2 in sales, it was none other than General Motors, which sold its cars, trucks, and other products to the tune of $66.3 billion. Ford Motor Company ranked fourth in 1979, with 43.5 billion in sales, and Chrysler seventeenth, with close to $12 billion.[10] The nature of the automotive-petroleum complex

---

[9]1972 is chosen as the base year because the OPEC embargo of 1973 signalled the beginning of the "energy crisis," a bonanza for big oil.

[10]The size and power of a particular corporation often buys protection from market forces. The financially troubled Chrysler Corporation slipped from number 10 in 1978 to number 17 on the *Fortune* list in 1979. However, Chrysler secured both Federal loan guarantees and a multi-billion dollar contract from the Defense Department to produce a new battle tank.

TABLE 5-6
Big Oil: Ranking by Sales in the *Fortune* 500 List: 1972 and 1979
(Billions of Dollars)

Company	Ranking by Sales		Sales	
	1972	1979	1972	1979
Exxon	2	1	$20.3	$79.1
Mobil	7	3	9.2	44.7
Texaco	8	5	8.7	38.4
Gulf Oil	11	7	6.2	23.9
Standard Oil of California	12	6	5.8	29.9
Standard Oil of Indiana	15	10	4.5	18.6
Shell Oil	17	13	4.1	14.4
Continental Oil (Conoco)	24	15	3.4	12.6
Atlantic Richfield	25	12	3.4	16.2
Tenneco	26	18	3.3	11.2
Phillips Petroleum	36	22	2.5	9.5
Occidental Petroleum	37	21	2.5	9.5
Union Oil of California	52	34	2.1	7.6
Sun	59	20	1.9	10.7
Cities Service	63	47	1.9	6.3
Ashland Oil	70	44	1.8	6.5
Standard Oil of Ohio	95	32	1.4	7.9
Amerada Hess	107	41	1.3	6.8
Marathon Oil	113	43	1.3	6.7

Source: "The *Fortune* Directory of the 500 Largest U.S. Industrial Corporations," *Fortune*, New York: Time-Life, Inc., 1972, 1980 (May).

is clear when one considers that in 1979 it accounted for the leading seven and eleven of the top fifteen industrials.

Of those considering their neighborhoods as "noisy" in a recent EPA survey, some 55 percent identified traffic as the chief source of destructive sound. (Rowse 1978, p. 509.) Nor can we avoid the "contribution" to air pollution of the petroleum-driven vehicle. As the following table makes apparent, gasoline and diesel fuel vehicles account for over 50 percent of the toxic substances causing respiratory disease, plant loss, and the general degradation of life quality. Most of these come from the passenger car.

Thus, as Charles Anderson has argued (1976, p. 21), "Any significant transformation in the use of the automobile would require nothing less than the reconstruction of the present American economy." Social change in transportation constitutes a frontal assault on corporate America.

Of course, the power of ideology is such that environmental concerns are frequently described as the cause of unemployment. If the concern for energy conservation, the argument goes, is allowed to diminish those industries which use a great deal of energy and/or produce energy inefficient products, then people are going to lose their jobs.

It is sometimes argued that energy conservation would inevitably lead to a slower rate of growth in real GNP (Gross National Prod-

**TABLE 5-7
Pollutants: 1975
(Million Tons per Year)**

	Total	Gasoline and Diesel Vehicles
Particulates	13.8	1.0
Sulfer oxides	32.8	.6
Nitrogen oxides	22.4	10.1
Hydro carbons	27.2	11.1
Carbon monoxide	93.4	76.6
	189.6	99.4

Source: EPA, Office of Air and Quality, *Planning and Standards*, Washington, D.C., 1978.

uct) and increase unemployment. *This is patently false.* Income not spent on energy or energy-intensive goods and services (such as the private automobile) would be available for other types of expenditures. Conservation would reduce the need to export goods to pay for imported oil, thereby permitting a larger share of domestic output to be consumed domestically. Furthermore, while conservation might reduce investment in conventional energy production and demand for energy-intensive products, conservation would stimulate investment in the exploitation of renewable energy sources, encourage spending for improvements in the energy efficiency of existing equipment, and spur the development of new products with superior energy-consuming characteristics (such as mass transit people movers). (United States House of Representatives, Committee on Science and Technology, pp. 171–72; parenthetical remarks and italics added)

When such industries close, how would workers move into new industries? What is required, of course, is a public commitment to retraining and relocation of displaced workers. Such involves social planning for labor utilization on a society wide basis. If realized, such would signal an end to the control of the labor force by owners and managers.

A national commitment to mass transit in densely populated urban areas would initiate a virtually infinite rippling effect. It would mean a drastic slowdown in the squandering of fossil fuels, which in turn would buy the time required for the full development of energy alternatives. It portends quieter cities, the substitution of pedestrian malls for parking lots and garages, and air fit to breathe. It would further mean less business for hospitals and morticians. Thus, our alternative vision of the ecological crisis begins with a redefinition of one of the master symbols of corporate society. In a sane and humanistic order, the automobile would perhaps be less a symbol of class status, sexual virility, or progress. Rather, it would be more a symbol for death, misery, and waste.

BIBLIOGRAPHY

Agran, Larry
1977   The Cancer Connection. Boston: Houghton Mifflin.

Albrecht, Stan
1976   "Legacy of the Environmental Movement." Environment and Behavior 8 (2) June: 147–68.

Anderson, Charles
1976   The Sociology of Survival. Homewood, Ill.: The Dorsey Press.

Barkley, Katherine, and
Weissman, Steve
1970   "The Eco-Establishment," in Eco-Catastrophe, Editors of Ramparts. San Francisco: Harper & Row.

Baron, Robert Alex
1970   The Tyranny of Noise. New York: St. Martin's Press.

Berland, Theodore
1970   The Fight for Quiet. Englewood Cliffs, N.J.: Prentice-Hall.

Blumenthal, Les
1980   "Power Tests Begin on N-Breeder Reactor." Spokesman-Review February 11:9.

Bowman, James
1977   "Public Opinion and the Environment," Environment and Behavior 9 (3) September: 385–416.

Brill, Harry
1980   "It Pays to Go Out of Big Business." The Progressive (August): 20–21.

Brown, Michael H.
1980   "Love Canal Dumpsite Gets Emergency Tag." Spokesman-Review, June 1:A-5.

Bryan, Rorke
1973   Much Is Taken, Much Remains: Canadian Issues in Environmental Conservation. Scituate, Mass.: Duxbury Press.

Burnham, David
1979   "Excerpts from Discussions on Accident at Reactor." New York Times, April 14:9.

The Calgary Herald
  1980   March 15:A22.

Carson, Rachel
  1962   The Silent Spring. Boston: Houghton Mifflin.

Catton, William R., and
Dunlap, Riley E.
  1978   "Environmental Sociology: A New Paradigm."
                           The American Sociologist 13 No. 1 February: 41–49.

Chandra, Satya, and
Shukla, Girja S.
  1978   "Manganese Encephalopathy in Growing Rats."
                           Environmental Research 15:28–37.

Commoner, Barry
  1976   The Poverty of Progress. New York: Alfred A.
                           Knopf.

  1979   The Politics of Energy. New York: Alfred A. Knopf.

Diamond, Robert S.
  1970   "What Business Thinks about the Environment."
                           In The Environment. Editors of Fortune. New
                           York: Harper & Row: 55–65.

Dotto, Lydia
  1980   "What Acid Rain Does to Our Land and Water."
                           Canadian Geographic, December/January: 36–41.

Douglas, William O.
  1969   "The Public Be Damned." Playboy Magazine, July.

Ehrlich, Paul and
Anne H.
  1970   Population, Resources, Environment: Issues in
                           Human Ecology. San Francisco: William Freeman
                           and Company.

The Energy Directory
  1974   New York: Environment Information Center.

Environmental Defense
Fund, and Boyle,
Robert H.
  1979   Malignant Neglect. New York: Alfred A. Knopf.

Environmental Protection
Agency
1978   "National Emissions Report for 1975." Washington,
D.C.: U.S. Government Printing Office.

Fortune Magazine
1972
1980   "The *Fortune* Directory of the 500 Largest U.S.
Industrial Corporations." New York: Time-Life.

Flowler, John
1975   Energy-Environment Source Book. Washington,
D.C.: National Science Teachers Association.

Freeman, Milton
1974   People Pollution. Montreal: Queens University Press.

Glass, D., and Singer, J.
1972   Urban Stress. New York: Academic Press.

Gomer, Robert
1968   "The Tyranny of Progress." In Changing Perspectives on Man. Ben Rothblett, ed. Chicago: University of Chicago Press, pp. 257–69.

Gouldner, A.
1970   The Coming Crisis of Western Sociology. New York:
Basic Books.

Hill, Gladwin
1978   "Giveway of Public Resources." New York Times.
Nov. 13.

Horsley, A. Doyle
1977   "The Effects of a Social Learning Experiment on
Attitudes and Behavior Toward Environmental
Conservation." Environment and Behavior 9(3)
September: 349–84.

Hunter, Lawson A. W.
1976   "Canada." In Energy Policies of the World. Gerald
J. Mangone, ed. New York: Elsevier.

Independent Record
(Helena, Montana)
1980   "Anaconda's Pullout Economic Disaster."
September 30: 1.

Klein, Jeffrey, and Leung,
Kenneth Ch'uan-K'ai
1976   The Environmental Control Industry. New York:
Elsevier.

Marvin, Ray C.
　1974　　　　　The Environmental Crisis and Corporate Debt
　　　　　　　　Policy. Lexington, Mass.: Lexington Books.

Martin, William F.
　1977　　　　　Energy Supply to the Year 2000. Cambridge, Mass.:
　　　　　　　　MIT Press.

Matsumoto, H., Koya, G.
and Takeuch, T.
　1965　　　　　"Fetal Minimata Disease: A Neuropathological
　　　　　　　　Study of Two Cases of Intrauterine Intoxication
　　　　　　　　by a Methylmercury Compound." Journal of Neuro-
　　　　　　　　pathological Experimental Neurology 29:563–74.

Micklin, Philip P.
　1977　　　　　"International Environmental Implications of
　　　　　　　　Soviet Development of the Volga River." Human
　　　　　　　　Ecology 5(2) June: 113–35.

Mills, C. Wright
　1943　　　　　"The Professional Ideology of Social Pathologists."
　　　　　　　　American Journal of Sociology 39 September:
　　　　　　　　165–80.

　1963　　　　　"The Structure of Power in American Society." In
　　　　　　　　Power, Politics and People. Irving Horowitz, ed.
　　　　　　　　New York: Ballantine.

Moody's Industrial Manual
　1980　　　　　Volume I. New York: Moody's Investor Service.

Nelson, Bryce
　1979　　　　　"Waste Dump Sites Pose Big Dangers." Spokesman-
　　　　　　　　Review, October 7:A12.

Newsweek
　1979　　　　　"Nuclear Accident." April 9:24–33.

New York Times
　1979　　　　　"A Chronicle of the Nation's Worst Nuclear Power
　　　　　　　　Accident." April 16.

Nuclear Regulatory
Commission
　1979　　　　　Nuclear Regulatory Commission Transcripts on
　　　　　　　　Three Mile Island. Washington, D.C.: ACE-
　　　　　　　　Federal Reporters.

Page, Richard
1977
"Noise and Helping Behavior." Environment and Behavior 9 September: 311–34.

Pawlick, Thomas
1980
"The Silent Toll." Harrowsmith vol. 4, no. 28, 33–49.

Peracchio, Adrian
1979
"Dioxin: A Few Parts per Trillion add up to a Dangerous Dose." Spokesman-Review, July 6:13.

Perdue, William D.
1979
"Noise: Attitudes and Action." Office of Noise Abatement, Environmental Protection Agency, Washington, D.C.: U.S. Government Printing Office.

Pierce, R. E.
1972
"Alkyl Mercury Poisoning in Humans: Report of an Outbreak." Journal of American Medical Association 220:1439–1442.

Pomeroy, William J.
1970
American Neo-Colonialism, New York: International Publishers.

Renzoni, Aristeo
1977
"The Increasing Number of Environmental-degrading Accidents in Italy." Environmental Conservation 4 (Spring): 21–26.

Ridgeway, James, and Conner Bettina
1975
New Energy. Boston: Beacon Press.

Rosenbaum, Walter A.
1974
The Politics of Environmental Concern. New York: Praeger.

Rowse, Arthur E., ed.
1978
Help: The Useful Almanac. Washington: Consumer News.

Schneider, Steven
1978
"Oil and Coal." The Progressive, April 22.

Scott, Marvin B., and Layman, Stanford M.
1968
"Accounts." American Sociological Review 33 December 1968: 46–62.

Sherrill, Robert
1979 "Energy 'Crisis' a Phony Emergency?" New York Times, October 21.

Silk, Leonard
1980 "Oil Companies Grow Rich on OPEC Prices." New York Times, June 13.

Sloan, Irving J.
1971 Environment and the Law. New York: Oceana.

Solomon, J.
1970 "Aural Assault." The Sciences, 10:26–31.

Spokane Chronicle
1980 "Underground Drinking Water Threatened." July 25:1.

Spokesman-Review
1979 "Trouble is Not a Stranger at N-Plants." April 15: A-6.

1980 "N-Plants Report 2,300 Incidents in a Year." July 14:10.

Tataryn, Lloyd
1979 Dying for a Living: The Politics of Industrial Presence. Toronto: Deneau and Greenberg.

Time Magazine
1976 "King Coal's Action: Wealth and Worry." March 1:45–47.

1980 "Where Is My Country?" February 25:20.

Tofler, Sid
1980 "Port Angeles Residents Buck Northern Tier Plan." The Calgary Herald March 17: A19.

United States Bureau of
the Census
1979 Statistical Abstract of the United States. Washington, D.C.: US Government Printing Office.

United States Congress
1977 "Surface Mining Control and Reclamation Act of 1977." Public Law 95–87. 95th Congress. Washington, D.C.: U.S. Government Printing Office.

United States Department
of the Interior
  1968

Man: An Endangered Species? Washington, D.C.:
U.S. Government Printing Office.

United States House of
Representatives,
Committee on Science
and Technology
  1977

Energy Demand, Conservation Potential and Probable Life Style Changes. 95th Congress. Washington, D.C.: U.S. Government Printing Office.

United States House of
Representatives,
Committee on the
Judiciary
  1980

Corporate Crime. 96th Congress, 2nd session.
Washington, D.C.: U.S. Government Printing
Office.

Wall Street Journal
  1972

"A Nationwide Survey of Environmental
Protection." New York.

Weisberg, Barry
  1970

"The Politics of Ecology." Liberation 14 (9)
January: 20–25.

White, Lynn
  1967

"The Historical Roots of Our Ecologic Crisis."
Science, vol. 155, no. 3767: 1203–7.

6

WHOSE LAW?
WHAT ORDER?

Abstract

The prevailing ideologies of law emphasize equality before the law and ignore the real threats to our freedom. Street crime and crimes against morality are identified as the most threatening types of lawlessness in our corporate society while white collar suite crime is viewed as much less harmful. However, this masks the ideological bias of a legal system that largely benefits corporate society, often to the detriment of basic human needs. An analysis of the *emergence, institutionalization,* and *maintenance* of the legal system in Western nation-states generally, and specific laws in particular, provides insight into the use of the legal system to support the imperatives of master institutions such as the corporate economy. An alternative view of justice can be found in different basic values and human rights being supported by law. This is reflected in the emergence of insurgency law and in the criminalization of organizations.

"Our citizenship is another occasion for pride! For the poor it consists in supporting and maintaining the rich in their power and their idleness. At this task they must labor in the face of the majestic equality of the laws, which forbid rich and poor alike to sleep under the bridges, to beg in the streets, and to steal their bread."
—Anatole France in The Red Lily

309

"Equality under the law" is the cornerstone of the legal ideology that prevails in Western societies. This, according to Anatole France, represents the "majesty of law." Of course the irony, or contradiction if you will, is apparent. The rich (or at least the more privileged) have no need to sleep under bridges, beg in the streets, or steal bread. Though the forms of "street crime" have changed since the mid-nineteenth century when this author wrote, justice under the law is still no substitute for broader social, economic, and political equality. Who truly benefits, at least in the greatest measure, from "law and order" is the subject of the following piece.

Viewpoint

Exerpted from "The Law School" by David N. Rockwell

Legal education trains people to fill the needs of the legal profession. The legal profession in turn has its needs defined by those interests which pay the highest price for the services of the profession. One of the primary functions of the legal profession is to support and defend the power and control of corporations and business interests. The top lawyers, in effect, represent the groups most concerned with the preservation of the status quo, that is, the protection of property and wealth. Besides this function, the legal profession, in cooperation with the legal system as a whole, operates in the lower economic and political levels to maintain the smooth transfer and accumulation of wealth without upsetting the essential quality of its distribution. The criminal justic system, for example, devoted as it is to the preservation of order, concentrates most of its energy in the fight to keep property rights secure. Those who suffer most in the criminal court processes are those who own the least. Making courts more efficient is proposed by reformists as a cheaper remedy than revising the social and economic institutions that are responsible for poverty, slums, and racism. Price-fixing and deceptive advertising, untouched by industry-dominated regulatory agencies, leave consumers virtually undefended. The lawyers' role in these matters, of course, has been crucial to the well-being of the corporate interests. Even with such significant and difficult problems arising from the growth of corporate capitalism and the concentration of wealth in corporate hands, the bulk of the legal profession continues to devote its main efforts to the protection of the social order, not to the development of meaningful and effective solutions.

The concerns and responses of the legal profession are reflected in the law schools. As long as corporations are the highest bidders for legal talent, the principal product of the law school will remain the lawyer who can best fulfill the needs of the corporate world. The law student, as a commodity, is thus expected to master not only the fundamentals of corporate planning, contract, and property law, but also the intricacies of antitrust law (to help the client steer clear of trouble and still achieve the desired goal of market dominance and stability), taxation (to locate and, in some circumstances, actively lobby for attractive loopholes and advantages in tax codes), and labor law (to satisfy the desires of both management and labor to maintain stability within their own framework of competing interests and yet not abandon maximum profits or wages). In addition, those who reap the financial rewards of the economic system determine the priorities of legal education in order to preserve their benefits; so law schools emphasize courses dealing with wills and estates. In short, the system of legal education, like the legal profession in general, has adapted itself to the demands of omnipresent and omnipotent corporate interests. Through, for example, specially trained and selected law professors, authoritarian teaching methods, the use of the "casebook" as the primary textbook, the limited nature of the curriculum, and the choice of persons who attend law school, the legal system ensures the preservation of the economic and political system.

Rockwell goes on to argue that at one of the premier law schools in the United States, it is recommended that all students

... take the "Big Four": Corporations, Taxation, Accounting, and Constitutional Law. "The case for a basic course in Corporations is a simple one: The corporate form of business enterprise is central to the economic system of the free world." Taxation and Accounting help in understanding and employing this "central" form. Constitutional Law is not only concerned with the rights of individuals but also with inter-state and international business conflicts. These second-year courses are prerequisites for numerous courses offered at Harvard in the third year. Taxation is a prerequisite for the following: Advanced Taxation—The Taxation of Business Enterprise; Taxation—Corporate Reorganizations and Distri-butions; Business Planning, Estate Planning; Taxation—Cur-rent Issues and Problems; and Land Development. Corpora-tions is required in order to take the following subjects: Business Planning; Securities Regulation; and Corporate Planning and Counselling. Accounting is a prerequisite for Business Planning. The extension of these basic courses into the third year shows the training of a business-oriented pro-fessional specialist; no courses are required to help the stu-dent develop a continuing concern for humanitarian needs.

The curriculum of a law school thus remains basically con-cerned with the protection and expansion of personal and corporate property, to the detriment of the problems and needs of the people who do not have even the wealth to feed, clothe, or house themselves, who are not free from discrimi-nation, and who cannot protect themselves in court.

If the legal profession is an extension of the corporate economy, it follows that those who are more the victims than the beneficiaries of such an order will have little or no defense when encountering the laws of the State. As this chapter will show, however, the question of justice tran-scends the legal question of competent counsel. For "crime" in corporate society is typically defined in property terms. Further, the official "crimi-nal" is one who reacts to, rather than one who perpetuates the inequalities of, property distribution. We argue for a redefinition of crime and the criminal, as the following discussion will show.

THE PREVAILING IDEOLOGIES

Street Crime

Most students of crime, like most citizens, take the crime problem as given. They assume that crime is self-evident and its dimensions therefore nor arguable. This common conception is embodied in the term "street crime." When we talk about the crime problem, we often assume a mean-ing that emphasizes offenses against the person, particularly crimes of violence such as robbery, assault, murder, rape. The imagery evoked by the concept "street crime" has long been a rallying cry for "wars on crime" by politicians, police officials, and other civic leaders. However, when one looks beyond the rhetoric of street crimes, one discovers that most murders, rapes, and assaults are not committed in the streets, but in homes, taverns, automobiles, and parks. Such a conception is even losing meaning regarding robbery. As one observer notes:

> I will deal here mainly with street crime, and particularly robbery. In fact the phrase "street crime" is a misnomer, at least in New York. Most robberies now occur inside, in hallways, elevators, shops, or subways. You are safer out on the sidewalk (Hacker 1973, p. 9).

In actuality, the large number of crimes in the streets are committed by vagrants, prostitutes, drunks, panhandlers, and auto thieves. It appears that if you want to increase your chances of avoiding murder, assault, rape, or robbery, it would be advisable to stay away from your home, family, friends, and local drinking establishment and be in the streets. Furthermore, crimes of violence are a very small proportion of criminal behavior. In Canada and the United States, crimes of violence account for less than 10 percent of all felonies (*Canada Year Book* 1973; Federal Bureau of Investigation 1975). While the rate of violent crime per 100,000 increased between 1965 and 1974, so did the rate of nonviolent crimes, which make the bulk (over 90 percent) of crimes in North America. However, what about this other 90 percent?

A cursory look at national and local criminal statutes attests to the diversity of behaviors defined as criminal. For example, the *Criminal Code of Canada* includes in its definition of crime offenses against public order (such as treason and other offenses against the Queen's authority and person, sedition, prizefights); offenses against the administration of law and justice (corruption and disobedience); offenses against public morals, sexual offenses, disorderly houses, gaming and betting (common bawdy house); offenses against the person and reputation (homicide, venereal diseases, blasphemous libel, hate propaganda); offenses against rights of property (theft, robbery, extortion, fraudulent transactions relating to contracts and trade [fraud, breach of contract]); willful and forbidden acts in respect of certain property (arson, cruelty to animals); offenses relating to currency (counterfeiting, defacing, or impairing); and attempts, conspiracies, or accessories regarding the above areas (Minister of Justice 1973). Since the United States has fifty separate jurisdictions, with each state having its own criminal code, it provides even more variety to definitions of crime.

> So far we have used the word "crime" in a broad sense. Like Humpty Dumpty I took it to mean what I meant it to be and yet I trust that we had a measure of mutual understanding. Already this is a

miracle in human discourse that a word as colorful, diverse and rich in shadings as the word "crime" should convey to us any meaning at all. It is a tribute to the breadth of the human mind, but also to its craftiness and sleight of hand. This does not really get any better as one enters the process of definition and you are all too familiar with the double-dealing, buck-passing, and circular reasoning that goes [sic] on. *Nullum crisen lege* is an old presumption and is still what most definitions come down to: crime is what the law says it is. This is no significant advance from Humpty Dumpty's argument because we are quite able to invent laws to fit what we want to call crime, although this is not often necessary (as in war crimes) since the fantastic elasticity of criminal laws covers pretty well all human behavior, which for one reason or another becomes a problem to us, or at least to some of us (Mohr 1972).

While in theory our freedom as citizens rests on the fact that no act is a crime unless so specified in law, in practice we have an enormous amount of behavior defined as crime in North America. In Canada this includes over 700 Criminal Code sections, 20,000 federal offenses, and 30,000 provincial offenses, excluding municipal laws (Law Reform Commission 1976), and in the United States even more laws are on the books. The sheer volume of statutes is staggering to the imagination. A theory accounting for both the emergence and administration of laws within the context of the nation-state is crucial to understanding the nature of crime in our society and will be addressed later in this chapter.

Suite Crime

While a great deal of attention is given to "street crime" and street criminals, relatively little attention is paid to "suite crime" and suite criminals. By "suite crime" we are referring to the illegal behavior that occurs in the business offices of the corporate, professional, and civil elites of society. Misrepresentation in advertising, price fixing, fraudulent financial manipulations, illegal rebates, misappropriation of public funds, splitting fees, restraint of trade, failure to maintain safety standards, and violation of human rights are all examples of suite crimes. Evidence suggests that such suite crimes are as pervasive, if not more so, as street crimes, and result in a great deal more financial loss, while also causing death and injury (Quinney 1975, pp. 131–161). However, we have almost totally ignored such offenses in North America. Data regarding street crime and street criminals are voluminous compared with that available on suite crime and suite criminals. The following news report is applicable:

> White-collar crime is evidently costing billions of dollars more per
> year than violent or street crime in the United States, yet there is no

comprehensive effort to keep track of it. . . . federal agencies concerned with crime are making few attempts to study white-collar crime, its magnitude or effects (Keep 1975).

While laws bearing on corporate crime are now on the books, the individualistic and privatized nature of Western Law greatly insulates the corporate offender from legal threat.

> The laws affecting the prescribed behavior of corporations has [sic] developed out of a body of laws addressed to "persons"; laws based on the acts of individuals, some of them crimes, others torts. The bridge between acts of individuals and an entity such as a corporation has been developed in part because many of the acts of corporations are acts that could be done by individuals, such as producing injurious goods, polluting the environment, bribing, or engaging in tax frauds. But it is hard to determine who might be injuring us—that is, even if we know that we have been injured by a particular product, we are faced with the difficult task of proving the extent of the injuries, and it is even more difficult to prove to what extent they were due to any specific source. Furthermore, the nature of the evidence that has to be evaluated by the court is far more complex and technical (U.S. Department of Justice, Law Enforcement Assistance Administration 1979, pp. 6–7).

Those who might hope for legislic solutions must also remember that the nature of corporation wrongdoing is frequently beyond the narrowly drawn language of the law. Bribery of foreign officials by agents of multinational corporations is not clearly illegal, though such behavior is clearly a method of neocolonialism: that is, the buying of the loyalties of Third World countries' elite, whose policies are not necessarily in the interests of the whole people. A recent pattern of bribery of foreign nationals by United States corporations is detailed in the following chart:

Ashland Oil	Admits paying more than $300,000 to foreign officials, including $150,000 to President Albert Bernard Bonga of Gabon to retain mineral and refining rights.
Burroughs	Admits that $1.5 million in corporate funds may have been used in improper payments to foreign officials.
Exxon	Admits paying $740,000 to government officials and others in three countries. Admits its Italian subsidiary paid $27 million in secret but legal contributions to seven Italian political parties.
Gulf Oil	Admits paying $4 million to South Korea's ruling political party. Admits giving $460,000 to Bolivian officials—including a $110,000 helicopter to the late President Rene Barrientos Orutno—for oil rights.

Lockheed Aircraft	Admits giving $202 million in commissions, payoffs, and bribes to foreign agents and government officials in the Netherlands, Italy, Japan, Turkey, and other countries. Admits that $22 million of this sum went for outright bribes.
McDonnell Douglas	Admits paying $2.5 million in commissions and consultant fees between 1970 and 1975 to foreign government officials.
Merck	Admits paying $3 million, largely in "commission-type payments," to employees of 36 foreign governments between 1968 and 1975.
Northrop	Admits, in part, SEC charges that it paid $30 million in commissions and bribes to government officials and agents in Holland, Iran, France, West Germany, Saudi Arabia, Brazil, Malaysia, and Taiwan.
G. D. Searle	Admits paying $1.3 million to foreign governmental employees from 1973 to 1975 to "obtain sales of products or services."
United Brands	Admits paying a $1.25 million bribe to Honduran officials for a reduction in the banana export tax. Admits paying $750,000 to European officials. Investigators say the payment was made to head off proposed Italian restrictions on banana imports.

Source: Conklin 1977, pp. 48–49.

Public Image of Crime

Why are our images of the crime problem only of street crimes? Where do we gain such perceptions? How are such images maintained? Our attitudes towards, and reaction to, crime are greatly affected by our perception of the nature of the crime problem, a perception largely related to our personal experiences and socialization. Since most of us do not experience rape, robbery, or other assaults, our perception of the nature and scope of "street crime" (in other words, *the* crime problem) is largely a product of the diffusion of conceptions of criminality and of criminal and social types. Our families, educational institutions, politicians, and the mass media paint such images for us of crime and the criminal. Newspapers, television, radio, magazines, movies, and official governmental reports continually define for us the nature and scope of the crime problem. Such headlines as "Violent Crimes up 10%," "Rape Increases 100%," "Murder Up 20%," "Serious Crime on the Upsurge" convey to citizens that the crime problem (street crime) is increasing at an alarming rate. Uniform Crime Reports in both Canada and the United States emphasize "street crimes." Therefore, such headlines as "Corporate Crime Up 100%," "Price Fixing Increase 50%," "Corporate Crimes Death Toll Rises" are not usually found in the media.

Furthermore, the mass media are replete with dramas depicting the crime problem and the actors involved in the "war against crime." Television provides almost daily doses of criminals, law enforcement officials, private investigators, judges, attorneys, and correctional personnel. Such conceptions are gross misrepresentations of the scope and nature of the crime problem and the criminal justice system.

> The misinformation available through the mass media . . . is overwhelming. Fiction about crime and criminal justice is ridden with formula and stereotype, its primary purpose being the satisfaction of the emotional needs of the viewing audience rather than the portrayal of crime in an authentic way. So also with crime news itself, which seldom portrays any but the most sensational and bizarre events (Henshel and Silverman 1975, p. 39).

In spite of the above limitations, the mass media provide most citizens with their conceptions of the crime problem. Fear of "street crime" is widespread while fear of "suite crime" is minimal.

The continual barrage of crime statistics we receive plays an important role in creating and maintaining a constant fear among the public and in reinforcing the belief that contemporary times are the most "crime infested" in history. Both the United States and Canada issue *Uniform Crime Reports* periodically during each year as the barometer on crime. While these reporting systems have been critically assailed for their methodological and substantive deficiencies, they are taken by the public as valid and reliable indicators of lawlessness (Wolfgang 1963; Silverman and Teevan 1975). Therefore, increases in crime noted in the media may incite the public, even though there may be little basis for such fears.

> In 1970 a Toronto survey team found that, for many, "concern with crime" was in part an artificial creation and that people were more concerned about crime in the abstract than about actually becoming a victim. Therefore, it appears that crime is to some extent an imaginary problem, manufactured in the minds of many people (Milakovich and Weis 1975, p. 2).

The traditional imagery of crime and the criminal stems from the official focus on a few selected offenses. The *Uniform Crime Reports* of the Federal Bureau of Investigation contains statistical reports from over 13,000 police stations throughout the United States. Of central importance is the fact that the FBI has selected seven *index crimes* to reflect the seriousness of "lawlessness" in the United States. These include criminal

TABLE 6-1

Total Estimated Arrests, United States, 1978

TOTAL³	10,271,000	Sex offenses (except forcible rape and prostitution)	69,100
Murder and nonnegligent manslaughter	19,840	Drug abuse violations	628,700
Forcible rape	29,660	Opium or cocaine and their derivatives	83,100
Robbery	148,930	Marijuana	445,800
Aggravated assault	271,270	Synthetic or manufactured narcotics	17,200
Burglary	511,600	Other dangerous nonnarcotic drugs	82,500
Larceny-theft	1,141,800		
Motor vehicle theft	161,400	Gambling	55,800
Violent crime²	469,700	Bookmaking	5,400
Property crime²	1,814,700	Numbers and lottery	8,200
		All other gambling	42,200
Crime Index total	2,284,400		
		Offenses against family	56,900
Other assaults	468,600	Driving under the influence	1,268,700
Arson	19,000	Liquor laws	376,400
Forgery and counterfeiting	77,200	Drunkenness	1,176,600
Fraud	262,500	Disorderly conduct	715,200
Embezzlement	8,100	Vagrancy	49,300
Stolen property; buying, receiving, possessing	118,200	All other offenses (except traffic)	1,883,800
Vandalism	235,300	Suspicion (not included in total)	22,900
Weapons, carrying, possessing, etc.	157,900	Curfew and loitering law violations	83,100
Prostitution and commercialized vice	94,200	Runaways	182,100

Source: U. S. Department of Justice, Federal Bureau of Investigation, *Uniform Crime Reports*, 1978 (Washington, D.C.: U.S. Government Printing Office, 1979), p. 186.

homicide, aggravated assault, forcible rape, robbery, burglary, larceny, and motor vehicle theft. As Table 6–1 demonstrates, however, only some 2.3 million of the total 10.3 million arrests in the United States in 1978 involved index offenses. Of these, some 321,000 were for crimes clearly against the person (homicide, rape, and assault) while the remainder of almost 2 million clearly were property offenses. If we count among crimes against the person the offense of robbery (which includes violence or the threat of violence) the picture is affected only slightly. Put another way, larceny and burglary arrests account for over 70 percent of the total index arrests while nonindex arrests account for some 80 percent of total arrests.

What is the picture of the "crime problem" when one examines crimes reported to police rather than arrest statistics? In 1978, there were over 11.1 million index offenses reported to police (compared with the 2.3 million arrests). For certain index offenses, specifically rape and assault, the actual incidence is suspected to be much greater. However, if we focus on reported crime, then in 1978 *fewer than 1.1 million* index offenses were violent as defined by the FBI (criminal homicide, forcible rape, aggravated assault, and robbery). Over *10 million* index offenses were larceny, burglary, or motor vehicle theft. Of these almost *6 million* were larceny theft.

318

Larceny-theft is the unlawful taking, carrying, leading, or riding away of property from the possession or constructive possession of another. It includes crimes such as shoplifting, pocket-picking, purse-snatching, thefts from motor vehicles, thefts of motor vehicle parts and accessories, bicycle thefts, etc., in which no use of force, violence, or fraud occurs (U.S. Department of Justice 1979, p. 27).

What conclusions can we draw from both arrest and report statistics as compiled by the FBI? First, it is apparent that there is an overwhelming emphasis on "street" offenses, whether one deals with property or violent crime, index or nonindex offenses. Therefore, this constitutes the "official imagery" of the crime problem, and is disseminated by the political and economic elite, law enforcement personnel, and the media. Secondly, if we focus on street offenses it is evident that property crime predominates. Thirdly, a close reading of the official report makes clear that over half of the "serious" (read "index") crimes were larcency-theft consisting of such capers as shoplifting, pocket-picking, purse-snatching, and bicycle theft. This fact appears to be lost on many both inside and outside the "crime control establishment." Finally, a large number of crimes against the person occur within the context of taking someone else's property. For example, 17 percent of the murders in 1978 "occurred as a result of some felonious act." Most such acts were property crimes. Further, 3.5 percent of the total number of murders resulted from arguments over property or money (U.S. Department of Justice 1979, p. 13).

Perhaps it is time to question which property crimes are in fact "serious" enough to be included in index crimes. Beyond this, however, looms a much larger question. It centers on the relationship of property to class inequality. This in turn bears not simply on "street" offenses but also on those of the upper world.

The Politics of Crime Statistics

It appears that we must distinguish between the actual problem of crime affecting those living in high crime areas, who are more likely to be victimized, and the political issue of crime among persons living in relatively safe areas. The latter may fear victimization due to public statements and mass media emphasis on crime. Increasingly, students of crime have looked at the variety of political functions crime statistics serve.

In the final analysis crime rates have to be understood as political devices. It is for political purposes that criminal statistics are gathered. And likewise it is according to political needs that criminal statistics are recorded and interpreted. For that reason, American crime rates are subject to great manipulation, from their inception to their use. It is impossible to know from any statistic the "true" rate of crime. Whether crime is increasing or decreasing in American society is a question that can never be answered objectively without considering the politics of the times (Quinney 1975, p. 23).

Crime statistics help to sell newspapers, aid law enforcement in obtaining more personnel and equipment, provide an issue for political campaigns, and maintain societal attention upon street crimes while diverting interest from suite crimes. Although these functions of crime statistics serve specific economic, political, and organizational interests, they tell us little about the true nature and scope of crime in society (Seidman and Couzans 1974).

The particular ideologies that define the scope and nature of the crime problem are largely based upon the general ideology of the corporate order. Accordingly, crime is supposedly committed by free-willed, rataional individuals (offenders) against the person or property of other individuals (victims), for which the offenders must be personally responsible. In spite of various factors that may reduce one's legal liability (legally mitigating factors), these are the basic ideological symbols used to explain crime. Thus, by legal definition in most industrial societies of the Western world, crime is a matter of private behavior. It is seldom viewed as a probable consequence of the way in which corporate society is organized.

Despite the current variety of types of crimes noted earlier, the public seems generally agreed on evaluating the seriousness of certain offenses. In a 1972 survey of Baltimore households, Rossi et al. (1974) found that respondents largely agreed on the relative seriousness of 140 crimes, with little variation by respondents' sex, race, or education. While this study can be criticized for the size of its sample, there appears to be accord across nation-states on the most serious crimes of murder, robbery, and assault (Newman 1976).

However, we should be aware that survey respondents are using narrow definitions of these crimes of violence, that even legal definitions as applied to street crimes will vary, and that such "street crimes" make up a relatively small proportion of all crime in society. The significance of these limitations will be apparent in subsequent discussion in this chapter. Finally, while there is a fairly strong street crime ideology among respondents in the Rossi study, actual enforcement practices frequently center on offenses not defined as serious by the general public.

As McDonald (1976, p. 233) concludes:

Clearly, the clientele of American police stations, courts, and prisons would be dramatically different if the priorities expressed in the Rossi survey were in fact the guide to practice. There would

TABLE 6-2
A Sampling from the Average Seriousness Ratings Given
to 140 Offenses in Baltimore Survey
(N is at least 100)

Crime	Mean	Variance
1. Planned killing of a policeman	8.474	2.002
2. Planned killing of a person for a fee	8.400	2.749
3. Selling heroin	8.293	2.658
4. Forcible rape after breaking into a home	8.241*	2.266
12. Kidnapping for ransom	7.930	3.844
15. Assassination of a public official	7.888	5.400
25. Manufacturing and selling drugs known to be harmful to users	7.653	3.280
26. Knowingly selling contaminated food which results in death	7.596	5.202
28. Using heroin	7.520	4.871
31. Beating up a child	7.490	3.840
33. Causing auto accident death while driving when drunk	7.455	3.904
63. Manufacturing and selling autos known to be dangerously defective	6.604	5.968
123. Engaging in male homosexual acts with consulting adults	4.736	9.396
124. Engaging in female homosexual acts with consulting adults	4.729	9.042
128. Selling pornographic magazines	4.526	7.826
130. Repeated refusal to obey parents	4.411	9.074
131. Joining a prohibited demonstration	4.323	6.486
136. Repeated truancy	3.537	7.658
137. Repeated running away from home	3.571*	6.342
140. Being drunk in public places	2.840	6.021

NOTE: Scores have a range of 9 (most serious) to 1 (least serious).
*Crimes rated by all members (200) of the Baltimore Sample.

be fewer unemployed alcoholics in the gaols, and fewer working-class children in reform school. Indeed there would be few children incarcerated at all.

There would be more car dealers, drug manufacturers and supermarket managers in prison or paying heavy fines. In place of the often unemployed petty vandals there would be overly prosperous merchants, apartment owners, and even butchers. There would be more drunks in public places, but fewer on the road. Pornography would be out as an offense, while child beating would be in.

Not Really Crimes

Criminologist Edward Sutherland noted some time ago that the criminality of corporations was like that of professional thieves in that corporations are persistent recidivists; their illegal behavior is much more extensive than the prosecutions and complaints indicate; the executives who violate the laws designed to regulate business do not customarily lose status among their business associates; business people customarily feel and express contempt for law, for government, and for governmental personnel; and corporate crime, like the professional thief, is highly organized

(1961). However, there are important distinctions between corporate criminality and that of the professional thief. The corporate criminal does not conceive of himself or herself as a criminal and neither does most of the public because such an individual does not fit the stereotype of the criminal. The professional thief's self-image is that of a criminal, and the general public accepts that view. While the professional thief has a "mouthpiece" (attorney) to argue against specific charges, corporations employ experts in law, public relations, and advertising. Such corporate "mouthpieces" serve a much wider range of functions than those of the professional thief. Their duties include influencing the enactment and administration of the law, advising clients on how to break the law with relative impunity, defending those few clients who have the misfortune to confront specific charges in court, and most importantly, building up and maintaining the corporations' status and image in the public's mind.

It is particularly those factors distinguishing the corporate criminal from the professional thief that help to maintain the appearance of non-criminality. The sharply dressed, neat-appearing corporate executive who pays taxes, contributes to local charities and juvenile delinquency funds, and is an elder in the church, fails to match the stereotyped image of the criminal who, with premeditation, earns a livelihood through victimizing the public. If the mass media stressed suite crime in the same manner it did street crime, there would likely be financial repercussions.

> Nearly all the advertising revenues of the newspapers and mass magazines, as well as of radio and television stations and networks, come from these same corporations and their smaller counterparts. . . . The newspapers have never, despite recent sociological revelations, ventured statistical summaries of the situation as they regularly do with lower-class, police-reported crimes—a marked case of class bias (Lundberg 1968).

Why do we tend to evaluate street crime so differently from suite crime? The direct, personal, face-to-face threat of physical violence—murder, rape, assault, robbery—is significant in street crimes. As one student of crime states,

> I realize that muggers take much less from us than do corporate, syndicate, and white-collar criminals. I have little doubt that the average executive swindles more on his taxes and expense account than the average addict steals in a typical year. Moreover, I am well aware that concentrating on street crimes provides yet another opportunity for picking on the poor, a campaign I have no wish to assist. It is a scandal that a bank embezzler gets six months while a hold-up man is hit with five years. Yet it is not entirely their disparate backgrounds that produce this discrimination.
>
> A face-to-face threat of bodily harm or possibly violent death is so terrifying to most people that the $20 or so stolen in a typical

mugging must be multiplied many times if comparisons with other offenses are to be made. I have a hunch that a majority of city dwellers would accept a bargain under which if they would not be mugged this year they would be willing to allow white-collar crimes to take an extra ten percent of their incomes. Of course we are annoyed by corporate thievery that drives up prices, but the kind of dread included by thuggery has no dollar equivalent or, if it does, an extremely high one (Hacker 1973, p. 9).

While there is obvious physical danger and harm from street crimes against the person, the belief that suite crimes are not violent is mistaken.

> Corporate crime kills and maims. It has been estimated, for example, that each year 200,000 to 500,000 workers are needlessly exposed to toxic agents such as radioactive materials and poisonous chemicals because of corporate failure to obey safety laws. And, many of the 2.5 million temporary and 250,000 permanent worker disabilities from industrial accidents each year are the result of managerial acts that represent culpable failure to adhere to established standards (Geis 1974).

However, when automobile accidents, airplane crashes, or industrial disasters occur, attention is usually focused upon the culpability of those directly responsible for the accident or disaster. In discussing the nearly 100,000 United States workers who die each year as a result of exposure to job health hazards, Swartz notes

> One of the more insidious tactics used by the corporate perpetrators of crime is to blame the victims for what happens to them. The National Safety Council, a corporation-funded institution, frequently runs "safety" campaigns. The point of these campaigns is always that the workers are careless and lazy, and do not take the measures necessary to protect themselves (wearing safety helmets, ear plugs, etc.). Never is the corporation held the culprit (Swartz 1975, p. 19).

When defects in manufacturing or violations of safety standards are investigated and found, it is usually interpreted as a quirk or accident with possible civil, but not criminal liability. (See Chapter Four on Work.) For example, while it appears that mercury poisoning from the Dryden Chemical plant in northwestern Ontario is evident among Native Americans in the area, it will not likely result in the laying of criminal charges. Such a decision is based largely upon a legal conception of causation, intent, and culpability, all of which mitigate corporate responsibility. Nonetheless, physical harm, injury, and often death result from this disease. Whether death or injury is at the hands of an assailant in a face-to-face encounter or traceable to an impersonal corporation through poisoning and disease, the end result is similar (Singer and Rodgers 1975).

The identification of victim(s) and offender(s) is one difference often noted in evaluating suite crime and violent street crime. While a visible, dramatic theft at gunpoint entails an obvious victim and criminal, the taking of millions of dollars from millions of people through fraud or price fixing is less direct, with a more diffuse victim and offender. For example, the theft of a worker's income tax, unemployment insurance, or pension deductions by an employer does not elicit the same response as bank robberies do, although it is a much more profitable type of crime. Failure by Canadian employers to remit payroll deductions in 1975 accounted for $7.9 million, while bank robbers, extortionists, and kidnappers gained a profit of only $5.17 million in the same year (Brecker 1976). In addition, it is more difficult to identify victim and offender. A significant factor in such evaluations is the nonhostile, nonthreatening nature of the setting and the fact that the offender is usually viewed as providing needed and legitimate goods and services.

> That we are daily victimized is not usually recognized because, for example, we do not view the grocery store or department store as an accomplice, the manufacturer as a criminal, and ourselves as victims of rising costs (Reasons 1974, p. 233).

Even when suite criminals commit "common crimes," they tend to be evaluated differently. For example, if a person breaks into another's premises and takes something, the usual definition is breaking and entering or burglary and the offender is subject to possible imprisonment. However, when the White House "Plumbers," CIA, FBI, RCMP, or federal narcotics agents commit such acts, they are likely to be evaluated in light of national defense and/or as necessary in the war against crime and therefore immune from prosecution. The innumerable offenses of former United States President Nixon were viewed by some as merely the legitimate exercise of authority by the Head of State (Dobrovir et al. 1974). The prevailing view of the abuse of office is that such is an individual fault. The structure of state power is not critically examined. To be clear, the articles of impeachment prepared by the Judiciary Committee of the House of Representatives cited such Watergate offenses as "obstruction of justice." Eliminated from consideration was the Administration's conduct of a "secret war" in Laos and Cambodia. Thus, legal issues that center on private behavior diverted attention from the structural issues involving the State and use of military force.

Furthermore, the imagery of the suite offender as a respectable business executive or civic official who contributes to the community and society is contrary to the stereotype of the criminal. The Churchill Forest Industries scandal in Manitoba attests to the significance of appearance and status in suite crime. In a multimillion dollar swindle against the people of Manitoba, one Dr. Kosser and his associates put over one of the greatest cons in the annals of crime. In the end, it was estimated by an investigative commission that Kosser made about $26 million in excessive fees and paid no Canadian taxes on more than $33 million in earnings by setting up a network of companies. Left holding the bag were business and government leaders and, of course, the taxpayers of Manitoba.

Our current perception and evaluation of suite crime has not always been with us. For example, antitrust legislation was passed in the United States in 1890 under pressure from an outraged populace who were concerned about oppressive and ruthless business practices, concentration of wealth and power, and government policies granting special privileges to big business (McCormick 1977). Nonetheless, subsequent lack of enforcement, combined with effective business and government propaganda, led to a change in concern with such crimes.

> By influencing visibility and reporting of offenses, manipulating community expectations through the propagandizing of themes focusing upon the necessity of a profit system, the role of business in combatting social problems, improvements in living standards, and affecting the organization and actions of enforcement agents, societal indignation and resistance directed toward illegal corporate activities have been steadily eroded (McCormick 1977, p. 37).

More critically, Sherman antitrust became a weapon to attack organized labor at the turn of the century. As a device to slow down economic concentration, it was ineffectual. (See Chapter Four on Work: Alienation and Freedom.)

Crime and Moral Depravity

In addition to "street crime" there is another element in the prevailing ideology of criminal offenses. Much of what is termed the criminal justice system (criminal law legislation, the judiciary, police, legal profession, and corrections) deals with the perpetrators of "victimless crimes." Thus, the law is used to mount crusades on "vice, sin, and depravity," all quite obviously examples of *private behavior*. As such, a social obsession with "evil" rarely leads to a structural critique.

Media images of crimes without victims depict them as inherently wicked and consequently dangerous. Stereotypes of the gambler, dope fiend, prostitute, homosexual, and drunk often present a frightful imagery that evokes both pity and fear among the "morally superior" (Reasons 1976). While most illicit drug users, prostitutes, gamblers, homosexuals, and the inebriated live relatively normal, law-abiding lives apart from their appetites, crimes of violence, personal psychopathology, and sordid environments are dramatized in the mass media as typical of such "kinds of people" and their behavior. Such representations fail to note that most of the limited violence and personal psychopathology that is evident is largely a product of restricted criminal policy, not of the behavior per se. In fact, the consequences of making and maintaining such behaviors as criminal are likely more harmful than removing them from the purview of the criminal law.

Report after report and study upon study have indicated that such "overcriminalization" produces the following negative consequences: (1) the creation of artificially high profits and criminal monopolies, (2) the emergence and maintenance of organized crime, (3) secondary crime such as theft among addicts to sustain their habit, (4) the creation and maintenance of criminal subcultures, (5) excessive expenditures of police and criminal justice resources, (6) corruption of agents of the criminal justice system, (7) contempt for the law and criminal justice system by offenders, (8) the infringement upon individual rights (Morris and Hawkins 1970).

Public policy criminalizing such behaviors is particularly subject to criticism within democratic societies.

> To some extent crimes without victims are outlawed because of a benevolent interest in protecting an individual from himself. The difficulties here are acute. For one thing, in a democracy freedom of an individual to determine what is best for himself as long as he does not interfere with a similar freedom of others, is a prime ingredient. For another, it is dubious that the force of the criminal law upon marijuana smokers, abortion-seeking women,[1] homosexuals and numbers players adds to the sum of their happiness and makes them better persons (Geis 1972).

Some students of crime are becoming increasingly aware of the ramifications of the trite observation that the formal cause of crime is the criminal law. The moral excesses in the criminal law can no longer be afforded. Overcriminalization in such areas as obscenity and pornography, unlawful gaming, and illicit drugs has produced more problems than it has solved. For example, social resources continue to be squandered to pay for law enforcement, judicial, and correctional personnel to "control" the drug user. The irrational and oppressive way agencies of the State respond to users of illicit drugs is hardly to be distinguished from the way witches were treated centuries ago. The "demonological" properties attributed to these drugs have little relation to their known effects, and state actions only appear to worsen the "drug problem" rather than ameliorate it (Brecher 1972). Clearly the answer is not to increase penalties and personnel in some sort of convoluted logic that there will be a decrease

[1] Though abortion has a specific legal standing in the United States today, antiabortion forces at this writing are organized and seeking more restrictive legal measures. (See Chapter Eleven, Sex and Sexism.)

in illicit drug use with an increase in social control agents. (See Chapter Nine, The Demonology of Drugs.)

EMERGENCE

When Wasn't There a Crime Wave?

The land is full of bloody crime and the city is full of violence.
—Ezekial 7:23

The above biblical quote belies the belief that street crime and violence are totally out of hand today and that in the past there was little to worry about. Such a perspective lacks a proper sense of history because since the emergence of crime as defined by the nation-state there have been periodic crime waves and public concern about personal safety. For example, during the first six decades of the Massachusetts Bay Colony there were three serious crime waves (Erikson 1966). These included the Antinomian controversy of 1636, the Quaker prosecutions of the late 1650s, and the witchcraft hysteria of 1692. While we may smugly assert that such behavior as questioning religious leaders, holding certain religious beliefs, or having presumed mystical powers are hardly criminal, at that time they were. These crimes had a great deal of impact on both the colony and the offenders. During a period of just a few months nineteen people were executed as witches, seven more were condemned, and one was pressed to death under a pile of rocks for standing mute at his trial.

Also, some tend to assume that increasing urbanization inevitably brings about more street crime, conventional violence, and moral depravity. However, such a view is arguable in light of historical analysis (Lane 1969, p. 469).

> America is now an urban nation, but Americans are still afraid of cities. There are many dimensions to this fear, but one of these is especially direct, and starkly physical. The current concern with "safety in the streets" echoes a belief, as old as the Republic, that the city is dangerous, the breeding ground of vice and violence. Observers of varying sophistication have pointed out that dark streets hide dark deeds, and that the anonymity and freedom of urban society, its temptations and frenzied pace, all contribute to encourage criminal behavior. From this it is easy to conclude that with metropolitan growth and the multiplication of all these conditions, the role of violent crime is inexorably multiplied also.
>
> But constant repetition of a myth is no substitute for proof. Under some circumstances it does in fact seem clear that migration to the

metropolis has been accompanied by disruption and violence. This does not mean that there is a necessary or inevitable connection between growth of cities and growth of crime. *In fact the existing historical evidence suggests the very reverse, that over a long term urbanization has had a settling, literally a civilizing, effect on the population involved.* (Emphasis added.)

Thus, the "good old days" may well have exhibited more conventional violence and street crime than contemporary times. In a classic work on violence, Georges Sorel suggested that increased intolerance and fear of physical assault are directly related to the more violence-free lives people are living. When violence and the threat of it are a constant daily possibility to the citizenry, it is accepted as a normal part of everyday life. However, with the decrease in the average citizen's exposure to the threat of personal physical attack it becomes something out of the ordinary and less tolerable. Therefore, the great preoccupation with crimes of violence and the fear of such crimes in North America may reflect a lessening of public tolerance for this sort of behavior rather than great increases in the number of such crimes. For example, political violence and assassination have received a great deal of scrutiny in the last few decades in North America. However, both the United States (Kirkham, Levy, and Crotty 1970) and Canada (Szabo 1970) have a long history of such activity.

> Thus, the notion (which is commonly held in all strata of our society) that the phenomenon of violence and assassination is something new, something "un-American," a peculiar product of the present day, is demonstrably and remarkably mistaken (Salisbury 1970, p. xvii).

Whose Law?

Two increasingly significant issues in contemporary criminology are: (1) do laws reflect some interests more than others? and (2) does the criminal justice system discriminate against some groups relative to other groups? Both of these issues are significant for students of law. While traditional criminology focuses largely upon characteristics of the offender, some criminologists are advocating that we study the way in which laws arise and how they operate. We are reminded again of a long-standing truism for students of the law: *The formal cause of crime is the criminal law*. Until recently, criminologists have largely neglected this observation. While criminology is often defined as the study of the sociology of law, causes of criminal behavior, and penology, relatively little of the discipline's attention has been given to the sociology of law. Hence, one may overlook the vital point that law is a social product reflecting both the imperatives in social structure and the general ideology that legitimizes those imperatives.

The study of law has recently been presented by students of crime who view social conflict and differences in power as significant factors in explaining crime in a society. These criminologists have explicitly recognized the importance of power, politics, and wealth in creating, sustaining, and shaping the more limited conditions identified by order theories of crime. For example, such factors as poverty, racial discrimination, inequality of opportunities, and others are often identified as "causes" of crime. However, the finding that poverty is associated with increases of certain kinds of street criminality and victimization might provoke the analyst to ask why large inequities in the distribution of wealth and goods exist in a "society of plenty." This might lead to a critical analysis of economic policy rather than of criminal characteristics (U.S. Congress, Joint Economic Committee 1976).

Increasing awareness regarding the political nature of crime and the law has arisen with heightened conflict between traditionally powerless groups (for instance, students and youth, poor and nonwhite) and those in power. Submerged in a consensus perspective of society, viewing the state as neutral, most criminologists have been unable to account for the increasing questioning of the legitimacy of specific laws and, ultimately, the authority of the State. However, some criminologists have begun to investigate critically the origin, enforcement, and administration of laws within the context of class interests, power, and conflict.

To understand the law, its enforcement, and its administration, we need to demystify the nature and function of law, placing it clearly in the context of conflict and ideology. Chambliss and Seidman (1971) suggest that the presentation of a "mythical" consensus perspective of the law is a normal occurrence in law schools, political science courses on law, criminology, and high school courses dealing with the law.

The Consensus View of Law A number of philosophical schools of jurisprudence, among them the natural, cultural, and historical schools, have denied that lawmakers have value choices in the creation of laws (Schur 1969). These schools of legal philosophy suggest that the law and its agents (including enforcers and administrators) stand apart from society, comprising a neutral body within which social struggle and conflict take place. This consensus perspective views the state as a value-neutral organ for the resolution of conflict. Order theories hold that although the adversary proceedings pit the state against the accused, trials occur within the "neutral" framework of the court. The judge supposedly epitomizes the evenhanded, nonbiased, neutral arbitrator of institutionalized conflict. This consensus perspective is widely diffused by the means of influence and is consistent with the prevailing ideology of the "blind" nature of justice and the equity of democratic political and legal systems. The presumed nonpolitical and unbiased character of the judicial system has obscured the basically political nature of crime and the law.

The Conflict View of Law Other schools of jurisprudence suggest that law is a legitimizing weapon of the highest order, and those making, enforcing, and administering laws are merely attempting to perpetrate the existing State and its social order (Chambliss and Seidman 1971). These schools have demystified the nature of laws by emphasizing that they are human products and State-given, not found in some supernatural realm beyond the influence and control of ordinary mortals. Rather than viewing the State and its legal actors as value-free, our ideological theory invests participants in the legal system with values, feelings, and biases that often subtly influence their actions. Rather than being a neutral framework for the collective interests of society, law is an instrument of those in power, used to maintain their position and privilege. Turk (1976, p. 276) argues that the conflict conception of law is superior to the neutral approach: "A superior alternative is the conception of law as power, i.e., a set of resources whose control and mobilization can in many ways . . . generate and exacerbate conflicts rather than resolving or softening them."

Therefore, viewing the law as an instrument of power has become a growing area of concern among criminologists. Quinney's text, *The Social Reality of Crime*, began to articulate what many dissident leaders of the 1960s suggested, that criminal law is largely made, enforced, and administered by powerful interest groups for their own gains. This text appeared in stark contrast to traditional criminology texts in theory and presentation. Through its focusing upon the political nature of criminal definitions, their application and enforcement, crime emerges as a product of power differentials and conflicting world views. Crime is a definition of behavior made by officials of the State and not inherent in an act. Those behaviors that are most offensive to the powers that be tend to be made crimes. At a later point, Quinney was to modify his theory of interests to center on class domination by means of law (1975).

Table 6–3 details the difference in order and conflict explanations of the causes and consequences of criminal law.

The order perspective views the criminal law as reflecting the common good and controlling the criminal, while the conflict perspective sees ruling-class interests as shaping criminal law to maintain class dominance.

The possibility that law does not reflect the common good means that we must look beyond and behind the public statements and proclamations on the necessity of law generally, and certain laws specifically. The law has emerged not as a mystical manifestation of the will of the people, but as an instrument that reflects the interests of power.

Today, law embodies the general ideology of corporate order, just as it reflected the rising mercantile interests that accompanied the decline of feudalism and the birth of trade capitalism. To be clear, the criminal

TABLE 6-3
Two Views of Criminal Law

	Cause	Consequence
Conflict Paradigm	Ruling class interests	Provide state coercive force to repress the class struggle and to legitimize the use of this force
Order Paradigm	Customary beliefs that are codified in state law	To establish procedures for controlling those who do not comply with customs

Source: Adapted from William J. Chambliss, *Functional and Conflict Theories of Crime* (New York: MSS Modular Publications, 1974).

law in its philosophy and statutory language centers on the individual as willful actor; crime becomes a private affair rather than a built-in feature of political and economic order; and all offenders are viewed as having equal opportunity in the sight of the law.

INSTITUTIONALIZATION

Having identified the interests behind the emergence of criminal law, it is appropriate to turn to the formal institutionalization of the law as a product of the nation-state. Criminal law is characterized by its public nature, state origin, and politically unifying role. To say that criminal law is inherently political is at once a trite truism and a blasphemous assertion. Such a statement is manifestly true if the criminal law purportedly reflects the desires and goals of a political unit (the nation-state), while it may appear to be a blasphemous assertion for those who divorce the law from politics. To provide a clearer picture of the political nature of the criminal law, one need only view the nation-state and subsequent criminal behavior as a relatively "new" creation in human history. How were "bad" behaviors dealt with prior to the emergence of the nation-state? How did the emergence of the nation-state affect justice?

The order paradigm views the criminalization of certain behaviors as a reflection of societal consensus and the expression of a common good. Law is viewed as functioning to maintain public order, facilitate cooperative action, confer legitimacy, and communicate moral standards (Berman and Greiner 1966). While the above functions may appear obvious and nondebatable, conflict theorists pose the questions: Public order for whom? Whose cooperative action? Legitimacy for whom? Whose moral standards? Such questions are particularly valid within the context of our large heterogeneous stratified urban industrial societies. As Quinney (1975, p. 38) notes,

> Definitions of crime are formulated according to the interests of those who have the power to translate their interests into public policy. Those definitions are ultimately incorporated into the criminal law. Furthermore, definitions of crime in a society change as the interests of the dominant class change. In other words, those who are able to have their interests represented in public policy regulate the formulation of definitions of crime.

From the order approach, law resulted from "double" institutionalization. That is, the law is an institution itself that represents "customary" institutions such as marriage, the family, religion. However, the historical record suggests that law through the coercion of the State, replaced custom and was often antagonistic toward custom. As one anthropologist notes,

> Efforts to legislate conscience by an external political power are the antithesis of custom; customary behavior comprises precisely those aspects of social behavior which are traditional, moral, and religious, which are, in short, conventional and nonlegal. Put another way, custom is social morality. The relation between custom and law is, basically, one of contradiciton not continuity (Diamond 1971, p. 31).

From Feudal to State Law

In Europe, beginning roughly with the fifth century A.D. and continuing on into the thirteenth century, a community form based on agriculture and caste prevailed. This community pattern, termed feudalism, can more accurately be defined as a social and economic system centered in land worked by *serfs* (workers bound to the land). The land was often held by *vassals* who pledged fealty to overlords. *Overlords* were often titled members of nobility who ruled feudal states, conferring land holdings on vassals in return for military and other services (Chambliss and Ryther 1975, pp. 172–197). Feudalism largely disappeared in medieval Europe due to a variety of historical forces including external conquest, the growth of central governments, surplus population, the loss of serfs' rights to common land and the rise of cities.

> In part as the legacy of the collapse of feudalism and in part as a consequence of the rise of institutions of capitalism which this

collapse afforded, individualism as a generalized social movement emerged from a fact of institutional chaos to a social philosophy and a normative order and transformed, as it grew, the whole of Western society and its culture. Early or late, it came eventually to find social expression in religion as Protestantism; in philosophy as empiricism and idealism; in scholastic inquiry as deductive and inductive methods of natural science; in economy as new institutions of private property, the market, entrepreneurship, rational accounting, and the redivision of labor along new social lines (Kennedy 1970, p. 20).

The feudal community based on shared responsibility was thus replaced by an emerging trade capitalism based on private property and bonded by a new ethic, that of *individualism*. Obviously, an economic system based on trade and markets required such things as roads and standardized currency. Also, the developing merchant class had no warrior caste (vassals) available to protect its interests. A central authority would have to provide the force of arms necessary to defend private interests. Such needs, together with others, gave rise to the *nation-state*, formally institutionalized in Europe in the post-fifteenth century period. With the establishment of the State, a transformation in law occurred, as is revealed in the following chart.

Changes from Feudal to State Law

Legal Factor	Feudal Law	State Law
Unit of justice	Family	State
Jurisdictional ties	Blood	Territory
Basis of responsibility	Collective	Individual
Method of dispute settlement	Feud or compensation	State court procedures: civil & criminal

Under the feudal system the family, based on blood ties, was the basic unit determining and administering justice. With the demise of the feudal system there emerged the nation-state, based on territorial ties, to determine and administer justice. For example, under feudal law if one took a person's life, the offender's kin would be collectively held responsible, not the individual killer. Subsequently, the victim's kin might attempt to settle the debt by taking the life of any member of the killer's family, not necessarily the offender. This might precipitate a feud that could go on for some time. Another possible method of retaliation was extracting compensation from the offending family. Such compensation might be in the form of valued goods paid for the deceased. Within the context of the nation-state by contrast, the killer was held individually responsible for the act and was punished by agents of the State. The nation-state does not allow for compensation as a means of resolving the harm even if the family of the deceased should agree to a settlement. This is because criminal behavior is viewed as an offense against the nation-state and not just against an individual.

Law versus Kinship   The laws that arose with the nation-state were in most instances unprecedented, and in opposition to the customary order of feudal society. They represented a new social power of the State—and the new goals of an interrelated census-tax-conscription system. The State's need for labor, an army, tax revenue, and the maintenance of a bureaucracy gave rise to the census of subjects and the subsequent emergence of civil law. Among the first civil laws were those against homicide and suicide, undermining the kinship system by establishing the individual as the property of the State (Diamond 1971). Thus, the State grew in power and influence as a consequence of a new economic order of private property and the increasingly powerful interests of property owners.

What occurred politically between the fifth and thirteenth centuries to bring about such a change in legal systems? In addition to the economic history surveyed earlier, political unification of heretofore separate feudal estates—largely due to civil wars among local military bands, the Danish invasion of the tenth century, and the acceptance of Christianity as the prevailing religion—greatly aided the rise of the nation-state. When William of Normandy became King of England in 1066, the Norman nobles replaced the Saxons in the ruling hierarchy and a system of common law emerged as law for all people of England. Subsequently, the State took the place of kin and no longer allowed private settlement of a criminal case.

> English criminal law came about to protect particular interests, primarily those of the King. The criminal law placed the affairs of his subjects under his jurisdiction. The powerful landholders and the church could no longer freely create and administer law in their own courts. Law that affected the nation was now the king's law, the nation's interests were those of the king (Quinney 1975, p. 47).

The above changes in legal systems are related to changes in the nature of societies. In the stateless society more emphasis was placed upon compromise of the "give a little, get a little" theory of dispute settlement (Chambliss and Seidman 1971, pp. 28–35). Such a means of resolving disputes usually occurs where an on-going relationship between disputants is anticipated. In other words, in a small, homogeneous society where continuing close relationships are the rule, compromise and negotiation are important. In complex, heterogeneous, stratified societies, the dispute-settling process determines that one party is right and one is wrong, that is, winner take all, or a zero-sum game. Thus, in contemporary North America the law and legal system are largely based upon determining victims and criminals, right and wrong, transgressed against and transgressor, based upon the "winner take all" philosophy. The development of this approach to conflict resolution is very much related to the extent of stratification in a nation-state.

> The more economically stratified a society becomes, the more it becomes necessary for the dominant groups in the society to enforce through coercion the norms of conduct which guarantee their supremacy (Chambliss and Seidman 1971, pp. 33–34).

Therefore, in our highly complex and stratified society one should expect the disproportionate representation of those in the lower classes in statistics on crime and the criminal justice system. Furthermore, as society grows more diverse and complex, an increase in the number of formal agents of social control follows. The interests of the dominant and powerful segments of the nation-state will be those incorporated into and protected by the law and legal system. What arose with the nation-state was the development of a legal ideology to enhance and subsequently protect the interests of the emerging bourgeoisie. As two legal scholars have noted,

> This tendency is reflected in the importance accorded lawyers and to legal training in all Western governmental structures and in all movements for social change which aim at seizing state power (Tigar and Levy 1977, p. 277).

An understanding of the dynamics of the State is crucial for the study of crime in contemporary society. The concept of the State stands for various specific institutions that are connected to one another and thus comprise the State. The system includes the following elements: (1) the government, (2) the administration, (3) the military and the police, (4) the judiciary, and (5) units of subcentral government (Miliband 1969, pp. 49–67). In capitalist nations such as the United States and Canada, the dominant economic class largely controls the State. Underlying a discussion of the role of the State in the study of crime is the realization that state interests represent dominant interests, and in capitalist society, this means largely economic elites[2]

---

[2]For a discussion of the role of law in socialist states, see Reasons and Rich 1978 and Kulcsar 1980.

Theft

A classic example of the role of dominant group interests in defining crime is the emergence of the law of theft (Hall 1952). Prior to the fifteenth century there was no legal conception of theft in the criminal law as we know it today. However, in the Carrier's Case of 1473 the legal concept of theft was established, and still flourishes in contemporary Western law. In the Carrier's Case, a transporter of goods took the wares he was entrusted with, converted them to his own use, and was subsequently charged with a felony. Prior to this case taking goods entrusted to one was not theft. The burden was upon those consigning commodities to others to find someone who was reliable and trustworthy. If you failed to get someone who could be trusted, you might lose quite a lot in goods. Thus, possession was ten-tenths of the law. However, in this case the King's judges ruled the transporter guilty of theft, contrary to all legal precedent. Why the dramatic change?

In fifteenth-century Europe the commercial revolution was taking place and the old feudal structure based upon agriculture was giving way to a new order based upon industry and trade. More significantly, the King was very much involved in royal commercial activities, including trade, and could not allow such wrongdoings. Since the courts were subservient to the wishes of King Edward IV, the decision against the dishonest merchant should have been anticipated. Notwithstanding prior common law, the State's (King's) interests were best served by expanding the definition of theft to better protect the commercial interests of the State and the new entrepreneurial class. As mentioned earlier in this chapter, contemporary emphasis upon theft as a working- or lower-class crime (street crime) rather than middle- or upper-class crime (suite crime) continues this protection of dominant interests.

Rape and Witchcraft

While rape laws may be thought to be in the interest of all citizens, an historical accounting suggests otherwise. In fact, Diamond (1971) describes how rape laws were invented by the State for conscription purposes. A specific category of the King's women in Dahomey were sent to local villages and men who had intercourse with them were charged with rape and upon summary trial were punished by conscription into the army. Therefore, rape began as a *civil* crime. Such behaviors would have been dealt with differently under feudal law; however, the King needed soldiers and this was one method to obtain them.

The emergence of rape laws in England reflect a sexist bias apparent in witchcraft laws. For some, the historical prosecution and persecution of witches portray a simple hatred of women and an attempt to maintain male hegemony. For example, the reasons given for the female nature of witchcraft reflected dominant male stereotypes. King James I explained in his *Demonologie*, 1597, why women were twenty times more likely than men to be witches. His explanation is based on three conditions women are supposedly more susceptible to: (1) curiosity, (2) revenge, and (3) greed due to poverty. Such a view was prevalent throughout the sixteenth and seventeenth centuries.

> Suffice it to say that witchcraft charges, at certain times, and under certain conditions become a useful method for men to keep women inferior and in fear (Geis).

Though it is tempting to view witchcraft as another male chauvinist plot, it is necessary to go beyond the apparent. Currie (1968) examined this phenomenon as it existed in Europe between roughly the fifteenth and eighteenth centuries. While women were most frequently identified as witches in England, on the continent of Europe men were often found guilty of the practice. Further, while most witches in England were lower class, many on the continent were propertied. Why the difference in the sex and class of witches? In Great Britain, the center of an emerging and increasingly strong mercantile capitalism, the sanctity of private property was ensured by law. Thus, the state could not confiscate the property of witches. On the continent, however, due to the less dramatic decline of feudal order, property could be confiscated. Consequently, there was a strong economic reason to identify men as well as women as witches provided of course they held property. Accordingly, the witch-hunting business was a virtual "industry" on the continent. On the island, at the same period of history it was little more than a "racket." Thus, what appears to be only sex-based discrimination may under closer examination assume somewhat the nature of economic exploitation.

Witchcraft trials ceased in Great Britain when religion became less of a powerful force in the State, medical practices improved, criminal procedures became fewer, and when humans began to explain disaster by something other than the evil forces within themselves or others. Nonetheless, other forms of sexual discrimination and oppression emerged since the underlying conflicts remained unresolved.

While witchcraft laws and trials are only historic curiosities today, rape remains as a significant social and political issue. Laws concerning rape in the twentieth century are largely based upon English common law. A major figure in defining legal approaches toward both witchcraft and rape was Sir Matthew Hale, a leading jurist of seventeenth-century England. His sexist bias was represented not only in witchcraft rulings, but also in rape cases. Rape laws arose to protect not women per se, but women as the property of fathers and husbands. From Hale emanated

337

the long-standing cautionary instruction that rape "is an accusation easily to be made and hard to be proved, and harder to be defended by the party accused, the never so innocent." Although this is an often quoted phrase, Geis shows it is entirely inaccurate. It has never been an easy charge to make and a difficult one to rebut. This is particuarly evident in the fact that the woman filing such a charge often becomes the defendant. (See Chapter Eleven, Sex and Sexism.) However, as will be discussed in a subsequent section, attempts are being made to change sexist laws.

Victimless Crimes

One of the more obvious areas of elite interest in crime may be found in victimless crimes such as pornography, obscenity, vagrancy, drunkenness, abortion, illicit drug use, gambling, and homosexuality. As noted in chapter nine, drug laws reflect class and racial interests. The other types of offenses also reflect class moral and economic interests. For example, vagrancy laws emerged in fourteenth-century England to supply labor for landowners. Subsequently, vagrancy laws were used to control criminal activities and "undesirable" elements in communities in England, the United States, and Canada (Chambliss 1964). In recent years such statutes have been attacked as unconstitutional and expunged, with other statutes substituted to control the under classes.

While drunkenness has been increasingly eliminated as a crime, historically it was established to uphold middle-class, rural, Protestant puritanical beliefs about drinking. In fact, such interests led to the "noble experiment" of Prohibition (Gusfield 1963). Not to be ignored is the historical fact that the temperance movement emerged during the post-Civil War period and continued on until the institutionalization of Prohibition in 1919. This was a time when the immigrant workers (men, women, and children) were savagely exploited in the urban factory system. The image of the drink-dependent workers seeking escape from toil was hardly comforting to the industrial elite. Thus, it is plausible to argue that Prohibition was more than a cultural victory for the "puritans." Rather, it was consistent with corporate industrial interests. The current movement toward decriminalization and involuntary civil lockup represents essentially the same moral interests but evidences the new ideology of the medical model rather than the criminal. The emphasis is still one of blaming the victim rather than examining the structural nature of alienation (see Chapter Four) and the relationship between a "privatized" society and alcohol abuse.

Juvenile Delinquency

We are constantly reminded by radio, television, newspapers, civic leaders, and criminal justice officials that juvenile delinquency is rapidly increasing and becoming a serious menace to society. However, if we look beyond the rhetoric of such assertions, we will find out that our contemporary problem of delinquency has an historical basis founded upon the needs and values of specific dominant interests and their ideology of social control.

While legal distinctions based upon age can be found in early Chinese society, our approach to juvenile delinquency today is based upon English common law. The case of Eyre *v*. Shaftsbury in 1722 established the principle of *parens patriae*, wherein the King (State) acts as parent in the best interests of the child. While such a principle apparently is humanitarian and benevolent, the facts of the case suggest other purposes. More specifically, the King had much to gain financially by managing the youth's (the Earl of Shaftsbury) land, so the young earl was made a ward of the court (Venable 1966). Subsequently, emphasis was placed upon wealthy youth who were judged dependent or neglected and in need of "protection."

In the nineteenth century there emerged a "child-saving movement" in the United States and Canada that was interested in child welfare, education, reformatories, labor, and other youth-related issues (Platt 1969). While many observers have characterized the antidelinquency reformers as humanitarians who were disinterested citizens representing an enlightened and socially responsible middle class, Platt (1974, p. 366) argues that:

> . . . the child-saving movement was a coercive and conservatizing influence, that liberalism in the Progressive era was the conscious product of policies initiated or supported by leaders of major corporations and financial institutions, and that many social reformers wanted to secure existing political and economic arrangements, albeit in an ameliorated and regulated form.

During the latter part of the nineteenth century major cities in the United States were teeming with immigrants who were struggling with poverty, deplorable housing, and miserable living conditions. Juvenile crime, like other social problems, was viewed by the middle and upper classes as generally a product of the city, and specifically of the poor and working-class immigrants. As part of the "Progressive Era," women primarily of the middle and upper classes, led the child-saving movement as an extension of the maternal role.

> For traditionally educated women and daughters of the landed and industrial gentry, the child-saving movement presented an

339

opportunity for pursuing socially acceptable public roles and for restoring some of the authority and spiritual influence which many women felt they had lost through the urbanization of family life (Platt 1974, p. 371).

The progressive period was characterized by nativism and racism largely directed at the urban working class, which was mainly immigrant. The attempts to control the youth of this class paralleled other efforts at manipulation such as birth control and eugenics. While their activities were legitimized as humanitarian, the child-savers reflected their class and ethnic position in society.

With the beginning of the juvenile court in the last decade of the nineteenth century in Chicago, a new era of social control was to begin. Although the court initially concerned itself with juvenile acts that violated existing criminal statutes, new "crimes" were to be developed that would greatly increase the scope of the court. These "status" offenses included vicious or immoral behavior; incorrigibility; truancy; roaming the streets; frequenting such places as pool halls, bowling alleys, dance halls, and movies, among others. While some of these "crimes" no longer exist, contemporary statutes censure:

> . . . children who engage in immoral or indecent behavior, exhibit immoral conduct around schools, engage in illegal occupations, knowingly associate with vicious or immoral persons, grow up in idleness or crime, patronize or visit policy shops or gaming houses, wander in the streets at night, habitually wander about railroad yards or tracks, are incorrigible, or deport themselves so as to injure themselves or others (Gibbons 1976, pp. 12–13).

Such delinquent behavior is principally found among the working class and poor and is falsely assumed to be a cause of subsequent criminality (Liazos 1974). The assumption by the child-savers was that "delinquent" behavior is correctable through treatment and rehabilitation. The new role of social workers was to aid greatly in the solution to this "problem." It was more than coincidental that women were instrumental in both the child-saving movement and the rise of the social work profession. Each represented a traditional view of women's place. Canadian delinquency legislation was also spearheaded by advocates of probation and the social welfare profession, many of whom were women (Hagen and Leon 1977).

Established along with the definition of delinquency and separate court processing was a whole new set of occupations for an emerging profession. The effects of this historical foundation for juvenile delinquency will be discussed later in this chapter.

Laws that are evidently directed to control those in the middle and upper classes are an *apparent* contradiction to the assumption that elite interests are the basis for law. There are innumerable laws governing professional, economic, and political sectors, among them laws concerning fraud, bribery, misappropriation of public funds, tax evasion, health and safety codes, and licensing. However, a careful analysis of such laws may reveal their symbolic importance and lack of subsequent enforcement. The Sherman Antitrust Act in the United States and the Combines Act in Canada are directed at protecting the public interest in economic competition through prohibiting various types of business activities (Reasons and Goff 1980). More specifically, they purportedly represent the values of free enterprise and a competitive marketplace. Thus, they are aimed at illegal mergers, monopolies, and price fixing, among other unfair practices.

Anticombines legislation in Canada was passed in 1899 to protect the "public interest." However, an historical analysis of the act suggests it was largely a product of business interests and concern (Goff and Reasons 1978). It was a law giving expression to the values of free enterprise and competition, but it had little effect upon the illicit practices it was supposed to control. The law's ineffectiveness is evident in the few prosecutions it has educed and the generally unenforceable nature of its provisions (Goff and Reasons 1976). Anticombines legislation appears to have emerged as a product of popular unrest and economic crises in order to assure certain discontented segments of the public that something was being done.

> Legislation was only introduced and amended when class conflict threatened the ruling class; that is, when the petit bourgeoisie felt squeezed out of the competition, or when working class discontent, intensified during periods of economic depression, threatened severe disruption (Young 1974, p. 73).

Antitrust legislation was passed in 1890 in the United States during a period of populism and antagonism to big business, particularly among farmers.

> Expressing his discontent through various agrarian third party movements, the typical small farmer placed the blame for falling prices, rising costs, increased debts, and massive foreclosures upon the monopolistic control of corporations and trusts. Big business was accused, with some justification, of massive manipulations of the marketplace, aided by such governmental favors as protective tariffs, import quotas, tax incorporation laws, currency and taxation policies, and access to government owned resources (McCormick 1977, p. 31).

341

In response to such agitation from a sizable and relatively powerful segment of the country, antitrust legislation was passed to reassert the value of free competition and free enterprise and, more importantly, give a symbolic, essentially hollow, victory to the "little person." The passage of such legislation helped to diffuse the rising class consciousness and class conflict, while imposing minimal inconvenience upon corporations. The nature of antitrust enforcement since 1890 gives evidence to the law's symbolic nature (McCormick 1977). Thus, while laws exist in both the United States and Canada to control certain business practices of the powerful, a careful analysis suggests these statutes are administered in the best interests of political and economic elites.[3]

Political Crime and Criminal Politics

Political crime is one of the oldest and most frequently recurring crimes in history (Kirchheimer 1961). While all crime is basically political, political crime is characterized as violations of laws created to protect the order of the state (Quinney 1964). The strictly legal definition includes direct offenses against the State such as treason, insurrection, rebellion, sedition, criminal anarchy, criminal syndicalism, and conduct interfering with government functions such as perjury, bribery, corruption, and criminal libel by publication (Packer 1962). The greater proportion of writing and societal attention has dwelt on the first category of offenses, those "threatening the very existence of the State." During the past two decades in North America, this "threat" has been variously defined by diverse officials to include the civil rights movement, the Black Panthers, American Indian Movement, Students for a Democratic Society, antiwar demonstrators, Communists, Anarchists, labor movements, antinuclear organizations, and the Parti Quebecois, among others.[4]

The history of attempts to outlaw certain "subversive" groups and ideas is the history of the use of the law to protect the State. All nations have such laws and use them at various times to prevent attempts to change the distribution of power in society. These statutes are by their very nature repressive of free communication, and have been the products of times of "national crisis." Examples of such efforts include the Sedition Act of 1798, which allowed the punishment of those who spoke in opposition to the government of the United States; criminal anarchy laws and criminal syndicalism laws enacted in the early twentieth century intended

---

[3]This is also true for England and Australia. See Reasons and Goff 1980. For an analysis of the enforcement of antitrust legislation, see Chapter Eight, The Crime Control Establishment.

[4]Political trials also, of course, take place in non-Western countries. See McConnell 1978.

to control "subversives"; the Smith Act of 1940, forbidding the overthrow of the government; the McCarran Act of 1950, requiring "Communists" to register; the "Rap Brown" portion of the 1968 Omnibus Bill, named after a black activist, which makes it a felony to travel in interstate commerce with the *intent* to incite a riot; the use of the War Measures Act in Quebec during the October Crisis in 1970, and the use of conspiracy and related statutes against the antiwar movement in the United States in the late 1960s and early 1970s (Quinney 1975, pp. 69–72; Allen 1974).

What about "conduct derived from unlawful state power" such as the criminal behavior of the State through its representatives (politicians, police, judges, legislatures)? The behavior of state officials (for instance, police brutality, denial of free speech, restriction of free assembly) that violates specific laws should be analyzed as political crime. Apart from the more dramatic crimes of politics such as the offenses of former President Richard M. Nixon (Dobrovir et al. 1974), there are many illegal actions perpetrated daily by officials of the State. For example, while laws exist to maintain safety standards in the work place, violations are frequent and enforcement rare. Such crimes are in part a product of government collusion with industry and lack of proper policing (Ashford 1976; Reasons, Paterson, and Ross 1981). While little attention has been given to this type of crime wave, there are increasing efforts to spotlight these areas (Lieberman 1973; Becker and Murray 1971; U.S. Department of Justice, LEAA 1979; Pearce 1976; Ermann and Lundman 1978).

The extent to which both definitions of illegality and enforcement of the law change will depend on the extent to which dominant interests can maintain current priorities.

MAINTENANCE

Once institutionalized, what does the law maintain or preserve? Who or what benefits from the continuation of the legal system? The need for social control through laws seems everywhere self-evident. People are continually reminded by the mass media, politicians, criminal justice personnel, and other experts that more and more laws are needed to ensure basic freedoms and security. Accordingly, universities are continuously graduating lawyers to interpret and act upon the multitude of laws written at the city, municipal, state or provincial, and federal levels. Hundreds of thousands of persons are employed in the business of making, interpreting, and enforcing various legal statutes. The necessity of law is a basic part of our ideology. Ours is a nation run by laws, not the whims of the powerful, or so the ideology goes. However, the nature of social control may not be as advertised.

The Maintenance of Racism

Since the establishment of the United States and Canada, the legal system has historically reflected the power relationships among the various races.

The history of the American legal structure in relationship to nonwhites in North America provides a clear example of the influence economic and political power has upon the scales of justice. One of the biggest obstacles to a frank national confrontation with the problems of race relations is that the original Constitution, together with the common and statutory law that followed, provided for racial inequality. Only within the last few decades has the American legal structure rid itself of the remaining *explicit* manifestations of racism in the law.

A Racist Constitution?   The United States Constitution did not make outright mention of slaves, slavery, or race. Nonetheless, it protected slavery in the states where it existed, provided for the return of escaped slaves to their masters, devised a formula for counting slaves in the apportionment of members of Congress, prohibited Congress from taxing slavery out of existence, and preserved the African slave trade for twenty years (Miller 1966). For example, Article 1, Section 2, paragraph 3 states:

> Representatives and direct Taxes shall be apportioned among the several states which may be included within this Union, according to their respective Numbers, including those bound to Service for a Term of Years, and excluding Indians not taxed, *three fifths of all other Persons.* (Emphasis ours.)

One need not be an expert in consitutional law to realize that "all other persons" referred primarily to the large number of black slaves at the time.

In the early part of the nineteenth century, the "free" states and territories erected barriers to blacks. By 1811, antiblack forces of the Indiana territorial legislature passed laws forbidding blacks to join the militia, testify in court against a white, or vote. Ohio excluded blacks from residence in the state unless they posted $500 bond for good behavior. In 1813, Illinois ordered every incoming "free" black to leave the territory under penalty of thirty-nine lashes repeated every fifteen days until he left. The chief argument against slavery in the North was that it would eventually produce a "free" black population (Woodward 1969).

In 1857, Chief Justice Taney of the United States Supreme Court handed down a landmark decision in a racist interpretation of the Constitution which, among other things, declared that the rights and privileges proclaimed in the Declaration of Independence and the Constitution did not extend to blacks at all. In addresssing this issue the Court said

We think they are not, and that they are not included, and were not intended to be included, under the word "citizen" in the Constitution, and can therefore claim none of the rights and privileges which that instrument provides for and secures to citizens of the United States. On the contrary, they were at that time considered as a subordinate and inferior class of beings, who had been subjugated by the dominant race, and whether emancipated or not, . . . had no rights or privileges but such as those who held power and the government might choose to grant them . . . [Dredd Scott *v.* Sandford, 19 How. 393 (1857), 17].

The opinion goes on to cite state statutes and societal mores as affirming the Court's decision. In fact given the social and legal precedents, how could the opinion have been otherwise?

Indian Genocide, Chinese "Inferiority"   Of course, blacks were not the only racial minority being dealt with by the legal structure. In Cherokee Nation *v.* Georgia (1831) Chief Justice Marshall suggested Indian tribes were "domestic dependent nations" whose relationships to the federal government resembled that of a "ward to his guardian." This decision was later to be implemented through the paternalistic colonialism manifest in the reservation system. However, a genocidal destruction of an estimated two thirds of the Native American population was first carried out in westward expansion. For example, one of the first debates in the Colorado legislature was over a measure to offer bounties for the "destruction of Indians and Skunks" (Willhelm 1969, p. 36). Furthermore, laws and treaties made by the United States government with the Native American tribes are infamous for their "flexibility" (Deloria 1969).

In 1849, a law in California provided that "no black, or mulatto person, or Indian shall be allowed to give evidence in favor of, or against a white man." In 1854 the chief justice of the California Supreme Court, a member of the Know-Nothings, ruled that Chinese were included as inferiors under law because

The anomalous spectacle of a distinct people, living in our community, recognizing no laws of this State except through necessity, bringing with them their prejudices and national feuds, in which they indulge in open violation of the law; whose mendacity is proverbial; a race of people whom nature has marked as inferior, and who are incapable of progress or intellectual development beyond a certain point, as their history has shown; differing in language, opinion, color, and physical conformation; between whom and ourselves nature has placed an impassable difference. . . .

Given the legal action prior to and after the Civil War, the altruistic image of the North's "white man's burden" interpretation of the conflict is a sorry mythology. It seems that C. Vann Woodward is correct in asserting that "the Union fought the war on borrowed moral capital and then repudiated the debt." The provisions of the Fourteenth and Fifteenth amendments were rapidly rendered impotent through a number of Supreme Court cases. The rise of "Jim Crow" statutes[5] received important support in the Plessey v. Ferguson decision by the United States Supreme Court in 1896. This decision gave its approval to the separate-but-equal doctrine. The demise of Jim Crow was not to begin until the 1954 Supreme Court decision Brown v. Board of Education in Topeka, which negated the separate-but-equal doctrine on the basis that it was inherently unequal; that to be set apart could not fail but label black children as socially inferior. This decision signaled the end of officially condoned, overt racism in legal statutes and judicial interpretations. Until that time the Constitution had been explicitly interpreted in a racist fashion. This, however, is not to say that race was no longer important legally.

Black Americans struggled for decades against laws that were explicitly racist in their denial of equal opportunity and treatment (Stampp 1970). Martin Luther King, Jr., and many other leaders of the civil rights movement in the 1950s and 1960s were fighting "unjust" laws that oppressed black people. In his "Letter from Birmingham Jail," King (1963) argued that it is one's obligation to disobey an "unjust law." Reflecting his humanistic Christian philosophy, he stated: "Any law that uplifts human personality is just. Any law that degrades human personality is unjust." Through their struggles, civil rights activists and their allies were subsequently able to eliminate the explicit racism in the law evident in various segregation statutes. Civil rights laws were passed nationally and locally, and human rights agencies were established. This entire effort signaled the end of centuries of explicit legal racism in the law. Thus, the "crimes" of integration and equal treatment were legally redefined. Illegality came to mean segregation and discrimination. Thus some two hundred years after incorporation in the Constitution of the United States, the Bill of Rights was finally being used on behalf of racial minorities. However, proclaiming "equality for all" in access to various areas does not change substantively the unequal economic and political situation of nonwhites.

For example, the law emphasizes that race should not be a factor in hiring, that candidates should be judged on their merit. However, since there are group advantages and disadvantages built up over centuries, the equal opportunity approach ignores the great group inequities. Affirmative action programs have been increasingly criticized as "reverse racism," even though such programs are largely symbolic. Under the law, individual racism is emphasized while institutional racism is largely ignored.[6] For example, the killing of black demonstrators by members of

---

[5]"Jim Crow" statutes were those designed to maintain racial segregation throughout public life. Thus, the races could be separated de jure in respect to everything from schools to drinking fountains.

[6]For a detailed analysis of individual and institutional racism, see Chapter Ten. Discussions of affirmative action programs are found in Chapter Ten, Race and Racism; and Chapter Eleven, Sex and Sexism.

the Ku Klux Klan is a criminal act, while the reduction of the life expectancy of black children in the ghetto through malnutrition and disease stemming from social and economic policies is not.

The Maintenance of Sexism

There have been increasing attacks in recent years upon the systematically unequal treatment given women in such areas as job classifications, wages, occupational advancement, credit purchasing and other consumer activities, rape laws, and prostitution laws, among others (DeCrow 1975). The proposed Equal Rights Amendment in the United States is designed to change the *legal* relationships between men and women, reflecting the current struggles undertaken on behalf of women's rights. While discrimination on the basis of sex is increasingly prohibited by state and provincial human rights acts, the extent of enforcement, prosecution, and conviction is neglible compared with "common crimes." In fact, such charges are generally handled through civil action and, if criminal, result in fines at most. More importantly the legal remedies for sexism continue to advance the prevailing ideology of equal opportunity. Wanting a larger piece of the pie is quite different from seeking to eliminate a structure of inequality. In a class-divided society, justice continues to be defined as competitive fairness in "getting ahead."

As was pointed out earlier in this chapter, rape laws arose to protect the property of men (chattelism) from "spoilage" by others, Rather than being an "easy charge to make and difficult to disprove," it has been quite the opposite. Rape cases often entail the woman's being put on trial. Efforts to change this have had certain limited results, reflected in changing definitions of permissible evidence. For example, in many states and provinces, the relevancy of the victim's past sexual behavior to the rape offense must be proven. Some change has occurred in certain jurisdictions through the elimination of rape as a distinct offense, defining it rather in terms of assault. Such a move takes the explicit sexual nature of the offense from the legal definition in an attempt to counter the mythology that sexual gratification is the essence of rape. Rather, the new laws focus on the threat and actuality of physical harm.

The Maintenance of Poverty

While laws in corporate society emphasize protecting people's property from the incursions of others, they do not hold the excessive accumulation of property as criminal. Nor do legal definitions find the social failure to meet basic human needs as illegal. Millions of people in the United States and Canada live in substandard housing, are malnourished, unemployed, or marginally employed in demeaning and dehumanizing jobs, yet these are not viewed as crimes perpetrated by the social system upon these victims (Manzer 1974; Miller and Roby 1970). Conversely, the fact that in both countries members of a self-perpetuating dominant class have accumulated and/or inherited millions of dollars for their own personal use is viewed largely as virtuous rather than abhorrent. By guaranteeing adequate levels of housing, food, health care, and other human needs society would open present values to question. Although we live in what has been called a Welfare State, the welfare of millions is neglected. Continued failure to institute adequate guaranteed-income legislation gives evidence to the general ideology of corporatism and its derivatives: rugged individualism, narcissism, and survival of the fittest (more moderately, equal opportunity). Such legislation would encroach upon the prevailing ideology by declaring that every person has the right to an adequate income regardless of his or her value in the labor market.

The Maintenance of Government and Corporate Crime

In addition to racism, law through commission or omission allows for the continuation of governmental and corporate crime. Government is increasingly big business in North America, with growing numbers of employees in ever-expanding services. Lawyer Jethro K. Lieberman (1973) has argued that violations of the law are pervasive throughout government, but they have not gained much attention until recently. He notes some of the benefits to government of its lawbreaking:

> When a man is fired from his job for telling the truth to Congress about the scandal in his federal office his boss has broken the law (but other employees have learned a lesson).

> When young children are forced into slavery by the warden of reformatories, no one can doubt the law has been at least politely overlooked (but someone gets free labor).

> When a judge increases the sentence of a convicted felon because the criminal wants to appeal his conviction, the Government has broken the law (but it has forestalled troublesome proceedings).

> When the Government decides that some polluters, but not all polluters, ought to be prosecuted, the Government as well as the polluters have violated the law (but the laudable ends are obvious).

When the governmental agencies choose to disregard their own regulations, on the theory that if you make them you can break them, they have violated law (but they do not undermine confidence in the administrative process—if no one finds out) (1973, pp. 20–21).

Government lawlessness becomes particularly evident during times of national crises. During the 1960s movements against the Vietnam War or for welfare rights, French-Canadian independence, black power, brown power, red power, and students' rights emerged in North America. Subsequent revelations have shown that both the United States and Canadian governments systematically violated the law in attempting to repress these efforts at social change. Burglaries, illegal wiretaps, agent provocations, surveillance, intimidating assaults and killings, mail opening, and bribery are just a few examples of the crime wave perpetrated by the government. Recently, the increasing surveillance as well as the restriction of personal privacy has been addressed by law. For example, a Freedom of Information Act was passed in the United States to aid citizens in knowing what "their" government is doing to them, for them, and/or about them. While such legislation is only minimally effective, requiring great patience for minimal information, it is evidence of citizen concern over the increasing power of government. A much more cumbersome and restrictive Freedom of Information Act became law in Canada in 1978. However, a limited right to know is more symbolic than substantive. It in no way means that the abuse of state power has been eliminated.

Illegal acts by corporations, as noted earlier, have been largely viewed as noncrimes. Thus, the failure of the State to control them clearly continues corporate criminality.

As already discussed, corporate acts or failure to act (omission) result in physical harm. For example, the use of thalidomide by pregnant women caused the deformation of between 8,000 and 10,000 babies before it was withdrawn from the market (Sjostrom and Nilsson 1972). At the time of this writing, about 3,000 asbestos workers die prematurely each year as a result of exposure to this substance in the work place (Ashford 1976, p. 324), and mercury effluent is poisoning many Native Americans in northwestern Ontario (Singer and Rodgers 1975). All of these tragedies are the consequence of specific organizations, conducting their normal business. Despite the gravity of the harm done, most organizations are subject to civil liabilities and fined, or at most, criminal liability, also with fines. For example, a construction company received a citation for failing to shore up a trench, which subsequently collapsed and killed an employee. Under the 1970 United States Occupational Safety and Health Act, the company was fined $3,500 for *not shoring up the trench*. The firm's conscious, willful violation of the law produced the death, but only a miniscule fine was imposed (Schrager and

Short 1977). In summary, the continuing failure of the criminal law to address corporation crime makes certain the continuation of a shadowy upper world.

CRIMINAL LAW: AN ALTERNATIVE VIEW

While the use of formal written law is highly developed in the United States and Canada, the People's Republic of China has few substantive rules. (One's initial response may be that since this is a Communist country, laws are not as important as in democracies. However, a cursory look at the Soviet Union or other Eastern European countries finds a well-developed use of formal written law.) In North America, the use of formal written law supports the ideological symbols of individualism (privatism), freedom of geographical and social movement (which ensures a mobile work force), and the need for professionalization of social control (expertise). The Chinese, on the other hand, lack a well-developed system of formal written laws. This reinforces their collectivist and cooperative orientation, the significance of group achievement and group advancement, and the desirability of citizens' working out their own local solutions to social issues and problems. While the official party directives in the People's Republic of China prescribe how decisions are to be made in the community (procedural rules), they do not indicate how each individual is to act. Therefore, the community groups decide how to accomplish party goals and aims. In North America, the formal written law prescribes what conduct is required by individual citizens (substantive rules). As Pepinsky notes (1975, p. 339),

> Rules of substantive conduct take decisions as to courses of action toward particular others out of the hands of individuals while directives as to how and why decisions must be made place responsibility for these decisions squarely in the hands of the citizen, while tending to take away responsibility for when and where the decisions are made.

A Jurisprudence of Insurgency

Traditional socialists, and particularly Marxists, have suggested that the law will wither away with the State. However, as it has a history of some 800 years, it appears safe to argue that the law and its accompanying legal institutions as we know them will survive for some time (Balbus,

1976). Thus, many advocates of change have sought to use the law more and more in recent times. A "jurisprudence of insurgency" has arisen that challenges the prevailing system of social relations. Therefore, understanding the law and legal ideology is being used in the struggle for social change.

> Claims for justice are being framed by dissident groups in terms of demands that the dominant legal ideology be interpreted in particular ways. In the domain of contract and property, claims to equal access to national wealth are being presented to tribunals and legislatures. These demands emphasize the antimonopoly, egalitarian values of the bourgeois legal ideology. In the domain of personal liberty, the dissidents cite the dominant legal ideology's claims of freedom of association and procedural fairness to protect their right to organize and proselytize, and to defend themselves against attack from the institutions of state power (Tigar and Levy 1977, p. 324).

Within recent years there have been attempts to redefine the nature of crime and the focus of the law and legal institutions. Thus, in some limited fashion, the legal weapons of the State have been turned against their maker. For example, legal attempts to change power relationships between ethnic groups in Canada is most evident in the case of French-Canadians and Native People. Historically, French Canada, specifically Quebec, has been largely dominated by English Canada (Morris and Laphier 1977). However, within the last few decades this has greatly changed. One of the most obvious examples is the Official Languages Act, which established Canada as a bilingual (French- and English-speaking) country. This, like civil rights legislation in the United States, was passed after violent demonstrations and much agitation and manifest conflict. It was official recognition of the rights, aspirations, and culture of French-Canadians. (Of course, the struggle continues both in the legal and non-legal areas and will be addressed in the chapter on racism.) Native People (Eskimos and Indians) in Canada are increasingly attempting to have their rights established in the law. Through legal insurgency, they are trying to establish their aboriginal claims to certain lands throughout the country (Mickenberg 1971). This essentially argues for acknowledging original title and undertaking subsequent negotiation regarding disposition and settlement of claims. If successful, such claims and possible compensation are explicit acknowledgment of the rights and dignity of Native People as a group (Price 1978). Of course, the government and many businesses have an economic incentive to fight such claims.

The reality of legal insurgency has sparked increasing debate among criminologists specifically and other citizens generally concerning the definition of crimes. In a now classic argument, Herman and Julia Schwendinger (1970) claim that criminologists should not be bound by

351

the definitions of crime developed by the State, but should develop a modern humanistic definition based upon explicit moral standards. These moral standards would be based upon universal human rights such as the right to be secure in one's own person, the right to speak one's mind, and the right to assemble freely. Rather than the liberal emphasis in corporate society upon equality of the right to compete, equality of circumstance would be guaranteed. Therefore, every person would have the right to food, shelter, clothing, medical services, challenging work and recreation, as well as security from predatory individuals or groups. These new freedoms would quite obviously affect the distribution of wealth and power in corporate society.

Based upon these new definitions of crime, social systems could be defined as criminal. That is, if social conditions produce criminal behavior, then changing such conditions is basic to reducing crime.

Of course, the nature of priorities will vary in different political systems. For example, in the Soviet Union, establishing conditions for full democratic participation in political life would be emphasized, while in the United States, establishing the right to economic well-being would be important. In using such a definition of crime, one would have to consider the specific period and nation to which it is applied.

From Rotten Apples to Rotten Barrels

Students of crime have traditionally viewed upperworld crime, or crime at the top, as white collar crime. That is, crime committed by a person in a position of trust for his or her personal gain. Therefore, emphasis has been upon individuals and their needs, goals, attitudes, and behavior. However, such a viewpoint has caused us to neglect the ever increasing impact of organizations upon our daily lives. It fails adequately to consider the physical harms resulting from organizational offenses, and does not deal with the special characteristics of illegal behavior in organizational settings.

> Organizational crimes are illegal acts of omission or commission of an individual or a group of individuals in a legitimate formal organization in accordance with the operative goals of the organization, which have serious physical or economic impact on employees, consumers or the general public (Schrager and Short 1978, pp. 411–12).

By making the distinction between white-collar and organizational crimes, we are recognizing the daily impact private and public organizations have upon our lives as workers, consumers, and members of the general public. Therefore, the behavior of individuals is seen within the context of the organization. For example, while an employee who embezzles from an employer is guilty of a white collar offense, the same employee may be involved in price fixing or misleading advertising as part of the policies, practices, and/or procedures of the organization. In the latter offenses, the white collar malefactor is carrying out organizational goals. Such a distinction forces one to look at changes and control of an enterprise as a means of redressing harm rather than solely at individual sanction. For example, penalizing a police officer for illegal entry or illegal mail opening may not alone stop the practice if the organizational goals and practices of the police reinforce such behavior.

Furthermore, organizational crimes are viewed as more serious among the public than criminologists have acknowledged. Schrager and Short (1980) have found that crimes with the same type of impact were rated similarly by respondents whether they were the misdeeds of individuals or organizations. Thus, organizational crimes that result in injury and death were viewed as similar to assault and homicide, while property destruction and theft did not receive as severe condemnation.

As the distinction between white-collar and organizational crime emerged (Gross 1978, 1980), varying types of organizational offenses have been noted. Schrager and Short (1978) identify three types of victims of organizational behavior based upon their relationship to the production of goods and services: (1) employees, (2) consumers, and (3) the general public. Reasons (1980) has divided organizational offenses on the basis of type of crime into three categories: (1) economic crimes, (2) human rights crimes, and (3) violent personal injury crimes. Combining both the aspects of the victim and nature of the offense provides a conceptual typology for categorizing organizational crimes, presented in Table 6-4. For example, it has been estimated that lost output arising from monopolies and shared monopolies run in the billions for the United States and Canada.

> A US study concludes that the overall cost of monopoly and shared monopoly in terms of lost production is somewhere between $48 billion and $60 billion annually. In Canada, lost output due to the same cause would be in the order of $4.5 to $6 billion dollars. The lost tax revenues alone from this wealth would go a long way towards ending poverty and pollution. The redistribution of income from monopoly profits that transfers income from consumers to shareholders is estimated at $23 billion annually in the US and $2 to $3 billion in Canada. Monopolistic firms thus contribute to inequality, inflation and unemployment. Unemployment results since monopolies, as noted, significantly reduce output, which in turn reduces the number of workers who would otherwise be producing (Gonick 1975, p. 22).

Concentration and monopolization are often the consequence of mergers. Aggregate concentration (the percentage of economic activity accounted

TABLE 6-4
Crimes of Organizations: A Typology

Nature of Offense

VICTIM	Economic	Human Rights	Violent
Employee	Failing to remit payroll deductions, pension fund abuse, violating minimum wage and other labor laws	Restrictions on political activity, dress and demeanor, union activity, public disclosure, e.g., Ellsberg and Pentagon Papers	Deaths and injuries in work place, industrial disease, e.g., asbestos-caused cancer
Consumer	Price fixing, monopolization, false advertising	Misuse of credit information, restrictions on credit based on political, sexual, racial, and class bias	Poor inspection, unsafe products, e.g., Ford Pinto case, thalidomide deformities
Public	Bribery, misuse of public funds, cost overruns, oil spills	Illegal surveillance, wiretaps, abuse of power by police, CIA, FBI, RCMP, military, e.g., Watergate	Police homicides, hazardous wastes, air and water pollutions, nuclear energy, e.g. Three Mile Island nuclear accident

Source: Reasons, 1981.

for by the largest firms in Canada) decreased from 1923 to 1975, while industrial concentration (the fraction of total activity in a given industry attributable to a fixed number of the largest corporations in that industry) increased in Canadian manufacturing industries from 1948 to 1972. Both aggregate and industrial concentration are higher in Canada than in the United States (Report 1978).

In the most recent and comprehensive analysis of corporate crime in the United States, Marshall B. Clinard and associates (1979) empirically investigated 582 of the largest publicly owned corporations in the United States, gathering data on all enforcement actions against them during 1975 and 1976. They note

> Before one considers any findings from a study of corporate violations it is essential that one recognize the significance of the small frequencies of corporate cases and why they must be evaluated differently from statistics on ordinary crimes such as assault,

larceny, or burglary. A single case of corporate law violation may involve millions and even billions of dollars of losses. . . . For example, in one case, the electrical price-fixing conspiracy of the 1960s, losses amounted to over $2 billion, a sum far greater than the total losses from the 3 million burglaries in any given year. At the same time, the average loss from a larceny theft is $165 and from a burglary $422, and the persons who commit these offenses may receive sentences of as much as five to ten years, or even longer. For the crimes committed by the large corporations the sole punishment often consists of warnings, consent orders, or comparatively small fines (Clinard 1979, p. xix).

Their findings were that more than 60 percent of these corporations had at least one enforcement action initiated against them during this period. More than three fourths of all actions were in the manufacturing, environmental, and labor areas of violation, with large corporations being more criminal than smaller ones. More specifically, they were cited in over 70 percent of the actions while making up less than one-half the corporations. The motor vehicle, drug, and oil refining industries accounted for almost one half of all violations, 40 percent of them serious or moderate in nature. Warnings and fines were the most prevalent sanctions, with 80 percent of the fines being $5,000 or less. There were fifty-six executives convicted federally, with 62.5 percent receiving probation, 21.4 percent obtaining suspended sentences, and 28.6 percent going to jail. The sixteen officers sent to jail were held for a total of 597 days, or 37.1 days per executive, with many having their sentence suspended after a few days of incarceration. Needless to say, such a record of combating crime would not do for "common crimes."

Other economic harms that may be justifiably made crimes include excessive profits, land speculation, and employer rip-offs. While prices increased 11 percent in 1978 in Canada and salaries approximately 7 percent, profits rose 21 percent to $9.3 billion. Business profits in the United States have also soared (Burns 1979). Also, an independent study recently released by the Economic Council of Canada concluded that customers contributed between $200 million and $500 million in excess profits to bank coffers between 1968 and 1973 (Oake 1979). This, coupled with the great increase in housing costs, has led to calls for antiprofiteering legislation. While bank robbers, extortionists, and kidnappers made off with $5.17 million in 1975 in Canada, employers received $7.9 million through such theft from workers (Goff and Reasons 1978, p. 11). Recently, the Canadian Imperial Bank was ordered by the Canada Labor Relations Board to pay salary increases withheld because employees signed union cards. The bank blatantly tried to intimidate its workers into not joining a union by giving a 9 percent increase only to nonunion employees (Conklin 1979). This brings us into the area of violations of human rights.

Human Rights Crimes

In a democratic society a fundamental right of the citizenry should be the right to know. Access to information upon which the government is making decisions and policies is essential to a government for the people. In Canada there is very little access to information that may be vital to citizens individually or collectively (Crump 1978). In 1971, former federal Solicitor General Jean-Pierre Goyer circulated among five of his fellow Cabinet members a list of some twenty-five Canadians who were believed to be "subversives." It contained mainly civil servants and university professors thought to be organizing for the overthrow of the government. Subsequent blacklists were revealed, although they were denied by the executive. Secret files on politicians, social activists, and others have been kept by the government. The Solicitor General's Department, RCMP Security Branch, and the Canadian Armed Forces deep files on political groups, business organizations, and individuals they regard as a threat to national security.

The United States Congress passed the Freedom of Information Act in 1966 to increase public disclosure of government information. However, it was largely ineffective until amended in 1974 because of bureaucratic discretion, delay, and cost. Subsequent to the 1974 amendments, thousands of requests for investigation have been made and numerous illegal acts by the government have been exposed, including CIA, FBI, and Department of Defense spying and disruption of domestic political groups (Prewitt and Verba 1979, pp. 444–45). For example, a Freedom of Information Act lawsuit uncovered extensive spying and other illegal activities by the CIA against the late Dr. Martin Luther King, Jr. (Burns 1980).

The police in a democratic society should be subject to the rule of law and to control by the citizenry and their representatives. Within the last few years there have been increasing revelations concerning illegal and questionable activities of the Royal Canadian Mounted Police, including illegal wiretaps, kidnapping, using agents provocateurs, illegal mail opening, burglary, theft, destruction of property, and surveillance of suspected political activists in universities, unions, native organizations, among others (Mann and Lee 1979). Throughout its history the RCMP has conducted surveillance of political and social activists, particularly among labor unions (Brown and Brown 1973).

A United States Senate Select Committee on Intelligence Activities disclosed that the CIA illegally opened 215,000 letters in one of four mail-intrusion projects and conducted domestic surveillance and prepared dossiers on United States citizens. All of these activities were illegal. The committee discovered that the National Security Agency scanned all overseas telephone calls and cables between 1967 and 1973 in order to control 1,680 citizens engaged in political dissent or suspected involvement in narcotics or of being potential threats to the President. The FBI publicly acknowledged committing 238 burglaries against domestic political activists, opening mail illegally, and harassing people belonging to certain organizations. The Internal Revenue Service established dossiers on 8,585 political activists and 2,873 political organizations, while military intelligence spied on thousands of dissidents between 1967 and 1970, preparing files on many citizens (Quinney 1979, pp. 164–68; Report of the Senate 1978; Commission on CIA Activities 1978).

Probably one of the most notorious crimes of this century is that of Watergate. Perpetrated largely from the office of the President of the United States, it entailed such offenses as obstructing justice, illegal wiretaps, burglaries, misuse of public funds, income tax fraud, and illegal surveillance and harassment of political dissidents and opponents (Douglas 1977). Due to these crimes, President Nixon resigned and several of his political aides were convicted and sentenced to prison.

Criminologists are just beginning to inquire into the crimes committed by public officials. However, as one recent text observes:

> The list of crimes committed by public officials is a long one and includes the dismissal of persons from their jobs for revealing governmental corruption; discriminatory prosecution on the basis of political opinions; the manufacturing of evidence, including the use of perjured testimony; unlawful sentencing; the premeditated and unlawful repression of legal dissent; entrapment; illegal wiretapping; illegal treatment of prisoners; illegal denial of the right to vote; illegal awards of state and federal contracts; bribery to influence the political process; unlawful use of force by the police; and military war crimes (Sykes 1978, p. 221).

The potential for abuse of civil rights and personal freedom is also evident in the increasing use of electronic eavesdropping. It appears that the Canadian Protection of Privacy Act introduced in 1974 is actually an erosion of the right of privacy (Title 1978). Unlike some other countries, evidence gained from illegal wiretaps may be admissible in a Canadian court and there is inadequate external review of the granting of legal wiretaps. Furthermore, legal wiretaps have largely been justified as combating organized crime, although the evidence does not confirm its worth in this area. In the United States, a study by the General Accounting Office estimated that only 1.3 percent of some 17,528 FBI domestic intelligence investigations in 1974 resulted in prosecution and conviction (Report of the Senate 1978, p. 171).

Finally, some criminologists and social critics are arguing for the criminalization of certain behaviors that have obvious harm. The issue of "victims without crimes" needs to be addressed (Schwendinger and Schwendinger 1970 and 1977). Individual and institutional discrimination on the basis of sex, age, race, ethnicity, sexual orientation, or class position is usually dealt with by civil, not criminal, laws. It is arguable that such practices strike at the very core of democratic egalitarian values and thus should receive the full attention of the criminal laws (Reiman 1979). For example, the history of racism in North America and its harmful effects on racial minorities are quite evident today (Blauner 1972; Hughes and Kallen 1974; Hill 1978).

Apart from legal discrimination there was both legally proscribed and/ or condoned violence against racial minorities (Reasons and Kuykendall 1972). This violence against minorities did not receive the attention of the criminal law, but the actions were surely criminal in moral terms (Graham 1969). For example, blacks were subjected to selective extermination in North America by lynching. Between 1882 and 1962, a total of 4,736 Americans were lynched, 73 percent of them black. Furthermore, approximately two thirds of Native Americans were exterminated in the "winning" of the West. Federal, state, and local social control organizations all contributed to this slaughter (Mouledoux 1967; Pinkney 1972). This brings us to the final category: crimes of violence.

Violent Personal Injury Crimes

While there is obvious physical danger and harm from some "street crimes" such as murder and assault, the belief that organizations' crimes are not violent is false. For example, Ford Motor Company has lost several civil suits and was indicted in Indiana for reckless homicide and criminal recklessness concerning the Pinto's fuel tanks.[6] More specifically, it has been revealed in court that the representatives of this organization calculated the costs of changing an unsafe gas tank were nearly three times the expected costs of suits arising due to deaths and injuries (Jacobson and Barnes 1978; Ford 1978). The following chart is based upon a Ford internal memo of 1972 that calculated the *benefits* of not making changes to their Pinto gas tank compared with the costs of making such changes. It was obviously cheaper to continue to build an unsafe automobile!

Thus, the policies and practices of the organization patently put profit over the saving of consumers' lives. Approximately 20 million serious injuries occur in the United States annually, permanently disabling 110,000 and killing 30,000 (Schrager and Short 1978, p. 415). An internationally known student of white collar crimes states that "commercial fraud kills more people than are murdered by acts that come to be listed as criminal homicide in the *Uniform Crime Reports*" (Geis 1975, p. 93). For example, aircraft manufacturers and drug companies, among others, have falsified test results in marketing unsafe products (McCaghy 1976,

[6]As written, North American criminal law is directed toward individual behavior—and individuals are often lost in the corporate organizational structure. An Indiana jury acquitted Ford of the criminal charges.

Benefits	Savings:	180 burn deaths, 180 serious burn injuries, 2,100 burned vehicles
	Unit Cost:	$200,000 per death, $67,000 per injury, $700 per vehicle
	Total Benefit:	180 x (200,000) + 180 x (67,000) + 2100 ($700) = $49.5 million
Costs	Sales:	11 million cars, 1.5 million light trucks
	Unit Cost:	$11 per car, $11 per truck
	Total Cost:	$11,000,000 x ($11) + 1,500,000 x ($11) = $137 million

Source: The *Sunday London Times*, February 12, 1978, p. 1.

pp. 213–14). Cosmetics, oral contraceptives, synthetic hormones, microwave ovens, childrens' sleepwear, pesticides, cleaning solutions and solvents, X-rays, among numerous other consumer goods have all been found to be unsafe and poorly regulated and/or marketed (The Environmental Defense Fund 1980). The number of deaths annually occurring from improper emergency care is twice that for homicide, while unneeded surgical operations cost an estimated $5 billion a year and 16,000 lives (Reiman 1979, p. 73). Whether it be in manufactured products, services, or accommodations, violence against the consumer may be the result of an organization's policies and practices.

The general public has been subjected to a variety of physical harms, principally through pollution, hazardous substances, and maintenance of unsafe structures. In one of the most tragic examples, a dam collapsed at Buffalo Creek, West Virginia, killing scores of people and destroying the fabric of a community (Erickson 1976). (While the "disaster" was a result of a company's knowingly maintaining an illegal dam, it is difficult to make a legal case given the problems of proving causation, foreseeability, and intent, among others.) Innumerable substances that are potentially hazardous, if not lethal, are illegally emitted into the air (The Environmental Defense Fund 1979). Arsenic poisoning of the general population of Yellowknife, Northwest Territories, is largely the consequence of two gold mining operations (Tataryn 1979). Lawyer Ralph Nader states, "Much more is lost in money and health through pollution than crimes of violence, yet only the latter is defined officially as violence." Current laws have minimal effect upon environmental pollution because it pays to violate the law (Eitzen 1980, pp. 11–12).

Possibly some of the largest crimes against the general public are crimes of war. The murder and ill-treatment of civilians and prisoners of war, destruction of nonmilitary targets, and illegal use of chemical warfare in Southeast Asia dwarf in magnitude the "garden variety" crimes of violence we are daily warned about (Quinney 1979, pp. 174–81). Reiman (1979, p. 64) concludes that:

> The most dangerous American crime ring since the days of Al Capone is the United States government. The Vietnam War, based on a history of deception predating even the lies we were told about the so-called Gulf of Tonkin incident, stands without peer in recent years in the annals of unnecessary carnage wrought by American hands.

Workers are daily assaulted on the job through unsafe working conditions and unhealthy chemicals (Reasons, Paterson, and Ross 1981). The number of annual deaths from industrial disease is at least 100,000 in the United States (The President's Report 1972), while the toll in Canada is undoubtedly in the thousands (Tataryn 1979). Many of these deaths are preventable through the control of the environmental level of dangerous substances. Despite this, corporations have knowingly exposed their workers to lethal and injurious levels of hazardous materials. For example, the United States Occupational Safety and Health Administration (OSHA) imposed one of its heaviest fines against the nation's largest lead producer, N.L. Industries. They had knowingly allowed workers to be exposed to lead levels that exceeded permissible levels by more than 100 times (Glasbeek and Rowland 1979, p. 591). Tataryn's book, *Dying for a Living: The Politics of Industrial Death*, documents the massive coverup by the asbestos industry of its knowledge since the 1930s of the harmful effects of asbestos. While this may be the subject of civil suits, criminal action is not available, although premeditated exposure to violent substances occurred.

Apart from the moral argument to criminalize these acts that entail "victims without crimes," it is arguable that current laws may be relevant. Glasbeek and Rowland (1979) make a case for the application of Canadian Federal Criminal Code charges (such as criminal negligence, duties of master to servant, assault, criminal breach of contract, traps likely to cause bodily harm, causing mischief, common nuisance, conspiracy, and murder) to violations of health and safety laws. For in the last analysis, a jurisprudency of insurgency will realize success only to the extent that predictable organizational harms acquire the criminal standing now reserved for acts of individual malice.

Allen, Francis A.
1974
The Crimes of Politics: Political Dimensions of Criminal Justice. Cambridge: Harvard University Press.

Ashford, Nicholas A.
1976
Crisis in the Workplace: Occupational Disease and Injury. Cambridge: MIT Press.

Balbus, Isaac D.
1977
"Commodity Form and Legal Form: An Essay on the 'Relative Autonomy' of the Law." Law and Society Review 11 (Winter):571–88.

Barron, Milton L.
1974
"The Criminogenic Society: Social Values and Deviance." In Current Perspectives on Criminal Behavior. Abraham S. Blumberg, ed. New York: Alfred A. Knopf, pp. 68–86.

Becker, Theodore L., and Murray, Vernon G.
1971
Government Lawlessness in America. New York: Oxford University Press.

Berger, Thomas R.
1977
Northern Frontier, Northern Homeland: The Report of the Mackenzie Valley Pipelines Inquiry Volume One. Ottawa: Printing and Publishing Supply and Services Canada.

Berman, Harold J., and Greiner, William R.
1966
The Nature and Functions of Law. Brooklyn: The Foundation Press.

Blauner, R.
1972
Racial Oppression in America. New York: Harper & Row

Brecker, Edward
1972
Licit and Illicit Drugs. Boston: Little, Brown.

1976
"Employer's Crimes Are Most Lucrative." The Calgary Herald, April 3:4.

Bullough, Vern L.
1964   The History of Prostitution. New Hyde Park, N.Y.: University Press.

Burns, P.
1979   "Business Profits Still Soaring in U.S." The Calgary Herald, May 19:C13.

1980   "CIA Tailed King." The Calgary Herald, February 20:B6.

Chambliss, William
1964   "A Sociological Analysis of the Law of Vagrancy." Social Problems 12 (Summer):67–77.

Chambliss, William J., and Seidman, Robert B.
1971   Law, Order and Power. Reading, Mass.: Addison-Wesley.

Chambliss, William J., and Ryther, Thomas
1975   Sociology: The Discipline and Its Direction. New York: McGraw-Hill.

Clinard, M.B., et. al.
1979   Illegal Corporate Behavior. Washington, D.C.: U.S. Government Printing Office.

Cohen, Warren H., and Mause, Phillip J.
1968   "The Indian: The Forgotten American." Harvard Law Review 81 (June):1818–1858.

Commission on CIA Activities within the United States
1978   "The CIA's Mail Intercepts." In Corporate and Government Deviance: Problems of Organizational Behavior in Contemporary Society. M.D. Ermann and R.J. Lundman, eds. New York: Oxford University Press.

Conklin, John E.
1977   Illegal but Not Criminal. Englewood Cliffs, N.J.: Prentice-Hall.

1979   "Contracts May Have Been Tied to Donations Chairman." The Calgary Herald, January 18, p. A22.

1979   "Court Orders Bank to Halt Pay Penalty." The Calgary Herald, December 8:B3.

Crump, Barry N.
1978   "Freedom of Information Legislation in Canada: Discretionary Secrecy, Political Deviance and Surreptitious Labeling." Paper presented to the annual meetings of the Canadian Sociology and Anthropology Association, London, Ontario, May 29–June 1.

Currie, Elliot P.
1968   "Crimes without Criminals: Witchcraft and Its Control in Renaissance Europe." Law & Society Review 3 (August):7–32.

Daniels, Roger, and
Kitana, Harry
1970   American Racism: Explanations of the Nature of Prejudice. Englewood Cliffs, N.J.: Prentice-Hall.

Deloria, Vine, Jr.
1969   Custer Died for Your Sins: An Indian Manifesto. New York: Macmillan.

Diamond, Stanley
1971   "The Rule of Law Versus the Order of Custom." Social Research 38 (Spring):42–72.

Dobrovir, William A.;
Gebhardt, Joseph D.;
Buffone, Samuel J.; and
Oakes, Andra N.
1974   The Offenses of Richard M. Nixon: A Guide to His Impeachable Crimes. New York: Quadrangle/The New York Times Book Co.

Douglas, Jack
1977   "Watergate: Harbinger of the American Prince." In Official Deviance: Readings in Malfeasance, Misfeasance, and Other Forms of Corruption. Philadelphia: Lippincott, pp. 112–20.

Eitzen, D. Stanley
1980   Social Problems. Boston: Allyn and Bacon.

Environmental Defense
Fund and R.H. Boyle
1980   Malignant Neglect. New York: Vintage Books.

363

Erikson, Kai
1966

Wayward Puritans: A Study in the Sociology of Deviance. New York: John Wiley.

1976

Everything in Its Path: Destruction of Community in the Buffalo Creek Flood. New York: Simon & Schuster.

Ermann, M.D., and
Lundman, R.J.
1978

Corporate and Governmental Deviance: Problems of Organizational Behavior in Contemporary Society. New York: Oxford University Press.

Feldman, E.
1967

"Prostitution, the Alien Woman, and the Progressive Imagination, 1910–1915." American Quarterly 19 (Summer):192–206.

Filliatreau, J.
1978

"Ford Is Indicted on Criminal Counts over Pinto Deaths." Globe and Mail, September 14.

Frideres, James
1974

Canada's Indians: Contemporary Conflict. Scarborough, Ont.: Prentice-Hall of Canada.

Geis, Gilbert
1972a

"Crimes—But No Victims." Reason 4 (September): 16–18.

1972b

Not the Law's Business? Washington, D.C.: U.S. Government Printing Office.

1974

"Deterring Corporate Crime." In The Criminologist: Crime and the Criminal. Charles E. Reasons, ed. Pacific Palisades, Calif.: Goodyear, pp. 246–59.

1975

"Victimization Patterns in White Collar Crime." In Victimology: A New Focus, Volume V: Exploiters and Exploited: The Dynamics of Victimization. I. Drapkin and E. Viana, eds. Lexington, Mass.: Lexington Books, pp. 89–105.

1979

"Lord Hale, Witches and Rape." British Journal of Law and Society.

Geis, G., and Stotland, E.
1980

White Collar Crime: Theory and Research. Beverly Hills, Calif.: Sage.

Gibbons, Don C.
1976

Delinquent Behavior. Englewood Cliffs, N.J.: Prentice-Hall.

Glasbeek, H.J., and Rowland, S.
1979

"Are Injuring and Killing at Work Crimes?" Osgoode Hall Law Journal, 17 (December):507–94.

Goff, Colin H., and Reasons, Charles E.
1976

"Corporations in Canada: A Study of Crime and Punishment." Criminal Law Quarterly 18 (August): 468–98.

1978

Corporate Crime in Canada: A Critical Analysis of Anti-Combines Legislation. Scarborough, Ont.: Prentice-Hall of Canada.

Gonick, D.
1975

Inflation or Depression. Toronto: James Lorimer.

Grabner, Gene
1973

"The Limits of Three Perspectives on Crime: 'Value-Free Science,' 'Objective Law' and State 'Morality.' " Issues in Criminology 8 (Spring):35–48.

Graham, Fred
1969

"A Contemporary History of American Crime." In The History of Violence in America. Hugh David Graham and Ted Robert Gun, eds. New York: Bantam Books.

Gross, E.
1978

"Organizational Crime: A Theoretical Perspective." In Studies in Symbolic Interaction. N. Denzin, ed. Greenwich, Conn.: JAI Press, pp 55–85.

1980

"Organizational Structure and Organizational Crime." In White Collar Crime: Theory and Research. G. Geis and E. Stotland, eds. Beverly Hills, Calif.: Sage, pp. 52–76.

Gusfield, Joseph
1963

Symbolic Crusade. Urbana, Ill.: University of Illinois Press.

Hacker, Andrew
1973

"Getting Used to Mugging." The New York Review of Books 20 (April 16):9.

Hagan, John, and Leon, Jeffrey
1977 "Rediscovering Delinquency: Social History, Political Ideology and the Sociology of Law." American Sociological Review 42 (August):587–98.

Hall, Jerome
1952 Theft, Law and Society. 2d ed. Indianapolis, Ind.: Bobbs-Merrill.

Henshel, Anne-Marie
1973 Sex Structure. Don Mills: Longman Canada.

Henshel, Richard L., and Silverman, Robert A.
1975 "Perceptions and Criminal Process." Canadian Journal of Sociology 1 (Spring).

Hill, D. G.
1978 Human Rights in Canada: A Focus on Racism. Ottawa: Canadian Labor Congress.

Hughes, D.R., and Kallen, E.
1974 The Anatomy of Racism: Canadian Dimensions. Montreal: Harvest House, Ltd.

Jacobson, P., and Barnes, J.
1978 "£66m in Damages: The Car that Carried Death in the Boot." The Sunday Times, February 12, pp. 4+.

Johnson, J.M., and Douglas, J.D.
1978 Crime at the Top: Deviance in Business and the Professions. Philadelphia: J.B. Lippincott.

Kennedy, Mark
1970 "Beyond Incrimination." Catalyst (Summer):1–37.

King, Jr., Martin Luther
1963 "Letter from Birmingham Jail." In Criminology: Power, Crime, and Criminal Law. John Galliher and James L. McCartney, eds. Homewood Ill.: Dorsey Press, 1977, pp. 15–31.

Kirchheimer, Otto
1961 Political Justice: The Use of the Legal Procedure for Political Ends. Princeton, N.J.: Princeton University Press.

Kirkham, James F.; Levy,
Sheldon, G.; and Crotty,
Williams J.
1970   Assassination and Political Violence. New York:
       Bantam.

Kulcsar, Kalman
1980   "Ideological Changes, and the Legal Structure: A
       Discussion of Socialist Experience." International
       Journal of the Sociology of Law 8:61–81.

Lane, Roger
1969   "Urbanization and Criminal Violence in the 19th
       Century: Massachusetts as a Test Case." In The
       History of Violence in America. Hugh David
       Graham and Ted Robert Gurr, eds. New York:
       Bantam.

Law Reform Commission
of Canada
1975   "White Collar Crime Ignored." The Calgary
       Herald, May 28:25.

1976   Our Criminal Law. Ottawa: Information Canada.

Lefcourt, Robert, ed.
1971   Law against the People: Essays to Demystify Law,
       Order and the Court. New York: Random House.

Liazos, Alexander
1974   "Class Oppression: The Functions of Juvenile
       Justice." The Insurgent Sociologist I (Fall): 2–8.

Lieberman, Jethro K.
1973   How the Government Breaks the Law. Baltimore:
       Penguin.

Lundberg, Ferdinand
1968   The Rich and the Super-Rich. New York: Bantam.

Mann, E., and Lee, J. A.
1979   RCMP v. The People. Dan Miles, Ontario: General
       Publishing Co. Limited.

Manzer, Ronald
1974   Canada: A Socio-Political Report. Toronto:
       McGraw-Hill Ryerson.

McCaghy, C.H.
1976   Deviant Behaviour. New York: Macmillan.

McConnell, W.H.
1978

"Political Trials East and West." In The Sociology of Law: A Conflict Perspective. Charles E. Reasons and Robert M. Rich, eds. Toronto: Butterworths, pp. 333–51.

McCormick, Jr., Albert E.
1977

"Rule Enforcement and Moral Indignation: Some Observations on the Effects of Criminal Antitrust Convictions upon Societal Reaction Processes." Social Problems 25 (October):30–39.

McCorry, C.
1972

Citizen Nader. New York: Saturday Review Press.

McDonald, Lynn
1976

The Sociology of Law and Order. Montreal: Book Center.

Mickenberg, Neil H.
1971

"Aboriginal Rights in Canada and the United States." Osgoode Hall Law Journal: 119–55.

Milakovich, Michael E., and Weis, Kurt
1975

"Politics and Measures of Success in the War on Crime." Crime and Delinquency 21 (January): 1–10.

Miliband, Ralph
1969

The State and Capitalist Society. London: Camelot Press.

Miller, Loren
1966

The Petitioners: The Story of the Supreme Court of the United States and the Negro. Cleveland: World.

Miller, S.M., and Roby, Pamela A.
1970

The Future of Inequality. New York: Basic Books.

Miller, Walter B.
1973

"Ideology and Criminal Justice Policy: Some Current Issues." The Journal of Criminal Law and Criminology 64 (June):141–63.

Minister of Justice
1973

Canada Criminal Code and Selected Statutes. Ottawa: Information Canada.

Mohr, J.W.
1972   "Facts, Figures, Perceptions and Myths—Ways of Describing and Understanding Crime." Canadian Journal of Criminology and Corrections 15 (July).

Morris, Nowal, and Hawkins, Gordon
1970   The Honest Politician's Guide to Crime Control. Chicago: University of Chicago Press.

Morris, Raymond N., and Lanphier, C. Michael
1977   Three Scales of Inequality: Perspectives on French-English Relations. Don Mills: Longman Canada.

Moulecloux, J.C.
1967   "Political Crime and the Negro Revolution." In Criminal Behavior Systems: A Typology. New York: Holt, Rinehart and Winston, pp. 217–31.

Newman, Graham
1976   Comparative Deviance: Perception and Law in Six Cultures. New York: Elsevier.

Oake, George
1979   "Large Corporate Profits Enrage Labor." The Calgary Herald, February 8, p. 1.

Packer, Herbert
1962   "Offenses against the State." Annals (January): 77–89.

Pearce, F.
1976   Crimes of the Powerful: Marxism, Crime and Deviance. London: Pluto Press.

Pepinsky, Harold E.
1975   "Reliance on Formal Written Law, and Freedom and Social Control in the United States and the People's Republic of China." The British Journal of Sociology 26 (September):330–42.

Platt, Anthony
1969   The Child Saviors. Chicago: University of Chicago Press.

1974   "The Triumph of Benevolence: The Origins of the Juvenile Justice System in the United States." In Criminal Justice in America. Richard Quinney, ed. Boston: Little, Brown, pp. 356–89.

369

President's Report on
Occupational Safety and
Health
   1972   Washington D.C.: U.S. Government Printing
Office.

Prewitt, Kenneth, and
Verba, Sidney
   1979   An Introduction to American Government, 3d ed.
New York: Harper & Row.

Price, John A.
   1978   Native Studies: American and Canadian Indians.
Toronto: McGraw-Hill Ryerson.

Punkey, A.
   1972   The American Way of Violence. New York: Vintage
Books.

Quinney, Richard
   1964   "Crime in a Political Perspective." American
Behavioral Scientist 8 (December): 19–22.

   1970   The Social Reality of Crime. Boston:
Little, Brown.

   1975   Criminology. Boston: Little, Brown.

   1977   Class, State and Crime. New York: David McKay.

   1979   Criminology, 2d ed. Boston: Little, Brown.

Reasons, C.E.
   1974   The Criminologists: Crime and the Criminal.
Pacific Palisades, Calif.: Goodyear.

   1976   "Images of Crime and the Criminal: The Dope
Fiend Mythology." Journal of Research in Crime
and Delinquency 13 (July):133–44.

   1980   "Crime and the Abuse of Power: Offenses and
Offenders Beyond the Reach of the Law." Paper
presented to the International Conference on Economic and White Collar Crime, Potsdam, N.Y.
(February).

   1981   "Organization Crime." In Sociology of Deviance.
M. Rosenberg, R. Stebbins, and A. Turowitz, eds.
New York: St. Martins Press.

Reasons, Charles E., and
Goff, Colin H.
1980   "Corporate Crime: A Cross-national Analysis."
In White Collar Crime: Theory and Research.
Gilbert Geis and Ezra Stollard, eds. Beverly Hills,
Calif.: Sage.

Reasons, Charles E., and
Kuykendall, Jack L., eds.
1972   Race, Crime and Justice. Pacific Palisades, Calif.:
Goodyear.

Reasons, C.E.; Paterson,
C.; and Ross, L.
1981   Assault on the Worker: Occupational Health and
Safety in Canada. Toronto: Butterworth.

Reasons, Charles, and
Rich, R.M.
1978   The Sociology of Law: A Conflict Perspective.
Toronto: Butterworth.

Reiman, J.H.
1979   The Rich Get Richer and the Poor Get Prison.
New York: John Wiley.

Report of the Royal
Commission on
Corporation Concentration
1978   Ottawa: Minister of Supply and Services, Canada.

Report of the Senate Select
Committee on Intelligence
1978   In Corporate and Governmental Deviance: Prob-
lems of Organizational Behavior in Contemporary
Society. M.D. Ermann and R.J. Lundman, eds.
New York: Oxford University Press, pp. 151–73.

Rockwell, David N.
1971   "The Education of the Capitalist Lawyer: The Law
School." In Law against the People. Robert Lefcourt,
ed. New York: Random House, pp. 90–104.

Rossi, Peter H.; Warte,
Emily; Base, Christine E.;
and Berk, Richard E.
1974   "The Seriousness of Crimes: Normative Structure
and Individual Differences." American Sociological
Review 39 (April):224–37.

Salisbury, Harrison
1970   "Special Introduction." In Assassination and Political Violence. James F. Kirkham, Sheldon G. Levy, and William J. Crotty, eds. New York: Bantam, p. xvii.

Schrager, Laura Shill, and Short, Jr., James F.
1977   "Toward a Sociology of Organizational Crimes." Paper presented at the American Sociological Association Meetings, Chicago.

Schur, Edwin
1969a   Law and Society. New York: Random House.

1969b   Our Criminal Society: The Social and Legal Sources of Crime in America. Englewood Cliffs, N.J.: Prentice-Hall.

Schwendinger, Herman and Julia R.
1970   "Defenders of Order or Guardians of Human Rights?" Issues in Criminology 5 (Summer):123–57.

1977   "Social Class and the Definition of Crime." Crime and Social Justice 7 (Spring-Summer):4–13.

Seidman, Robert, and Couzans, Michael
1974   "Getting the Crime Rate Norm: Political Pressure and Crime Reporting." Law and Society Review 8 (Spring):457–93.

Short Jr., James F.
1980   "How Serious a Crime? Perceptions of Organizational and Common Crimes." In White Collar Crime: Theory and Research. G. Geis and E. Stotland, eds. Beverly Hills, Calif.: Sage, pp. 14–31.

Silverman, Robert A., and Teevan, Jr., James, eds.
1975   Crime in Canadian Society. Toronto: Butterworth.

Singer, Gail, and Rodgers, Bob
1975   "Mercury: The Hidden Poison in the Northern Rivers." Saturday Night (October):15–22.

Sjostrom, Henning, and
Nilsson, Robert
  1972   Thalidomide and the Power of the Drug Companies. Middlesex, England: Penguin.

Smigel, Erwin O., and
Ross, H. Lawrence
  1970   Crimes against Bureaucracy. New York: Van Nostrand Reinhold.

Snider, D.L.
  1978   "Corporate Crime in Canada: A Preliminary Report." Canadian Journal of Criminology 20 (April):142–68.

Sorel, George
  1950   Reflections on Violence. New York: Free Press.

Stampp, Kenneth M.
  1970   The Civil Rights Record: Black Americans and the Law, 1849–1970. New York: Thomas Y. Crowell.

Stern, Gerald M.
  1976   The Buffalo Creek Disaster: The Story of the Survivors, Unprecedented Lawsuit. New York: Random House.

Sutherland, E.H.,
  1961   White Collar Crime. New York: Holt, Rinehart and Winston.

Swartz, Joel
  1975   "Silent Killers at Work." Crime and Social Justice 3 (Summer):15–20.

Sykes, G.M.
  1978   Criminology, New York: Harcourt Brace Jovanovich.

Szabo, Dennis
  1970   "Assassination and Political Violence in Canada." In Assassination and Political Violence. James F. Kirkham, Sheldon G. Levy, and William J. Crotty, eds. New York: Bantam, pp. 700–14.

Tataryn, L.
  1979   Dying for a Living. Toronto: Deneau and Greenberg.

Tigar, Michael E., and
Levy, Madelein R.
1977   Law and the Rise of Capitalism. New York:
        Monthly Review Press.

Title, M.M.
1978   "Canadian Wiretap Legislation: Protection or
        Erosion of Privacy?" Chitty's Law Journal 26:
        47–49.

Turk, Austin
1976   "Law as a Weapon in Social Conflict." Social
        Problems 23 (Febuary):276–91.

U.S. Congress
1976   "Achieving the Goals of the Employment Act of
        1946—Thirtieth Anniversary Review." Joint Eco-
        nomic Committee, Paper No. 5: "Estimating the
        Social Costs of National Economic Policy: Impli-
        cations for Mental and Physical Health and
        Criminal Aggression," October 26. Washington
        D.C.: U.S. Government Printing Office.

U.S. Department of
Justice
1975   "Crime in the United States, 1974," FBI Uniform
        Crime Reports. Washington, D.C.: U.S. Govern-
        ment Printing Office.

1979a   "Crime in the United States, 1978," FBI Uniform
        Crime Reports. Washington, D.C.: U.S. Govern-
        ment Printing Office.

1979b   "Illegal Corporate Behavior." Law Enforcement
        Assistance Administration, National Institute of
        Law Enforcement and Criminal Justice. Wash-
        ington, D.C.: U.S. Government Printing Office.

Venable, Gilbert T.
1966   "The Parens Patriae Theory and Its Effect on the
        Constitutional Limits of Juvenile Court Powers."
        University of Pittsburgh Law Review (June):
        892–914.

Willhelm, Sidney M.
1969   "Black Man, Red Man, and White America: The
        Constitutional Approach to Genocide." Catalyst
        (Spring):1–62.

Wolfgang, Marvin E.
1963   "Uniform Crime Reports: A Critical Appraisal."
University of Pennsylvania Law Review 111
(April):708–38.

Woodward, C. Vann
1969   "Our Racist History." The New York Review of
Books 12 (February 27):338–52.

Young, Bert
1974   "Corporate Interests and the State." Our Generation 10 (Winter-Spring):70–83.

375

7

EXPLAINING CRIMINAL BEHAVIOR

Abstract

The search for the causes of crime has led to the investigation of biological characteristics of crimininals, the study of their psychological makeup, the analysis of their family background and employment record. The explanation of criminal behavior has been in terms of the characteristics of criminals and, thus, fits the dominant corporate societies' emphasis upon individualism and blaming the victim. The institutionalization and maintenance of programs and policies based upon explanations of *kinds of people* or *kinds of environment* ensure that a critical questioning of the master institutions will not be evident. The alternative explanation of crime arising from a *power/conflict* conception of causation has radical implications for social policy in this area. We do know some of the sources of crime and have the ability, if not the desire, to change its nature and scope in our society.

A criminological doctrine which regards crime as a phenomenon deeply embedded in the structure of society will naturally concentrate its proposals for reform on fundamental changes in the social structure. Broad social policy will be its primary concern. In contrast, a criminological doctrine which sees the sources of crime in the individual will advocate a programme including specific proposals for the reform of the criminal law and procedure and above all the penal system. The first approach will be more closely identified with social reform, the second with penal reform. —Leon Radzinowicz

Viewpoint

In 1902, the famed trial lawyer Clarence Darrow was asked by the warden of the Cook County jail to address the inmates. The following exerpts from that speech suggest that its broad thrust is still applicable some eight decades later. Though turn-of-the-century trusts have been replaced by interlocking giant corporations, and the "robber barons" of that age have given way to a less-visible, less flamboyant corporate elite, these are changes in form rather than substance. The historical specifics have been altered but the social consequences of inequality still include the "traditional" crimes of the poor and the often overlooked crimes of the upper world.

"CRIMES AND CRIMINALS"
ADDRESS TO THE PRISONERS IN
THE COOK COUNTY JAIL
1902

By Clarence Darrow

If I looked at jails and crimes and prisoners in the the way the ordinary person does, I should not speak on this subject to you. The reason I talk to you on the question of crime, its cause and cure, is that I really do not in the least believe in crime. There is no such thing as crime as the word is generally understood. I do not believe there is any sort of distinction between the real moral conditions of the people in and out of jail. One is just as good as the other. The people here can no more help being here than the people outside can avoid being outside. I do not believe that people are in jail because they deserve to be. They are in jail simply because they cannot avoid it on account of circumstances which are entirely beyond their control and for which they are in no way responsible.

I suppose a great many people on the outside would say I was doing you harm if they should hear what I say to you this afternoon, but you cannot be hurt a great deal anyway, so it will not matter. Good people outside would say that I was really teaching you things that were calculated to injure society, but it's worthwhile now and then to hear something different from what you ordinarily get from preachers and the like. These will tell you that you should be good and then you will get rich and be happy. Of course we know that people do not get rich by being good, and that is the reason why so many of you people try to get rich some other way, only you do not understand how to do it quite as well as the fellow outside.

There are people who think that everything in this world is an accident. But really there is no such thing as an accident. A great many folks admit that many of the people in jail ought to be there, and many who are outside ought to be in. I think none of them ought to be here. There ought to be no jails; and if it were not for the fact that the people on the outside are so grasping and heartless in their dealings with the people on the inside, there would be no such institution as jails.

I do not want you to believe that I think all you people here are angels. I do not think that. You are people of all kinds, all of you doing the best you can—and that is evidently not very well. You are people of all kinds and conditions and under all circumstances. In one sense everybody is equally good and equally bad. We all do the best we can under the circumstances. But as to the exact things for which you are sent here, some of you are guilty and did the particular act because you needed the money.

While you would not have the least thing against me in the world, you might pick my pockets. I do not think all of you would, but I think some of you would. You would not have anything against me, but that's your profession, a few of you. Some of the rest of you, if my doors were unlocked, might come in if you saw anything you wanted—not out of any malice to me, but because that is your trade. There is no doubt there are quite a number of people in this jail who would pick my pockets. And still I know this—that when I get outside pretty nearly everybody picks my pocket. There may be some of you who would hold up a man on the street, if you did not happen to have something else to do, and needed the money; but when I want to light my house or my office the gas company holds me up. They charge me one dollar for something that is worth twenty-five cents. Still all these people are good people; they are pillars of society and support the churches, and they are respectable.

When I ride on the streetcars I am held up—I pay five cents for a ride that is worth two-and-a-half cents, simply because a body of men have bribed the city council and the legislature, so that all the rest of us have to pay tribute to them.

If I do not want to fall into the clutches of the gas trust and choose to burn oil instead of gas, then good Mr. Rockefeller holds me up, and he uses a certain portion of his money to build universities and support churches which are engaged in telling us how to be good.

Some of you are here for obtaining property under false pretenses—yet I pick up a great Sunday paper and read the advertisements of a merchant prince—"Shirtwaists for 39 cents, marked down from $3.00."

When I read the advertisements in the paper I see they are all lies. When I want to get out and find a place to stand anywhere on the face of the earth, I find that it has all been taken up long ago before I came here, and before you came here, and somebody says, "Get off, swim into the lake, fly into the air; go anywhere, but get off." That is because these people have the police and they have the jails and the judges and the lawyers and the soldiers and all the rest of them to take care of the earth and drive everybody off that comes in their way.

A great many people will tell you that all this is true, but that it does not excuse you. These facts do not excuse some fellow who reaches into my pocket and takes out a five-dollar bill. The fact that the gas company bribes the members of the legislature from year to year, and fixes the law so that all you people are compelled to be "fleeced" whenever you deal with them; the fact that the streetcar companies and the gas companies have control of the streets; and the fact that the landlords own all the earth—this, they say, has nothing to do with you.

Let us see whether there is any connection between the crimes of the respectable classes and your presence in the jail. Many of you people are in jail because you have stolen something. In the meaning of the law, you have taken some other person's property. Some of you have entered a store and carried off a pair of shoes because you did not have the price. Possibly some of you have committed murder. I cannot tell what all of you did. There are a great many people here who have done some of these things who really do not know themselves why they did them. I think I know why you did them—every one of you; you did these things because you were bound to do them. You could not help it any more than we outside can help taking the positions that we take. The reformers who tell you to be good and you will be happy, and the people on the outside who have property to protect—they think that the only way to do it is by building jails and locking you up in cells on weekdays and praying for you on Sundays.

I think that all of this has nothing whatever to do with right conduct. I think it is very easily seen what has to do with right conduct. Some so-called criminals—and I will use this word because it is handy, it means nothing to me—I speak of the criminals who get caught as distinguished from the criminals who catch them—some of these so-called criminals are in jail for their first offenses, but nine tenths of you are in jail because you did not have a good lawyer and, of course, you did not have a good lawyer because you did not have enough money to pay a good lawyer. There is no very great danger of a rich man going to jail.

There are more people who go to jail in hard times than in good times—few people, comparatively, go to jail except when they are hard up. They go to jail because they have no other place to go. They may not know why, but it is true all the same. People are not more wicked in hard times. That is not the reason. The fact is true all over the world that in hard times more people go to jail than in good times, and in winter more people go to jail than in summer. Of course, it is pretty hard times for people who go to jail at any time. The people who go to jail are almost always poor people—people who have no other place to live, first and last. When times are hard, then you find large numbers of people who go to jail who would not otherwise be in jail.

Long ago, Mr. Buckle, who was a great philosopher and historian, collected facts, and he showed that the number of people who are arrested increased just as the price of food increased. When they put up the price of gas ten cents a thousand, I do not know who will go to jail, but I do know that a certain number of people will go. When the meat combine raises the price of beef, I do not know who is going to jail, but I know that a large number of people are bound to go. Whenever the Standard Oil Company raises the price of oil, I know that a certain number of girls who are seamstresses, and who work night after night long hours for somebody else, will be compelled to go out on the streets and ply another trade; and I know that Mr. Rockefeller and his associates are responsible and not the poor girls in the jails.

There is a bill before the legislature of this state to punish kidnapping children with death. We have wise members of the legislature. They know the gas trust when they see it and they always see it—they can furnish light enough to be seen; and this legislature thinks it is going to stop kidnapping children by making a law punishing kidnappers of children with death. I don't believe in kidnapping children, but the legislature is all wrong. Kidnapping children is not a crime; it is a profession. It has been developed with the times. It has been developed with our modern industrial conditions. There are many ways of making money—many new ways that our ancestors knew nothing about. Our ancestors knew nothing about a billion-dollar trust; and here comes some poor fellow who has no other trade and he discovers the profession of kidnapping children.

This crime is born, not because people are bad; people don't kidnap other people's children because they want the children or because they are devilish, but because they see a chance to get some money out of it. You cannot cure this crime by passing a law punishing by death kidnappers of children. There is one way to cure it. There is one way to cure all these offenses, and that is to give the people a chance to live. There is no other way, and there never was any other way since the world began; and the world is so blind and stupid that it will not see. If every man and woman and child in the world had a chance to make a decent, fair, honest living, there would be no jails and no lawyers and no courts. There might be some persons here or there with some peculiar formation of their brain, like Rockefeller, who would do these things simply to be doing them; but they would be very, very few, and those should be sent to a hospital and treated, and not sent to jail; and they would entirely disappear in the second generation, or at least in the third generation.

I am not talking pure theory. I will just give you two or three illustrations.

The English people once punished criminals by sending them away. They would load them on a ship and export them to Australia. England was owned by lords and nobles and rich people. They owned the whole earth over there, and the other people had to stay in the streets. They could not get a decent living. They used to take their criminals and send them to Australia—I mean the class of criminals who got caught. When these criminals got over there, and nobody else had come, they had the whole continent to run over, and so they could raise sheep and furnish their own meat, which is easier than stealing it. These criminals then became decent, respectable people because they had a chance to live. They did not commit any crimes. They were just like the English people who sent them there, only better. And in the second generation the descendants of the those criminals were as good and respectable a class of people as there were on the face of the earth, and then they began building churches and jails themselves.

A portion of this country was settled in the same way, landing prisoners down on the southern coast; but when they got here and had a whole continent to run over and plenty of chances to make a living, they became respectable citizens, making their own living just like any other citizen in the world. But finally the descendants of the English aristocracy who sent the people over to Australia found out they were getting rich, and so they went over to get possession of the earth as they always do, and they organized land syndicates and got control of the land and ores, and then they had just as many criminals in Australia as they did in England. It was not because the world had grown bad; it was because the earth had been taken away from the people.

Let me illustrate: Take the poorest person in this room. If the community had provided a system of doing justice, the poorest person in this room would have as good a lawyer as the richest, would he not? When you went into court you would have just as long a trial and just as fair a trial as the richest person in Chicago. Your case would not be tried in fifteen or twenty minutes, whereas it would take fifteen days to get through with a rich man's case. Then if you were rich and were beaten, your case would be taken to the Appellate Court. A poor man cannot take his case to the Appellate Court; he has not the price. And then to the Supreme Court. And if he were beaten there he might perhaps go to the United States Supreme Court. And he might die of old age before he got into jail.

It's easy to see how to do away with what we call crime. It is not so easy to do it. I will tell you how to do it. It can be done by giving the people a chance to live—by destroying special privileges. So long as big criminals can get the coal fields, so long as the big criminals have control of the city council and get the public streets for streetcars and gas rights, this is bound to send thousands of poor people to jail. So long as men are allowed to monopolize all the earth, and compel others to live on such terms as these men see fit to make, then you are bound to get into jail.

The only way in the world to abolish crime and criminals is to abolish the big ones and the little ones together. Make fair conditions of life. Give men a chance to live. Abolish the right of private ownership of land, abolish monopoly, make the world partners in production, partners in the good things of life. Nobody would steal if he could get something of his own some easier way. Nobody will commit burglary when he has a house full. No girl will go out on the streets when she has a comfortable place at home. The man who owns a sweatshop or a department store may not be to blame himself for the conditions of his girls, but when he pays them five dollars, three dollars, and two dollars a week, I wonder where he thinks they will get the rest of their money to live. The only way to cure these conditions is by equality. There should be no jails. They do not accomplish what they pretend to accomplish. If you would wipe them out there would be no more criminals than now. They terrorize nobody. They are a blot upon any civilization, and a jail is an evidence of the lack of charity of the people on the outside who make the jails and fill them with the victims of their greed.

"Too radical" was the comment of one prisoner when a guard later asked him what he thought of the speech.

Darrow's friends, too, were distressed when they heard about the talk. "Your theories might be true, Clarence," they insisted, "but you should never have told them to criminals in a jail."

Darrow's reaction to his friends' thinking is best expressed in the introduction to the lecture which he had printed in pamphlet form.

Wrote Darrow: "realizing the force of the suggestion that the truth should not be spoken to all people, I have caused these remarks to be printed on rather good paper and in a somewhat expensive form. In this way the truth does not become cheap and vulgar, and is only placed before those whose intelligence and affluence will prevent their being influenced by it."

The pamphlet sold for five cents.

Arthur Weinberg, ed. "Attorney for the Damned" New York; Simon & Schuster.

THE PREVAILING IDEOLOGIES

The Villainous Family

Why did she or he do it? This question has been repeatedly asked by millions of people in their attempts to explain the aberrant behavior of others, particularly their "criminal" behavior. The prevailing tendency is to assume that law-abiding, conforming behavior is "natural." One rarely asks, Why did she or he *not* steal, lie, cheat, injure, or otherwise commit a crime? While the focus in the preceding chapter is on law, the concern here is with criminal behavior. Both are social products best understood when related to societal structure.

The usual range of explanations of criminal behavior includes:

1. The criminal chose to commit a crime through free will.

2. The criminal was born that way.

3. The criminal is mentally ill (sick).

4. The criminal is from a bad family.

5. The criminal was influenced by a bad group of friends.

6. The criminal was forced to commit crime because of poverty and/or ethnic status.

While many other explanations can be presented, these generally cover the range of reasons noted by most of the public and many students of crime. In a United States national poll concerning the causes of criminal behavior, parental laxity was identified as the major cause of crime, with bad environments and economic conditions listed next. The poll results are seen in Table 7–1.

However, there is quite a difference between the views of black and white respondents. Black respondents emphasize environmental conditions (particularly economic such as poverty, welfare, and subsequent alcohol abuse) more than parental laxity, while whites overwhelmingly stress a breakdown in parental responsibility. This is undoubtedly a product of socially situated explanations, with blacks more subject to poverty, unemployment, bad environments, and other disadvantages while whites are much less likely to face such conditions and thus place the blame on the parents.

So we see that social being determines social consciousness in seeking explanations for crime. Emphasis upon lack of discipline in the home, lack of respect for law, broken homes, drugs, and alcohol were the most

TABLE 7-1
National Poll

What Are the Main Reasons Why People Become Criminals?

	Total[a]	Negro Respondents	White Respondents
Parents too lax			63%
Bad environments			16
Poverty		25	14
Unemployment	12		11
Lack of education	12		11
Young people have no morals	12	9	12
Alcohol	10	18	9
Drugs; narcotics	10	9	10
Broken homes	9	7	10
Not enough recreation for young	9		10
For kicks	9	13	8
People have too much; spoiled	7	4	8
Too many on welfare	7	13	6
Lack of religion	7	8	7
Courts too lenient; don't prevent crimes	5		5
Time of unrest	4	5	4
Kids see violence on TV	4	2	4
Mentally ill	3	1	3
Too many restrictions on police	3	—	3
Other	8	7	8
Not sure	3	5	3

[a] Figures add to more than 100 percent as some respondents gave more than one answer.

Source: From Louis Harris and Associates, *The Public Looks at Crime and Corrections* (Washington, D.C.: Joint Commission on Correctional Manpower and Training, 1968), p. 5.

frequently noted causes of crime in a Toronto, Ontario, study (Courtis 1970). It appears that family conditions play an important part in the general public's explanation of the origins of lawlessness. Given the ideological component of "familism," this is theoretically consistent. As corporate society fractures community support, the ideology of the family is offered instead. "Good" families supposedly make for law-abiding citizens; "bad" families are portrayed as the breeding grounds for crime. What such "explanations" overlook is that the family in its turn is shaped by powerful social forces. Nonetheless, certain populations, at least to some extent, identify broader conditions of environment, particularly economic factors.

Stereotyping the Criminal   Since most of us do not personally experience the crimes of violence that are of major concern, our understanding of the causes of such crimes is primarily gained from the media, criminal justice officials, and more generally, the prevailing ideology. Most of us learn as children about heroes and villains, good guys and bad guys, good and evil.

> The villain is a functional character, and a ritual is a social device for repeating his functions again and again. He often serves society, for example, as a scapegoat or safety valve for aggression, or as a perfected hate-symbol building morale for law enforcement and others' actions. Oddly, he serves society by deviating from its mores (Klapp 1962, p. 51).

Most of us carry around in our heads a conception of the "criminal type" generally, and of specific types of criminals. One researcher (Simmons 1965) found that public stereotyping of deviants is quite prevalent. Marijuana smokers were viewed as insecure escapists, looking for kicks and without self-control, while homosexuals were identified as perverted and mentally ill, and adulterers were characterized as promiscuous, insecure, and immoral. Traits imputed to all types were irresponsibility and lack of self-control. In a more recent study (Shoemaker et al. 1973), researchers found that the public has definite stereotypes of what a murderer, a robber, and a treasonous person look like and use such images in attributing guilt. Stereotypes of crime and the criminal are also to be found in the mass media (Reasons 1976a; Gordon 1971; Friendly and Goldfarb 1968; Hess and Mariner 1975), among academics and among agents in the criminal justice system (Henshel and Silverman 1975). A recent study of stereotypes in the criminal justice system found one such violent offender was designated as the "normal primitive."

> While treated as diagnostic category, the designation "normal primitive" constitutes a *social* description of a group of people whose behavior, *within their own social setting*, is best described as normal. The "normal primitive" comes largely from the foreign-born and black populations. Their lives are characterized by impoverished economic conditions which, as with their behavior, may be described as "primitive." Occupational achievements center around unskilled, menial labor, and these careers are often sporadic. Educational levels are minimal and testing indicates borderline to low-average intelligence. While the children of the foreign-born do acclimate to a less "primitive" existence, the offspring of the black population seem unaffected by improved educational and social opportunities (Swigert and Farrell 1977, p. 19).

The above description was taken from clinical records in a court serving a large urban area in the northeastern United States. This conception of criminality combines both racial and class characteristics as "causing crime." It further combines biological, psychological, and social factors that have been used by students of crime. As an ideology of criminal explanation, such a description focuses attention on the intimate reasons for deviant behavior, not the more removed problems of social structure.

A More Realistic View We might better visualize explanations of crime as emphasizing (1) the personal characteristics of the criminal; (2) the characteristics of the situation; (3) the criminal's family life; (4) the offender's social position as determined by ethnicity, employment, education; (5) his or her political position in terms of the definition of crime and the administration of justice; and/or (6) the offender's economic standing.

Figure 7-1. Circle of Explanations of Criminal Behavior

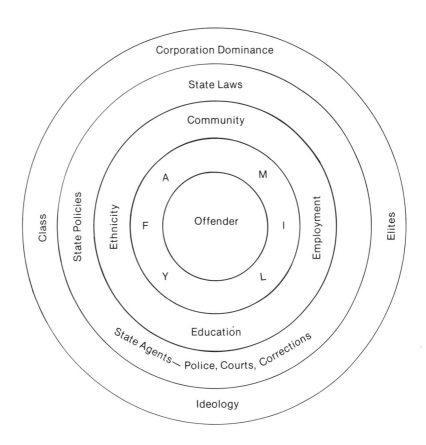

These various emphases in explanation can be identified as kinds of people, kinds of environment, and power/conflict explanations of criminal behaviors (Reasons 1975). "Kinds of people" explanations emphasize the biological or psychological characteristics of the criminal in explaining crime, while "kinds of environment" explanations stress the characteristics of the offender's family and community as major causes. "Kinds of people" and "kinds of environment" explanations focus on personal or social characteristics of criminals, but "power/conflict" explanations emphasize differences in power and economic control. Such differences influence which behaviors (street or suite) will be defined as crime and which people will be defined as criminal through the criminal justice process. For example, how would you explain the following observations?

> Nationally, 58% of the inmates in federal and state correctional institutions were white in 1970, compared to 41% black and 1% Native American. If one considers peoples of Spanish origin as an ethnic/racial group (which we do), then only 51% of the incarcerated population is white, with 7% being of Spanish origin (Mexican, Puerto Rican, Cuban, other). For these racial/ethnic groups the ratio of their representation in prisons compared to their representation in the US population is White .6; Blacks, 3.7; Indian 3.4; Spanish origin 1.8. The disproportionate incarceration rate of nonwhites is greatest in state institutions and the least in federal. The above ratios remain essentially the same for local jails and workhouses in 1970! (Reasons 1974, p. 5.)

Does the preponderance of nonwhites in correctional institutions mean that blacks, Chicanos, and Native Americans tend to be "born criminals"? Or perhaps their families and subcultures have taught them the "wrong" values? If both of these are victim blaming, then it seems logical to address the intersection of race or ethnicity and class inequality. If it is true (and it is) that nonwhites are overly represented among the poor, the underemployed, and the unemployed, is there a connection between these social conditions and the racial and class composition of the prison population?

As will become evident later, different emphases suggest different "solutions" to the crime problem. For example, the family appears to be identified by most of the public as the cause of criminal behavior; thus, particular family environments, such as single-headed households, those with working mothers, or those lacking discipline are thought to produce certain kinds of people, namely, delinquents and criminals.

The Criminal Type

There are thousands of behaviors that are against the law, with many different persons committing them. More specifically, Clinard and Quinney (1973) have developed a typology of criminal behavior systems that includes eight types of offenses. They classify each type according to offender's career, group support, extent of correspondence with legal behavior, societal reaction, and specific legal inclusive offenses. The public's images of the crime problem and criminals are largely based upon violent personal crime, occasional property crime, and conventional

TABLE 7-2
Typology of Criminal Behavior Systems

Classification Characteristics	Violent Personal Crime	Occasional Property Crime	Occupational Crime	Political Crime
Criminal Career of the Offender	Low Crime not part of offender's career; usually does not conceive of it as criminal	Low Little or no criminal self-concept, does not identify with crime	Low No criminal self-concept, occasionally violates the law; part of one's legitimate work, accepts conventional values of society	Low Usually no criminal self-concept; violates the law out of conscience; attempts to change society or correct perceived injustices; desire for a better society
Group Support of Criminal Behavior	Low Little or no group support, offenses committed for personal reasons, some support in subculture	Low Little group support; individual offenses	Medium Some groups may tolerate offenses; offender integrated in groups	High Group support; association with persons of same values; behavior reinforced by group
Correspondence between Criminal Behavior and Legitimate Behavior Patterns	Low Violation of values on life and safety	Low Violation of value on private property	High Behavior corresponds to pursuit of business activity; "sharp" practices respected; "buyer beware" philosophy; hands off policy	Medium Some toleration of protest and dissent, short of revolution; dissent periodically regarded as a threat (in times of national unrest)
Societal Reaction	High Capital punishment; long imprisonment	Medium Arrest, jail; short imprisonment, probation	Low Indifference; monetary penalties, revocation of license to practice, seizure of product or injunction	High Strong disapproval; regarded as threat to society; prison
Legal Categories of Crime	Murder, assault, forcible rape, child molesting	Some auto theft, shoplifting, check forgery, vandalism	Embezzlement, fraudulent sales, false advertising, fee-splitting, violation of labor practice laws, antitrust violations, black market activity, prescription violation	Treason, sedition, espionage, sabotage, radicalism, military draft violations, war collaboration, various protests defined as criminal

390

Typology of Criminal Behavior Systems (continued)

Public Order Crime	Conventional Crime	Organized Crime	Professional Crime
Medium	Medium	High	High
Confused self concept, vacillation in identification with crime	Income supplemented through crimes of gain; often a youthful activity, vacillation in self-concept; partial commitment to a criminal subculture	Crime pursued as a livelihood, criminal self-concept, progression in crime; isolation from larger society	Crime pursued as a livelihood, criminal self-concept, status in the world of crime; commitment to world of professional criminals
Medium	High	High	High
Partial support for behavior from some groups, considerable association with other offenders	Behavior supported by group norms, status achieved in groups; principal association with other offenders	Business associations in crime, behavior prescribed by the groups; integration of the person into the group	Associations primarily with other offenders, status gained in criminal offenses; behavior prescribed by group norms
Medium	Medium	Medium	Medium
Some forms required by legitimate society; some are economic activities	Consistent with goals on economic success, inconsistent with sanctity of private property; behavior not consistent with expectations of adolescence and young adulthood	Illegal services received by legitimate society; economic risk values; large scale control also employed on legitimate society	Engaged in an occupation; skill respected; survival because of cooperation from legitimate society; law-abiding persons often accomplices
Medium	High	Medium	Medium
Arrest; jail; prison; probation	Arrest; jail; probation; institutionalization; parole; rehabilitation	Considerable public toleration; arrest and sentence when detected; often not visible to society, immunity through politicians and law officers	Rarely strong societal reaction, most cases "fixed"
Drunkenness, vagrancy, disorderly conduct, prostitution, homosexuality, gambling, traffic violation, drug addiction	Robbery, larceny, burglary, gang theft	Racketeering, organized prostitution and commercialized vice, control of drug traffic, organized gambling	Confidence games, shoplifting, pickpocketing, forgery, counterfeiting

Source: Marshall B. Clinard & Richard Quinney, "Criminal Behavior Systems: A Typology," 2nd ed. New York: Holt, Rinehart & Winston, 1973

crime. The public sees the persons committing these types of crime as psychologically and socially maladjusted, coming from a faulty family background, poor, young, male, and disproportionately nonwhite.

> As a social type, the "criminal" can be understood by the observer as one who has attributes believed to characterize a class of people. The criminal, as socially typed, is a construct incorporating a description of what such people are like, why they act as they do, and how they should act in the future. All that is associated with crime can be categorized by the public (Quinney 1975, p. 263).

North American evaluations of the causes of criminal behavior still largely reflect the traditional puritan concept of order. By this heritage, crime becomes an act against the balance of nature caused by some pre-destined flaw in personal character (Erickson 1966). The puritan assumption of the irreversibility of human nature still underlies the prevailing ideology of crime, thus effectively blocking rehabilitation.

> Now as then, we leave few return routes open to people who try to resume a normal social life after a period of time spent on the community's boundaries, because most of us feel that anyone who skids off into the more severe forms of aberrant expression is displaying a serious defect of character, a deep blemish which cannot easily be erased. We may learn to think of such people as "sick" rather than "reprobate," but a single logic governs both of these labels, for they imply that nothing less than an important change of heart, a spiritual conversion or a clinical cure, can eliminate that inner seed which leads one to behave in a deviant fashion (Erickson 1966, p. 204–5).

Those crimes that are viewed as most threatening to the established moral values are commonly explained as irrational and psychopathological. Crimes that are believed to be particularly destructive of the basic foundation of society will often be explained as quite distinct aberrations committed by particularly "unique" or "different" types of individuals. Therefore, murder, assassination, political kidnappings, and other political crimes are perpetrated by "evil" and "wicked" persons. For example, during what was termed the Watergate episode in the United States, political officials such as Nixon, Mitchell, Haldeman, and Ehrlichman among others, violated the law. However, the prevailing ideology was that these were the deeds of men who were somehow warped, or otherwise quite different from other politicians (see Chapter One, Section on Idiosyncratic Explanations). The "bad apple" theory implies that to prevent such crimes you have to be more careful about the kinds of people you get into office, and use more thorough screening and testing. However, if such actions are found to be pervasive and commonplace, rather than changing individuals there might be a need for changing the structure of the political system. If murder and physical assault were seen to be normal, logical consequences of societal emphasis upon toughness and aggression as resolutions to interpersonal conflict, there might be more emphasis upon understanding violence at the state level (such as that inflicted by the military, police, personnel in asylums, and so on). If the State advances dominant class interests through, for example, military force, what is the message sent to the alienated, the outcasts, and the hopeless?

Crime: An Irrational Behavior?   The assumption of irrationality, lack of self-control, and improper socialization is often found in explanations of criminal behavior. This evaluation of the causes of criminal behavior is in part a product of Social Darwinism.[1] The belief in the "survival of the fittest" suggests that the law-abiding persons are the fittest and criminals are somehow lacking. Those who have achieved some semblance of success and survival (white collar and corporate criminals) are evaluated differently from "common criminals" because they have many of the attributes of respectability. Therefore, such violations of the law may be viewed as a momentary or temporary aberration in a generally upstanding and respectable life. In fact, given the general ideology of triumph of the will that embraces such ideas as "rugged individualism," "competition," "survival of the fittest," and "winning," one who has achieved success financially, occupationally, and in social status is assumed to be of "good character." While the achiever is considered a rational, purposive actor, those who do not succeed are characterized as irrational and defective in character. Crime committed by the poor, young, and/or nonwhites is often explained as a "normal" consequence of their biological, psychological, or social characteristics. In other words, what can you expect from "them"?

Crime: A Rational Response   Although criminal behavior is generally thought of as irrational, one economist has suggested that much crime is largely a "rational" response to one's economic circumstances.

> . . . nearly all crimes in capitalist societies represent perfectly *rational* responses to the structure of institutions upon which capitalist societies are based. Crimes of many different varieties constitute functionally similar responses to the organization of capitalist institutions, for those crimes help provide a means of survival in a society within which survival is never assured (Gordon 1973, p. 170).

[1] Social Darwinism is a set of ideas that holds that social inequality reflects biological inequality. Thus, those at the top are the "fittest" while those on the bottom are the biological "inferiors." These ideas were popular in social science and constituted a part of the prevailing ideology of corporatism at the turn of the twentieth century.

Gordon argues that ghetto, organized, and white collar crime represent clearly "rational," that is predictable and expected, behavior given the barriers of structural inequality. The most prevalent ghetto crimes such as theft, robbery, drug dealing, gambling, and prostitution are to be expected in light of the absence of alternative economic opportunities for ghetto residents. Such activities bring in decent wages compared with the typical low-paying, demeaning, and temporary "legitimate" work sporadically available. Likewise, organized crime activities such as gambling, prostitution, and sale of illicit drugs are a normal consequence of the way in which corporate society is organized. There is a *demand* for often illegal goods and services and therefore, enormous *profits* are to be made from their sale. Further, as Daniel Bell (1953) has argued, organized crime has been a form of upward mobility (a step up) for some members of repressed minority groups at different periods of American history including the Irish, Eastern European Jews, and the Italians. Finally, corporate crime is a "rational" response to the goal of corporations, which is to protect and add to the capital of their owners. Thus, monopolies, price fixing, briberies, and other illegal activities help create more capital with almost no chance of detection, prosecution, conviction, and incarceration. If this analysis is correct, then most crime is sensible and sane, given basic social conditions. The tendency to explain crime as "irrational conduct" on the part of social deviants, of course diverts attention from the economic and political respectables who quite rationally manage the corporate order.

EMERGENCE

Knowledge is a social product. It is bound to a historical context and reflects the events of an era. As a specific form of knowledge, the explanations for criminal behavior also emerge in a historical setting, advanced by scholars and influentials who are responsive to the prevailing ideologies.

Before the Age of Enlightenment and Reason in the seventeenth and eighteenth centuries, deviant behavior was largely given a demonological explanation. Those who committed crimes were thought to be possessed by demons and driven by the Devil. Various rituals and procedures were derived to determine guilt or innocence, all based on the assumption that "other-world" powers were operating. Compensation for crime and for sin; trial by battle; trial by ordeal; testimony under oath; miraculous "signs" or omens indicating guilt or innocence all bespoke belief in a supernatural order (Vold 1958). For example, in a trial by battle, the accused fought the accuser and it was presumed that the innocent person would win out through divine favor. Trial by ordeal also was based upon demonological assumptions. It has been described in the following terms:

It was popular among prosecutors because it eliminated the unpleasant chances of battle. The accused person, being bound hand and foot, was thrown into a pond. If he "swam," as it was expressed, he was taken out and dealt with as guilty. If he sank and drowned, his innocence was manifest and he was buried with all decency and respect. . . . A not unreasonable dissatisfaction was felt among the criminal classes, which at that time constituted the bulk of the population (Block and Geis 1970, p. 424).

The interpretation of trial by ordeal requires an understanding of the feudal society in which such a test was carried out. For under feudalism, the dogma of the Church was the basis for criminal law. Thus, to swim or float indicated that one was rejected by the waters that symbolized baptism. Baptismal "acceptance," as is evident, often exacted a heavy price.

Classical School

With the decline of the feudal order and the emergence of trade capitalism during the Middle Ages, secular explanations came to replace religious ones. More emphasis was given to viewing the human being as a calculating, free-willing actor who is the master of his or her fate. Therefore, rather than being driven by other-worldly forces, human behavior was seen as a product of choice. The historical stage was thus set for the emergence of the classical school of criminology in the eighteenth century. Such writers as Blackstone, Bentham, and Becarria helped to establish the basic ideas of the classical tradition. They held that people are reasoning, rational beings,[2] possessors of a will that regulates and controls behavior. Further, they saw the will as free in that there were no limitations to the choices an individual could make. Finally, for the classicists the fear of pain was the principal instrument to control the will and was to be provided by punishment through the criminal code (Vold 1958, pp. 14–26). As a calculating, rational, free-willed actor, a human being selects that behavior that minimizes pain and maximizes pleasure. Given these primary ideas, the classical school held that punishments should be rationally fixed to outweigh the pleasure derived from the criminal act. If such is accomplished, the human actor will not commit a crime.

[2]"Rational" for the classicists had a different meaning than for Gordon, whose work we examined in an earlier section. For the classicists, people choose from among alternatives on the basis of the "pleasure or pain" consequences of their choice. For Gordon, given structural inequality, criminal choice is conditioned and expected. Thus, the classicist emphasis is on free will, while Gordon centers on a political and economic system that stacks the deck, producing suite crime by the upper world and street (survival) crime by those of the under classes.

These classical school ideas were in response to the arbitrary, cruel, and oppressive nature of the criminal justice system. The school's adherents argued that such principles should be the basis of the penal code and justice should be meted out equally, without favor or variation. While the notion of equal justice for all is an appealing doctrine, the practical application of this approach ran into disfavor in the French Code of 1791 discussed later in this chapter.

The practical problems this approach encountered were substantial: ignoring individual differences and the significance of situational factors; treating first and repeat offenders alike; and viewing as purely rational decision makers the intellectually and emotionally handicapped, minors, and others of diminished capability. Such deficiences gave rise during the first half of the nineteenth century to the neoclassical school of criminology. These reformers brought about modification of the Doctrine of Pure Reason by noting exceptions such as incompetence and insanity, and such mitigating factors as age, imbecility, or social situation. While this neoclassical approach modified "free will" through noting individual and situational differences, it still was based upon the assumption that most behavior is rational, autonomous, and calculating. (As will be evident in subsequent discussion, the assumption of rationality underlies much of our legal system.) Nonetheless, this tradition recognized circumstances and conditions that reduced one's legal responsibility for one's actions. Such legal distinctions as necessity, self-defense, insanity, juvenile delinquency, among others, become part of the definition of legal responsibility and the explanation of criminal behavior. Thus, a child of seven or under could not have a criminal mind or intent (*mens rea*) because of immature reason. Increasingly, the notions of free will and rationality as the bases of human behavior came under attack in the nineteenth century. It came to be argued that human behavior was instead determined by biological, psychological, and/or social factors.

Positive School

As the social sciences emerged in the nineteenth century, the methods of the natural sciences were increasingly used to study human behavior. It was believed that nature was a closed system with universal rules, and, thus, one could predict and understand in positive fashion the "laws" of human behavior. Human behavior, in this view, was determined not by other-world forces but by universal laws that could be discovered through scientific techniques. Human behavior was not a matter of free choice but was produced by internal and external forces and dynamic processes discoverable through science. If one could ascertain the causal laws of human behavior, one could shape and direct that behavior to be law-abiding.

Taken together, these ideas were the basis for the positive school. Positivism is characterized by (1) the denial of free will, (2) the divorce of science and law from morals, (3) the priority of science in explanation and belief in the existence of invariable social laws, (4) an emphasis on the unity of scientific methods for both the social and natural sciences, (5) a focus on criminal *behavior*, (6) an emphasis on quantitative research, and (7) the assumption that causality and determinism are of paramount concern and are best discerned through observation (Mann 1960). This positivist emphasis led to the study of the personal and social characteristics of criminals and the incorporation of such characteristics both into theories explaining criminal behavior and into public crime control policies.

The Born Criminal

Students of crime, like many other citizens, have focused much of their time and effort on studying the criminal to find the causes of crime. This has led to many different explanations of criminal behavior all looking for its causes in the kinds of people who are identified as criminal. In the early part of the twentieth century such "kinds of people" theories held that there were *born criminals*. Generally it was believed that the born criminal was the cause of crime; more particularly, this problem was attributed to foreign races and nationalities. The belief in the existence of innate differences between a criminal's behavior and that of a noncriminal reflected an era of Social Darwinism, imperialism, and racist ideology. In the United States, the president of the California State Law Enforcement League epitomized the public concern in a 1925 article that stated:

> It is the law-breaking foreigners who we are talking about now. Schooled in low standards of morality, they seek to impose their European customs upon their newfound Land of Liberty. . . . foreigners are predominant in all the big movements of lawlessness and these movements aim at anarchy (Grant 1925).

Similar ideas were prevalent in Canada as exemplified by the attitude towards the Chinese at the turn of the century: ". . . these Chinese are nonassimilative and have no intention of settled citizenship, are in moral, social, sanitary status below the most inferior standard of Western life. . . ." (*Report of the Commissioners* 1902, p. 2). Furthermore, one student of the drug problem in early twentieth-century Canada notes

> Previously attacked for their work habits, the Chinese were assailed as being selfish, slothful, weak, diseased, inefficient, untrustworthy and emasculated. In company with the racial assault

against the Chinese, vivid descriptions of the opium dens were invariably released to the horrified Canadian populace (Chapman 1976, p. 3).

The belief in the biological basis of human behavior was prevalent in the nineteenth and early twentieth centuries (Fink 1938). Charles Darwin's book, *The Origin of Species* (1859), was subsequently used by others to promote the ideas of Social Darwinism. They reasoned that if, as Darwin claimed, Homo Sapiens evolved from earlier forms of life through natural selection,[3] could not this be the reason for some achieving more than others? Essentially, the argument was made that those on top through wealth, education, power, and status were there because they were the "fittest." Those who were poor, illiterate, criminal, "uncivilized," and so forth were the lesser of the species. Such arguments became widespread in justifying a class system, imperialism, and the subjugation of the "white man's burden" throughout the world. The great extremes in wealth and the degradation of people on the basis of cultural and racial differences were explained as "natural processes" and outcomes. When "they" committed crimes it was taken as evidence of their inferior genetic endowment.

The XYY Chromosome Anomaly   The contemporary belief in the "born criminal" is found in the XYY chromosome anomaly. Since there is an extra male (Y) chromosome in some, it has been claimed that a "super male" is created who is prone to criminality, particularly violence (Jacobs 1965). There does not appear to be much good evidence to support such beliefs (Baker 1970; Sarbin and Miller 1970; Amir and Berman 1970; Cullition 1974). The XYY explanation does not account for the increasing involvement of women in crime. (See Chapter Eleven, Sex and Sexism.) Further, in another context violence may be the occasion for a medal of valor. And perhaps most important, the institutionalized forms of violence that occur inside the corporate structure are the analytic casualties of the "born criminal" explanation. Nonetheless, this particular explanation for criminal behavior emerged in the ideological context of class inequality. It is perhaps comforting to "discover" that criminals and other deviants are somehow fundamentally different from noncriminals and nondeviants. Besides seeming to fulfill the naive hope for a simple, single source of criminality, ". . . it also provides a convenient moral advantage for both the community at large and those personally responsible for the offender's welfare, for all are relieved from blame for the behavioral consequences of what is a purely biological accident" (Fox 1971, p. 71–72).

Not surprisingly, in spite of evidence to the contrary, many people

---

[3]The term "survival of the fittest" was not used by Darwin. By "natural selection" Darwin meant that some species were able to adapt to change and survive while those that could not, perished.

want to believe in such an ideologically transparent explanation and thus an apparently easy solution to the crime problem. For example, a professor in the Department of Genetics at the University of Alberta proposed the following "solution" in (*Science* 1969, p. 1117): "All boys and men who are under lawful restraint should be classified into XY and XYY categories so that the best treatment can be ascertained and carried out. . . . The probability factor makes the criminal XYY a predictably dangerous person and the standards of the duty to take care should accordingly be raised." As will be evident in a subsequent section, such ideas have become institutionalized to some extent. For example, former President of the United States Richard Nixon advanced such a scheme for identifying potential criminals. This was of course before he resigned from office rather than face impeachment charges for the obstruction of justice.

Are Criminals Psychologically Different? One of the most widely accepted "kinds of people" positions today centers on the belief that those committing crime are psychologically different from the rest of us. A great deal of research and many rehabilitation programs are based upon this assumption (see the following section on rehabilitation). Although such beliefs are quite compatible with the general ideology of corporatism (individualism and personal culpability), it presents somewhat of a dilemma for the offender. While legally responsible for personal actions, he or she is treated for the malady that supposedly caused the deviant behavior through psychiatric or psychological methods of casework, probation, and parole. More importantly, we simply do not have good evidence supporting the assumption that criminals differ significantly from noncriminals psychologically. One criminology student describes the circular reasoning (tautology) evident in such explanations.

> The medical model has prompted a long and futile search for the psychological counterparts of germs and tumors. Unfortunately there are no infected organs or disease entities that can be identified as the causes of deviant behavior. Instead we infer deviant personality types and emotional disorders from our observations of behavior. Then we use our psychological constructs to explain the very phenomena from which they were inferred in the first place. In short, deviance, including delinquency, is fundamentally different from physical illness. It has no existence apart from the judgments people make about particular kinds of behavior (Balch 1975, p. 117).

Despite the lack of supporting data for the psychological abnormality theory, it still receives a great deal of professional and public support. Since psychological positivism, like the biological approach, emphasizes the nature of the criminal, such an approach seems quite appealing ideologically.

Radzinowicz notes the ideological appeal of "kinds of people" explanations.

> This way of looking at crime as the product of society (kinds of environment) was hardly likely to be welcome, however, at a time when a major concern was to hold down the "dangerous classes." The concept of the dangerous classes as the main source of crime and disorder was very much to the fore at the beginning of the nineteenth century. They were made up of those who had so miserable a share in the accumulated wealth of the industrial revolution that they might at any time break out in political revolt as in France. At their lowest level was the hard core of parasites to be found in any society, ancient or modern. And closely related to this, often indistinguishable from it, were the "criminal classes."
>
> It served the interests and relieved the conscience of those at the top to look upon the dangerous classes as an independent category, detached from the prevailing social conditions. They were portrayed as a race apart, morally depraved and vicious, living by violating the fundamental law of orderly society, which was that a man should maintain himself by honest, steady work. In France they were commonly described as nomads, barbarians, savages, strangers to the customs of the country. English terminology was, perhaps, less strong and colourful, but the meaning was fundamentally similar (1966, pp. 38–39).

Thus, the positivist emphasis remains, in spite of paltry evidence, due to its ideological appeal. First, it is based upon a consensus world view that does not question the law or social order. Also, since the criminal's behavior is supposedly determined by forces beyond his or her control, no one could possibly choose it. Given the adequate socialization of the noncriminal (normal person), by definition such an individual could not find criminal behavior attractive. Finally, since positivism operates as a science, it is a powerful weapon to justify therapy and treatment, and thus qualifies frequently as a method of blaming the victim.

> For the politician and the planner, positivism provides a model of human nature which, in its consensual aspects, allows the world "as it is" to remain unquestioned and, in its determination notion of human action, offers the possibility of rational planning and control (Taylor, Walton, and Young 1973, p. 35).

The Bad Environment

While "kinds of people" explanations have predominated in positivist analysis, "kinds of environment" thought has increasingly gained influence in the twentieth century. Here, the explanation for criminal behavior is located in factors like peer group influence, family, and/or community conditions such as poor housing, inadequate education, and unemployment (Reid 1976, pp. 173–182).

The notion that criminal behavior is learned from others is often advanced as a reason for crime. When parents warn their children not to play with "undesirables," they implicitly embrace the idea that their offspring will learn "bad" things. E.H. Sutherland, a major figure in North American criminology, formulated a "theory of differential association" emphasizing that criminal behavior, like noncriminal behavior, is learned.

While this theory has been criticized for its vagueness and difficulty in testing, it has probably been one of the most influential theories in this century. It explains criminal behavior as a product of bad companions, and is quite consistent with the privatized thrust of general corporate ideology. It is also evident in various policies in the criminal justice system and in crime prevention programs.[4]

What one learns or does not learn in the family has been a major explanation of delinquency and criminality. As noted earlier in this chapter, parental laxity and permissiveness are often identified by the public as the causes of criminal behavior. Calvin J. Frederick, a psychologist with the Center for Studies of Crime and Delinquency at the United States National Institute of Mental Health notes

> Another factor is a breakdown of the home which has us oriented toward a "do your own thing" philosophy. That kind of indifference given to a juvenile is too much to handle too soon. The key is teaching responsibility at an early age (*Crime* 1974, p. 34).

Throughout this century, and even earlier, students of crime have observed that most criminals and delinquents have come from certain types of homes.

> The homes from which delinquent children come are frequently characterized by one or more of the following conditions:
>
> (a) other members of the family criminalistic, immoral, or alcoholic,
> (b) absence of one or both parents by reason of death, divorce, or desertion,
> (c) lack of parental control because of ignorance or illness,
> (d) home uncongeniality, as evidenced by domination by one member, favoritism, oversolicitude, overseverity, neglect, jealousy, crowded housing conditions, interfering relatives,

[4] We do not quarrel with the simple observation that behavior is learned. However, what is learned from one's "associates" is learned in a specific structural context. For example, one might discover that definitions learned in a ghetto or in a corporation suite favor violation of the law. Perhaps a more important question, however, is what are the social forces that produce both ghetto and corporation?

(e) racial or religious differences, differences in conventions and standards, foster home, or institutional home,

(f) economic pressures such as unemployment, poverty, mother working.

(Sutherland and Cressey 1970, p. 204)

The significance of the family in explaining crime is apparent in various programs, policies, and practices in crime prevention and treatment. Big Brother, Big Sister, and Uncle programs, among others, are directed at youth who do not have certain family relationships. Of course, emphasis on family history and situation has also played a significant role in the determination of wardship in the juvenile justice system. These and other policy ramifications of this explanation of crime will be discussed in the next section.

Ecological Theories of Criminal Behavior The analysis on a community basis of the distribution of such homes and related characteristics is found in "ecological theories" of criminal behavior. Here the distribution of crime and delinquency is mapped out within cities to identify the characteristics of communities with various crime rates. In everyday lay terms, these are the places in the city where most of the crimes occur. Thus, in every city of substantial size, there are places where a large proportion of *official* crime takes place and which are known about by the local citizens. Ecological analyses have generally found that an unduly high amount of official delinquency occurs in areas of the city that are relatively poor, have a disproportionate number of ethnic and/or racial minorities, high unemployment, overcrowded population, poor housing, and higher incidences of the home problems noted above (Shaw and McKay 1972). One of the more recent analyses concludes

(1) the total urban and unemployment rate has a positive influence on the rates of burglary and larceny, (2) the male unemployment rate exerts a positive influence on the robbery rate, and (3) both the male and female unemployment rates have a positive effect on the rate of rape (Kvalseth 1977, p. 109).

The analysis of the distribution of official crime and delinquency has implications for programs, policies, and practices aimed at dealing with the problem.

A cursory look at arrest rates, as well as the prison population in North America, attests to the fact that economic position, age, and ethnic/racial status are related to *officially recognized* criminal behavior. Such observations have led to explanations emphasizing cultural differences between and among classes, ethnic/racial groups, youth, and adults. For example, Miller (1958) explains lower-class delinquency as a product of the "focal concerns" of the lower class. These are areas or issues of major attention and involvement, including trouble, toughness, smartness, excitement, fate, and autonomy. He suggests that these "focal concerns" are distinctive to the lower class as part of their cultural system of values, separating them from the middle and upper class. Therefore, the subculture characteristic of the lower class supposedly conflicts with that of the middle and upper class.

A Conflict of Cultures Some have explained the different rates of delinquency purely by ethnic/racial culture conflict. Sellin (1938) accounted for the higher incidence of ethnic/racial minority crime by the fact that these segments of society have different norms of behavior than the dominant group and thus come into conflict with the law. Also, the excessive involvement of youth with the law has been explained as a product of the youth subculture, with its differing values and emphases. Whether class, race/ethnicity, or youth subculture, the policies based on these explanations attempt to achieve some form of cultural assimilation whereby the offenders are to be brought into the "mainstream" (through athletics, dances, summer jobs, and the like). Further, the above three factors (youth, poverty, and minority status), combine to give the public and control agents an image of "crime" and the "criminal."

> Most of us have become sufficiently urban, for example, so that if we (whatever our race) had to fantasize an Agent of Violence, he would probably turn out to be a young black mugger (*Harper's* 1975, p. 5).

Throughout the various kinds of environment explanations, economic conditions constantly appear. In a recent book co-authored by the former Executive Director of the Canadian Criminology and Corrections Association, W. T. McGrath, such an approach is emphasized in a discussion of "the roots of crime": "The corrosive effects of substandard or slum areas in our cities should be understood, since they are areas of infection which may corrupt all our children" (Kirkpatrick and McGrath 1976, pp. 156–57).

We would agree that the condition of poverty is closely related to street delinquency and crime. The implications of this finding logically call for fundamental change in the corporate economic system, which by definition is a system of inequality. However, as the prevailing ideology emphasizes individualism and self-help, efforts to change the nature of inequality are largely directed to changing the poor. Work training programs are consequently a major facet of the attack on poverty. In the area of rehabilitation of "street" criminals, much attention is given to providing some type of job training and/or experience for the offender. Seldom are attempts made to change the nature of the economic system in order to lessen inequalities as a preventive measure in the fight against crime. The Law Reform Commission of Canada addresses this issue by proposing that laws on property offenses be simplified and reassessed with regard to the role of property. "Some property offenses are a product of the unjust distribution of property in our society and such 'crimes' call not for criminal law and punishment, but rather for some genuine social reform" (1978, p. 15). This observation has quite radical implications for social change in our society, but most "kinds of environment" theories focus upon changing the offender to fit within the current conditions of society. For example, while much has been said and written about the relationship between poverty and crime, most rehabilitation programs based upon "kinds of environment" theories emphasize dubious change of the individual to fit into the current economic system rather than changing the nature of jobs and work obligations to fit the needs of individual citizens. Despite the rehabilitative good sense of making sure prisoners can reenter the economic order, corporate society can make no such guarantee even to those *without* a criminal record. Thus the general problem of unemployment confounds rehabilitation policy.

If structural conditions are the causes of criminal behavior, then society must consider how to change these conditions. Ramsey Clark (1970, pp. iii–xiv), former attorney general of the United States, explains it this way:

> If we are to deal meaningfully with crime, what must be seen is the dehumanizing effect on the individual of slums, racism, ignorance and violence, of corruption and impotence to fulfill rights, of poverty, and unemployment and idleness, of generations of malnutrition, of congenital brain damage and prenatal neglect, of sickness and disease, of pollution, of decrepit, dirty, ugly unsafe, overcrowded housing, of alcoholism, anxiety, fear, hatred, hopelessness and injustice. These are the fountainheads of crime.

Power/Conflict

Both the "kinds of people" and the "kinds of environment" theories of criminal behavior compare criminals and noncriminals in order to discover the correlates and ultimately the causes of crime. Both are consistent with the prevailing ideologies of corporate order. The power/conflict explanation differs from these traditional positivistic approaches in its emphasis on the political-economy of crime. Accordingly, we are concerned with such things as class influence, an elite of power, ideology and the significance of the State in defining what is criminal, and determining the emphasis of the criminal justice system.

While poverty, broken homes, and ethnic minority status are noted in most texts as significant causes of crime, what can be said about the corporate executives who violate the law? They do not live in poverty, and in most cases have stable homes and family lives and are members of the majority ethnic group. This suggests that the previously noted relationship between crime and certain "kinds of environments" is only applicable to certain types of offenses. Again we must become aware of the multitude of behaviors defined as criminal and realize that most of society's attention is given to "street crime" and thus "street criminals." Therefore, relationships between and among social class, ethnicity, family life, and crime are due to a selective definition of crime. That is, the attention of law enforcement and the general public is focused upon "street crimes" such as robbery, auto theft, and murder, which do take place more frequently within the under classes and oppressed ethnic groups. However, such economic trespasses as fraud, price fixing, income tax evasion, and such violent offenses as lack of safety standard maintenance; systematic production of defective products; poisoning of the air, water, or food gain little public or law enforcement attention.

The Law Reform Commission of Canada observes that in theory the principle of justice dictates that equal treatment be given throughout the criminal justice system without regard to social class, ethnicity, or other "irrelevant traits." However:

> In practice, the penalty often depends, not on the nature of the crime, but on the person who commits it. Our prison population, for example, contains a quite unrepresentative proportion of poor, of disadvantaged and of native offenders. The richer you are, the better your chance of getting away with something. *Is it that rich men make the laws and so what rich men do is not a crime but simply shrewd business practice? Or is it that position and wealth protect the rich against intervention? . . . For all the respect we pay to justice and equality, we still have one law for the rich and another for the poor* (1976, p. 12, emphasis added).

Reactions based upon the power/conflict level of explanation call for major changes in the social structure to reduce criminal behavior. Such suggestions are as diverse as eliminating "victimless crimes" from criminal law; defining "harms" committed by the powerful as serious crimes; establishing community control of justice; permitting prisoner unionization; all the way to the elimination of capitalism and the creation of a socialist society. In a Marxist analysis, most criminal behavior of the poor and working class results from the condition of capitalism and are crimes of accommodation and resistance (Quinney 1977). While the power/conflict exploration of criminal behavior is increasingly being advanced by some criminologists and members of society at large, the institutionalization of such an explanation into policies, practices, and procedures has been minimal.

Corporate society by its nature sorts people into political and economic categories, thus bestowing different power and wealth. The corporate imperatives of profit maximization and growth bring this economic entity into conflict with those laws and policies (such as they are) that may seek to address issues like worker safety, product reliability, monopolization, and other matters of the public interest. Thus, corporate crime is a matter of corporate structure. Beyond this understanding, however, is a more important point. The concentration of power and wealth undeniably impacts those below.

The creation of a more or less permanent underclass, fed by the rejects of a class-based educational system, together with the reality of unemployment for millions and the threat of joblessness for many more are clear indicators that meaningful work for all is not a priority of corporate society (see Chapters Three and Four, on Inequality and Work, respectively). As Braverman (1975) has demonstrated, corporations employ, but on their own terms and in accordance with their own imperatives. The success of the corporation is measured by return on investment for shareholders, not by reductions in the rates of unemployment.

A Crisis of Survival   Given such conditions, it is altogether obvious that a continuing crisis of survival will beset those considered superfluous to the contemporary needs of the corporate labor market. Many of the unemployed constitute a "reserve industrial army," whose presence means the ready availability of cheap labor. Further, such a force provides a clear and chilling reminder to those with jobs of their expendable station in the social order. In other words, the threat of unemployment quite logically has a "cooling off" effect on the disaffected, if employed person. Thus, workers may rather bear the ills they have than quit, file complaints, or organize.

It should come as no surprise to find that those most vulnerable to economic failure are disproportionately represented among street offenders. When such misdeeds are examined, the male, the young, and the black are most often singled out for official attention. For example, considering only the arrests for index crimes considered "serious" by the FBI (all of which are the street variety), males outnumbered females four to one. With regard to age, 72 percent of those arrested nationwide were under twenty-five. More striking is the fact that 58 percent were under twenty-one (U.S. Department of Justice 1979, p. 185). Further, while constituting some 12 percent of the total population in the United States, blacks in 1978 constituted 49 percent of the total arrests for criminal homicide. For forcible rape the corresponding statistic was 48 percent; for robbery 59 percent; for aggravated assault 39 percent; for burglary 29 percent; for motor vehicle theft 27 percent; and for larceny, some 30 percent (U.S. Department of Justice 1979, pp. 7–34).

Institutionalized Racism   Such statistics must be tempered by the realization that the criminal justice system represents institutionalized racism. Thus, one must admit the probability that crimes perpetrated by nonwhites will be more zealously cleared by arrests than those perpetrated by whites. Further, if street crime reflects a disproportionate black involvement, the reverse can be said for corporate crimes, which is predominantly a white affair. However, as demonstrated earlier, corporate crime is virtually ignored. The police power of the State is by its structural nature geared to street offenders. The same holds for police (FBI) statistics.

How do arrest statistics compare with unemployment statistics? *In 1977 in the United States, the official unemployment rate for black males ages 16–19 was 37.0 percent, and for those ages 20–24, the rate was 21.7 percent. For young white males, the corresponding percentages were 15.0 and 9.3, respectively* (U.S. Bureau of the Census 1978, p. 401). *Such figures compare with an average unemployment rate of 6.2 percent for the total male labor force in 1977.* As official unemployment statistics systematically understate the extent of unemployment, such figures may be considered conservative on all counts. Still, when all is said and done, those groups disproportionately represented in the arrest statistics for conventional crime are also the clearest victims of the structural unemployment of the corporate order.[5]

INSTITUTIONALIZATION

Demonology

While a number of different ways have emerged to explain criminal behavior, only some become the basis of society's programs, policies, and practices to reduce the magnitude of crime. Thus, the early notion that demons or the Devil caused crime by possessing one's body and mind was institutionalized into trials by battle and ordeal. The execution or banishment of criminals served to rid the community of such unredeemable persons. During the Middle Ages in France various forms of torture and execution were commonplace. Quartering was probably the most horrible.

> The victim would first be put through preliminary torture, such as the burning of his limbs. Then the executioner would attach a rope to each of his four limbs and fasten each rope to a bar to which a strong horse was harnessed. First, the horses would be made to give short jerks, but as the victim cried out in agony, the horses would be suddenly urged on rapidly in different directions. If the

---

[5] Though the unemployment rate for women was greater than that for men for these age cohorts, men still dominate the arrest statistics. However, inflationary pressures together with corporate interest in cheap labor are pushing women into the lower echelons of the work force in increasing numbers. Thus, as more and more women work to survive, they assume the burdens and frustrations of economic pressures that earlier were more a male prerogative. Predictably, then, the level of property crime committed by women is increasing at a faster rate than that for men.

limbs were not dismembered, the executioner would finish the job with a hatchet, put all the limbs in front of the torso (which might still show some signs of life, for this method took a long time), and burn them (Reid 1976, p. 105).

During the sixteenth and seventeenth centuries it has been estimated that 200,000 witches were executed in Europe. Burning offenders alive or after their death was believed to destroy the evil spirits in them. Furthermore, purification ceremonies and rituals were practiced to ward off evil spirits and the Devil. The emergence of the penitentiary was based upon the notion of doing penance for one's sins. If one was locked up to think about and ask forgiveness for his or her sins, this might appease God and cleanse the culprit's soul. Of course, confessions and remorsefulness are still integral parts of justice. The religious notions of redemption, salvation, and rebirth are found in the concepts of rehabilitation. Rehabilitation is to "restore a dependent, defective, or criminal to a state of physical, mental, and moral health through treatment and training" (*Webster's* 1964, p. 649). Its moral basis is the religious concept of "falling out of grace," and a subsequent absolution. The impact of demonology can still be observed in the growth of religious revivalism and the emphasis upon religion as both a protector from sin (including crime) and cleanser of sinners (religion in corrections). Dramatic "conversions" of such famous criminals as Eldridge Cleaver, former official of the revolutionary Black Panther Party, and Charles Colson, a member of the Nixon inner circle in the Watergate era, attest to the continued existence of demonological explanations.

Pure Reason

The classical school notion that the human being is a rational, calculating, free-willed person who selects actions on the basis of pleasure and pain underlies many of our current criminal statutes. This is embedded in the legal concept of *mens rea*, or criminal state of mind, and the belief that appropriate punishment acts as a deterrent to criminal behavior. The definition of causation in the law reflects these assumptions.

> It must appear that the accused criminal act was the *legal cause* of the injuries for which the state is seeking to impose penal sanctions. The defendant is not liable for remote and indirect consequences which a reasonable man would not have foreseen as likely to have flowed from his act (Rutter 1972, p. 17).

The ideas of the classical school were incorporated into the Declaration of the Rights of Man, passed in France on August 26, 1789. The institutionalization of these ideas came soon after in the French Penal Code of 1791 and allowed no judicial discretion, with predetermined penalties applied unswervingly to all violations of the law.

The belief in the calculating nature of human beings, free will, and the idea that justice means equality before the law mirrored the decline of feudal order with its reliance on custom and caste, and the emergence of mercantile capitalism with its emphasis on private interests secured by the power of the State. The emphasis on calculation and free will separates the individual from society while "equality before the law" replaces as an ideal a "society of equals." Such individualistic and fragmented concepts of human beings are the cornerstones of emergent corporate nation-states and their legal systems. The approach is evident in the judicial ceremony of the defendant's pleading, where, on one's own volition and free will, one pleads either guilty or not guilty. Further, arguments given for mandatory penalties are often based on deterrence. That is, the anticipation of sure and certain punishment supposedly prevents crime. This is the rationale for mandatory minimum sentences for offenses in which a gun is used, various drug offenses, and conviction of murder.

Deterrence is the most commonly advanced argument in support of the death penalty. The evidence, however, suggests that capital punishment does not act as a general deterrent. The existence of the death penalty and the extent of its use do not affect the murder rate (Tepperman 1977, pp. 68–75).

The classical explanation for criminal behavior is evident in various crime prevention programs. For example, if reason and free will prevail, then bringing ex-convicts and reformed addicts into schools to talk to students about the horrors of crime and punishment or addiction will deter youngsters from crime and drug use. School-officer programs in which police are invited in are based upon the same view of human nature. It also follows that placing signs in stores ("shoplifters will be prosecuted"), windows of residential homes ("neighborhood watch"), on machines ("minors will be prosecuted"), and elsewhere, will thwart potential criminals.

Such signs, together with media warnings directed toward bank robbers, shoplifters, car thieves, juveniles, and various police "crime check" and "neighborhood watch" programs must be partially understood as ideological devices. They are intended to unite the "law-abiding" against marauding street criminals while ignoring, of course, systematic corporate crime. For example, in the United States financial institutions have sponsored a media campaign encouraging listeners to "rat on a rat," that is, a bank robber. Needless to say, few public service commercials suggest that exorbitant interest rates are a form of "thievery." Perhaps the conventional bank robber is reversing the natural order of things.

While there are many other examples, the view that the behavior of people is chosen by them from a number of alternatives has been institutionalized. It follows that human beings are individually responsible for their choice, unless of course there are mitigating factors.

The notion that mitigating factors may reduce responsibility for one's behavior is evident in the neoclassical school. Because the classical school failed to consider individual differences, it appeared cruel and harsh. In reaction, there arose the idea that such factors as age, mental state, situation, among others, reduced a person's culpability. Today we find this in the criminal law concerning the defenses relating to capacity (infant, delinquent, insanity, intoxication), to criminal intent (ignorance or mistake of fact of law, duress and related offenses, entrapment) and defenses related to justification (self-defense, defense of others or of property, law enforcement, victim's consent, condonation, negligence or criminality of injured party) (Rutter 1972, pp. 104–22). Since the beginnings of these modifications of the classical school explanations for criminal behavior in the early part of the nineteenth century, the notions of free will and pure reason have been increasingly attacked by the social sciences generally, and the positivistic philosophy specifically.

Kinds of People

The belief that criminal behavior was inherited was part of the eugenics movement for enforced sterilization. For example, the Human Betterment Foundation of California argued during the 1930s and 1940s that there was a definite relationship between sterilization and reduction of criminality.

> They posited that criminals should be sterilized, not because they are criminals, but because they are insane or feebleminded. The sterilization of the insane and the feebleminded would, of course, prevent the birth of persons who are more like to become criminals (Fong and Johnson 1974, p. 108).

The Human Betterment Foundation favored the retention in some twenty states of sterilization laws. Such laws represented the institutionalization of the "born criminal" form of positivistic explanation. These statutes arose in the first two decades of the twentieth century, specifically legalizing the sterilization of sex offenders. The first such statute was passed in Indiana in 1907. It provided for the sterilization of "male criminals and other defectives" (Reid 1976, p. 166). Although it was declared unconstitutional in 1921, a subsequent law passed in 1927 permits sterilization of the insane, feebleminded, or epileptic persons in mental hospitals or other state institutions and remains in effect at the time of this writing. While compulsory sterilization of criminals has been eliminated, sterilization laws still plague the poor and predominantly nonwhite (Fong and Johnson 1974, p. 111). Restrictive immigration laws in the 1920s in the United States were oriented toward those racial groups thought to be criminally inclined, particularly Orientals (Reasons and Kuykendall 1972). Proposed restrictions on immigration into Canada imply that certain types of immigrants (specifically nonwhites) are the cause of social problems in general and crime in particular.

The use of lobotomy for violent offenders and shock aversion "therapy" and castration for sex offenders are further examples of biological explanations incorporated into state policy. While supposedly based on the learning theories of Pavlov, Watson, Thorndyke, and Skinner, *behavior modification* often intersects a biological conception of human behavior.

> In other programs across the country, drugs, hypnosis, electroconvulsive shocks, brainwashing and psychosurgery have been added to an arsenal of therapies prison officials are labeling behavior modification. To psychologists, the term refers to principles of learning theory developed largely through experiments with animals. In essence, the idea is that behaviors that are rewarded tend to recur; those that are punished tend to cease. The behaviorists have spent many years punishing and rewarding flatworms, rats and pigeons, and now have them going in and out of mazes at their bidding. Wardens, eager to do as much for prisoners, are revamping American penitentiaries with behavior schemes so elaborate and eclectic that behavior modification behind the walls has come to connote just about any procedure that aims to modify behavior (Sage 1974).

The basis for criminal responsibility as biological is seen in two groups of offenders: children and women. Age is defined as the measure of maturity. Thus, a child seven years or younger is not considered capable of committing a crime, while those within the legal category of "juvenile delinquents" are believed to have a lesser degree of culpability. Sex is also a relevant biological category institutionalized in policy. For example, prostitution has generally been defined as an offense committed by women, while rape is committed by men. Infanticide has been defined in Canada as a crime only perpetrated by women due to their biological nature.

> A female person commits infanticide when by a willful act or omission she causes the death of her newly born child. If at the time of the act or omission she is not fully recovered from the effects of giving birth to the child and by reason thereof or of the effect of lactation consequent on the birth of the child her mind is then disturbed (Minister of Justice 1973).

Psychology and Crime The most widely accepted "kinds of people" view today is that those committing crimes are psychologically different from the law-abiding. A great deal of research and many of our programs of rehabilitation are based upon this explanation. Thus the notion of psychological difference has been institutionalized. In fact, it would be correct to say that most contemporary programs of rehabilitation rest on the notion that the offender is somehow psychologically "sick." The fact that accused offenders can be ordered by the court to take tests of mental competency and that a plea of "insanity" (although used infrequently) may make one not responsible for his or her actions testifies to its institutionalization.

Although only about 2 percent of the cases that come to criminal trial in the United States plead a defense of insanity (Morris and Hawkins 1970, p. 178), it has been the topic of much public concern and media attention. The defense of insanity arose in Britain during the nineteenth century in response to the classical notions of rationality and free will. In the murder trial of one Daniel McNaughton, a rule of insanity was formulated that still pervades Western criminal law. In order to form criminal intent, one must understand the consequences of one's deeds, and the difference between "right and wrong" at the time of the act.

The establishment of the insanity plea in the McNaughton case (1843) began the increasing infusion of mental illness notions into the use of penal sanctions and treatment of the offender. As psychiatry became a legitimate and increasingly powerful profession (Szasz 1970), forensic psychiatry arose to proclaim that much criminal behavior could be explained on the basis of psychological determinism. Hence appeared the view that people were not always rational but rather frequently driven by unconscious or other psychological forces. Increasing efforts were made to discover such forces in order to correct "defective" personality. While psychiatrists and psychologists employ the medical model of diagnosis, prognosis, and treatment, the illness is not organic.

Laws concerning sexual psychopaths and dangerous offenders are based upon this "kinds of people" approach. Legislation in Canada and the United States provides that a person judged a sexual psychopath may be committed to a state institution until cured. Furthermore, a person may be determined a "dangerous offender" after a certain number of crimes, for instance, three felony convictions, and sent to prison indefinitely. In the case of sexual psychopaths there is a diagnosis of psychopathology (a nebulous term indeed), and prognosis of possible correction through treatment, while dangerous offenders are diagnosed as "sick" and not curable. Both categories are vague in definition and persons so labeled have not been shown to be treatable. Further, psychodiagnosis involves predictions of future behavior that are inadequate and inaccurate. Nonetheless, such psychological categories become institutionalized upon the assumption that there are distinct "criminal types" that can be diagnosed (Reid 1976; Klein 1976).

Psychodiagnosis is also institutionalized in the presentence investigation that establishes a person's social and psychological profile. In determining sentence, the prognosis the judge derives from the presentence report, defendant's demeanor, and nature of the act, among other factors, may be stated in terms of treatment and/or punishment. For example, the judge may view the offender as incorrigible and impose a prison sentence as punishment, or see the offender as treatable through probation or programs at a particular institution.

Throughout the correctional system the psychological model is evident. From diagnosis inside the institution to group therapy programs, the thrust of such emphasis is to "turn the offender's head around." Increasingly, correctional institutions state their goals in terms of "rehabilitating" the offender through various treatment programs. This is evident in reality therapy, self-help clubs, T groups, drug groups, self-expression groups, among others, where the emphasis is upon changing an inmate's essential character. While the psychological model is still very evident in institutionalized policy, "kinds of environment" explanations have been gaining in significance in this century.

Kinds of Environment

Probably of major significance in popularizing the "kinds of environment" explanation was the institutionalization of the juvenile justice system. "Child-savers" believed that young people were delinquent and subsequently criminal because of the harsh living conditions of their early lives. Therefore, statutory definitions of delinquency included growing up in idleness and crime, frequenting pool halls and immoral places, associating with vicious and immoral people, among other "offenses" (Platt 1977). Subsequently, many youth were declared wards of the State and sent to foster homes, group homes, reformatories, industrial schools, or other such facilities because of their "bad home environment."

The theory of "differential association" has also been institutionalized and underlies restrictions placed upon the behavior of accused or convicted offenders. An accused may be told by the court not to associate with certain individuals or frequent specific places before the case is concluded. Conditions of probation and parole often explicitly define certain persons and places the offender is to avoid during the probation or parole period. Furthermore, correctional facilities may prohibit certain persons from visiting an inmate on the grounds that it is not conducive to rehabilitation. Certain books, magazines, speakers, films, clubs, or organizations may be deemed harmful to a proper environment. Conversely, emphasis upon making contacts with law-abiding, "normal" citizens is to be found in such things as Junior Chamber of Commerce groups in prisons, Take a Lifer to Dinner, sponsors for day parole, among others. The definition of a good environment is usually spelled out in the criteria for parole, including employment and family and home conditions upon release.

The significance of the immediate environment in causing criminal behavior is found in such defenses as duress and necessity. For example, the defense attorneys for Patty Hearst, the American newspaper heiress abducted by the revolutionary Symbionese Liberation Army in 1074, argued that she committed crimes under the compulsion (duress) of her captors. Also, the defense for Lt. William L. Calley, Jr., on trial for the systematic execution of certain civilian inhabitants of My Lai 4 in Vietnam, 1968, argued that his actions were taken under the compulsion to follow orders of superiors. Both the Hearst and Calley cases are more recent examples of the common law defense of committing offenses under duress (Rutter 1972).[6]

A variety of programs in corrections are based upon this notion. For example, job training and various educational and cultural programs within correctional institutions are justified as creating a proper environment for rehabilitation and equipping inmates with salable skills so they do not have to return to their preconviction circles of influence. The assumption that inmates lack discipline, training, and proper motivation is countered in the strict codes and regulations in corrections institutions. Learning to obey rules, follow orders, complete tasks, and work hard are emphasized as parole authorities believe the learning experiences of their charges were deficient in these respects.

This attitude is also epitomized in behavioral approaches to the treatment of offenders (Braukmann et al. 1975). For example, a penal institution may use a token economy where a prisoner is given so many tokens for correct behavior and loses tokens for unacceptable conduct. The accumulated tokens may be used to purchase a treat such as candy or cigarettes, or gain a pass, more TV time, recreational time, longer visiting hours, or other liberties. The same notion of reinforcement is found in the contingency contract. By this, an inmate agrees to implement a plan of rehabilitation (such as completing an auto body course in a specific period of time) and various privileges or inducements are attached to completion of the contract conditions. Such behaviorist approaches emphasize manipulation of a person's environment (rewards and punishments) to direct behavior.

Capturing the ideology of familism, a variety of programs such as Big Brothers, Uncles, Big Sisters, summer camps for the disadvantaged, Boys' Clubs, neighborhood gyms, and Positive Peer groups, among others also represent the institutionalization of the "kinds of environment" explanation. Police patrol practices also operate upon the assumption that certain kinds of environments breed crime. Thus, police patrol poorer and working-class ethnic/racial areas more heavily. More specifically, certain bars, hotels, and other establishments are identified as breeders of criminal behavior and closely watched. Urban renewal,

[6]Patricia Hearst was convicted of bank robbery and spent less than two years in prison. Lieutenant William Calley was convicted by a military tribunal of premeditated murder, and sentenced to twenty years in prison in 1971. At this writing, he works as a salesman at a jewelry store in Georgia. Despite a military policy of "Search and Destroy Missions" no higher ranking officer was charged for My Lai or similar incidents.

neighborhood watch, inner-city youth programs, summer job programs, among others often are cited as fighters of crime.

The institutionalization of explanations of criminal behavior has largely emphasized the nature of the offender as described above. When other factors are considered, they tend to be those that do not implicate corporate and state power.

> Finally, is it not possible that searches for the causes of crime are, for the most part, wastage of effort? Insofar as they focus on something about the criminal that causes him to commit crimes do they not miss most of the picture? Shouldn't we also ask what other causes of crime there are other than the criminals—like victims who do not take reasonable care of their persons and property; the lack of protective devices such as well-lit streets and burglar alarms; criminal justice systems that are so overburned that their deterrent effect is drastically lessened—and whose efforts at rehabilitating are in most cases a failure; and the easy availability of weapons which make violent crime a realistic possibility even for the young and weak, just to name a few (Kaplan 1973, p. 657).

Such ideas have brought about crime prevention programs such as education of the public regarding securing your house; not leaving the keys in your car; installation of various devices to prevent burglaries of businesses; improvements in lighting, openness and visibility, among other changes. The view that the criminal justice system generally, and correctional institutions specifically, create more street criminals (Reasons and Kaplan 1975) has led to an emphasis upon alternatives to institutionalization. The movement towards community-based corrections arises from the notion that treatment institutions make things worse. Further, this development implies that as criminal behavior is produced in the community, it must be treated in the community. This has led to an increase in the number of halfway houses, residential treatment centers, work release centers, and other types of community correctional programs. While still based upon the medical model, emphasis is upon treatment in the community rather than in an isolated institutional setting (Reasons 1976). A dramatic example in the last decade of this deinstitutionalization was the tearing down of the reformatories in Massachusetts. The head of the state's system declared that if they did work then they should not be kept (Ohlin, Coates, and Miller 1974).

Power/Conflict

Whether the explanations for criminal behavior are biological, psychological, or free will, all center on the actor, by and large disengaging the human being from a social context. As far as institutionalized explanations are concerned, any recognition of social causation is only of the most limited sort, that is, the "kinds of environment" emphasis on subcultural and family circumstances. Thus what has been institutionalized in law and policies is an alienated form of thought that splits personality from social structure, the private from the public, and the biographical from the historical. We believe an undue emphasis on individuals and only their most immediate environments is a reflection of the prevailing ideologies of privatism and familism. To the extent that social conditions are viewed as problematic at all, it is only in the sense of subcultural barriers to equal opportunity. Such explanations divert attention from the structural concerns of power and conflict.

The emphasis upon deinstitutionalization is part of a larger movement to reduce the negative effects of labels upon people. The stigma of being labeled a delinquent or criminal and separated from normals can merely produce more of the same unwanted behavior. The damaging effects are particularly disturbing since the power to avoid apprehension and subsequently official labeling is based upon nonlegal factors like social class, ethnicity, and family background. The fact that criminal behavior is widespread throughout the social structure suggests that whether one is poor or rich, nonwhite or white, weak or powerful influences the types of crime (robbery or embezzlement) one commits and whether one's offenses are detected or pursued in the legal system. Finally, if one has more influence in defining crime than others, one may eliminate or create crime in accordance with the way one behaves.

In *Radical Nonintervention*, Schur (1973) argues that the juvenile justice system creates more problems through attempts to deal with delinquency than it solves. Thus, the State should largely leave kids alone unless they commit offenses that are criminal for adults. The emergence of certain "due process" rights for juveniles and adults recognizes that the accused is relatively powerless against the State and must be entitled to at least the minimal protection due all citizens, including the right to counsel.

The "prisoner rights" movement is based upon the notion that prisoners are without influence in basic conflict with institutional authorities, and are hence entitled to civil rights. Ultimately, convicts are in prison as much for their powerlessness as for their criminal behavior. Power/conflict explanations of criminal behavior largely deal with issues beyond the specifics of the criminal justic system, such as changes in the social and economic institutions of society. As our analysis of crime is structural we invite the reader to examine carefully Chapters Three (Inequality) and Four (Work). For inequality and alienation are at the root of any sophisticated and meaningful explanation of criminal behavior.

MAINTENANCE

Who benefits from the particular "kinds of people" and "kinds of environment" explanations institutionalized in policies, programs, and systems? While there are a variety of explanations for criminal behavior, the one most evident in our penal practice is the notion that the criminal is psychologically sick. As noted above, the idea that through psychological diagnosis, prognosis, and treatment one can "cure" the criminal is found throughout the criminal justice system in testing, screening, presentence reports, parole, probation, and in correctional institutions. Implementing this idea has led to increases in the number of counselors and other treatment staff in correctional facilities, the building of more institutions, including those for the criminally insane, and more probation and parole officers to help the offender to "get his or her act together." While this remains the major approach to explaining crime, it is increasingly being questioned by competitors seeking legitimacy for new explanations.

Biological Determinism

There further appears to be a revival of biological determinism that is gaining some support from the government. As previously discussed, the XYY chromosomal theory has produced certain research efforts and even an attempt at using it as an argument for defendants (Reid 1976). The more general area of the biological basis of human behavior has seen a resurgence in science generally, and criminology specifically. For example, Professor C.R. Jeffery,[7] noted criminologist and president of the American Society of Criminology, emphasizes the need to pursue these areas (Jeffery 1977, pp. 284–85).

> The genetic bases for behavioral disorders, including criminality, have been demonstrated by Kety, Mednick, and others. The role of the brain and the neurotransmitter system has been demonstrated for an array of disorders from schizophrenia to manic depression, alcoholism, drug addiction and other forms of antisocial behavior.

The increasing medicalization of deviance, and crime, suggests more attempts to find the surgical or chemical "solution." For example, hyperkinesis (popularly known as hyperactivity) has increasingly been treated through drug therapy (Conrad 1975). Established as a medical diagnosis

---

[7]For an extended criticism of biosocial criminology and analysis of the ideological foundations to Jeffery's criminology, see Platt and Takagi 1979.

only within the last two decades, it is being viewed more and more as a cause of delinquency and crime. It is only one of a multitude of youthful "disorders" labeled "learning disabilities."

> The social effects of learning disability aren't yet fully known, although they are perceived as serious. As one illustration, some studies suggest that anywhere from 70 to 90 percent of all juvenile delinquents have adopted antisocial attitudes as a reaction to continual failure ("Disability Centre," 1977, 23).

The delegates of the First Canadian Conference on Learning Disabilities in 1977 were told that 40 percent of institutionalized youth, as opposed to 3.5 percent of nonincarcerated youth have learning disabilities (Liaison 1977, p. 16). The appeal of the biological solution to crime is partly due to the great breakthroughs and advances in medical science generally, the prestige of the medical profession, and the failure of rehabilitation. While it may appear more human and less condemnatory to say criminal behavior is due to biological problems, such an explanation ignores certain issues. Firstly, medicalizing crime would give the medical profession a monopoly over it. As will be evident in subsequent discussion, the medicalizing of criminal behavior in psychological terms did create such power and control but without the expected results. Since most crime is not easily distinguished as biological in nature, defining it as such excludes alternative definitions. This will produce medical social control (like in psychiatry) where various forms of "treatment" (genetic control, psychosurgery, drug therapy, to name a few) will be justified as "good" for the patient. Such an approach focuses on the causes of crime as existing in the person and, thus, fails to acknowledge social causes. It may be that criminal behavior points to defects in society rather than the individual. In this individualization of causes through medicine, the issue is depoliticized. Therefore, the rapist may come to be viewed as compelled by biology rather than one asserting his "masculinity" in a society that emphasizes the domination (intellectually, politically, socially, and physically) of men over women. The ultimate policy implications of such an approach are to be found in George Orwell's *1984* and Anthony Burgess's *Clockwork Orange*. Both of these futuristic views of social order present the realization of societies in which behavior is managed, manipulated, and controlled. The question is: In whose image? Jeffery (1977, p. 285) notes a probation department that routinely screens offenders for hypoglycemia. It is possible that the test tube sample will replace the personality inventory in the diagnosis of criminality. More likely they will operate together in explaining and testing criminal behavior.

Again we must be sensitive to the selective picture of crime provided by the medical model. In other words, it is necessary to do ideological analysis. Thus we note that the medical model does not address crimes among the powerful. Are the directors and chief executives of the major corporations of Canadian and American societies "psychopathic"? Should they be treated with amphetamines as are hyperactive children? Are they possessors of XYY chromosomes? Should they receive genetic counselling, psychosurgery, and chemotherapy? It should be clear that the medical model maintains the street imagery of crime.

The medical model has been increasingly attacked as an inappropriate explanation of criminal behavior, particularly since it has failed to rehabilitate. As one professor at John Jay College of Criminal Justice in New York City observes,

> For the basic flaw of the medical model is its basic premise: that the offender is "sick" when in fact he is far more likely to be as "normal" as most nonoffenders but inadequately, negatively, or contraculturally socialized, at war with a world he never made, a world in which he has been subjected to *abuse, brutalization, discrimination, and exploitation.* No program of education, vocational training, medical or psychiatric therapy is relevant to his "cure" and none is likely to reverse his twenty or thirty years of antisocial condition (MacNamara 1977, p. 441, italics added).

The Return of Free Will

In their controversial review of the effectiveness of correctional treatment, Lipton, Martinson, and Wilks (1975) conclude that treatment of offenders is irrelevant and ineffective. Since most treatment approaches are based upon psychological "kinds of people" explanations, the work of these scholars is largely a rejection of this type of explanation. The failure of rehabilitation has produced calls for the elimination of forced rehabilitation and treatment; the reduction of judicial sentencing discretion; the reduction in the number of offenders going to prison for "treatment"; the abolition of parole; the elimination of the indeterminate sentence; the acceptance of a deterrent-sentence; the establishment of a retributive-punitive rationale for dealing with offenders; and the enunciation of minimum civil and human rights for prisoners.

> The new penologists posit a basic conflict between a medical model maintaining that crime is the product of individual defects and disorders that can be corrected in a program of medical, psychiatric, and social rehabilitation and a re-adjusted or reformed offender returned to his rightful place in society *versus* a justice model based on the more classic doctrine of the free moral agent and of individual responsibility for one's criminal behavior (MacNamara 1977, p. 446).

The "new" justice model is based upon the same old classical notion of the free-willed, rational actor who selects criminal behavior from a variety of options. Thus, its proponents advocate the deterrent-retributive-punitive approach (Fogel 1975). Swift and sure punishment is advanced as a deterrent to criminal behavior. For the "justice model" advocates, a sentence of incarceration should only be justified as a means of protecting society and punishing the offender, with most property offenders supervised in the community. Supporters of this approach push the elimination of parole, institutional treatment, and indeterminate sentencing, citing the failure of the rehabilitation ideas underlying these practices. Undoubtedly, such proposals conflict with the interests of those espousing a medical model, from treatment staff to parole board employees.

Many prisoners' and ex-prisoners' organizations and representatives are also asking for the above changes, with the added element of minimal civil and human rights for inmates. John Irwin (1970) points out that inmates have always disagreed with the "sick" diagnosis imposed upon them in prison. The great majority of inmates are not "sick" psychologically speaking, and would rather be treated as individuals who have violated the law and are being punished by their incarceration. Thus, the free will conception of human nature is a lesser evil. Accordingly, while prisoners desire some sort of counselling, therapy, education, skill training or other outlet, such help should be available and voluntary, not mandatory. Most importantly, rather than being given "therapy" prisoners should be treated as adult human beings who have certain rights: freedom from physical violence from other inmates or staff; decent levels of medical care; food; sanitary living conditions; the right to minimum wages; a degree of privacy; and general treatment as citizens who have committed crimes, rather than as an entirely different species.

Some prisoners are rejecting the ideologies and programs of both the pure reason and medical models. The emergence of prisoner unions and the more political nature of prison riots suggest that the power/conflict explanation is being seriously entertained.

> Prisoners—especially Blacks, Chicanos, and Puerto Ricans—are increasingly advancing the proposition that they are political prisoners. They contend that they are political prisoners in the sense that they are largely victims of an oppressive political-economic order, swiftly becoming conscious of the causes underlying their victimization (David 1971, p. 37).

The Role of Social Control Agents

If labeling and abusive and discriminatory treatment cause criminal behavior, then programs in diversion and attempts at controlling police and correctional personnel are significant in terms of policy. "Diversion" has been heralded as part of the "new" penology, one that will protect the offender from the negative effects of a criminal label. Through police and court screening an attempt is made to handle offenders less formally and less officially. For example, more youth may be placed on informal probation for first offenses or non-serious law violations. Therefore, they would not have to go through regular court processing and labeling. However, it appears that diversion still has the effect of negative labeling and may well increase rather than decrease the number of people coming under the authority of formal social control agents. The number formally processed has not declined while a large number of people are being informally controlled. It follows that workers in the social control industry will be the primary beneficiaries of the "new" peneology.

Ironically, control itself may breed rather than reduce disorder. A major precipitating factor in the riots and civil unrest in black communities in the 1960s was police behavior (*Report of the National Advisory Commission* 1968). A similar statement can be made concerning the antiwar movement in that same decade (Walker 1968). In fact, there is a long history of civil disorders that have been sparked by the actions of social control agents (Paulsen, Whitebread, and Bonnie 1970). However, there is a crucial difference between precipitating events and structural causes. Although a ghetto disturbance may be precipitated by police action, the ghetto itself is a product of the institutionalization of racially based economic and political exploitation. While police behavior may constitute the spark, we must look to the broader ground of history to understand the powder keg. (see Chapter Ten, Race and Racism.)

If our behavior is to some extent reflective of social conditioning and conditions, then the best way to change behavior (including criminal behavior) is to change such criminogenic conditions. However, this sort of change is difficult to undertake since it demands structural changes that would affect all of us, not just criminals or other "problem" groups. For example, it is humanly possible to largely eliminate slums, poverty, poor housing, inferior schools, unemployment, and in general greatly to reduce economic and social inequality in society.[8] However, this would require changes in structure and ideology. Movement towards a state that seeks to promote the general welfare means movement away from a warfare state. Other changes would redirect tax money from more highways to public transportation; reduce the great variations in personal income; deemphasize material wealth and the accumulation of goods (the large house, two cars, and all that goes with them); change the emphasis from competition and individualism to cooperation and communalism; redefine success as sharing and giving rather than hoarding and getting, among other changes. The values of success and monetary

[8]While not necesssarily representing a model for change that fits the specific history of North American society, the massive changes in the institutions of such countries as Cuba and China indicate that only in societies of structured inequality is a greater measure of equality considered as "impractical" ideal. See such works as: Kozol 1978; Zeitlin 1967; Andors 1977.

wealth move both the ghetto hustler and the corporate executive. To say that any society gets the criminals it deserves is to recognize the significance of criminogenic conditions in explaining the scope and nature of crime in a society. Since a significant number of citizens (far more likely, a number of significant citizens) want to have their cake and eat it too, they will continue to explain crime by the characteristics of offenders. By divorcing ourselves from structural "causes" and focusing upon the offender, we participate in the maintenance of a Criminogenic Corporate Order.

> The problem of "street" crime should be approached not only as a product of the unequal distribution of wealth and chaotic labor market practices, but also as an important aspect of the demoralizing social relations and individualistic ideology that characterize the capitalist mode of production at its highest stage of development (Platt 1978, p. 33).

ALTERNATIVE

In a sense it is difficult to offer an "alternative explanation" to conclude a chapter that deals with explanations of crime. This is because alternative thought is interwoven throughout the previous discussion. Nonetheless, a criminologist has recently pointed out how we could reduce crime if we really wanted to; however, we persist in presenting three erroneous excuses (Reiman 1979, pp. 18–35).

The first excuse is that crime inevitably emerges in heavily populated, diverse, industrialized societies. Therefore, as we become more urbanized and industrialized, we will have more crime. Like death and taxes, crime is here to stay. Such a fatalistic perspective fails to consider that there are highly industrialized, complex, urbanized societies that have lower crime rates than ours, evidence less increase, and, in fact, may occasionally show decreases. For example, Japan and West Germany have much lower crime rates than the United States, and Canada has much less violence and murder than its neighbor to the south. In a recent case study entitled *Cities with Little Crime: The Case of Switzerland,* Clinard (1978) describes a nation that is highly industrialized and urbanized, but has relatively little street crime. The above examples suggest the nature and extent of crime are not inevitable with urbanization and industrialization.

Apart from cross-national differences, we can look at differences within countries that dispel this simple logic. For example, the murder rate in metropolitan New York in 1977 was 17.1 per 100,000 while it was 21.9 in Fresno, California, and 18.1 in Albany, Georgia. During the same year the violent crime rate was only 825.6 per 100,000 in Detroit as against 908.6 in Charleston, South Carolina (*The World Almanac* 1979, p. 967). The highest rates of crime in Canada are in the least industrialized and urbanized provinces—the Northwest Territories and the Yukon. What these various data suggest is that the belief that urbanization plus industrialization equals more crime is not true. As Reiman shows in his statistical analysis, there is a lack of correlation between a city's crime rate and its population density (1979, 23).

The second excuse that is often presented is that the crime problem is largely caused by young people, their proportion of the population has grown, therefore crime inevitably will increase. While youth fifteen to twenty-four years old are disproportionately found in "street" crime statistics, there is no exact relationship between the increase in this type of crime and proportional increases in the youthful population. Furthermore, many criminal acts such as income tax evasion, embezzlement, fraud, price fixing, and other upper world crimes are committed primarily by mature people. Finally, this "explanation" fails to consider the fact that in some countries such as Switzerland, youth are not disproportionately represented in crime (Clinard 1978). Clearly, there is not some inevitable causal connection between being young and stealing cars anymore than there is between being middle-aged and cheating on your taxes.

Finally, experts and others say, "Alas, we simply are not yet smart enough to solve the problem. We need some research money, studies, discussion, and time and someday we will find the answer." Like the person who failed to see the forest because the trees were in the way, most of us are resigned to letting the experts solve the problem. Of course, we can spend billions on building atomic weapons, developing the most sophisticated technology for conventional spying, policing, and warfare besides developing the technology of the nuclear age. We can land men on the moon, generate life in a test tube, and create innumerable devices and products to satisfy the needs of those who can afford them. The ultimate cop-out of the student of crime and the politician is that we really do not know enough.

We do know that poverty, unemployment, and slums spawn crime; therefore, we can do something about these human-made conditions. Those young people who disproportionately fill our jails are largely from the poor, unemployed, ethnic/ minority groups who would be helped by a state policy of assuring everyone of a meaningful and useful job. We do know that prisons and jails really do not correct and, in fact, may actually create crime. We do know that handguns are easy to get and easier to resort to in resolving disputes. We do know that illegal drugs are a source of crime, even though they are no more dangerous than legal drugs. Finally, we know that providing justice on a fee for service basis promotes unequal justice, cynicism, corruption, and despair in our class-based, stratified society. Reiman concludes,

> In summary, then, American criminal justice has failed to reduce crime. The failure cannot be excused by claiming that our growing crime problem is intractable or impossible to solve. The failure cannot be excused by claiming we do not know what to do to reduce crime. Both of these excuses fly in the face of the obvious fact that the crime rate varies under different social conditions and that there are some things we really do know about reducing crime. The second excuse also asks us to believe that the makers of criminal justice policy are more ignorant than we can possibly imagine. Therefore, if a solution is possible and we know it and we can institute it and we do not, what are we left to believe? It must be that we do not want to "solve" the crime problem, or at least some people who are strategically placed do not want to. And if this is so, *the system's failure is only in the eye of the victim: for those in control, it is a roaring success!* (1979, p. 35).

BIBLIOGRAPHY

Amir, Menachen, and
Berman, Yitzchak
1970

"Chromosomal Deviation and Crime." Federal Probation 34 (June):55–62.

Andors, Stephen
1977   China's Industrial Revolution. New York: Pantheon Press.

Baker, Brian C.
1970   "XYY Chromosome Syndrome and the Law." Criminologica 7 (February):2–25.

Balch, Robert W.
1975   "The Medical Model of Delinquency." Crime and Delinquency, April, pp. 116–30.

Bell, Daniel
1953   "Crime as an American Way of Life." The Antioch Review 13 (June):131–54.

Bloch, Herbert A., and
Geis, Gilbert
1970   Man, Crime and Society. 2d ed. New York: Random House.

Braverman, Harry
1975   Labor and Monopoly Capital: The Degradation of Work in the Twentieth Century. New York: Monthly Review Press.

Braukmann, Curtis J.,
et al.
1975   "Behavioural Approaches to Treatment in the Crime and Delinquency Field." Criminology 13 (November):299–331.

Chapman, Terry L.
1976   The Drug Problem in Western Canada 1900–1920. Unpublished master's thesis, the University of Calgary.

Clark, Ramsey
1970   Crime in America. New York: Pocket Books.

Clinard, Marshall B.
1978   Cities with Little Crime: The Case of Switzerland. Cambridge, England: Cambridge University Press.

Clinard, Marshall B., and
Quinney, Richard
1973   Criminal Behavior Systems: A typology, 2d ed. New York: Holt, Rinehart and Winston.

Conrad, Peter
1975   "The Medicalization of Deviance in American Culture." Social Problems 23 (October):12–21.

425

Courtis, M.C.
1970

Attitudes to Crime and the Police in Toronto: A Report on Some Survey Findings. Toronto: Centre of Criminology, University of Toronto.

"Crime: A High Price Tag that Everybody Pays."
1974

U.S. News and World Report, December 16, pp. 32–40.

Cullition, Barbara J.
1974

"Patients' Rights: Harvard Is Site of Battle Over X and Y Chromosomes." Science 186 (November); 715–17.

Darrow, Clarence
1902

"Address to the Prisoners in the Cook County Jail." In Attorney for the Damned, Arthur Weinberg, ed. New York: Simon & Schuster.

David, Brian
1957

Homicide in American Fiction, 1798–1860: A Study in Social Values. Ithaca: Cornell University Press.

Davis, Angela Y.
1971

If They Come in the Morning. New York: The New American Library.

Davis, F.J.
1952

"Crime News in Colorado Newspapers." American Journal of Sociology 57 (January):325–30.

"Disability Centre"
1977

The Calgary Herald, October 3, p. 20.

Erickson, Kai
1966

Wayward Puritans: A Study in the Sociology of Deviance. New York: John Wiley

Fink, Arthur E.
1938

Causes of Crime: Biological Theories in the United States, 1800–1915. Philadelphia: University of Pennsylvania Press.

Fogel, D.
1975

We Are the Living Proof: The Justice Model for Corrections. Cincinnati: W. H. Anderson.

Fong, Melanie, and
Johnson, Larry O.
1974   "The Eugenics Movement: Some Insight into the
Institutionalization of Racism." Issues in Criminology 9 (Fall):89–115.

Fox, Richard G.
1971   "The XYY Offender: A Modern Myth." The Journal
of Criminal Law, Criminology and Police Science,
March: 71 + .

Friendly, Alfred, and
Goldfarb, Ronald L.
1968   Crime and Publicity: The Impact of News on the
Administration of Justice. New York: Vantage
Books.

Gordon, David M.
1973   "Capitalism, Class and Crime in America." Crime
and Delinquency, April: 163–86.

Gordon, Michael
1971   Juvenile Delinquency in the American Novel
1905–1965: A Study in the Sociology of Literature.
Bowling Green: Bowling Green UniversityPress.

Grant, Edwin
1925   "Scum from the Melting Pot." American Journal
of Sociology 30 (May): 641–51.

Harper's Magazine
1975   "Villians: Who's to Blame?" January: 5–12.

Henshel, Richard L., and
Silverman, Robert A.
1975   Perception in Criminology. New York: Columbia
University Press.

Hess, Albert G., and
Mariner, Dorothy A.
1975   "On the Sociology of Crime Cartoons." International Journal of Criminology and Penology
3:253–65.

Hooton, E. A.
1939   The American Criminal: An Anthropological Study.
Cambridge, Mass: Harvard University Press.

Irwin, John
1970   The Felon. Englewood Cliffs, N.J.: Prentice-Hall.

Jacobs, P. A.
1965   "Aggressive Behavior, Mental Subnormality, and the XYY Male." Nature 208 (December): 13–51.

Jeffery, C. R.
1977   "Criminology: Whither or Wither?" Criminology 15 (November):283–86.

Kaplan, John
1973   Criminal Justice: Introductory Cases and Materials. Mineola, N.Y.: The Foundation Press.

Kirkpatrick, A. M., and McGrath, W. T.
1976   Crime and You. Toronto: Macmillan of Canada.

Klapp, Orrin E.
1962   Heroes, Villains and Fools. Englewood Cliffs, N.J.: Prentice-Hall.

Klein, John F.
1976   "The Dangerousness of Dangerous Offender Legislation: Forensic Folklore Revisited." Canadian Journal of Criminology and Corrections 18 (April): 109–22.

Koblick, Steven
1975   Sweden's Development from Poverty to Affluence. Minneapolis: University of Minnesota Press.

Kozol, Jonathan
1978   Children of the Revolution. New York: Delacorte Press.

Kvalseth, Tarald O.
1977   "A Note on the Effects of Population Density and Unemployment on Urban Crime." Criminology 15 (May): 105–110.

Law Reform Commission of Canada.
1976   Our Criminal Law. Ottawa: Information Canada.

Liaison: A Monthly Newsletter for the Criminal Justic System
1977   "Learning Disabilities and the Law" 3 (November): 15–18.

Lipton, D.; Martinson,
R.; and Wilks, J.
1975   The Effectiveness of Correctional Treatment. New York: Praeger.

Lombroso, Cesare
1911   Crime, Its Causes and Remedies. Translated by H.P. Horton. Boston, Mass.: Little, Brown.

MacNamara, Donald
E. J.
1977   "The Medical Model in Corrections: Requiescat in Pace." Criminology 14 (February): 439–447.

Mannheim, Herbert
1960   Pioneers in Criminology. Chicago: Quadrangle.

Marx, Gary T.
1970   "Civil Disorder and the Agents of Social Control." **Journal of Social Issues, Winter: 19–57.**

Miller, Walter B.
1958   "Lower Class Culture as a Generating Milieu of Gang Delinquency." Journal of Social Issues 14 (June):5–19.

Minister of Justice
1973   Criminal Code and Selected Statutes. Ottawa: Information Canada.

Moran, Richard
1977   "Awaiting the Crown's Pleasure: The Case of Daniel McNaughton." Criminology 15 (May):7–26.

Morris, Norval, and
Hawkins, Gordon
1970   The Honest Politician's Guide to Crime Control. Chicago: The University of Chicago Press.

National Commission
on the Causes and
Prevention of Violence
1970   Law and Order Reconsidered. New York: Bantam.

Nettler, Gwynn
1974   Explaining Crime. New York: McGraw-Hill.

Ohlin, Lloyd E.;
Coates, Robert B.;
Miller, Alden D.
1974

"Radical Correctional Reform: A Case Study of the Massachusetts Youth Correctional System." Harvard Educational Review, February: 74–111. 74–111.

Paulsen, Monroe G.;
Whitebread, Charles;
and Bonnie, Richard
1970

"Securing Police Compliance with Constitutional Limitations: The Exclusionary Rule and Other Devices." In Law and Order Reconsidered. National Commission on the Causes and Prevention of Violence, pp. 310–436.

Platt, Anthony
1977

The Child Savers: The Invention of Delinquency. 2d ed. Chicago: The University of Chicago Press.

1978

"Street Crime. A View from the Left." Crime and Social Justice 9 (Spring/Summer):26–34.

Platt, Tony, and
Takagi, Paul
1979

"Biosocial Criminology: A Critique." Crime and Social Justice 11 (Spring/Summer): 5–13.

Quinney, Richard
1975

Criminology. Boston: Little, Brown.

1977

Class, State and Crime. New York: David McKay.

Radzinowicz, Leon
1966

Ideology and Crime. New York: Columbia University Press.

Reasons, Charles E.
1974

"Racism, Prisons and Prisoners' Rights." Issues in Criminology 9 (Fall):3–20.

1975

"Social Thought and Social Structure: Competing Paradigms in Criminology." Criminology 13 (November):332–65.

1976a

"Images of Crime and the Criminal: The Dope Fiend Mythology." Journal of Research in Crime and Delinquency 13 (July):133–44.

1976b
"Toward Community-Based Corrections." Crime and Social Justice 4 (August/November): 108–14.

Reasons, Charles E., and Kaplan, Russell L.
1975
"Tear Down the Walls? Some Functions of Prisons." Crime and Delinquency 21 (October):360–72.

Reasons, Charles E., and Kuykendall, Jack L.
1972
Race, Crime and Justice. Pacific Palisades, Calif.: Goodyear.

Reid, Sue Titus
1976
Crime and Criminology. Homewood, Ill.: The Dryden Press.

Reiman, Jeffrey
1979
The Rich Get Richer and the Poor Get Prison. New York: John Wiley.

Report of the Commissioners Appointed to Inquire into the Subject of Chinese and Japanese Immigration into the Province of British Columbia
1902
Sessional Papers 54:2.

Report of the National Advisory Commission on Civil Disorders
1968
New York: Bantam.

Rutter, William A.
1972
Criminal Law. 9th ed. Gardena, Calif.: Gilbert Law Summaries.

Sage, Wayne
1974
"Crime and the Clockwork Lemon," Human Behavior, September.

Sarbin, Theodore R., and Miller, Jeffrey E.
1970
"Demonism Revisited: The XYY Chromosomal Anomaly." Issues in Criminology 5 (Summer): 195–207.

Schur, Edwin
1973   Radical Nonintervention. Englewood Cliffs, N.J.:
                        Prentice-Hall.

Science
1969   164:1117[+].

Sellin, Thorsten
1938   Culture Conflict and Crime. New York: Social
                        Science Research Council Bulletin No. 41.

Shaw, Clifford R., and
McKay, Henry D.
1972   Juvenile Delinquency and Urban Areas. Rev. ed.
                        Chicago: The University of Chicago Press.

Shoemaker, Donald J.;
South, Donald R.; and
Lowe, Jay
1973   "Facial Stereotypes and Guilt." Social Forces 51
                        (June):427–33.

Simmons, J. L.
1965   "Public Stereotypes of Deviants." Social Problems
                        13 (Fall):223–32.

Sutherland, Edwin H.
1947   Principles of Criminology. 4th ed. Philadelphia:
                        Lippincott.

Sutherland, Edwin H.,
and Cressey, Donald R.
1970   Criminology. Philadelphia: Lippincott.

Swigert, Victoria L.,
and Farrell, Ronald A.
1977   "Normal Homicides and the Law." American
                        Sociological Review 42 (February):16–32.

Szasz, Thomas
1970   The Manufacture of Madness. New York: Dell.

Taylor, Ian; Walton, Paul;
and Young, Jack
1973   The New Criminology: For a Social Theory of
                        Deviance. London: Routledge and Kegan Paul.

Tepperman, Lorne
1977   Crime Control: The Urge Toward Authority.
                        Toronto: McGraw-Hill Ryerson.

United States Bureau of the
Census
    1978   Statistical Abstract of the United States. Washington, D.C.: U.S. Government Printing Office.

United States Department
of Justice
    1979   Uniform Crime Reports. Federal Bureau of Investigation, Washington, D.C.: U.S. Government Printing Office.

Vold, George B.
    1958   Theoretical Criminology. New York: Oxford University Press.

Walker, Daniel
    1968   Rights in Conflict. New York: Bantam.

Webster's New World
Dictionary of the
American Language
    1964   College Edition. New York: World.

World Almanac and
Book of Facts, 1980
    1979   New York: Newspaper Enterprise Association.

Zeitlin, Maurice
    1967   Revolutionary Politics and the Cuban Working Class. Princeton, N.J.: Princeton University Press.

8

THE CRIME CONTROL ESTABLISHMENT

Abstract

The prevailing ideologies of the criminal justice system includes "Support your local police," equal justice for all, and deterring crime through correcting offenders. The emergence, institutionalization, and maintenance of the criminal justice system reflect one of the major goals of the master economic institution—peace and order. The economic inequality that is a consequence of our corporate society is reflected in *class-based justice* throughout the criminal justice system. The gap between prevailing ideologies and social reality has produced alternative suggestions for policing the police, dispensing justice, and correcting corrections.

Indeed, the whole system resembles a vast machine sucking people in one end, spewing them out the other and then sucking them back in again—a self-generating mechanism, certainly not a human process.—Law Reform Commission of Canada in Our Criminal Law

The United States National Advisory Commission on Criminal Justice Standards and Goals (1973) has identified two criminal justice systems in operation. Criminal Justice System I is what most people think when they are asked to identify the components of this system. These agencies include law enforcement personnel, judges, prosecutors, defense attorneys, correctional institutions, and probation and parole agencies. However,

435

the Advisory Commission also notes a second Criminal Justice System, consisting of public and private agencies and citizens outside the traditional system who are directly or indirectly involved in reducing and preventing crime.

> A State legislature, for example, becomes part of this larger criminal justice system when it considers and debates any proposed law that might affect, even remotely, any area of criminal justice activities. So also the executive agencies of the State, educational administrative units, welfare departments, youth service bureaus, recreation departments, and other public offices become a part of Criminal Justice 2 in many of their decisions and actions. Moving outside the State and local governments, community organizations, union offices, neighborhood action groups, and employers may also be important functionaries in the second system (National Advisory Commission 1973, p. 1).

The focus of this chapter will be upon Criminal Justice System 1. Nonetheless, aspects of Criminal Justice System 2 will be presented where pertinent, particularly when discussing social change. As will become evident in subsequent discussion, much of the impetus for changes in the criminal justice system has come from persons and organizations who are not part of the multibillion dollar crime control establishment. The crime control establishment consists of the criminal justice institutions and their leaders, who are given the authority to influence and shape the definition of the crime problem and appropriate measures to deal with it (Silver 1974). As always, such influentials operate in an ideological context. As always, the crime control agencies of the State are not independent of the existing economic order.

PERSPECTIVE

Dismantling the System[1]

The title of this paper—"Dismantling the System"—is suggestive of conclusions that some people at least have reached in regard to our billion-dollar criminal justice industry. The industry analogy is helpful. In some provinces expenditures within the crime industry exceed or equal the combined government outlays for environment, natural resources, recreation and culture, and housing.

When the industry's budgetary outlays are plotted on a graph, the

[1]Adapted from Keith B. Jobson, "Dismantling the System," *Canadian Journal of Criminology and Corrections* 19 (July 1977): 254–60.

results show a dramatic and straight-line increase from $0.6 billion in 1966 to an estimated $1.5 billion in 1976. The industry has more than doubled its growth in the last ten years.

The industry is made up of several interrelated but somewhat autonomous branches or sectors: the police sector, the courts sector (including prosecutorial and defense services), and the corrections or prisons sector including the parole "plant." Projected expansions within the prison sector again underline the large capital requirements of the industry and its high operating costs. New prison plants, built to security specifications, cost from $70,000 to $100,000 per cell or bed space. Once constructed, operating costs are not cheap. In British Columbia in 1976–1977, the estimated budgetary requirement for the adult prison sector was approximately $22,000,000. That money was needed to provide for the 1,950 bed spaces for adult offenders; that works out to a little less than $12,000 per bed. It is disturbing that 20 percent of these expensive beds are taken up by persons awaiting trial—waiting from one to five months at the present time. It is also disturbing that it costs so much to hand out relatively minor punishment: 65 percent of prison terms are for six months or less. Admittedly, short terms mean that prison beds can be "recycled" several times in the course of a year. This cycle of use, however, does nothing to reduce the overall costs of almost $1,000 a month per bed—an amount all the more distressing in light of the fact, as shown later in the paper, that the industry is not producing either reform, deterrence, or prevention, as it has promised.

The crime control industry, that is the formal part of the industry set up to deal with crime, is big and expensive. In large part, it is an industry teetering on the edge of bankruptcy: its liabilities are many, its assets few.

Failure of the Crime Control System   It is not a question of needed infusion of capital, nor of hiring more professional management teams, nor even of staff retraining. Overhaul of the industry along such lines cannot alter the basic fact that the industry does not now have the technological capacity to deliver on its promises, namely,

1. To reform criminals;

2. To deter persons from committing crimes;

3. To prevent crimes.

The industry's claims to crime prevention are particularly suspect when viewed in the reality of low clearance rates, lack of certainty of punishment, and the ineffectiveness of punishment generally in reducing recidivism rates. The claims are suspect, too, when viewed in the light of other facts:

1. Crime rates and unemployment rates tend to be correlated;

2. Apprehended offenders tend to be poorly educated;

3. Almost 80 percent of persons appearing in court are under twenty-five years of age;

4. Irrespective of sentence, persons drop out of the crime industry as they get older or join the work force;

5. Recidivism at the penitentiary level over the years is about 45 percent.

Can the industry claim that it prevents crime among the elderly, the affluent, the middle class, and females, or is the relative lack of "criminality" in these groups due to factors other than the influence of the criminal justice industry? Moreover, with respect to violent offenses, the industry already admits it has little capacity to deliver on its promise to prevent them. Even increased police patrols have been shown to be ineffective in lowering crime rates.

Finally, it cannot pass unnoticed that the industry itself generates a measurable amount of crime that in turn is fed back into its own system at the usual costs to the shareholders. Included here is the violence that wracks the prison sector through riots and suicides as well as the lesser forms of violence suffered daily by workers and prisoners alike within the institutions. In addition, breaches of probation and parole, not based on any violation of criminal law, result in revocations that send persons back into the prison sector.

Not only has the industry promised delivery much beyond its capacity, it has also promoted and extended its services far into fields that can be equally or more profitably serviced by competing industries or by individual efforts.

An Industry Overextended   Thus, the industry finds itself servicing noncrime areas. Particularly is this true in the areas of juvenile "crime" and regulatory "offenses" where pseudocrimes or noncrimes are euphemistically referred to as "delinquencies" or "quasi-criminal" offenses and, thus packaged, become eligible for entry into the criminal justice industry. Noncrimes such as "truancy," "incorrigibility," and so on gained early entry on a promise by the industry to deliver a reformative product. Since the product cannot be delivered, these cases should no longer qualify for inclusion as crimes and should be rejected. It is to be noted that the proposed reforms to the Juvenile Delinquents Act would follow this course: under the proposals the young offender would be liable only for those offenses that appear in the Criminal Code. This leaves untouched the question of whether or not pseudocrimes have crept into the Code as well.

Another example of overextension of the crime industry is in the area of regulatory offenses such as those relating to parking, consumption and sale of beverages and foods, stray dogs, beekeeping, and many other minor infractions. It is estimated that there are more than 42,000 regulatory type offenses in addition to the "real crime" included in the Criminal Code. This estimate does not include the numerous offenses covered in municipal bylaws. The criminal justice industry should abandon its operations in some of these areas and leave the field to alternative servicing mechanisms such as administrative boards.

Public drunkenness and other abuses of alcohol or drugs are another example of overextension of the industry. Some rational control over the industry's expansion is needed. One limiting factor in determining such expansion has often been cited as "proven public harm." In short, the industry should not extend or carry on operations in fields absent of public harm. In the case of marijuana and some other drugs, the expansion initially took place on an unproven assumption of harm and a promise that the industry through its intervention, could "prevent" the continuation or spread of the supposed public injury. The evidence now shows an absence of the supposed harm and also shows for consumption of both alcohol and drugs not a reduction but a widespread growth, undermining again the industry's claims to be able to deliver a deterrent service.

For many unfortunate years the industry has allowed itself to be cajoled into offering a service ("free"—at tax-payers' expense) in any theft or fraud, no matter how minor the loss. Thus we have the spectacle of the industry processing $1.49 thefts. Again, the error in judgment leading to this extended service may have been made under the mistaken belief, prevalent at the time, that the industry could deliver a deterrent or preventive effect. The hanging of scores of nonviolent offenders for minor thefts in England did not deter pickpockets from plying their trade at these public exhibitions, and showed the industry, as early as a hundred years ago, its incapacity to prevent or deter crime.

THE PREVAILING IDEOLOGIES

How is the criminal justice system perceived by the public? Do most citizens have a conception of the role and functions of the police, courts, and corrections? How are these perspectives gained and changed? Actually, there is the officially presented ideology of the criminal justice system and then there is the actual operation. Similar to our perception of the nature and magnitude of the crime problem and the causes of criminal behavior, much of our information regarding the criminal justice system comes from the media, public leaders, and other social institutions and their representatives. This is the offical version of how the system is run, including conceptions of the roles of various participants such as police officers, lawyers, judges, guards, counselors, criminals, convicts, and others. This is, one fears, an idealized version of the criminal justice system.

The Thin Blue Line

Despite historical flurries of criticism and the feeling among police that the public is hostile to them, law enforcement personnel, as we shall soon demonstrate, enjoy widespread public confidence. Police are popularly conceptualized as a "thin blue line" who function "to protect and to serve" the law-abiding. That police defend "us" from the violent and the profane continues as an engrained stereotype despite the evidence that less than 5 percent of the total arrests made by police in the United States in 1978 were for violent crime, that is, criminal homicide, forcible rape, robbery, and aggravated assault (U.S. Department of Justice 1979, p. 186). Further, 37.5 percent of all "violent" robberies were of the "strong-armed" variety, which means that the offender was not armed with a gun, knife, or other weapon (ibid, p. 19). Police action is by and large directed against property offenders and those whose behavior constitutes a violation of public "decency or morality." In 1978, police in the United States arrested a total of 469,700 persons for violent crime. In that same year they arrested 445,800 for marijuana offenses, and 1.2 million for drunkenness (ibid, p. 186).

As subsequent data will point out, emphasis in the criminal justice system in both personnel and funding is upon law enforcement. The majority of citizens have contact with the police at some point in their lives, whether it be asking directions or receiving a traffic warning or citation. A person's perception of the criminal justice system generally, and the police specifically, is influenced by such contacts and by various other factors such as age, sex roles, social class, race, newspapers, and television.

Public Perception of Police   Our view of the police is gained in the early stages of our socialization. One researcher found that third graders had definite conceptions of the police (Derbyshire 1968). Children in three elementary schools in Los Angeles, representing varying social class and ethnic populations, were asked to draw a picture describing the police officer at work. The analysis of the pictures by four independent professionals found that the perceptions of lower-class black and lower middle-class Chicano youths had differed significantly from that of upper middle-class white third graders. More specifically, the black and Chicano drawings showed more concern with aggressive and negative police behavior such as fighting, chasing, shooting, giving tickets, while the white anglo third graders displayed a high emphasis upon neutral, non-aggressive, and positive police behavior such as talking with children, giving directions, riding in a car, or directing traffic. Differences in the perception of the police were thus found to be based on social class and ethnicity.

Undoubtedly, one develops an understanding of the police in part from childhood socialization and subsequent experiences. It may be that as a child, one's perception of the police is greatly affected by being a member of the school patrol or having an officer visit class as part of a school-police program. Thus police contact may be positive and the image that results is that of a nice person who helps children across the street and catches bad guys. However, negative experiences with the police may also influence a youngster's perceptions. For example, blacks living in the inner city are more likely to see the police stopping or arresting someone, searching a person, or generally disrupting the day-to-day routine. Furthermore, the police are more likely to be visible by both their color and number. The white youth growing up in a middle-class suburban area is less apt to observe such behavior or have contact with others who have had such confrontations. Since official crime rates and police patrol practices reflect conditions in poorer and nonwhite areas, the attitudes of the third graders are not surprising. As will be discussed later, such differences are also found among adults in their evaluation of the criminal justice system.

Many of us gain our images of the police, courts, lawyers, and correctional work from the mass media. Since over 95 percent of the households in North America have television sets, this is a major source of people's ideas about crime and criminal justice. Many television series concern crime and criminal justice. Most of them deal with police work, fewer concern lawyers and the courts, and only rarely has there been one portraying corrections. Given the fact that police are most visible to the public and that this criminal justice agent is most likely to have contact with the average citizen, it is understandable that more attention would be given to this area. However, television generally presents an erroneous picture of the nature of both police work and of crime and criminals. While their number is legion, one early program became the historical prototype for police series.

Dragnet began in 1949 as a radio program, followed by the television series in 1952. It was one of the most popular media events of the first decade of television. Subsequently, it was revived in 1966 and ran into the 1970s. This program represents a case study in police ideology. Produced with the cooperation and approval of the Los Angeles Police Department, *Dragnet* presented the police perspective on the problem of law enforcement in contemporary society. In an extensive analysis of this program, one student of the media concludes:

> Through the *Dragnet* television series (and ones similar to it) one interest group in the debate—the police—are provided access to an audience of millions to whom they can present, in the context of a documentary drama, their side of the story (Varni 1974).

In his thorough analysis of *Dragnet*, Varni shows how the series presents the police view on social order and how it portrays their conception of the nature and causes of deviance and deviants. Finally, he describes the professional role of the police as presented in the series. That role portrays the police as servants of the people and the public will, the latter supposedly embodied in the law. The *Dragnet* officers and their contemporary media descendants appear as objective and apolitical agents of law enforcement. They maintain their emotional distance and do not engage in illegal or unethical activity. They also are careful to observe procedural laws that emphasize the rights of the accused. *Dragnet* officers did not make deals with deviants for this was viewed as a violation of the police role and as corrupting.

> Taken altogether, the police officer on *Dragnet* is portrayed as an altruistic martyr, a self-effacing and humble man who provides an unpopular, yet necessary, service for his fellow human beings, persevering against the slings and arrows of outrageous fortune heaped upon him by hostile courts, liberals, and the dregs of humankind. While today's media cop may be more "realistically presented" to an adult audience, the deals made with deviants as well as renegade police behavior are typically presented as necessary under the circumstances (Varni 1974, p. 21).

Public Confidence in the Police   Given media and official support by national and community leaders, it should come as no surprise to find that police enjoy a high degree of public confidence. Table 8–1 presents 1975 ratings of police in thirteen selected United States cities. This study supports the findings from other studies in both the United States and Canada showing that the large majority of citizens approve of the job the police are doing. However, there are some significant differences among various populations. Both nonwhites and younger persons are less favorable toward the police than whites and older people. This perhaps reflects such groups' larger number of negative contacts and fewer positive contacts with police. Youth and nonwhites are heavily represented in arrest statistics for a variety of offenses and are thus more likely to have bad experiences with law enforcement. Furthermore, the lower the income the more likely that the individual will give a poor rating to local police. Given the fact that the law and legal system are more accessible for those with money, it is not surprising that those with over $20,000 in annual income give local police the highest rating. While police rate fairly high with those under $5,000, a large proportion of this income cohort is 65 years of age or older. This age group gave police the highest rating among all respondents. Evidently police enjoy the respect of the elderly poor, but not the poor in general.

Attitudes toward the police do not exist in a vacuum; they are part of a larger set of interrelated attitudes. Negative evaluations of the police are closely related to negative evaluations toward the court system, to a belief that wealth and power are overly concentrated, and generally to feelings of political alienation and powerlessness (Albrecht and Green

TABLE 8–1
Ratings of Local Police, by Respondents' Characteristics in 13 Selected American Cities (aggregate), 1975

Question: Would you say, in general, that your local police are doing a good job, an average job, or a poor job?
(Percent)

	Good	Aver- age	Poor	Don't Know	No Answer	Number of Respondents[a] (millions)
Thirteen-city total	40%	41%	12%	7%	0%	15,386,699
Sex						
Male	40	41	13	5	0	6,882,142
Female	40	40	11	8	0	8,504,193
Race						
White	47	37	9	7	0	10,872,109
Black and other	24	50	19	7	0	4,514,226
Education						
Less than 9 years	46	33	11	11	0	2,959,807
Some high school	37	43	14	6	0	3,039,822
High school graduate	39	42	12	6	0	5,093,778
Some college	38	43	13	6	0	2,250,349
Four years of college and more	39	43	10	7	1	2,026,193
Not ascertained	32	50	10	8	0	8,230
Income						
Under $3,000	40	36	14	10	0	1,304,699
$3,000 to $4,999	41	36	13	9	0	1,593,365
$5,000 TO 7,499	38	40	14	7	1	2,016,131
$7,500 to $9,999	38	43	13	6	0	1,587,500
$10,000 to $11,999	39	43	12	5	0	1,570,004
$12,000 to $14,999	41	42	12	5	0	1,839,205
$15,000 to $19,999	42	42	11	4	0	1,799,727
$20,000 to $24,999	42	43	9	5	0	940,742
$25,000 or more	45	41	9	6	0	1,074,675
Not ascertained	36	40	13	11	1	1,660,690
Age						
16 to 19	25	52	18	5	0	1,477,445
20 to 24	29	48	16	6	1	1,857,174
25 to 34	34	45	15	6	0	2,975,189
35 to 49	40	42	13	6	0	3,228,509
50 to 64	48	36	9	7	0	3,397,629
65 years or older	53	28	6	11	0	2,390,388

[a]Base on which percentages were computed.

Source: Table constructed from data provided by the National Criminal Justice Information and Statistics Service of the Law Enforcement Assistance Adminstration.

1977). As will become evident in this chapter, youth, the poor, and non-whites represent a subjugated population. Since they have less chance to obtain justice and are more subjects of the law and legal system than participants in it, they will be more negative in their evaluations.

While the local police are viewed well among the general public, the FBI suffered a rapid decline in public favor between 1965 and 1975. Although the Bureau is considered by many to be the elite in law enforcement, the great reduction in the highly favorable rating is likely due to revelations concerning its political activities. More specifically, the Federal Bureau of Investigation has been implicated in spying on civilian civil rights and antiwar activists, disrupting their activities, putting agents provocateurs in their ranks, committing break-ins and illegal wiretaps, and generally carrying out various forms of repression against social and political dissidents. It appears that the FBI has a long history of engaging in such repression, even when its public image was more favorable. However, the various crises of the Nixon years set the stage and the Bureau, with the death of its patriarch, J. Edgar Hoover, became vulnerable as an idiosyncratic scapegoat (Unger 1976). Although the Royal Canadian Mounted Police (RCMP) have played a similar role in antisubversion activities in Canada, their image has received less critical public scrutiny than has that of the FBI (Brown 1972). However, revelations in the late 1970s concerning their involvement in illegal break-ins, mail opening, frameups, political surveillance of "subversive" groups including unions, and other questionable activity may cause some shift in public support in the 1980s. Without the development of a Canadian "Watergate" with RCMP complicity, this organization will probably continue to enjoy a primarily positive image.

Although the FBI lost much of its strong support during the 1965–1975 period, it still kept a high rating relative to other organizations in the United States. A 1973 public opinion poll in this country had citizens rate sixteen widely known organizations. The FBI and local police were only

TABLE 8–2
Respondents Rating the FBI "Highly Favorable,"
United States, Selected Years
(Percent)

	Highly favorable
1965	84
1970	71
1973	52
1975	37

Sources: George Gallup, *The Gallup Poll* cited in *Current Opinion*, Williamstown, Mass.: The Roper Public Opinion Research Center, vol. 1, pp. 93, 94; vol. 4, pp. 7, 8.

TABLE 8–3
Sentiment of General Public toward Local Police and Other Well-Known Organizations

Organizations	Mean Sentiment	Rank of Mean Sentiment	Percent of Nonresponses
*United States	9.11	1	03%
FBI	8.18	2	04
Local Police	8.03	3	03
*AMA	7.67	4	06
*Congress	7.37	5	06
*Supreme Court	7.33	6	07
*The Press	7.10	7	04
*CIA	6.89	8	14
*NAM	6.68	9	30
*AFL-CIO	6.52	10	06
*CORE	6.47	11	27
*NAACP	6.46	12	08
*ACLU	6.35	13	28
*Russia	5.08	14	10
*John Birch Society	3.67	15	22
*Ku Klux Klan	2.22	16	08

*Groups for whom the mean sentiment is different (at .05 level or beyond) from the mean sentiment toward local police.
Source: Peek et al. 1978.

surpassed by the love of country. There were no statistically significant differences between the FBI and local police in their evaluation by survey respondents. A further analysis by age and race found that the youngest and oldest black respondents were most negative toward local police, while rating the FBI fifth. Old and young blacks hold only Russia, the John Birch Society, and the Ku Klux Klan in significantly less regard than the local police. As the authors point out, both the favorable and unfavorable ratings are largely a function of the nature and extent of contact with the police (Peek et al. 1978). This study suggests police not only are highly evaluated, but are also rated better than a number of other organizations.

The prevailing ideology that pertains to police and police power consists of widely shared supportive beliefs (especially among the more established and advantaged). Consistent with media imagery, the agents of law enforcement are seen as neutral defenders of social order. Thus, those representing the "thin blue line" are accepted as protecting the insiders and law-abiding from the outsiders and law-deriding. Beyond this, support for police represents support for police *work*. And what is the nature of police work? The criminal justice system, including its law enforcement component, is geared to a war on street crime. To look with acceptance on police work means more than an insensitivity to occasional police lawlessness. It is rather to adopt a view of crime (that is, street offenses by the dregs of society) that is clearly in the particular interests of police and the more general interests of a criminogenic corporate order.

Blind Justice

As the prevailing image of the police presented in the media emphasizes the detached, objective, fair, and equal application of the law, so the ideological portrait of the courts emphasizes the fair and even-handed application of procedural and substantive law in determining guilt or innocence. The media drama is stereotyped: the accused, protected by legal counsel, enters into combat with the prosecutor, while the judge, an agent of the supposed neutral state, represents an impartial, disinterested arbitrator of the conflict. Thus, the adversary proceedings, sometimes presented in the context of a jury trial, are assumed to set two opponents of equal size against one another in search of truth and justice. The extent to which such imagery reflects reality will be addressed in a later section. Nonetheless, this is the portrayal of the administration of justice most often given in media programming concerning the judicial system.

What about public evaluation of the administration of justice? Social surveys consistently show a high rating for judges. However, when pressed for specific beliefs, many citizens are at least somewhat suspicious of the ideology of "blind justice." For example, a 1972 national study in the United States (Blumenthal et al. 1972) found that 79 percent of the public thought that the courts treat rich people better than poor people, with 86 percent of the blacks in the sample holding this view. Also, 40 percent of the sample believed that whites are treated better than blacks, while 66 percent of the surveyed blacks agreed. Another study, in Missouri, found that 33 percent of the nearly 3,000 interviewed subjects did not think they would get a fair trial if accused of a crime, with those having some experience in court or knowledge of how courts operate being less positive (Missouri Bar 1963). In an extensive review of survey research literature, Sarat (1977) summarized the following findings:

1. Black and young people are least likely to consult a lawyer;

2. Income is directly related to support for lawyers;

3. The willingness to use lawyers is directly related to income, education, and attitudes toward lawyers;

4. The more contact one has with lawyers, the less positive one's attitudes toward them;

5. The higher one's education and occupational status, the more positively one views lawyers;

6. Family income and property ownership are highly correlated with the use of lawyers.

The above survey reflects the fact that access to the law and legal services is largely a matter of money. One's ability to retain legal counsel is based on economic worth. It follows that those who are poorer, including a disproportionate number of nonwhites, will not have equal access to the law.

The Ideology of Deterrence

Last and least in media presentation is corrections. Correctional institutions, parole and probation systems are the least systematically presented facets of the criminal justice system. When they are portrayed they tend to be discussed in their crisis aspects such as prison escapes or riots, and probation and parole violations. The prevailing public attitude toward such institutions is one of "out of sight and out of mind." While the police are visible and the courts are accessible, correctional institutions not only keep the inmates locked up, but outsiders locked out. Access to corrections is the most difficult and, given their location and security, one must rely heavily upon media accounts for an understanding of their operation.

What about the ideology of corrections? Correctional programs and practices are largely justified today on the basis of rehabilitating or correcting the offender. The term rehabilitation means "to restore to lost standing." Yet to which standing do we refer? As already demonstrated, most prisoners come from backgrounds of economic and racial exploitation. If this be true, perhaps the rehabilitation should be directed more toward the conditions outside than the attitudes and behaviors inside. Rehabilitation aside, the aim of the corrections system is often to make an example of criminals so that others will not be tempted to commit crime. The latter objective is termed general deterrence.

By deterrence one means that punishment "deters" an offender from future criminal behavior. Further, the benefits of punishment supposedly go beyond the offender in that others are supposedly deterred. If punishment deters, however, then how is one to explain the phenomena of recidivism and repeat crime? Approximately half of those released from prison come back again, while some 80 percent of serious crime is committed by those convicted of earlier offenses (Gordon 1973). Further, the rate of prisoners in federal and state prisons per 100,000 population in the United States continues to climb (110.3 in 1950 to 123.1 in 1976. *Statistical Abstract of the United States* 1978, p. 197). This, although the sentences meted out in this country are the harshest in the Western world. Despite such a generous test of the deterrence hypothesis, the official rate of all categories of serious crime continues to grow (U.S. Department of Justice 1979, p. 35).

Although capital punishment has been eliminated in most industrial

Western nation states, including Canada, the United States still provides for execution of certain offenders. A 1977 Harris survey (*Chicago Tribune* 1977) in the United States found that 59 percent of the sample believed that capital punishment of murderers acts as a general deterrent, while 34 percent said it did not have much effect, with 7 percent not sure. Sociological research suggests that capital punishment does not act as a general deterrent (Reid 1976, pp. 480–92).

It is apparent that the notion that prison and/or other forms of punishment rehabilitate, correct, or deter offenders stands without evidence. Only ideological analysis can explain the popularity of such beliefs, for to focus on offenders and their behavior is to reduce the public issue of a criminal political-economy to a private trouble of individual deviants. Thus, the prevailing ideology is that biographical solutions can be found to historical problems of structure. One does not address class inequality and racism through behavior modification, psychosurgery, and chapel.

Table 8–4 shows how correctional officials evaluate programs of rehabilitation. A majority of administrators, supervising adults and juveniles, disagree with the statement that institutional programs have low recidivism. Both sets of administrators believed that community programs are more effective at rehabilitation than institutional programs. However, while the public position of corrections officials is one advocating rehabilitation, the reality of contemporary prisons is one of obsession with control (Mitford 1974).

A New Consciousness?

Public opinion polls are coming to reflect a selective skepticism toward certain aspects of the criminal justice system. Some believe that this may signal the awakening of a general crisis of confidence in major institutions in North American society.

> Young or old, black or white, male or female—not one group crossed the midpoint in agreement with the statement about police officers' honesty. Not one group was in less than extreme disagreement with the statement, "In the courts a poor man has the same chance as a rich man," while everyone clearly did agree that court decisions could be bought by money or influence. On the other hand, those questions that referred to personal honesty elicited responses that were much more positive. Everyone agreed that one should tell the truth, no one agreed that it was O.K. to lie. These measures suggest that confidence in the integrity of the individual, notably expectations of personal truthfulness, were quite high; *it was the system and its servants that were perceived as dishonest and inequitable* (La Kind et al. 1977, p. 336; emphasis added).

TABLE 8-4
Adult and juvenile correctional administrators' views on the relative effectiveness of community and institutional programs in rehabilitating offenders, 1975

Question: Do you think that community programs are more effective at rehabilitating offenders than institutional programs?

	Yes		No		Don't Know		For Some Offenders	
	Number	Percent	Number	Percent	Number	Percent	Number	Percent
Adult administrators	24	48%	4	8%	9	18%	13	26%
Juvenile administrators	23	48	2	4	7	15	16	33
All responses	47	48	6	6	16	16	29	30

Source: Michael S. Serrill, "Is Rehabilitation Dead?" *Corrections Magazine* 1 (May/June 1975), p. 5.

However, one should be wary of hailing the development of counter-ideologies purely on the basis of public opinion polls. Prevailing ideologies die slowly. A concern with the *unfairness* of control organizations may merely reflect the element of general ideology termed *equal opportunity*, or more particularly, *equal justice under law*. If so, public criticism of the criminal justice system is restricted to the lament that the system should work more fairly, in accordance with the rule of the law, to control the (street) criminal. On the other hand, our theory of ideology requires one to draw a connection between structural inequality in corporate society and that same inequality reflected in the criminal justice system. Thus, the criminal justice system is a microcosm of the corporate order. Laws reflecting the interests of the "haves" more than the "have-nots" are enforced and administered by middle-level agents of state power, with the propertyless serving by and large as fodder for the system. Accordingly, "unfairness" is to be expected and will be difficult to eradicate until the inequalities in power and privilege in the broader society are recognized and reduced.

What about the evaluation of the criminal justice system by those going through it? Research suggests that prisoners' attitudes toward the law are predictably unfavorable. However, those who retained their own private counsel are generally more positive toward the police, the law, and the judicial system than those who were assigned a public defender. This reflects income and the ability to buy justice. Also, nonwhites are more likely to view the police, the law, and the judicial system more negatively than whites. The police appear to be most disliked, with the law and judicial system evoking less hostility, and lawyers receiving the most positive evaluation (Alpert and Hicks 1977). It also appears that parolees have a negative attitude toward the police, courts, and lawyers. While blacks appear more negative than whites toward the police and courts, the two show no significant differences in their more positive evaluation of lawyers (Berman 1976).

Generally, a person's evaluation of the criminal justice system and its agents reflects his or her age; social class; ethnic/racial identity; occupation, and experience with, and learning about, the law and its administration. The fact that persons who are poorer, younger, and disproportionately nonwhite have a less positive view of the police, courts, and corrections reflects the fact that they or members of their cohort are more likely to have had more negative contacts with the law and its agents. Thus, they are less apt to be persuaded by the prevailing ideologies of equal justice under the law and the deterrent value of punishment.

EMERGENCE

The basis for the contemporary criminal justice system in North American society can be found largely in the period of the enlightenment. Before the emergence of police, courts, and corrections, there were various other ways to deal with those who offended.

From Constabulary to Police

Who dealt with offenders before the professional police arose? In early England, and subsequently in Canada and the United States, the military and constabulary system preceded the emergence of the police as we know them today. The army or nobility under the King enforced the King's laws in early England and its colonies in North America (Kelly 1976). In the reign of Edward I (1272–1307) the first official sheriffs appeared in the large towns of England. This policing was based upon the system of constables (reeves) appointed by noblemen to enforce laws in a local area and subsequently larger areas called "shires"; thus the office of "shire-reeve" was created. These constables were charged with protecting property between sunset and daybreak (Quinney 1979). By the eighteenth century, there were increasing demands for more democratic participation in social institutions, including law. During this time the "night-watch" system of constables spread in England, requiring civilians to patrol city streets "slowly and silently and now and then listen" (Kelly 1976, p. 137). It was difficult to compel citizens to take their turns at this graveyard shift (9 P.M. to sunrise) since many had day jobs. Although day watches arose in England with urbanization, they were eventually to give way to the establishment of the professional police force in 1829.

Like England, the American colonies established the constabulary based upon the collective responsibility of all able-bodied men. It was such a thankless job that as early as 1653 those who refused to serve were fined. They served only in the day, with a citizens' watch, or nightwatch, in the evening. The day constable basically responded to citizens' complaints of lawbreaking, while the nightwatch patrolled for fires, reported the time, and described the weather (Parks 1970).

The constabulary worked in a consensually based, homogeneous community where most agreed on the rules and the need to obey them. However, with the heightened visibility of social, cultural, and economic differences in urban areas, the constabulary was to find social control increasingly difficult. Charles Reith observed that the basis for the constabulary was voluntary observance of the law. Such

> . . . can be seen to have never survived in effective form the advent of community prosperity, as this brings into being inevitable differences in wealth and social status, and creates, on this basis, classes and parties and factions with or without wealth and power and privileges. In the presence of these divisions, community unanimity in voluntary law observance and the maintenance of authority and order must be found (1952, p. 210).

Old Time Justice

Our contemporary process of determining guilt through the "adversary proceeding" emphasizes the combative model of justice. Accordingly, the accused is pitted against the accuser (the State or Crown) with the judge representing the arbitration of the dispute. Before the emergence of the State, dispute settlement entailed a blood feud where an injured party exacted justice from the accused or his kin mainly through restitution or battle. It was a private matter to be settled by the parties involved. During the early period of the Anglo-Saxon state, the courts merely oversaw a dispute settlement and did not rule on laws. In fact, such statutory law hardly existed. Given the small, homogeneous nature of the earlier societies, everyone knew the rules and it was merely for the court to determine if there had been an offense against the commonly accepted code. Thus, common law preceded statutory law and emphasized private prosecutions. Under this approach, there had to be a victim to initiate prosecution, an ascertainable harm done, and a norm violated that the victim believed he or she had a right to redress. William the Conqueror introduced trial by combat between the injured party and the accused, which emphasized the private nature of that adversary process (Chambliss and Seidman 1971). In this case, the two parties would enter into combat to determine guilt and redress harms under the eye of the King, who merely made sure the rules of the game—the procedural norms—were followed. It was presumed that the innocent person would win due to divine favor. Trial by ordeal, described in Chapter Seven, also existed to determine guilt and innocence.

Subsequently the King and the State came to represent the accuser. Thus a crime was not only an offense against the individual, but also against the King and State. Thus, the representative of the State would present the case against the accused before a judge or judges, who were to arrive at a verdict.

The current emphasis upon the legal rights of the accused arose because of great abuses against citizens. For example, during the Middle Ages in France, sentencing decisions were made in secret and there were no restrictions on judicial verdicts. Further, the accused had no right to defense and often trials were secret. The secretiveness and arbitrariness of the administration of justice in France contributed to that country's revolution. Paralleling France during this same period, English justice was corrupt, severe, and unjust. Only "men of blood" (the nobility) could be trained in law, and the courts were subject to money and the monarch's power. The Star Chamber existed wherein the accused had no rights and would be interrogated or tortured. While the judicial procedures were arbitrary and corrupt, the penalties were swift and severe. It was during the eighteenth century that reformers paid increased attention to the unequal and cruel system of justice. Reacting against both the debased system of justice and harsh penalties, the classical school of criminology argued for equality in the administration of justice (Reid 1976).

Eye for an Eye

Before the emergence and widespread use of imprisonment, fines, probation, and parole as correctional measures, there existed a wide variety of ways to punish the offender. Most of these were corporal, or physical, forms of punishment. Many involved torture and death. In the Middle Ages and later in France quartering was a particularly vicious form of capital punishment. This type of punishment, meted out by a secret and corrupt judiciary, was inflicted until the French Revolution.

The English Code of the eighteenth century has often been called the "Bloody Code" since it was one of the harshest in history. More than two hundred offenses brought the death penalty, including cutting down trees in an avenue or park, setting fire to a cornfield, shooting a rabbit, or demolishing a turnpike gate (Reid 1976).

Other forms of corporal punishment once practiced in North America included mutilation and branding, the ducking stool, and the stocks and pillory. Mutilation might mean severing the hand of a thief, or the tongue of a person guilty of heresy or treasonous remarks. Branding might include a letter indicating the type of crime on the forehead of the offender. In ducking, a person was attached to a chair and submerged in water. Stocks were holes in a wooden frame where the victim was secured by the ankles, neck, and/or arms while onlookers were entitled to throw refuse at the culprit. The pillory was called the "stretch neck" and would often be driven through town with the offender attached to humiliate the person further. Probably the most popular form of corporal punishment was flogging. Such whipping has been, and still is, used by parents and schools, as well as by public officials dealing with criminals. Flogging has only recently been eliminated from most penal codes in the United States and Canada, although some parents and school officials still resort to it.

Besides inflicting corporal punishment, many countries have forced the offender to leave the society through exile, banishment, and transportation. Many European societies developed outlaw communities made up of persons banished from their homes and forced into exile. Until the sixteenth century, offenders would often be cast out of the society to work on galleys as slaves. With the introduction of sails, rowing slaves were no longer needed and deportation became popular. England deported many criminals to its colonies. By 1775, approximately 2,000 convicts arrived yearly in the American colonies as indentured servants. Also, persons were transported to the Bermudas, England, New South Wales, Van Diemen's Land (Tasmania), and Australia. Legislation was passed in Canada in 1802 providing for banishment of people convicted of crime. One society's misfits sometimes became another society's establishment. As the *Colonial Times* of Australia reported on April 7, 1840; "We learn that the Canadian political convicts are men of good sense and good conduct, and are anything but in their proper position in gangs on public roads" (Edmison 1976, p. 353).

After the American Revolution, England sent about 100,000 convicts to Australia. Although deportation was good business for shipowners and colonists who needed labor, the conditions surrounding it were as abhorrent as on African slave ships, and intensified the reformist efforts of humanitarians. Deportation continues to be used by the United States and Canada for "undesirable aliens." As the number of new territories to populate with deported criminals dwindled and as colonizers no longer needed such labor, imprisonment with hard labor became an alternative.

INSTITUTIONALIZATION

The State has two major agents of social control, the military and the police. As previously noted, prior to the emergence of the professional police force, the military and constabulary enforced the laws. In 1829, the London police force was created, providing the basic model of policing for contemporary North American society.

With the spread of urbanization and industrialization and the increasing class inequality, it was becoming more difficult to rely on the constabulary system of enforcement. The disparities in income, wealth, and living conditions were becoming more visible and resentment sharpened toward the military and constabulary based upon their attachment to the propertied and wealthy class. Furthermore, social and political protest, in the form of "illuminations," was increasing. In these demonstrations, citizens would march in the streets and verbally attack policies or practices of the government or others in power. Citizens who were for the marchers' position would place light in the window (illumination) in support. If the windows remained dark, the house was subject to stoning. This and other forms of protest reflected an upsurge in the ideology of democracy and social justice. It was difficult to use the military to quell such disturbances because of mobilization and training problems, but most significantly, such force merely increased resistance to the government. Needless to say, the constabulary lacked the ability and legitimacy to control such situations. Thus, the professional police force arose to provide order. The question remains: order for whom?

Why Police?

The creation of the professional police force served a number of important functions:

1. It relieved the propertied classes of the task of controlling "riots" (political protests);

2. Ordinary citizens no longer had to perform basic police duties;

3. The military did not have to be used for policing;

4. It insulated the rich from the popular violence in the streets;

5. It made the police rather than those in power the focus of animosity and attack; and,

6. It separated constitutional authority from social and economic dominance (Silver 1967).

The final point is particularly important, for the more legitimacy given to the law and its agents, the less likely that there will be collective action against such authority. The professional police came to be viewed (falsely, we believe) as apolitical, neutral enforcers of the law, rather than as manifest representatives of the propertied and wealthy.

Essentially the same process of professionalization occurred in the United States. Increasing economic inequality and class stratification in urban areas, combined with riots, brought about the emergence of professional police in the United States (Parks 1970). New York City adopted the London plan in 1844 and subsequently other major urban centers created police forces so that by the early 1900s most cities had professional controllers.

> The paramilitary form of early police bureaucracy was a response not only, or even primarily, to crime per se, but to the possibility of riotous disorder. Not crime and danger, but the "criminal" and "dangerous classes" as part of the urban social structure led to the formation of uniformed and military organized police. Such organizations intervened between the propertied elites and the propertyless masses who were regarded as politically dangerous as a class (Bordua and Reiss 1967, p. 276).

Today in the United States there exist police agents at the federal, state, county (sheriffs), and city levels, plus thousands of private police. Also, law enforcement leaders (such as sheriffs or state attorneys general) may be elected by citizens at the local or state level.

In Canada, policing is basically carried out by three police forces: federal (Royal Canadian Mounted Police), provincial, and municipal. The municipal forces include those of cities, towns, counties, villages, and townships, and are the largest policing body in Canada. The first professional force began in 1833 in Quebec City, with other major cities following suit. Only the provinces of Ontario and Quebec operate their own police forces, while the other eight provinces use the Royal Canadian Mounted Police (RCMP). Thus, the federal police in Canada provide much of the day-to-day control in small towns and rural areas of the country, while this type of policing is carried out largely by county and state forces in the United States. The RCMP was formed in 1873 to police the Northwest Territories. Its major functions included controlling the Indian population and aiding the Canadian Pacific Railway in its expansion together with the subsequent settlers who moved into the area (Brown and Brown 1972). Canada, like England, emphasizes an appointed professional civil service approach toward the selection and retention of law enforcement leaders, rather than the local, popularly elected approach evident in the United States.

The police institution became an important factor in the maintenance of colonial rule, along with the military. For example, the Texas Rangers gained their notoriety through the control of Mexican-Americans in that state, while the RCMP is known for its control of the Native American population. The legacy of colonialism in North American policing today is found in the policing of the reserve, reservation, ghetto, and barrio, where an often hostile population views the police as an internal, domestic colonizer. As the black writer James Baldwin notes:

> The only way to police a ghetto is to be oppressive. None of the police commissioners' men, even with the best will in the world, have any way of understanding the lives led by the people; they swagger about in twos and threes patrolling. Their very presence is an insult, and it would be, even if they spent their entire day feeding gumdrops to children. They represent the force of the white world, and that world's criminal profit and ease, to keep the black man corralled up here, in his place (1962, p. 65).

The legacy of colonialism is to be found in other countries as well. For example, former British colonies in Africa and Asia still have problems with regard to legitimacy for the law and its agents as social change continues. As occurred under British domination, the police are used to suppress political dissent and quell protest.

> At present police do not contribute adequately to the national development of countries previously under colonial rule, largely because they have been greatly affected, and to some extent handicapped, by the ideologies and police practices of the colonial administrations (Clinard and Abbott 1973, p. 216).

The Basis of Justice

Justice in the colonies in North America came to be based upon common law practices in England. Among these were the right to be brought swiftly to a magistrate to hear the charges against you, to be able to speak on your own behalf, a privilege against self-incrimination, and the right to trial by a judge and/or jury. The English system emphasized national uniformity and control over the administration of justice, with prosecutors being civil servants representing the Crown. After the American Revolution, the new country established certain procedures in its Constitution reflecting its concern about government power. These include the Fifth Amendment protection against unreasonable searches and seizures, and the Sixth Amendment right to a speedy and public trial by an impartial jury. Further, the accused must be notified of the charges; allowed to confront witnesses and call his or her own; extended the right to counsel; and protected by the Eighth Amendment prohibition of excessive bail, excessive fines, and cruel and unusual punishment (Newman 1975).

Jurisdiction emphasizes localism and particularism, with the United States having a dual court system (state and federal). Since most substantive criminal law is contained in state statutes, most criminal cases (85 to 90 percent) are tried in state courts. Basically, lower courts deal with less serious crimes (misdemeanors) while felony cases are heard in higher trial courts (Reid 1976, pp. 424–40). Federal crimes are prosecuted in federal courts, consisting of United States district courts for initial trial, United States appellate courts for appeals, and the United States Supreme Court, which has judicial review over state decisions as well as federal ones. Due in large part to its revolutionary past and suspicion of government power and authority, the United States has established more extensive procedural norms governing police action and court proceedings than Canada. For example, the right to be informed of one's right to remain silent as well as the right to counsel is not present in the Canadian version of due process (Tepperman 1977, p. 47). Exclusionary rules (by which evidence obtained through improper police procedures is ruled inadmissible) operate in the United States but not in Canada.

Let's Make a Deal

Under corporate ideology, social relationships tend to be contractual in nature. That is, they are often the subject of bargaining or negotiation. This is clearly seen in the Criminal Justice System. Generally, procedural rights are much more elaborate in the United States than in Canada. However, in both countries the great majority of persons (nearly 90 percent) convicted of crimes plead guilty and do not invoke such norms.

The following is typical of the process when a defendant appears before the judge:

> Judge: You want to plead guilty to _____ .
> Defendant: Yes, Sir.
> Judge: Your plea of guilty is free and voluntary?
> Defendant: Yes, Sir.
> Judge: No one has promised you anything?
> Defendant: Yes.
> Judge: No one has induced you to plead guilty?
> Defendant: No.
> Judge: You're pleading guilty because you are guilty?
> Defendant: Yes.
> Judge: I'll accept your plea of guilty to _____ and refer it to the probation department for a report and sentencing.
>
> (Newman 1966, p. 83)

The emphasis upon the free and voluntary nature of the guilty plea arises from the fact that historically, and contemporarily, persons have been physically and psychologically coerced to confess to crimes they did not commit. While much of the physical coercion has been reduced, psychological coercion still is found in the plea bargaining process.

Plea bargaining is a compromise worked out between the prosecutor and defendant (or defendant's counsel). It is an exchange between the two where each party supposedly receives something from the other for mutual cooperation. However, it should be remembered that the accused has only one thing to trade away—a plea of innocent to the charge. Therefore, to bargain one must plead guilty to obtain a reduction in the number of charges, a reduction in the status of the offense (lesser charge), or sentence leniency. The prosecutor, and more generally the court system, benefit by going through cases swiftly and in the most efficient manner, thus eliminating the cost and time of a trial. This system of exchange emerged in England in the seventeenth and eighteenth centuries, when prosecutors were given much discretion in charging because most felony charges carried the death penalty. This allowed them to reduce the charge so that the defendant would not be executed. While rights of the accused have since been institutionalized in common law and in statute, the guilty plea remains as the basis for processing of criminals. By pleading guilty, the nature of the investigation, extent of evidence, and other factors relevant in a trial are not addressed. Hence, the process of plea bargaining has become a significant institutionalized practice for the judicial system.

Lock 'Em Up

In the middle of the sixteenth century imprisonment in houses of correction arose in England. By a parliamentary act of 1576, each county was to have such a house for "vagabonds, lewd and idle," and other criminals. Emphasis was upon hard work as a form of rehabilitation and a source of cheap labor (Sutherland and Cressey 1974).

Confinement appeared with the rise of mercantilism and the weakening of the feudal economy. As a surplus population of agricultural workers could no longer be supported on the feudal estate, many people were uprooted. Given the emerging industrial order's need for labor, landowners were in an increasingly disadvantageous position to keep laborers on the estate. Thus, vagrancy laws arose to control the poor. Workers who flocked to the cities were subject to arrest if they had no job. Such laws and confinement were in the interests of landowners. Idleness and poverty were viewed as immoral and criminal; therefore, poorhouses and jails were established to put the jobless poor to work (Chambliss 1964).

By the end of the seventeenth century most persons confined were laboring as punishment and to maintain the penal institution, under the ideology of work as a moral imperative. During the eighteenth century prison labor was largely repressive and nonproductive, an attempt to deter the "dangerous classes." With the French Revolution and increasing agitation by the masses, the number of capital offenses was increased and imprisonment with hard labor arose. All of these were part of the effort to keep the poor in their place. By the end of the eighteenth century, reformers began to demand more humanitarian sentencing and punishment.

In England, the United States, and Canada there was growing opposition to capital punishment and other forms of corporal punishment in the eighteenth and nineteenth centuries. Partly as an alternative, jails, which initially were used to detain persons awaiting trials, became places of confinement as a form of punishment. Subsequently, penitentiaries and reformatories arose to provide places for the convicted offender (Sutherland and Cressey 1974). They were also supposed to provide for the rehabilitation of the offender through hard work, which contributed in turn to state and private coffers.

Pennsylvania and Auburn Systems

Jails were the first form of imprisonment in North America and were often characterized in negative ways. For example, the following is a description of the Walnut Street Jail in Philadelphia at the end of the American Revolutionary War:

> It is represented as a scene of promiscuous and unrestricted intercourse, and universal riot and debauchery. There was no labor, no separation of the accused but yet untried, nor even of those confined for debt only, from convicts sentenced for the foulest crimes, no separation of color, age or sex, by day or night; the prisoners lying promiscuously on the floor most of them without anything like bed or bedding. As soon as the sexes were placed in different wings, which was the first reform made in the prison, of thirty or forty women then confined there, all but four or five immediately left it, it having been a common practice, it is said, for women to cause themselves to be arrested for fictitious debts, that they might share in the orgies of the place. Intoxicating liquors abounded, and indeed were freely sold at a bar kept by one of the officers of the prison. Intercourse between the convicts and persons without was hardly restricted. Prisoners tried and acquitted were still detained till they should pay jail fees to the keeper, and the custom of garnish was established and unquestioned, that is, the custom of stripping every newcomer of his outer clothing, to be sold for liquor, unless redeemed by the payment of a sum of money to be applied to the

459

same object. It need hardly be added, there was no attempt to give any kind of instruction, and no religious service whatsoever (Gray 1848, pp. 15 16).

Under the ideology of rehabilitation, larger and more secure institutions (that is, state prisons) arose, beginning in New York in 1796. Emphasis was upon "labor, silence and penitence." For example, Philadelphia Quakers became involved in prison reform initially through their concern with the Walnut Street Jail. The Quakers developed the penitentiary in Pennsylvania based upon the assumption that imprisonment was a severe enough punishment and rehabilitation should be the aim of the institution. The penitentiary emphasized solitary confinement to eliminate the negative effects of association with other types of criminals and to force criminals to reflect on their crimes and thus be reformed. A select number of specific persons were allowed to visit the inmate to facilitate the person's efforts to change.

After attempting to follow the Pennsylvania system in its prisons, New York built Auburn Penitentiary in 1816. It divided prisoners into three classes, with the oldest and most heinous offenders kept in solitary confinement, and the others allowed to mix. The emphasis was on hard work and discipline. These two systems, Pennsylvania and Auburn, became the models for others. European visitors favored the Pennsylvania system, while other American states favored the Auburn system. The Auburn system had the advantages of economy, since congregated confinement is less costly than solitary confinement and permited more efficient utilization of convict labor.

Reformation of the inmate was a major argument by proponents of the prison. Early supporters of the penitentiary saw it as "a grand theatre, for the trial of all new plans in hygiene and education, in physical and moral reform" (Rothman 1971, p. 85). The Reverend James B. Finely, chaplain at the Ohio Penitentiary, stated in his memoirs in 1851,

> Could we all be put on prison fare, for the space of two or three generations, the world would ultimately be the better for it. Indeed, should society change places with the prisoners so far as habits are concerned, taking to itself the regularity, the temperance, and sobriety of a good prison, the goals of peace, right and Christianity would be advanced. As it is, taking this world and the next together, the prisoner has the advantage (Rothman 1971, pp. 84–85).

Established in Kingston in 1835, the Kingston Penitentiary is the oldest in Canada and its annual report for 1856 reflects the rehabilitative goals. The padre reported the following responses to questions required of discharged inmates, "Do you go out a better or worse man?"

Go out improved morally	55
Go out much better	7

Better in	1
Inclined for the better	1
Not much better	1
Not better	1
Neither better nor worse	2
About the same	1
Better in a great many ways	1
Not any worse	1
Cannot say whether improved	3
Is not better	1
Got out worse	2
No definite answers	5

Those responses prompted the padre to conclude, "that the discharged convicts, generally, leave prison morally benefitted" (Edmison 1976, p. 360). In the eyes of reformers, the great correctional fortresses had become cathedrals.

A Place for Everyone
and Everyone in Their Place

Since the development of jails, specialized facilities have emerged to deal with offenders according to characteristics such as sex, age, mental capability, physical condition, seriousness of the crime, and unit of jurisdiction. The desire to "reform" criminals was particularly influential in bringing about juvenile institutions. The mixing of hardened felons with first offenders was viewed as contributing to youthful degeneration. Therefore, segregation in jails and prisons gave rise to institutions for juvenile delinquents. New York City opened the first juvenile institution in 1825, and today there are hundreds of "reformatories" in North America (Sutherland and Cressey 1974). Inmates of such institutions are defined by "child-savers" old and new as "salvageable" offenders. Today there are institutions for juveniles, women, men, youthful offenders, the criminally insane, the physically handicapped, and sex offenders. Such facilities may be operated at the federal, state, or local level. Generally, in the United States persons convicted of state offenses are committed to state institutions, while if convicted of federal offenses one goes to a federal institution. Of course, it depends on the seriousness of the offense, with those guilty of more serious crimes going to state prisons rather than local jails. In Canada, those sentenced to two years or more are sent to federal penitentiaries, while a sentence of less than two years earns a stay in provincial jails. In both countries there are gradations of facilities from

461

relatively open institutions with minimum security, to very closed and heavily guarded maximum security fortresses. The varying degrees of specialization and division of labor in correctional institutions are related to the purposes of rehabilitation, deterrence, incapacitation, and punishment. The extent to which they fulfill these stated goals will be addressed in the next section.

MAINTENANCE

In the selection at the beginning of this chapter, Jobson emphasizes that the criminal justice system has largely failed in its responsibility to prevent crime, deter and correct criminals, and contribute to the domestic tranquility. While unsuccessful in achieving its official objectives, the criminal justice system has realized other less apparent ends.

The criminal justice system can be viewed as a vast industry that employs millions and costs billions in North America. In the fiscal year 1975, the United States expended more than $18 billion for criminal justice activities. In Figure 8–1, we find that these funds are expended principally at the local level, followed by state and federal government appropriations for police, the courts, corrections, and other services. Increases in criminal justice expenditures at the federal level have been dramatic during the 1970s, as Figure 8–2 vividly portrays. Furthermore, the criminal justice industry employs over one million persons in various activities at the local, state, and federal levels. Millions of persons come in contact with and are processed through the various components of the criminal justice system.

In Canada, federal expenditures for the criminal justice system in fiscal 1975/1976 were over $2 billion a year and were projected to more than double in constant dollar expenditures by 1986. Furthermore, as in the United States, the largest proportion of the expenditure is for the police. Policing and corrections expenditures as a proportion of the whole have increased from 1880 to 1974, while the proportion spent on the courts has decreased over this period (Ministry of the Solicitor General 1976, pp. 157–67).

Although the continuation of the crime control industry is clearly in the interest of those who plan, direct, and execute its mission, its structural nature must be understood. For the crime control industry represents more than the perpetuation of a massive bureaucracy; in a class-divided society, it dispenses class-based "justice."

When one speaks about protecting the rights of the accused, one invokes the individual model of justice that dominates Western law; that is, protecting the individual from abuse by the State and its agents. However,

**Figure 8–1. Expenditure for Criminal Justice Activities,
by Level of Government and Type of Activity,
United States, Fiscal Year 1975.**

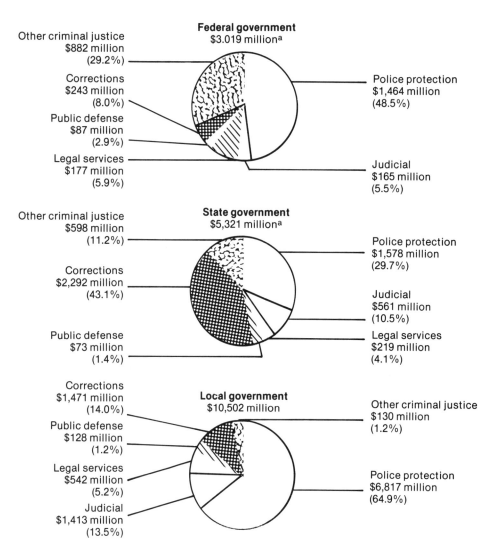

Other criminal justice
$882 million
(29.2%)

Corrections
$243 million
(8.0%)

Public defense
$87 million
(2.9%)

Legal services
$177 million
(5.9%)

Federal government
$3.019 million[a]

Police protection
$1,464 million
(48.5%)

Judicial
$165 million
(5.5%)

Other criminal justice
$598 million
(11.2%)

Corrections
$2,292 million
(43.1%)

Public defense
$73 million
(1.4%)

State government
$5,321 million[a]

Police protection
$1,578 million
(29.7%)

Judicial
$561 million
(10.5%)

Legal services
$219 million
(4.1%)

Corrections
$1,471 million
(14.0%)

Public defense
$128 million
(1.2%)

Legal services
$542 million
(5.2%)

Judicial
$1,413 million
(13.5%)

Local government
$10,502 million

Other criminal justice
$130 million
(1.2%)

Police protection
$6,817 million
(64.9%)

[a] Because of rounding, detail may not add to total.

Source: U.S. Department of Justice, Law Enforcement Assistance Administration and U.S. Bureau of the Census, *Expenditure and Employment Data for the Criminal Justice System 1975* (Washington, D.C.: U.S. Government Printing Office, 1977), p. 5, Fig. 3; p. 7, Fig. 5; p. 9, Fig. 7.

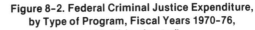

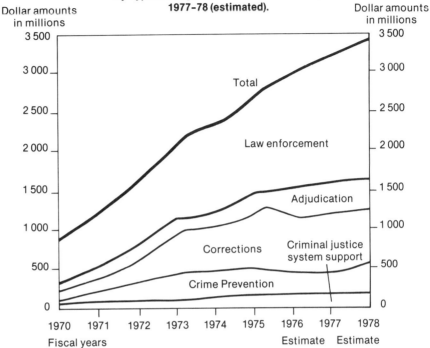

Figure 8-2. Federal Criminal Justice Expenditure, by Type of Program, Fiscal Years 1970–76, 1977–78 (estimated).

Source: Executive Office of the President, Office of Management and Budget, *Special Analyses, Budget of the United States Government Fiscal Year 1978* (Washington, D.C.: U.S. Government Printing Office, 1977), p. 255.

one can talk also about group justice in terms of social class, race, age, and the like. It becomes evident by looking at statistics for the criminal justice system that the system processes a disproportionately large percentage of poor persons, nonwhites, and youth, particularly for common law crimes. Given the sacred standing of property in corporate society, the large proportion of crimes deal with property and its theft. Given the unequal distribution of goods in corporate society, the have–nots are more likely to be nonwhite, young, unemployed, or marginally employed at low wages. Thus, the excessive representation of these latter groups in prisons is a product of class differences in access to wealth. While justice, or some approximation of it, is available to persons with money, those without it are more likely to meet injustice. This can be seen by looking at two models of law enforcement and the administration of justice, and how they are applied.

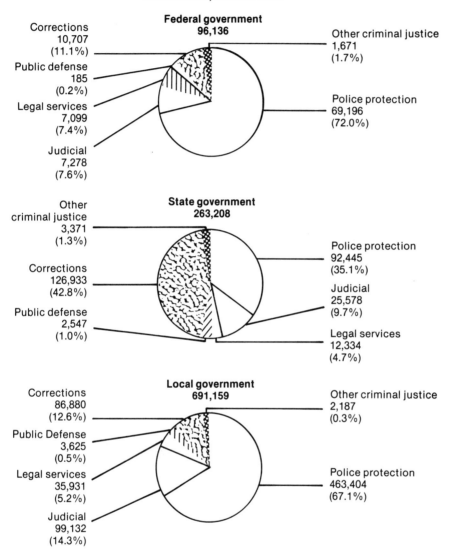

Figure 8–3. Full-time Equivalent Employment in Criminal Justice Activities, by Level of Government and Type of Activity, United States, October 1975.

Federal government
96,136

Corrections
10,707
(11.1%)

Public defense
185
(0.2%)

Legal services
7,099
(7.4%)

Judicial
7,278
(7.6%)

Other criminal justice
1,671
(1.7%)

Police protection
69,196
(72.0%)

State government
263,208

Other
criminal justice
3,371
(1.3%)

Corrections
126,933
(42.8%)

Public defense
2,547
(1.0%)

Police protection
92,445
(35.1%)

Judicial
25,578
(9.7%)

Legal services
12,334
(4.7%)

Local government
691,159

Corrections
86,880
(12.6%)

Public Defense
3,625
(0.5%)

Legal services
35,931
(5.2%)

Judicial
99,132
(14.3%)

Other criminal justice
2,187
(0.3%)

Police protection
463,404
(67.1%)

Source: U.S. Department of Justice, Law Enforcement Assistance Administration and U.S. Bureau of the Census, *Expenditure and Employment Data for the Criminal Justice System 1975* (Washington, D.C.: U.S. Government Printing Office, 1977), p. 5, Figure 4; p. 7, Figure 6; p. 9, Figure 8.

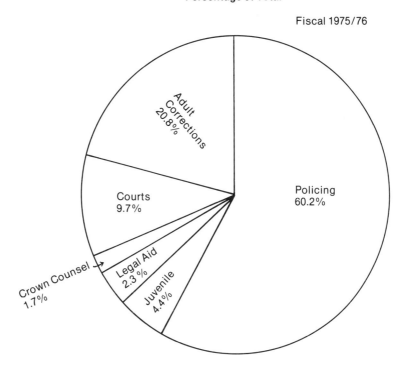

Figure 8–4. Justice Expenditures in Canada
Percentage of Total

Fiscal 1975/76

Policing 60.2%

Adult Corrections 20.8%

Courts 9.7%

Crown Counsel 1.7%

Legal Aid 2.3%

Juvenile 4.4%

Crime Control and Due Process Models

Law enforcement agencies are bureaucratic organizations that, like other bureaucratic organizations, tend to substitute for the official goals and norms of the organization, policies, and activities that maximize rewards and minimize strain for the organization.

This goals substitution is made possible by

1. An absence of motivation to resist pressure toward such goal substitution;

2. The pervasiveness of discretion among law enforcement officials; and

3. The relative absence of effective sanctions to adhere to formal organizational rules.

The extent to which such goal substitution exists depends in part upon its visibility and who observes it. Competing goals and demands are found in the crime control and due process models of the criminal process.

The crime control model emphasizes the repression of criminal activity as its highest priority. Within this approach there is an attempt to sanction as much criminal behavior as possible, including the searching out of crime through such means as patrolling, and undercover agents. Accused persons are assumed to be guilty and speedy handling of cases is deemed necessary. On the other hand, the due process model emphasizes the protection of the citizen from the power of the State through various procedural safeguards. The suspect is assumed innocent until proven guilty by the court. While protection of the rights of the individual are formally required of law enforcement personnel, the informal norm is to process as many persons as possible in order to deter and suppress crime (Chambliss and Seidman 1971, pp. 272–74).

The crime control model is the major approach of most law enforcement agencies, although both models will be used depending on the nature of the offense and offender. Due in part to the real and potential power of the middle- and upper-class citizen, plus the police's identification with those classes, the due process model will more likely be used with the more affluent. For obvious reasons, the demeanor of the police officer becomes important in maintaining his or her legitimacy among those who have potential power. Also, the due process model will more likely prevail in those "significant cases" in which the evidence is substantial and the need for conviction is greatest. On the other hand, in lesser offenses such as drunkenness and petty theft that will more likely involve a person of less potential power, the crime control model will probably be used (Reasons 1974, pp. 263–64). Therefore, persons who have less real or potential power such as the poor, nonwhite, and youth will more likely be subject to the crime control model. Furthermore, since they are less likely to have legal representation and more likely to plead guilty, the practices of the police in dealing with these groups will not ordinarily be subject to judicial review.

Police Violence

As one might expect, most instances of police violence involve the use of the crime control approach. The underlying assumption is that you have to deal with crime in any way possible, including excessive force. From this perspective the use or threat of violence may be felt to be a deterrent without formally charging a person with an offense. Most cases of police brutality and excessive force are against the young, poor, and nonwhite who are not as likely to pursue a grievance (Reiss 1968). From both an organizational and individual standpoint this is understandable, although not acceptable. The police are caught in the middle between the demands of the middle and upper class for protection of property and the demands of the poor for equality of distribution of property.

The police are thus put squarely in the middle. The control of the disinherited, who are regarded as potentially dangerous, from the perspective of the police can be most efficiently accomplished through the arbitrary use of force and coercion. But these methods, when applied to the privileged, bring forth public criticism and censure. The simple and most often practiced solution is to adopt a dual standard. Crime-control practices prevail in dealing with the poor, and due process is observed in dealing with the privileged (Chambliss and Seidman 1971, p. 359).

Undoubtedly significant in the use of the double standard is the fact that "crime in the streets" such as robberies, muggings, and assaults are of top priority to community leaders and thus, pressure is placed upon the police organization to produce arrests and suppression of such crimes. Since such crimes are disproportionately committed by the poor, nonwhite, and youth, they are subject to the crime-control model. However, the embezzler, income tax cheater, antitrust violator, or manufacturer of unsafe cars is treated carefully according to the due process model.

The fact that these differing approaches are applied to different types of people committing certain types of crimes in certain areas of town explains why most citizens can honestly say they have no experience with police violence. However, many of the youth, poor, and nonwhites will just as honestly say that they have experienced police brutality. If you are raised in a middle-class neighborhood and continue to live your life in suburbia, it is likely you will not view police violence. Those who grow up and live in poorer, minority areas of towns are more likely to have such experiences. There would most likely be a surge of protest if the surveillance and interrogations used in "those areas" were used in suburbia.

Crime Control Strikes the Middle Class   In recent years a number of middle-class people have come to experience the crime-control model of law enforcement. Many middle-class citizens participated in the United States Civil Rights Movement activities in the 1950s and 1960s and gained a new understanding of police power (Mouledous 1967). The fact that the police were often supporting the racist standards of segregation was evident in their use of excessive force to control demonstrations. Also, many middle-class youth were active in the antiwar movement in the United States and Canada during the 1960s and early 1970s. Many of these protests and demonstrations found police or other agents of the state using excessive force, leading to homicides on the campus of Kent State, Greensborough State, and Southern University (Stone 1970). An official United States government report concluded that the excessive use of force by police against antiwar demonstrators at the 1968 National Democratic Convention was a "police riot" in which officers took off their badges and randomly brutalized hundreds of demonstrators (Walker 1968). Other evidence confirms that local officers or informants became agent provocateurs who advocated and participated in violence to discredit the protestors (Karmen 1974). Finally, many middle-class youth joined the counter-culture in the 1960s and their long hair and use of illicit drugs often brought them harassment and assaults from the police. Revelations of federal, state, and local police violence, illegalities, and general surveillance of these groups are continuing in the late 1970s in the United States. In Canada, the federal police (Royal Canadian Mounted Police) have committed a number of illegal acts such as mail opening, breaking and entering, kidnapping, and destruction of property, plus the surveillance of "subversive" groups (those advocating radical change). Many of these activities were aimed at the struggle of French-speaking Quebec to gain power in Canada (Lewis 1979).

Crime Control: A Political Weapon The result of the above experiences and revelations is that many middle-class youth have gained a different view of the function of the police. Of course the poor, nonwhite, and dispossessed, particularly their youth, knew such behavior before it affected kids from the suburbs. Further, as minority groups began collectively to struggle for more power and control, they constantly were confronted with the State's front-line troops—the police. When the police, often with the help of the military, have to quell and/or control social and political protests, their roots in the strife of nineteenth century London again are evident. The manifest political nature of crime control becomes apparent when, as frequently happens, police become the shock troops protecting the values, property, and peaceful existence of the privileged in society (Marx 1970, pp. 19–57).

An extensive analysis of police killings of civilians in the United States found the rate for blacks to be thirteen times that for whites from 1950 to 1968. Over half (57 percent) of the citizens killed by police in the United States were members of national minorities (blacks, Chicanos, Native Americans, and Asians) (Harring 1977). James Q. Wilson (1975) notes that 5 percent of all blacks (over a million people) report themselves unjustifiably beaten by the police at least once. The national report on the urban riots in 1967 in the United States pointed out that ghetto dwellers wanted *both* better protection by the police *and* better protection from police abuse and violence (Report of the National Advisory Commission 1968).

The three-day riot in Miami in May 1980 was sparked by the police killing of a 33-year old black insurance salesman. Underlying the rage which brought 16 dead and 400 injured were long-standing grievances against the police. When four policemen were acquitted of all charges connected with the beating death of Arthur McDuffie, the frustration broke loose ("The McDuffie Case," *Newsweek* June 2, 1980, p. 39). In a nationwide telephone survey of black adults conducted May 21, 1980, *Newsweek* obtained the following responses concerning justice for blacks in America ("The Mood of Ghetto America," 1980, p. 33).

Do you think there is any police brutality where you live?

Yes, a great deal	10%
Yes, a fair amount	16%
Yes, only a little	18%
No	50%
Don't know	6%

Do you think blacks and whites usually receive equal justice in the courts in the area where you live?

Yes	31%
No	54%
Don't know	15%

Both the police and the courts have a long way to go according to black Americans.

Maintaining Corporate Order:

Symbolic Enforcement and Incestuous Relationships

Though police power is often viewed in the context of conventional crime, such a focus does little to help us understand the relationship between the government and corporation illegality. We believe history confirms that the police power of the State only lightly addresses suite crime.

Commencing with the Sherman Antitrust Act of 1890 and followed by the Clayton and Federal Trade Commission acts of 1914, the government of the United States began an essentially *symbolic* venture of corporate regulation.[2] By symbolic we mean that the State is less an adversary and more an instrument of corporate interests. As evident from the materials on interlocks presented in Chapter Two, those prominent in the corporation ranks of executives are well represented in the highest echelons of government. Still, corporate spokespersons commonly address the evils of governmental regulation. The reasons for this are not altogether clear. It may be that members of the corporate elite, who heavily influence state affairs, fear the potential that a still-unrealized representative democracy has for meaningful public control. Also, it must be acknowledged that corporate influence on the State, while immense, is not total. Thus state laws and regulations can be considered at least an annoyance for those who manage economic empires. Finally, one of the consequences

[2] For a parallel view of Canadian history, see Chapter Six for a discussion of Anticombine legislation in Canada.

of "regulation rhetoric" is to give at least the appearance that government is supporting the interests of the "little person." Whatever the reasons behind it, a specific ideology exists that seeks to deny the criminal nature of corporate violations of the law. (The authors are indebted to Silk and Vogel, 1976, for their study of views expressed by leading executives in confidential interviews.) This ideology is as follows.

Not Really Crime

1. "Caveat emptor": The hallmark belief of that corporate ideology that denies the necessity of laws and regulations. In short, this tenet holds that the consumer must be expected to take responsibility for his or her own choices in the marketplace. The truly rugged consumer does not need the government to protect his or her personal interests.

2. "Government regulations mean an end to free enterprise": Corporations must be free to conduct business without interference, responsible only to the demands of the marketplace and the standards set by competitors. (Marketplace demand is manipulated by advertising, while monopolies and oligopolies leave little room for competition. See Chapter Three, Inequality.)

3. "Government regulation as criminal motive": The corporate belief that regulations cut into profits and are therefore violated with justification.

4. "We didn't mean to do it": If in fact criminal, the corporate action represented a simple mistake, with no criminal intent.

5. "And besides, the regulated behavior is unimportant": The belief that occupational health, ecological safeguards, shoddy or dangerous merchandise, and so forth require no legal intervention.

6. "Spreading the grief": The corporate belief that although cases affecting many consumers may involve a great deal of money, single consumers are not hurt very much.

7. "Anyway, it didn't work": If a violation of the law produces no increase in profits, then the violation is irrelevant.

8. "Everybody does it": One's competitors do it (fix prices, rig bids, bribe foreign officials, ignore or minimize compliance with safety regulations, and so on), so such behavior is necessary to survive in the marketplace.

9. "We don't do that anymore": The final belief identified here is that of corporate reform. Frequently associated with ceremonial change at the top, such "rehabilitation" provides assurances that the practices of the past are no longer tolerated. (Our argument, developed throughout Chapters Four, Five, and Six, is that the corporate imperatives of growth and profit produce socially and environmentally injurious practices. While it is not our intention to argue that certain illegal practices cannot be halted, we do contend that all practices, criminal or not, that yield important growth and profitability will persist despite a change in leadership. This is the only argument permitted by a structural analysis.[3])

Ideology as Reality: Law Enforcement and the Corporate World

In sum, the ideology portrayed above contends that corporate crime is not really crime, that corporate offenses are not as serious as those of the street variety. We have challenged elsewhere the legitimacy of this argument. However, it is fair to state that the weak enforcement of laws and regulations centering on corporate crime is quite consistent with the position that the practices in question are not as serious as traditional offenses.

Regulatory agencies, delegated authority by Congress, seek to control corporate crime in the United States. Usually directed by a small commission, whose members are appointed by the president, each agency has rule-making powers that it attempts to enforce in specific economic areas. Examples of regulatory commissions include the Interstate Commerce Commission (ICC), the Federal Trade Commission (FTC), and the Securities and Exchange Commission (SEC). The Environmental Protection Agency (EPA), among newer agencies, is not headed by a commission (U.S. Department of Justice 1979, p. 29).

Enforcement of Regulations   The enforcement divisions of the specific regulatory agencies are charged with investigating the violations that fall within their respective agency's jurisdiction. After completing their investigation, enforcement officials present a report of their findings to the commission or chief administrator, who initiates one or more of three courses of action: administrative action, criminal referral, and/or civil prosecution (Bequai 1978). Administrative action means that an agency "in-house" hearing is conducted in which the agency's attorneys prosecute

[3] For a clear discussion of "structural transgressions," see Chapter Five, Environmental Contradictions.

the case while the corporation is represented by its own counsel. An agency hearing examiner sits in judgment. Any decision can be appealed to the commission for that agency or to the United States Court of Appeals. If an agency chooses the path of criminal referral, a "criminal referral memorandum" is sent to the Department of Justice, where attorneys make a decision as to prosecution. Agencies are also free to conduct a civil prosecution employing their own attorneys. However, criminal referrals and civil prosecutions are rare. The most common resolution consists of an agreement known as a consent decree by which the corporation agrees to no further law violations, *without admitting guilt* (U.S. Department of Justice 1979, pp. 29–30). It is estimated that over 90 percent of all agency actions result in consent decrees (Bequai 1978, p. 143). Unlike the "plea bargaining" engaged in by traditional offenders, corporate offenders need not plead guilty in exchange for considerations. They must simply agree not to transgress in the future.

The penalties available to regulatory agencies include primarily fine, injunctions, and, in the case of criminal behavior on the part of individual executives, prison sentences. An injunction is a court order prohibiting or requiring a certain course of action. Fines vary widely from $10,000 for an Occupational Safety and Health Agency violation to $1 million for antitrust violations. Prison terms range from six months (OSHA violators), to three years (antitrust). We should hasten to add that even in those cases (antitrust) where monetary penalties seem high, we are dealing with an organization that may have billions of dollars in assets and yearly sales. One student of corporation crime compared the $437,500 fine levied against General Electric Corporation for antitrust violations in the 1960s with a parking ticket for many citizens (Geis 1973, p. 196). We should also remember that there is a broad gap between those penalties available to regulatory agencies and those actually imposed.

In a recent study conducted by Marshall Clinard and others (U.S. Department of Justice 1979, p. 141), 328 monetary penalties were levied against parent manufacturing corporations during 1975 and 1976. Some 293 of these punitive actions were against large corporations (annual sales of $1 billion and over), 22 involved medium-sized corporations (annual sales of more than $500 million but less than $1 billion). However, for the large corporations, the monetary penalty was less than $5,000 in some 84 percent of the cases. For medium-sized corporations, the corresponding percentage was about 68, and for small, almost 54. In other words, although large corporations received most of the monetary penalties, they were little more than a slap on the wrist in most instances. More severe financial penalties were meted out to smaller corporations. In 1975 and 1976, a total of only fifty-six executives were convicted of federal offenses. Of these, sixteen actually spent some time in jail and their sentences were often suspended after some part was served. "The average prison sentence for all those convicted, whether or not they went to prison and regardless of the offense, averaged 2.8 days." The study continues,

Problems of modest sentence following criminal conviction of corporate executives may lie with the statutes and the judges, but there are other difficulties in securing a prison sentence. *Businessmen may have sought legal advice as to how to circumvent the law even before they committed the offense, and this advice may be cited as evidence of good faith in avoiding any violation of the law* (Clinard 1979, p. 209; italics added).

Skilled corporate attorneys cite possible health problems, the absence of previous convictions, and the unlikely nature of recidivism to sympathetic judges. They are also able to introduce numerous precedents showing that corporate officers charged with a similar offense were not incarcerated. Corporate counsel will also succeed in restricting evidence to conceal other offenses. Finally, in a form of corporate plea bargaining, the Justice Department's legal staff may agree not to charge *individual* corporate officers with criminal offenses in return for other concessions that implicate the corporation as an *organization* (such as a heavy fine or agreeing to halt the practice in question) (U.S. Department of Justice 1979, p. 208–12).

One is forced to conclude that in the area of law enforcement centering on corporate crime, those with the gold make and break the rules, virtually with impunity.

ALTERNATIVE

Policing the Police

Given the real and potential use and abuse of violence by the police, how can this be controlled? Some alternatives call for the upgrading of personnel, community relations, and legal remedies.

A major contemporary effort to reduce tensions between the police on one side and youth and nonwhites on the other, while simultaneously enhancing the legitimacy of the state, has been police-community relations programs. Although some aspects of police-community relations programs have existed for quite some time, since the late 1960s there has been a proliferation of these activities (Kreps 1973). According to the United States President's Commission on Law Enforcement,

> Police-community relations have two essentially different aspects. First, the substantial majority of Americans respect its police force, support its actions, and look to it for protection. Second, a significant number of people, largely the poor or members of minority groups, fear and distrust the police (1967, p. 150).

Police-community relations programs may include police-community relations units, citizen advisory committees, and/or special programs that bring the police into continuing positive contact with the community. A national survey of police-community relations units in the United States found that while most of them were formed in response to increasing conflict with the poor and minorities, many of their programs dealt with the well-off and majority (Reasons and Wirth 1975). Although the various programs have differing degrees of success (Johnson and Gregory 1971) the extent to which the poor and nonwhite will be satisfied largely depends upon how their grievances concerning harassment and brutality are appeased.

Most police departments, like other organizations, would prefer to police themselves. Therefore, internal controls are usually found, with citizens' complaints being registered with and adjudicated by the department itself. However, this has been largely ineffective because those most likely to be abused (youth, poor, and nonwhites) are least likely to register a complaint. First of all, most persons don't know (1) that they can register a complaint, (2) how to do it, and (3) if it will make a difference. Those with the most distrust and antagonism for the police and least social and political power are not likely to go to the station to file with the police a complaint against members of the force (Chambliss and Seidman 1971, pp. 370–73). Therefore, a department may pride itself on the few official complaints it receives, while this may be irrelevant to the actual abuses occurring.

Weapons Against Police Abuse   There are four basic ways of legally combating police abuse of authority:

1. Criminal prosecutions;
2. Civil actions;
3. Injunctions and
4. Exclusionary rules. (Paulsen et al. 1970)

Increasingly, citizens are pursuing criminal prosecutions for police violence.

> Bulletins issued by the Department of Justice show that police officers have been indicted in every region of the United States for acting under the color of law, unlawfully shooting the victim, taking away his constitutional right not to be deprived of liberty without due process of law (Takagi 1974).

The major difficulties in pursuing criminal sanctions against lawless police are that police and prosecutors work together; the violence often occurs without other witnesses; those abused are often not given credibility as witnesses; and the courts generally give a wide latitude. Nonetheless, through such charges citizens are showing their increasing concern.

Although civil actions by citizens have been largely ineffectual, they appear to be on the rise. Injunctions prohibiting certain police practices are rare. However, exclusionary rules have been more readily applied. By exclusionary rules we mean the courts may find that police failed to follow legal procedures in enforcing the law. If the proper procedures are not followed in searches, seizures, interrogation, or other practices, the case may be thrown out of court. While this form of control has gained much public attention, with some arguing that it handcuffs the police, it does not appear to greatly affect most cases. This is because less than 10 percent of the cases reach trial, with 90 percent of the convictions on guilty pleas. Also, police are mainly concerned with clearing crimes by arrest, not necessarily convictions (Chambliss and Seidman 1971, pp. 376–79).

External Controls   Forms of external control of the police, other than legal action, include police commissioners, civilian review boards, and ombudsmen (Chambliss and Seidman 1971, pp. 379–91). Many cities, particularly in Canada (Grossman 1976), have a board of police commissioners appointed by the mayor to oversee the police. However, these bodies are largely ineffectual in addressing major issues, and tend to go along with the police professionals. Civilian review boards have existed in a number of United States cities. While the notion of an independent civilian review board is appealing to many, these bodies have failed for the most part because of a lack of power and resources and because of organized opposition. Given the power to impose punishment and publicize wrongdoings, such boards would likely have more effect upon law enforcement agencies and police behavior. The ombudsman is another potentially viable agent of social control if independent and possessing adequate procedural and investigative powers, plus the power of media access. Perhaps the only real solution is community control exerted through neighborhood participation in both policing the community and policing the police. Thus, blacks would police black communities, and elected officials in each neighborhood would control local policing (Waskow 1969). Through combining external control mechanisms with legal action, the police can be made more accountable to those they oversee. However, the realization of accountability requires a goal that remains of interest primarily to the powerless.

The Underside of Justice

Like the police, the judicial system operates on both a crime control and due process model. The due process model supposedly prevails in those few cases that reach trial by judge or jury, while the crime control model governs the over 90 percent of the convictions based upon pleas of guilty.

In the less than 5 percent of cases that reach criminal trial, the due process model is apparent as the prosecutor and defense battle it out in an effort to win their respective cases (Senna and Siegel 1978, pp. 283–309). Here the right to counsel, self-representation, speedy trial, to confront and cross-examine witnesses, and other rights are dramatically evident. The trial is the epitome of the ideals of justice. Righteousness is supposedly determined before one's peers and in the dispassionate setting of the court, with the defendant protected by legal safeguards from the power of the State. However, the guarantees of due process may be more apparent than real.

Hurry Them Along   Since over 90 percent of convictions are based on a plea of guilty, we should gain an understanding of what happens prior to the selection of cases that reach trial. A lawyer/sociologist has noted that while the image officially promoted is one of an adversary-combative type of system, the reality is that of a cooperative, consensual system largely based upon organizational needs (Blumberg 1967). While the official ideology emphasizes due process, the court reality emphasizes crime control assumptions of guilt and the need to process clients as quickly as possible. Hence, the overwhelming majority of convictions merely involve sentencing after a negotiated plea of guilty. The organization of the court defines the defense lawyer's role differently from that of the official ideology. Rather than being a person who will fight long and enduring battles, using every legal tactic to get justice for a client, the defense lawyer has greater ties and obligations to the court and its personnel than to the client, who, after all, is just passing through. According to Blumberg, all court personnel are agent mediators who help the accused redefine the situation so that it becomes compatible with a guilty plea. Emphasis is upon maximum "production"; therefore, bargaining is important to getting cases processed and closed. This is particularly true for clients with little money, because legal fees are high and those with fewer resources will get less time. Blumberg concluded that most defense lawyers act as double agents who want to limit the scope and duration of the case. The negotiated plea is economical and efficient timewise for the court as an organization; helps in the prosecutor's conviction statistics; gives the appearance of justice to the defendant since his lawyer did "make a deal"; keeps police activity beyond review; and does not necessitate police appearance at a trial.

However, bargain basement justice makes a mockery of the professed ideals of equal justice since those who cannot afford to spend the time and money to go to trial are largely the poor and powerless. It may "pay" the defendant to plead guilty even if he or she is not. The advice of an attorney to a client is telling: "Don't be a fool—if you buck us you will wait six months in jail for your trial. Now if you take a plea you'll get six months and at the end of that time you'll be a free man" (Dash 1951, p. 392).

Since the ability to make bail and obtain a good lawyer is class related, the impact upon the financially weak weighs most heavily. Therefore, bail on personal recognizance and public defender systems have emerged to provide legal band-aids for those unable to afford justice. The inability to make bail means one loses liberty, often a job, and family contact. Further, those denied bail are more likely to be convicted and receive longer sentences. In the United States in 1966 and in Canada in 1972, Bail Reform Acts generally allowed more accused to be released while awaiting court appearance because of the inability to make bail. In another abuse, the inability to make bail has been used as preventive detention during civil disorders venting social and political protests (Balbus 1973).

The public defender system arose after the Progressive Era as "a means of avoiding burdensome safeguards, protections, and loopholes utilized during the nineteenth century by an almost exclusively white population" (Barak 1975, p. 4). Basically, it helped the court be more efficient while giving the appearance of equal justice. If one has a choice between a public defender and a renowned criminal lawyer, there is not much choice. Obviously, public defenders are for those with no choice.[4]

Race has been an important factor both in the access to justice, and the nature of justice meted out. Until the mid-twentieth century, blacks, Chicanos, and Native Americans experienced legally sanctioned segregated justice (Reasons and Kuykendall 1972). There existed separate systems of justice for whites and nonwhites coupled with more severe sentences and penalties and continued oppression of these minorities.

While it appears that individual racism has somewhat diminished in recent years (at least as measured by public opinion polls), institutional racism still mars North American society. For example, there are institutional policies and practices of the legal system generally, and the courts, specifically, that burden nonwhites more heavily than whites. For example, cultural bias built into the legal system puts nonwhites at a disadvantage. The white middle- and upper-class nature of court personnel do not represent the culture of the poor nonwhite. Furthermore, a jury drawn from voter polls is likely to reflect the dominant culture rather than that of the minority group member. Also, institutionalized policies regarding bail and quality of counsel weight more heavily upon nonwhites, who are disproportionately poor. Likewise, the language and dialect of the courtroom are likely to be foreign for those from the ghetto, barrio, or reserve. These, among other factors, mean that minority group members are particularly disadvantaged in the administration of justice (Swett 1969).

Struggles for better justice for minority group members have included attempts to change the complexion of the jury and bar, change the rules concerning courtroom practices, and broaden the extent of community control and participation in the administration of justice. Real change is

[4] It has been the pleasure of the authors to work closely with practitioners of "poverty law." Their efforts are often heroic. However, as noted by Platt and Pollack (1974), the caseloads are enormous, as are the pressures to make a deal. Most, sooner or later, "burn out" and leave.

dependent upon increasing the power minority communities have over institutions in their neighborhoods.

Correcting Corrections

Today in North America, there are hundreds of thousands of persons serving time in jails and prisons. In a ranking of fifteen countries on the basis of their imprisonment rate per 100,000 population, the United States stood first and Canada sixth (Waller and Chan 1974). In both these countries, correctional institutions are largely populated with the poor, unskilled, and nonwhite. In the United States 51 percent of the incarcerated population in federal and state institutions are white, while nonwhites make up the remaining 49 percent (Reasons 1974, p. 5). The great majority of inmates are from the lower and working classes (Chiricos and Waldo 1975). In Canada, Native Americans and the members of the poor and working classes are also disproportionately found in prisons (Schmeiser 1974). From arrest to incarceration the population becomes progressively poorer and darker. Because the legal system largely views the offenses of the poor and nonwhite as more threatening, and the administration of justice is biased economically and culturally, correctional institutions represent a not surprising microcosm of class and racial repression. Thus, besides being sources of slave labor for the State, correctional institutions reduce unemployment rates and control poor and nonwhite people (Reasons and Kaplan 1975).

The ideologies of rehabilitation and deterrence are an integral part of our correctional policy in North America and may survive in spite of findings that neither goal is realized. Besides employing hundreds of thousands of persons, the rehabilitative ideal allows for social control and manipulation under the guise of humanitarianism. Various forms of "treatment," such as surgical operations, electroshock conditioning and behavior modification, may in fact be punishment.

While some fairness may be attempted in the criminal justice system, it will only reflect the extent of justice in the larger society (Clarke 1978). In highly stratified nations such as Canada and the United States there are basic injustices in the distribution of goods and services, and thus in human and civil rights. The extent to which these inequities and injustices are addressed will greatly affect the institutions of society, including the criminal justice system.

It goes without saying that any realistic attempt to control corporate crime awaits a broadly based movement whose ideals and objectives are independent of the considerable influence of corporate ideology. Such a movement would most probably view the phrase "corporate crime" as redundant. However, in the Mannheimian sense of utopian thought (counterideology), a central concern of such insurgency would center on the expansion of public ownership of vital industries.

The press toward a more "just" justice must be evidenced on a number of simultaneous fronts.

> Every step toward domestic disarmament, toward decriminalization of heroin and "victimless crimes," toward criminalization of the dangerous acts of the affluent and vigorous prosecution of "white-collar" crimes; every step toward creating a correctional system that promotes human dignity, toward giving ex-offenders a real opportunity to go straight, toward making the exercise of power by police officers, prosecutors, and judges more reasonable and more just, toward giving all individuals accused of crime equal access to high-quality legal expertise in their defense; every step toward establishing economic and social justice is a step that moves us from a system of *criminal* justice to a system of criminal *justice*. The refusal to take those steps is a move in the opposite direction" (Reiman 1979, p. 203).

BIBLIOGRAPHY

Albrecht, Stan L., and
Green, Miles
1977   "Attitudes Toward the Police and the Larger Attitude Complex." Criminology 15 (May):67–86.

Albert, Geoffrey P., and
Hicks, Donald A.
1977   "Prisoners' Attitudes Toward Components of the Legal and Judicial Systems." Criminology 14 (February 1977):461–82.

Atkins, Burton M., and
Glick, Henry R.
1972   Prisons, Protest and Politics. Englewood Cliffs, N.J.: Prentice-Hall.

Balbus, Isaac D.
1973   The Dialectics of Legal Repression: Black Rebels before the American Criminal Courts. New York: Russell Sage Foundation.

Baldwin, James
1962   Nobody Knows My Name. New York: Dell.

Barak, Gregg
1975   "In Defense of the Rich: The Emergence of the Public Defender." Crime and Social Justice 3 (Summer):2–14.

Bequai, August
1978   White Collar Crime: A 20th Century Crisis. Lexington, Mass.: D.C. Heath.

Berman, John J.
1976   "Parolees' Perception of the Justice System." Criminology 13 (February):507–20.

Block, Herbert Spencer, and Geis, Gilbert
1970   Man, Crime, and Society. New York: Random House.

Blumberg, Abraham S.
1967   Criminal Justice. Chicago: Quadrangle.

Blumenthal, Monica; Kahn, Robert; Andrews, Frank; and Head, Kendra
1972   Justifying Violence. Ann Arbor, Mich.: Ann Arbor Institute for Social Research, University of Michigan.

Bordua, David, and Reiss, Albert, J.
1967   "Law Enforcement." In The Uses of Sociology. **Paul F. Lazarsfield et al. eds. New York: Basic** Books, pp. 275–303.

Boydell, Craig L.; Whitehead, Paul C.; and Grindstaff, Carl F.
1974   The Administration of Criminal Justice in Canada. Toronto: Holt, Rinehart and Winston of Canada.

Brown, Lorne and Caroline
1972   An Unauthorized History of the R.C.M.P. Toronto: James Lorimer.

Chambliss, William J.
1964   "A Sociological Analysis of the Law of Vagrancy." Social Problems 12 (Summer): 67–77.

Chambliss, William J., and Seidman, Robert B.
1971   Law, Order, and Power. Reading, Mass.: Addison-Wesley.

Chicago Tribune
1977   Harris Survey, page 1.

Chiricos, Theodore G.,
and Waldo, Gordon P.
1975

"Socioeconomic Status and Criminal Sentencing: An Empirical Assessment of a Conflict Proposition." American Sociological Review 40:753–72.

Clarke, Dean H.
1978

"Marxism, Justice and the Justice Model." Contemporary Crisis 2:27–62.

Clinard, Marshall B., and
Abbott, Daniel J.
1973

Crime in Developing Countries. New York: John Wiley.

Clinard, M.B. et al.
1979

Illegal Corporate Behavior. Washington, D.C.: U.S. Government Printing Office.

Dash, Samuel
1951

"Cracks in the Foundation of Criminal Justice." Illinois Law Review 56 (July/August):385–406.

Derbyshire, Robert L.
1968

"Children's Perceptions of the Police: A Comparative Study of Attitudes and Attitude Change." Journal of Criminal Law, Criminology and Police Science 59 (June): 36–56.

Edmison, J. Alex
1976

"Some Aspects of Nineteenth-Century Canadian Prisons." In Crime and Its Treatment in Canada. W. T. McGrath, ed. Toronto: Macmillan, pp. 347–69.

Fairchild, Erika S.
1977

"Politicization of the Criminal Offender." Criminology 15 (November): 287–318.

Geis, Gilbert
1973

"Deterring Corporate Crime." In Corporate Power in America. Ralph Nader and Mark J. Green, eds. New York: Grossman, pp. 182–97.

Gilman, David
1975

"The Sanction of Imprisonment: For When, What and How." Crime and Delinquency 21 (October): 337–47.

Glaser, David
1964

The Effectiveness of a Prison and Parole System. Indianpolis, Ind.: Bobbs-Merrill.

Gordon, David M.
1973   "Capitalism, Class and Crime in America." Crime and Delinquency (April):163–86.

Greenberg, David F.
1975   "Problems in Community Corrections." Issues in Criminology 10 (Spring):1–33.

Gray, F.C.
1849   Prison Discipline in America. London: J. Murray.

Grossman, Brian
1976   Police Command. Toronto: Macmillan of Canada.

Harring, Sid et al.
1977   "The Management of Police Killings." Crime and Social Justice 8 (Fall/Winter):34–43.

Johnson, Deborah, and Gregary, Robert J.
1971   "Police-Community Relations in the United States: A Review of Recent Literature and Projects." Journal of Criminal Law, Criminology and Police Science (March):94–103.

Karmen, Andrew
1974   "Agents Provocateurs in the Contemporary U.S. Leftist Movement." In the Criminologist: Crime and the Criminal. Pacific Palisades, Calif.: Goodyear, pp. 209–26.

Kelly, W.H.
1976   "The Police." In Crime and Its Treatment in Canada. Toronto: Macmillan of Canada, pp. 136–78.

Kreps, G.A., and Weller, J.M.
1973   "The Police-Community Relations Movement." American Behavioural Scientist 16:402–12.

Lewis, Robert
1979   "The Parliament Hill Mob." MacLean's 90 (July 11):14–16.

Martinson, Robert
1974   "What Works?—Questions and Answers About Prison Reform. The Public Interest 35 (Spring): 22–54.

Marx, Gary T.
1970   "Civil Disorder and the Agents of Social Control." Journal of Social Issues (Winter): 19–57.

Ministry of Solicitor
General of Canada
Statistical Handbook
1976   Selected Aspects of Criminal Justice. Ottawa:
        Ministry of the Solicitor General of Canada.

Mitford, Jessica
1974   Kind and Usual Punishment. New York: Vintage.

Mouledous, James C.
1967   "Political Crime and the Negro Revolution." In
        Criminal Behavior Systems: A Typology. Marshall
        B. Clinard and Richard Quinney, eds. New York:
        Holt, Rinehart and Winston, pp. 217–31.

National Advisory
Commission on
Criminal Justice
Standards and Goals
1973   Criminal Justice Systems. Washington, D.C.:
        U.S. Government Printing Office.

Newman, Donald J.
1966   Conviction: The Determination of Guilt or Inno-
        cence without Trial. Boston: Little, Brown.

1975   Introduction to Criminal Justice. Philadelphia:
        J.B. Lippincott.

Newsweek
1980a   "The McDuffie Case." June 2:39.

1980b   "The Mood of Ghetto America." June 2:32–33.

Pallas, John, and
Barber, Bob
1972   "From Riot to Revolution." Issues in Criminology 7
        (Fall):1–19.

Palmer. Ted
1976   "Martinson Revisited." In Rehabilitation, Recid-
        ivism and Research. Robert Martinson, Ted
        Palmer, and Stuart Adams, eds. Hackensack, N.J.:
        National Council on Crime and Delinquency,
        pp. 41–62.

Parks, Evelyn L.
1970   "From Constabulary to Police Society: Implications
        for Social Control." Catalyst 6 (Summer): 76–97.

Quinney, Richard
1979   Criminology. 2d ed. Boston: Little, Brown.

Reasons, Charles E., and
Kuykendall, Jack L.
1972   Race, Crime and Justice. Pacific Palisades, Calif.:
Goodyear.

Reasons, Charles E., ed.
1974   The Criminologist: Crime and the Criminal.
Pacific Palisades, Calif.: Goodyear.

Reasons, Charles E.
1974   "Racism, Prisons, and Prisoners' Right." Issues
in Criminology 9 (Fall):3–20.

1976   "Toward Community-Based Corrections." Crime
and Social Justice (November):108–14.

Reasons, Charles E., and
Wirth, Bernard A.
1975   "Police-Community Relations Units: A National
Survey." Journal of Social Issues 31:27–34.

Reasons, Charles E., and
Kaplan, Russell L.
1975   "Tear Down the Walls? Some Functions of
Prisons." Crime and Delinquency (October):360–72.

Reid, Sue Titus
1976   Crime and Criminology. Hinsdale, Ill.: The
Dryden Press.

Reiman, Jeffrey
1979   The Rich Get Richer and the Poor Get Prison.
New York: John Wiley.

Reiss, Albert J., Jr.
1968   "Police Brutality—Answers to Key Questions."
Trans-action (July/August):10–19.

Reith, Charles
1952   The Blind Eye of History: A Study of the Origins
of the Present Police Era. London: Farber and
Farber.

Report of the National
Advisory Commission on
Civil Disorders
1968   Washington, D.C.: U.S. Government Printing
Office.

Rothman, David J.
1971   The Discovery of the Asylum. Boston: Little, Brown.

Sarat, Austin
1977
"Studying American Legal Culture: An Assessment of Survey Evidence." Law and Society Review (Winter):427–88.

Schmeiser, Douglas A.
1974
Native Offenders and the Law. Ottawa: Information Canada.

Senna, Joseph J., and Siegel, Larry J.
1978
Introduction to Criminal Justice. St. Paul, Minn.: West Publishing Company.

Silk, L. Howard, and Vogel, David
1976
Ethics and Profits: The Crisis of Confidence in American Business. New York: Simon & Schuster.

Silver, Allan
1967
"The Demand for Order in Civil Disorder: A Review of Some Themes in the History of Urban Crime, Police and Riots." In the Police: Six Sociological Essays. David Boradua, ed. New York: John Wiley.

Sutherland, Edwin H., and Cressey, Donald R.
1974
Criminology. 9th ed. Philadelphia: J.B. Lippincott.

Spece, Ray G., Jr.
1972
"Conditioning and Other Technologies Used to Treat? Rehabilitate? Demolish? Prisoners and Mental Patients." Southern California Law Review (Spring):616–81.

Stone, I.F.
1970
The Killings at Kent State. New York: Vintage Books.

Swett, Daniel H.
1969
"Cultural Bias in the American Legal System." Law and Society Review (August):79–110.

Sykes, Gresham M.
1978
Criminology. New York: Harcourt Brace Jovanovich.

Takagi, Paul
1974
"A Garrison State in a Democratic Society." Crime and Social Justice 1 (Spring-Summer).

Tepperman, Lorne
  1977   Crime Control. Toronto: McGraw-Hill Ryerson.

Unger, Sanford J.
  1976   F.B.I. Boston: Little, Brown.

U.S. Bureau of the Census
  1978   Statistical Abstract of the United States, 99th ed.
                          Washington, D.C.: U.S. Government Printing
                          Office.

U.S. Department of
Justice
  1979   F.B.I. Uniform Crime Report. Washington,
                          D.C.: U.S. Government Printing Office.

Varni, Charles
  1974   **Images of Police Work and Mass Media Prop-**
                          aganda: The Case of Dragnet. Unpublished PhD
                          dissertation, Washington State University.

Walker, Daniel
  1968   Rights in Conflict. New York: Bantam.

Walker, Irving, and Chan,
Janet
  1974   "Prison Use: A Canadian and International
                          Comparison." Criminal Law Quarterly 17
                          (December):47–71.

Waskow, Arthur R.
  1969   "Community Control of the Police." Trans-action
                          7 (December):4–7.

Wilson, James Q.
  1975   Thinking About Crime. New York: Basic Books.

Wright, Erik Olin
  1973   The Politics of Punishment: A Critical Analysis of
                          Prisons in America. New York: Harper & Row.

9

THE DEMONOLOGY
OF DRUGS

Abstract

The distinction between legal and illegal drugs is
based largely upon ideology rather than actual differences in harmful effects. The prevailing ideologies
of drug abuse, puritan ethic, and dope fiends has led
to minority and class suppression. An historical
analysis of the development of drug problems indicates that the status of users, as well as economic
and class interests, shape the definition of the "drug
problem" at any given time. The legal institutionalization and political-economic maintenance of our
contemporary drug problem ensures increasing corporate profits in the drug industry and expansion of
the drug education-enforcement complex. A rational
view of the problem entails elimination of our criminal
approach, adequate education, and legal, regulated
distribution of drugs. Such a policy will have less
detrimental consequences than that currently in
operation.

*It is a discriminating demonology which posits more devil per
drop in some preparations than in others. Aspirin, tobacco, barbiturates and tranquilizers are of little concern, alcohol occupies a
middle ground, the amphetamines, which once were of little importance, are now growing worrisome, but it is heroin, cannabis, LSD,
and other hallucinogens which are deemed most devilish—that is,
awesome, seductive, and menacing. Such a discrimination is a bit*

489

awkward on strictly pharmacological grounds, but if the characteristics of users and settings are considered, we see that the attribution of menace is linked closely to the degree to which the committed users of each drug advertise their escape from the fold.—Richard Blum

In the above statement, Richard Blum has concisely presented the nature of the "drug problem" today. It is not the objective properties of the drug that are most threatening but rather the characteristics of users and their settings. Joel Fort's medical research further substantiates the argument that on purely pharmacological grounds, current drug policies do not make sense. Fort (1973) analyzes drugs by several dimensions of "hardness," including resulting brain and organic damage, insanity, addiction, violence, vehicular accidents, and death. Using these criteria he arrives at the following categories that form a continuum ranging from greatest to least harm: (1) alcohol, barbiturates, amphetamines, nicotine, and cocaine; (2) all narcotics and hallucinogens; (3) caffeine, aspirin, and marijuana. Alcohol and nicotine are seen to be more harmful than opiates; however, they are easily available and acceptable while the opiates are rarely available and largely socially taboo. In comparing narcotics with alcohol, Fort observes,

> Like alcohol and sedatives, these drugs can produce addiction and are more likely to do this, but in the dimension of physical damage to the body narcotics are "safer" drugs than alcohol. Even years of heavy use produce no permanent damage to the liver, brain, or other body organs (1973, p. 75).

How does one explain the disparity between known effects of a drug and social policy? One must look to the area of subjective meanings and their importance for the drug problem within the context of corporate society.

Viewpoint

"The Scapegoat as Drug and the Drug as Scapegoat"
by Thomas Szasz (1974)

Thousands of years ago—in times we are fond of calling "primitive" (since this renders us "modern" without having to exert ourselves further to earn this qualification)—religion and medicine were a united and undifferentiated enterprise; and both were closely allied with government and politics— all being concerned with maintaining the integrity of the community and of the individuals who were its members. How did ancient societies and their priest-physicians protect people from plagues and famines, from the perils of impending military encounters, and from all the other calamities that threaten persons and peoples? They did so, in general, by performing certain religious ceremonies.

In ancient Greece (as elsewhere), one of these ceremonies consisted of human sacrifice. The selection, naming, special treatment, and finally the ritualized destruction of the scapegoat was the most important and most potent "therapeutic" intervention known to "primitive" man. In ancient Greece, the person sacrificed as a scapegoat was called the *pharmakos.* The root of modern terms such as pharmacology and pharmacopeia is therefore not "medicine," "drug," and "poison," as most dictionaries erroneously state, but "scapegoat"! To be sure, after the practice of human sacrifice was abandoned in Greece, probably around the sixth century B.C., the word did come to mean "medicine," "drug," and "poison." Interestingly, in modern Albanian *pharmak* still means only "poison."

The "modern" reader might be tempted to shrug off all this as etymological curiosity. The magic in which his ancestors believed he considers "nonsense." He doesn't believe in magic. He "believes" only in facts, in science, in medicine. Insofar as this critical characterization of the modern mind is accurate, it shows us starkly two things: first, that just as human anatomy and physiology have changed little if at all during the past, say, three thousand years, so social organizations and the principles of social control have also changed little if at all; and second, that, in some ways at least, modern man may be more "primitive" than was ancient man. When the ancients saw a scapegoat, they could at least recognize him for what he was: a *pharmakos,* a human sacrifice. When modern man sees one, he does not, or refuses to, recognize him for what he is; instead, he looks for "scientific" explanations—to explain away the obvious. Thus, to the modern mind, the witches were mentally sick women; the Jews in Nazi Germany were the victims of a mass psychosis; involuntary mental patients are sick people unaware of their own need for treatment; and so on. I submit, and will try to show, that among the long list of scapegoats which the insatiable human appetite for *pharmakoi* seems to demand, some of the most important today are certain substances—called "dangerous drugs," "narcotics," or "dope"; certain entrepreneurs —called "pushers" or "drug traffickers"; and certain persons who use certain prohibited substances—called "drug addicts," "drug abusers," or "drug-dependent persons." This pseudo-scientific and pseudomedical language is both the cause and result of the shocking modern insensibility concerning scape-goating, and insensitivity toward scapegoats. Civilized man, in contrast to his primitive forebear, "knows" that opium is a dangerous narcotic; that people who sell it are evil individuals, properly analogized with, and treated as, murderers; and that persons who use it are sick and sinful, and should be "treated" against their will for their own good—in short, he "knows" that none of them is a scapegoat (1974, p. 19–20).

For Thomas Szasz, in certain modern societies the State has come to exercise control over the lives of people by means of "therapeutic power." Rather than relying purely on the enforcement of criminal laws, the agents of the modern State may employ versions of the "medical model" by which dissident individuals or groups may be effectively "treated." Thus, sickness of a "mental sort" legitimates the taking of liberty by force.

Szasz is also concerned that drug "abusers" as well as the "mentally ill" have become modern-day satanists and that drugcraft has replaced witchcraft as a popular explanation of the ills of society. Thus an ideology of drug abuse, together with those human beings known as "addicts" become scapegoats for social ills. And as always, scapegoats consist of those on the outside whose conditions mark them not simply as different, but as powerless.[1]

Accordingly, drugs and drug abuse appear as "devils" to be exorcised. They emerge as grand symbols of what is "wrong" with the order of things. As shall be demonstrated later in this chapter, while the respect-able drug industry (the distillers, the tobacco products manufacturers, and the pharmaceutical houses) have been pushing their products, the disrespectables (organized crime, dope fiends, street pushers, and dealers) have become the focus of the unending war on drugs.

---

[1] Thomas Szasz is a well-known libertarian who views state power as a threat to individual freedom. While the authors respect his views, we believe it impossible to examine the State apart from corporate order in North American society. We readily acknowledge the con-tradictions in the definition of the "drug problem." We also agree that the drug usage of the outsider is more often the target of political crusades than are the drugs used by the insiders. However, our focus will be expanded to include the corporate influence of respect-able pharmaceuticals and other components of the drug industry. In this sense, the following discussion is system-specific.

THE PREVAILING IDEOLOGIES

Clearly evident in the general ideology of corporate society is the emphasis on rationalism, freedom of choice, and willpower. The social universe becomes a rather private affair. One must therefore meet its challenges armed only with individual resources. Thus, that which appears to threaten the imagery of pure reason will become the target of specific ideologies that define the "danger." Certain chemical agents (not all) come to acquire the standing of "demons" that supposedly threaten the reason, assertiveness, and aggression necessary to sell, grow, and prosper. For example, million-dollar transactions may be conducted over the three-martini lunch. However, the imagery of passing around a joint has yet to acquire such legitimation. Beyond this, one is compelled to recognize that an obsession with *chemical* controls effectively channels attention from other sorts of institutionalized (or "legitimate") influence. The latter include but are not necessarily restricted to the corporate media and the agencies of the State (see Chapter Two).

The societal context of drug use greatly influences drug definitions, drug effects, drug-related behavior, and the drug experience. As with other social problems, a specific ideology for drugs exists that reflects the prime ideological symbols of corporate society. It should follow that some drugs will be seen as problems and others will not; some users will be openly acknowledged and others denied; certain harmful effects will become a part of the conventional wisdom while others do not reach public consciousness. Such is the power of ideas and the means of influence that shape and disseminate them. For example, the "chemicalistic fallacy," which presumes that drug A causes harm B, fails to explain adequately why some drugs (such as heroin, LSD) are viewed with revulsion and horror while others (alcohol, tobacco, Librium, Valium, and so on) are not (Goode 1972). An examination of terminology will provide more vivid evidence that the definition of "dangerous" drugs is based on an ideological process, not a pharmacological one.

Drug Abuse

What is a drug? What do we mean by a drug user? How does one define drug abuse? Broadly defined, a drug is "any chemical agent that affects living processes . . ." (Fingle and Woodbury 1970, p. 1). Such a definition includes a glass of water, a shot of 150 proof rum, or even a bullet fired from a gun.

Canada's federal commission on the nonmedical use of drugs states:

"A drug is considered to be any substance that, by its chemical nature, alters structure or function in the living organism" (Commission of Inquiry 1973, p. 278). This definition is also spacious. A narrower definition is "any biologically active substance used in the treatment and prevention of illness" (Fort 1973, pp. 4–5). Such a definition moves from pharmacological properties of the substance to a specific use, namely, medical. This is similar to Webster's definition:

> drug (drug) n. o Fr. *drogue* 1. any substance used as or in a medicine. a. a narcotic, hallucinogen, etc. (1971, p. 171).

Webster's second definition is the one most of the general public means when discussing the "drug problem." When we speak of drug users, drug takers, and drug pushers, we usually are not referring to our own daily dose of caffeine, nicotine, or alcohol; or to the liquor and grocery stores and their salespersons. No, it is the user and seller of certain demonological drugs, such as heroin, marijuana, cocaine, LSD, who most of us are talking about.

Goode suggests that any definition of drugs should meet two criteria: (1) it should group together all the things that share a given relevant trait, and (2) it should set apart those things that do not share that trait. As he notes:

> In actuality, the term "drug" is a social fabrication. The fact is that no formal, objective pharmacological characteristic of chemical agents will satisfy both criteria of an adequate definition simultaneously. There is no effect common to all drugs that, at the same time, is not shared by substances not considered drugs. . . . This does not mean that drug effects are not "real." Drugs, of course, have chemical and pharmacological properties; they do act on human tissue. But the way they act has relatively little to do with how they are viewed and defined. Society's attitudes toward a given substance have very little to do with its laboratory identified properties and a great deal to do with sentiment and emotion. Society, or rather certain segments of society, define what a drug is, and the social definition, the linguistic device, largely determines our attitudes (1974, p. 165).

The general public considers a substance a drug because of assumed specific behavioral effects and social contexts of use apart from any common chemical properties. Examples of public definitions of drugs are provided by the Marijuana Commission. In a nationwide probability sample, respondents were asked, "What do you think is a drug?" As Table 9–1 indicates, illegal drugs are considered "drugs" while legal socially acceptable drugs are largely "nondrugs." Thus, drugs are generally characterized by their illegality, a demonstration of the powerful force of law in shaping public imagery.

**TABLE 9-1
Substances Regarded as Drugs
(Selected from a list)**

	Adults 2411	Youth 880
Heroin	95%	96%
Cocaine	88	86
Barbiturates	83	91
Marijuana	80	80
Amphetamines	79	86
Alcohol	39	34
Tobacco	27	16
No opinion	1	1

Source: National Commission on Marijuana and Drug Abuse, Vol. 1, 1973, p. 512.

Like the term drug, most other terms relating to drugs and their use largely reflect ideologies based on power and wealth. Such judgments are evident in social problems texts as well as popular literature. For example, most social problems texts distinguish between drugs, their use and abuse on the one hand, and alcohol use and abuse, on the other, often having one chapter on drugs and another on alcohol and alcoholism, or one chapter such as "Drugs and Alcohol: Their Use and Abuse."

Many students of social problems have taken for granted the artificial distinction made by those in positions of power in the "hierarchy of credibility." The "hierarchy of credibility" means that some people have more power to define what is true than others do (Becker 1967). Therefore, if legislators, law enforcement agents, and medical spokespersons label a chemical substance dangerous, it must be so. For example, on March 6, 1971, Dr. Wesley Hall, president of the American Medical Association, was quoted as saying that an AMA study left very little doubt that marijuana caused considerable reduction in sex drive, and hinted that certain evidence demonstrated that it caused birth defects. These "findings" presented by such an "authority" received wide publicity. Approximately three weeks later, Dr. Hall said he had been misquoted, but added:

> I don't mind . . . if this can do some good in waking people up to the fact that, by jingo, whether we like to face it or not, our campuses are going to pot, both literally and figuratively. . . . If we don't wake up in this country to the fact that every college campus and high school has a problem with drug addiction, we're going down the drain not only with respect to morality, but . . . the type of system we're going to have (Drugs and Drug Abuse Education 1971, pp 6–7).

In the "war" against drugs, all is fair.

Another example of this sleight of hand is found in the concepts of drug addiction, dependence, and abuse. In pharmacological terms, an addictive drug makes cells dependent on that drug. As Joel Fort has noted, this includes alcohol and narcotics. A case may also be made for nicotine as an addictive drug (Brecher 1972). However, the popular definition deals only with narcotic addiction through illicit drugs.

According to the World Health Organization:

> Drug addiction is a state of periodic or chronic intoxication detrimental to the individual and to society, produced by the repeated consumption of a drug (natural or synthetic). Its characteristics include: 1) an overpowering desire or need (compulsion) to continue taking the drug and to obtain it by any means, 2) a tendency to increase the dosage, and 3) a psychic (psychological) and sometimes physical dependence on the effects of the drug. (In Szasz 1973, p. 134.)

Szasz points out that "these judgments have nothing whatever to do with medicine, pharmacology, or psychiatry. They are *moral judgments*" (italics added).

While earlier official statements labeled such drugs as marijuana "addicting," contemporary language in the hierarchy of credibility is "drug dependence." The World Health Organization devised new terminology in the 1960s to encompass "abuse" of all drugs, not just addicting drugs. They adopted the following definition of "drug dependence":

> A state of psychic dependence or physical dependence, or both, on a drug, arising in a person following administration of that drug on a periodic or continued basis. The characteristics of such a state will vary with the agent involved, and these characteristics must always be made clear by designating the particular type of drug dependence in each specific case. . . . *All of these drugs have one effect in common: they are capable of creating in certain individuals, a particular state of mind that is termed "psychic dependence."* In this situation, there is a feeling of satisfaction and psychic drive that require periodic or continuous administration of the drug to produce pleasure or to avoid discomfort (Goode 1972, p. 22; emphasis added).

Goode notes that the intent of this definition is patently ideological in nature and attempts to discredit as many nonaddictive drugs as possible. Another sociologist has commented on the "psychic dependence of marijuana":

> What does this phrase mean? It means that the drug is pleasurable, as is wine, smoked sturgeon, poetry, comfortable chairs, and *Trans-action* (Freidson 1968, p. 75).

In the definition of drug abuse, ideology plays a major role, as noted by the first report of the National Commission on Marijuana and Drug Abuse.

> Drug abuse is another way of saying drug problem. Now immortalized in the titles of federal and state governmental agencies (and we might add, in our own), this term has the virtue of rallying all parties to a common cause: no one could possibly be for abuse of drugs any more than they could be for abuse of minorities, power or children. By the same token, the term also obscures the fact that "abuse" is undefined where drugs are concerned. Neither the public, its policymakers nor the expert community share a common understanding of its meaning or of the nature and phenomenon to which it refers. The Commission has noted over the last two years that the public and press often employ drug abuse interchangeably with drug use. Indeed, many drug abuse experts, including governmental officials, do so as well (1972, pp. 11–12).

In their surveys of the public regarding their beliefs about the meaning of drug abuse, the 1972 and 1973 Reports of the National Commission on Marijuana and Drug Abuse in the United States emphasize that to the public, drug abuse usually means drug usage for a nonmedical purpose. Of course, if a substance is not identified as a drug, such as alcohol and tobacco, its nonmedical use is irrelevant. The taking of drugs for pleasure is often connected with drug abuse. However, as we shall see, the pleasure thesis, while important, is not sufficient to explain the drug problem.

The Puritan Ethic

The evaluation of substances as drugs or nondrugs, addictive or nonaddictive, abused or nonabused is essentially based upon the values of the dominant interests in society and their establishment in public policy through the law. It is often argued that puritan ideas have been the prototype for beliefs and practices regarding drugs, illicit users, and the treatment of "addicts." If our puritan forebears are responsible, then the use of certain drugs is wrong because of the ethical and philosophical foundations of religious culture. Rationality and inner discipline both negate drugs, and the philosophical and legal doctrines of free will are believed to be lessened by certain drug use. Must the reaction to drugs therefore be understood in terms of Judeo-Christian tradition? Should the puritanical aversion to pleasure also be an important facet of the moral interpretation of drug use? While we currently view nicotine, caffeine, and alcohol as sociable drugs that are largely accepted, they once were viewed as antisocial, hedonistic, self-indulgent drugs just like heroin, LSD, and marijuana today.

In his classical work, *The Protestant Ethic and the Spirit of Capitalism*, Max Weber (1958) noted that puritan asceticism (self-denial) was the foundation for a work ethic, which in turn produced the very life, will, and soul of a historically emerging capitalism. For Protestants, hard work was mandatory and material success indicated God's pleasure. The accumulation of wealth, considered by some an indicator of greed, thus found religious sanction. Weber attempted a comparative study to show that capitalism thrived more in predominantly Protestant as opposed to Catholic societies. (One must note that the emergence of European mercantile capitalism preceded the sixteenth-century Reformation, which resulted in the establishment of Protestant churches, by some 300 years [Kennedy 1970]. Further, it appears that Catholic, Jews, agnostics, and atheists, as well as the religiously disinterested, have numbered among them numerous successful capitalists.)

Has the tradition of asceticism surfaced in current drug laws and policies? This is doubtlessly true. However, the "puritanical argument" leaves important considerations untouched. It should be pointed out, for example, that alcohol and tobacco also produce states of pleasure and "altered consciousness." Why are these drugs seldom included when contemporary conversation turns to "drugs"? While there still are numerous "dry" areas in the southern United States that necessitate elaborate schemes of "private clubs" and "bootleggers," even within the "Bible Belt" liquor bans are ceremonial, symbolic, and ineffective. (At one time in a "dry" Southern state, bootleggers advertised in the Yellow Pages.) As we shall soon see, historically, powerful industries have grown up around alcohol, tobacco, and tranquilizers. As such, they have come to wear a badge of legitimacy. The same cannot be said for heroin, LSD, marijuana, and other "dangerous" drugs.

Although there is not much belief in witches today, the conceptual basis exists. Demons found in certain drugs serve as excuses for otherwise unacceptable actions and states of mind. The power in substances labeled drugs is believed to be such that those identified as users are immediately reclassified socially as "dope fiends." Have witches turned to technology, whereby they lurk in heroin, LSD, and other materials? Once possessed by a devil, so the theory goes, people themselves become devils capable of all manner of inhuman actions (Blum 1969). The user is often characterized as both the victim and the criminal. The helpless individual succumbing to the ruthless and relentless pressure of the pusher, is also the violent, psychopathic, moral degenerate spreading the evil.

The Dope Fiend Mythology

While much attention has been given to the causes of drug abuse, treating the user, and educating the public regarding the ills of illicit drugs, little systematic investigation has been made of drugs and users as portrayed in the mass media. The presentation of myths concerning the nature and effects of drugs has received scant attention (Smith 1966; Blum 1971).

The social reality of the drug problem appears to have largely emanated from the diffusion of a specific ideology about drug users. One of the earliest scientific investigators to suggest that the presentation and perpetuation of misconceptions regarding drugs should be investigated was Alfred Lindesmith. A renowned student of drugs, he suggested in 1940 that a "dope fiend" ideology had been constructed about the addict justifying the severe treatment generally accorded the drug user, and was being used by vested interests to frighten the public into appropriating increased funds to combat the "dope menace" (Lindesmith 1940). Furthermore, he asserted:

> The "dope fiend" mythology serves, in short, as a rationalization of the status quo. It is a body of superstition, half truths and misinformation which bolsters up an indefensible repressive law, the victims of which are in no position to protest. . . . The treatment of addicts in the United States today is on no higher plane than the persecution of witches of other ages. . . .

The "dope fiend" mythology included the following four myths:

1. The drug addict is a violent criminal.

2. The drug addict is a moral degenerate.

3. The drug peddler wants to convert nonusers into addicts.

4. The drug addict wants to convert nonusers into addicts (1940a, p. 200).

A fifth myth can be included from another article by Lindesmith (1940b).

5. The drug addict takes drugs because of inferior and abnormal personality.

The above stereotypes of drug users are distortions of reality that provide preconceived, standardized, group-shared ideas regarding a whole category of persons—"dope fiends." While most of these images have some basis in fact, they are simplifications of drugs and drug users. Though some addicts commit crimes to support their addiction, this is not an effect of the drug, but rather an outcome of exhorbitant prices, as has been noted repeatedly by many students of drugs and crime (Schur 1962). Ironically, the most consistent and persistent relationship is found between alcohol and violent crimes, resulting in thousands of deaths and injuries each year. Of course, even this is not a direct, inevitable product of the drug per se, but also of the individuals and situations involved. Likewise, although the other myths have a degree of factual basis, they are largely erroneous interpretations that have subsequently been refuted (Brecher 1972; Kaplan 1970; Weil 1973; Goode 1972; Waldorf 1973). Nonetheless, such images undoubtedly have an important role in shaping the public conception of the drug problem (Reasons 1976).

The image of the "user" plays an important part in the evaluation of the drug, notwithstanding the pharmacological properties of the substance. While alcohol and nicotine have been directly related to many more diseases and deaths than heroin, LSD, cocaine, and marijuana, it is the latter group of drugs that are perceived as most dangerous and threatening to society. The image of the user greatly influences the evaluation of the drug. The users of illicit drugs have been characterized as being out of society's mainstream. As will be evident in subsequent analysis, the emergence of this image in North America largely paralleled minority repression, with the drugs viewed as a symbol of the inferiority of out-groups. More recently, the use of certain drugs, particularly marijuana and the psychedelics (hallucinogens), has been associated with a number of volatile issues. John Kaplan (1971) points out that a great deal of the objection to marijuana use is based upon the life-style associated with it, not upon the effects of the drug.

Some view the life-style as a result of marijuana use. Issues such as radicalism, permissiveness, disrespect for authority, law and order, the generation gap, and intercultural conflict are intertwined with the "drug problem."

The first report of the National Commission on Marijuana and Drug Abuse identifies the symbolic aspects of marijuana as possibly being "at the heart of the marijuana problem."

> The threat which marijuana use is thought to present to the dominant social order is a major undercurrent of the marihuana problem. Use of the drug is linked with idleness, lack of motivation, hedonism and sexual promiscuity. Many see the drug as fostering a counter-culture which conflicts with basic moral precepts as well as with the operating functions of our society. The dropping out or rejection of the established value system is viewed with alarm. Marihuana becomes more than a drug; it becomes a symbol of cherished values (1972, p. 9).

Prescription Dope

While marijuana and other hallucinogens seize the public consciousness, legal psychoactive agents represent an increasingly lucrative commodity. In the United States, some 120 million prescriptions (an estimated 8.3 billion doses) of "tranquilizers" were consumed in 1977. The market value of these psychoactive drugs amounted to some $2 billion. Almost half of the prescriptions and 39 percent of the total doses were for Valium. This drug was implicated in over 900 deaths and 54,000 cases of emergency room treatment between May 1976 and April 1977 (Hughes and Brewin 1979, pp. 8–9). How do Valium and other tranquilizers escape inclusion in the "dope fiend" ideology?

Valium, and its chemical cousins Librium and Dalmane, were dispensed in a total of 85 million prescriptions (4.5 billion pills) in 1977.

> All these drugs are manufactured by the same company, Hoffman-La Roche, a Swiss-based multinational giant with US headquarters in Nutley, New Jersey. These three drugs all belong to the same chemical class, the benzodiazepines, and since the first drug of the class, Librium, was introduced in 1960, the benzodiazepines have dominated the growing tranquilizer field.
> . . . Considering that almost half a billion Valium prescriptions have been written since the drug was introduced, it is estimated that Roche profits run in the billions. . . . (Hughes and Brewin 1979, p. 9).

Valium, of course, constitutes only the tip of the iceberg. Prescription drugs, psychoactive and otherwise, represent an enormous industry. The Pharmaceutical Manufacturers Association estimates that the global sales for US manufacturers in 1977 amounted to $16.7 billion (Hughes and Brewin 1979, p. 191). And as might be expected, the advertising industry plays a major role in the selling of cures, tranquility or others. Advertisers meet the legal standards for "factuality" more often than not. However, such standards are seldom effective, given the centrality of the advertising industry in corporate society. (See Chapter Two, and DeBakey 1977).

Through little known but highly influential health advertising entities (such as Healthmark, Marshall Smith, Sudler & Hennessey, and *Medical Economics*), the legal drug industry pushes and promotes its wares. Included in these are psychoactive drugs. According to the Commerce Department, tranquilizers alone accounted for some 25 percent of the $8 billion prescription drug market in the United States in 1977. The drug giants (including Roche; Eli Lilly; Pfizer; Parke, Davis; A.H. Robbins; Abbot; Ayerst; Upjohn; Squibb; Searle; Sandoz; Ortho) spend some 25 cents of every revenue dollar on promotion compared with 15 cents on research. The advertising of "legitimate" drugs worldwide would thus amount to a $4 billion expense (1977) for US manufacturers alone (Hughes and Brewin 1979, p. 191).

The target of such influence is of course the medical profession. To reach the some 200,000 high prescribers (among the 370,000 active physicians in the United States in 1978) the drug companies and their advertising agencies that year spent roughly $7,500 per doctor. The drug education of the medical profession has been left to the drug suppliers. In the late 1970s, only half of the nation's 123 medical schools had specialists in the area of clinical pharmacology (Hughes and Brewin 1979, p. 194).

The selling of tranquility reads like a wonderland, even in corporate America: (1) Drug companies underwrite the costs of "educational symposia" on psychoactive and other drugs. For such "updating" of professional skills, physicians may receive continuing education credit required by their professional associations. (2) The pharmaceuticals further work to define ordinary anxiety as a problem requiring a chemical solution. Roche Laboratories in 1979 launched a $3 million "Consequences of Stress" program as a means of pushing Valium. (3) In the same year, the Physicians' Radio Network, a communiation service for doctors, reached more than 80,000 clients in thirty-five cities with professional news and of course drug "information." (4) For Pfizer Laboratories, what passes as education consists of videotape claims that depression is underdiagnosed and Sinequan (Pfizer's tranquilizer) is the answer. (5) And finally, in 1978, McNeil Laboratories promoted its tranquilizer, Haldol, as a method for controlling nursing home patients. Its ad included a picture of a smiling and alert patient (in the fine print in the corner, it was admitted that the patient pictured was *not* using Haldol) (Hughes and Brewin 1979, pp. 191–227). Perhaps the legitimation of marijuana awaits the attention of Madison Avenue.

EMERGENCE

The emergence of drug crusades has greatly varied historically and cross-culturally. Tobacco was almost universally prohibited across Europe in the seventeenth century with many severe penalties. The Sultan Murad IV decreed the death penalty for smoking tobacco in Constantinople in 1633.

> Whenever the Sultan went on his travels or on a military expedition his halting-places were always distinguished by a terrible increase in the number of executions. Even on the battlefield he was fond of surprising men in the act of smoking, when he would punish them by beheading, hanging, quartering, or crushing their hands and feet and leaving them helpless between the lines (Brecher 1972, p. 212).

Furthermore, the first of the Romanoff czars, Michael Feodorovitch, prohibited smoking in 1634 under such dire penalties as slitting of the nostrils. An edict in 1603 also prohibited smoking in Japan. Thus, the negative evaluation of tobacco by those in positions of power brought swift and harsh penalties. In spite of these attempts to curb the nicotine habit, no country that has ever learned to use tobacco has given up the practice. In time, many of those in positions of power became addicted to nicotine, and subsequently the drug becomes socially acceptable.

Between 1895 and 1921, fourteen of the United States completely banned cigarette smoking. Of course, such laws were ultimately repealed and today the drug, nicotine, remains a major means of euphoria, despite the United States Surgeon General's Report in 1964 and subsequent medical findings (Neuhring and Markle 1974). Medical research notwithstanding, the lack of strict controls and regulations regarding this addictive drug attest to the significance of power, politics, and the tobacco industry in the making and shaping of the drug problem.

The introduction of caffeine drinks into countries not previously acquainted with this drug—like the introduction of other exotic drugs such as nicotine and marijuana—initially aroused a deep sense of moral outrage and evoked efforts to repress the new substance. One author notes that when coffee was first introduced in sixteenth-century Egypt, "the 'coffee bugaboo' . . . caused almost as much fuss as the 'marijuana bugaboo' in the contemporary United States. Sales of coffee was prohibited; wherever stocks of coffee were found they were burned. . . . All this fuss only had the result of interesting more people in the brew and its use spread rapidly" (Brecher 1972, p. 197).

One of the first major "wars" on drugs in North America was the anti-alcohol movement in the nineteenth century in the United States. While drinking habits were well established in the early colonies, the great influx of immigrants in the nineteenth century brought about a change in consumption standards and reactions from the dominant moral order. The rural, native-born American Protestant of that era respected temperance ideals, adhering to a culture in which self-control, industriousness, and impulse renunciation were both praised and made necessary. These were the essentials of the "spirit of capitalism." The temperance movement represented the effort of urban, native-born Americans to consolidate their middle-class life-styles while condemning those of the mostly immigrant working class. The national Prohibition Movement was largely Protestant, rural, and activist, and subsequently came to oppose Catholics, immigrants, and urban dwellers, most of whom toiled in the factory system (Gusfield 1963). During this same period concern arose about the opium problem.

Emergence of the "Opium Problem"

In the nineteenth century preparations containing opium were readily available and could be purchased in any pharmacy or grocery store without prescription. In fact, until the turn of the century, the use of opium and its derivatives was generally less offensive to public morals than the smoking of cigarettes and the consumption of alcohol (Isbell 1963). In the 1870s and the 1880s medical men warned that opiate addiction was claiming people who craved the effect of a stimulant, but would not risk their reputation for temperance by taking alcoholic beverages. The addictive qualities of opium were not generally recognized at the time and its use was widespread throughout the social structure. In fact, it seems that white middle- and upper-class women accounted for a disproportionate share of such use (Terry and Pellens 1928). The opium evil of the period was associated with "smoking opium," practiced extensively by Chinese. It was through international affairs that the "opium problem" first came to public attention.

International Concern

The major "reform" movements concerning drugs included those in China in the late nineteenth centuries, the antiopium agitation in England in the late nineteenth century, and the organized opposition of reformers in the United States to the use of liquor, opium, and other "vices" among peoples in so-called pagan lands.[2] While the antiopium movement began in China and England prior to its emergence in Canada and the United States, Americans were influential in those earlier movements. In fact, an American missionary in China, Reverend Hampden D. DuBose, was instrumental in starting an antiopium campaign in China in the late 1800s. A general movement subsequently emerged with missionaries playing the major role.

Missionaries were the most constant and vigorous supporters of the antiopium movement. American church workers in the Far East played the greatest role in inducing the United States to take the lead in the movement against the drug trafficking. According to Taylor:

> So great was their role, invoking the inauguration of the movement, and in promoting the early work once the movement had been started, that in its early stages the international campaign might appropriately be referred to as a missionary movement—or better still missionary diplomacy (1969, p. 29).

Thus, while Karl Marx decried the fact that religion was the opiate of the people, the missionaries seemed to believe that opium was the religion of the people. It appears that the Chinese themselves were distraught about the effects of *both* Christianity and opium on their people.

Through agitation and the creation of popular unrest, antiopium societies were formed in England. Again, Anglo-Saxon Protestant missionaries,

[2] This section is drawn largely from Taylor 1969, and Lowes 1966. Much of the subsequent discussion will focus upon the United States, which has a much greater volume of literature concerning this subject.

many from the United States, were instrumental in beginning the campaign. The Committee of the Anti-Opium Society listed the principles of Christian and commercial opposition in one of their earliest publications in 1840. The Society for the Suppression of the Opium Trade was founded in London in 1874. It and other subsequent organizations published books, pamphlets, and reports on every phase of the opium question. Members wrote reviews, delivered lectures, and circulated petitions. While such agitation failed to affect the British policy significantly, it did have an impact on American diplomacy. By the end of 1906, the American government was committed through treaties, legislation, and a resolution of Congress, and by representatives to foreign governments to the principle of international action to control the traffic in both alcohol and opium for the benefit of unprotected peoples.

Emanating out of the general humanitarian movement of the nineteenth century, with particular emphasis upon the "white man's burden"[3] and missionary zeal, was a specific social movement to limit the spread of "evil drugs." Societies were formed, ideologies were enunciated, and leaders emerged. Through agitation, development of morale, the formulation of an ideology, and operating tactics, the movement gained international momentum and recognition. Two important personalities in this international campaign were Americans, the Right Reverend Charles Brent and Dr. Hamilton Wright.

The Right Reverend Brent, Episcopal bishop in the Philippine Islands, brought about the Shanghai Opium Convention of 1908 through a letter to President Roosevelt. Although born and raised in Canada, he was part of the United States establishment, and was able to provide continuity through the early years of the international movement. He was unanimously elected president of both the Shanghai meeting in 1908 and the Hague International Opium Convention of 1912. By instituting and presiding over the first two major conferences on the "drug problem," Bishop Brent fathered an important aspect of the international movement, that is, periodic conferences.

Brent first became interested in the opium problem while a bishop in the Philippine Islands. He was appointed to work on the Philippine Opium Committee prior to the Shanghai meeting. This gave him the idea for the international meeting that followed. Brent epitomized the moral entrepreneur, attacking the problem with missionary zeal. He regarded opium use as essentially a moral question and transactions in the drug as a social vice—a crime.

Prior to World War I the most energetic American participant in the antidrug campaign was Hamilton Wright. Wright's appointment to the United States opium commission for Shanghai marked a turning point in

---

[3]By "white man's burden" we refer to a specific ideology of the eighteenth and nineteenth centuries that held that the higher gifts of Western civilization (typically, Christianity and venereal disease) should be brought to native populations whose souls (and resources) were to be "saved." Thus, such beliefs represented a basic defense of colonialism.

his career. A medical doctor, educated in Canada, he devoted the remainder of his life to the antinarcotic campaign after the Shanghai conference. Until his unexpected death in France in 1917, he was almost continuously in charge of the State Department's antiopium work. Dr. Wright developed a possessive attitude toward American drug policy and practice. This is not difficult to understand since not only was he largely entrusted with forming and carrying out United States foreign policy regarding traffic in narcotics, but he also was given the job of drafting domestic antinarcotic legislation.

It was Wright who was largely responsible for the discovery of the domestic "drug problem." Through correspondence and personal interviews with police officials, state health and pharmaceutical boards, drug manufacturers and their organizations, firms dealing in the various forms of opium, and members of the medical profession, he concluded in his *Report* for the Shanghai Opium Commission that the United States had a "drug problem" of its own. His thoroughness and energetic concern are well characterized by Lowes:

> Someone with Dr. Wright's burning zeal to get things done would certainly not underestimate the extent of a problem he was asked to report upon and it may be that, fanatical crusader for a cause that he was, Dr. Wright might have been guilty of some hyperbole. Be that as it may, his driving energy was exactly what the movement needed to get it started both nationally and internationally (1966, p. 100).

Although Dr. Wright's early death brought an end to his campaign, he left a lasting impact upon both international and national drug policy. His influence upon domestic legislation will be readily apparent in subsequent discussion of the institutionalization of the drug problem.

Minority Oppression

While Wright was the major figure to influence domestic concern and particularly legislation, this does not mean that North America was not already aware of a "drug problem." Increasing urbanization, immigration, racism, and a nativistic spirit marked the early part of the twentieth century. Concern with a number of moral evils, including prostitution and the use of narcotics and alcohol, brought about federal attempts to control these "demons." All of these practices violated the ethical and philosophical foundations of the dominant religious and moral culture. Narcotics use, like alcohol use, led to a lack of rationality and self-control. More than the cornerstones of proper "WASP" behavior, such were the essence of corporation commerce. Indulgence in "escapism" by immigrant workers, whatever the drug, represented a clear and present danger to the labor requirements of the factory system and westward expansion. Beyond these concerns, however, stories about alcohol and drug use portrayed minority workers as depraved and subhuman; hence, legitimate objects of exploitation.

Opium and "The Yellow Peril" The association of the "drug problem," and specifically opiate addiction, with racism was particularly acute during the first few decades of this century. Opiate addiction was linked with the "yellow peril" and was felt to be incompatible with white morality and superiority. The issues arising around the use of opium for smoking became part of a larger effort to stigmatize the Oriental as dangerous and insidious, to be condemned and isolated. (As a specific ideology, "the yellow peril" rationalized the low wages and danger that often accompanied what was disparagingly termed "coolie labor.") "Anti-drug" became a rallying point for racists and nativists, who felt themselves in the throes of life-and-death struggle with alien forces. Such racist appeals were significant in the definition of the drug problem in Canada as well as the United States. Both in the House of Commons Debates regarding narcotics and in popular literature, the "drug problem" was largely viewed as originating with degenerate Chinese and negroes (Cook 1969). In a widely read and quoted Canadian book on the drug problem, Judge Emily Murphy noted:

> It is claimed also, but with what truth we cannot say, that there is a well-defined propaganda among the aliens of color to bring about the degeneration of the white race. . . . It is hardly credible that the average Chinese peddler has any definite idea in his mind of bringing about the downfall of the white race, his swaying motive being probably that of greed, but in the hands of his superiors he may become a powerful instrument to this very end . . . whatever their motive, the traffic always comes with the Oriental, and . . . one would, therefore, be justified in assuming that it was their desire to injure the bright-browed races of the world. . . . Some of the Negroes coming into Canada . . . have similar ideas, and one of their greatest writers has boasted how, ultimately, they will control the white man (1922, pp. 186–89).

In Canada, the major figure in the antidrug campaign in the early part of this century was Mr. Mackenzie King (Cook 1969). In 1907, Mr. King was sent to Vancouver as deputy minister of labor to supervise compensations to Chinese and Japanese after anti-Asiatic rioting. He was shocked by two claims from Chinese opium manufacturers whose stocks had been destroyed in the riots. Subsequently, when he found that he could purchase opium over the counter, he initiated successful antiopium legislation. During the second decade of this century, Mr. King continued to lead the war on drugs as a member of the federal cabinet.

It appears clear from the record of history that the oppression of minority groups formed the context within which antidrug movements emerged and drug abuse laws, policies, and control agencies became institutionalized. As we shall shortly demonstrate, the efforts of specific agencies of the State to promote their interests through shaping law and policy can be extremely important. However, one cannot view bureaucratic inertia in isolation. Bureaucracies have not been so successful when their targets have been large-scale corporations. However, when the "menace" consists of the behaviors of various elements of an essentially powerless working class, the responsibility for controlling that behavior has quickly passed to agencies of the State (Galliher and Walker 1978).

When racial and ethnic minorities are the objects of state attention, it is often tempting to explain this simply in cultural terms. After all, the customs and values of the "out-group" appear strange, perhaps producing an uneasiness among insiders. We do not doubt the often powerful conflicts stemming from cultural differences. However, there appears to be much historical support for an alternative explanation. To be clear, the emergence of drug crusades, laws, and agencies reflects more a conflict of classes than a conflict of values. Minority oppression has perhaps more to do with imperialism, profit, and depressed wages than with the simple preservation of custom.

The English Opium Pushers The origin of widespread Chinese opium use began not in China, which became the most notable market for the drug, but in India in the state of Bengal, where the English became the dominant political power in the middle of the eighteenth century. It was in Bengal that the English established a monopoly over the opium industry and began to supply China. The command of this market was the basis of British opium policy throughout the nineteenth century.

The specific monopolist in the opium arrangement was the Honorable East India Company, as trade between Great Britain and China was its exclusive preserve. Pressured by British rulers, Indian landowners reluctantly converted more and more land to poppy production. The intention of course was to provide more opium profits for the East India Company and more tax revenues for the Crown. In the fourth decade of the nineteenth century, the predictable happened. The vast shipments of opium to China began to glut the marketplace. The response of the British was to cut the price. Between 1830 and 1839, opium prices averaged approximately 50 percent of those of the previous decade. Cheaper prices attracted more consumers. Thus, the pattern was set for one facet of British colonialism that was to continue through the century: pushing opium on an international level. Although the trade was finally halted in 1917, local production emerged (Owen 1934). Thus, the opium problem remained a colonial legacy in China, successfully controlled only with the coming of the Chinese Revolution in the latter half of the 1940s.

The Chinese began to emigrate to the United States in large numbers in the 1850s. Two decades later a serious crusade against opium use began during a period of economic depression. The press widely disseminated the imagery of opium-crazed Chinese who were supposedly a threat to "American" institutions. Native members of the working class blamed their grim economic condition on the unfair competition of Chinese immigrant labor. Thus, the "yellow peril" represented more than a symbol of cultural and racial bigotry. It was rather a specific ideology that diverted attention from the failure of the economic system, fragmented the working class, and preserved the interests of the higher circles (Helmer 1975).

The "Mexican Menace"   In the section that follows, detailed attention is given to the role of the Federal Bureau of Narcotics as an instrument in the development of the Marijuana Tax Act of 1937. However, it is vital to understand the historical period within which this legislation emerged. This was the decade of America's greatest (not only) depression (see Chapter Four). As with the decade of the 1870s, markets collapsed, industrial production sagged, and unemployment was rampant. Once again, a specific ideology of drugs emerged. This time opium and the yellow peril were replaced by marijuana and the "Mexican menace."

In 1928, the Benito Juarez Mutual Aid Society was founded as one of the first labor unions in California. It provided a storm warning for corporate agriculture and landowning interests in that state. The reason for this is clear. Agribusiness in California was built on cheap Chicano labor. The centrality of that labor was evident in the opposition by growers to immigration quotas for Mexicans. However, the coming of the Depression meant a surplus of cheap labor, especially in the urban areas (Los Angeles was a prime example).

In times of economic downturn, the propensity for scapegoating increases. The presence of Chicano workers as well as their use of cannabis as a peasant cure produced no great moral crusades or legislative efforts when economic times were good. However, with the onset of the Great Depression, the Chicano labor force was cast as a threat to the growing legions of unemployed. The use of marijuana became a symbol of evil. Users were supposed to commit violent crimes including the shooting of police. Salvation from the menace required "repatriation" (deportation) and jail for the "enemy deviants" (Helmer 1975). Thus, on a cultural level the marijuana menace was in part a nativistic phenomenon pitting Anglo against Chicano. As we shall shortly demonstrate, on the bureaucratic-political level, the "problem" became a reason for being for a specific government agency and countless other law enforcement interests. However, the societal foundation or infrastructure for both of these developments proves to be primarily the requirements of economic order.

509

INSTITUTIONALIZATION

In North America those antidrug movements with specific ideals consistent with corporate ideology helped to move the drug problem into an institutional phase. With the creation of an antidrug climate, drug restrictions assumed the force of law. Initial attempts to control opium were at the local level. The first antiopium law passed was a city ordinance in San Francisco in 1875. Virginia City, Nevada, followed suit in 1876. According to Terry and Pellens:

> As so frequently happens in social reform, it required this more spectacular method of opium use (smoking), the character of the places in which it was smoked, chiefly in Chinatown, and the attendant social evils, to awaken public and official interest (1928, p. 808).

This astute observation provides insight into the social circumstances surrounding drug use. The institutionalization of the problem was largely a response to the imagery surrounding those who used drugs. By the early part of the twentieth century, most states in the United States and most municipalities in North America had passed laws to counter the "drug problem." These early prohibitions against opium smoking can be viewed in light of ethnic inequality. The laws were a symbolic gesture to indicate the superiority of whites over Orientals in a time of great concern about the "yellow peril." More than "status politics," however, such laws, as we have seen, were instrumental in the exploitation of Chinese labor. The true "yellow peril" from the standpoint of such dominant interests as the railroads was that Oriental workers might organize and diminish the profits of westward expansion.

The first federal law in North America directed at opium use in general, and the Chinese specifically, was the 1908 Opium Act in Canada. It prohibited the importation, manufacture, and sale of the drug for other than medical purposes. Subsequently, the Opium and Drug Act of 1911 prohibited smoking opium and the nonmedical use of cocaine, morphine, and eucaine. Such legislation criminalized the user of these drugs.

> By undertaking an anti-opium smoking campaign on both racial and class lines, the middle class tries to disassociate themselves from such a vice. Since historically, the Japanese did not indulge in the use of opium, primarily due to their government's strict action against opium users, the Chinese bore the brunt of the criticism levied against such a habit. Upholders of Canadian public morality believed that once Oriental immigration was curbed, then the problem of the nonmedical use of opium would follow suit. By 1922, 65 percent of all illicit traffic in drugs was attributed to the presence of the Chinese in Canada. Canadians refused to admit that the problem of opium use for other than medicinal purposes

was in existence before the entry of the Chinese into the Canadian West. The presence of white opium addicts was blamed on the Chinese for their introduction of the opium smoking habit (Chapman 1975, p. 70).

Because of both domestic concern and international obligations, the United States Congress passed "an Act to prohibit the importation and use of opium for other than medicinal purposes" on February 9, 1909. It specifically prohibited opium prepared for smoking, while allowing other forms to be imported for medicinal purposes only. This law was passed largely in response to the investigation made by Hamilton Wright's American Opium Commission during the summer and autumn of 1908.

The initial concern expressed by medical and drug interests regarding the scope of such legislation was soon appeased and no hardships were imposed upon the manufacturers. Like its Canadian counterpart, this early legislation did not infringe upon medical and drug economic interests; therefore, opposition was slight.

While this act began to control smoking opium, it failed to control interstate traffic in other habit-forming drugs. Therefore, Hamilton Wright suggested that legislation was needed against these. As mentioned earlier, a vigorous movement was begun in the early part of the twentieth century in the United States against habit-forming drugs in general, and opium in particular. While state and local statutes were being initiated or revised, agitation was increasing for more federal control.

Both medical and drug interests were greatly concerned with the content of such control. Although Dr. Wright favored such legislation in Congress in 1910, it was not until December 17, 1914, that the major bill, the Harrison Narcotics Act, was approved. Numerous hearings were held before the Ways and Means Committee of the House. It appears that representatives of the drug trade and medical interests needed some time to modify the bill, notwithstanding pressures to get it passed (Reasons 1974).

In the final bill, evidence of the efforts of medical and drug interests were readily apparent. Two doctor senators, Gallinger and Lane, provided amendments that freed doctors, dentists, and veterinarians from the bill's restrictions. Exempted was "the dispensing or administration of these drugs to a patient by a physician, dentist, or veterinary surgeon in the course of his professional practice and for legitimate medical purposes." Thus, the above professionals were allowed to continue their administration of such drugs based upon their medical judgment. However, the phrase "for legitimate medical purposes" would prove to be a point of controversy in the near future.

The National Drug Trade Conference managed to delete a provision requiring the registration of manufacturers and of dealers in hypodermic syringes. Probably the most important amendment to the act that the drug trade obtained was the following exclusion: from "Certain preparations containing not more than two grains of opium, one-fourth grain of morphine, one-eighth grain of heroin or one grain of codeine or any preparations of them. . . ."

Thus, the medical and drug industries fared well in the establishment of this bill. The medical practitioner was assured that his professional duties would not be infringed upon, and the drug industry saved many of its cough medicines and other remedies from control.

While the Harrison Bill was lauded as a necessary step in eradicating this evil, some saw such deletions as not in the public interest. Dr. Harvey W. Wiley, vociferous critic and persistent crusader for adequate food and drug legislation, responded to the exemption of certain "medical preparations" in no uncertain terms:

> What more, may I ask, can any victim of the drug habit demand than to be able to get unlimited quantities of his drug in this diluted form? . . . Satan himself must rub his hands and smile with satisfaction when he reads such a section and such a proviso as that. . . . We need not expect to get a measure which really protects the public against the wiles of the mercenary manufacturer and vendor so long as the interests that acquire gain by the manufacture or distribution of these so-called remedies are allowed a controlling voice in the formation of the laws (Wiley and Pierce 1914, p. 398).

He further cited the fact that spent coca leaves were exempted primarily for benefit of the cola industry, additional confirmation of his position that the Harrison Act was largely fashioned for commercial interests. Thus, according to Dr. Wiley, such exemptions "are due to direct efforts of interested parties who are content to sacrifice public welfare to personal and corporate gain."

Interestingly enough, the above aspects of the bill were those under major criticism, while the medical practitioner's provisions went relatively unchallenged. As will become apparent, this was largely because the conception of the problem was primarily a medical one. Nonetheless, this aspect of the bill was to become the focal point of many subsequent battles between doctors and the United States Treasury Department. The medical interests were victorious in this initial battle.

Ostensibly, the main object of the Harrison Act was to provide certain definite legitimate channels through which the prescribed drugs should pass from the time of their importation to the time of their consumption, and to permit verification of this through specific machinery permitting a checking and tracing of the drugs. This was the manifest instrumental purpose of the law. Symbolically, it represented a reaffirmation of certain subsets of corporate ideology: rationality, self-control, and individual responsibility. An insight into an important latent function of the bill is provided by Dr. Wright in his description of the measure to Congress:

> It is designed to place the entire interstate traffic in the habit-forming drugs under the administration of the Treasury Depart-

ment. It is the opinion of the American Opium Commission that it would bring this whole traffic and the use of these drugs into the light of day and thereby *create a public opinion against the use of them that would be more important, perhaps, than the act itself.* (Italics are the author's.) (In King 1957, p. 116.)

Thus, Wright felt the bill and subsequent attention to it would further arouse the public and create a negative feeling towards the use of drugs.

A major point of concern after the passage of the act was the status of the addict. The Harrison Act left this indeterminate, neither outlawing addiction nor authorizing or forbidding doctors to prescribe drugs for addicts regularly. In fact, the Harrison Act did not mention the addict. So, while the "drug problem" was institutionalized, it needed further clarification. This was forthcoming shortly in a series of administrative decisions and court cases.

Criminalization of the Addict

With agencies of the State now fully activated, the control of drugs had moved from the movement or emergence phase. Accordingly, bureaucratic forces were formally involved in the institutionalization of the "dope menace" through legislation.

In 1919, the Narcotics Division of the United States Treasury Department began a two-pronged campaign of "informing the public" and instigating court cases. In a report dated June 1919, a committee appointed by the Treasury Department to study narcotics reported that there were 237,655 addicts in the United States treated by physicians; that there were over 1 million addicts; that there was extensive addiction among children; that narcotics were harmful to health and morals; and that these drugs were directly connected with crime and abject poverty (Dickson 1968). It appears that the intention of the Narcotics Division was to create widespread disgust toward narcotics users and generate support for state intervention. The image of the user, and subsequently of the "drug problem," was being changed and shaped.

Prior to, and immediately after, the Harrison Act, the addict was generally perceived as one who was enslaved and needed to be converted and salvaged through benevolent goodwill and humanitarian efforts. Thus, the major effect of drugs—moral degeneration—would only be halted by concerted efforts of those who care. Addiction was seen in medical terms as a disease that should be handled by physicians.

The addict through a specific ideology became both a "sick deviant" and a "repentant deviant." The sick image relates to the conception that addiction is an illness and many of those addicted contracted the illness

513

while under medical care, often by unscrupulous doctors, or through seduction by evil associates. The image of the addict as a "repentant deviant" emanates from the belief that the addict held allegiance to the major societal norms but through moral weakness or personal circumstances slipped into the depths of evil. It was believed that such a person desired to renounce this devil and hold to the values that it threatened.

Up to this time most users were believed redeemable. In a 1916 article a doctor suggested treatment for the social users, who comprised 70 percent of a group of addicts, as well as for another 10 percent who became dependent when drugs were used to treat illness. Thus, 80 percent of the users were felt salvageable through treatment, with the 20 percent defined as criminal and delinquent needing the services of the penologist and criminologist (Terry and Pellens 1928).

It appears that important changes in the image of the addict were brought about by changes in the way such persons were handled. A major attack was instigated against the medical profession through court cases in the United States. While the medical profession had come under attack for dereliction of professional duties in prescribing drugs indiscriminately after the Harrison Act, doctors continued to prescribe based upon the "legitimate medical purposes" clause. In Webb v. United States, the Supreme Court affirmed the following Treasury decision, dated March 20, 1919, restricting the physician's conduct:

> An order purporting to be a prescription issued to an addict or habitual user of narcotics, not in the course of professional treatment in an attempted cure of the habit, but for the purpose of providing the user with narcotics sufficient to keep him comfortable by maintaining his customary use is not a prescription within the meaning and intent of the act, and the persons filling and receiving drugs under such an order, as well as the person issuing it, will be regarded as guilty of violation of the law (Terry and Pellens 1928, p. 756).

This Supreme Court decision was the first of three that would shape the future of the "drug problem" in the United States. The subsequent two decisions would totally eliminate the doctor as a source of narcotics for the addict. In Jin Fuey Moy v. United States in 1920, the Supreme Court ruled that a doctor could not legitimately prescribe drugs "to cater to the appetite or satisfy the craving of one addicted to the use of drugs." Finally, in Behram v. United States in 1922, the Supreme Court ruled that such prescriptions were illegal regardless of the purpose the doctor may have had (Lindesmith 1965). This decision denied the addict all access to legal drugs.

Beginning with the Treasury decision and the Webb case, there had been continual conflict between enforcement personnel and medical practitioners regarding whether a "criminal approach" or a "medical approach" toward the addict was appropriate. Narcotics clinics were opened in 1918 to provide the addict with a medical resource. However, newspaper accounts portrayed them as "sinful places where the addict could go to satisfy his morbid desires and pursue the thrills and pleasures of narcotics." The addict would be subsequently viewed as an "enemy" deviant, indulging in drugs for personal pleasure in defiance of corporate ideology with its reliance on willpower and competitive individualism. Furthermore, such an individual was increasingly perceived in criminal terms as a threat to the personal safety and moral well-being of good citizens. While the early imagery was primarily one of a moral degenerate, the user's affiliations with the criminal class was increasingly emphasized. The user of drugs came to be associated with the "dangerous classes" and was viewed as manifesting disrespect for the imperatives of growth, progress, and hard work. This change in imagery is related to change in the type of user. While in the first decade the addict population was portrayed as relatively evenly spread over the social classes, by 1920 media reports held that most users were from the disrespectable underbelly of social order.

In a reaction to sensational journalistic coverage and the Treasury Department's pressure, the narcotics clinics were closed abruptly in 1922 (Duster 1970). The above decisions by the Supreme Court and the Treasury Department, together with the closing of treatment facilities in 1922, completed the transformation of addiction and the addict from a "medical" to a "criminal" problem. The addict's image was transformed rapidly from the "sick" and "repentant" deviant to the "enemy" deviant.

The "medical approach" was partially vindicated in Linder v. The United States in 1925, which found that a physician was not precluded by earlier decisions from giving an addict moderate amounts of drugs to relieve conditions related to the addiction. However, the Narcotics Division and other law enforcement officials did not include this decision in policy. Few reputable doctors cared to challenge existing enforcement practices since many of their colleagues were being convicted and jailed. Bowing to propaganda, enforcement policies, and public opinion, lower federal courts would not follow the implications of the Linder decision. Fearful of persecution through prosecution, the medical profession largely acquiesced to the "criminal approach," often being literally "handcuffed" in their efforts. While there remained a group of vociferous critics of the handling of the problem, the American Medical Association and most of its members came around to the Bureau's "way of thinking" and ceased to deal with addicts altogether. While the "medical approach" versus the "criminal approach" would still be debated in both professional and lay circles, the "criminal approach," propagated by the Narcotics Division, would reign through both propaganda and intimidation. The image of the addict, and subsequently of addiction, was reshaped and would determine policy for quite some time (Reasons 1975).

515

Banning Booze

Before continuing with an historical account of the criminalization of what are still considered "dangerous drugs," it is important to look for a moment at another substance. For in the same year (1919) that marked the public antidrug information campaign of the Narcotics Division of the United States Treasury Department, another event of some significance occurred. The rise and fall of state enforcement of alcohol "temperance" represents an important parallel in the history of drug control.

The first temperance organization, the Union Temperance Society, was founded by a physician in 1808. By 1836, the American Temperance Union was a national organization of more than 8,000 local chapters. They were largely antiworking class, antisaloon and anti-immigrant. During the latter half of the nineteenth century, the German immigrant became associated with the "evils" of alcohol and socialism. Thus, the prohibitionist movement was in this respect a defense of corporation capitalism. "Nativism" became an ideological rationalization for depressed wages, which in turn contributed to profit maximization. The anti-German facet of the prohibition movement became crucial during World War I. Anything German was degraded and portrayed as evil, including their drinking habits.

The Women's Christian Temperance Union (WCTU) was organized in 1874 in Cleveland with delegates from seventeen states. During the same year the Anti-Saloon League was founded. Over the next four decades, the temperance movement was to work in the historical context of expanding corporation power and economic control. Like the specific ideology of racism, which sought to legitimate slavery through casting the African (and others) as less than human, the specific ideology of temperance legitimated the exploitation of immigrant workers through depicting them as morally inferior. Such ideology was of course to be popular with native-born American workers whose hopes for better conditions appeared threatened by immigrants who were even more desperate than themselves. Thus, "nativism" was to fragment the working class and convert the immigrant into a scapegoat for a depressed wage structure. Cheap labor is of course in the interest of corporate profit maximization.

The temperance movement, consistent with the imperatives of corporate society, flourished and Prohibition was formally institutionalized with the passage of the Eighteenth Amendment by Congress in August 1917, and the subsequent completion of its ratification by thirty-six states by January 1918. Congress passed the enabling legislation, the Volstead Act, in October 1919. The enforcement of Prohibition was assigned to the Treasury Department on the grounds that it was a revenue act and $2 million was appropriated to implement the law. Events of the next decade, however, were to prove that the temperance movement had gone too far.

The "noble experiment" of Prohibition had not so noble consequences. The Volstead Act went into effect on January 16, 1920, and by 1924 the federal prison population had doubled, with most of the new inmates violators of the act. Arrests peaked in 1928 at 75,000, with 58,000 convictions. With Prohibition came an era of gangsterism, organized crime, much law enforcement corruption, and a great disrespect and/or disregard for the law and the legal system (Goshen 1973).

Notwithstanding the disaster of Prohibition, law enforcement officials praised the crusade and its consequences. After documenting the inability of the government to stem payoffs and corruption among prohibition agents, Goshen notes:

> Nevertheless, in 1922, Hayes, the New Commissioner of the Prohibition Unit, praised the new era of "clean living" that had prevailed since Prohibition had gone into effect and stated that there were no significant enforcement problems. He claimed, for instance, that 17,500,000 former alcoholics had given up drinking, thus making the whole experiment worthwhile. This blindness to reality was echoed many times later during the Twenties and has continued to be the dominant theme in the drug enforcement area today. Throughout both the alcohol and the drug prohibition eras, there has been a perpetual tendency for leaders in the enforcement area to misconstrue good intentions as actual practice (1973, p. 38).

By 1930, many organizations, including the American Legion, American Bar Association, and Women's Organization for National Prohibition Reform, among others, began supporting repeal of the Volstead Act. The experiment had ended in failure, with the speakeasy and bootlegging of the Twenties a fitting epitaph. More critical perhaps for the demise of temperance legislation were the shock waves of the Great Depression. The "New Deal" promised by the Democratic Party's candidate for the presidency in 1931 would require a massive and unprecedented exercise in state power. Prohibition had given rise to state corruption and thus was expendable. Franklin Delano Roosevelt campaigned on a "wet" platform and, upon assuming office in 1932, he called for the repeal of the Volstead Act. Subsequently the Eighteenth Amendment was repealed in 1934.

Reefer Madness

The demise of alcohol prohibition did not spread to the related area of "drug control." The Narcotics Division, placed within the Bureau of Prohibition from 1920–1930, had succeeded in institutionalizing its definition of the "drug problem" in national policy. The success of these efforts is to be found in increases in both arrests for federal narcotics violations and budgetary appropriations.

In August 1930, a separate Bureau of Narcotics was formed, no longer associated with the Bureau of Prohibition. Early in 1930 a federal grand jury revealed the padding of arrest records by narcotics agents and their collusion with illegal sellers; and the Bureau of Prohibition underwent immediate reorganization (Meisler 1960). The creation of the Federal Bureau of Narcotics (FBN) also appears to be related to the evident failure of the attempt to prohibit alcohol. While the outlawing of liquor was increasingly recognized as both a moral and bureaucratic failure, the elimination of narcotics would remain a national concern, partially filling the moral void created by the repeal of the Volstead Act. Harry J. Anslinger, assistant commissioner of the Bureau of Prohibition, was named the head of the new Bureau of Narcotics. Anslinger was to have an enormous impact upon national drug policy for the next thirty-two years. In fact, it may be said that subsequent to 1930 the Federal Bureau of Narcotics would be a personification of the "Anslinger philosophy." An essential ingredient in this specific ideology is that the addict is an "immoral, vicious, social leper," who cannot escape responsibility for his or her actions, who must feel the force of swift, impartial punishment. Thus, the "criminal approach" became the cornerstone of the FBN.

In 1923, marijuana was added to the schedule of the Narcotic Drugs Act in Canada. During the 1930s the United States Bureau of Narcotics became aware of a new "drug problem"—marijuana. Initially, the Bureau discounted it as a national threat requiring federal action, noting that the "publicity tends to magnify the extent of the evil and lends color to an inference that there is an alarming spread of the improper use of the drug, whereas, the actual increase in such use may not have been inordinately large" (U.S. Bureau of Narcotics 1932). However, the report also mentions that use was primarily among the Mexicans in the Southwest. At that time the Bureau suggested state legislation as a remedy. Coincidentally, the agency was sending out special representatives to campaign for a uniform state narcotics law, which included control of marijuana. In its report covering 1933, it notes: "A disconcerting development in quite a number of states is found in the apparently increasing use of marijuana by the younger element in the larger cities" (U.S. Bureau of Narcotics 1934). Thus Chicanos and youth, groups outside the mainstream of corporate society, were targeted for "salvation."

An increase in newspaper and magazine "revelations" concerning the negative effects of marijuana and its spread to the nation's youth aroused the public. According to Schaller:

> Middle-class white America of the 1930's had almost no contact with marijuana. Instead, it was subjected to a vicarious familiarity through the medium of hysteria-provoking stories that marijuana was a "killer drug" which inspired crimes of violence, acts of sexual

excess, impotency, insanity, and moral degeneracy. Special attention was given to its supposed effects on school children, lured by
insidious pushers to try the drug in the shadow of the school building (1970, p. 62).

The United States Federal Bureau of Narcotics was to become one of
the primary sources in shaping and sustaining such demonology. In its
report covering 1936, the Bureau first began its continuous presentation
of the specific ideology of the "violent addict." In a section entitled "Marijuana Crimes," brutal murders and other violent attacks were vividly
presented. In a continuation and exaggeration of the dope fiend imagery,
the Bureau's publications detailed the homicidal tendencies and the general debasing effects supposedly deriving from marijuana use.

The spread of "reefer madness" imagery can be related to the effort of
the Bureau of Narcotics. However, this specific ideology was consistent
with the general ideology of corporatism and so was publicized by the
media. The popular literature of the day became a forum for a new
crusade to save the republic from dramatized degenerate forces. Accordingly, the Marijuana Tax Act was passed in 1937, placing a prohibitively
high tax on marijuana and creating a whole new class of "criminals."
Anslinger personally provided information for two articles that appeared
in *Hygeia*, published by the American Medical Association. He describes
the history of marijuana use as a record of "crime, bestiality, and insanity" and notes that its users are all "degenerates" (Mandal 1966). Many
articles that appeared in professional and police journals can be traced
back to the Federal Bureau of Narcotics.

MAINTENANCE

Whose interests have been served historically by the war on selected
drugs? The Marijuana Tax Act was approved by Congress on June 14,
1937, and signed by President Roosevelt on August 2, 1937. A whole new
group of outsiders had been created and would provide a reason for being
for the Bureau of Narcotics agents. For example, in 1938, one fourth of
all federal drug and narcotics convictions were for marijuana offenses.
Furthermore, a decline in budgetary appropriations for the Bureau of
Narcotics was halted by the new marijuana prohibition. Schaller provides
a cogent summary of the preceding events and their subsequent effect:

> In law, the Federal Bureau of Narcotics had completely routed
> the forces of evil. It had shaped a law to its liking and had even
> triumphed over the scientific method which presumed to question
> the moral truths of the Bureau. The atmosphere was so clouded

that serious investigations into marijuana remained stifled for almost 20 years. The dedicated entrepreneurs within the Bureau had sold their beliefs not only to Congress and the public, but to a large part of the scientific establishment as well (1970, p. 74).

Thus, marijuana became the new peril in America. Anslinger declared:

> In the fight against narcotics, each victory leads to a new field of battle. Our most recent enemy is marijuana, the use of which as a narcotic drug was virtually unknown in the United States a decade ago. It is a new peril—in some ways the worst we have met and it concerns us all. . . . I believe that informed public opinion is the most powerful weapon with which to fight this dangerous public enemy (U.S. Bureau of Narcotics 1939, p. 57).

Indeed, through public appearances and publications, the "Anslinger philosophy" would continue to "inform" the public.

Postwar attention to the "drug problem" increased tremendously in the early 1950s. In 1951, the United States Kefauver Committee on Crime turned its attention to narcotics and marijuana, evoking a flurry of public apprehension. Articles in numerous popular magazines warned that drug addiction was on the increase and had captured elementary schoolchildren and teenagers. Anslinger provided much of the information concerning this alleged rise of drug use. In his statement before the Kefauver Committee in 1950, he had noted that although there had been an historical decrease in addiction, a recent reversal in this trend was manifest, with addiction rising among "young hoodlums." He recommended stiffer penalties for offenders and increased personnel for the Bureau. Lawmakers vying for public recognition as saviors in the face of this well-publicized menace introduced dozens of "tough" measures in the Eighty-first Congress. Both the addict and the pusher were identified as "enemy deviants." In fact, in this era of McCarthyism the "drug problem" became associated with the major evil of the time—communism, just as the use of alcohol had earlier been linked to socialism (U.S. Senate 1955). Somewhat ironically, during this same period the United States Army was experimenting with hallucinogenic drugs upon soldiers, among others (Calgary Herald 1975). This activity was not defined as the "drug problem," even though some apparently died from such experiments.

Two major pieces of "get tough" legislation were passed in the 1950s. The Boggs Amendment of 1951 attached mandatory minimum sentences to narcotics violations, with no probation or suspension for repeaters. The 1956 Narcotics Control Act extended this "get tough" approach with even more severe and inflexible penalties. The Federal Bureau of Narcotics and other law enforcement agencies were instrumental in pushing such legislation through Congress.

The Bureau noted the positive effects of the legislation and supported the additional punishment in the Narcotics Control Act of 1956. This further entrenched the "tough" approach, which subsequently was instituted in state statutes. During this period of heightened fears concerning the "drug problem," addiction per se was made a crime. Anslinger personally sent a congratulatory letter to the Chairman of the Board of Supervisors of the city of San Diego after it had passed an ordinance prohibiting addiction per se.

Bureau under Attack

While the Bureau continued to emphasize the positive effect of the no-nonsense approach, increasing criticism was heard during the late 1950s. Discussion of the "medical approach" as an alternative to the "criminal approach" was widespread. Probably the most controversial material to come out at this time was the Joint American Bar Association-American Medical Association report on drug addiction. In 1955–1956, the ABA and AMA appointed a joint committee to explore the problem. The committee presented an interim report in 1958, with a final report in 1959. Both the interim and final reports were published in 1961 by Indiana University Press under the title *Drug Addiction: Crime or Disease?* (Joint Committee 1961).

The interim report (1958) elicited a swift and vehement response from the Bureau of Narcotics. The most frightening aspects to the bureau were the suggestions by the joint committee that outpatient experimental clinics be established for the treatment of drug addicts and the conclusion that law enforcement was not the answer to the problem. In response, Anslinger appointed an advisory committee composed of "distinguished experts" in the field of narcotics, such as Hale Boggs, anti-communist congressman from Louisiana, to respond to the ABA-AMA report. The report (Advisory Committee 1959) was largely a personal attack upon those who served on the ABA-AMA committee and the sources cited in their report. It consisted of eclectic gathering of vehement, emotional responses to the "un-American" approach. (In fact, publication of the report was delayed due to its irrational attack upon the Supreme Court.)

While few copies of the ABA-AMA report were initially available, the Advisory Committee Report was printed in bulk and widely distributed. When the Indiana University Press was to publish the ABA-AMA position in 1961, an agent of the Federal Bureau of Narcotics was sent to the campus to "investigate" its publication. Thus, the Bureau was continuing its efforts to intimidate those whose views were contrary to its own. Nonetheless, criticism of the "criminal approach" was mounting.

In August 1962, Anslinger retired from the Bureau and Henry L. Giordano was appointed the new head. While he was a less vehement and vociferous critic of opposing perspectives, the "criminal approach" was still "the approach."

A New Challenge: Kids and Dope

It appears that public attention to the drug problem greatly increased in the second half of the 1960s. Much of this concern stemmed from the increased use of illicit drugs, primarily nonopiates, among the youth of the nation. Apprehension was particularly acute regarding marijuana, as evidenced in the 1966 *Annual Report of the Bureau of Narcotics:*

> The dangerous rise in illicit marihuana traffic and the increased use of marihuana and narcotic drugs by college age persons of middle and upper economic status became more evident at the close of 1966. These facts present a new challenge which must and will be met for the welfare of the country (U.S. Bureau of Narcotics 1967, p. 2).

This threat was to pose an increasingly more difficult problem for the Bureau, for besides being "enemy deviants," many users were "nonconformists" who openly attacked the laws as unjust and corrupt, and even proselytized the use of such drugs.

In response to those asserting that marijuana is no more harmful than alcohol and tobacco, the Bureau began to plan a program of counterattack in 1966: "to refute this misinformation and to convince or reaffirm the knowledge that marijuana is, indeed, a harmful and dangerous drug" (U.S. Bureau of Narcotics 1967, p. 25). A "Marijuana Task Force" of four agents specially trained in the abuse and dangers of pot was formed. Through speeches, conventions, seminars, symposiums, conferences, and resolutions, they began to get the message across to the American public. The bureau had a new and more insidious "enemy" to combat, the open and flagrant proselytizer of drugs.

The Enlightenment

In 1968, there was a reorganization of the agencies responsible for control of narcotics and other dangerous drugs in the United States. Under the reorganization plan the drug enforcement agencies of the Department of Health, Education, and Welfare and the Treasury Department (except those involved with customs) were merged and transferred to the Department of Justice as the Bureau of Narcotics and Dangerous Drugs. This move was designed to consolidate agencies for more efficient and effective law enforcement. Indeed, it seems befitting that the "drug problem" should be invested in the Department of Justice, given the "criminal approach" that has been emphasized. The Annual Report—*Traffic in*

Opium and Other Dangerous Drugs—was replaced with a new *Bureau of Narcotics and Dangerous Drugs Bulletin.* A new director, John E. Ingersoll, was appointed and he instituted a more enlightened, academic approach to the "drug problem." Social scientists were increasingly relied upon to present evidence and conduct studies concerning drugs, and the perpetration of the classical "dope fiend" mythology is not apparent in the bulletin. Thus, a new "era of enlightenment" seems to have been instituted within the department. However, the "criminal approach" remains the paramount method of handling the "drug problem" in the United States. This became apparent in later major federal legislation.

On October 27, 1970, President Nixon signed into law the Comprehensive Drug Abuse Prevention and Control Act. This can be said to be the most important legislation of this sort since the Harrison Act. The statute removes the tax base of control and eliminates the Harrison Act, Opium Smoking Act, Marijuana Tax Act, Narcotics Control Act, and others as the basis for controlling drugs. Although penalties have been generally reduced, reflecting a more informed perspective, the law still maintains essentially a "criminal approach" to the problem. Senator Harold Hughes proposed an alternate bill that would have created a new federal agency to coordinate drug abuse prevention, treatment, and rehabilitation. While the senator's bill had the support of doctors and health experts outside of government, it was attacked by administration supporters. Bureau director Ingersoll said the Justice Department strongly opposed the bill, with particular reference to a generalized finding that drug dependence is "an illness or a disease rather than a crime. This broad finding goes far beyond existing court decisions and might be a serious impediment to criminal prosecution" (Packer 1970).

Hughes's bill was not adopted, and the medical and scientific community attacked certain provisions of the administration's bill, particularly those putting control of drug classification, research funds, and research into drug abuse and medical practice under the purview of the attorney general. This concern was evident when the Committee for Effective Drug Abuse Legislation testified before the House Ways and Means Committee. Dr. Roger Meyer, lecturer at Boston University School of Medicine and former chief of the Center for Studies of Narcotic and Drug Abuse at the National Institute of Mental Health, states that such opposition:

> . . . was not from some fringe group of hippies' allies advocating the overthrow of traditional American values and the "turning on" of our young people. This was the health establishment, with views ranging from liberal to conservative, urging that mistakes of the past be avoided and that Congress legislate a public health approach to the drug problem consistent with several Presidential commissions and consistent with the intent of Congress in involving the medical community in the drug abuse and alcoholism areas (Reasons 1975, p. 26).

Nonetheless, the "criminal approach" was maintained as the Comprehensive Drug Abuse Prevention and Control Act became a law.

Youth Versus The Dominant Order   Of particular significance throughout the hearings was the great emphasis administration supporters placed upon youth and drugs. Such a focus brings out an important symbolic function of the act. The significant moral forces behind such action, particularly in the scheduling, or categorizing, of drugs, call on more than medical and scientific criteria. The scheduling is based primarily upon potential for abuse, medical benefits, and harmful effects. Marijuana is found in Schedule 1, "most dangerous." As was cogently pointed out by Director Ingersoll in discussing the attorney general's power to designate drugs for control, "An affirmative decision to control involves more than medical and scientific determinations. It has important policy, legal and enforcement implications as well" (U.S. Congress House of Reps. 1970, p. 220). Such behavior as permissiveness, immorality, irreverence, and self-indulgence was assailed in the congressional hearings as both cause and effect of drug use among youth. Particularly with reference to marijuana, this bill represented the victory of corporate ideology (triumph of the will, progress, conspicuous consumption) over the "hippie youth culture." In fact, marijuana remains a symbol of the youth culture, identified with an ongoing symbolic attack on the status quo. Discussion of marijuana often evokes in those who represent the dominant moral order visions of illicit sex, long hair, poor personal hygiene, and radicalism in politics. According to Erich Goode:

> The problem is one of hegemony, of legitimating one distinctive view of the world, and discrediting competing views (1969, p. 182).

An interesting fact relating to conflict between youth and the dominant moral order is that while between 1960 and 1969 total arrests for those under eighteen years old increased 105.4 percent, during the same period drug violations rose by 2,453 percent (males increased 2,281 and females 3,468 percent). In 1965, of the arrests for narcotic law violations 35 percent were for heroin or cocaine, while in 1969 this figure dropped to 29 percent. Between 1967 and 1971 there was a 400 percent jump in arrests for violations of state and federal drug laws. In 1978, a total of 596,940 arrests for drug abuse violations were reported to the Federal Bureau of Investigation. Of these, some 71 percent were for marijuana offenses. In other words, over 423,000 arrests in this year remained as the legacy of the Marijuana Tax Act in particular, and of the war on those who threaten the dominant ideology in general. Broken down, some 366,000 arrests were for possession while slightly more than 57,000 were for sale or "manufacturing" (that is, growing). Only 13.2 percent of all drug arrests (approximately 79,000) in 1978 were for heroin or cocaine violations. Of this total, some 22,000 were for sale or manufacture while approximately 57,000 were for possession. *For all drug arrests, 18 percent were for sale or manufacture; and 82.0 percent for possession* (U.S. Department of Justice 1979, pp. 187, 184, respectively). Statistics in Canada are similar. Marijuana was the unlawful substance in 92 percent of the convictions under the Canadian Narcotic Control Act in 1970, 93 percent of the convictions in 1971, and 91 percent in 1972 (Commission of Inquiry 1973). In summary, the statistical picture suggests that the war on drugs is primarily a war on marijuana and the fight against organized crime, pushers, and dealers is in reality more the persecution of users.

Pharmaceuticals: A Relaxed Crusade While the war on demon drugs has served the interests of law enforcement agencies, the plight of the pharmaceutical industry has been somewhat less grievous. The government agency charged with the protection of the public health in the area of "legitimate" (that is, corporate manufactured) drugs is the Federal Drug Administration (FDA). In a manner consistent with the structural imperatives of corporate society, the FDA has developed an intimate and supportive relationship with the pharmaceutical industry.

> This pro-industry bias comes not out of malice but from an attitude that places more emphasis on friendly cooperation with the industry than on public advocacy. The effect of this within the agency itself is to make the public the adversary and the industry the friend. This friendly working relationship between the FDA and the drug companies works well for the industry, as the following statement by C. Joseph Stetler, president of the Pharmaceutical Manufacturers Association, testifies: "As I look back over three or four years, we have commented on 60 different proposed regulations. At least a third were never published in final form. And every one, without exception, picked up a significant part of our suggestions (Hughes and Brewin 1979, p. 229).

The "working approach" results in ongoing "concern" for corporate problems, a positive approach to the introduction of new drugs, and the demoting of medical reviewers who believe in an adversative policy vis-a-vis the industry. One other structural observation common to the political bureaucratic elite also pertains to the FDA. In the not uncommon revolving door reality, top agency administrators frequently leave government to assume positions with the pharmaceutical industry they have been overseeing (Hughes and Brewin 1979, pp. 228, 254).

The Corporate Connection

While the 1970 legislation was a triumph over the long-haired hippie "dope fiend," it was also a victory for the American pharmaceutical industry. One observer notes that:

> The lawmakers who have declared that possession of marijuana is a serious crime have simultaneously defended and protected the profits of the amphetamine pill-makers. The comprehensive Drug Abuse Prevention and Control Act of 1970 in its final form constitutes a victory for that alliance over compelling, contrary evidence on the use of amphetamines . . . the end result is a national policy which declares an all-out war on drugs which are not a source of corporate income. Meanwhile, under the protection of law, billions of amphetamines are overproduced without medical justification (Graham 1972, pp. 14–15).

While amphetamines dwarf heroin and marijuana in use and potential abuse, they were placed in Schedule III, where they were exempt from quotas and were subject to lesser penalties and controls. Thus, present drug policies and laws do more than maintain the drug enforcement establishment. They also serve other interests, primary among them those of the "corporate connection."

In our earlier discourse on the prevailing ideologies that shape the definition of the drug problem, we undertook an examination of the pharmaceutical industry and its advertising influence. The standing of this particular business is greatly enhanced as medical practitioners become, in effect, the providers of psychoactive drugs. It goes without saying that the present definition of the drug problem diverts attention from the legitimate manufacturers of psychoactive chemical agents. As the statistics cited earlier confirm, this industry continues to expand. The corporations involved are multinational, and it should be noted that the quest for profit has led to unhealthy and unethical (if not strictly illegal) practices abroad. To be specific, psychoactive drugs such as antipsychotic tranquilizers and antidepressants (as well as other drugs) are marketed with "indications for use" as well as "contraindications and warnings" and "adverse reactions." An examination of this information, which is dispensed to doctors, reveals that the indications for use are *far more numerous* in Mexico, Central America, Brazil, and Argentina than in the United States. Further, the list of contraindications, warnings, and possible adverse reactions is *much smaller* in these Latin American nations. Thus, physicians in these countries are led to overestimate potential benefits and underestimate potential harms (Silverman 1976). However, the maintenance of the corporate connection does not end with the pharmaceuticals.

Where There's Smoke . . .   In 1964, the first report of the surgeon general in the United States on smoking and health noted the presence of seven carcinogens, in addition to a number of cancer promoters, in tobacco smoke. This report also cited a 70 percent increase in the age-specific death rate for male smokers (Environmental Defense Fund 1979, pp. 174–75). Government reaction was remarkably restrained. No new prohibitions were written into law. The persecution of tobacco users did not spawn a new enforcement bureaucracy. Rather, in 1971, a ban was placed on radio and television advertising of cigarettes while packages and print advertising began to carry a warning that "smoking may be hazardous to your health."

Despite the overwhelming evidence that cigarette smoking is a prime factor in lung cancer and other life-threatening diseases (Environmental Defense Fund 1979, pp. 173–79), this particular drug seems to produce little of the hysteria associated with marijuana. The answer to this riddle does not reside in toxicology or other biological sciences. It is found rather in the considerable influence of corporate power together with the revenues generated by tobacco for the coffers of the State.

The production, distribution, and sale of tobacco and tobacco products represents a $15 billion a year industry in the United States (Environmental Defense Fund 1979, p. 173). In 1970, the year before the television and radio ban on cigarette advertising, the tobacco industry spent $19 million on newspaper, $65 million on magazine, and $51 million on television advertising (*Statistical Abstract of the United States* 1972, pp. 758–59). Six years later (1977), the industry spent some *$234 million* for newspaper and *$194 million* for magazine ads, signaling a massive switch from broadcasting to print advertising (*Statistical Abstract of the United States* 1978, p. 855).

The Most Abused Drug Similar arguments can be presented with regard to the most abused drug in North America (Fort 1973). Heavy alcohol consumption produces the destruction of cells and the accumulation of fat in the liver. This medical condition is known as cirrhosis, a disease ranked fourth as the cause of death for those between twenty-five and forty-five in the United States. Alcohol abuse is also a causal factor in memory impairment as heavy drinking inhibits the production of ribonucleic acid and proteins by brain cells. The social costs of this legal drug were estimated at some $25 billion in the United States in 1974 through losses in work time, traffic accidents, and illness (Thio 1979, pp. 317–41).

Despite the record, the alcohol industry has indeed recovered from whatever indignities it may have suffered during the Prohibition Era in the United States. In 1977, expenditures for the personal consumption of alcoholic beverages in the United States topped $28 billion (*Statistical Abstract of the United States* 1979, p. 440). The alcohol industry also spent enormous sums associating alcohol use with the typical gamut ranging from sex and beauty to success and prosperity. In 1977, the cost to the industry of newspaper, magazine, and television advertising totaled over $465 million (*Statistical Abstract of the United States* 1979, pp. 596–97). It should come as no surprise to find that the per capita consumption of beer rose from 16.7 to 22.5 gallons between 1968 and 1977, a 35 percent increase. Also, between 1962 and 1977, the per capita consumption of distilled spirits rose by over 65 percent to a level of almost 3 gallons for each adult in the United States (*Standard and Poor's Industry Surveys* 1979, pp. B67 and B71).

Not to be overlooked in this scenario are the tax revenues that swell government treasuries. In 1977, state governments received over $2.1 billion in taxes on alcoholic beverages as well as some $3.5 billion from taxes on tobacco products. Federal excise taxes for these drugs in 1978 amounted to $5.6 billion and $2.5 billion, respectively (*Statistical Abstract of the United States* 1979, pp. 300, 264).

A Look at the Future

Because of its consistency with corporate and bureaucratic interests, it appears that the "criminal approach" will remain dominant. Table 9–2 shows that United States federal expenditures for drug law enforcement increased from $20.5 million in 1969 to over $226 million in 1973.

Increases in expenditures and law enforcement personnel are also evident in Canada. The Royal Canadian Mounted Police (RCMP) expanded its federal drug squad from 106 in 1969–1970 to 311 in 1972–1973, while local police forces were also evidencing increases (Commission of Inquiry 1973, pp. 82–89). Present enforcement costs continue to rise if not so dramatically.

A number of arguments have been marshalled to point up the irrational nature of most drug legislation in North America. For example, the marijuana prohibition produces a number of negative results: (1) at least one third of the younger generation are turned into criminals; (2) hostility toward the police is greatly increased among youth; (3) federal, state, provincial, and local governments expend great amounts of money and labor to enforce the laws and administer justice; (4) marijuana laws tend to make a mockery of drug education; and (5) by keeping marijuana illegal without eliminating it, the system funnels profits to those in the illicit drug market (Kaplan 1971).

An additional collateral effect is the "secondary" crime necessitated by the high cost of hard drugs. Addicts steal, not to pay for an inherently expensive drug, but for the incredible premium added through its criminalization. In England, in 1972, the pharmacy cost of heroin was 4 cents per grain. In the United States the street price was $30 to $90 per grain. (Szasz 1974, p. 211). Furthermore, the assumed need for no-knock laws, informants, and relaxed search-and-seizure regulations wears away at the basic rights of every citizen to be secure from the power of the State. An example of the excesses that our current drug policy fosters is the rash of erroneous break-ins. In a number of raids, narcotics agents have illegally broken into houses and abused the residents, who were innocent victims of mistaken identification. Several such forays have had tragic results—the death of innocent suspects or the shooting of obtrusive narcotics agents (*New York Times* 1973). Finally, illegal drugs and their higher tariff have produced much corruption in law enforcement personnel.

TABLE 9-2
Federal Expenditures for Drug Law Enforcement

Agency	Fiscal Year				
	1969	1970	1971	1972	1973
Justice:					
LEAA	$ 0	$ 0.6	$ 2.2	$16.6	$30.3
BNDD	16.8	25.8	41.3	59.7	71.2
Other	0.3	1.3	3.5	0.3	4.8
Treasury:					
IRS	0	0	0	7.6	18.9
Customs	3.1	12.4	30.2	46.8	54.3
State	0.3	1.3	1	1.0	1.6
Aid	0	0	4.4	20.7	42.7
Agriculture	0	0	0	2.1	1.8
Department of Transportation	0	0	0	0.5	0.5
Law enforcement, total	20.5	41.4	81.6	155.3	226.1

0 means less than $100,000.

Source: Second Report of the National Commission on Marihuana and Drug Abuse. *Drug Use in America: Problem in Perspective,* Washington, D.C.: U.S. Printing Office, 1973, p. 227.

Similar excesses have been noted in Canada. The Interim Report of the Canadian Government's Le Dain Commission observed:

> During the intitial phase of our inquiry, we have heard bitter complaints and criticism of the use of entrapment and physical violence to obtain evidence. We have not verified the particular circumstances of these complaints and criticisms, so that we make no charge of any kind at this time but we deplore the use of such methods to the extent that they may be resorted to on occasion. We believe that such methods are not only a serious violation of respect for the human person, but they are counterproductive in that they create contempt for law and law enforcement. The price that is paid for them is far too great for any good that they may do (1970, p. 250).

While the law enforcement model has yielded irrationalities and contradictions, it has served well to protect corporate ideology in general and the legalized drug industry in particular. It has also served to provide a growing bureaucratic domain with a continued reason for existence. However, as we came to understand in Chapter Two, a reductionist focus need not employ a "criminal approach." There are other ways to draw attention to those drugs that have no corporate constituency. Like the law enforcement model, the *treatment approach* encourages one to look away from the structural imperatives of profit and growth and how these operate in the tranquilizing of North America.

The Drug Treatment—Education—Industrial Complex

Jerome Jaffe, former head of the federal program to deal with drug use in the United States, noted in 1970, "It's getting to be a major industry. Either you sell dope or you cure addicts" (Buckley 1970). More recently, in discussing the consequences of the drug hysteria in the United States, the National Commission on Marijuana and Drug Abuse observes:

> The recent result has been the creation of ever larger bureaucracies, ever increasing expenditures of monies, and an outpouring of publicity so that the public will know that "something" is being done. Perhaps the "major" consequence of this ad hoc policy planning has been the creation, at the federal, state and community levels, of a vested interest in the perpetuation of the problem among those dispensing and receiving funds. Infrastructures are created, job descriptions are standardized, "experts" are created and ways of doing business routinized and established along bureaucratic channels. During the last several years, drug programming has become a multibillion dollar industry, one administering to its own needs as well as to those of its drug-using clientele. In drug use, this society may have inadvertently institutionalized it as a never-ending project (Second Report 1973, p. 27).

While most of the effort in the "war on drugs" has been expended through the law enforcement approach, a variety of "treatment" approaches have gained recognition and, more importantly, political and financial support. Geis (1972) reviews four major rehabilitative themes for narcotics addicts: (1) the community approach, (2) communal treatment programs, (3) treatments with a religious stress, and (4) chemotherapy regimens.

The community approach attempts treatment in the community environment, with hope that the user will cease to use drugs. This approach is difficult unless larger structural changes occur, such as eliminating the urban decay and deterioration that plague those corporate societies in which planning is seldom found. The communal treatment approach uses group pressures to bring about change among drug users. Synanon, a self-help treatment program for one-time addicts, operated by abstaining addicts, was heralded by some as a panacea to the drug problem. However, it treats very few addicts and its success rate is low. During its first seven years of operation it returned fewer than 100 persons to the community. Nonetheless, such an approach has wide appeal.

While religious involvement may provide a means for addicts of various "drugs" (caffeine, nicotine, alcohol, opiates) to establish a new identity and create a relatively drug-free existence, this has not been shown to be "the" answer. As with Synanon and other communal treatment programs, the religious "cure" of addiction depends on whether one remains in the supportive environment of the program. Those who leave typically relapse. Chemotherapy regimes are attempts to synthesize a drug having the effects of a narcotic but not producing physical addiction. Like the nonnicotine cigarette, decaffeinated coffee, nonalcoholic beer, and diet candy, there is an attempt to provide the euphoria of consumption without its negative consequences. A major attempt at such substitution has been "methadone maintenance." However, methadone is addictive. Further, it addresses only one facet of the problem. As one critic observes:

> The drug treatment business has entered the major leagues in the United States. It is now proposed that the federal government alone will spend about $1 billion over the next three years in an effort to stem the tide of the urban drug crisis. Its major treatment approach will be the widespread use of methadone, a typically American answer to a large-scale American problem—the use of a synthetic chemical to cure a complex socially rotted disease. Methadone has the benefit of being cheap and easy to administer, but is also the basis of a new bureaucracy within a whole new field in which to create a bureaucratic empire. For the addict it is a substitute addiction. Correctly administered, it can be the beginning of a new life for him, but only if methadone is recognized as a first step in the treatment process instead of a final solution—a legal addiction to replace an illegal one (Heyman 1972, p. 15).

Mandatory treatment, like the use of substitute drugs, can be oppressive. Thomas S. Szasz (1963), a psychiatrist, claims that "most of the legal and social applications of psychiatry, undertaken in the name of psychiatric liberalism, are actually instances of despotism and there is a danger in our society of tyranny by therapy." The use of the "civil commitment" of addicts to mandatory treatment has been a means of punishing the drug user. "Programs of civil commitment represent ways of punishing addicts under the guise of treatment; what is new in these programs is the vocabulary rather than the practices" (Lindesmith 1968, p. 240). In 1962, the United States Supreme Court ruled that punishing a person merely for being an addict, not for possession or some other substantive offense, was "cruel and unusual punishment." Therefore, civil commitment became the means of circumventing this ruling. The rate of failure for the methadone program is similar to others under correctional auspices (more than 80 percent). In addition, these have failed to provide the "accused" with the few safeguards available in the legal sphere.

Millions of dollars are being spent annually on drug education, and wherever this type of money is available, there will be many "innovative" responses to meet the challenge. Such corporations as American Telephone and Telegraph, Lockheed, Raytheon, and the 3M Company have contributed to drug education. A *Journal of Drug Education* has been established and many "authorities" have emerged to lead the educational campaign. While drug education is big business, there is no evidence to suggest it is a deterrent. In fact, the corporate interest in drug education is transparent. Beyond the obvious public relations and tax write-off benefits, corporate America gains through the subsidization of a specific drug ideology. For example, a Gallup Poll (1973) reported that the most common "explanation" for a perceived increase in crime was "increased use of drugs." Thus, once again reductionist "kinds of people" reasons divert attention from a structural focus. Street crime and other problems (including the truly serious abuse of psychoactive drugs) may constitute reactions to pronounced inequality and alienation, which are in turn the natural consequences of corporate society. And within corporate society, the state continues to play a primary role in "drug education."

> The state, defining drug use and addiction as a problem, has conditioned the public to respond by condemning the drug user, rather than questioning the kind of social order that makes drug use a viable alternative to everyday reality. Being taught to believe that the problem is in the drug user's morality or physical condition, rather than in the social order's pathology, those who rule maintain order without any threatening changes. The existing order is secured by legislating morality. The moral order and the social-economic order are inseparable; they serve each other (Quinney 1975, p. 91).

ALTERNATIVE

The British Approach

The Dangerous Drug Act of 1920 in England, like the Harrison Act of 1914 in the United States, allowed British physicians to prescribe drugs to patients based upon their professional judgment (Schur 1962). In 1970, London had approximately 3,000 addicts while New York had approximately 100,000. The United States criminalized the addict subsequent to the Harrison Act, thus contributing to the creation of a drug subculture, high prices, organized crime, and accessory crime for maintaining the habit, whereas Britain continued a medical approach toward addiction and suffered fewer deleterious consequences. While the "drug problem" increased in the 1960s and 1970s in Britain, the negative policy consequences were minor compared with those of North America. Heroin addicts lead "normal" productive lives while being maintained on their drug (Barbara and Morrison 1975). Many critics of North American policy have suggested trying the British approach, but the government and law enforcement agencies have constantly disparaged its positive effects, while expounding on its faults. The Consumers Union Report on *Licit and Illicit Drugs* notes that "review of the literature, moreover, has turned up no other country in the world, except Canada, which tolerates anything approaching the heroin black market in the United States" (Brecher 1972, p. 129). A similar statement might be made concerning American pharmaceuticals.

An increasingly large segment of society is calling for heroin maintenance programs for a pragmatic reason: to stop associated crime. For example, the oldest citizens' crime-fighting organization in the United States, the National Council on Crime and Delinquency, issued a policy statement nearly a decade ago supporting heroin maintenance:

> Therefore, until we understand our society better—until we determine why drugs are wanted in the first place and then remove those causes—heroin should be provided to those who need it by hospitals, clinics, and doctors under government regulations. This may not cure addiction, but it greatly enhances our ability to control the distribution of heroin. It will cut down the enormous profit now reaped by the underworld, and it will cut down the crime committed by addicts. Heroin maintenance is worth considering (Rector 1972, pp. 241–42).

While heroin maintenance may be a more humane method of handling narcotic addicts, what of the great proportion of the illicit drug-using population, the marijuana users? The treatment "solutions" discussed above have been largely aimed at narcotics users, while explicit proposals regarding "treatment" of the marijuana user are less evident. With the general trend in North America to lessen penalties for possession and use of marijuana, there is increasingly an acknowledgment that the user of pot does not need to be treated for an "illness." The assumption that the user of illicit drugs is sick, abnormal, emotionally ill, or weak of character is erroneous.

A society which does a better job of distributing rewards, influence, and dignity among all its people would be less prone to provide the motivation and market for various forms of serious escapism. However, an interim measure might bring more immediate relief.

Following the logic that a part of a loaf is better than none, the authors believe

1. That the British approach to heroin addiction is more rational than the present persecution method in North America.

2. That the use and possession of drugs should not be considered a crime.

3. That the commercial advertising of all drugs (alcohol, tobacco, prescriptions, and so forth) be banned. Such a restriction would apply to advertising in medical journals and by drug salespersons.

4. That periodic refresher courses on pharmacology offered under the auspices of certified medical schools be mandatory for all physicians and pharmacists.

5. That a new public interest agency be created to regulate the production and marketing of opiates, hallucinogens, and psychoactive prescription drugs. The FDA, an historical ally of the drug industry, would no longer serve in this area. The new agency would not be directed by career bureaucrats. Those entitled to representation would include, but not necessarily be restricted to, pharmacologists, legal specialists, consumer groups, and experts in the human sciences. This agency would be charged to provide reliable scientific information to consumers. As with alcoholism, treatment for other drug "problems" (primarily opiate) should be widely available but not compulsory. Such treatment should be covered by a national health care program that provides medical care at little or no fee.

Of course, the most important specific change would be structural, which in turn would largely encompass the other suggestions. We propose simply that the drug industry (including alcohol, tobacco, hallucinogens, and prescription drugs) be nationalized under the regulation of a public interest agency as described above.

It goes without saying that the drug phenomenon cannot be seen in isolation. Implicit in the five points above is the contention that "public" servants and agencies can somehow free themselves of the power of corporate imperatives and ideology in general, and the influence of the pharmaceutical industry in particular. For in order to implement such changes, the State would have to operate in this specific area in a manner contrary to the golden rule of political-economy.

As always, one must be concerned with the logical connections of given arguments. Although these propositions address drugs, they also threaten the advertising industry (what of caffeine in coffee, aspirin, and the additives in sugar-coated cereals?). They further challenge the marketplace "freedom" of physicians to decide their own professional training, and the continued domination of the economy by private corporate interests. Our proposals also imperil entrenched drug enforcement agencies. Perhaps their fate, as well as that of wider alternatives, rests with an enlightened populace.

BIBLIOGRAPHY

Advisory Committee to
the Federal Bureau of
Narcotics
1959

Comments on Narcotic Drugs: Interim Report of the Joint Committee of the American Bar Association and the American Medical Association. Washington, D.C.: U.S. Government Printing Office.

Barbara, John, and
Morrison, June
1975   "If Addiction is Incurable, Why Do We Try to Cure It?" Crime and Delinquency, January: 28–33.

Becker, Howard S.
1967   "Whose Side Are We On?" Social Problems 14 (Winter): 239–47.

Blum, Richard
1969   Society and Drugs. San Francisco: Jossey-Bass.

1971   "Drug Pushers: A Collective Portrait." Trans-action 8 (July/August): 18–21.

Brecher, Edward M.
1972   Licit and Illicit Drugs . Boston: Little, Brown.

Buckley, Tom
1970   "The Fight against Drugs Is in a Mess." New York Times, March 22.

Calgary Herald
1975   "Drug Death Claim Asks $8.5 Million." September 4: 2.

Chapman, Terry
1975   Opium Addiction in the Canadian West, 1900–1920. Unpublished thesis, University of Calgary, Department of History.

Commission of Inquiry into
the Non-Medical Use of Drugs
1973   Final Report of the Commission of Inquiry into the Non-Medical Use of Drugs. Ottawa: Information Canada.

Cook, Shirley, J.
1969   "Canadian Narcotics Legislation, 1908-1923: A Conflict Model Interpretation." Canadian Review of Sociology and Anthropology 6 (February): 36–46.

DeBakey, Lois
1977   "Happiness Is Only a Pill Away: Madison Avenue Rhetoric without Reason." Addictive Diseases, Vol. 3 (2): 273–86.

Dickson, Donald
1968   "Bureaucracy and Morality: An Organizational Perspective on a Moral Crusade." Social Problems 16 (Fall): 143–56.

Drugs and Drug Abuse
Education
1971
"AMA Officials Pot Shots Disputed; Taken out of Context, but I Don't Mind." March: 6–7.

Duster, Troy
1970
The Legislation of Morality. New York: Free Press.

Environmental Defense
Fund and Boyle, Robert
1979
Malignant Neglect. New York: Alfred A. Knopf.

Filler, Lois
1950
Crusades for American Liberalism. Yellow Springs, Ohio: Antioch Press.

Fingle, Edward, and
Woodbury, Dixon M.
1970
"General Principles." In The Pharmacological Basis of Therapeutics, 4th ed. Louis S. Goodman and Alfred Gilman, eds. New York: Macmillan.

Fort, Joel
1973
Alcohol: Our Biggest Drug Problem. New York: McGraw-Hill.

Freidson, Eliot
1968
"Ending Campus Drug Incidents." Trans-action 5 (July/August): 75–81.

Galliher, John F., and
Walker, Allynn
1978
"The Politics of Systematic Research Error: The Case of the Federal Bureau of Narcotics as a Moral Entrepreneur." Crime and Social Justice 10 (Fall–Winter): 29–33.

Gallup, George
1973
"Crime is Rated Worst Urban Problem." The Washington Post, January 16: A3.

Geis, Gilbert
1972
Not the Law's Business? An Examination of Homosexuality, Abortion, Prostitution, Narcotics and Gambling in the United States. Washington, D.C.: U.S. Government Printing Office.

Good Housekeeping
Magazine
1911
"Insidious Drug Habit in the Home." July: 55–56.

Goode, Erich
1969   "Marijuana and the Politics of Reality." Journal of Health and Social Behavior 10 (June):83–94.

1972   Drugs in American Society. New York: Alfred A. Knopf.

1974   "The Criminology of Drugs and Drug Use." In **Current Perspectives on Criminal Behavior:** Original Essays on Criminology. Abraham S. Blumberg, ed. New York: Alfred A. Knopf, pp. 165–91.

Goshen, Charles E.
1973   Drinks, Drugs and Do-Gooders. New York: Free Press.

Graham, James M.
1972   "Amphetamine Politics on Capitol Hill." Transaction 9 (January): 14–20.

Gusfield, Joseph R.
1963   Symbolic Crusade: Status Politics and the American Temperance Movement. Urbana: University of Illinois Press.

Helmer, John
1975   Drugs and Minority Oppression. New York: Seabury Press.

Heyman, Florence
1972   "Methadone Maintenance as Law and Order." Society 9 (June): 15–25.

Hughes, Richard, and Brewin, Robert
1979   The Tranquilizing of America. New York: Harcourt Brace Jovanovich.

Isbell, H.
1963   "Historical Development of Attitudes toward Opiate Addiction in the United States." In Man and Civilization: Conflict and Creativity. Seymour M. Farber and Rodger H.L. Wilson, eds. New York: McGraw-Hill, pp. 154–70.

Joint Committee of the American Bar Association and the American Medical Association on Narcotic Drugs
1961   Drug Addiction: Crime or Disease? Bloomington, Ind.: Indiana University Press.

Kaplan, John
1970   Marijuana: The New Prohibition. New York: World,

Kennedy, Mark
1970   "Beyond Incrimination." Catalyst 6 (Summer): 1–37.

King, Rufus
1957   "Narcotic Drug Laws and Enforcement Policies." Law and Contemporary Problems 22 (Winter): 113–31.

Le Dain Commission
1970   Le Dain Commission Interim Report. Ottawa: Information Canada.

Lindesmith, Alfred R.
1940a   "Dope Fiend Mythology." Journal of Criminal Law, Criminology and Police Science 31 (July-August): 199–208.

1940b   "The Drug Addict as a Psychopath." American Sociological Review 5 (December): 914–20.

1965   The Addict and the Law. Bloomington, Ind.: Indiana University Press.

1968   Addiction and Opiates. Chicago: Aldine.

Lowes, Peter D.
1966   The Genesis of International Narcotics Control. Geneva. Switzerland: Librarie Droz.

Mandal, J.
1966   Hashish, Assassins, and the Love of God." Issues in Criminology 2 (Fall): 149–56.

McCoy, Alfred W.
1972   The Politics of Heroin in Southeast Asia. New York: Harper & Row.

Meisler, S.
1960   "Federal Narcotics Czar." The Nation, February 20: 159–62.

Murphy, Emily
1922   The Black Candle. Toronto: Thomas Allen.

National Commission on Marijuana and Drug Abuse
1972   Marijuana: A Signal of Misunderstanding. Washington, D.C.: U.S. Government Printing Office.

1973a   The Technical Papers of the Second Report of the
             National Commission on Marijuana and Drug
             Abuse, Volume I, Patterns and Consequences of
             Drug Use. Washington, D.C.: U.S. Government
             Printing Office.

1973b   Second Report of the National Commission on
             Marijuana and Drug Abuse, Drug Use in America:
             Problem in Perspective. Washington, D.C.: U.S.
             Government Printing Office.

1973c   The Technical Papers of the Second Report of the
             National Commission on Marijuana and Drug
             Abuse, Volume 2, Social Responses to Drug Use.
             Washington, D.C.: U.S. Government Printing
             Office.

New York Times
  1973   "Violent Drug Raid against the Innocent Found
             Widespread." June 25, p. 1.

Nuehring, Elaine, and
Markle, Gerald E.
  1974   "Nicotine and Norms: The Re-Emergence of a
             Deviant Behavior." Social Problems 21 (April):
             511–26.

Owen, David E.
  1934   British Opium Policy in China and India. New
             Haven, Conn.: Yale University Press.

Packer, H.
  1970   "A Guide to Nixon's New Crime Control." New
             York Review of Books, October 22: 26–37.

Pekkonen, John
  1973   The American Connection: Profiteering and
             Politicking in the "Ethical" Drug Industry.
             Chicago: Follett.

Quinney, Richard
  1975   Criminology. Boston: Little, Brown.

Reasons, Charles E.
  1974   "The Politics of Drugs: An Inquiry in the Sociology
             of Social Problems." The Sociological Quarterly
             (Summer): 381–04.

  1975   "The Addict As a Criminal: Perpetuation of a
             Legend." Crime and Delinquency 8 (January):
             19–27.

1976 "Images of Crimes and Criminals: The Dope Fiend Mythology." Journal of Research in Crime and Delinquency 13 (July): 133–44.

Rector, Milton G.
1972 "Heroin Maintenance: A Rational Approach." Crime and Delinquency 18 (July):240–42.

Schaller, M.
1970 "The Federal Prohibition of Marijuana." Journal of Social History 4 (Fall): 61–74.

Schur, Edwin
1962 Narcotic Addiction in Britain and America. Bloomington, Ind.: Indiana University Press.

Silverman, Milton
1976 The Drugging of the Americas. Berkeley, Calif.: University of California Press.

Smith, R.
1966 "Status Politics and the Image of the Addict." Issues in Criminology 2 (Fall): 157–75.

Standard and Poor's
1979 Industry Surveys. New York: Standard and Poor's Corporation, July.

Szasz, Thomas S.
1963 Law, Liberty and Psychiatry: An Inquiry into the Social Uses of Mental Health Practices. New York: Macmillan.

1973 "The Ethics of Addiction." In Readings in Social Problems. '73–'74, Guilford, Conn.: Dushkin, pp. 134–40.

1974 Ceremonial Chemistry. Garden City: Anchor Press.

Taylor, Arnold H.
1969 American Diplomacy and the Narcotics Traffic, 1900–1939: A Study in International Humanitarian Reform. Durham: Duke University.

Terry, Charles E., and Pellens Milfred
1928 The Opium Problem. New York: Bureau of Social Hygiene.

United States Bureau of
the Census
 1972
 1978
 1979

Statistical Abstract of the United States. Washington, D.C.: U.S. Government Printing Office.

United States Bureau of
Narcotics
 1932–1968

Traffic in Opium and Other Dangerous Drugs for
the Years 1930–1967. Washington, D.C.: U.S.
Government Printing Office.

United States Department
of Justice
 1979

Uniform Crime Reports. Federal Bureau of
Investigation. Washington, D.C.: U.S. Government
Printing Office.

United States Senate
 1955

"Communist China and Illicit Narcotics Traffic."
Hearings before the Subcommittee to Investigate
the Administration of the Internal Security Law
of the Committee on the Judiciary, 84th Congress,
1st session.

Waldorf, Don
 1973

Careers in Dope. Englewood Cliffs, N.J. Prentice-
Hall.

Weber, Max
 1958

The Protestant Ethic and the Spirit of Capitalism.
New York: Scribner's.

Webster's New World
Dictionary
 1971

Webster's New World Dictionary of the American
Language, paperback ed. New York: Popular
Library.

Weil, Andrew
 1973

The Natural Mind. Boston: Houghton Mifflin.

Wiley, H. W., and
Pierce, A.L.
 1914

"The Cocaine Crime." Good Housekeeping,
March: 393–98.

Wright, Hamilton
 1910

Report on the International Opium Commission
and on the Opium Problem as Seen within the
United States. Washington, D.C.: U.S.
Government Printing Office.

541

10

RACE AND RACISM

Abstract

Although the concept of race has been given various definitions during the last few centuries, it has historically meant the exploitation and subjugation of people. A product of state imperialism and corporate growth, racism in Canada and the United States has not been squarely confronted. The prevailing ideologies such as *blaming the victim* and/or *individual prejudice and discrimination* have largely failed to address *institutional racism.* The history of state policies give evidence of institutional racism, including genocide. It remains for workers and minority groups acting together to provide effective alternatives to dominant policies and practices. The liberation movements of blacks, Indians, Chicanos, and French-Canadians are as much *class-based struggles* as they are racially founded.

It is difficult to let others see the full psychological meaning of caste segregation. It is as though one, looking out from a dark cave in a side of an impending mountain, sees the world passing and speaks to it; speaks courteously and persuasively, showing them how these entombed souls are hindered in their natural movement, expression, and development; and how their loosening from prison would be a matter not simply of courtesy, sympathy, and help to them, but aid to all the world. One talks on evenly and logically in this way but notices that the people passing do not hear; that some thick sheet of invisible but horribly tangible plate glass is between them and the world. They get excited; they talk louder; they gesticulate. Some of the passing world stop in curiosity; these gesticulations seem so pointless; they laugh and pass on. They still either do not hear at all, or hear but dimly, and even what they hear, they do not understand. Then the people within may become hysterical. They scream and hurl themselves against the barriers, hardly realizing in their bewilderment that they are screaming in a vacuum unheard and that their antics may actually seem funny to those outside looking in. They may even, here and there, break through in blood and disfigurement, and find themselves faced by a horrified, implacable, and quite overwhelming mob of people frightened for their own very existence. —W.E.B. DuBois

Racial and ethnic minorities have been increasingly assertive in demanding equality in North America in the last forty years. Blacks, Chicanos, and Indians in the United States and Indians and French-speaking people in Canada have become fairly well organized and political since World War II. Such movements have largely been a consequence of the growing awareness among these minorities that their individual fate is tied to their collective fate, and as a group their life chances are much poorer than those of dominant group members. When we analyze income, occupation, employment, housing, health, and wealth, we find sharp differences between racial groups.

A Shorter, Poorer Life

Perhaps the most meaningful approach to the nature of racism in North America is to understand its relationship to life expectancy. Many have focused, as does the passage from DuBois, on the psychological bondage that remains after the chains disappear. However, inequality in the United States for nonwhites means more than a psychic form of death. In 1977, the death rate per 1,000 live births for white males was 13.98 and for white females 10.75. The corresponding rates for nonwhites were 23.91 and 19.73 (*Statistical Abstract of the United States* 1979, p. 71).

Turning to other indicators, in Table 10–1 we find that blacks are consistently behind whites in income in the United States, but much more heavily represented in unemployment and poverty. While there was a slight gain in the income ratio through 1975, this is somewhat deceptive since it is based on families. Black families are larger than white, more blacks are unrelated, and more blacks, particularly the poor, are not included in the mail census (Jhabzala 1977).

Further, black income compared with white income has slipped significantly in the last two years (as specified in the table) so that the ratio in 1977 was only slightly better than that of 1966. Unemployment and poverty have remained fairly constant during this twenty-five year period. By 1977, median black family income was only 61 percent of

TABLE 10-1
Racial Inequality over Time, 1950–1977

Year	1[a] Black Income White Income	2[b] Black Unemployment White Unemployment	3[c] Black Poverty White Poverty
1950	.54	1.8	n.a.[d]
1951	.53	1.7	n.a.
1952	.57	1.9	n.a.
1953	.56	1.7	n.a.
1954	.56	2.0	n.a.
1955	.55	2.2	n.a.
1956	.53	2.3	n.a.
1957	.54	2.1	n.a.
1958	.51	2.1	n.a.
1959	.54	2.2	2.9
1960	.55	2.1	3.1
1961	.53	2.1	3.2
1962	.53	2.2	3.4
1963	.53	2.2	3.3
1964	.56	2.1	3.3
1965	.55	2.0	3.5
1966	.60	2.2	3.5
1967	.62	2.2	3.4
1968	.63	2.1	3.4
1969	.63	2.1	3.3
1970	.64	2.0	3.2
1971	.63	1.8	3.1
1972	.62	2.0	3.5
1973	.60	2.1	3.5
1974	.62	2.0	3.3
1975	.65	1.8	3.0
1976	.63	1.9	3.2
1977	.61	2.1	3.3

[a] Col. 1: Median black family income/median white family income.

[b] Col. 2: Percent of black labor force unemployed/percent of white labor force unemployed.

[c] Col. 3: Percent of black population living in poverty/percent of white population living in poverty.

[d] n.a. means not available.

Sources: Through 1974: Cols. 1 and 3 from U.S. Bureau of the Census, "The Social and Economic Status of the Black Population in the U.S., 1974," *Current Population Reports,* Series P–23, Number 54, July 1975, pp. 25 and 42, respectively. Col. 2 from *Manpower Report of the President,* 1974, (Washington, D.C.:U.S. Government Printing Office, 1975), p.230. From 1975–1977: *Statistical Abstract of the United States,* 1978, pp. 452, 408, 466.

white family income, while the gap in absolute dollars grew from $2,846 in 1959 to $6,300 in 1976 (Ritzer, Kammeyer, and Yetman 1979, p. 365). While blacks comprise over ten percent of the United States population, they are second-class citizens in income, employment, and poverty.

Indians are Canada's largest "racial" minority and have a per capita income per year about 25 percent of that for Euro-Canadians. Over 80 percent of the Indian population lives in poverty. Jobs held by native

Americans are primarily unskilled and their unemployment rate is three times that of the total Canadian labor force. The infant mortality rate for children in their first year is three times higher among native children, and eight times higher for babies up to two years of age. In 1970, the average life span of an Indian was thirty-four years compared with seventy-two for the average white (Frideres 1974). The situation for native people in the United States is hardly any better (Price 1978; Bahr et al. 1972). It is safe to say that of all North American minorities the Native population has been the most oppressed in income, housing, occupation, education, health, and the other indicators of well-being.

French-Canadians are the largest ethnic minority in Canada, comprising approximately 30 percent of the population for over a hundred years. As a dominated ethnic minority group, they have experienced discrimination primarily in education and employment, a fact reflected in their underrepresentation in white collar and higher occupations (Manzer 1974, pp. 206–33).

The position of nonwhites in the United States occupational structure is presented in Table 10–2. While nonwhites have made apparent gains in white collar and skilled blue collar work, they remain greatly overrepresented in laboring and service jobs. As the income data suggest, this has not really affected their position relative to whites.

The apparent contradiction between better jobs and continuing income disadvantage can be resolved if one takes notice of the true meaning of job titles. Historically, in Western corporate societies various occupations have been "upgraded" by agencies of the State (such as the Bureau of the Census and the Department of Labor), which means that additional skill requirements have been "identified" for certain kinds of work. However, a careful look at the record suggests that much of this upgrading is more a matter of definition than of substance. Blacks and other nonwhites as social categories (irrespective of individual exceptions) have become the beneficiaries of the increased "status" of occupational labels without the income to show for it. Accordingly, nonwhites are participating disproportionately in a process termed by one economist "the degradation of work in the twentieth century" (Braverman 1975).

One must remember that job titles as occupational categories are neither objective nor clear-cut. In the United States, the term "white collar" is most accurately applied to clerks, as they account for the largest subdivision within that occupation (36 percent in 1978) (*Statistical Abstract of the United States* 1979, p. 415). Another example is found in the blue collar categories of "operatives" (typically factory workers) and "laborers." This distinction is based on the misleading definition by agencies of the State that the former occupation is "semiskilled" while the latter is "unskilled." "Semiskilled" workers are distinguished only by receiving brief on-the-job training (ranging from a few hours to a few weeks). Thus, one has an apparent as opposed to a real increase in the skills of the working class (Braverman 1974, pp. 428–33).

	1940	1950	1960[b]	1965[b]	1970[b]	1977[b]
White Collar:						
Professional, technical, and kindred workers	.36	.40	.49	.55	.64	.78
Managers, officials, and proprietors, except farm	.17	.22	.23	.25	.33	.45
Clerical and kindred workers	.12	.29	.46	.53	.76	.90
Sales workers		.18	.23	.29	.34	.41
Blue Collar:						
Craftworkers, foremen, and kindred workers	.27	.38	.49	.52	.64	.69
Operatives and kindred workers	.57	.94	1.08	1.15	1.34	1.33
Laborers, except farm and mine	2.06	2.56	2.59	2.40	2.18	1.66
Service workers:						
Service workers, except private household	1.53	2.00	2.02	1.94	1.77	1.68
Private household workers	4.66	5.92	5.46	4.10	3.89	3.23
Farm						
Farmers and farm managers	1.31	1.22	.78	.58	.45	.24
Farm laborers and foremen	2.57	2.28	2.46	2.25	1.68	1.29

Source: For 1940-1960, Glenn, 1963: Table 1. Ratios for 1965 and 1970 are computed from basic data in Department of Labor, Bureau of Labor Statistics, *Monthly Labor Review* and *Employment and Earnings Report on the Labor Force.* Ratios for 1977 are computed from data in *Statistical Abstract of the United States* 1978, pp. 418-19.

[a] The "expected" proportion of nonwhites in each occupational category is the proportion of all workers in that category. For instance, in 1965, 12.3 percent of all employed workers in the United States were professional, technical, and kindred workers, and therefore one would "expect" 12.3 percent of the employed nonwhites to be in that occupational category. However, only 6.8 percent of employed nonwhites were actually so employed. Thus, the ratio of actual to expected is .55, that is, 6.8/12.3 = 0.55. If nonwhites were proportionately represented, the ratio would be 1.00. A ratio of more than 1.00 indicates overrepresentation, and a ratio of less than 1.00 indicates underrepresentation.

[b] Inclusion of nonwhites in Hawaii accounts for a small part of the changes after 1950.

What is perhaps crucial is that *occupational classification is not necessarily related to income.* For example, blue collar craftworkers had a median weekly income of $279.00 in 1978, compared with $232.00 for white collar clerical workers (*Statistical Abstract of the United States* 1979, p. 420). Further, there is obviously enormous variation in earnings within occupational categories. Both physicians *and* nurses are health care *professionals.* In short, there is general tendency in corporate economy toward a fragmented division of labor, with a continuing erosion of skills required for many white and blue collar jobs. When this is connected with the absence of any clear association between broad occupational categories and earnings, the only conclusion to be drawn is that job title "uplift" for workers in general and minority groups in particular constitutes little more than illusion. In recent history, nonwhites have come to partake of a greater share of the prevailing fiction.

One economist has calculated how far behind blacks are from whites in certain indicators of well-being (Table 10-3). He states that this does not mean that blacks are catching up but merely gives an indication of

TABLE 10-3
Years Blacks Are behind Whites

Indicator of Well-Being	Approximate Number of Years that Blacks Are behind Whites
Income	30
Employment	50 or more
Education	over 20
Housing	20 to 30
Health	from 20 to 30
Wealth	over 100

Source: Jhabzala 1977, p. 159.

TABLE 10-4
Black Population as a Percentage of the Total Population of the Twelve Largest U.S. Cities: 1920, 1950, 1970

City[a]	1920[b]	1950[b]	1970
New York	2.7%	9.8%	21.1%
Chicago	4.1	14.1	32.7
Los Angeles	2.7	10.7	17.9
Philadelphia	7.4	18.3	33.6
Detroit	4.1	16.4	43.7
Houston	24.6	21.1	25.7
Baltimore	14.8	23.8	46.4
Dallas	15.1	13.2	24.9
Washington, D.C.	25.1	35.4	71.1
Cleveland	4.3	16.3	38.3
Indianapolis	11.0	15.0	18.0
Milwaukee	.5	3.6	14.7

[a] These were the 12 largest cities in 1970.
[b] Figures pertain to "nonwhite" population.

Source: U.S. Census of 1920 and 1950, "Characteristics of the Population," *Statistical Abstract,* 1972, pp. 21–23.

the significant gap between the conditions of white and black. Therefore, white income thirty years ago is comparable to black income today, while white wealth (net wealth and assets) over one hundred years ago is similar to the position of blacks today (Jhabzala, 1977). Since there has been practically no change in the relative position of blacks and whites since World War II, equality appears to await a fundamental alteration in the political economy of corporate society.

Increased Racial Consciousness Further contributing to the increased racial consciousness of minority group members is their sharing of mutual problems, particularly in large urban areas. The ghetto, barrio, or urban Indian neighborhood provides a base for collective efforts. As Table 10–4 indicates, the complexion of major cities in the United States has dramatically changed in this century.

The increased visibility and concentration of minorities in large cities has undoubtedly affected the way in which race is perceived. While racial conflict is usually seen as a dilemma of the United States, the following *Perspective* points out that Canada also has problems of racial conflict and oppression. This is because the roots of race-related ideology and oppression can be traced to similarities in the historical development of the North American economic order. As we shall soon discover, racism has proven to be an invaluable weapon for justifying colonialism—old and new, international and domestic.

Viewpoint

"A CAUSE FOR CONCERN"*   **by Daniel G. Hill**

In 1973, the United Nations proclaimed the start of what it called the Decade for Action to Combat Racism and Racial Discrimination. For Canada, the timing was ironically appropriate. In the ensuing few years, a series of racial traumas rudely forced many Canadians to recognize festering racial problems here of a scope that few people previously acknowledged. We were finally made to re-examine our complacency and confront the clear evidence of racism throughout Canada.

*From *Human Rights in Canada: A Focus on Racism*, Ottawa: Canadian Labour Congress, 1978.

THE IDEOLOGY OF SOCIAL PROBLEMS

If Canadians are disturbed or shocked by revelations of racism in their society, that is as it should be. If they are surprised or puzzled by it, however, that demonstrates an abysmal lack of awareness—of the less creditable aspects of Canadian history. Racist themes originate deep in Canada's past, reverberate through the country's development and ring clearly in many of our contemporary social conditions and institutional practices.

Among the earliest acts of willful racism recorded in Canadian history—although rarely mentioned—was the slaughter of Beothuk Indians of Newfoundland in the 18th century. A Newfoundland government tourist brochure quaintly attributes the disappearance of the Beothuks to killings that resulted from "misunderstandings" and starvation resulting from Europeans "unknowingly" blocking Beothuk hunting routes. However, evidence exists to show that Beothuks were often killed on sight, sometimes captured for display, and indeed, starved out by white settlements that served to dry up food sources.

During roughly the same period, the slave trade was thriving in Canada, although Canadians like to think of slavery as distinctly an American institution. In fact, the first slave was brought to New France in 1628 from Madagascar. In the St. Lawrence and Niagara regions of Upper Canada, slaves were brought by the United Empire Loyalists during and after the American Revolutionary War. Indeed, at least six of the sixteen legislators in the first Parliament of Upper Canada owned slaves.

Slave holdings in all parts of the emerging Canada grew in the ensuing decade, so much so that in New Brunswick and Nova Scotia a "removal" program was instituted. The British government paid the Sierra Leone Company to transport 1,180 freed men and women, all of whom had asked to go, to the new African colony of Sierra Leone.

By 1833 slavery was finally abolished throughout the British Empire, but life was destined to be hard for illiterate blacks who were freed but required to apply minimal farming skills on the largely barren lands on which they were settled. The effects of their poverty would be felt well over a century later, and they would find that freedom from slavery was not freedom from racism.

School segregation, for example, was legally established in 1849 under the euphemistically titled Act for the Better Establishment and Maintenance of Public Schools in Upper Canada. (Ironically, Canadians were inclined to feel morally superior when the civil rights movement assailed southern U.S. school segregation in the early 1960s, but it was not until 1965 that the last segregated school in Ontario was closed.)

By the mid-1800s, the Metis, a people of mixed Indian and French Catholic origins, were also feeling the effects of mounting racism. Having struggled under the leadership of Louis Riel to establish their claim to the Red River area of Manitoba, they eventually found their leader exiled and their lands taken over by anti-French, anti-Catholic, anti-Indian squatters from the East. Moving west to new lands promised them by the government, they soon found those lands taken as well. Returning from exile, Riel found the government unwilling to take measures necessary to resolve Metis grievances. As a consequence, he set up a provisional government for Metis areas in Saskatchewan, but that action ultimately provoked a series of battles between the Metis and government troops. The Metis were defeated and Riel was hanged as a traitor to Canada in 1885. Subsequently, most Metis agreed under treaty to accept cash instead of land as a settlement with the government, but the money was soon spent. Again, poverty complicated by racism, this time afflicting the Metis, became part of the Canadian social fabric.

Meanwhile, the pattern of treatment that would ultimately lead to Indian deprivation was also being established in the 1800s. Indian interests in lands were being "alienated" through treaties; Indians themselves were being assigned to reserves and a government department was assuming charge of Indian affairs.

It was an arrangement whereby, theoretically, Indians were to be protected and eased into white civilization. In fact, it served to get them out of the way—to allow for the expansion of white society and to remove them from the mainstream of economic, social, and political life.

Other "civilizing" efforts and "protective" measures under the Indian Act have also been revealed as less than beneficient. Ralph Steinhauer, the Indian who became Lieutenant-Governor of Alberta, has written of having his rear kicked for daring to speak Cree on his school playground when he was a child. He also recalls Alberta's Social Credit government of the 1930s offering a prize to the Grade 12 student with the highest academic standing; one year an Indian girl won, but then was told Indians did not qualify. And until relatively recently, native people throughout Canada were denied the right to vote.

But blacks and natives were not the only objects of white Canadian racism and exploitation. Some of the most shameful episodes in Canadian history deal with the treatment of Chinese, Japanese, and East Indians.

In many respects, the experience of these groups in Canada was roughly parallel. Each can trace its origins in the country back to the end of the 1800s. Each was imported as much-needed labour—to build railroads or man lumber mills of the developing west. Each, when its job was done, was subjected to treatment that clearly demonstrated the Canadian Majority society's contempt often fostered by what should have been liberalizing forces—labour, churches, politicians.

For example, in 1895, the government of British Columbia denied the right to vote to Chinese, Japanese, and East Indians. By doing so, the province also effectively barred them from the federal franchise—since the Dominion Elections Act automatically denied the vote to anyone who did not have it provincially. This restriction was not lifted for Chinese and East Indians until 1947 and for Japanese until 1948. While in force, this law also effectively barred these groups from certain occupations for which licenses were required since having one's name on a voters' list was a prerequisite for getting a license. Meanwhile, of course, these groups were still subject to taxation.

Such restrictions and the perpetual threat of violence—a threat often translated into action—were hazards common to all groups. But each had its own special discriminatory burdens to bear as well. New Chinese immigrants for many years had to be males capable of hard physical labor; women were simply not admitted. Furthermore, the immigrants were subjected to a $500 head tax in 1904 and, by 1924, the legislation was passed barring them altogether until the law was eased in 1947. Japanese-Canadians were physically removed from British Columbia coastal areas in 1942 in the name of wartime security; most were interned and their properties were taken in "trusteeship" and sold, for the most part, at scandalously low prices.

In 1908 the government moved to cut down East Indian immigration by requiring that anyone who came from India had to do so by "continuous passage"; in 1914, however, 376

Sikhs fulfilled this requirement, arriving aboard the *Komagatu Maru;* their ship was made to wait in Vancouver Harbour for three months before being turned away.

Ironically, though, while the Canadian and B.C. governments were so industriously guarding Canada against the imaginary "hordes of Asia," a far more real and distasteful force made its way into Canada from the United States in 1920. The Ku Klux Klan, that coven of anti-Semitic white supremacists given to wearing bedsheets and burning crosses at night, set up shop in Montreal and spread across Canada. By 1932 the Klan was even provincially chartered in Alberta. Although it lost the charter in 1952, it was revived there in 1972.

By the end of the Second World War, however, the nature of racism and discrimination in Canada changed—it had softened in some ways and had become more subtle in others. Legislation against discriminaton was passed and, over the years, gradually strengthened. Discrimination lost its public respectability. But it certainly did not disappear.

The Francophone Situation

It was also in the postwar period that many Canadians began to characterize the relationships between the country's English- and French-speaking peoples as racist. Not that these two groups could be defined anthropologically or biologically as races, but their actions and attitudes towards one another—particularly anglophones towards francophones—were strongly racist in nature.

The signs of this kind of racism were clearest, of course, in Quebec. For almost two centuries, the minority anglophones there had maintained rigid economic, social, and, indirectly, political domination over the majority Quebecois. However, it was not until the so-called Quiet Revolution of the early 1960s that most Canadians began to recognize the fact. Only then, for example, did they start to understand how systematic had been the exclusion of francophones from the corporate boardrooms and executive suites of Montreal, the financial heart of what was known as French Canada.

Subsequently federal and provincial programs, ostensibly

aimed at redress, were undertaken, but these often seemed to be too little too late, or, ultimately, even strongly anti-anglophone in a few instances.

Meanwhile, antifrancophone feeling was being manifested in other parts of Canada. In the early 1960s, residents in a suburban Toronto community protested vehemently an experiment in the use of French on street signs. In 1976, fans at an international hockey game at Toronto's Maple Leaf Gardens booed when announcements first made in English were repeated in French. In 1977, teenaged hockey players from Quebec were subjected to physical and verbal abuse at a game in Edmonton. And, all too frequently, francophones were unable to secure the right to use French in dealings with courts or other public institutions in many parts of Canada.

But it was the Federation of Francophones Outside Quebec who, in 1977, most poignantly demonstrated that, whether by virtue of ill will or apathy, anglophone Canada was acquiescing in their demise as a cultural entity—indeed, as a people. In a two-volume research report, the federation documented claims that many of their communities across Canada had no access to French schools or French-language broadcasting. They showed that, as a group, their incomes were substantially lower than those of Canadians at large. They concluded that "it is not surprising that we are in the process of assimilating ourselves," a particularly sad cry in a Canada that had rejected the melting-pot concept of cultural uniformity and proudly proclaimed its adherence to the more egalitarian concept of cultural pluralism.

Whatever its origins, however, we know from experience in Canada that discrimination becomes overt when two factors —economic insecurity and increased visibility of racial minorities—coincide. In the 1970s we have seen unemployment rise to unprecedented levels. Inflation has reached critical heights. The tendency in many quarters is to look for causes and easy answers. Immigration is the cause often identified, immigrants—especially those most visible because of their colour—the culprits most often blamed. Little thought is given to the fact that most immigrants, far from being a burden on the economy, contribute to it.

Perhaps, though, when it comes down to taking action, it is less important that we know why racism exists than how discrimination is practiced. In any war, defense is based not only on why the enemy is hostile, but how he vents that hostility.

Overt Discrimination

There probably is little that one need say about the kind of discrimination that is practiced openly. It labels itself frankly, unashamedly appealing for support to negative racial stereo-types. It is as readily apparent as the sign that appeared in Kingston, Ontario, in 1976. "To let," the sign said, "2 bedroom apartment . . . Aryan Caucasian Adults Only."

"Nice Guy" Discrimination

There is something peculiarly Canadian about the way a good deal of discrimination—perhaps most of the direct discrim-ination—is practiced here. If one can ascribe characteristics to national groups, one would probably call Canadians "nice" people, conservative people who do most things quietly and dislike making a fuss. We like our diplomacy quiet; we like our economic and political life comparatively quiet; we cer-tainly like our discrimination quiet. Consequently, much of it is practiced subtly, quietly, by people who do not consider themselves bigots but who discriminate in order to avoid dis-turbing what they see as the established social order.

Such people are the landlords who, professing their own freedom from prejudice, refuse to rent to members of visible minorities because their other tenants presumably would move out. Or the employers who reject minority group job applicants for fear of the negative reactions of other employ-ees, or businesses which exclude patrons of racial groups for fear of a general loss of revenue.

Of course, these people will seldom admit their motives; they would not wish to embarrass those who seek their jobs, accommodation or services; so they cloak their discrimina-tion in excuses—the job, the apartment is gone.

The disastrous consequences they claim to fear seldom materialize. Indeed, petitions circulated in the 1960s among tenants in buildings where landlords argued in this manner demonstrated that the overwhelming majority of the tenants either did not care, or welcomed minority group neighbours.

However, even if there were some cost to employers, landlords or business people associated with the extension of fair play to minorities, could that be accepted as a justification for discrimination? Society demands that such entrepreneurs take all manner of costly safeguards to protect the public. Surely the preservation of dignity and a just social order is worth some cost.

Institutional Discrimination

There probably is no more subtle form of discrimination, none more pervasive, none more difficult to combat, than institutional discrimination. With its roots buried deep in Canadian social history, it makes many of our major institutions—notably our businesses and schools—operate to the detriment or exclusion of racial minorities. Meanwhile, many of the people involved in the life of these institutions are unaware that their operating techniques and criteria for judgment are racist in character and functionally discriminatory. In short, what they do is not motivated by racism, but it has the same effect.

Perhaps the problem is best demonstrated with reference to the educational system. Education in Canada is fundamentally based on the white, middle-class, largely urban population's experience, cultures, and values. The models that teachers present to their students—indeed, the models personified by the teachers themselves—are seldom ones with which non-whites from an impoverished and often non-urban background can identify. There is nothing in education for them, nothing that reflects the culture of heroes of their heritage, nothing that evokes their interest or self-respect.

In fact, examinations of textbooks in several parts of Canada indicate that the opposite is the rule. *Teaching Prejudice*, a 1971 report on a study of 400 textbooks in Ontario, revealed, for example, that nonwhite groups were frequently referred to as bloodthirsty, primitive, cruel and savage, while often contrasted with saintly and refined Europeans. With only a few and passing exceptions, natives, blacks or Asians who had contributed to Canadian development in significant and positive ways were omitted from reference. In addition, major events in the sad history of Canada's mistreatment of minorities—the extinction of the Beothuks, the treatment of Japanese-Canadians during the Second World War, the abuse of Metis and Indians throughout Canada—were barely touched, if at all. Being subjected to such a school system, it is small wonder that minority group persons often got little out of the educational process.

As if the burden of inadequate education were not enough of a handicap, members of visible minority groups meet other institutionalized impediments when they enter the job market. For example, employment tests which job applicants may be required to take usually contain a cultural bias that screens out nonwhites and nonurban people.

Employers may apply residential criteria that native people who live on remote reserves or in isolated communities may not be able to meet. Again, the intention is not necessarily discrimination; but the result is.

Legislative Discrimination

For the most part, legislation of an overtly discriminatory nature has been gradually phased out in Canada since the Second World War. That phasing-out took a long time in some instances. For example, until the early 1960s, Canada's immigration laws were distinctly racist—directly so at first, disallowing immigration of certain racial groups; then indirectly, setting up criteria that militated largely against nonwhite immigration. In fact, during the early 1960s Alabama's Governor George Wallace, asked by a CBC interviewer about his racist policies, was able to reply:

> You folks are pretty smart. You got your immigration laws fixed so that you don't let anybody come into your country but who you want to let in.

Over the ensuing years Canadian immigration law was liberalized. But even as late as 1977, as the government moved to redraft its laws and when nonwhite immigration was under serious public fire, there was concern about whether government effort would sufficiently protect against discrimination, as some of the rules could be used adversely against non-white travellers.

Labor's Role

Throughout the 1950s and into the 1960s, labour played a prominent role in the drive for human rights legislation, particularly in the areas of race, colour, creed and nationality. When at the end of the sixties, labour had achieved its goal of having human rights legislation passed and commissions established in all jurisdictions of Canada, some labour human rights committees became inactive. Minority groups and religious organizations now assumed a higher profile in the area of racial discrimination. Although labour continued to be involved in such areas as native people's rights, other aspects of human rights, such as the rights of women, the elderly and the handicapped became the focus of attention. Indeed, labour's involvement in other social concerns received greater emphasis.

Today, racism is once again evident in Canada and the early legislative approaches are proving to be less sophisticated and effective than initially expected. Revitalized local human rights committees could be a means of combatting this dangerous trend.

Formerly, labour's human rights committees had four general areas of responsibility: human rights education for the local's members, support of people who suffered discrimination on the job or in the community, pressure for anti-discrimination laws or bylaws, and negotiation of anti-discrimination clauses in collective agreements. Today's human rights committees might bear those same responsibilities, but their main thrust in many areas of the country would be for affirmative action programs.

The local's human rights committee, as part of its responsibility for an affirmative action program, could:

• Persuade the local's executive and membership that affirmative action is necessary, morally legitimate, and legal.

- Recruit minority group members into union membership through contact with their community leaders, organizations and educational institutions.

- Ensure that location and operation of hiring halls are easily accessible to minority group members living in remote areas, especially when work is to be done in those areas.

- Document cases of discrimination and racism within their community and exert public pressure on government for its elimination.

Without union support, affirmative action in many of Canada's key industries is virtually impossible. With it, the chances of a program succeeding are immeasurably enhanced. The local human rights committee seems the ideal vehicle through which that support could be provided.

What Daniel Hill documents as the development of racism in Canada, others have found for the United States. As we shall soon discover, although specific minority groups may differ as one crosses the national boundary, the development of corporate continentalism has given rise to a parallel history in the political economy of racism for the United States and Canada.

THE PREVAILING IDEOLOGIES

A Confusion of Tongues

The concept of race has been the apparent center of much human conflict. Nevertheless, it remains as confused a term today as through history. For example, the idea of "race" has been used to describe differences in language, culture, religion, and national origin. Other usages have focused on color and physiognomy.

One definition of race used by physical anthropologists emphasizes phenotypical and genotypical traits such as body build and blood type. There are differences of opinion among scientists as to whether there really are distinct races based upon such characteristics. Montague (1953) argues that there is no such thing as race from the standpoint of a physical anthropologist. Many people use the word "race" to describe people who

559

share certain cultural characteristics such as language or religion. Thus, one has heard of the French race and the Jewish race. (Social scientists today usually identify these as ethnic groups on the basis of shared *cultural characteristics*). Race has also been used as a synonym for the species as a whole (Homo Sapiens) such as the human race. Finally, the term has been applied to a group that is *socially defined* on the basis of physical differences, particularly skin color. This is the usual layperson's meaning of the word, and while there may not be real differences between people from a physical anthropology approach, people do make distinctions on the basis of visible group differences. We must conclude that though the term "race" is without serious biological meaning, it has acquired a social, political, and economic meaning. When institutionalized, false conceptions of human potential can have devastating consequences.

Although the meaning of "race" is imprecise, the definition of racism is somewhat clearer. Racism is an ideology that holds that organic, genetically transmitted differences among human groups are intrinsically associated with the presence or absence of certain socially relevant abilities or characteristics such as intelligence, temperament, morality, or culture. Therefore, differences between whites and Indians or blacks in IQ scores, educational attainment, murder rates, suicide rates, mental illness, disease, sexual activity, divorce, unemployment rates, athletic abilities, or musical talents are explained by inborn traits. "They" are different because "they" were born that way.

Frequently the term racism is used for the lesser known term, "ethnocentrism." For purposes of analysis, it is useful to distinguish between the former, which indicates a falsely presumed genetic or hereditary advantage, and the latter, which refers to a faulty assumption of cultural superiority. One respected scholar in the field notes that while notions of cultural superiority are virtually universal, "Only a few human groups have deemed themselves superior because of the content of their gonads" (van den Berghe 1967, p. 12).

The Media Is the Message: Blaming the Victim

It appears that children learn about race by the time they are three or four years old, subsequently adding to their initial perceptions. Many of the images that develop of minority group members are stereotypes. Stereotypes are a form of prejudgment (prejudice) that exaggerate certain characteristics, invent others, suppress favorable attributes, fail to show how majority group members also have the same undesirable characteristics, ignore the causes of the trait, and leave little room for change or individual variation (Simpson and Yinger 1965). For example, the stereotype of the lazy, shiftless, irresponsible American black was presented for years in the media and through other socialization agencies to maintain dominance over this minority. Also, the racist stereotypes of Chicanos presented in the media and various texts emphasized their supposed passive, fatalistic, lazy, oversexed, and criminally prone nature (Wagner and Haug 1971). Finally, North American Indians have been characterized as savage, warlike, scalping, lusting for white women, humorless, simple minded, and prone to drunkenness (Price 1978).

Turning specifically to the television industry, several variations of corporate ideology can be identified that are specifically relevant for minority groups. In the first complete decade of commercial television, programming of the Fifties portrayed nonwhites in explicitly negative fashion.

> Blacks appeared most often in comedy and variety shows; Native American roles were limited to the television western; Asian Americans appeared primarily in Fu Manchu and Charlie Chan movies. People of Spanish origin, usually Mexican Americans, appeared primarily as bandits in television westerns or in reruns of movies such as *The Treasure of Sierra Madre* (U.S. Commission on Civil Rights 1977, p. 4).

Perhaps the most patently offensive depiction of blacks was a program entitled Amos 'n' Andy. Beginning as a radio broadcast in 1929, this "comedy" focused on the humor of black character and culture (as seen by some whites). The creators and players of the leading roles were two white men (Freeman Gosden and Charles Correll). Although black actors and actresses were necessarily featured when the program was converted into a television series in the early 1950s, the National Association for the Advancement of Colored People unsuccessfully demanded its removal in 1951. The NAACP noted that "every character in this one and only TV show with an all-Negro cast is either a clown or a crook" (U.S. Commission on Civil Rights 1977, p. 4). The show survived on network television until 1953, and was in syndication and widely shown throughout the decade (Fife 1974, pp. 9–10).

While the Fifties constituted a decade of negativism, the Sixties introduced an era of tokenism. Set against the historical background of the civil rights movement led by Martin Luther King, and the increasing United States involvement in the Vietnam War (which meant more nonwhites were needed in military combat), the decade saw the inclusion of blacks in medical stories, police dramas, and comedies. The first situation comedy about blacks since *Amos 'n' Andy* was Diahann Carroll's *Julia*, which featured the trials of a nurse and mother. The central failing of this hit series had to do with what was *omitted*. While not patently offensive, the program fluffed over the realities of racial oppression at a time when ghettos were going up in smoke (Fife 1974, p. 13).

While nonwhites came to be featured in more roles in the Sixties, television, especially during the latter years of the decade, proved to be more a vehicle for "socially relevant melodrama." Such programming featured the young, minorities, and women (sometimes combined in the same role) who could be depended on to side with the underdog. Thus, stories about "hip" cops, whether or not official (*Mod Squad*, *Get Christie Love*, and in the early Seventies, *Shaft* and *Tenafly*); groovie lawyers (*The Young Lawyers*, *Storefront Lawyers*); antiestablishment doctors (*The Young Interns*); and empathetic teachers (*Mr. Novak* and *Room 222*) plagued the airways. Most such programming was based on the premise of working within the system in order to save it (U.S. Commission on Civil Rights 1977, pp. 15–16).

As saviors, the characters in series and special programming faced and defeated the true "baddies":

> . . . militants were not angry revolutionaries but paranoics or agents of hostile countries; draft evaders, not really opponents of the war but neurotics rejecting their fathers in return for having been rejected by them; bigots, not true haters but merely persons who lived too long in isolation from other races; drug users, not disenchanted but victims of ghoulish weirdos and organized crime. Television faced the gut issues with false characters, and instead of shedding light on the ailments of the social system and the divisions within it the playlets distorted the questions and fudged the answers (Brown 1971, p. 308).

The most effective ideological message is to portray those most victimized by corporate order as dedicated to its continuation.

Television programming during the 1970s came to feature the triumphant minority. Situation comedies such as *Good Times* and *The Jeffersons* demonstrated that through family strength, good humor, and the power of the will, nonwhites could defeat the despair of the ghetto or escape it altogether. While the ideological symbols of privatism, triumph of the will, and familism are evident in various forms, perhaps the most important example of the decade came on those eight January evenings in the winter of 1977 when the American Broadcasting Corporation presented the television version of Alex Haley's *Roots*.

Roots

Roots was quite correctly described as the "saga of an American family." The book and the subsequent television mini-series dealt with a black author's search for his origins and touched off a wave of interest in genealogy. Through tales handed down orally to members of his family over two centuries, Haley received clues that initiated his quest for his African ancestor, Kunte Kinte, a victim of the traffic in slaves, brought in chains to the southern United States and sold into bondage. The final televised episode of *Roots* was viewed by 80 million Americans, the largest TV audience in the history of the medium (*New York Times* 1977, 22:1).

As with other media fare, the importance of *Roots* lay more with ideology than its accurate depiction of the origins and perpetuation of racism. True, the stereotypes had become positive. Haley's ancestors had supposedly conquered despite the savagery of whip, nightriders, murder, and all forms of degradation. Here were heroic figures enduring the barbarism of slavery through the strength provided by family ties. While we do not doubt that a knowledge of one's family history and cultural origins may provide some sense of biographical meaning, to offer these as psychological armor protecting the wearer from the ravages of institutional racism is an unfounded claim. Further, there is simply no evidence that knowledge of genealogy or culture somehow affects the distribution of wealth, income, and power. Slavery and the plantation system together with the feudal society they represented were not victims of the discovery of genealogy or cultural heritage. They fell with the advent of an industrial order, punctuated only by the Civil War.

In summary, the record of images for minorities on television is a clear reflection of what we have termed corporate ideology. Blacks (and others) were portrayed as failing because of character flaws in the 1950s. They became the beneficiaries and promoters of a white liberal version of the established order in the Sixties. In the past decade, they have triumphed through superhuman, larger-than-life effort. All of these stereotypes represent what we have termed "reductionist" thought. None find the center of racism in contemporary institutions.

Individual Racism

Among the specific racist ideologies that prevail must be counted the many apparently "tolerant" views that have emerged in more recent times. Today in North America it is not uncommon to find the disadvantaged positions of nonwhites frequently acknowledged by members of the higher corporate and political circles. However, it is the particular *explanation* for racism or, perhaps more important, the level at which the problem is explained that must command our attention.

Given a more liberal version of corporate ideology today, one might expect to find an emphasis on such things as "equal opportunity" and "affirmative action," which shall be examined in due course. However, what remains a constant feature of the dominant ideology is the element of *privatism*. When this is applied to the popular explanations for racism, the result is an emphasis on individual-centered "reasons." Thus, the problem of racism is falsely presented as a matter of individual attitudes (racial *prejudice* or prejudgments of individuals based on group identity) or behavior (racial *discrimination* or the differential treatment of persons depending on group association). Given such explanations, the argument must follow that if a society is successful in reducing or eliminating prejudice and discrimination, then the problem of racism will be largely resolved. The position taken here is that such a conception distorts the origin of the problem, thus perpetuating it. It logically follows that the perpetuation of racism through false explanations, despite what may be good intentions, stands as a form of racism.

A simple example should make the above distinction clear. If the form of racism evident in the plantation system of the pre-Civil War South is explained at an individual level of abstraction, then one would be required to *isolate* the bigoted attitudes and brutal practices of slaveholders, overseers, and others from the *structure* of plantation society and the institution of slavery fundamental to the continuation of that system. As we shall make clear at a later point, *the ideology of racism together with its attitudinal (prejudice) and behavioral (discrimination) dimensions have been a logical consequence of the economic arrangements prevailing at specific periods of history.*

The individualization of racism is predictably reflected in traditional sociology. Robert K. Merton, whose views of society are grounded in the order paradigm, has described the relationship between prejudice and discrimination (Table 10–5). Although it is interesting to note that attitudes and action may not be consistent, the focus is purely individual.

When racism, or the "minority problem," is recognized at all in North American society, elimination of the "prejudiced discriminator" is the primary focus. But what about the nonprejudiced person who discriminates simply in response to company or governmental policy? Also, under what conditions do persons who are prejudiced refrain from discriminating? Official segregation in South Africa and, until recently, in the United States, forced persons to discriminate because it was the law. As we shall

**TABLE 10–5
Relationship between Prejudice and Discrimination**

	Prejudice	Nonprejudice
Discriminating	prejudiced discriminator	nonprejudiced discriminator
Nondiscriminating	prejudiced nondiscriminator	nonprejudiced nondiscriminator

Source: Adapted from R.K. Merton, *Social Theory and Social Structure,* rev. ed. New York: The Free Press, 1937.

see, more subtle yet powerful forms of institutional practice continue. Nonetheless, the private focus remains. For example, words or actions come under close scrutiny. Political candidates may be embarrassed if a representative of the media overhears an ethnic joke. However, the same candidate can support a structure of inequality that means less income, fewer jobs, and restricted influence for minorities without fear of being called "prejudiced." One must pose the question: Which is more serious?

For conflict sociologists, racism will best be understood as a matter of social structure. As one student of race relations states:

> Institutional racism can be defined as those established laws, customs, and practices which systematically reflect and produce racial inequities in American society. If racist consequences accrue to institutional laws, customs, or practices, the institution is racist, whether or not the individuals maintaining those practices have racist intentions. . . . Institutional racism can be either overt or covert (corresponding to de jure and de facto, respectively) and either intentional or unintentional (Jones 1972, p. 35).

Most institutional racism today is covert. For example, using the standard of a high school diploma for employment systematically eliminates the majority of Indian people due to group differences in formal educational attainment. While the requirement is "evenly" applied to all applicants, it is inherently discriminatory because of group differences in opportunity for education.

When an attempt is made truly to understand institutional racism, it is necessary to operate in a historically specific fashion. In corporate society, one is struck by the social reality of class. As our argument unfolds, it should be clear that race and racism cannot be separated from the structure of inequality that marks a society of classes. Viewing racism in historical isolation or dealing with it as more or less a personal problem means that one cannot examine the political-economy of corporate society. Marx identified this type of error over a century ago.

> Every industrial and commercial center in England now possesses a working class divided into two hostile camps, English proletarians and Irish proletarians. The ordinary English worker hates the Irish worker as a competitor who lowers his standard of life . . . feels himself a member of the ruling nation, and so turns himself into a tool of the aristocrats and capitalists of his country against Ireland, thus strengthening their domination over himself. He cherishes religious, social, and national prejudices against the Irish worker. His attitude towards him is much the same as that of the "poor whites" to the "niggers" in the former slave states of the U.S.A. (Marx 1970, p. 136).

Thus, a more sophisticated understanding of race and racism causes one to go beyond the lines of color, religion, and culture to explore the ways in which the economic system works. Today we need not confine the intraclass struggle born of job scarcity to impoverished blacks and whites. Substitute white for English and black for Irish and the above observation represents more than a little truth.

> The American worker's job is his stake in the American Dream. He works hard so that he can make the "easy payments" on a car, a TV, a hi-fi, a speedboat. And he is ready to defend his job with the same determination that the United Fruit Company, for example, is ready to defend its property investments in Central America. So the Negro struggle for equality, taking place at a time when there is a general decline in the number of jobs, threatens the white worker with expropriation in much the same way as the colonial struggle for national independence threatens the expropriation of the property of the imperialists (Boggs 1970, p. 14).

While the number of jobs may not be declining in an absolute sense in North America, the scarcity of those that minimally offer hope of survival and advancement is always at issue (see Chapter Four). Further, in terms of the unemployment rate, the white male worker has traditionally enjoyed most-favored status. For example, in 1978, the "official" unemployment rate for white males was 4.5 percent and for black males, 10.9 percent. The corresponding figures for women were 6.2 percent and 13.1 percent (*Statistical Abstract of the United States* 1979, p. 396).

A careful reading of the history of the plantation period in the southern United States reveals that landowners often justified slavery on the grounds that their slaves were no worse off in a material sense than the predominantly white urban working class of the time (Genovese 1974, pp. 68–69). While this might have been true for living conditions alone, racism then as now must be considered a unique evil.

> What did it mean to be a slave? It is hard to imagine it today. We think of oppression beyond all conception: cruelty, degradation, whipping, and starvation, the absolute negation of human rights; or on the contrary, we may think of the ordinary worker the world over today (1935), slaving ten, twelve, or fourteen hours a day, with not enough to eat, compelled by his physical necessities to do this and not to do that, curtailed in his movements and his possibilities; and we say, here too, is a slave called a "free worker," and slavery is merely a matter of name.
>
> But there was in 1863 a real meaning to slavery different from that we may apply to the laborer today. It was in part psychological, the enforced feeling of inferiority, the calling of another Master; the standing with hat in hand. It was the helplessness. It was the defenselessness of family life. It was the submergence below the arbitrary will of any sort of individual. It was without doubt worse

in these vital respects than was that which exists today in Europe or America (W.E.B. DuBois, quoted in Genovese, 1974, pp. 68–69).

It was in part the failure of progressive labor movements at the turn of the century to understand the particular brutality of racism, whether institutionalized as slavery or as more subtle economic and political exploitation, that prevented the emergence of a white/black worker coalition. During the first two decades of this century, the Socialist Party attempted to appeal to black workers by asking them to forget "race" and join a class-based movement. At the same time, it sought to appeal to white workers (especially in the South) by promising that the rise of socialism would not bring about the social equality of the races (Foner 1977, pp. 320–21). Needless to say, the "strategy" was stillborn.

Eugenics: Re-creating the Master Race

Perhaps the clearest example of that form of racism that holds that genetic or hereditary factors produce racial superiority (or inferiority) is found within the so-called eugenics movement. In 1980, Robert K. Graham, an Escondido, California, millionaire who made his fortune developing plastic lenses for eyeglasses, established a "sperm bank" for the preservation of seminal fluid from Nobel prizewinners. Volunteers from women with "high IQs" were selected for breeding and several were impregnated (Cornell 1980). This is a contemporary example of efforts supposedly designed to improve the human species by controlling heredity. As we shall see, this movement historically has contributed to the ideology of racism.

One of the believers in the "stud theory of eugenics" who contributed his sperm was William Shockley, a physicist convinced that intelligence is primarily hereditary (as opposed to environmental), an assertion that is simply unproven. Perhaps the most discrediting aspect of contemporary eugenics is the naive tendency in some quarters to embrace "intelligence tests" as a measure of the innate ability to learn. Further, the scores on intelligence tests are no measure of social usefulness. Though we give critical attention to the views of Shockley and others elsewhere (see Chapter Four), it should be noted here that he advances the notion of hereditary black intellectual inferiority because blacks do not do as well as other races on the "intelligence tests" of the dominant culture.

Ironically, both Shockley and Graham appear to overlook recent research in genetics not based on culturally bound definitions of intelligence. The probability of giving birth to a child with Downs Syndrome, a severe form of mental and physical retardation, increases with the age of both the mother and father, especially if the latter is past fifty-five. Nobel prizewinners tend to be older; Shockley, for example, at the time of his sperm contribution was seventy (*Time* 1980, p. 49).

Pseudoscience, a Source of Racism   This "kinds of people" genetic explanation of racial differences is an example of academic racism where the authority and prestige of science are used to legitimate differences in educational opportunity and attainment between blacks and whites. Actually, science has historically been a major source of racist beliefs and ideologies (Gosset 1963). The foundations of the "Eugenics Movement" were developed during the nineteenth and early twentieth centuries. For example, pseudoscientific justification for racial oppression was taken from Charles Darwin's *The Origin of the Species*. Although Darwin did not support such racist notions in this work, social and political writers developed a theory of social Darwinism. This belief system, essentially legitimated the position of those on top and those on the bottom as a consequence of biology. The elite found it convenient to believe that the political, social, and economic worlds operated on the principle of "survival of the fittest." Therefore, those who "make it" are of "better character" than those who do not. Such thought was used not only to justify differences among individuals and races, but also among nations.

The social Darwinism that prevailed in early twentieth century American sociology is widely refuted today. So, too, are the more contemporary examples of academic racism such as the views of Arthur Jensen and William Shockley. However, as we shall discover at a later point, racist ideologies regardless of their shoddy scholarship have proven to be powerful political devices, justifying oppression ranging from discimination to extermination.

To illustrate, a French historian by the name of Arthur de Gobineau (1816–1882) wrote a four-volume work on the nature of race in the mid-nineteenth century (Sorokin 1964, pp. 222–29). He argued that at the onset of human history there were three pure races: white, yellow, and black. According to de Gobineau, the most talented and creative was the white, especially its so-called Aryan branch. Derived from the word for "noble" from Sanskrit, the classical literary language of ancient India, the term "aryan" is without meaning as regards a race, ethnic group, nation, or culture. This idea of a master race lived on in the work of the English historian Houston Stewart Chamberlain (1885–1926), who in his *The Foundations of the Nineteenth Century* advanced the idea of white Aryan superiority while decrying the supposedly injurious effect the Jews had on "Western civilization" (Sorokin 1964, pp. 222–23). In the late nineteenth century the Aryan myth was further nurtured in the work of Otto Ammon and G. V. de Lapouge, both anthropologists. It remained, however, for Karl Pearson, a turn-of-the-century mathematician who pioneered in the area of correlation, to reveal the power of racism clothed in the garments of eugenics as a tool for political and economic domination.

How many centuries, how many thousands of years, have the Kaffir or the negro held large districts in Africa undisturbed by the white man? Yet their intertribal struggles have not yet produced *a civilization in the least comparable with the Aryan.* Educate and nurture them as you will, I do not believe that you will succeed in modifying the stock. History shows me one way, and one way only, in which a high state of civilization has been produced, namely, in the struggle of race with race, and the survival of the physically and mentally fitter race. (Quoted in Sorokin 1964, p. 260; italics added.)

In a series of books relating eugenic racism to the welfare of the modern State, Pearson argued that the white "should go and drive out the inferior race" (Sorkin 1964, p. 260). Given these views, his position on social class is not surprising.

Let there be a ladder from class to class, and occupation to occupation, but let it not be a very easy ladder to climb. . . . The gradation of the body social is not a mere historical anomaly; it is largely the result of long continued selection, economically differentiating the community into classes roughly fitted to certain types of work. (Quoted in Sorokin 1964, p. 261.)

If Pearson provides a service, it is to demonstrate the logical connection between racism and inequality. As we shall soon see, it remained for a white self-styled "Aryan civilization," in the 1930s to carry the idea of "the survival of the physically and mentally fitter race" to its terrifying conclusion.

Cultural Imperialism

A more popular evaluation of the race problem in the modern era is that of individual deficiencies caused by family and environmental factors. For example, these reductionist arguments typically hold that blacks, Indians, and Chicanos have obtained less education because their cultures do not emphasize education, their parents do not promote education, their family environment is not conducive to education, and their achievement motivation is lower than that of whites. The bottom line is that the racial minorities are culturally or otherwise deficient in certain characteristics that can be remedied by programs to help family stability, early childhood education, tutoring, busing, or other tactics. This evaluation of the racial problem identifies it as mainly a minority group problem, although prejudice and discrimination should also be combated. At bottom, this view demands that the minority group should "fit" into dominant group institutions.

Assimilation, or the shedding of unique cultural traits and identity and the adoption of dominant group traits, is a goal of majority group policies. From the point of view of minority races and ethnic groups, a better description of the process is cultural imperialism. By this we mean that unique languages, customs, belief systems, and life-styles are systematically disvalued, stigmatized, and eliminated. Existing institutions and their practices as well as the dominant culture are judged appropriate, and largely go unquestioned. Another obvious difficulty for racial minorities is that they cannot change their skin color, which continues as a barrier even if they attempt to assimilate. In fact, this has been the basis of a crucial misunderstanding when people attempt to compare assimilation of ethnic groups such as the Irish or Germans with that of a racial group such as blacks or Indians. While white immigrants to North America like the Germans, English, Poles, Czechs, Irish, Ukrainians, or others can melt into the majority group, nonwhites do not have that option.

From the conflict perspective, racial and ethnic differences in social and economic indicators are evaluated as a consequence of differences in power. For some who hold with this model, the black problem, Indian problem, or Chicano problem becomes the white problem, since whites control the power and resources and have established and continue to perpetrate inequalities through institutional policies and practices. It therefore follows that to understand the nature of the contemporary situation of minorities in Canada and the United States, the first step may be to analyze historically and contemporarily, the policies and practices of *white* society and its institutions. In so saying, however, we do not embrace an inverse racism that argues that whites are genetically prone to racial exploitation. Most whites are also victims of inequality in North America. It is the particular brutality suffered by minorities of color that sets them apart. Often visible by their color, brought to the continent in chains or gathered in reservations, ghettos, and barrios, stigmatized by the ideologies of racism, ethnic and racial minorities have been and continue to be more vulnerable to the structural inequality of class society.

To solve the racial problem, minority self-determination and collective struggle are necessary. Rather than the "solution" of assimilation, a consciousness of class position on the part of minorities and whites, together with a mutual respect for cultural pluralism by which distinctive customs and traits are preserved, is required. A comparison of order/assimilationist and conflict/pluralist analysis is provided in Table 10-6.

EMERGENCE

At the outset of this text, the authors expressed a preference for a sociology of knowledge approach to prevailing ideologies. In short, ideas and idea systems cannot be viewed in historical isolation. The academic views

TABLE 10–6
Order/Assimilationist and Conflict/
Pluralist Theories of Racial Problems

	Order/Assimilationist	Conflict/Pluralist
Cause of Problem	Minority group member's failure to adopt majority group standards adequately and some prejudice and discrimination among a few majority group individuals	Dominant class restrictions and oppression through institutional racism that prohibits minority group advancement.
Solution to Problem	Programs to help individual minority group members assimilate and to stop individual prejudice and discrimination through education and human rights laws.	Consciousness of class position leading to collective action by minority group members and allies to change oppressive institutional policies and practices.

Those who focus purely on cultural enhancement, separating the problem of racism from class, do not address structural origins. The intention of the Conflict/Pluralist approach is to retain and develop cultural *enrichment*—not the unemployment, disease, and early death associated with minority standing.

on social Darwinism, the Aryan race, and the functional necessity of social inequality were bound to the material events of history at the time they were put forward. Ideas such as those of the eugenics movement were part of the prevailing ideologies of their time, reflecting and reinforcing global economic and political practices.

Thus, the emergence of the concept of race and the growth of racism were outgrowths of European imperialism, slavery, and nationalism. Before the sixteenth century there was little consciousness of race. Conflict between peoples of the word was due to political, economic, cultural, religious, and linguistic differences (Snyder 1962). Beginning in the sixteenth century, Europeans conquered and colonized native populations throughout the world. Whites soon dominated black, brown, and red people and exploited their labor and their land. Black slaves in Africa, Indians in North America, and brown people of Mexico, Central, and South America became subjugated and part of white-dominated empires.

Racism and Colonialism

In searching for the historical origins of racism, some might take issue with the contention that such ideas were rooted in European colonialism. Indeed, a number of other societies without colonial empires gave evidence of some crude association between physical properties such as skin

571

color or height and social superiority (van den Berghe 1967, pp. 12–13). However, we are not so much concerned with identifying the magic moment of ideological creation. The concern here is with the cultivation and spread of this peculiar ideology.

> . . . it remains true that the Western strain of the virus has eclipsed all others in importance. Through the colonial expansion of Europe, racism spread widely over the world. Apart from its geographical spread, no other brand of racism has developed such a flourishing mythology and ideology. In folklore, as well as in literature and science, racism became a deeply ingrained component of the Western *Weltanschauung*. Western racism had its poets like Kipling, its philosophers like Gobineau and Chamberlain, its statesmen like Hitler, Theodore Roosevelt, and Verwoerd; this is a record not even remotely approached in either scope or complexity by any other cultural tradition (van den Berghe 1967, p. 13).

Indeed it was the colonial expansion of capitalistic European nation-states that set the historical stage for the ideology of racism. As always, the objective of colonization was exploitation of human and natural resources. Despite the colonizer's "concern" for the soul of the "heathen" as well as the often expressed desire to "uplift" the native population, subjugation was in the interest of the master (Noel 1972, pp. 163–64).

However, exploitation in and of itself is not sufficient to explain the emergency of racism. The historical treatment of the working classes, particularly at the zenith of the Industrial Revolution, is ample testimony that whites can exploit whites. However, when such processes occur in societies with egalitarian ideals such as political democracy, the Judeo-Christian ethic, and the eighteenth-century enlightenment, ideologies that legitimate such obvious inconsistencies are required. As the colonial process and the institution of slavery were obviously subhuman, the dilemma was neatly resolved by declaring the victim also subhuman (van den Berghe 1967, pp. 16–18; Noel 1972, pp. 164–65). And what racism provided for the justification of colonialism, the plantation system and slavery, social Darwinism, the functionalist theory of stratification, and the ideological components of corporate order have achieved for the subjugation of workers.

As we have seen, by the late nineteenth century academics were distinguishing between "higher" and "lower" races, with European whites being judged the highest race. This provided a "scientific" justification for the exploitation and subjugation of nonwhite peoples. The "white man's burden" became a popular phrase expressing the colonial attitude of the British Empire that although the "civilizing" of subjugated populations was a difficult task, the British would persevere (Gosset 1963).

The social-psychological consequences of colonialism, like those of slavery, cannot be ignored. Frantz Fanon, a psychiatrist born on the island of Martinique as a French colonial subject, observed:

When we consider the efforts made to carry out the cultural estrangement so characteristic of the colonial epoch, we realize that nothing has been left to chance and that the total result looked for by colonial domination was indeed to convince the natives that colonialism came to lighten their darkness. The effect consciously sought by colonialism was to drive into the natives' heads the idea that if the settlers were to leave, they would at once fall back into barbarism, degradation, and bestiality (1968, pp. 210–11).

Such paternalism (caring for the childlike) was very much a part of the rampant nationalism of the eighteenth, nineteenth, and early twentieth centuries. Races were confused with nationalities, which prompted the "discovery" of the Norman (French), the Teutonic (German), and the Anglo-Saxon (English) races. This wedding of racism and nationalism helped to justify the imperialism culminating in the French Empire, British Empire, and German conquests, including the rise of the Third Reich.

The belief that nonwhites were innately inferior to whites was evident in the practices and policies of the French and British toward the Indian population in North America. The native population was colonized and subsequently subject to hundreds of years of colonial control. Racism also justified the practice of slavery in Canada and the United States and the oppression of black people.

The Slave Trade

With the rise of plantation agriculture in the New World, the traffic in human cargo grew from modest beginnings to a flourishing trade in the eighteenth century (Mannix and Cowley 1970). As many as 14 million Africans were ripped from their native land to provide merchandise for the international slave trade. An estimated 10 million died during passage (Jacobs et al. 1971, p. 91).

Slavers held to one of two positions with regard to the transportation of their "cargo." For the "loose-packers," it made sense to provide additional room and better food so as to reduce the mortality rate and deliver a healthier product. The "tight-packers" had the slaves laid side by side in rows on platforms constructed one on top of the other. There was little room to move and no choice but to lie in one's excrement. Though the mortality rate was greater, larger numbers usually meant a greater net survival. Accordingly, the "tight-packers" were most commonly found among the slavers.

Given the hideous circumstances, slavers lived in constant dread of revolt or suicide. Chains, whips, and guns were used to prevent both successful rebellion and most suicides, though some succeeded in throwing themselves into the sea. A more common method of suicide was refusing to eat.

> "Upon the Negroes refusing to take food," says Falconbridge (a witness), "I have seen coals of fire, glowing hot, put on a shovel and placed so near their lips as to scorch and burn them . . . but if the Negroes still refused, they were flogged day after day. Lest flogging prove ineffective, every Guineaman was provided with a special instrument called the "speculum oris," or mouth opener. It looked like a pair of dividers with notched legs and with a thumb-screw at the blunt end. The legs were closed and the notches were hammered between the slave's teeth. When the thumbscrew was tightened, the legs of the instrument separated, forcing open the slave's mouth; the food was poured into it through a funnel" (Mannix and Cowley 1970, p. 30).

Stolen from their native land, denied the support of community, family, and ritual, treated as beasts without soul or reason, many slaves developed what was termed "fixed melancholy," losing the will to live. Thus, the death of the body was no more than an epilogue for the spiritual passage already endured (Mannix and Cowley 1970, p. 31).

By the mid-eighteenth century, slavery dominated the economy of the southern United States. From this base grew the social world of the South.

> White society in the South shaped its laws, religion, and institutions around slavery, and the blacks shaped their lives the best they could around surviving in a society that denied them the fundamental rights of manhood and womenhood: the right to marry, to be parents, to have sexual choice. Human beings, even slaves, had enjoyed these rights in almost every other civilization known in the history of the world (Jacobs et al. 1971, p. 97).

Evidence of the foregoing can be pulled from history. Many of the framers of the Declaration of Independence and the Constitution of the United States were slaveholders. White American legislators, frequently committed to the "rights of man" embodied in the eighteenth-century enlightenment, did not make application of these principles to their human chattel (Jacobs et al. 1971, pp. 97–98). In 1820, Representative Charles Pinckney of South Carolina, who had worked to create the Constitution, articulated the rationalization for slavery, a line of reasoning that remains familiar wherever there is human bondage.

> If we are to believe that this world was formed by a great and omnipotent Being, that nothing is permitted to exist here but by his will, and then throw our eyes throughout the whole of it, we should form an opinion very different indeed from that asserted, that slavery was against the law of God. . . .

> Have the Northern states any idea of the value of our slaves? At least, sir, six hundred millions of dollars. If we lose them, the value of the lands they cultivate will be diminished in all cases one half, and in many they will become wholly useless. And an annual income of at least forty millions of dollars will be lost to your citizens, the loss of which will not alone be felt by the non-slaving states, but by the whole union (Jacobs et al. 1971, pp. 133–34).

It appears that religion and property are powerful ideological forces.

Ironically, even those who later favored the emancipation of slaves could not free themselves of the prevailing historical ideology. From the words of Abraham Lincoln:

> *Springfield, Illinois, October 11, 1854:* My first impulse would be to free all the slaves, and send them to Liberia, to their own native land.

> *Charleston, September 18, 1858:* I will say then that I am not, nor ever have been, in favor of bringing about the social and political equality of the white and black races: that I am not, nor ever have been, in favor of making voters or jurors of negroes, nor of qualifying them to hold office, nor to intermarry with white people . . .

> . . . While they (the races) do remain together there must be the position of superior and inferior, and as much as any other man I am in favor of having the superior position assigned to the white race.

> *Annual Message to Congress, December 1, 1862:* I regret to say such (black) persons contemplating colonization do not seem so willing to migrate to those countries as to some others, nor so willing as their interest demands. I believe, however, opinion among them in this respect is improving; and that ere long there will be an augmented and considerable migration to both these countries from the United States.

And finally, in the Emancipation Proclamation Lincoln stated that granting freedom to slaves was "warranted by the Constitution upon military necessity," and "as a fit and necessary war measure for suppressing (the Southern) rebellion . . ." (Jacobs et al. 1971, pp. 159–61).

The Foundations of Fascism

As we have seen, the emergence of the slave trade cannot be separated from the institutionalization of the plantation system. With the fall of the Confederacy, agrarian-based slavery came to an end in North America. However, an examination of the political-economy of racism cannot be confined to pre-twentieth-century history. For there emerged in the modern era of the "Old World" another social order for which the practice of racist policy became an imperative.

During the 1930s a Great Depression struck most of the Western capitalist world. Not unexpectedly, economic decline prepared the way for political movements that promised an end to the hardships. In the United States the programs, policies, and laws that constituted the "New Deal" of the Democratic Party brought some reform, created evidence of national solidarity, and bought time until the economic salvation of the Second World War. However, the European experiences did not follow similar lines.

Europe and the Great Depression   The economic impact of global depression was severely felt in the societies of eastern and southern Europe. Many of these nations (Spain, Portugal, Hungary, Poland, Romania, Bulgaria, Yugoslavia, Greece, the Baltic States), together with several Latin American countries, which were also not well-industrialized, saw the birth of an agrarian form of "fascism." The more developed industrial powers of Germany, Italy, and Japan were to follow a different course. As Chirot notes (1977, pp. 98–101), the events of the Great Depression created for Germany conditions that had already become severe for Italy and Japan during the previous decade. All three nations (which came to comprise the "Axis Powers" during the Second World War) were developing in an industrial fashion *without the control of native or colonial resources*. Such conditions set the stage for the development of militarism and the emergence of imperialist conquest.

The form of "industrial fascism" (Chirot 1977, p. 100) represented by Germany is of particular concern because of the critical role played by racism in this complex political ideology. Unlike the United States, Great Britain, and France, Germany had no colonial empire. As the major loser of the First World War, this country was also without the neocolonial[1] advantages some Western powers enjoyed before the war. In short, in the Germany of the 1920s and 1930s the severity of the Great Depression could not be lessened through guaranteed external resources. Conditions were ripe for the rise of the Nazi (National Socialist) party under the leadership of Adolph Hitler.

---

[1] By neocolonialism we mean the substantial control of the economy and political order of an underdeveloped or developing nation by an industrial power without the "official" possession of the country as a colony. In the post-World War II era, Western multinational corporations have been the central beneficiaries of neocolonial arrangements. Such arrangements predictably have been secured through the power of the State in corporate society. The means of control include military force; political subversion through the use of "intelligence" agencies; military and other grants, loans, and sales; and substantial foreign investment; all of which are critical sources of influence in small, frequently poor countries.

The Nazi form of racism cannot be isolated from its political base. Fascism in Germany came to mean many things: belligerent nationalism, militarism supported by a war economy, international conquest, the highly organized control of social institutions by the State, and the systematic cultivation of anti-Semitic racism. It mattered not that the designation of Jews as a separate "race" was a fiction. The concept of an Aryan race was also fiction. Yet in Nazi Germany, the doctrine of racial supremacy became the official policy of the State.

To explain the racism that prevailed in Germany requires the prior explanation of Nazi Facism. It is not enough to say that the historical stage was set: it is also important to identify specific factors that precipitated the rise of the Third Reich, a period of rule Hitler promised would last a thousand years. Inlcuded among these must be the role of the wealthy industrialists, the allegiance of the new middle classes, the control of workers' socialism, and the cultivation of powerful Nazi ideology.

The development of state control of the economic order began with the appointment of Hitler as Chancellor of Germany in 1933. Realizing the need for the support of the industrialists, he met with key figures within three weeks of taking office.

> . . . Goering and Hitler laid down the line to a couple of dozen of Germany's leading magnates, including Krupp von Bohlen, who had become an enthusiastic Nazi overnight, Bosch and Schnitzler of I.G. Farben, and Voegler, head of the United Steel Works . . .

> . . . they responded with enthusiasm to the promise of the end of the infernal elections, of democracy and disarmament. Krupp, the munitions king, who, according to Thyssen, had urged Hindenburg on January 29 not to appoint Hitler, jumped up and expressed to the Chancellor the "gratitude" of the businessman "for having given us such a clear picture." Dr. Schacht then passed the hat. "I collected three million marks," he recalled at Nuremberg (Shirer 1960, pp. 189–90).

The cooperation of capital was to be well rewarded. The State quickly moved to subsidize the economy in the form of armament credits, amounting to "about 62 percent of total government expenditures, or over 16 percent of total national income by 1938" (Schoenbaum 1967, p. 116).

For popular support, the Nazi party drew heavily from what G.D.H. Cole describes as "the new middle classes." Elsewhere (Chapter Four) we have termed the more privileged technicians, professionals, and administrators, who exist primarily on salaries, as a new working class. Whatever the description, these together with small landowners and business interests formed a political vanguard for the Nazi party. It was this middle segment of the society that had been devastated by the inflation coming in the wake of the First World War. It was also this class that greatly feared the emergence of a workers' socialism that would sweep away their claim to higher status and their dreams of moving up the class ladder (Cole 1973).

What of the working classes? When Hitler came to power, they were organized, well-educated, and strong. They had actually carried out a wartime strike during the First World War. Yet there was no organized resistance to Nazism (Schoenbaum 1967, p. xii). In the end it appears that working-class socialism in Germany collapsed partly through a united industrialist middle class front, and partly from a weakness in ideology. (It must also be noted that the Nazi regime demonstrated remarkable ability to eliminate potential sources of opposition. For example, Hitler's agents set fire to the Reichstag in 1933 and blamed the communists.) Fervent nationalism proved very effective in the destruction of working-class interests. Socialist political ideology based purely on a discussion of objective or material contradictions in a decaying capitalism became the clear loser. Despite the essential accuracy of the view that depressed conditions could not be isolated from an economic order continuing to favor the wealthy and exploit the worker, the *Nazis were saying the same thing* to the working masses while assuring the upper classes that they had nothing to fear.

However, they went much further. Nazi ideology elevated spiritualism to the level of a historically unique political force (Reich 1977). More specifically, downtrodden, frequently unemployed and hungry people still suffering from the humiliating loss of the First World War, were to find their dignity restored through the rhetoric of racial mysticism. True Germans, those with untainted blood, were the supposed descendants of the mythical Aryan master race. How then did those of superior biological heritage come to find themselves in such desperate conditions? The full-blown racist ideology of the late nineteenth and twentieth centuries in combination with Hitler's own virulent anti-Semitism were to identify the "internal enemy," who threatened racial purity, Aryan morality, and economic order. The period of Nazism in Germany saw the conversion of the Jewish people into a state-sanctioned scapegoat. And as we shall later see, the implementation of that ideology went far beyond the goals of national morale and solidarity, and the enrichment of the coffers of the State through expropriation.

INSTITUTIONALIZATION

Nation-states have adopted a variety of policies to deal with majority/minority relations. These policies include: (1) assimilation, (2) pluralism, (3) legal protection of minorities, (4) population transfer, and (5) extermination (Simpson and Yinger 1965, pp. 20–26).

Assimilation

Assimilation is the adoption by the minority group of the dominant group's culture, thereby eliminating the cultural differences. It can be forced assimilation where, for example, one is not allowed to speak other than English in school or at work. Also, it can be permitted assimilation in which the minority group members can adopt the majority's ways at their own pace. Many of the institutionalized practices in Canada and the United States have employed forced assimilation. For example, the fact that English is the only language spoken (outside of Quebec) means that non-English speaking people must adopt English for school and for work. In spite of Canada's being a bilingual nation, for all practical purposes it is largely unilingual outside of French Quebec.

Pluralism

Pluralism exists where the dominant groups permit cultural variety within the nation-state. As noted, in Canada, French-Canadians have established pluralistic policies in language. There is a French-speaking province, Quebec, where French is the official language, while in the other nine provinces English prevails. Also, the Quebec legal system is based upon French civil law rather than English common law like the rest of the provinces. Only in recent history did the dominant English government accede to French-Canadian demands for bilingualism and biculturalism (Hiller 1976). In 1963, a Royal Commission on Bilingualism and Biculturalism was appointed and the Offical Language Bill was passed in July 1967 stipulating that the "English and French languages are the official languages of Canada" and that they "possess and enjoy equality of status and equal rights and privileges as to their use in all the institutions of the Parliament and Government of Canada" (*Statistics Canada* 1978, p. 53).

Given the fact of heavy post-World War II immigration to Canada largely from Europe, there exists a great number of diverse ethnic groups with differing cultures and languages, among them Dutch, Germans, Hungarians, Italians, Poles, Russians, Scandinavians, and Ukrainians. While the Canadian government has an official policy of multiculturalism, many of these immigrants are being assimilated through the educational system and the workplace (Valle 1975).

The United States has never really emphasized pluralistic policies, excepting in the tragic case of the Indian reservation. Its major institutions have been basically English/White/Anglo-Saxon, supported by both forced and permitted assimilation. Until the last few decades, racial segregation was the official government policy toward blacks, Indians, and Chicanos. However, while these minorities had their separate schools, they were oriented to teaching forced assimilation to the dominant group standards. Only within recent years have federal, state, and local governments attempted to adjust institutional policies and practices to fit the culturally different. Therefore, in Los Angeles, New York, San Antonio, and other cities with sizable Spanish-speaking populations, Spanish is taught in the schools and there are media in Spanish, including radio and TV stations and newspapers. While non-English media have existed for some time in certain United States urban centers, the government is now supporting such expressions of culture. These efforts at fostering divergent cultures have largely been in response to the collective protests and activities of minority groups, although the predominant policy remains one of assimilation. We hasten to add that cultural gains have not brought dramatic movement away from political and economic repression. Institutional concessions to minority customs are easier to achieve than the elimination of the structural inequality of corporate order.

Legal Protection

Related to the policy of pluralism is the legal protection of minorities. This entails specific laws that protect minority groups from majority oppression. The history of the United States legal system has been mainly one of sanctioned oppression of racial minorities. Termed de jure segregation, the separation of the races was required *by law*. Furthermore, the original Constitution and both common law and statutory law thereafter provided for inequality along racial lines. Only within the last few decades has the legal system of the United States rid itself of the remaining explicit manifestations of racism in the law.

The United States Constitution did not specifically mention slaves, slavery, or race. However, it protected slavery in the states where it existed, provided for the return of escaped slaves to their masters, devised a formula for counting slaves in the appointment of members of Congress[2], prohibited Congress from taxing slavery out of existence, and preserved the African slave trade for twenty years (Miller 1966a; 1966b).

In the early part of the nineteenth century, the "free" states and territories erected legal barriers against blacks. By 1811, antiblack forces of the Indiana territorial legislature passed laws forbidding blacks to join the militia, testify in court against a white, or vote. Ohio forbade blacks to live in the state unless they posted $500 bond for good behavior. In 1813, Illinois (home of Abe Lincoln), ordered every incoming "free" black to

[2]The "formula" was the 3/5 rule which meant that five slaves were to count as three persons.

leave the territory under penalty of thirty-nine lashes repeated every fifteen days until departure. The chief argument against slavery among Northerners was that it would eventually produce a "free" black population competing for jobs and resources when none were assured (except of course for those who had amassed large amounts of wealth). Working whites in Northern states feared being "overrun" by blacks and thus supported efforts to keep them out (Woodward 1969).

In an extensive analysis of racism in California from 1769 to 1942, Daniels and Kitano (1970) vividly portrayed the use of the law and other institutions in support of racism against Indians, Chicanos, blacks, Chinese, and Japanese.

Contemporary mythology interprets the Civil War as a struggle over slavery and racial oppression when in fact it principally concerned states' rights and economic factors (Woodward 1969). The marshalling of technology under the ever-growing corporate economy in the industrial North was inevitably to clash with an agrarian somewhat feudal order whose historical time had passed. After the Civil War the Fourteenth and Fifteenth amendments were enacted eliminating slavery and giving blacks the right to vote; these provisions, however, were emasculated through a number of Supreme Court cases. The institutionalization of racism through Jim Crow statutes began in the North in the early 1800s and spread to the South after the Civil War. Such laws established segregation in churches, schools, housing, jobs, restaurants, public transportation, sports, prisons, hospitals, military service, courtrooms, funeral homes, morgues, cemeteries, and many other facilities (Woodward 1969). Thus, legal culture was a constant reminder of the inferior status of blacks remaining in effect in many southern states until the 1960s. Not until the 1954 Supreme Court decision—Brown v. Board of Education of Topeka—was the doctrine of separate-but-equal judged to be inherently unequal. After this decision the Jim Crow statutes met increasing challenges and were subsequently eliminated by the 1970s. While the Bill of Rights and the United States Constitution were designed to protect the rights of property owners from state abuses, it has only been within the past few decades that these rights have been extended to racial minorities.

The Canadian Bill of Rights was passed in 1967, and has subsequently been used to address racism. As in the United States, laws representing an essentially symbolic (rather than substantive) repudiation of racism came after World War II. Racial discrimination acts and human rights legislation were enacted in the 1950s and 1960s. Prior to World War II, laws ignored the fact that Canada had a well-established history of racism against Native Americans, blacks, French-Canadians, and other minority groups (Hill 1978).

We analyze elsewhere the legislative history of such concepts as "civil rights," "equal opportunity," and "affirmative action" for women and workers (see Chapters Four and Eleven). Similar arguments can be made for racial and ethnic minorities. In short, these legislative remedies have sought to substitute "equality under the law" for "equality." Such legislation in the past two decades has had minimal impact in improving minority jobs and income. However, it does serve to convince unemployed or nonpromoted whites that others receive preferential treatment. Its real consequence is class division.

Population Transfer

A variety of measures have been used by nation-states to move specific populations. The original inhabitants of North America were continually moved by colonizing powers. As the French and English conquered various parts of North America, native people were relegated to a smaller portion of the land. Subsequently, through conquest, they were concentrated on reservations and reserves that were established primarily on undesirable lands. As of December 31, 1975, there were 282,762 registered Indians in Canada in 574 separate Indian bands on 2,284 reserves and speaking forty-six languages (*Statistics Canada* 1978, p. 46). In the United States the Indian and Eskimo population is about 880,000, with 550,000 living on or near reservations. The Bureau of Indian Affairs has some jurisdiction over 266 Indian land units including reservations, pueblos, rancheros, colonies, and communities and thirty-five groups of scattered public-domain allotments and other off-reservation settlements. There are also twenty-six newly established state reservations (Price 1978, pp. 130–46).

Perhaps the most eloquent and symbolic action in the recent history of Native Americans occurred in late 1969. For two years, Alcatraz Island in San Francisco Bay, the site of an abandoned federal maximum security institution, was occupied by Indians of various tribes. Their proclamation speaks well to historical reservation policy.

> We feel that this so-called Alcatraz Island is more than suitable for an Indian Reservation, as determined by the white man's own standards. By this we mean that this place resembles most Indian reservations in that:
>
> 1. It is isolated from modern facilities, and without adequate means of transportation.
>
> 2. It has no fresh running water.
>
> 3. It has inadequate sanitation facilities.
>
> 4. There are no oil or mineral rights.
>
> 5. There is no industry and so unemployment is very great.

6. There are no health care facilities.

7. The soil is rocky and nonproductive; and the land does not support game.

8. There are no educational facilities.

9. The population has always exceeded the land base.

10. The population has always been held as prisoners and kept dependent upon others.

Further, it would be fitting and symbolic that ships from all over the world, entering the Golden Gate, would first see Indian land, and thus be reminded of the true history of this nation. This tiny island would be a symbol of the great lands once ruled by free and noble Indians (Alcatraz Indians 1972, pp. 166–67).

One of the most infamous population transfers was the forced removal of the Cherokee Nation from their native land, named Georgia by the colonizer, to the wilderness west of the Mississippi. The trek brought severe hardship and thousands of deaths. As recounted earlier, in 1831 in Cherokee Nation v. Georgia, United States Supreme Court Justice Marshall suggested Indian tribes were "domestic dependent nations" whose relationship to the federal government resembled that of a "ward to his guardian" (Cohen and Mause 1968). Although he subsequently ruled that the Cherokees be recognized as a self-governing people, he had no way to enforce the ruling. Under the insistence of President Andrew Jackson, Congress had already passed the Indian Removal Act of 1830 and the forced march, The Trail of Tears, was carried out by the United States military (David 1972, pp. 36–37).

From the beginning of slavery, blacks were subjected to continuous population transfer. Viewed as property, they were brought from Africa and distributed according to the market demands for labor. When "freed," as previously mentioned, there were restrictions on their movement. Hemmed in by such racially specific tactics as Jim Crow legislation and Ku Klux terrorism, together with the general tendencies in a society of classes to concentrate the poor out of sight and out of mind, blacks have remained separate and unequal (Clark 1965).

Chinese and Japanese were originally brought to North America because of the obvious advantage cheap labor represented to the property owning class. Various inducements such as free transport were used to attract Oriental workers. However, once they began to move away from the harsh and less desirable jobs (such as railroad construction) to compete for better jobs and to establish small farms and businesses, immigration regulations arose. In the 1920s legislatures in both Canada and the United States passed racist immigration regulations prohibiting Chinese and Japanese from moving to North America. Prior to that time bonds and head taxes were levied to keep out the "yellow peril" (Hughes and Kallen 1974; Daniels and Kitano 1970).

Before 1953, the Canadian Immigration Act included the criteria of "climatic unsuitability" for prohibiting entrance. This was a form of institutionalized racism primarily barring people from Third World countries.

A disgraceful example of racist population transfer was the imprisonment of Americans of Japanese descent in concentration camps during World War II in North America. As the war news worsened after the December 7, 1941, attack on Pearl Harbor, there was a growing public demand to do something about the "dangerous" Japanese living in the United States. Although people could distinguish between a "good" and "bad" German or Italian, all Japanese were condemned. Lieutenant General J.L. DeWitt, chief of the United States Western Defense Command, called for the relocation of all Japanese, proclaiming that a "Jap was a Jap" whether alien or native born. President Roosevelt gave the green light to this proposal and more than 100,000 innocent people were uprooted and put in these prison camps. Interestingly enough, many isolated Japanese outside of the West Coast were not confined. For example, most Japanese in Hawaii were free to go about their business. As Justice Murphy of the United States Supreme Court observed, the sanctioning of the relocation was "legislation of racism" (Daniels and Kitano 1970).

> It is enough to say that national security had little to do with these acts. Rather, it was a classic case of repression in which some groups stood to benefit economically from the action. In spite of fantastic discrimination and unfair legislation, the West Coast Japanese had done well economically. . . . Japanese youth were going to college in higher numbers than any single ethnic group in the United States. . . . The Federal Reserve Bank of San Francisco estimated that the land confiscated during the internment period amounted to about $400 million. Since the land was claimed by prosperous whites, the group that benefited from these acts of repression became clear (Wolfe 1978, pp. 99–100).

In the province of British Columbia, Canadians also reacted with racist policies. Japanese people were identified as a subversive "fifth column" and subject to official persecution. Included was the relocation of all persons of Japanese origin to the interior of Canada in concentration camps. After the Japanese surrendered to the Allies in 1945, the Canadian government ordered the deportation to Japan of all persons of Japanese ancestry. Although rescinded in 1947, nearly 4,000 Japanese-Canadians left the country. During the war, most Canadians were fighting Germans; however, Canadians of German origin, with the exception of the Hutterite religious minority, were not singled out for official persecution. Obviously racism was the major element in such repression (Hughes and Kallen 1974, pp. 144–46).

The current segregation of blacks, Natives, and Chicanos in the ghetto, reserve, or barrio is testimony to the history of subjugation and control by the white majority.

Extermination

The ultimate form of oppression of a minority group is extermination. The United States destroyed approximately two thirds of the Indian population through such policies (Simpson and Yinger 1965, p. 25). An indication of the systematic and premeditated nature of this genocide was the Colorado legislation offering bounties for the "destruction of Indians and Skunks" (Reasons and Kuykendall 1972, p. 3). Another example is the historical treatment of the Yaki Indians near Sacramento, California, who were hunted down and virtually eliminated in 1864. The murder of these 2,000 innocent people was legally sanctioned and carried out by parties of armed whites (Daniels and Kitano 1970).

Perhaps the clearest single episode of a massacre perpetrated by the United States government against a native people was not uncovered for almost a century. By 1890, many plains Indians mired in reservation poverty and degradation, experienced a revival of messianic religion. Fearing an uprising, the army arrested the Sioux chief Sitting Bull and he was shortly assassinated. Fearful and starving (due to government restrictions on food rations), Chief Big Foot and his Minneconjou Sioux left the Cheyenne River Reservation to travel to another at Pine Ridge for safety. They were intercepted by the Seventh Cavalry at Wounded Knee Creek after a 150-mile march in the harsh Dakota winter. The Sioux camped for the night. The next morning they were disarmed. Supposedly instigated by an ensuing gunshot the soldiers opened fire. Almost 300 men, women, and children were slain (Brown N. David, 1972:91–92).

> It was the fourth day after Christmas in the Year of Our Lord 1890. When the first torn and bleeding bodies were carried into the candlelit church, those who were conscious could see Christmas greenery hanging from the open rafters. Across the chancel front above the pulpit was strung a crudely lettered banner: PEACE ON EARTH, GOOD WILL TO MEN (Brown 1972, p. 98).

Blacks in North America were subjected to selective extermination by lynchings. Researchers from Tuskegee Institute report that between 1882 and 1962 there were 4,736 Americans lynched, 73 percent of them black and 27 percent white. While four fifths of black lynchings occurred in the South, only the New England states, Arizona, Idaho, Nevada, South Dakota, Wisconsin, Alaska, and Hawaii have no records of the lawless execution of blacks. Although most lynchings were of persons accused of homicide, assault, robbery, or rape, black people have been lynched for such "offenses" as "peeping in a window," arguing with a white man, trying to vote, attempting to get work at a restaurant, using offensive language, being boastful, or violating racial etiquette" (Pinkney 1972). A dramatic example of the lawless nature of such action is the fact that the mayor of Omaha, Nebraska, was killed trying to stop a lynch mob in 1919. The local newspaper described it as follows:

> Several men sprang out of the window with the rope in their hands, and others shoved the half dead brute out the window. Then the most fearful work ever witnessed at the hands of a mob in Omaha, up to that time, was performed amid the piercing yells of thousands of desperate men.
> The rope was grasped by nearly a hundred men, who ran down to Seventeenth and Harney Streets. The accused Negro was dragged by the neck all the way and was nearly dead before he had been dragged 100 feet. The mob rushed upon him, kicking and jumping upon him as he was jerked down over the rough pavement, his clothing being almost torn from his body and the skin and flesh bleeding in a shocking manner (Ginzeburg 1962, p. 128).

The day after the lynching an estimated one fifth of Omaha's 10,000 blacks fled to Kansas City, St. Louis, and St. Joseph, Missouri, while the rest armed themselves for self-defense. Although many have participated in lynchings, few have ever been charged with violating the law. For example, in 1930 tens of thousands of people joined lynch mobs, with only forty-nine indicted and four sentenced. The reality has been that in most instances local officials, including law enforcement, encouraged or tacitly approved of such killings (Pinkney 1970). Historically lynching has been used to keep blacks in their place and continue their subjugation. It appears to have been particularly prevalent when white supremacy was being challenged (Inverarity 1976).

Undoubtedly the most horrendous twentieth-century example of racist extermination was the systematic murder of an estimated 6 million Jews by the Nazis between 1933 and 1945.

Holocaust

Their names are not that well known in North America: Auschwitz; Buchenwald; Dachau; Mauthausen; Sachsenhausen; Treblinka; but these were some of the Nazi concentration centers better termed death camps. These chambers of horror were placed under the control of Hitler's elite SS (Schutzstaffel), whose death's head insigna came to be more than ordinarily symbolic (Shirer 1960, p. 272).

Before the invasion of Poland on September 1, 1939, and the beginning of the Second World War, Nazi concentration camps had no more than twenty or thirty thousand inmates. While they were brutal, their existence served primarily to punish enemies of the State and to strengthen the party through terror (Shirer 1960, 271). However, with the coming of the war years, the concentration camps grew in size and number, assuming such functions as slave labor and "scientific" research. The latter involved subjecting specimens of "inferior races" (primarily Jews, but also some Polish and Russian prisoners of war) to such "experiments" as injections of typhus and jaundice; being shot with poison bullets, being given gas gangrene wounds, and determining the length of time one could live on salt water (Shirer 1960, pp. 979–91). The logical conclusion of master race ideology was to be institutionalized, however, in the implementation of the "final solution."

The Final Solution

In an address to the German legislature on January 30, 1939, Hitler had warned of the annihilation of the Jewish people. He was to repeat that message publicly at least five other times (Shirer 1960, p. 964). The innocent term "final solution" was adopted by Hitler's chief lieutenants, including Himmler and Goering, to refer to the systematic extermination of European Jews.

With terrifying variety, a plan of mass extermination was implemented. Overall, the murder processes revealed an increasing efficiency. The methods of execution included the early use of lethal injections, vans rigged as carbon monoxide gas chambers, and shooting. In the latter stages, the poison gas Zyklon B was developed. One death camp commander (Hoess) speaks of his concern for minimizing effort, expense, and waste.

> So when I set up the extermination building at Auschwitz, I used Zyklon B, which was a crystallized prussic acid which was dropped into the death chamber from a small opening. It took from three to fifteen minutes to kill the people in the death chamber, depending upon climatic conditions.

> We knew when the people were dead because their screaming stopped. We usually waited about a half hour before we opened the doors and removed the bodies. After the bodies were removed our special commandos took off the rings and extracted the gold from the teeth of the corpses.

> Another improvement we made over Treblinka was that we built our gas chambers to accommodate 2,000 people at one time, whereas at Treblinka their ten gas chambers only accommodated 200 people each. (Quoted in Shirer 1960, p. 968.)

The concern for efficiency did not stop here. The disposition of the corpses evolved from mass burial to cremation in giant furnaces. Once the crematoria (usually located adjacent to the gas chambers) had done their job, the remains were often ground to fine ash by a milling process and sometimes sold as fertilizer.

In an attempt to forestall revolt, details of the extermination process were not made public. And despite the overwhelming evidence, including the stench of burning bodies, few asked questions. Jews were rounded up and concentrated in large urban ghettos. They were then transported out, most frequently by rail, ostensibly to work camps. Indeed, the gates to the notorious Auschwitz carried the slogan "Arbeit Macht Frei" (Work Makes Freedom). Once at the camp, the victims were told they were to be given showers or deloused. The gas chambers were surrounded by grass and flowers and often equipped with dummy showerheads. Signs at the entrances read *Baths*, and live music was frequently played as men, women, and children lined up to play out their role in the final solution (Shirer 1960, pp. 963–79).

MAINTENANCE

To understand who or what benefits from contemporary race relations in North America, it is necessary to have a historical framework for analysis. While the preceding section provides some historical background, here we will place racism in a theoretical context.

We believe that the continued oppression of racial minorities has in part been a special case of exploitation of labor. While most white ethnic immigrants have experienced some upward movement, that mobility in this century (as well as that of other workers) has been basically intraclass rather than interclass (Braverman 1974, pp. 424–429). Further, few white immigrants were brought to this continent in chains. Nor were they among the native populations standing in the way of westward expansion. Today, in a class-divided society where freedom from want is not assured, those in similar social positions continue to define their ills in purely racial, ethnic, sexual, or other terms. Race and skin color have been a basis for assigning "inferior" labor and status thus ensuring a reserve industrial army and depressed wages. It might be more appropriate to compare our native peoples, Chicanos, and blacks to colonized people. If racial groups have been colonized, they cannot be understood in the terminology of immigration and assimilation. Like other Third World peoples, colonized persons became part of a society through force or violence, while immigrants enter a country under different circumstances. The issue is one of specific historical analysis (Blauner 1972).

Colonial Model

In an analysis of Indian and white relations in Canada, Frideres (1974) identifies seven facets of the colonial model: (1) forced entry; (2) destruction of indigenous institutions; (3) external political control; (4) economic dependence upon the colonizer; (5) inferior social services provided to the colonized; (6) racism based upon belief in the innate inferiority of nonwhites; (7) a color line based upon skin pigmentation allowing groups to be quickly and easily identified. This model can be used to explain both the historical and contemporary situations of native people, black people, Chicanos, and (in part) French-Canadians in North America.

Native people in both Canada and the United States were conquered and subsequently dominated as a logical consequence of the colonial practices of Western capitalism (Noel 1972, pp. 153–55). Their political, religious, and social institutions have been largely destroyed and they are controlled externally by Bureaus of Indian Affairs. Through the paternalistic policies of the government, Indians have become economically dependent while the social services they receive have been inferior to those provided to the rest of the population. Racism, based upon skin color, still provides a rationale for paternalism and oppression. Contemporary reserves are the manifestations of colonial policy, still the dominant approach toward native peoples in North America (Frideres 1974; Price 1978; Hughes and Kallen 1974).

Black people were forced into North America through slavery, and treated as mere pieces of property. Their prior culture was almost completely destroyed and they were controlled politically and economically through racist policies and practices. The contemporary ghetto represents colonialism in that it is largely dependent on external political and economic control (Blauner 1972, 82–110). The social services in ghetto areas such as medical care, police protection, education, and sanitation are inferior to those in other areas and have been identified as important causes of riots (Knowles and Prewitt 1969; Report of the National Advisory Commission 1968).

The second largest minority group in the United States is the census category defined as "Spanish-speaking" persons. Americans of Hispanic background numbered 11.3 million in 1977. In that year, Chicanos (Mexican-Americans) comprised nearly 60 percent of this population, with the rest primarily from Puerto Rico and Cuba (*Statistical Abstract of the United States* 1978, p. 32). Located primarily in the southwestern states, Chicanos are burdened with poor health, housing, income, occupation, and education when compared with Anglo-Americans (Wagner and Haug 1971).

Mexicans became part of the United States by being conquered. The Mexican War ended in 1848 with one half of Mexico under control of the United States. The ideology of "manifest destiny" was the basis for expansion to the Pacific Ocean, and like the "white man's burden" it rationalized domination of native and Mexican peoples. Chicano institutions and culture, including language, were subsequently dominated and repressed by white society, and the urban barrio is the contemporary colony in American cities (Moore 1970).

Until 1941, French-Canadians were identified as a race. The British conquered the French on the Plains of Abraham in 1759 and subsequently the province of Quebec developed as a French colony in a British-dominated nation. The principal method of domination has been through economic institutions and numerous studies have noted French-Canadians' historically inferior socioeconomic status (Porter 1968; Manzer 1974). In recent years, however, the Quebecois (Quebecers) have intensified their struggle to rid themselves of colonial status (Milner 1973).

The significance of the colonial model in analyzing the situation of all these minorities is that we come to understand the historical basis for contemporary inequality. Also, the current struggles for liberation by these minority groups gain more meaning if we have a grasp of the underlying basis for their grievances.

In conclusion, domestic and global colonialism has historically been in the interest of those who have profited by and large from the systematic usurping of land and resources, both human and natural. In most European colonial systems, a civil service apparatus was developed to control the native population. For North American domestic colonialism, a clear parallel is the development of a welfare and law enforcement bureaucracy that although not restricted to controlling minority groups, certainly provides disproportionate services for them. More specifically, the development of Bureaus of Indian Affairs gives ample testimony to what continues to be maintained by the prevailing definition of the "racial problem."

ALTERNATIVE: MINORITY LIBERATION

The entire history of colonial status has been that of institutionalized inferiority. Since dominant institutions and policies have oppressed minority groups, some have attempted to establish a power base. At this historical period, the base is frequently fragmented on the basis of cultural, ethnic, and racial identity.

Black Power

Black Power entails the mobilization of blacks' political, social, and economic resources for their collective struggle to control their own destiny (Carmichael and Hamilton 1967). It is an ideology consisting of a philosophy, an ethic, strategies, and programs that relate black people to society in a historical context (Franklin 1969). As a philosophy it is directed at the white power structure, and emphasizes coracial politics rather than coalition (white-dominated) politics. As an ethical norm it opposes the goal of integration since that acknowledges the superiority of whites. Black power strategy is that of self-direction, self-support, and self-ownership of institutions in the ghetto (community control). By stressing the individual's positive self-image (black is beautiful) and identity with the movement and struggle, this alternative holds that black people will develop self-respect, self-discipline, and increased control over themselves and their community.

A Leader Before His Time   The black liberation movement in the United States got much of its impetus from W.E.B. DuBois in the early part of this century. DuBois, the first black to receive a PhD degree in the United States (1895), stated that America's major problem of the twentieth century was that of the race/color line. Unlike Booker T. Washington, who identified the problem as a black problem, DuBois focused on white domination and the subjugation of blacks. He advocated black pride and black power (economic, political, and social) long before the contemporary struggle took form (DuBois 1903). He helped form the Niagara Movement in 1905 to combat racism. Subsequently, in 1909, he participated in establishing the National Association for the Advancement of Colored People (NAACP). DuBois was labeled a "radical" by white society because he blamed white society for the "Negro problem," advocating black power while later centering the specific problem of race in the more general framework of class inequality (DuBois 1970, pp. 335–53). Questioning the basic tenets of corporate ideology, he bore the brunt of slander and repression, eventually leaving the United States and becoming a citizen of Ghana, where he died in 1965.

Following World War II, blacks in the United States increased their collective efforts to gain equality. Since the United States was now a world power, its leaders came to have increasing difficulty explaining how Nazi racism had been fought with segregated troops. Blacks had opposed racism and oppression overseas only to return to legally segregated housing, jobs, education, and Jim Crow. Finally, African nationalism was gaining momentum as a global force and the long night of colonialism continues today to pass away (Rotberg 1971).

Nonviolence: A New Weapon   Martin Luther King, Jr., assumed leadership of a Montgomery, Alabama, boycott of segregated busing in 1955, which led to his becoming a symbol of black, nonviolent civil disobedience, and eventually his assassination. A minister with a PhD in theology, King left the quiet comfort of the pulpit to lead blacks and sympathetic whites in marches and demonstrations against racist segregation. A dedicated humanitarian and student of the philosophy and practice of non-violence, King believed that showing the degradation and inhumanity of segregation and racial oppression to all of white society would awaken the conscience of America. Unfortunately, many Americans viewed the "black" struggle for equality as the problem. As King increasingly found opposition, he came to see racism related to economic oppression and war. With the State escalating its war in Vietnam (while de-escalating its war on poverty and racism at home) he increasingly spoke out against both the Southeast Asian conflict and inequality. In April 1968 Martin Luther King, Jr., was assassinated while in Memphis, Tennessee, to give a speech in support of striking garbage collectors. While the conspiratorial nature of this murder may never be solved, it is clear that he had come into increasing disfavor among whites during the 1960s because of his "militant" posture (U.S. House of Representatives, Select Committee on Assassinations 1979).

The militant nature of white resistance to black power led to the formation of various organizations expressing a stronger demand for community control. The Black Panthers were formed in Oakland, California, in 1965 largely to provide community protection from the police (Foner 1970). Since it threatened the ultimate social control of white society over the ghetto (by police), it was subsequently attacked politically and physically and by the early 1970s many of its leaders were dead or in jail. In the 1980s, the Black Panther Party has continued to work for community control by more conventional political channels, seeking, for example, to influence local government.

Red Power

Within recent years native people have increasingly challenged the ability and legitimacy of whites to run their affairs. Such spokesmen as Vine Deloria (1969) in the United States and Harold Cardinal (1969) in Canada have presented a compelling case against white domination. While Indian organizations have been in existence for some years (Frideres 1975), it has only been recently that Native Americans began to militantly assert their rights. In both Canada and the United States the American Indian Movement is a symbol of such militancy (Price 1978, pp. 226–39).

The American Indian Movement was founded in Minneapolis, Minnesota, in 1968 to help native Americans and other poor people in trouble with the law. Like blacks and Chicanos, native people are often in conflict with white legal institutions (Reasons and Kuykendall 1972). From Minneapolis the movement established itself in other areas. Because its leaders were outspoken and emphasized confrontational tactics, agents of the State saw it as "radical" and a threat to society. Emphasizing Indian economic, political, and social power and self-determination, AIM has focused public attention on the plight of Indians. Through marches, sit-ins, and other forms of protest, it has helped to create a sense of self-pride and self-worth among many native people, including those who do not necessarily agree with its tactics. Much of the real and potential power of native people in North America resides in their claim to land. Various Indian organizations are increasingly recognizing and pursuing this (Frideres 1975; Mickenberg 1971). Native protest is likely to become stronger in Canada than the United States because Indians are the largest racial minority in Canada; their proportion of the population is greater in Canada than in the United States (2.5 percent and .4 percent of the population, respectively); there is greater cultural contrast in Canada, where natives follow a more traditional life-style; and Canada's Indians have a stronger potential economic and political base in their reserves (Reasons 1978).

Brown Power

For Chicanos, the concept of La Raza, or "the race," provides ethnic pride and a common bond (Steiner 1970). The Brown Berets began in 1968 in Los Angeles with various educational demands, including bilingual instruction (Moquin and Van Doren 1971). Also important to Chicanos has been the effort of Cesar Chavez in organizing farm workers in California to better their situation. The honor and reputation he has earned among Chicanos place him with such famous Mexicans as Juarez, Zapata, and Villa (Steiner 1970, p. 242). His struggles have further dramatized the oppression of Chicanos and provided increased political consciousness and action. The United Farm Workers' Organizing Committee, led by Chavez, has greatly helped the struggles of migrant and agricultural laborers specifically, and Chicanos generally.

The tactics used by various Chicano organizations are similar to those of other minority protest groups—sit-ins, strikes, and marches. Violence, when it occurs, is frequently a reaction to police practices. For example, the Texas Rangers and the Federal Border Patrol have been notorious historically for their tactics of search, seizure, and detention. (Turner 1977, pp. 267–74.) While the former organization finally became a public embarrassment and had its budget and personnel substantially reduced, the latter continues to harass "illegal aliens" rather than the growers who exploit their labor.

French-Canadian Power

As previously mentioned, French-Canadians were colonized and subsequently became an oppressed minority within English-dominated Canada. Their collective struggle to gain more power began in earnest during the 1960s. The radical wing of the movement was the Federation for the Liberation of Quebec (FLQ) which used such tactics as bombing, kidnapping, and one assassination. These violent practices cannot, of course, be understood in historical isolation. Like other movements confronted daily by the "legitimate" force of the State (the police and the military), the FLQ reacted to the institutionalized violence of state power, corporate inequality, and domestic colonialism. Their major aim was to create an independent nation of Quebec that would be socialist and for the workers. While FLQ leaders were subsequently captured and prosecuted, the movement for a separation of Quebec from English-speaking Canada gained momentum and legitimacy. In the 1970 provincial election the separatists won 23 percent of the vote and in 1975 René Lévesque of the separatist Parti Quebecois was elected Premier of Quebec. English Canada was shocked by the realization that this previously "radical fringe" party was now governing Quebec with the mandate of the popular vote. Subsequently, Quebec Bill 22 was passed, making French the offical language of the province and further alienating many English-Canadians.

Since emerging victorious in Quebec, Lévesque has led his party in an attempt to secure independence for the French-speaking province. In 1980, a majority of Quebec's voters voted "no" on the question of separatism. However, at this writing the question of a free Quebec is certainly not resolved.

The Struggle Continues

Efforts by minority groups to better their collective fate are continuous and usually uphill battles. Resistance takes the form of indifference, legal obstacles, and individual and collective violence against minority group members. For example, the history of race riots has largely been that of whites attacking minority persons. Only since World War II have riots been directed largely at white property by black urban dwellers, who have suffered far more casualties than the predominantly white forces of control. Before that time, race riots usually consisted of whites indiscriminately beating and killing blacks (Baskin 1969), largely in efforts to maintain the status quo. Besides lynchings, systematic terrorism has a long history in the United States through a vigilante tradition (Brown

1969). Such a tradition cannot be separated from its structural context. For example, until recently, agricultural, ranching, and mining interests promoted and supported such actions to control Chicano workers in the southwestern United States (Lohman 1966, p. 55). Such oppression has been directed at both ethnic and racial minority groups (Myers 1960).

While the term militant is often used with reference to minority groups, "white militancy" has a long tradition.

> The historical record, however, indicates that considerably more disorder and violence have come from groups whose aim has been the preservation of an existing or remembered order of social arrangements, and in whose ideology the concept of "law and order" has played a primary role (Skolnick 1969, p. 210).

The Ku Klux Klan is a prime example of a racist organization attempting to oppress nonwhites through terrorist tactics. Starting in the 1880s to protect "Americanism" (WASP), it has at times been a powerful social and political force. In the 1920s the Klan's preaching of hatred toward blacks, Catholics, and Jews helped it spread through the United States. During this time its membership rose to several million and it became influential at the local, state, and federal levels (Skolnick 1969, pp. 216–17).

The Ku Klux Klan and other racist organizations such as the White Citizens Councils drew adherents as the civil rights movement made gains. Evident in Canada as well, the Ku Klux Klan reminds us that racist and inhumane ideologies and organizations are still active in today's "enlightened" world. For example, in June 1979 nine Ku Klux Klansmen were convicted in Alabama of terrorizing blacks (Calgary Herald 1979).

While organizations such as the Ku Klux Klan have a long history of open brutality and virulent racism, one must be careful not to conceptualize racism along such dramatic lines. The stereotype of the poorly educated inarticulate white mouthing venom against minority groups is received with contempt by most people. If the problem of race and racism were confined to such symbols of hate, it would be easier to resolve. However, in contemporary North America the Klan is simply out of time and place. The torch of racism has been passed to the more devastating if subtle social forces of institutionalized inequality—in work, in education, in power, in wealth. That those who are central to the political-economy of control may join in the open denunciation of the Klan does little to threaten the prevailing form of stratification.

Minority struggles for increased power are related to the struggles of other groups, such as the poor, the aged, and women, and their collective success will be a measure of the extent to which we live in a truly just society.

BIBLIOGRAPHY

Alcatraz Indians
1972   "Proclamation of the Indians of Alcatraz by Indians of All Tribes." In The American Indian: The First Victim, Jay David, ed. New York: William Morrow, pp. 165–67.

Bahr, Howard M.;
Chadwick, Bruce A.;
and Day, Robert C.
1972   Native Americans Today: Sociological Perspectives. New York: Harper & Row.

Blauner, Robert
1972   Racial Oppression in America. New York: Harper & Row.

Boggs, James
1970   Racism and the Class Struggle. New York: Monthly Review Press.

Boskin, Joseph
1969   Urban Racial Violence in the Twentieth Century. Beverly Hills, Calif.: Glencoe Press.

Braverman, Harry
1974   Labor and Monopoly Capital: The Degradation of Work in the Twentieth Century. New York: Monthly Review Press.

Brown, Dee
1972   "Bury My Heart at Wounded Knee." Excerpted In The American Indian: The First Victim. Jay David, ed. New York: William Morrow, pp. 92–98.

Brown, Les
1971   Television, the Business behind the Box. New York: Harcourt Brace Jovanovich.

Brown, Lorne and Caroline
1972   The Unauthorized History of the RCMP. Toronto: James Lorimer.

Brown, Richard Maxwell
1969   "The American Vigilante Tradition." In The History of Violence in America. Hugh Davis Graham and Ted Robert Gun, eds. New York: Bantam, pp. 154–226.

Calgary Herald
1979   "Nine Klansmen Convicted of Terrorizing Blacks."
June 15, p. D25.

Cardinal, Harold
1969   The Unjust Society: The Tragedy of Canada's
Indians. Edmonton, Alberta: Hurtin.

Carmichael, Stokely and
Hamilton, Charles V.
1967   Black Power: The Politics of Liberation, New York:
Vintage Books.

Chirot, Daniel
1977   Social Change in the Twentieth Century. New
York: Harcourt Brace Jovanovich.

Clark, Kenneth
1965   Dark Ghetto. New York: Harper & Row.

Cohen, Warren H., and
Mause, Phillip I.
1968   "The Indian: The Forgotten American." Harvard
Law Review 81 (June): 1818–58.

Cole, G.D.H.
1970   "The New Middle Classes and the Rise of Facism."
In Problems of Industrial Society. William Chambliss, ed. Reading, Mass.: Addison-Wesley.

Cornell, George W.
1980   "Religion, Ethics, Scholars Blast Sperm Bank Project." Spokesman-Review. March 9, p. E2.

Daniels, Roger, and
Kitano, Harry
1970   American Racism: Explorations of the Nature of
Prejudice. Englewood Cliffs, N.J.: Prentice-Hall.

David, Jay
1972   The American Indian: The First Victim. New York:
William Morrow.

Deloria, Vine, Jr.
1969   Custer Died for Your Sins: An Indian Manifesto.
New York: Macmillan.

DuBois, William E.B.
1903   The Souls of Black Folk. Chicago: McClurg.

1940   Dusk of Dawn. New York: Harcourt Brace
Jovanovich.

1970   "The Negro and Socialism." In W.E.B. DuBois: A Reader. New York: Harper & Row, pp. 335–53.

Fanon, Frantz
1970   The Wretched of the Earth. New York: Grove Press.

Fife, Marilyn Diane
1974   "Black Images in American TV: The First Two Decades." The Black Scholar, November: 9–13.

Foner, Philip
1970   The Black Panthers Speak. Philadelphia: J.B. Lippincott.

1977   American Socialism and Black Americans. Westport, Conn.:Greenwood Press.

Franklin, Raymond S.
1969   "The Political Economy of Black Power." Social Problems 16 (Winter): 286–301.

Frideres, James S.
1974   Canada's Indians: Contemporary Conflicts. Scarborough, Ontario: Prentice-Hall of Canada.

Genovese, Eugene
1974   Roll, Jordan, Roll. New York: Random House.

Ginzburg, Ralph
1962   100 Years of Lynching. New York: Lancer Books.

Glenn, Norval D.
1963   Occupational Benefits to Whites from the Subordination of Negroes. American Sociological Review 28 (June): 443–48.

Gonzalez, Nancie L.
1970   "Alianza Federal De Mercedes." The Mexican Americans: An Awakening Minority. Beverly Hills, Calif.: Glencoe Press.

Gossett, Thomas
1963   Race: The History of an Idea. Dallas, Tex.: Southern Methodist University Press.

Hill, Daniel G.
1978   Human Rights in Canada: A Focus on Racism. Ottawa: Canadian Labour Congress.

Hiller, Harry H.
1976
Canadian Society: A Sociological Analysis. Scarborough, Ontario: Prentice-Hall of Canada.

Hughes, David R., and
Callen, Evelyn
1974
The Anatomy of Racism: Canadian Dimensions. Montreal: Harvest House.

Hunt, Chester L., and
Walker, Lewis
1974
Ethnic Dynamics: Patterns of Intergroup Relations in Various Societies. Homewood, Ill.: Dorsey Press.

Inverarity, James M.
1976
"Populism and Lynching in Louisiana 1889–1896: A Test of Erickson's Theory of the Relationship Between Boundary Crisis and Repressive Justice." American Sociological Review 41 (April): 262–80.

Jacobs, Paul; Landau,
Saul; and Pell, Eve
1971
To Serve the Devil, Volume 1: Natives and Slaves. New York: Random House.

Jhabzala, Firdaus
1977
"The Economic Situation of Black People." In Problems in Political Economy: An Urban Perspective, 2d ed. David M. Gorden, ed. Lexington, Mass.: D.C. Heath, pp. 153–60.

Jones, James M.
1972
Prejudice and Racism. Reading, Mass.: Addison-Wesley.

Kitano, Harry H.L.
1969
Japanese Americans: The Evolution of a Subculture. Englewood Cliffs, N.J.: Prentice-Hall.

Knowles, Louis L., and
Prewitt, Kenneth
1969
Institutional Racism in America. Englewood Cliffs, N.J.: Prentice-Hall.

Lohman, J.D.
1966
The Police and the Commuity. Berkeley, Calif.: President's Commission on Law Enforcement and Administration of Justice. Field Survey No. 4.

Mannix, Daniel, and
Cowley, Malcolm
1970   "Middle Passage." In The Slavery Experience in the United States. Irwin Unger and David Reimers, eds. New York: Holt, Rinehart and Winston.

Manzer, Ronald
1974   Canada: A Socio-Political Report. Toronto: McGraw-Hill Ryerson.

Marx, Karl
1970   Letter on the Conditions of Irish Workers in England. In Dynamics of Social Change. Howard Sellman, David Goldman, and Harry Martel, eds. New York: International Publishers.

Merton, Robert K.
1957   Social Theory and Social Structure. rev. ed. New York: The Free Press.

Mickenberg, Neil H.
1971   "Aboriginal Rights in Canada and the United States." Osgoode Hall Law Journal, pp. 119–55.

Miller, Loren
1966a   "Race, Poverty and the Law." In The Law of the Poor. Jacobus Tenbroek, ed. San Francisco: Chandler, pp. 62–82.

1966b   The Petitioners: The Story of the Supreme Court of the United States and the Negro. Cleveland, O.: World.

Milner, S.H., and
Milner, H.
1973   The Decolonization of Quebec. Toronto: McClelland and Stewart.

Montagu, Ashley M.F.
1953   Man's Most Dangerous Myth: The Fallacy of Race, 3d ed. New York: Columbia University Press.

Moore, Joane
1970   "Colonialism: The Case of the Mexican-American." Social Problems 17 (Spring):463–72.

Moquin, Wayne, and
Van Doren, Charles
1971   A Documentary History of the Mexican Americans. New York: Bantam.

Myers, Gustavus
1960   History of Bigotry in the United States. New York: Capricorn.

Myrdal, Gunnar
1944   An American Dilemma: The Negro Problem and Modern Democracy. New York: Harper & Row.

New York Times
1977   "Nielsen Ratings for Roots," February 2, 22:1.

Noel, Donald L.
1972   The Origins of American Slavery and Racism. Columbus, O.: Charles E. Merrill.

Pinkney, Alphonso
1972   The American Way of Violence. New York: Vintage.

Porter, John
1968   The Vertical Mosaic. Toronto: University of Toronto Press.

Price, John A.
1978   Native Studies: American and Canadian Indians. Toronto: McGraw-Hill Ryerson.

Reasons, Charles E.
1978   "Two Models of Race Relations and Prison Racism: A Cross-Cultural Analysis." In The Sociology of Law: A Conflict Perspective. Charles E. Reasons and Robert M. Rich, eds. Toronto: Butterworth, pp. 367–89.

Reasons, Charles E. and
Kuykendall, Jack L.
1972   Race, Crime and Justice. Pacific Palisades, Calif.: Goodyear.

Reich, Wilhelm
1977   "The Mass Psychology of Fascism." In The Psychology of Society. Rich Sennett, ed. New York: Random House, pp. 183–292.

Report of the National
Advisory Commission
on Civil Disorders
1968   New York: Bantam.

Ritzer, George; Kammeyer,
Kenneth C.W., and
Yetman, Norman R.
1979

Sociology: Experiencing a Changing Society.
Boston: Allyn and Bacon.

Rotberg, Robert I., ed.
1971

Rebellion in Black Africa. New York: Oxford
University Press.

Schoenbaum, David
1967

Hitler's Social Revolution. New York: Doubleday.

Shirer, William
1960

The Rise and Fall of the Third Reich. New York:
Simon & Schuster.

Simpson, George Eaton,
and Yinger, J. Milton
1965

Racial and Cultural Minorities. 3d ed. New York:
Harper & Row.

Skolnick, Jerome
1969

The Politics of Protest. New York: Simon &
Schuster.

Snyder, Louis L.
1962

The Idea of Racialism: Its Meaning and History.
Princeton: D. Van Nostrand.

Sorokin, Pitirim A.
1964

Contemporary Sociological Theories. New York:
Harper & Row.

Stampp, Kenneth M.
1970

The Civil Rights Record: Black Americans and the
Law. New York: Thomas Y Crowell.

Statistics Canada
1978

Canada Handbook. Ottawa: Minister of Supply and
Services Canada.

Steiner, Stan
1970

La Raza, the Mexican Americans. New York:
Harper & Row.

Time Magazine
1980

"Super Kids? A Sperm Bank of Nobelists," March
10:49.

Turner, Jonathan H.
1977   Social Problems in America. New York: Harper & Row.

United States Bureau of the Census
1979   Statistical Abstract of the United States. Washington, D.C.: U.S. Government Printing Office.

United States Commission on Civil Rights
1977   Window Dressing on the Set: Women and Minorities in Television. Washington, D.C.: U.S. Government Printing Office.

United States House of Representatives, Select Committee on Assassinations
1979   Investigation of the Assassination of Martin Luther King. Vols. 1–12. Washington, D.C.: U.S. Government Printing Office.

Vallee, Frank G.
1975   "Multi-Ethnic Societies: The Issues of Identity and Inequality." In Issues in Canadian Society: An Introduction to Sociology. Dennis Forcese and Stephen Richer, eds. Scarborough, Ontario: Prentice-Hall of Canada, pp. 162–202.

van den Berghe, Pierre
1967   Race and Racism: A Comparative Perspective. New York: John Wiley.

Wagner, Nathaniel N., and Haug, Marsha J.
1971   Chicanos: Social and Psychological Perspectives. St. Louis, Mo.: C.V. Mosby.

Wolfe, Alan
1978   The Seamy Side of Democracy. New York: Longman.

Woodward, C. Vann
1966   The Strange Career of Jim Crow. 2d rev. ed. New York: Oxford University Press.

1969   "Our Racist History." The New York Review of Books 12 (February 27, 1969):5–11.

11

SEX AND SEXISM

Abstract

Consistent with the organization of this text, Chapter Eleven begins with a discussion of the *prevailing ideologies* that bear on the problems associated with sexism. Powerful symbols serve to channel women into a subordinate place in North American society. Under corporate order, the economic salvation of most women proves to be marriage. Without this institution, women frequently find themselves impoverished.

The historical *emergence* of the women's movement finds a consistent commitment to the "contractual solution," represented by such things as the vote and legislative action. Thus, the thrust of the women's movement has been directed toward the *institutionalization* of equal opportunity, affirmative action laws, and executive orders. However, an examination of the data shows that such gains are more image than substance as the political and economic conditions of women as a whole have benefited little. With regard to *maintenance,* it can be argued that sexism, like racism, is inequality's imposter. In other words, the same system that separates the classes separates the races and the sexes. Having large pools of poorly paid workers who frequently serve as members of a surplus labor force (sometimes employed, but always vulnerable to job loss and layoff) serves the corporate economic system.

For her world is her husband, her family, her children and her home. . . . We do not find it right when the woman presses into the

605

world of the man. . . . The man upholds the nation as the woman upholds the family. . . . Reason is dominant in man. He searches, analyzes and often opens new immeasurable realms. —Adolph Hitler

Today we experience the swelling tide of a new frontier of human liberation. Women in rising numbers in North America and other societies, have formed a movement intended to shake the foundations of traditionally male-centered social institutions. The differences in rights and privileges accorded men and women have come to be defined in many quarters as a fundamental basis for political and economic conflict. Increasingly, sex has joined class and race as a preeminent symbol of inequality.

As we trace the definitional and ideological concerns associated with sex and sexism, we discover a new interpretation of humanity. To be fully human has been redefined as something more than finding one's predetermined niche in the social order. Indeed, the concept of a "place" for women has acquired the same negative connotation associated with the special statuses reserved historically for racial, ethnic, and age minority groups.

A Woman's Place Is . . .

Ironically, the measure of tolerance was once tied to the recognition of a special place. One who possessed an "open mind" could often be heard to remark that members of a certain social group should be treated with kindness as long as they stayed in their place. Needless to say, the "place" of a subject population is clearly beneath that of a dominant social category. For many, the modern women's movement is directed toward the obliteration of that "special" standing. Thus, the argument that women should not bear the burden of the complexities of political and economic life has been interpreted critically. To speak of "women's place" in such a way, even if that standing involves home and pedestal, is to argue that those who do not direct a society need not understand it.

At the point of birth, the enormous biological similarities of male and female are lost to a social definition that is primarily based on one's gonads. From the beginning of existence outside the mother's womb, a sex-related process of socialization begins. New parents can be expected to experience a mysterious sense of discomfort when the sex of the infant (or perhaps later, the toddler) is mistaken. Thus, we wrap one sex in pink and the other in blue. One sex is expected to be aggressive, to inquire, to initiate. The other is trained to be passive, to listen, to respond. To cry or be affectionate is "feminine." Those who hold their tears, deny their pain, and remain in "control" are little men.

Sex-role socialization involves more than emotional shaping. In a sense, a virtual caste system is being erected. As girls mature, they are taught more than how to be wife, mother, grandmother. They are taught that they must *be* taught. The bearer of truth, of course, is typically the male, ever enshrined as an authority figure, never a peer.

This is not to imply that the definitional process is always successful. Women increasingly are seeking a new standing free of sex-based barriers to confidence and the fully flourishing human life. However, the ideologies that seek to confine women's arena of action are strong and traditional. Further, they do not exist in a social-political vacuum. Consistent with the thrust of this text, we shall seek to clarify the structural origins of those ideologies that create the social place of women. It follows that we will not merely examine the stereotypes that are the content of sex-role socialization. Rather, we will also examine the political and economic ends served by sex-imposed limitations. For women, as for any oppressed group, freedom is more than a state of mind. It is a state of being.

Viewpoint

"BARBAROUS RITUALS"*   by Robin Morgan

Woman Is:

_____ kicking strongly in your mother's womb, upon which she is told, "It must be a boy, if it's so active!"

_____ being tagged with a pink beaded bracelet thirty seconds after you are born, and wrapped in pink blankets five minutes thereafter.

_____ being confined to the Doll Corner in nursery school when you are really fascinated by Tinker Toys.

_____ wanting to wear overalls instead of "frocks."

_____ learning to detest the words "dainty" and "cute."

*From *Sisterhood Is Powerful*, New York: Random House, pp. 161–69.

____being labeled a tomboy when all you wanted to do was climb that tree to look out and see a distance.

____learning to sit with your legs crossed, even when your feet can't touch the floor yet.

____hating boys—because they're allowed to do things you want to do but when your brother does the same thing, it's "spunky."

____wondering why your father gets mad now and then, but your mother mostly sighs a lot.

____seeing grownups chuckle when you say you want to be an engineer or doctor when you grow up—and learning to say you want to be a mommy or a nurse, instead.

____wanting to shave your legs at twelve and being agonized because your mother won't let you.

____being agonized at fourteen because you finally have shaved your legs, and your flesh is on fire.

____being told nothing whatsoever about menstruation, so that you think you are bleeding to death with your first period, or:

____being told all about it in advance by kids at school who titter and make it clear the whole thing is dirty, or:

____being prepared for it by your mother, who carefully reiterates that it isn't dirty, all the while talking just above a whisper, and referring to it as "the curse," "being sick," or "falling off the roof."

____feeling proud of and disgusted by your own body for the first, but not last, time.

____dying of shame because your mother makes you wear a "training bra" but there's nothing to train, or:

____dying of shame because your mother won't let you wear a bra and your breasts are bigger than other girls your age and they flop when you run and you sit all the time with your arms folded over your chest.

_____ feeling basically comfortable in your own body, but gradually learning to hate it because you are: too short or tall, too fat or thin, thick-thighed or big-wristed, large-eared or stringy-haired, short-necked or long-armed, bowlegged, knock-kneed, or pigeon-toed—something that might make boys not like you.

_____ wanting to kill yourself because of pimples, dandruff or a natural tendency to sweat—and discovering that commercials about miracle products just lie.

_____ dreading summertime because more of your body with its imperfections will be seen—and judged.

_____ tweezing your eyebrows/bleaching your hair/scraping your armpits/dieting/investigating vaginal sprays/biting your nails and hating that and filing what's left of them but hitting the quick instead.

_____ liking math or history a lot and getting hints that boys are turned off by smart girls.

_____ getting hints that other girls are turned off by smart girls.

_____ finally getting turned off by smart girls, unconsciously dropping back, lousing up your marks and being liked by the other kids at last.

_____ having an intense crush on another girl or on a woman teacher and learning that that's unspeakable.

_____ going to your first dance and dreaming about it beforehand and hating it, just hating it afterwards: you didn't dance right, you spilled the punch, you were a wallflower in anguish (or: you were popular but in anguish because your best friend was a wallflower), you said all the wrong things.

_____ being absolutely convinced that you are a clod, a goon, a dog, a schlep, a flop, and an utter klutz.

_____discovering that what seems like everything worthwhile doing in life "isn't feminine," and learning to just delight in being feminine and "nice"—and feeling somehow guilty.

_____masturbating like crazy and being terrified that you'll go insane, be sterile, turn into a whore or destroy your own virginity.

_____getting more information any way you can, and then being worried because you've been masturbating clitorally, and that isn't even the "right way."

_____swinging down the street feeling good and smiling at people and being hassled like a piece of meat in return.

_____having your first real human talk with your mother and being told about all her old hopes and lost ambitions, and how you can't fight it, and that's just the way it is: life, sex, men, the works—and loving her and hating her for having been so beaten down.

_____having your first real human talk with your father and being told about all his old hopes and lost ambitions, and how women really have it easier, and "what a man really wants in a woman,"—and loving him and hating him for having been beaten down—and for beating down your mother in turn.

_____brooding about "how far" you should go with the guy you really like. Will he no longer respect you? Will you get— oh God—a "reputation"? Or, if not, are you a square? Being pissed off because you can't just do what you feel like doing.

_____being secretly afraid that you'll lose your virginity to a tampon, but being too ashamed to ask anyone about it.

_____lying awake wondering if a girl really can get pregnant by the sperm swimming through her panties.

_____having a horrible fight with your boyfriend who keeps shouting how he's frustrated by not "doing it"—it never occurring to him that you might be climbing walls, too, which you maybe don't even dare to admit.

_____ finally screwing and your groin and buttocks and thighs ache like hell and you're all wet and maybe bloody and it wasn't like a Hollywood movie at all but jesus at least you're not a virgin anymore, but is this what it's all about? —and meanwhile he's asking "Did you come?"

_____ finding that the career you've chosen exacts more than just study or hard work—an emotional price of being made to feel "less a woman."

_____ finding that almost all jobs open to you pay less for harder work than to men.

_____ being bugged by men in the office who assume that you're a virginal prude if you don't flirt, and that you're an easy mark if you are halfway relaxed and pleasant.

_____ learning to be very tactful if you have men working "under you." More likely, learning to always be working under men.

_____ becoming a woman executive, for God's sake, and then being asked to order the delicatessen food for an office party.

_____ finding out how difficult it is to get hold of "easily accessible" birth-control information.

_____ chasing the slippery diaphragm around the bathroom as if in a game of frisbee the first time you try to insert it yourself, or:

_____ gaining weight, or hemorrhaging, or feeling generally miserable with the Pill, or just freaking out at the scare stories about it, or:

_____ going on a cross-country car trip in a Volkswagen, during which the Loop or the Coil becomes dislodged and begins to tear at your flesh.

THE IDEOLOGY OF SOCIAL PROBLEMS

_____wondering why we can have live color telecasts of the moon's surface, but still no truly simple, humane, safe method of birth control.

_____going the rounds of showers, shopping, money worries, invitation lists, licenses—when all you really wanted to do was live with the guy.

_____quarreling with your fiance over whether "and obey" should be in the marriage ceremony.

_____secretly being bitched because the ceremony says "man and wife"—not "husband and wife" or "man and woman." Resenting having to change your (actually, your father's) name.

_____having been up since 6:00 A.M. on your wedding day seeing family and friends you really don't even like and being exhausted from standing just so and not creasing your gown and from the ceremony and reception and traveling and now being alone with this strange man who wants to "make love" when you don't know that you even like him and even if you did you desperately want to just sleep for fourteen hours, or:

_____not getting married, just living together in "free love," and finding out it's just the same as marriage anyway, and you're the one who pays for the "free."

_____playing the role to the hilt, cooking special dishes, cleaning, etc.—and knowing you'll never make it as _Good Housekeeping's_ "ideal," or:

_____"dropping out" together to a "hip, groovy" commune— and cooking brown rice instead of Betty Crocker.

_____having menstrual cramps each month quite normally, cramps and/or headaches and/or nausea that would put a "normal" man out of commission for two weeks—and going on with your job or chores, etc., so no one will be inconvenienced.

612

_____finding out that you're bored by your husband in bed.

_____faking an orgasm for the first time: disgust, frustration—and relief (because he never even knew the difference).

_____feeling guilty for not having an orgasm: what is wrong with you?

_____finding out that you bore your husband in bed. Getting desperate—where have you failed?

_____wanting desperately to know what special things he wants you to do to him in bed—and being afraid to tell him what you'd want him to do; or telling him hints that he promptly forgets forever after.

_____wanting to be the power behind the throne and finding out either that he's not a great man after all, or that he doesn't need your support.

_____being jealous and hating yourself for showing it.

_____hating certain books that you might have loved—all because he read them first and told you all about them. Feeling robbed. This goes for movies, too.

_____wanting to go back to school, to read, to join something, do something. Why isn't home enough for you? What's wrong with you?

_____coming home from work—and starting in to work: unpack the groceries, fix supper, wash up the dishes, rinse out some laundry, etc., etc.

_____feeling a need to say "thank you" when your guy actually fixes himself a meal now that you're dying with the flu.

_____getting pregnant, hearing all the earth-mother shit from everyone, going around with a fixed smile on your terrified face.

_____having men on the street, in cabs and busses, no longer (at least) regard you as an ogle-object; now they regard you as Carrier Of The Species.

____knowing there must be some deep-down way to enjoy this that maybe women in some "primitive" tribe feel, but being elephantine, achy, nauseated—and kvetched at having to be cheerful.

____wanting your husband with you, or wanting natural childbirth, and either he won't, or the doctor or hospital won't —and you're on your own, or:

____maybe you're lucky and he's not afraid or disgusted and the doctor approves and you go through it together and it's even beautiful—and you hear another woman screaming in solitary labor next door.

____feeling responsible for more lives—your kids, as well as your man's—but never, never your own life.

____learning to hate other women who are: younger, freer, unmarried, without children, in jobs, in school, in careers —whatever. Hating yourself for hating them.

____trying desperately not to repeat the pattern, and catching yourself telling your daughter one day that she "isn't acting like a lady," or warning your son "not to be a sissy."

____knowing that your husband is "playing around" and wanting to care, but not even being able to.

____being widowed, or divorced, and trying to get a "good" job—at your age.

____claiming not to understand the "revolt" of your kids, but understanding it in your gut and not being able to help being bitter because you think it's too late for you.

____still wanting to have sex but feeling faintly ridiculous before your husband, let alone other men.

____being patronized and smirked over by your own children during the agonizing ritual of widowhood dating.

____getting older, getting lonelier, getting ready to die—and knowing it wouldn't have had to be this way, after all.

"Barbarous Rituals" captures the conflict and despair, pathos and tragedy, that together represent the tragicomedy of sex-role socialization. Each of these is a vignette, a small-scale theatrical production that speaks intensely to basic human questions. While not all women see themselves as the central character in these episodes, it is the contention here that the baring of such rituals is a collective experience with which many identify. The mothers and grandmothers of today's university women perhaps feel more uncomfortable than their progeny with such explicit introspection. Such fears have traditionally been unspeakable. However, one consequence of a social movement designed to alter the social standing of an oppressed population is the transformation of private conflict into public debate.

THE PREVAILING IDEOLOGIES

Taken together, the introductory remarks and the rituals described in this chapter's Viewpoint confirm that differing definitions apply to the social standing of women. As we consider the social construction of the problem of sexism, we invite the reader to remember that the only historical constant is change. What may be perceived as blatant discrimination on sexual grounds has been defined at other periods, and indeed for many in this enlightened age, as "reasonable." Unfortunately, what is considered reasonable may be perceived as such only because it complements the status quo.

Aristotle argued that some were born to be masters, others to be slaves. His conception of the natural order of things grew from the observation that there were *in fact* superordinate/subordinate relationships. Such were *obviously necessary* (functional), else why would they exist? The philosophy of Aristotle is quite consistent with the order model of society described in our introductory chapter. When applied to the subjugation of women, Aristotelean order confuses what *is* with what *must be* and mistakes existing order for natural order. Horkheimer identifies the problem well:

> The father thus has a moral claim upon submission to his strength, but not because he proves himself worthy of respect; rather he proves himself worthy by the very fact that he is stronger. . . . The self-control of the individual, the disposition for work and discipline, the ability to hold firmly to certain ideas, consistency in practical life; application of reason, perseverance and pleasure in constructive activity could all be developed, in the circumstances, only under the dictation and guidance of the father whose own education had been won in the school of life. (In Sennett 1977, p. 186.)

615

The argument is that paternal domination as a subset of male domination is altogether proper. After all, it is *he* who is both strong and experienced; it is *he* who has truly lived. What is overlooked by this functionalist interpretation is the possibility that strength, in its important aspects of confidence, self-assuredness, and firmness as well as expanded life experiences is related to an expanded social role, not biological gender. Thus, the social containment of women is taken as evidence of their natural submission and the worldly involvement of men as proof of their natural superiority. If one group is shorn of political power while another monopolizes decision making, it may appear reasonable to argue that such a division of labor is part of the natural order of things. The question remains, however: Whose reason? Whose order?

Sexism Defined　Before continuing, we should pause to consider the meaning of "sexism." At first, the term appears deceptively simple. Patterned after "racism," it seems that sexism means discrimination or prejudice based on an individual's sex. Indeed, to study how and why people treat people differently, or prejudge them on the basis of gender, may represent a beginning point for analysis. However, simple differential treatment is not automatically problematic nor are all sex-related judgments sexist. The difficulty begins when the opportunity to develop our human potential fully is stunted by social obstacles, including those of powerful stereotypes.

Our discussion of "sexism" should not end here, however. In the language of Chapter One, prejudice and discrimination are *reductionist* (that is, low-level) terms when taken in isolation. (See assumption Number Nine of the Order Paradigm). The former suggests an attitude and the latter an act. We believe there is more underpinning sexism than fixed mental pictures and rigid prejudgments. Further, if discrimination is manifested only in individual behavior, then it follows that we can identify the "sexists" among us who are betrayed by *their* language, *their* refusal to hire women, and *their* domination of key political and economic positions. Identified, the offenders can be reeducated, cured, or purged. However, the contention here is that sexism is an ideology, and as such follows the lines of the argument developed in Chapters One and Two. In short, rather than identifying *who* the sexists may be, it is more important to understand that in a society of structured inequality, a number of ideologies including *sexism* will be found that justify, rationalize, and legitimate such social division.

For purposes of definition, sexism here refers to an interdependent system of beliefs structural in origin that rationalize the differences in the psychological, social, political, and economic standing of women and men. As an ideology, sexism asserts the natural superiority of the male in the sphere of power, influence, and work, while locating the role of women in marriage, motherhood, and select maternal and subordinate occupations. As with any ideology, sexism has implications for socialization, self-concept, life chances, and the functioning of social institutions. Also as with any ideology, specific beliefs rest not on logic or evidence but on conviction.

The ideology of sexism is not without its "silver-lining." Reminiscent of the racism that portrays blacks as inherently athletic, masters of music and dance, and content to live carefree lives unbothered by the tedium of political and economic control, is the celebration of the softer side of femininity.

> Feminine virtues are indeed extolled in the most extravagant manner by precisely those who insist that woman cannot, because of her nature, aspire to the status and heights of achievement in politics or intellectual or artistic work attained by a man. The charm of women, their gentleness and their sensitivity to the sufferings of others are invariably held up as qualities special to their sex and moreover as qualities so attractive that they more than make up for women's lesser abilities in other areas" (Amundsen 1977, p. 101).

To continue, we believe that the various phases of the definitional model introduced earlier in Proposition Five (Chapter Two) develop within an ideological context. For example, the perception of sex role as a social problem will be directed by specific ideologies consistent with the general ideology of corporatism. It follows that these ideologies will divert attention from the structural properties of the corporate system. To be specific, certain idea-systems will deny the problem of sexism altogether. Others will glorify the traditional place of women. Still others will constitute a vigorous attack on the liberation of women.

Fascinating Womenhood

In the early 1960s, a self-improvement program directed toward women concerned with recovering or discovering marital bliss began in California. Directed mainly toward middle-income career housewives, *Fascinating Womanhood* is a course founded without apology on the premise that the husband is lord and master. Women are given responsibility for the preservation of marriage and home through self-denial. The course teaches that domesticity is bliss, that manipulation through "feminine" wiles (a toss of the head, a stamp of the foot) is preferable to challenging male superiority, and that what might be termed "macho" is not to be contained but cultivated. By the mid-1970s some half a million women had paid a fee to take the course.

The originator of *Fascinating Womanhood* was Helen B. Andelin, mother of eight, who wrote a "textbook" to enable others to teach the principles of how to behave like Scarlett O'Hara. When Andelin and her husband could not interest a publishing house in the book, they published it on their own. By the middle of the Seventies, more than a million copies of *Fascinating Womanhood* had been sold, evenly divided between the hardcover edition brought out by the Andelins and a Bantam paperbook.

Another "save your marriage" course for women was developed by Marabel Morgan in Florida in 1971. *Total Woman* is different from *Fascinating Womanhood* in name only. The ideological content is virtually identical. Women are taught to follow the four As in the daily struggle to improve the marital relationship. In short, the husband is to be accepted, admired, adapted to, and appreciated. Unlike Helen Andelin's experience, a religious publishing house convinced Marabel Morgan to reduce the principles of her course to writing. *Total Woman* quickly climbed to the top of the 1974 nonfiction best-seller list, selling some 575,000 copies.

As both book and course, *Total Woman* (1973) and its 1976 sequel, *Total Joy*, make incessant reference to biblical precepts to support the ideology of female submissiveness. In this respect, both *Fascinating Womanhood* and *Total Woman* are identical. United by a heavenly connection, two enterprising women have followed the lead of countless men in enshrining God as the author of masculine dominance. Neither, we suppose, would be amused by the question: Suppose God is a woman?

Total Joy is chosen here for analysis as a more recent example of unabashed sexism. In so doing, we do not hold that his book is more important than many others that extol the virtues of male leadership. Indeed, the King James Version of the Bible might successfully contend for preeminence as the all-time historical best-seller and leading purveyor of the natural subordination of women. However, Morgan's work is representative of a strong if changing current in North American social life.

In *Total Joy* she argues that too many wives expect their husbands to reform.

> Seven years ago, Charlie and I weren't romantic, or polite, or hardly even talking to each other. My quest for marriage survival began in earnest—my project: change Marabel (Morgan 1976, p. 16).

The road to change is not without signposts. Morgan blends Protestant Christianity and Existentialism with their telling emphasis on the mastery of individual will (see Chapters One and Two). The author clearly embraces the existentialist principle of the acceptance of responsibility for one's own being. The advice is simple: "Bloom where you're planted." The book concludes with twenty-nine biblical references. Thus, armed with the self-determination to execute God's master plan of male dominance, the wife is supposedly ready to experience an ever emerging "totality."

Morgan argues that the total woman is the *real* woman, the *authentic* female who understands that there is no escape from biological pre-destination. One critic of sexism defines the "anatomy is destiny" stereotype as follows:

> The mere facts that she bears children and has menstrual periods make her the prey to hormonal influences that shape her temperament and abilities in certain distinct ways. Woman is supposed to be more emotional than man, less able to apply logic to problems and situations, more conforming, and less aggressive, but also more devious and superior, naturally, in possession of that mysterious "feminine" quality, intuition (Amundsen 1977, p. 100).

It is perhaps obvious that the *total* woman is complete only when defined in relationship to a man. Otherwise, she is doomed to live a fragmented and despairing life, desperately envying the complete wife and mother, and perhaps in bitterness joining some organization of feminists in order to deny her loneliness. Critics would argue, however, that totality really means that women must be plugged into another's source of strength and energy or else be denied existence. Totality for Morgan's critics is redefined as alienation (see Chapter Four), and the place of the fascinating woman is nothing more than prone in the home.

Fascination is Economic   The popularity of "traditional" sex role ideology cannot be simply dismissed as opportunistic or wrong thinking. Nor does this sexist thought spring from the Andelins or Morgans or even the Bible. What should be considered is the possibility that the concerns women hold about home and marriage reflect some very real fears born of sex-based inequality in North American societies. For many women, the marriage state remains an economic estate. Given a structure of limited opportunity, a marriage failure may be seen for many women as tantamount to a financial death sentence.

The following table presents the marital status of adult men and women in the United States.

TABLE 11-1
Marital Status of the Population: 1977
(Thousands)

Sex	Number Total	Single	Married	Widowed	Divorced	Total	Percent Distribution Single	Married	Widowed	Divorced
Male	70,328	15,380	49,889	1,887	3,172	100.0%	21.9%	70.9%	2.7%	4.5%
Female	77,947	12,151	50,912	10,028	4,859	100.0	15.6	65.3	12.9	6.2

Source: *Statistical Abstract of the United States* 1978, p. 41.

A careful perusal of the statistics indicates that in 1977 almost 15 million American women were in the widowed or divorced category. Collectively, they are known as "displaced homemakers." Many of these, especially those who are widowed or divorced at middle age, are without work experience and skills.

When women find themselves as the female head of a family unit, or living alone without familial status, poverty is frequently their companion.

It is important to note that in the United States in March 1978 there were some 57.2 million family units. Only 8.2 million (some 14.3 percent) were headed by women. Yet families headed by women accounted for 9.2 million of the nation's 19.5 million persons in family units living below the poverty line. Unrelated women accounted for another 3.4 million of the nation's poor. Thus, 51 percent of those below the poverty standard in the United States lived in homes without a man (*Statistical Abstract of the United States* 1978, p. 459). In Canada, nearly half of the female-headed households are in poverty compared with 15 percent of the male-headed households (Manzer 1975).

Women's place is therefore not merely one of a fanciful "natural subordination." Rather, it is one of extreme economic disadvantage outside the marriage state. The virtually insatiable market for courses, books, and magazine articles on "how to save your marriage while losing yourself" must be understood within the broader context of economic dependency.

Fear of Estrangement   Certainly there is more to the fear of marital disintegration than its financial consequences. The primary form of family life in North American society is frequently described as nuclear. This family structure consists of one or two generations. It is geographically mobile and somewhat geared to the socialization of children, due to the transference of other social functions (work, education, perhaps religion) outside the home. The nuclear family is a privatized unit, cut

**TABLE 11–2
Persons Below Poverty Level, By Family Status
and Sex of Head: 1977**

	Number (millions)	Percentage
Male Head	10.3	6.2%
Female Head	9.2	36.2
Unrelated Male	1.8	18.0
Unrelated Female	3.4	26.1

Source: *Statistical Abstract of the United States* 1978, p. 466.

apart from collective and community support. Accordingly, the fear of marital disintegration is the fear of social and psychological estrangement.

> As countless books and articles on the problems of divorcees reveal, very seldom is there a retinue of friends standing by, only rarely does a newly single woman get invitations to social gatherings, and hardly ever are there other acceptable and socially promising organizations for her to join. A woman on the loose in her mature years is a social handicap, a potential threat, and a dreaded embarrassment to the couples she used to see socially with her former mate (Amundsen 1977, p. 25).

In privatized society, the alternative to family life is to be alone among strangers.

Motherhood and Apple Pie

Certainly one of the more powerful specific ideologies shaping the perception of woman's place is motherhood. Superseded by no other standing (though gracefully exchanged for grandmotherhood), a boon to Gerber, Hallmark, and your FTD florist, the bearer of the species inspires hymns, prose, and tears. Today the accelerating forces of inflation, unemployment, and institutionalized thirst for profit suggest perhaps a crack in the corporate economy. Such pressures, moving in coincidental fashion with a rising divorce rate (one marriage in every three) and the insistence among some for a measure of self-actualization and independence, have driven large numbers of women into the work force. However, motherhood as a prime ideological symbol has not surrendered its dominant position. It is a part of the traditional culture surrounding woman's place. Accordingly, women who work frequently contend with a burden of guilt perhaps best described as the "neglect syndrome."[1]

The origins of the ideology of woman's place can best be examined later when we pose the question of maintenance or "who benefits?" At this point, it is enough to recognize that women are expected to marry, and married women to care for their husbands, have children and care for them.

Given this prime ideological directive, those who enter the work force can expect to have to cope with a degree of moral anxiety. Often a woman must combine the traditional role of wife and mother with that of the worker. In so doing, she escapes to some extent the accusations of significant "others" (or perhaps "mothers") and the pangs of conscience that accompany "neglect" of her family.

[1] Supposedly, working mothers generally neglect children, home, spouse (while working men generally do not).

Inside the household, husbands are given special treatment. It is clearly understand that even though both are wage earners, at home Mom is still Mom and Pop is still Pop. The care and feeding of the children is Mom's job and so is the care and feeding of Pop. Thus, Super Mom hurries home from work to bathe the children, feed them, read to them, help them with their homework, and put them to bed. This is the children's hour and it is so sacred. If Mom fails to observe it, or lets Pop take over, the children will be traumatized for life, or at the very least, Mom will feel that she failed as a "real woman, fulfilling her natural role" (Bedell 1977, p. 242).

A woman achieves this superhuman status at significant personal costs. However, our purpose is to show not simply the social psychological consequences of the motherhood ideology, but to understand its broader implications. In the first place, this symbol and others that confirm the traditional place of women serve to define woman's work outside the home as secondary. Accordingly, woman's work is seen as less important, and consequently worth less in the labor marketplace. Furthermore, the distinctive importance of this symbol is revealed in that it captures a state of alienation. As with the "fascinating woman," the supermother is without personal identity. In the language of Simone de Beauvoir, she is "the other."

> The category of the other is as primordial as consciousness itself. In the most primitive societies, in the most ancient mythologies, one finds the expression of a duality—that of the Self and the Other. This duality was not originally attached to the division of the sexes; it was not dependent upon any empirical facts. It is revealed in such works as that of Granet on Chinese thought and those of Dumezil on the East Indies and Rome. . . . Otherness is a fundamental category of human thought (1977, p. 73).

Frequently those who hold that motherhood is the most demanding, important, and fulfilling of roles simultaneously argue that women are by their nature dependent on the strength and reason of a man. There appears to be a basic contradiction in this argument. If motherhood is a challenging and difficult role, then it is not ably executed by inferiors. If it is not a life-consuming career, then women should be able to do other things as well. It should be remembered that the modal number of children per family in North American society is two. Given the early entry of children into the public school system, motherhood as a full-time career comes to a close before many mothers reach thirty.

There are often unanticipated or unrecognized consequences that follow logically the symbols of legitimation identifying the traditional place of women. To be explicit, when motherhood is extolled it may well be that the role of the father is shortchanged in the process. While women demonstrate femininity through the tasks of reproduction and the caring for children, men supposedly confirm their manhood through work.

SEX AND
SEXISM

> We have defined this role almost exclusively as that of provider, and nearly everything else about him as a human being depends on how well he performs that one function. If he does well in that role he can get away with almost anything else in the bosom of his family. . . . But let him cease to be a good provider and no other virtue will compensate for his failure. Everything else collapses, including his manhood (Bernard 1975, p. 220).

Bernard goes on to question the role of specialization described above. Citing the work of the anthropologist Malinowski, she notes that in preindustrial society women contributed substantially as providers. Fishing, gathering, the domestication of animals, and gardening were functions carried out by early women. "Only since provisions have had to be purchased with cash in a market have men become so exclusively specialized in the provider role; they were the members of the family who had the money with which to purchase provisions" (1975, p. 224). We need not journey into the past to find evidence of women as providers. Women today constitute over 40 percent of the labor force in the United States and Canada. As Table 11–3 shows, married women have greatly increased their participation in the labor force in Canada. Further, the proportion of women (married and unmarried) in the Canadian work force rose from 36.5 percent in 1969 to 45 percent in 1976 (*Canada Year*

TABLE 11–3
Female Labor Force Participation: Census Years 1931–1971[a]
(Percent)

| Year | Participation Rate | | | | Married women as a percentage[b] of total women in labor force |
	Married	Single	Other	Total	
1931	3.5%	43.8%	21.3%	19.3%	10.0%
1941	4.5	47.2	17.3	20.3	12.7
1951	11.2	58.3	19.3	24.1	30.0
1961	22.0	54.1	22.9	29.5	49.8
1971	37.0	53.5	26.5	39.9	59.1

[a]Statistics from the 1931 Census are for the age group 10 and over. Statistics from the 1931–1951 Census are for the age group 15 and over. Statistics from the 1961 and 1971 Census are for the age group 15 and over. Figures exclude those on active military service; Newfoundland is included from 1951 on; the Yukon and Northwest Territories are not included.

[b]Including those permanently separated.

Sources: DBS, 1961 Census, Advance Report N. AL-1. Table from Spencer & Featherstone 1970, p. 12, and *Statistics Canada,* 1971 Census, Vol. 3.

Book 1978–1979). In the United States it is predicted that two of every three mothers will hold jobs by 1990. Already in 1980, fewer than one third of American mothers were full-time homemakers raising children (Smith 1980).

Malinowski's work, in concert with that of other anthropologists, also establishes that men can play central child-rearing roles. Again, it is not necessary to rely on tribal examples. Today, men are invading the traditional bastion of motherhood with increasing success. More and more fathers are being awarded custody of minor children. Though accurate national statistics are lacking on paternal custody, attorneys are no longer automatically content to advise the father seeking divorce simply to accept the visitor's role and start over (Levine 1976, p. 47).

In another indication of role revision, the former Prime Minister of Sweden, Olaf Palme, described the problem of sex-role socialization as a problem in human liberation, not simply an affair pertaining to women. Citing the "risks to boys of growing up in the traditional female world," Palme argues:

> There is a risk that the boys, by means of T.V., comic strips, and other mass media, create a false and exaggerated picture of what it means to be a man. The men are tough and hard-boiled Wild West heroes, agents, supermen, soldiers. The boys compensate their lack of contact with kind and everyday men by looking upon media men as their ideal. (In Levine 1976, p. 158.)

Accordingly, Sweden has adopted a program of reeducation designed to eliminate sex-role stereotypes. The government also sponsors a program of parental leave that allows *either* mother or father to remain at home for the first seven months of a newborn's life, or to divide the time between them, at 90 percent of salary.

Sexism in Science

The perception of sexism as a social problem is not molded exclusively in the realm of popular culture. To the contrary, academic argument and theory are replete with examples that confirm the traditional ideology of woman's place. Sociologists have long been aware that there is no necessary division between the major values of a society and what is presented as knowledge by scientists who inquire into the human condition. Knowledge is a social product. It is intricately bound up in a distinct historical context. If women occupy a subordinate political and economic place, it follows that experts on social and personal life will find it difficult to construct a knowledge challenging that subordination.

Over the past decade, explanations that emphasize the biological divisions of the sexes have been subjected to critical inquiry. Such skepticism must be accounted for, at least in part, by the ascendancy of the women's movement. For example, Freud argued in the *Psychology of Women* that the penis was the origin of conflict for both sexes. One was anxious of what he might lose (castration anxiety), the other forever compensating through feminine vanity for what she could not have (penis envy). These and other aspects of "the anatomy is destiny" argument indicate that what may appear "obvious" to some (especially those trained in traditional Freudian psychoanalytic theory) will not survive the scrutiny of science.

> Consider Freud. What he thought constituted evidence violated the most minimal conditions of scientific rigor. In *The Sexual Enlightenment of Children*, the classic document which is supposed to demonstrate empirically the existence of a castration complex and its connection to a phobia, Freud based his analysis on the reports of the father of the little boy, himself in therapy, and a devotee of Freudian theory. . . . It is remarkable that only recently has Freud's classic theory on the sexuality of women—the notion of the double orgasm—been tested physiologically and found just plain wrong (Weisstein in Morgan, 1970, pp. 209–10).

What is termed "double orgasm" might best be called shifting orgasm. In *Three Essays on the Theory of Sexuality*, Freud held that for young girls the clitoris was the dominant erogenous zone. The successful movement into mature womanhood supposedly brought the shifting of the dominant erogenous zone from the clitoris to the vagina. Thus, the notion of the shifting orgasm must be viewed in part as ideology. If correct, the vaginal orgasm portends that women will be sexually gratified by the same sexual behavior that commonly produces the male orgasm. In 1966, Wiliam H. Masters and Virginia E. Johnson in a landmark study reported that all female orgasms are centered in the clitoris.

Despite the shallow nature of the Freudian position and the destruction by Masters and Johnson in *Human Sexual Response* of the myth of the vaginal orgasm, traditional psychoanalysts tend to describe career women as masculine, castrating, and neurotic (Whitehurst 1977, pp. 68–69).

Others in the social sciences have argued that if the career women is disturbingly aggressive, it is because the well-integrated female identity awaits the coming of Mr. "Right" who, along with his offspring, will become the focus of her being. According to psychologist Erik Erikson, a woman's identity should shift from that of "other" in the father's family to that of "other" for her chosen. For Erikson, the cornerstone of feminine being is the womb (Erikson 1968).

Sociologists have also contributed strongly to the enshrinement of "otherness" as the primary status for women. Whitehurst (1977) argues correctly that family theory through much of the 1960s was influenced by the functionalist view presented earlier. For Talcott Parsons, an important systems (functionalist) theorist writing in 1955, men were to execute the "task" role while women were masters of the "expressive" role. Men were thus vested with the responsibility of the "provider" and authority. Wives on the other hand furnished emotional support and care for children. This division of labor was to prevent the competition for status that might occur if women left their "place." Thus, the marriage would survive in a state of order.

> Parsons admitted this division of functions also could be a source of strain for women, who were not allowed to compete on an equal basis with men. He felt that many women succumbed to their conflicts through neurotic illness or compulsive domesticity. To Parsons, however, it was functional for society to define half the population as the homemakers and childrearers, and the other half as the breadwinners, achievers, policymakers, and leaders, despite individual strains. Marital roles were therefore complementary, or "separate but equal" (Whitehurst 1977, pp. 15–16).

In the language of the Vietnam War, it became necessary to destroy the country in order to save it. In the language of sexism, it is necessary to sacrifice women in order to save womanhood.

Male Chauvinism and Social Inequality

Nicolas Chauvin was a legendary French soldier, famous for his devotion to his emperor, Napoleon Bonaparte, and his homeland. Though the term chauvinism applied originally to an exaggerated nationalism or a blind form of patriotism, it has been generalized over the years to refer to any extreme devotion or partiality to a group or place to which one belongs. Chauvin's views on women are not known to the authors. However, those of his emperor are a matter of record.

> Nature intended women to be our slaves . . . they are our property; we are not theirs. They belong to us, just as a tree that bears fruit belongs to a gardener. What a mad idea to demand equality for women! . . . Women are nothing but machines for producing children (Napoleon Bonaparte, quoted in Morgan 1970, p. 34).

The blatant notion of the natural superiority of the male is perhaps representative of what today is termed *male chauvinism*. This particular term has come to represent an assortment of beliefs and/or practices sometimes flagrant, more often subtle. It would represent an enormous task to begin to list the components. Perhaps at base, however, we would find some version of the Orthodox Jewish prayer: "I thank thee, O Lord, that thou hast not created me a woman."

Earlier, we identified the ideology of sexism. On the surface, much of what was discussed as sex-based differences in important talents might be simply referred to as male chauvinism. However, this term is somewhat deficient as a guide to social analysis. The reasons for this are clear, if interrelated.

1. First of all, the term suggests an exaggerated sense of masculinity. The chauvinist is the "macho man," captured by his own magnified vision of virility and strength. The "macho" prototype, while offensive to those concerned with human liberation, is often a convenient fiction that allows people to individualize the problem of sexism.

2. *Male* chauvinism implicitly argues that the oppression of women is fundamentally a problem of male psychology. Accordingly, if we change the personality of male offenders, we eliminate the problem.

3. Finally, and most important, the popular use of the term suggests that women are controlled as property by men; hence men must hold ownership and power. While it appears logical to argue that there is no slave without a master, the particular social properties that confer mastery are sometimes incorrectly defined. To be clear, Napoleon's statement of the functions of women could have almost as easily been said about his soldiers, even the loyal Chauvin! It follows that both sexes may be victimized, not by male attitudes of dominance or female attitudes of subservience, but by a system of inequality. By its nature, such a social order sorts people into boxes, giving rise to ideologies that rationalize such boundaries as "natural."

Men: The Other Victims of Sexism If the portrait of a woman chained to housework, marriage, childbearing, and underpaid work outside the home is grim, so too is the picture of the provider male bound to the assembly line or trying to get a nose ahead in the rat race. If the fear of assertiveness, a crisis of confidence, and the expectations of emotional expressiveness are burdens for women, so too for men are the wearisome demands to be strong, the imperative to be right, and the distance from the feelings for self and others. Male chauvinism falsely defines men as "devils." Our point is that men too are victimized by sexism. The nature of the trap is different and in some ways not as vicious. Men do have wider occupational representation, more pay, more privilege. But most are definitely not free.

> In return for all this stress and effort, the male prototype tends to expect rewards that, in the main, fail to materialize. First, he finds that his work, which he has been taught should constitute the alter

ego of self, is by and large meaningless. In Richard Yates' *Revolutionary Road*, the antihero Frank defines his condition as "one of hundreds of tiny pink men in white shirts, forever shifting papers and frowning into telephones." This is what work is for millions of men in America today. Clearly a life spent in such a paltry activity, if it has at the same time been identified as the core of vital sex performance, is bound to lead to a sadly diminished sense of masculinity. As C. Wright Mills has written, "a bureaucracy is no testing field for heroes" (Reeves 1971, p. 26).

Perhaps it is time to consider the nature of the inferno, rather than simply debating which level we are on.

As a final illustration, let the reader consider this riddle. An important executive for a large corporation is working with a secretary on the job late at night. After the task is done the man, who is notorious for his sexual aggressiveness, considers an advance, quickly becomes fearful, and leaves. Why? The logical answer, that the man is the secretary, reveals more than the answer to a riddle. It also reveals more than our inability to think of women as executives or, on a variation of the theme above, of a woman as sexual initiator. Rather, this answer suggests that some of the ordinary circumstances confronted by women are matters of *power relationship, not gender.*

The solution to the broader dilemma implied by our riddle is not, as some argue, simply more women executives. Until structural change is realized, we may well applaud the advance of women within the existing order. However, the conclusion that more women should find room at the top still seeks an answer in gender. Only in this case, more women become the leaders of more men. To the contrary, perhaps the ultimate problem is a social structure that consists of top and bottom. The sexual composition of top and bottom notwithstanding, as long as one class dominates and controls the conditions of life for the other, liberation is denied.

Despite the above limitations, psychological variations of male chauvinism are commonplace. Frequently, when behavioral scholars unmask the pompous supermale, they reveal the ever present inferiority complex.

> In my clinical practice, I noticed that insecure men, unachievers, men who are pushed around on their jobs, men who felt they were not respected by their colleagues and associates, have been prone to discriminate against women. It seems this was the only area where they could show their nonexistent power. . . . In practically all cases of men who beat their wives or daughters . . . the men were cowards who would never stand up to other men (Wolman, in Denmark 1974, p. 49).

Tempting as it may be to brand Mr. Macho as suffering from feelings of inadequacy and venting his frustrations on scapegoats, this sort of explanation is subject to the first two arguments developed earlier in this section. Thus, we have weak individual males to blame. Further, when the question of who discriminates against women is answered empirically, the answer appears to cover broad ground indeed. One study (Goldberg, in Denmark 1974) concluded that sexist attitudes and behavior are pervasive to the point that a particular personality type that is prejudiced against women is impossible to find.

> If we are right, then, in our suggestion that sexism approaches being a culturally fixed and almost universal attitude, then it would seem that final explanations of the phenomenon are not profitably to be looked for at the level of individual psychology. Indeed, neither explanation nor solution is likely located there, though the price of sexism is paid for person by person (1974, p. 64).

If the reference to "culturally fixed and almost universal attitude" were changed to "prevailing ideology," Goldberg's conclusion would be strongly consistent with the thrust of this chapter. The term "attitude" is best reserved for the "level of individual psychology."

Sexist Socialization

Another form of ideology related to the interpretation of sexism centers around the socialization argument. At first glance, the contention that we are what we are taught to be is both compelling and simple. As the twig is bent, so grows the tree. Likewise, if our children are exposed to ideas and role models that present and reinforce a sex-based division of labor, then they shall teach them to their children and on *ad infinitum*.

A concern with sexist socialization has encouraged studies of the advice given by influentials in the care and rearing of children. Though he has demonstrated a changing and, we believe, more accurate world view in later life, the advice of the noted pediatrician Benjamin Spock affected strongly the rearing of post-World War II babies in the United States and Canada.[2] In *Decent and Indecent*, Dr. Spock wrote that sex imposes innate temperamental differences:

> Very few girls right from birth seem to have as much striving and restlessness as the average boy. Even at one year of age I think

[2] Dr. Spock dedicated *Decent and Indecent* written at the zenith of the Vietnam War and the Civil Rights Movement "to the young people, black and white, who are being clubbed, jailed, and even killed for showing us the way to justice." We believe that justice commands the recognition that the specific ideology of innate sex-related temperament legitimates the subordination of women in class society. Such is not to deny anatomical and physiological differences. However, we do mean to deny the exaggeration of their importance.

boys have a greater interest in mechanical objects that can be investigated and manipulated. Girls as toddlers are more compliant than boys; they can be toilet trained more easily. More girls get high grades in school and college, because they are inclined to accept the instructor's word as long as it is reasonable. . . . Women on the average are more ready to make the multiple adjustments of marriage. . . . Women are usually more patient in working at unexciting repetitive tasks. . . . Women on the average have more passivity in the inborn core of their personality. . . . Boys and men have potentially much more aggressiveness, though this can be thoroughly controlled and curbed by upbringing. Even at two or three years they sense the general spirit of pistol play, long before they have any knowledge of death or ballistics (Spock 1970, pp. 45–46).

When such views are coupled with his advice to new mothers to put that role above all others, it is not difficult to see why Dr. Spock came under fire from feminists in the Sixties and Seventies.

As the chief transmission agents of the norms of a society and as primary role models, mothers and fathers, together with the family as a social unit, have come under examination. Whitehurst (1977) notes that sex-related differences in the behavior exhibited toward children are so ingrained in our society that many parents are not fully conscious of their actions. In the choice of color for clothing and nursery, selection of toys, roughhousing with boys and caressing of girls a sex-based socialization is implemented. In addition to the obvious differences centering around who does the housework, who brings home the bacon (or the larger share of it), who has major responsibility for the children, other learning experiences are singled out. Little girls, within the learning laboratory of the home, acquire the "social expectations" that

. . . specify that a female should marry a male who is taller, stronger, older, better educated, wealthier, more sexually experienced, and potentially successful. This arrangement compounds maleness with other variables which define dominance and increases the probability that the male should be considered the superior of the two (Mintz 1974, p. 20).

Beyond experts and parents, the media have been identified as important makers of image and stereotype. In her paper submitted to the Joint Economic Committee, Congress of the United States, Gaye Tuchman (1977) pointed out that an incessant barrage of messages confines and distorts woman's place in society. To illustrate, a quantitative content analysis of television fare reveals that women are typically cast as family oriented or as objects of romance or sex. Furthermore, programming in which violence is common systematically sends the following messages:

1. Single women work; married women do not.

2. Single working women are more likely to encounter evil because they are not protected by a man.

3. Single working women are more likely to do evil and so depart from stereotypes of soft, appealing femininity.

4. By implication, TV content recommends that a woman should both marry and stay out of the labor force in order to retain her femininity (Tuchman 1977, p. 254).

The view of woman's place as in the home is disseminated by public television as well.

Predictably, positions of control in the media are "manned." To be specific, the American Society of Newspaper Editors as of the spring of 1977 had 803 members. Only 22, or 3 percent were women. At the same time, among newspapers with a daily circulation of 40,000 and above, only 30 women were in policy-making positions compared with 1,128 men. In 1976, the Producers Guild had 590 members, 20 of whom were women, and the Directors Guild had 4,500 members, 288 of them women. In like fashion, men dominate the upper echelons of commercial and public television and radio stations. In sum, the media reflect in microcosm the realities of the broader society. However, the phrase "it's a man's world" should be rewritten. The world *of the elite* is predominantly male.

Much of human learning is in symbols, symbols that are infinitely rich because of language. The importance of language in socialization has prompted increasing inquiry into "linguistic sexism." By now most are familiar with the studious attempts to avoid using the masculine as a generic term. Students of symbolic socialization remind us that the controversy is not one of "mere words."

> Legal, political and religious language: the words, names, labels, phrases, definitions we use when we talk and write to and about each other influence how we see ourselves and how others perceive us. If the words of the law say that the woman has lesser rights than the man, then our attitude and behavior towards women will be different from that towards men. If the words of our religion place women in a status inferior to men, our beliefs and behavior towards the female will be different from those towards the male (Bosmajian 1977, p. 77).

Thus the traditional terms for the salutation of women (Mrs., Miss) are political in that they define a woman by her relationship to a man. The use of the term "Miss" for the unmarried woman connotes incompleteness. She is not yet actualized. Centuries ago "Miss" was short for mistress and commonly referred to a prostitute or "kept" woman. Either way, the title is a form of stigma, an often daily reminder of the *ultimate* destiny of the true woman.

Socialization creates a pattern of expectations. Though there is more to growth and survival than the simple establishment of goals, the limitations of objectives lessens the prospect of failure. It was the French sociologist Emile Durkheim (1951) who argued in 1897 that the norms of a society serve to limit our expectations. When these standards begin to break down (anomic), people expect too much. Consequently, they are doomed to disappointment and, most importantly, turn on the institutions of society or on themselves. Consequently, when the female sex is taught to aspire only to certain occupations, or not to expect to achieve as much as males academically Durkheim's call to conserve the existing order is being obeyed. Further, as Rosen and Aneshensel (1978) have shown, adolescent expectations are shaped more by the parent of the same sex. Thus, until mothers alter their expectations, it is more difficult for their daughters to redefine their own place.

Understanding the somewhat revolutionary potential of "great expectations" is the beginning of our brief critique of the socialization form of evaluation. The problem is that sensitivity, even oversensitivity, to the discriminatory nature of sex-based socialization, is not an end in itself. Sociology is about the formulation of logical connections between the immediate social-psychological world and the broader structural network of social institutions. We cannot be content to note the differences in what is taught. It is imperative that we search out the origin of those differences. Socialization research frequently does not go far enough, as the section on "Maintenance" will later show.

A Piece of the Action

The quest for interpretation, the development of judgments concerning sexism, often touch lightly on the topic of social institutions. In short, critics of tradition point with disapproval to the denial to women of a piece of the action. In so doing, they assign to women "minority" status. In sociology, the term *minority* has little to do with numbers.

The applicability of the minority construct to the problem of sexism was well developed in a landmark article by Helen Hacker (1951). The concerns of minority standing are: the barring of full participation or disenfranchisements; the restriction of opportunities; and the nonrecognition of individual merit. Accordingly, studies evolving from this starting point will seek to demonstrate the denial of mainstream status for women.

Frequently, "piece of the action" research concerns a specific manifestation of sexual discrimination in an institutional context. For example, Joan Abramson's work on the *Invisible Woman* (1975) is a study of discrimination in the academic profession. She notes that women professors are more frequently found in small colleges than large universities, that they are in the lower ranks, and are frequently underpaid relative to their male colleagues. However, most work in this tradition focuses on the position of women in the broader economy and politics.

In 1977 in the United States, 40.5 percent of those employed were women. They accounted for 42.6 percent of the "professional, technical and kindred" workers. However, a deeper look reveals that women are concentrated occupationally in this and other categories in jobs carrying the "maternal mystique." By maternal mystique we mean the particular qualities of nurturance and stroking traditional ideology attributes to women. The argument is straightforward. When women leave the home to enter the job market, they are channeled into occupations that represent a simple extension of the skills of wife, homemaker, and mother.

Women's Jobs   As evidence of this, in 1977 women constituted 96.7 percent of the 1.06 million *registered nurses* in the United States and 70.9 percent of the K–12 *schoolteachers*. The care of children, a component of the maternal mystique, is clearly revealed in a breakdown of the teaching profession. Women comprised 98.7 percent of the prekindergarten and kindergarten teachers, 84.2 percent of the elementary teachers, 51.2 percent of the secondary teachers, and 31.7 percent of the college and university faculties. As the development of intellectual mastery supplants nurturance, men replace women in the teaching profession. Such a reality cannot be lost on those who spend an enormous share of their childhood and adolescence in the classroom.

Continuing with the statistical record for 1977, of the managers and administrators (nonfarm), 22.3 percent were women. Within this occupational category, 58.0 percent of all *office managers* were women, bearing central responsibility for the supervision of primarily female clerks and secretaries. This was the single managerial category in which women represented a majority. Women also comprised 43.3 percent of the sales-workers, but again within this broader occupational category they accounted for 70.4 percent of the retail sales clerks.

Further, women represented 78.9 percent of the *clerical* and kindred workers, but only 5 percent of the craftworkers. However, within this latter category, 39.6 percent of *bakers* were women. Among operatives, women comprised 98.3 percent of the nonfactory *dressmakers and seamstresses* and 95.2 percent of the *sewers and stitchers* in the garment industry. Although they constituted 29.4 percent of farm laborers and supervisors, women make up 67.8 percent of those farm laborers who are *unpaid family workers*.

When we look at service occupations, we note that women represented 58.3 percent of service workers. Within this category, they constitute 95.2 percent of the *child care workers* (except private household) and 90.4 percent of the *waiters*. (Note: The United States Bureau of Labor Statistics still terms those who serve food "waiters," even though over 90 percent are "waitresses.") Finally, women represented 97.0 percent of *private household workers* (providing child care or working as a maid or servant).

Playing the sexist numbers game in a slightly different way, if a woman is a professional by occupation she is most apt to be a teacher of children at the elementary level or below or a nurse. If she is a manager, she is most apt to manage an office. If she is in sales, the probability is greatest that she is a retail clerk. If she is a clerical worker, the most likely option is that of secretary (99.1 percent of the 3.42 million secretaries in 1977 were women).

Continuing, if a woman is a craftworker the most frequent occupation is that of baker, if an operative she is sewing and stitching, if in transport she drives a bus (42.2 percent of the total). Women are also preeminent in serving tables, caring for other people's children, and taking care of other people's houses (*Statistical Abstract of the United States* 1978, pp. 419–21). It appears that even outside the home women continue to wear the scarlet letter *M* (for maternal).

Womanpower   Minority status evaluations frequently attempt an analysis of the political institution. The ultimate political question has to do with the distribution of power. Though often mystified by politics in the abstract, people begin to address the question of power when they ask: "Who decides?" When women are conceptualized as a political minority, a number of topics may be raised.

> When a particular group (such as women or minorities) lacks representation in legislative bodies, it may be assumed that that group cannot speak for itself and that its interests are not being made known. Such groups traditionally have lacked their own power base, being obliged to rely on the good graces of those who are in power (Whitehurst 1977, p. 77).

One should keep in mind the nature of the pluralist ideology that is the basis for the "minority group" form of explanation. As always, pluralist ideology embraces the master institutions of society. According to this view, the problem for minorities, in this instance women, is that they have not been brought on board to share in the benefits enjoyed by the majority. Accordingly, the redress of oppression will be cast in terms of voting, gaining public office, and seeking legislative reform.

As a statistical majority, women should be a political force to be reckoned with. Indeed, they constitute a definite majority of registered voters and tend to vote about as frequently as men. In 1976, of the male voting-age population 67.1 percent were registered to vote, and 59.6 percent reported they did vote. For women, the comparable figures were 66.4 percent and 58.8 percent, respectively. This translates into a 45.6 million to 41.1 million advantage for women (*Statistical Abstract of the United States* 1978, pp. 520, 521).

Recent data continue to confirm Whitehurst's argument (1977) that women do not use the vote to elect women. For the Ninety-Fifth Congress in 1978, only 18 of 417 representatives (4.3 percent) and 1 of the 100 senators (1 percent) were women. (*Statistical Abstract of the United States* 1978, pp. 516–17). As of early 1981, there were no elected women governors in office.[3]

The vote, as we shall soon see, galvanized the suffragettes, and has historically been the cornerstone of pluralist ideology. Women are the only minority in American history who could control the ballot box. Yet they remain disenfranchised. This contradiction represents the severest test of pluralist ideology, not merely for women but for all minority groups who have seen the vote as their key to political power.

A final concern of those who evaluate women as a political minority is seeking justice through the law. The "emergence" element of our model will show that historically the women's movement has had legalistic reason for being. Minority groups in general have traditionally looked to the majesty of the law to strike down discrimination. For those conceptualizing women as a minority group, political power is to be found in civil rights legislation, the redefinition of women's legal status (as an independent party), and recently the Equal Rights Amendment of the United States. Indeed, the movement developed in the context of a faith in equal justice under the law, the impartiality of the State, and the democratic vision of the sharing of power. It should be obvious that "piece of the action" ideology leads to some important findings. Inquiry into "institutionalized sexism" reveals similarities to "institutionalized racism." In other words, in a predictable, systematic, and enduring fashion, the major institutions (economic, political, and educational) of North American society have promoted and sustained a subordinate place for women. However, in sociology it is necessary to go beyond the obvious, to think beyond the limitations of the existing order.

To be direct, those who opt for the "piece of the action" position assume that the "action" (in other words, system) is legitimate; that promises are not false; that there should be room at the top, or at least away from the bottom, for more women. With the latter sentiment, we heartily agree. However, in the long view there are other important questions. Perhaps going first-class is small consolation if the ship is sinking. What if the mainstream turns out to be a whirlpool, incessantly dragging most of the majority down? And what if the "majority" that presidents, prime ministers, and countless others assure us hold power, turns out to be a tiny political and economic elite? True, Hitler's Gestapo was not an equal opportunity employer. Women certainly did not constitute 50 percent of its membership. But perhaps there is more to oppression than being denied a "fair share." The ultimate question is, "What do we wish to share?"

---

[3] One woman governor, Dixie Lee Ray of Washington State, lost in her bid to gain her party's nomination in 1980. Another, Ella Grasso of Connecticut, resigned due to poor health.

EMERGENCE

As we leave the subjective realm of ideology and turn to the movement phase of our model, the concern with organization and action is once again paramount. However, two important points should be kept in mind. First, the definition of sexism as a *social problem* is possible only when those prevailing ideologies that legitimate the traditional place of women are questioned. Further, the dominant interpretations, judgments, and values that have shaped the women's movement, hold that women are a minority group, denied the political standing of the majority.

> The women's rights movement, however, did not grow out of the trade-union struggles of women. It was never closely associated with trade-union activities nor particularly interested in the problems of working women. This may seem contradictory unless you keep in mind that the women's movement was primarily a fight for legal, not economic, rights (Cowley 1970, p. 5).

Involvement in the political process was therefore seen as the key to the emancipation of women. As we shall see, such a concern ties the early suffragettes and their single-minded obsession with the vote to the later feminists who have sought justice through changing the law. According to this ideology, in the wake of general political involvement and specific legal reforms would come new economic opportunities, changes in sexist education and socialization patterns, and an end to male chauvinism.

Thus, we can best understand the major thrust of the women's movement within the framework of an "assimilation model of equality" (Rossi 1970). The essence of assimilation is captured in the "melting pot" description of early twentieth-century historians. It means that through a gradual process of absorption, sometimes requiring several generations, minority groups exchange their culture and traditions for those of the "majority." In the process, a synthesis of culture supposedly occurs so that the majority adopts certain minority traditions. Equipped with certain cultural advantages of the majority (education, customs, life-style), the minority can supposedly begin the climb upward.

With the goal of assimilation embraced and the political/legal arena selected as the place to do battle, the women's movement was defined. It followed that the movement was to obey a basic ideological imperative: that of the *contractual solution*. By contractual solution, we mean the following:

1. Controversies of most sorts can best be resolved through a process of negotiation leading to binding contracts.

2. The terms "contract" and "negotiation" should not be interpreted in a limited and concrete fashion. A contract may be a formal document, as with a collective bargaining agreement. In an abstract sense, however, law is a contract that specifies the rights and obligations of the people and the State. In similar fashion, negotiation may be a formal process occurring in a bargaining situation involving workers and the managerial representatives of owners. It may also include that general political process by which lawmakers come to conclusions on statutory content. In these and numerous other examples the parties to a contract resolve differences and reduce the negotiated agreements to a binding decision.

3. The question of what is "right," "moral," and "ethical" is replaced by the formal language of the binding agreement, which is subject to interpretation. Thus, the civil contract between parties may carry remedies for breach (what you shall lose if you do not live up to your part of the agreement). The criminal law may specify penalties for noncompliance within the context of due process (someone accused of violating the law is entitled to an orderly procedure that ensures a defense).

4. Although sometimes a collective instrument, the "contractual solution" also contains the entitlement by the individual to negotiate standing and rewards on the basis of supposed merit and talent. Denial thereof is an indication that the individual is a member of a group without contractual standing.

5. The negotiation of an agreement, which in an abstract sense may include seeing one's interests written into law, requires organization and influence. (For a discussion of contracts, see Wolfe 1977; Mill 1977; and Chambliss and Ryther 1975.)

Early Contractualism: Suffrage

With an understanding of the ideological nature of the women's movement in hand, it is possible to turn to the historical record. The problem here, as with many powerless groups in North American society, is that women have been hidden by historians. Perhaps heavily influenced by Carlyle's "Great Man" explanation of history, those who tell the story of humankind in Western civilization have made two cardinal errors. First, the emphasis on giants from the past who tower above the masses, molding political systems and building the economic order is an example of romanticized elitism. Fully compatible with individualistic ideology, history often reads as if Washington were at Valley Forge alone, Carnegie made his own steel, and Rockefeller worked on a drilling platform. Beyond this, women and the vanquished Native Americans, blacks, and Chicanos join the "common" fold as losers without official past (Sochen, Volume I 1974).

Though it is certainly plausible to trace the origins of the women's movement to earlier periods, it was only toward the middle of the nineteenth century that the voices of feminists began to be heard in England and the United States and, at the end of the century, in Canada (Strong-Boag 1977). Earlier, Mary Wollstonecraft wrote *A Vindication of the Rights of Women* in 1792. However, it proved to be simply a vanguard statement more or less ignored for half a century.

The crystallization of the women's movement in the United States during the nineteenth century is deserving of explanation. Some have suggested that feminists were moved by the great revolutionary currents in England and North America; that the rise of egalitarianism and liberal democracy together with the massive force of the Industrial Revolution had implications for male as well as aristocratic dominance. However, such arguments ignore two historical realities. First, in America the initial step toward organization was not taken until 1848, with the first women's rights convention meeting at Seneca Falls, New York. This was over seventy years past the signing of the Declaration of Independence. Moreover, if the Industrial Revolution represented a boon for feminism in that it opened many occupational opportunities outside the home, why were the most prominent leaders of the women's movement not gainfully employed (O'Neill 1971)?

Change in the Family In a particularly cogent analysis of an important book by Phillippe Aries entitled *Centuries of Childhood*, O'Neill suggests that the origins of the women's movement resided not with libertarian ideals or the Industrial Revolution. Rather, one can trace the roots of feminism to the revolutionary shift occurring in family life with the passing of medieval feudal society. Simply put, prior to the sixteenth century the family was not considered the center of social existence. Rather, people were attached to the broader society. The family, though large and identifiable, was not an isolated and fragmented unit with a being unto itself.

This earlier family type offered more freedom to women.

> Standards of conduct were broader and more flexible, for noblewomen positions of great authority were not unusual, and even lower class women enjoyed substantial economic opportunities in certain crafts and trades (O'Neill 1971, p. 17).

However, the rise of capitalism saw the shift of production from the home and feudal estate to the cities with their centers of trade and beginnings of a factory system. Predictably, law replaced custom, and private ownership of land supplanted the estate with its well-defined place for all levels from nobility to serf. The social world came to be marked by the emergence of classes. Owners and workers of various sorts replaced ruling families, warriors, and serfs; and the Church, the master institution of feudal society, gave way to the State.

Within this context of political and economic change, the nature of the family could not remain the same. The women of the working class often left the home in search of wage employment. The women of the old nobility saw the formal heritage of title; the inheritance of position, challenged by a new code of standing: the extent of private holdings and personal wealth. Wives of men who were small landowners, operators of modest businesses, or employed in positions of trust by the economic elite found a new role. Their husbands caught up in a profit/wage economy, their children no longer apprenticed out, and their work options outside the home grim and foreboding, the women of the middle class became the fulcrum for the newly developed privatized family. Caught in the web of domesticity, middle-class wives and mothers saw an external social world develop without them. The role of "homemaker" became intense and demanding. The ideal wife was one who equipped her husband for economic warfare and sustained her children through prolonged childhood and adolescence (childhood had ceased in medieval society about age six). Her single salvation was to be spared the class distinction of being a "working woman."

Given our argument to this point, it follows that women were vulnerable to the loss of political and economic rights. Middle-class women, however, defined their losses by legal standing, not by opportunities in the workplace. Accordingly, early feminism was prepared historically to react to the appeal of suffrage. It was a safe road for the

> . . . overwhelming majority of suffragists—white middle-class women who accepted most of the society's attitudes toward a women's role. These women agreed that the family was sacred, and they accepted the praise for their higher moral nature which is the reverse rhetoric of sexism: "We who are more virtuous will have a purifying effect on politics" (Brown and Seitz 1970, p. 19).

In the United States, the official birth year for the women's movement is 1848, when several hundred women and a few men convened at Seneca Falls, New York. The conference was called by two women tied to both the abolition of slavery and the cause of feminism, Lucretia Mott and Elizabeth Cady Stanton. There the delegates framed a clear and compelling statement, the *Seneca Falls Declaration of Rights and Sentiments*. The language of that document fits well the ideological critique made earlier in this chapter. Eloquent, moving and important, this declaration nonetheless identifies the source of oppression as "Him." The introductory statement reads, "The history of mankind is a history of repeated injuries and usurpations on the part of men toward women, having in direct object the establishment of an absolute tyranny over her (sic)." The list of grievances clearly fit the "piece of the action" interpretation. However, first on the list is "He has never permitted her to exercise her inalienable right to the elective franchise."

Seven decades after the Seneca Falls declaration, in 1919, the Congress of the United States passed the suffrage amendment. Canadian women had won the vote in 1918. Nellie L. McClung, leader of the women's movement in Canada, was often invited to speak to United States organizations (Strong-Boag 1977). The Nineteenth Amendment, after ratification by the required two thirds of the states, became law in 1920. Women had won the "inalienable right to the elective franchise." Now they could choose—most frequently between two white Anglo-Saxon males from privileged class position. However, to choose is one thing, to determine the range of choice is quite another. The latter is the measure of power.

Later Contractualism: Civil Rights

The "woman question" was certainly not a dead issue following the realization of suffrage. However, for the next quarter-century the historical spotlight shifted to other social issues. During the Twenties, the United States suffered the customary postwar economic problems and, following the nature of the corporate order, people were encouraged to spend their way free. Progress was ordained for those who dreamed, and the nature of their dream was fashioned by the burgeoning advertising industry. It was in this context that the ghost of the suffragettes passed into history and women emerged as consumers, a caste of shoppers oblivious to the fact that they were "the only unpaid workers in a money economy" (Sochen 1974, p. 290). It was during this period, as Sochen notes, that three women were well on their way to becoming millionaires—predictably in the cosmetics industry. They were Helena Rubenstein, Elizabeth Arden, and Madame C. J. Walker (who manufactured skin preparations and hair-straightening agents for black people).

The "consumptive" role for women became incongruous with the coming of the Great Depression. Officially born in the fall of 1929 with the collapse of the stock market, the Depression saw the nation plunge into chaos. Capitalism, a crisis economy, is no stranger to "peaks and valleys." However, between 1929 and World War II, this mode of production fell into an abyss. "Women's place" was described by Anne O'Hare McCormick, winner of the 1937 Pulitzer Price for Journalism.

. . . traveling around the country, (she) wrote about the nobility of American women who worked the land in Idaho, scrimped and saved from their meager incomes, and made do with their limited resources. Full of faith in the economic richness of the system, she encouraged her women readers to participate in local politics and help improve community life (Sochen 1974, p. 316).

The fictional power of women as family treasurers was to have minimal effect on the contradictions of the corporate economy. Such deep-rooted structural problems were also beyond the remedial adjustments sought by Franklin Delano Roosevelt's New Deal programs. Salvation awaited the coming of the Second World War and the enormous impetus given the economy by defense spending. (See Chapter Three and Chomsky 1973)

Women were subjected to a new ideological definition during the war years. Because of the drain on the nation's manpower, the new symbol of patriotism became "Rosie the Riveter." Women who were supposedly too frail for much of the work done by men before the war were redefined in a renaissance of the "pioneer woman." Predictably, women were supplanted when their men came home. However, after the inert Twenties when women who had fought singlemindedly for the vote seemed confident they had won an important victory; after the simple obsession with national survival during the Depression and war years; and after the stagnancy of postwar life, the women's movement was reborn. The general struggle for the civil rights of black people and the movement to end the war in Southeast Asia formed the backdrop for action.

As stated earlier, what is termed the women's movement in the United States has historical ties to the cause of black liberation. Early suffragettes were often abolitionists. As their political progeny entered the decades of the 1950s, they were to be affected by legal victories for blacks that were perhaps more apparent than real. In 1954, the United States Supreme Court ruled in Brown *v*. the Board of Education, Topeka, Kansas, that "separate but equal" education was a thinly disguised racist doctrine destructive of black self-image. Then came the Montgomery, Alabama, bus boycott.

> The emergence of the modern civil rights movement can be traced to the December day in 1955 when Rosa Parks refused to move to the back of a Montgomery bus and was arrested as a result. The next day the black community of Montgomery responded with a total boycott of the city's bus lines (Chafe 1977, p. 89).

The boycott was to provide a center stage for a local minister who emerged as a charismatic leader. Professing and practicing Gandhi's doctrine of nonviolent civil disobedience, Martin Luther King was to lead his people in the pursuit of contractual justice until his assassination in 1968. (See Chapter 10).

Our opinion that the ends of the movement were incorrectly defined is based on our contention that there is no political power of substance until there is economic power of substance. However, this should not detract from the heroic proportions of the civil rights crusade of the Sixties and the role played in it by women, especially black women.

> As white women from the South joined the movement, they were continually inspired by examples of black women who, in Sara Evans' words, "shattered cultural images of appropriate female behavior." . . . in every Southern town . . . there were "Mamas" who provided the organizational base for action against the white power structure, coordinating food, shelter, transportation, jail visits, and other life-support activities. The result of all this, as one white Southern woman observed, was that "for the first time I had role models I could respect" (Chafe 1977, pp. 109–110).

The inclusion of guarantees against sex-based discrimination in civil rights legislation is an appropriate topic for the institutionalization phase of this chapter. However, it is worthwhile to recall that the feminist movement and the movements directed against racism in the United States have been united philosophically and tactically in a quest for what we have defined as a contractual solution. Such a reality means a general confidence in the potential justice offered by the existing order. By its nature, the contractual promise is that the system is the solution. Following this, we can better understand the view of the media-selected leaders of the current women's movement in the United States.

Betty Friedan, founder of the National Organization for Women (NOW), authored *The Feminine Mystique* in 1963. It is widely regarded as a manifesto for the modern women's liberation movement. This pivotal book is a well-written attempt to conceptualize the "problem that has no name." For Friedan, the dilemma is captured in the question posed silently by women suffering through cosmetic bliss—"Is this all there is?" The evident conclusion to be reached by the reader is that the void for the middle-class, unactualized housewife can be filled somewhere beyond the pedestal of home and family.

A Phi Beta Kappa graduate of Smith College, named "Woman of the Year" in 1971 by Theta Sigma Phi (a national sorority for professional women), and founder of *MS* magazine, Gloria Steinem proved a natural for media stardom. In 1970, she called for the breaking down of traditional sex roles, equality in opportunity, and suggested that a divorce represents an event analogous to the dissolution of a business partnership. All of these are contractual concerns. More to the point, she centered squarely on the loss of civil rights for women that occurs as a consequence of marriage laws. This demand, that women should have independent legal standing, has been the rudder of the women's movement since 1848.

Due to the nature of class society, those who have spoken to and written about the oppression of women seldom identify with the working-class. There is, however, a real, silent, media-ignored struggle that occurs daily in factories, department stores, and offices. Perhaps what we hear most often are the voices of those who are not as opposed to the concept of class-based inequality as they are opposed to the lack of a female elite.

A final statistical example serves as evidence for the popularity of the contractual solution. In 1972, only 3.8 percent of some 320,000 lawyers and judges in the United States were women. By 1977, the corresponding percentage was 9.5 percent of a total 462,000. Such statistics represent a laudable movement away from sex-restricted occupational choice. It also represents for many women a confirmation of the hope that the law is an ally. We shall now examine the evidence for that hope.

INSTITUTIONALIZATION

The assimilative direction of the women's movement has had a number of consequences. As we shall see, the language of the law has undergone some revision and some women have realized the promise of contractualism: the freedom to negotiate a more favored position in a system of inequality.

In point of fact, we have already dealt with the first evidence of the institutionalization of sexism as an "official" social problem.

> After the 1920 ratification of the Nineteenth Amendment, granting women's suffrage, the legislative status of women in the United States changed very little until the 1960s. The Women's Bureau of the Department of Labor began collecting data and publishing statistical reports on the status of women after the passage of the Nineteenth Amendment, but it was not until 1964 that the differential treatment of women and men documented in these reports became a legal issue (Whitehurst 1977, p. 78).

The Civil Rights Act of 1964 was in effect political compensation for the brutality suffered by workers in a movement seeking the elimination of racial injustice. However, as an afterthought, Title VII of this legislation was amended to add "sex" to the list of social categories that were to be henceforth an illegal basis for the denial of employment. (Others were race/color, religion, and national origin.)

Whitehurst, Rossi, and other feminists place this "victory" in historical context. Curiously, the strongest political support for the amendment came from the land of the Southern belle. Such regional backing was seen as a maneuver on the part of those who opposed civil rights legislation to broaden the scope of discrimination and thereby weaken the act's enforcement potential.

Title VII gave birth to the Equal Employment Opportunities Commission (EEOC), which was to create policy and enforce the federal ban on job discrimination. Though the women's movement had nothing of the magnitude of the predominantly black 1963 march on Washington, which many observers believed to be the precipitating force for the 1964 Civil Rights Act, women were quick to take advantage of the contractual solution. Sex discrimination soon became the most frequently lodged complaint with the EEOC.

The Women's Movement and Civil Rights

In some ways, it was the civil rights movement with its essential trust in the potential of the law that contributed greatly to a rising consciousness on the part of women. Such consciousness went beyond the century-old realization that basic human rights were denied on grounds other than race. It was rather forged in the contradictions of the movement itself. Men, black and white, committed to racial equality would rarely extend that concern to women. Thus, many women in both the civil rights and antiwar movements had to battle with a restricting ideology: a belief system that cast the liberation of women purely in terms of sexual freedom.

It is for this reason that we cannot separate the civil rights movement from later political gains scored by women. Not only did women come to recognize the caste relationship between sex and race, but their growing numbers also suggested to those in office that a stronger potential for social turmoil resided with a statistical majority. Accordingly, executive orders as well as legislation addressed the legal chains of sexism. In 1965, Executive Order 11246 made all Title VII criteria for nondiscrimination *except sex* binding on holders of federal contractors. In 1967, Order 11375 *added* the deleted criterion and established an "affirmative action" requirement.

Civil action claiming sex discrimination has been most frequently found in colleges and universities (Whitehurst 1977). This is to be expected as the law is most frequently a remote and abstract tool for those in underclass positions. Shrouded in controversy for over a decade, affirmative action guidelines call for employers to establish goals and timetables to overcome institutionalized discrimination in the occupational sector. We suspect that *affirmative action* is a symbol directed primarily toward the specific needs of a frustrated elite of women who have been shackled by their sex and denied advancement. Affirmative action is not designed to improve the conditions of the overwhelming number of women workers. For that reason, statistical data presented later will show that more than a decade of affirmative action has done little for women as a category. It has, as intended, extended an occasional promise to the well-educated individual who might otherwise take the lead in questioning the very roots of the corporate system.

The Equal Rights Amendment

The above does not constitute an exhaustive list of legislation and executive orders bearing on sexual discrimination. Others include the State and Local Fiscal Assistance Act of 1972, which provided that "no person in the United States shall on the ground of race, color, national origin or sex be excluded from participation in, be denied the benefits of, or be subjected to discrimination under any program or activity funded in whole or in part with funds made available under this Act." Title IX of the Education Amendments Act (1972) forbade discrimination on the basis of sex for schools receiving federal funding. However, perhaps a milestone in contractual solutions was reached in March 1972, when Congress approved the Equal Rights Amendment (ERA) and submitted it to the states for the required three-fourths approval by state legislative bodies. At this writing, 35 states have approved the amendment and Congress has extended the deadline for its ratification to June 1982. However, there appears little hope that the additional three state ratifications will be secured.

The language of the ERA is straightforward. It declares that "equality under the law shall not be denied or abridged by the United States or any state on account of sex." However, in the late 1970s supporters of the amendment began to encounter strong resistance, much of it in the form of the "Stop ERA" countermovement championed by Phyllis Schafly. The countermovement has argued that ERA is a threat to family life and marriage, as it encourages women to leave the home. Other charges are that should ERA pass, women would lose alimony, child custody, and child support. ERA has also been cast as "pro" prostitution, obscenity, adultery, homosexuality, and unisex toilets.

The dire consequences foretold by anti-ERA forces strain credulity. However, the prediction of pro-ERA supporters that this constitutional amendment will achieve for women what the Nineteenth did not is also subject to serious doubt. Passing laws is not a magical ritual. The ills spoken to by the language of legislation do not simply disappear with the passage of a bill. The controversy surrounding ERA is more in the nature of what Joseph Gusfield (1963) terms a "symbolic crusade."

Frequently, groups representing social and cultural differences seek some widespread affirmation of the "rightness" of their ideologies and customs. The "traditional woman" described earlier fits well the prototype of the anti-ERA movement. The "pedestal" status of home, motherhood, and protection seems to be challenged by women who are demand-

645

ing actualization in the broader society. Those desiring a bigger "piece of the action" see ERA as a symbol attesting to the real problem of sex-based discrimination. Each side wants its view of woman's place written into law. Symbolism, however, should be differentiated from substance.

The fate of the ERA appears inextricably bound with the state of the economy. A study drawn from survey data of two Illinois random samples in 1976 and 1977 revealed that the perceived effect ERA would have on jobs was a critical determinant of one's position on the amendment. (Those who felt their jobs might be threatened by ERA tended to oppose it.) It appears difficult to approve even symbolically the democratic concept of equality within a context of structural unemployment and work alienation (Huber et al. 1978).

Our Bodies, Ourselves

A final concern for women seeking a contractual solution can be referred to simply as "our bodies, ourselves." It is important to realize that women have suffered cruelly at the hands of a medical and judicial order that has traditionally been unresponsive to the specific needs of "the other sex." A legal milestone was passed in 1973 when the United States Supreme Court ruled that during the first trimester of pregnancy a woman in consultation with her physician could decide to abort the fetus. The laws of the several states were not to infringe upon this right. However, state law could regulate procedures for performing abortions in the second trimester. State law could also prohibit an abortion during the third trimester, provided the woman's life was not endangered.

Once again, the legal victories do not apply uniformly to all. On the last day of June 1980, the United States Supreme Court declared that federal Medicaid funds for the poor need not be used to pay for abortions if such be the will of Congress. At present, highly restrictive criteria must be met. Federal Medicaid abortion law stipulates that federal money can be used for abortions only if (1) the mother's life would be endangered if the fetus were carried to term, (2) the pregnancy resulted from rape or incest promptly reported to a law enforcement agency, or (3) two physicians certify that the continuation of the pregnancy would produce "severe and long-lasting physical health damage to the mother" (Spokesman-Review 1980).

In addition to abortion, women's groups have shown increasing interest in the crime of rape, correctly understanding that the offense is primarily one of violent assault rather than one of passion. Wisconsin and Michigan have changed their sexual assault laws in order to increase both the incidence of reporting by victims and the decision to prosecute. Severe penalties for rape such as life imprisonment deter juries from conviction.

Those seeking the revision of rape laws have called for graduated degrees of sexual assault and a corresponding range of punishments. Laws in a number of states, including Oregon, Iowa, and Wisconsin, make sexual assault by a spouse a crime. Oregon's law permits a spouse to be prosecuted even if the two are living under the same roof. In 1978, Greta Rideout accused her husband of rape under Oregon law. A jury acquitted the husband. However, the first conviction for marital rape in the United States followed shortly in Salem, Massachusetts, in 1979.

Although legal reform in the area of sexual assault is to be applauded, its results are most likely to remain symbolic. Rape may be reported more frequently, and the rapist subjected to prosecution, but it is doubtful that the incidence of sexual assault will diminish significantly. Centuries of changing laws and punishments have met with little success in other areas. Capital punishment has not proven a deterrent to homocide, Prohibition did not prevent alcoholism, and, after more than a century of civil rights legislation, nonwhites are still not free. The violence perpetrated against women, whether in the form of sexual assault or wife battering, cannot be separated from the chattel status of women in the corporate society. When combined with the continual attack on self-worth to which many men are subjected, the results are potentially explosive. The rapist does not assault a person. He violates a commodity, an object, a thing. (See the discussion on alienation in Chapter four.)

Keeping in mind the view that the law has been defined historically within the women's movement as a tool of assimilation, other feminist concerns logically follow. Women have been urged to work for the elimination of sex-based discrimination in insurance coverage (Sydlaske 1975), seek employment in "nontraditional" jobs (that is, crafts and trades), and take full advantage of vocational training (Roby 1977). In all of these, the law is described as a tool to force compliance.

The Restricted Vision:

Equal Opportunity Is Not Equality

Contractual promises notwithstanding, the law has never embraced the objective of *equality*. The Civil Rights Act of 1866 provided for *nondiscrimination* in employment and public accommodations during the reconstruction period and for the next 100 years thereafter. The Pendleton Act of 1883 established the principle of *merit employment* for federal government employees, and vested responsibility for fair promotions in the Civil Service Commission. The Civil Service Regulation, Rule VIII (1883), outlawed religious *discrimination* in federal employment. Under Franklin Delano Roosevelt, the Unemployment Relief Act of 1933 forbade *discrimination* on the basis of race, color, or creed. Roosevelt's Executive Order 8587 (1940) forbade racial discrimination in federal employment and promotion. His Executive Order 8802 created the *Fair* Employment Practice Committee, and a later order (9346), in 1943, created a new *Fair* Employment Practice Committee. In 1948, President Truman issued Executive Order 9980, which provided more precise machinery in the federal government to deal with *discrimination* based on race, color, creed, or national origin through a Civil Service Commission *Fair* Employment Board. In 1961, President Kennedy issued Executive Order 10925, creating the President's Committee on Equal Employment *Opportunity*. And finally, in 1963 Congress passed the Equal Pay Act, which expanded the "equal pay for *equal work*" demand beyond the federal government to all employers subject to minimum wage requirements.

Though the above did not specifically focus on eliminating discrimination based on sex, our point is that *avoiding* the issue of "equality" is firmly entrenched in the political order of the corporate society. Perhaps such is to be expected, as in 1972 the top 1 percent of the population in the United States held 24.1 percent of the wealth. More to the point, and as was pointed out in Chapter Three, this same 1 percent held 56.5 percent of the corporate stock, 60 percent of the bonds, 52.7 percent of the debt instruments (notes, mortgages, security credit, etc.), and 89.9 percent of the trusts. These are the means of economic control (*Statistical Abstract of the United States* 1978, p. 476). Accordingly, the institutionalized rhetoric is that of "nondiscrimination," "merit," "fair," and "opportunity." Following a century of such euphemisms, a new rhetoric was discovered: that of "affirmative action." After 115 years of the former and over a decade of the latter, women and blacks still make only some 60 percent of the income of men and whites, respectively. (Tables 11–4 and 11–5 test the impact of law on earnings.)

Over the past quarter-century, women have entered the work force in increasing numbers.

TABLE 11-4
Work Force Composition by Sex: Selected Years

	Male Workers (millions)	Female Workers (millions)	Women as Percentage of the Labor Force
1955	44.5	20.5	32%
1960	46.4	23.2	33
1965	48.3	26.2	35
1970	51.2	31.5	38
1975	55.6	37.0	40
1978	58.2	41.1	41

Source: Compiled from data in the *Statistical Abstract of the United States* 1978, pp. 398–99.

However, most crucially, in the United States in the Seventies the median (midpoint) dollar gap between the earnings of men and women, both wage and salary workers, continued to grow.

SEX AND
SEXISM

TABLE 11-5
The Dollar Gap: Median Weekly Earnings by Sex for
Full-Time Wage and Salary Workers: Selected Year

	1967	1970	1973	1974	1975	1976	1977
Male	$125	$151	$188	$204	$221	$234	$253
Female	78	94	116	124	137	145	156
Gap	$47	$57	$72	$80	$84	$89	$97

Source: Compiled from data in the *Statistical Abstract of the United States* 1978, p. 423.

It appears that the major reason for hiring women remains a matter of economics, not of law. It is easier to pass "equal opportunity" legislation and issue "affirmative action" executive orders than it is to raise the salaries and wages of women who work. Of course, class position is very much related to the proportion of women working. For example, in Canada a disproportionate number of married women who work have husbands whose wages are low (Table 11-6). The same is true for the United States (Turner 1977, p. 300). Thus, the notion that women simply want to "actualize" themselves through careers is a myth for all save the more affluent.

Of course, the force driving increasing numbers of women into the work force is inflation. As economist Richard Parker (1979) cogently argues, the declining purchasing power of the dollar has spared few of the

TABLE 11-6
Labour Force Participation Rates of Married Women,
Husbands Present, by Family Income Excluding
Wives' Earnings: Canada

Family Income Exluding Wives' Earnings	Participation Rate of Wives
$3,000 or less	47%
$3,000–$5,999	44
$6,000–$8,999	44
$9,000–$11,999	38
$12,000–$14,999	33
$15,000 or over	27

Source: Special 1971 Census tabulations from *Statistics Canada*.

working class. Consequently, the second income is the only thing currently keeping the "middle class" afloat. The question of course is: What next?[4]

Parker correctly ties inflation to its structural origin. In corporate society, the specific ideology that seeks to account for inflation places the blame on "wasteful consumers." For example, people's driving habits are scorned without considering the absence of adequate public transportation (see Chapter Five). In point of fact, as Parker notes, the production of cancer-producing herbicides and essentially useless plastics accounts for much more energy waste than "pleasure driving."

The prevailing ideologies present other ways of countering inflation. A common one presses for the elimination of government waste (usually meaning welfare services). In point of fact, the 50 million persons at the bottom of the heap in American society receive only 5 percent of the nation's total income. As detailed in Chapter Three, "wealthfare" is much more costly. When we examine structural inequality, we find the income of the upper 7 percent of the population to be over $400 billion dollars (Parker 1979). If consumer spending fuels inflation, perhaps we should look at those who can afford to spend wildly. If government spending is related to inflation, perhaps we should look at the superrich and the centers of economic power who truly benefit from a socialism for the elite.

There are a number of rational beginnings to resolving inflation. These call for lids on profits, prices, and wages; conservation; the development of renewable energy sources such as solar energy and wind power (a strategy that would create more jobs than similar investment in the fossil fuel industry); direct marketing of food; and the development of public worker-controlled organizations to provide energy, health care, and other needed services. Needless to say, these alternatives run counter to the dominant ideology of corporatism and those it serves. While inflation during the 1970s was ravaging the security of most members of North American society, some were doing quite well. In the United States in this decade, the number of millionaires increased from 100,000 to 500,000, an increase only partially explained by inflation (Parker 1979).

MAINTENANCE

The issue of maintenance once again raises the question of "who benefits?" by the particular definition of the "woman issue" that prevails. We have seen that the solution to "sexism" continues to be defined by assimilation. Accordingly, the women's liberation movement has pushed for a legal form of contractual solution. This has led to the passing of

[4]A partial answer to this question may be had from the increasing entry of adolescents into the part-time service economy (for example, as fast-food workers).

laws and the establishment of compliance machinery to enforce them. However, economic data serve to question the contention that women as a category have made significant gains as a consequence of either the Nineteenth Amendment or "rights" legislation. Who or what, then, are the benificiaries?

Professional and Managerial Women

Much has been written of women's penetration into the more desirable kinds of jobs in the United States. There is some evidence to support this contention. However, as the following table demonstrates, an emphasis on occupational representation may be misleading in two respects.

First of all, as the economy expands, the number of jobs available to women will also expand. However, an emphasis on growth in professional and managerial jobs held by women may divert attention from the fact that the greatest increase in jobs for women between 1972 and 1977 was in the *clerical* field. Furthermore, the rise in number of service jobs for women (waitresses, hairdressers, etc.) far outstripped the increases in the managerial positions. In the second place, we should be careful in speaking generally of "professions" or "management" when addressing the question of opportunities for women, because the Bureau of Labor Statis-

TABLE 11-7
Employed Persons by Sex and Occupation:
United States 1972 and 1977

Occupation	1972		1977		Increase in Number of Women
	Total Employed	Percent Female	Total Employed	Percent Female	
Professional/ Technical	11,459,000	39.3%	13,692,000	42.6%	1,479,000
Nurses, Dietitians, Therapists	949,000	92.6	1,285,000	92.8	313,000
Teachers (except college)	2,841,000	70.0	3,024,000	70.9	155,000
Managers/Admin- istrators	8,031,000	17.6	9,662,000	22.3	742,000
Clerical	14,247,000	75.6	16,106,000	78.9	2,014,000
Service (except private household)	9,529,000	57.0	11,234	58.3	1,117,000

Source: Compiled from the *Statistical Abstract of the United States* 1978, pp. 419–721.

tics includes a wide range of jobs under these major occupational headings. In fact, the two professional occupations demonstrating the greatest growth for women were nursing (or something related) and non-college teaching. The managerial category also categorizes such occupations as upper-level corporate executives and university presidents with office managers. Whatever the occupational category, women dominate the lower echelons.

There is other information that leads us to predict that the women beneficiaries of the movement as presently defined will be the already advantaged few who simply "want in." In testimony before a subcommittee of the House on the issue of women in business, the following argument was made by the National Association of Women Business Owners:

> Economic independence for women is seldom expressed in terms of entrepreneurship. Until recently, economic gains for women have been seen in terms of job equality, promotional opportunity, and entry into formerly segregated job classifications. However, more and more it has been recognized that the virtual absence of women from American Business is a measuring rod for just how little equality has been achieved for women (United States Congress 1977, p. 2).

A concluding remark about occupational penetration: As long as the success of the feminist movement is gauged by the gains made by an advantaged occupational category, the movement will appear irrelevant to the millions of working-class women. In the United States in 1977, women constituted 36.7 million of 90.5 million employed workers. Of these, 12.7 million were clerical and 6.5 million were service workers. These two categories comprise over 52 percent of employed women. They are indeed a "silenced majority."

Supporting the Bureaucracy

By contractual standards, the United States now has a broad legal foundation calling for the elimination of sex-based discrimination. However, even those who favor legal reform as the road to changing woman's place agree that the enforcement of laws and executive orders has been weak and ineffective.

> One reason why voluntary compliance with the laws appears so weak is the failure of enforcement agencies to use their sanctions. Most women filing charges must wait years for agency action, to say nothing of the time required for legal action if that becomes necessary.

The EEOC (Equal Employment Opportunity Commission) complaint backlog in the spring of 1976 topped 100,000. And sex discrimination complaints filed in 1970 with the HEW Office for Civil Rights were still waiting for processing six years later (National Commission on the Observance of International Women's Year 1976, p. 49).

Along the same line, in 1976 the EEOC marked 75,000 cases "resolved." The average length of time for resolution was two and one-half years (Rowse 1978, p. 22). Further, the EEOC has hardly been vigorous in attempting to oppose broad patterns of discrimination on the part of large employers. As noted in Chapter Two, the "incestuous relationship" between government and the corporate order is not confined to EEOC or to the Department of Health and Human Resources' Office for Civil Rights (Wolfe 1977).

Enforcement failure notwithstanding, the various directives from Congress and the Executive have created a reason for being for a number of federal agencies.

> The *Civil Service Commission* CSC), under the EEO Act of 1972, is responsible for equal employment opportunity programs in Federal employment. . . .
>
> In addition, the Intergovernmental Personnel Act of 1970 (Section 208) requires the Commission to ensure that all federally aided State agencies maintain a merit system plan, wherein EEO is an integral part. . . .
>
> *The Equal Employment Opportunity Commission* (EEOC) derives its enforcement status from the Equal Employment Opportunity Act of 1972. Under the act, the Commission is responsible for investigating complaints of employment discrimination in labor unions, the private sector, State and local government, higher education institutions, and elementary and secondary schools. . . .
>
> *The Department of Justice* derives its major EEO enforcement status from the Civil Rights Act of 1964 and the 1973 Crime Control Act. Under Title VII of the Civil Rights Act of 1964, the Justice Department is responsible for the enforcement of nondiscrimination in employment. . . .
>
> As a result of Executive Order 11764, the Department also has responsibility for the coordination of agency enforcement of Title VI, nondiscrimination in federally funded programs. . . .
>
> *The Department of Labor* obtains its enforcement authority from the 1963 Equal Pay Act, 1967 Age Discrimination in Employment Act, and the 1973 Comprehensive Employment and Training Act as well as the Vietnam Era Veteran's Readjustment Assistance Act and the Rehabilitation Act of 1973. . . .
>
> Executive order 11246 issued in 1965 by President Johnson assigns responsibility to the *Office of Federal Contract Compliance Programs* (OFCCP) within DOL (Department of Labor) to establish regulations and standards for Federal agencies which make contracts with private employers. . . .

The State and Local Fiscal Assistance Act of 1972 confers upon the Treasury's Office of Revenue Sharing responsibility for enforcement, ensuring there is nondiscrimination in the use of federal financial assistance provided to State and local governments . . . (U.S. Commission on Federal Paperwork 1977, pp. 21–24).

We must beg the reader's forgiveness for this litany of legislation, orders, and agencies but perhaps they will make the point crystal clear. When one adds state and local bureaucracies to the partial federal list designated above, it cannot be denied that the quest for nondiscrimination has spawned an awesome bureaucratic leviathan. This ensures that the cause of women's rights (as well as those of other minority groups) will be preserved. However, that cause will be preserved in the sense of equal *opportunity*. Such a definition while supporting a civil rights bureaucracy does not ultimately threaten a society of haves and have-nots, those who own and those who toil, those who decide and those who are acted upon.

Another form of bureaucratic maintenance can be traced to the broader involvement of women in the economy. This has led to an increase in the level of property crime perpetrated by females. The rate of such crime attributable to women is rising, specifically in the area of larceny/theft and fraud/embezzlement. (Some popular accounts notwithstanding, the gap between male and female rates of violent crime show no evidence of narrowing [Steffensmeier 1978].) Accordingly, it appears that the law enforcement agencies have an additional reason for being.

Women and the Corporate Economy

Beyond bureaucratic maintenance is the more serious sphere of supporting the economic order. In this respect, twentieth-century women have served the corporate economy long and well. In *The Theory of the Leisure Class*, Thorstein Veblen identifies ostentatious consumption as the master status symbol in class society. He argues that maintaining a conspicuous life-style as a means of showing one's pecuniary standing began with the upper classes. However, such a pattern in the course of time came to be emulated by those in other classes. Women, assuming they were married to men who could afford it, became the mainstays of a subsidiary or derivative leisure class. To be clear, women in affluent families became ceremonial consumers, thus affirming their leisured, or successful position. However, such women (Not in the industrial work force) consumed only *vicariously*. The leisure of the servant (wife) was not to be confused with the leisure of the master. Women became a sort of commodity, adorned in the latest fashion, participating in the proper social events, and testifying to their husbands' success by demonstrating that they "did not have to work." Some position-conscious women today who fear that an occupation other than ceremonial consumer is a threat to social standing still apologize for being in the labor force.

Our argument is that the traditional concept of women's place is not simply an expression of male chauvinism. It is rather a direct reflection of the importance of the consumptive role in the corporate economy.

> In addition, both advertising and education institutions have attempted to stress the importance of the middle-class woman's roles as mother, housewife, and consumer in an effort to invest women with a sense of productivity. Much of the advertising directed to women in the Twentieth Century, for example, has attempted semantically to turn consumption into production. The housewife managing her home has been compared to the businessman running his firm. "Through her dealings as business manager of the home," one advertisement in the 1920s read, "the modern woman brings sound commercial sense to bear on her judgment of a Ford closed car." "Retail buying is a productive act," wrote one praiser of the new economic order (Gordon et al. 1973, p. 51).

Consumption is so vital to the health of the corporate economy that its artificial stimulation supports an industry of enormous magnitude. As Table 11–8 shows, the estimated expenditures for advertising in the United States grew from $5.7 billion in 1950 to $38.1 billion in 1977.

TABLE 11–8
Advertising—Estimated Expenditures: 1950 to 1977
(Millions of Dollars)

Year	Total	National	Local	Year	Total	National	Local	Year	Total	National	Local
1950	$ 5,700	$ 3,260	$ 2,440	1968	$18,090	$10,800	$ 7,290	1973	$25,120	$13,775	$11,345
1955	9,150	5,380	3,770	1969	19,420	11,400	8,020	1974	26,780	14,760	12,020
1960	11,960	7,305	4,655	1970	19,550	11,350	8,200	1975	28,230	15,410	12,820
1965	15,250	9,340	5,910	1971	20,740	11,775	8,965	1976	33,720	18,585	15,135
1966	16,630	10,150	6,480	1972	23,300	13,030	10,270	1977	38,100	21,090	17,010
1967	16,870	10,210	6,660								

Source: *Statistical Abstract of the United States* 1978, p. 854.

Certainly a major share of this industry is directed primarily, if not exclusively, toward women. For example, in 1977 about $3.6 billion was spent on national network advertising. Of this total, $99 million was spent to proclaim the virtues of apparel, footwear, and accessories; $89 million on department and discount stores, $626 million on food and food products; $182 million on household equipment, supplies, and furnishings; $80 million on jewelry, optical goods, and cameras; $279 million on laundry soaps, cleaners, and polishes; $104 million on pet products; $334 million on proprietary medicines (such as Geritol); and a whopping $576 million dollars on toiletries (*Statistical Abstract of the United States* 1978, p. 857).

Leaders of the women's movement, consistent with the contractual solution, have sought in recent years to pressure those controlling the media to change the "dippy portrayal" of the housewife. In so doing, they rightfully challenge the stereotypical woman who is ecstatic over products that attack "rings" whether around the collar or the toilet bowl. There is some evidence of response in the industry. Ads in the future can be expected increasingly to portray the successful working mother and the professional/managerial woman. However, perhaps what should be questioned is the broader ground of the advertising world. As detailed in Chapter Two, advertising substitutes the magical properties of the product for self-actualization; thus the commodity becomes the measure of self-worth. The commodity also is portrayed as filling the gap in social relationships, becoming the vehicle by which togetherness, sex appeal, and motherhood can be realized. Advertising teaches that humanity can be had in the marketplace—for a price (see Proposition Two and the discussion of commodification).

Earlier we documented the penetration of some women into traditionally male-dominated occupations. Such change is frequently regarded as a measure of success for those who argue that women should have a stake in the system. Before one goes too far, however, it is necessary to remember that it is relatively easy to create new job titles and descriptions. Moreover, the appeal of cheap labor has never been lost on those directing the course of the corporate economy. There does exist a contradiction between wages and profits. We must therefore be sensitive to the possibility that job titles can mask economic exploitation. Tables 11–9 and 11–10 speak to this point. In all occupational categories, women's earnings trail those of men substantially.

Those seeking to convince employers to expand the range of opportunities for women often argue that hiring a woman makes good business sense. It certainly does.

A final argument can be developed on the support by women of the corporate system. Given the prevailing ideologies, we are often led to believe that certain laws and programs exist to help the unfortunate, the outcasts, and the victims of discrimination. What is frequently overlooked is a category of hidden beneficiaries. In the United States, food stamps for the poor are also food stamps for agribusiness; thus the program is administered by the Department of Agriculture. FHA 245 housing for the moderate income family is a boon to the construction industry, the real estate business, and the many connected occupations. In like fashion, laws seemingly written to help women often prove to be a stimulus to the economic order. Two examples confirm this point.

Legislation we might have included as an example of institutionalization is the Equal Credit Opportunity Act of 1975. It was designed to prohibit sex or marital status discrimination in the securing of credit. This law has not only added to the responsibilities of the Federal Reserve Board, which issues credit regulations, it also speaks to the potential *market women represent for lending institutions.* In this case, we do not believe that lenders' commitment to human equality is nearly so great a

TABLE 11-9
Ratio of Female Earnings to Male Earnings,[a]
All and Full-Time Earners, by Occupation,
Canada 1961 and 1971

Occupation	1961 Census[b]		1971 Census	
	All wage earners	Full-year[c] Full-time	All wage earners	Full-year[c] Full-time
Manager/professional[d]	.46	.56	.49	.56
Clerical	.61	.74	.59	.67
Sales	.35	.45	.34	.49
Service	.47	.47	.37	.50
Primary	.43	.60	.38	.47
Blue collar[e]	.53	.59	.47	.53
Other	—	—	.47	.55
All occupations	.54	.59	.50	.59

[a]Earnings figures are for wage and salary earners and exclude those self-employed in unincorporated businesses. Ratios for 1961 and 1971 are not strictly comparable. In 1961, wage and salary data were collected, with fine breakdowns to the income level of $12,000, with an openend class of $15,000 or more. For calculating averages, all incomes of $15,000 or more were given the value of $15,000. This means that for occupations that had any incomes of $15,000 or more, the averages are too low. The groups most likely to be affected are the managerial and professional; in 1971 actual earnings were collected, so that the same bias does not exist in 1971 data.

[b]1961 occupation groupings are based on the 1951 Census categories and are not directly comparable with the 1971 figures, which are based on the CCDO groupings.

[c]Worked 49–52 weeks for 35 or more hours per week.

[d]Figures for 1961 are an unweighted average of the ratios for managers and professional and technical, used because the two groups had approximately equal numbers in 1961.

[e]Ratios for 1961 are a weighted average of the ratios for transportation and communication with craft, production, and related workers. The latter ratio was weighted by 3 to reflect the fact that there were approximately 3 times as many craft, production, and related workers as transportation and communication workers. Figures for 1971 consist of CCDO occupations 81–95, which include crafts, production, transportation, communication, and construction workers.

Sources: Data for 1961 derived from Sylvia Ostry, *The Female Worker in Canada.* Ottawa: Queen's Printer, 1968, Table 16. Data for 1971 are from special 1971 Census tabulations from *Statistics Canada.*

TABLE 11–10
Median in the United States: 1977
Full-time Workers, by Occupation and Sex

Occupation	Annual Earnings		Women's Earnings as Percentage of Men's
	Women	Men	
Professional and technical	$11,995	$18,224	65.8%
Managers and administrators	9,799	18,086	54.2
Sales workers	6,825	16,067	42.5
Clerical workers	8,601	13,966	61.6
Craft and kindred workers	8,902	14,517	61.3
Operatives, except transport	7,350	12,612	58.3
Laborers, except farm	7,441	10,824	68.7
Service workers, except private household	6,108	10,332	59.1
Farm workers	1,635	6,412	25.5

Source: U.S. Department of Commerce, Bureau of the Census, *Current Population Reports,* P–60, No. 118.

motivator as their desire to collect a high rate of interest. Sex discrimination in lending is paralleled by sex discrimination in the insurance industry. In 1974, Americans spent a staggering $120.8 billion seeking financial security against possible accident, disability, loss of property, or death (*Statistical Abstract of the United States* 1978, p. 857). When members of the National Commission on the Observance of International Women's Year called in 1977 for a "Women's Insurance Bill of Rights," they clearly called for assimilation. The declaration demands an end to sex-based discrimination in all phases of coverage, as well as equal employment opportunities in the industry and the regulatory bureaucracies supposed to monitor it.

The authors wish to state clearly that women are entitled to credit and insurance. We merely wish to point out that such entitlements will most probably be realized because they represent stimuli to two of the cornerstones of the corporate economy. Beyond this, the energy-consuming drive to participate diverts attention from the recognition that credit and insurance reflect in microcosm the contradictions of the existing order. The credit system is fundamental to the ability to pay the inflated prices of goods in the marketplace. As such, it is a vital dynamic of the inflationary spiral. Insurance is unnecessary for the rich, absent for the poor, and a drain on the resources of the middle class. It represents a crazy quilt of overlapping coverage and confusing promises and makes a commodity out of human tragedy. It is the corporate world's substitute for the planned, socially assured allocation of collective resources and new opportunities to all members of a social order who might suffer misfortune.

ALTERNATIVE

Beyond Sisterhood

Once again, a number of alternatives to the "problem" at hand might be posed. However, as we examine the oppression of women we must grasp the *context* of the realities and ideology of sexism. Such an effort requires that we see the connections between the problem at hand and the larger, frequently global, forces of history. Rosemary Brown, a Canadian feminist, addresses the specific issue of women and the economy (1978). Her portrayal of the relationships between the United States and Canada, the impact of technological forces, and the specific problems of women clearly suggests new symbols for the women's liberation movement.

Brown begins by noting the "gradual absorption of Canada into a U.S. dominated economic and cultural framework." She identifies Canada as something of a neocolony of the United States. It provides resources while decisions affecting the national destiny are made outside its boundaries. Further, she identifies "cultural continentalism" as an inevitable by-product of the domination of the Canadian economy. One specific example of this is the enthusiasm with which Canadian property owners met California's Proposition 13. (This measure, passed in 1978, placed a ceiling on property taxes, resulting in a loss of revenues for social programs, public services, and education in Calfornia.)

The point for both Canadians and Americans is that, as the economic problems of the corporate society intensify, the historically familiar revolt of the middle classes may follow. Profits for the giant corporations ensured by the ever present tax loopholes will most probably remain inviolate in the 1980s. It logically follows that those of the middle classes will seek to keep their heads above inflation's waters through demanding tax relief. Should these events occur, the State will respond through the rollback of domestic programs designed to provide some minimal services for the impoverished and disadvantaged minorities.

> The effect on many—especially women—will be disastrous. As health services, social assistance, transition houses and proliferation of other programs specifically useful to the most powerless women are cut back, the inequities and inequalities of our society as well as the alliance between government and the corporations will be exposed (Brown 1978, p. 32).

Brown then continues on, showing the impact of technological change. In so doing, she shows technology not as an "evil" unto itself but as a tool, whose uses are socially determined. For example, the traditional coal miner in Appalachia was displaced not simply by the technology of strip mining but by the absence of rational, society-wide planning to retrain and replace workers whose jobs are made obsolete by technology. The same obsession with short-term profit maximization can be expected to impact the traditional "female job ghettos."

> Standardization of products can not only eliminate job opportunities, but also entrench the ghettos. The development of fast-food outlets means fewer skilled cooks and more underpaid counter girls. Simplification of work skills can lead to mere machine tending. For example, the "correctable typewriter" has virtually eliminated the need for highly skilled typists. Clerical workers are being transformed into assembly line workers who simply "process words" or stuff data into computer systems. As these electronic gadgets absorb skills, the position of the (mostly female) workers is degraded. And such workers are more vulnerable to layoffs (Brown 1978, p. 33).

The importance of this type of analysis is that it clearly indicates a shift in direction from the contractual solutions sought by more privileged women in America. We offer this as we believe that a viable women's movement, better yet a human movement, must be constructed around the concerns of women of the working class.

> The differences in economic roles and personal expectations between working-class women and middle-class women were also reflected in the feminist movement in the early part of the century. Working-class women were generally apathetic to the goals of the organized feminist movement. They did not see the movement as furthering their collective aims of better conditions and unionism. . . . Then, too, working women generally did not regard obtaining the vote as a tangible improvement in their condition, while middle-class suffragists often saw the vote as the only important goal of the movement (Gordon et al. 1973, p. 44).

The problem is that we see things not as they are but as we are. There is a reality but it must be *defined* and the definitions of our reality will be shaped by our position in the social order. The skepticism with which working women viewed suffrage seems vindicated by history. Perhaps their view from the sweatshops of early twentieth-century North American society to the garment plants, department stores, and offices of today constitutes a more promising beginning.

In taking this position, there are two myths to avoid. The first is that middle-class women cannot escape the contractual solution. Human beings have the potential for *vicarious* experience. Should the "more fortunate" use their frequent educational advantage to study the failure of more than a century of civil rights legislation, perhaps they will seriously challenge the assimilative strategy. The second myth is that working-class women have escaped or are somehow immune to the contractual solution. To the contrary; for the few workers who are affiliated with trade unions, the ultimate contractual form—the collective bargaining agreement—is often accepted as an end unto itself. The difference is that working-class women have had some experience historically with collective organizing to promote the common good. Middle-class women, aspiring to a place in the professional or managerial strata, see the contractual solution as a guarantor of *individual* negotiation. It matters greatly whether one is concerned with the forces holding *women* in general back *or* the forces holding the supposedly *talented and deserving* women back.

It should be clear that there is more to the solidarity of women than the mystique of "sisterhood." Simply having similar gonads will not tear down the boundary lines of class. Anatomy is still not destiny. Attempts at erasing these lines are not without historical precedent. In the early part of this century, the "consumer league movement, the union label organizations and the women's labor groups like the Women's Trade Union League" attempted to develop boycotts and purchasing habits by which middle-class women could support women in the working class (Gordon et al. 1973, p. 46). This brief flirtation with interclass cooperation did not succeed. Neither has over a century of North American feminism.

BIBLIOGRAPHY

Abramson, Joan
1975   The Invisible Woman. San Francisco: Jossey-Bass.

Amundsen, Kirsten
1977   A New Look at the Silenced Majority. Englewood Cliffs, N.J.: Prentice-Hall.

Andrews, Margaret W.
1977   "Attitudes in Canadian Women's History, 1945–1975." Journal of Canadian Studies 12, 4 (Summer):69–78.

Bedell, Madelon
1977   "Supermom." In Sex Equality. June English, ed. Englewood Cliffs, N.J.: Prentice-Hall, pp. 239–77.

Bernard, Jesse
1975

Women, Wives, Mothers: Values and Options. Chicago: Aldine.

Bosmajian, Haig
1977

"Sexism in the Language of Legislatures and Courts." In Sexism and Language. Alleen Nilson et al. eds. Urbana, Ill. National Council of Teachers of English, pp. 77–104.

Brown, Connie, and Seitz, Jane
1970

"You've Come a Long Way, Baby: Historical Perspectives." In Sisterhood Is Powerful. Robin Morgan, ed. New York: Random House.

Brown, Rosemary
1978

"Women and the Economy: Bleak Prospects." Perception. Ottawa: Canadian Council on Social Development.

Chafe, William H.
1977

Woman and Equality. New York: Oxford University Press.

Chambliss, William, and Ryther, Thomas
1975

Sociology: The Disciple and Its Direction. New York: McGraw-Hill.

Chomsky, Noam
1973

"At War with Asia." In Problems of Industrial Society. William Chambliss, ed. Reading, Mass.: Addison-Wesley.

Connelly, Patricia M.
1979

"The Economic Context of Women's Labour Force Participation in Canada." In Economy, Class and Social Reality. John Allen Fry, ed. Toronto: Butterworth, pp. 206–23.

Cowley, Joyce
1970

"Pioneers of Women's Liberation." In Voices of New Feminism. Mary Lou Thompson, ed. Boston: Beacon Press.

de Beauvoir, Simone
1977

"The Second Sex." In Sex Equality. June English, ed. Englewood Cliffs, N.J.: Prentice-Hall.

Decrow, Karen
1974   Sexist Justice. New York: Random House.

Durkheim, Emile
1951   Suicide. Translated by John A. Spalding. New York: The Free Press.

Erickson, Erik
1968   Identity: Youth in Crisis. New York: Norton.

Firestone, Shulamith
1970   The Dialectic of Sex. New York: William Morrow.

Gordon, Ann D.; Buhle, Mari Jo; and Shron, Nancy E.
1973   "Women in American Society." Radical American 5(4): 1–69.

Goldman, Philip A.
1974   "Prejudice toward Women." In Who Discriminates Against Women? Florence Denmark, ed. Beverly Hills, Calif.: Sage.

Gusfield, Joseph
1963   Symbolic Crusade: Status Politics and the American Temperance Movement. Urbana, Ill.: University of Illinois Press.

Hacker, Helen
1951   "Women as a Minority Group." Social Forces 30 1 (October): 60–69.

Horkheimer, Max
1977   "Authority and the Family." In The Psychology of Society. Richard Sennett, ed. New York: Random House.

Huber, Joan; Rexroat, Cynthia; and Spitze, Glenna
1978   "A Crucible of Opinion on Women's Status: ERA in Illinois." Social Forces 57 (December) (2): 549–65.

Levine, Janet, A.
1976   Who Will Raise the Children? Philadelphia: J. B. Lippincott.

Manzer, Ronald
1975   Canada: A Socio-Political Report. Toronto:
McGraw-Hill Ryerson.

Masters, William H., and
Johnson, Virginia E.
1966   Human Sexual Response. Boston: Little, Brown.

McDonald, Lynn
1979   "The Gap between Women and Men in the Wages
of Work." In Social Stratification: Canada. James
E. Curtis and William G. Scott, eds. Scarborough:
Prentice-Hall of Canada, pp. 340–46.

Mill, John S.
1977   "The Subjection of Women." In The Psychology
of Society. Richard Sennett, ed. New York: Random
House, pp. 171–78.

Mintz, Ellen
1974   "The Prejudice of Parents." In Who Discriminates
Against Women? Florence Denmark, ed. Beverly
Hills, Calif. Sage, pp. 9–23.

Morgan, Marabel
1976   Total Joy. Old Tappan, N.J.: Fleming H. Revell.

Morgan, Robin
1970   Sisterhood Is Powerful. New York: Random House.

National Commission on
the Observation of Inter-
national Women's Year
1976   "To Form a More Perfect Union." Washington,
D.C.: U.S. Government Printing Office.

O'Neill, William L.
1971   The Woman Movement. Chicago: Quadrangle.

Parker, Richard
1979   "Inflation Can Destroy U.S." Los Angeles Times:
August 19.

Parsons, Talcott, and
Bales, R.F.
1955   Family, Socialization, and Interaction Process.
New York: Free Press.

Reeves, Nancy
1971   Womankind. Chicago: Aldine-Atherton Press.

Roby, Pamela
1977   "Vocational Education." In American Workers in
                              a Full Employment Economy. Submitted to the
                              Sub-committee on Economic Growth and Stabili-
                              zation. Washington, D.C.: U.S. Government
                              Printing Office.

Rosen, Bernard C. and
Aneshensel, Carol S.
1978   "Sex Differences in the Educational-Occupational
                              Expectations Process." Social Forces 57 (September):
                              164–86.

Rossi, Alice S.
1970   "Sex Equality: The Beginnings of Ideology." In
                              Voices of the New Feminism. Mary Lou Thompson,
                              ed. Boston: Beacon Press.

Rowse, Arthur, ed.
1978   Help: The Useful Almanac. Washington, D.C.:
                              Consumer News.

Smith, Ralph, ed.
1980   The Subtle Revolution: Women at Work.
                              Washington, D.C.: The Urban Institute.

Sochen, June
1974   Herstory, Volumes I and II. Sherman Oaks, Calif.:
                              Alfred.

Spock, Benjamin
1970   Decent and Indecent: Our Personal and Political
                              Behavior. New York: The McCall Publishing
                              Company.

Steffensmeier, Daniel J.
1978   "Crime and the Contemporary Woman." Social
                              Forces 57 (December):566–85.

Steinem, Gloria
1970   "What It Would Be Like if Women Win." In
                              Women's Liberation. Michael E. Adelstein and
                              Jean G. Pival, eds. New York: St. Martin's Press,
                              pp. 142–48.

Strong-Boag, Veronica
1977
"Canadian Feminism in the 1920's: The Case of Nellie L. McClung." Journal of Canadian Studies 12 (Summer):58–63.

Spokesman-Review
1980
"Court Ruling on Abortion Ignites Furor." July 1:1.

Sydlaske, Janet
1975
"Gender Classification in the Insurance Industry." Columbia Law Review 15(7).

Tuchman, Gaye
1977
"The Impact of Mass Media Stereotypes Upon the Full Employment of Women." In American Workers in a Fuller Employment Economy. Submitted to the Subcommittee on Economic Growth and Stabilization. Washington, D.C.: U.S. Government Printing Office.

United States Bureau of the Census
1978
Statistical Abstract of the United States. 99th ed. Washington, D.C.: U.S. Government Printing Office.

United States Commission on Federal Paperwork
1977
"Equal Employment Opportunity." Washington, D.C.: U.S. Government Printing Office.

United States Congress
1977
"Women in Business." Report of the Subcommittee on Minority Enterprise and General Oversight of the Committee on Small Business. Washington, D.C.: U.S. Government Printing Office.

Veblen, Thorstein
1953
The Theory of the Leisure Class. New York: Menton Books Edition.

Whitehurst, Carol A.
1977
Women in America: The Oppressed Minority. Santa Monica, Calif.:Goodyear.

Weisstein, Naomi
1970

" 'Kinder, Kuche, Kirche' as Scientific Law: Psychology Constructs the Female." In Sisterhood Is Powerful. Robin Morgan, ed. New York: Random House, pp. 205–20.

Wolfe, Alan
1977

The Seamy Side of Democracy. New York: Longman.

Wolman, Benjamin B.
1974

"On Men Who Discriminate against Women." In Who Discriminates Against Women? Florence Denmark, ed. Beverly Hills, Calif.: Sage.

12

AGE AND AGEISM

Abstract

Consistent with the theoretical position which
organizes this text, we begin our examination of
the problem of aging in North America through an
overview of the *prevailing ideologies*. These include
among others the popular beliefs that the nuclear
family cares adequately for its elders; that aging
brings rapidly deteriorating mental and physical
capabilities; and that retirement represents the
"best years of our lives." Academic theories of aging
also have their ideological aspects. Thus, the major
works in gerontology argue that the relegation of the
aged to less demanding roles benefits the total
society, or that the aging willingly "disengage" to
prepare for their demise and death, or that "modernization" or the industrialization of society automatically displaces and disvalues the elders.
  In the *emergence* phase, we will discover that
aging is a problem without a movement—at least,
without an organized power base consisting of the
older members of society. Social insurance programs providing some minimal benefit for the elders
have either been *institutionalized* in a time of economic crisis and unemployment, or as with the case
of medicare in the United States, have been offered
instead of a comprehensive care system for all citizens. In the latter instance, the entrepreneurial
interests of the medical profession continue to be
maintained. In the 1980s the corporate society's
"solution" to the problem revolves around legal

remedies which address age discrimination. However, such approaches do not address the structural roots of ageism: The corporate economy and its class based system of stratification which leaves those who are old useless and powerless because their labor is declared of no further value.

During a long, hard winter a husband and wife decided they could no longer afford to provide a home for the man's aging father. They prepared a basket of food and instructed their small son to find a blanket for his grandfather to protect him from the cold. The youngster soon returned, but with only half a blanket. Angrily, the father demanded to know why the boy had torn the blanket in two. "Because," replied his son, "I am saving the other half for you."—Russian parable

The term "minority group" has been expanded in recent history. Formerly embracing only racial and ethnic groups, the roster of outcasts was expanded in the 1950s to include women. The most recent social category broadly defined as deficient in power, influence, and economic standing is the aging. The emergence of growing old as a "social problem" was announced informally by the appearance of such terms as "senior citizen" and "older American." Formal recognition has taken the form of political action ranging from hearings to laws and programs. Predictably, in the last few years, courses on aging and related topics such as death and dying have found currency in college and university curricula.

The definition of the older members of a society as a special problem has occurred within a context of powerful social forces. The most commonly found explanation for the upsurge in interest in aging is that the populations of industrial societies are growing progressively older. Such a common demographic contention must be seriously qualified, however, as we shall demonstrate in due course. Beyond this, one must approach this topic with an understanding of the fragmentation of the family together with a pattern of early exit from the labor force. The former signals increasing, though not yet typical, erosion of family support for the elders. The latter cannot be dissociated from the structural question of worker alienation, health, and safety (see Chapter Four).

Academic interest in aging is centered in the field of gerontology. Historically, the study of gerontology has been founded in the functionalist paradigm with its order model of society (see Chapter One). The dominant assumption in gerontology is that the institutions that comprise the existing order are basically sound, legitimated through popular consent. If there is a failing, it is to be found in the unintentional and unfortunate exclusion of a few minority groups from the full promise of the mainstream society. For order theorists the "good life" is here—it only has to be extended to outcast groups such as the aged.

The traditional focus in much gerontology includes an emphasis on *image enhancement*. Thus, the task is to gain acceptance for the aging while seeking to integrate them into the existing order. The very terms "senior *citizen*" and "older *American*" are cases in point. These are attempts to create an imagery of the law-abiding and patriotic who have been somehow lost or overlooked rather than systematically excluded. Further, there appears an overriding concern with *intimate social and psychological support systems*. The family as a caring network continues to receive major attention, as does the improvement of self-concept particularly through age-specific "activity" programs. A third focus has to do with detailed inquiry into the specific political programs bearing on the old, a concern that might be termed *elderfare*. Finally, gerontology centers on adjustment or *coping*. In this instance, much attention and research are directed toward how the aging cope with physiological change, the traumas of death and personal loss, social change, natural disasters, and institutionalization.

All of the above are important. The aging in North American and other industrial societies do suffer from negative stereotypes. Frequently, they must endure the absence of family support, a degrading sense of uselessness, as well as forced idleness. Admittedly, the older members of society are devoid of power and disproportionately poor, and problems of trauma and change are important as at any time of life. However, a telling criticism of such traditional concerns is that they tend to compartmentalize the issue of aging: separating consequences from causes, personal troubles from public incongruities, and the elderly from those of other exploited groups who suffer lifelong structural exclusion.

To think sociologically requires that we search for connections. We can easily identify an ideology of "ageism" built from negative stereotypes that cast the old as somehow inferior to the young. But the questions remain: What are the origins of such an ideology? Whom or what does it sustain? The family indeed is subject to profound and frequently disrupting forces. The nuclear family as a social unit grows increasingly privatized. Individual families are shattered in great numbers, but the disaffected members frequently find themselves seeking out a new marriage, a reconstituted family. What are the forces that alter and sometimes destroy the family unit and then bring those affected into the same sort of social entity but with different individuals? How do such undercurrents separate out those who in other times and places represent the wisdom to which reverence is due? In like fashion, what are the forces that leave many who have worked a lifetime in poverty and without influence? And precisely with what are the aging expected to cope? *Adjustment assumes a necessary and legitimate set of social conditions.* It is, therefore, the individual who must bear the burden of change. Perhaps attention should be directed toward the inherent contradictions of the social order. Perhaps the problem of aging is not a problem of the aged. Perhaps change is required of the corporate society, not its victims.

Viewpoint

"AGE, CLASS, AND SOCIAL INEQUALITY"*
by James J. Dowd

The personal troubles associated with growing old are experienced earlier and more frequently among those at the bottom of the class hierarchy than among those at the top. This simple observation is not made clear, however, in recent analyses of age stratification that relate age and class only inasmuch as they constitute two distinct means of analyzing social status. Foner and Kertzer (1978), for example, propose to analyze rites of passage and generational succession in terms of "age conflicts and tensions" just as Marx analyzed social change in terms of class conflict. Although the age-stratification literature has contributed much to our understanding of age-related phenomena, we must eventually move beyond the restrictions imposed by this approach and attempt to integrate the concepts of age stratum and social class within a single perspective. In reality, the social world resists such facile categorization as the arrangement of stratification hierarchies in neat, discrete, juxtaposed columns marked "age" and "class"; but it is my contention that the individual experience of growing old and the nature of age relations vary so significantly by social class that there is a need for unified analysis in which both age *and* class are considered.

It is also necessary to integrate the concepts of age stratum and social class when one examines issues that encompass more than the relations and problems of individuals. For example, the problems of inequality of social classes within a particular age stratum (class stratification) and inequality of different age strata (age stratification) involve the same issue; if one talks about inequality in one case, one will have to touch on inequality in the other. This is not to suggest that age stratification and class stratification share similar origins or persist for similar reasons. However, both age strata and social classes are defined by the possession or lack of valued resources and the degree of access to the means of acquiring

*From *Stratification Among the Aged*. Monterey, Calif.: Brooks/Cole Publishing Company, pp. 12–22.

these resources. As a result, membership in a particular age stratum or social class facilitates a certain style of life and world-view.

Interaction patterns are also affected by the stratum or class membership of the actors involved: interaction among people of equal status proceeds from a basis of greater common understanding and is, therefore, potentially less structured than interaction involving actors from different classes or strata. In other words, interaction among status equals is less likely to involve the exercise of *deference.* In studies of social class, the actors involved are usually about the same age; in studies of age stratification, the principal parties are of different ages. However, deference means the same in both cases: one actor (individual or group) defers to the greater power of another. The key element is neither age nor social class but the *power* that one's age and social status confer.

As Dowd suggests in the Viewpoint above, the issue of power is central to the standing of the elders in society. We believe that in North America, the relationship between age and class can best be understood as a logical consequence of the position of labor in corporate society. To be explicit, labor represents simply an element in the cost of production. The term alienation applies here as it describes the arrangements whereby one is unable to influence the conditions of work, but is rather a part of the machinery or the bureaucratic process. It therefore follows that those of the traditional (blue collar) or new (white collar) working class simply carry their disvalued status with them into retirement.

The conditions of retirement are of course more negative because of income shortfall, reflecting the general problem of inequality in corporate order. The observation that members of the owning class or the political, military, and economic elite do not suffer the same loss of standing or resources with age as do retired workers confirms that the problem of aging cannot be separated from the problems of class and power in the United States.

THE PREVAILING IDEOLOGIES

A Family Affair

Before a problem is recognized, a number of ideological symbols or accounts must be discarded. Aging has no standing as a social problem unless it is so defined. One prime ideological barrier to the perception of the aging problem is the master symbol of family responsibility. The conventional wisdom has it that the well-integrated and loving family is the bedrock of social order. It is the fundamental reason for positive achievement and the ultimate social security. The declaration that the care and well-being of the aging are primarily a family affair is especially popular with those who see government programs for the aging as contributors to inflation. Before one decides, however, that the aging are having their needs met by the modern family, it is necessary to evaluate critically the nature of that family.

For many who emphasize the importance of the family in contemporary society, the proper role for those growing old is that of "grandparenting."

> Becoming a grandparent for the first time is a big emotional experience, usually first met in middle age. But if we had more than one child and they married at different times, the appearance of new grandchildren and, eventually, great-grandchildren is an experience covering many years. Welcoming in a new generation is, take it from me, an almost dizzying experience. As I walked out of the hospital that morning of the first grandchild, I knew at last what the word "giddy" means. My feet seemed not quite to touch the ground (Carlson 1977, p. 95).

The Myth of the Modern Family Though many writing formally in the field stop short of enshrining grandparenthood as a "giddy" experience, the virtues of the modern family are extolled by many contemporary gerontologists. Their defense of the nuclear family typically involves the destruction of the historical "myth" of the extended family. According to this "myth," multiple generations lived together as members of a strong and self-sustaining social unit. In this context of mutual support, the old ones enjoyed the respect of the young; contributed their wisdom, experience, and skill; and were essentially secure throughout their lives. Those who attack the "myth," see this portrait as romanticized nostalgia (Puner 1974). They point out that the nuclear (two-generational) family became primary no later than the turn of the century in the United States.

Admittedly, the extended family in the nineteenth century was a crumbling institution. Mumford (1961) and de Beauvoir (1972) clearly document the vicious impact of the Industrial Revolution on family and personal life. Capitalism in Europe had begun to replace a sagging feudal order as early as the twelfth century. Centered in urban areas, this mode of production assumed gigantic proportions with the coming of the machine and the factory system. As people were pulled into the cities from the countryside, an army of industrial workers grew while the number of peasants declined. The factory system ensured the acceleration of the concentration of wealth, the establishment of a wage system, and destitution for the working class. The cities quickly became densely populated warrens of poverty, disease, and death. Similar processes were to occur in turn in the great urban centers of the United States and Canada. Taken together, then, the works of Mumford and de Beauvoir document the relationship of the more intimate circles of social life to economic order. This does not portray the nuclear family as somehow "more solidly based than ever" (Puner 1974, p. 128). For de Beauvoir and Mumford, it appears that the extended family was more victim than myth.

That is not to say that the extended family did exist in its idealized form. Rather, we believe it is more important to address the possibility of mythmaking associated with the *modern nuclear family.* The origin of such mythmaking is to be found in the functionalist interpretation, which is widely accepted in gerontology. Since the nuclear family prevails, it must be *necessary* for the social good; it must contribute in an essential way to the societal equilibrium. The modern family is portrayed as a source of mutual assistance for the aging (Sussman and Burchinal 1962), as the foundation for enduring human relationships (Shanas and Sussman 1977), and as the primary social support system for the elderly (Shanas 1979). We shall question such views in the discussion which follows.

In 1887, Ferdinand Toennies published his classic work, *Gemeinschaft und Gesellschaft.* In it he sought to trace the conversion of social life from the intimate and primary relationships of the *community (Gemeinschaft)* to the impersonal and secondary forms of the *society (Gesellschaft).* With the decline of community, temporary associations born of common and partial interests prevail, the law supplants custom, and the bureaucracy usurps the function of family.

Functionalist gerontologists today hold to a *Gemeinschaft* vision of human association, which accords centrality to the family. However, Toennies was describing the profound structural changes signaling the emergence of the privatized and nuclear family from the Industrial Revolution (1957). This point seems to be lost on those modern gerontologists who cling to the *Gemeinschaft* vision in our social order, where the contract has replaced the handshake and the law has supplanted trust. Those gerontologists who hold to the centrality of the modern family are quick to deny its decline. According to them, the "bureaucracy" and beyond that demon, the larger one of the "state" must never be considered a substitute for the family.

Professional ideology aside, however, to what extent is the nuclear family able to meet the needs of the aging in the area of social support? Has the increasing privatization of the family resulted in the increasing separation of family members? The evidence cited to support the argument that the family continues as a primary system of aid for the elderly is subject to differing interpretations. Shanas (1979a, p. 6) argues that "the proportion of old people living either with a child or living within ten minutes distance of a child has remained fairly constant over 10 years." However, her data show that the figure for this category has in fact declined from 59 percent to 52 percent between 1957 and 1975. In other words, in less than two decades the number of aging persons living with a child or within ten minutes' distance has declined by 7 percentage points. Further, the percentage of the elderly living in the same household had declined from 36 percent in 1957 to 18 percent in 1975, a drop of 50 percent of the total.

Distant and Alone Along these same lines, three older persons in four in 1975 lived in the same household with one of their children or within a thirty-minute distance (Shanas 1979a, p. 6). However, this means that one elder in four does not enjoy this geographical nearness. Specifically, one of every five noninstitutionalized persons over 65 in the United States *does not have living children* (Shanas 1979a, p. 6). In 1957, moreover, 83 percent of parents over the age of 65 saw at least one child during the week before they were interviewed. The corresponding figure for 1975 was 77 percent (Shanas 1979a, p. 6). Functionalist gerontologists and certain family sociologists are fond of the term "intimacy at a distance." By it they mean that the family continues as a support system for the aging even though older people no longer necessarily live in the same household with children or other relatives. We believe the trend data support the observation that the future portends intimacy at a *greater* distance.

In another article, Shanas (1979b, p. 173) argues correctly that "the immediate family of the old person, husbands, wives, and children is the major support of the elderly in time of illness." Once again, what may be true for a majority is not true for a sizable minority. The author again cites survey data showing that one of every four noninstitutionalized persons age 65 and over said he or she had spent one or more days in bed due to sickness *with no help at all.* Furthermore, older women who outlive their spouses are "from two to three times as likely as men to say that no one helped them during their illness" (Shanas 1979b, p. 173). When extrapolated to a population 65 and over of 23.48 million in 1977, this 25 percent amounts to almost 6 million persons who were sick and alone at some time during that year.

It should be noted that when the family is reported as a support system for the elderly, *the basic support person is the spouse* (Shanas 1979b). Such a simple observation has profound implications because when the spouse dies, an increasing number of the elderly live alone.

TABLE 12-1
Persons over 65 Living Alone (Millions)

Year	Number Alone	Total Number 65 and Over	Percent Living Alone
1960	2.9	16.6	17.5%
1970	5.1	20.0	25.4
1977	6.5	23.5	27.6

Source: Compiled from *Statistical Abstract of the United States* 1978, pp. 29 and 50.

One cannot help but be struck by the statistical coincidence revealed by even a casual examination. One elder in four lived alone in 1977. In 1975, one elder in four reported spending one day or more sick in bed with no one to aid. In Canada the data are essentially the same, with nearly 30 percent of the elderly living alone in 1976 (*Statistics Canada* 1976).

We believe the trends point to certain sociological and demographic realities. As older people come to constitute an increasing percentage of the population, as the birth rate declines (from 25.0 per thousand population in 1950 to 14.8 per thousand in 1976), and as the divorce rate continues to grow (ten marriages for every one divorce in 1910 to ten marriages for every five divorces in 1977), the capability of the family to serve as a major support system for the aging will continue to decline (*Statistical Abstract of the United States* 1978, p. 59).

The Over-the Hill Gang

In our theoretical chapter two, a discussion on "blaming the victim" was presented. "Blaming the victim" is to find the source of an individual's predicament in his or her personal shortcomings. This often results in the development of rigid stereotypes used to characterize groups whose conditions represent an embarrassing gap between their expected and actual accomplishments.

Perhaps the harshest type of "blaming the aged victim" is the senility stereotype.

> Senility is an archaic, general term that was used in the past to refer to mental infirmities thought to be the result of aging. We now know that the symptoms formerly associated with aging, and called *senility*, are in fact symptoms of specific, and often treatable diseases (Atchley 1977, p. 33).

In short, senility implies the bumbling and failing return to childhood and is popularly portrayed as a biological consequence of aging. Although vital organs decline along with the ability of the body to withstand disease (immunological deterioration), such obvious changes in no way support the senility argument. To the contrary, biological aging (senescence) varies greatly, not only from one person to another but also from organ to organ and process to process within the same individual. Given such a range, the best evidence is that *chronological age has little value as an indicator of biological age* (Atchley 1977, pp. 33–39).

A more specific aspect of the senility stereotype is the supposed decline in intelligence. Research conducted between the 1930s and the 1950s suggested that mental ability peaks in early adulthood and begins to diminish sometime between the ages of thirty and forty. The reader should not assume however that those past thirty quickly become candidates for the "over-the-hill gang." Contemporary research has termed the relationship between aging and IQ "the myth of the twilight years" (Balties and Schaie 1974). For example, when subjects ranging in age from twenty-one to seventy were tested in 1956 and retested in 1970, the only age-related area of decline was in "visuomotor flexibility." This dimension of intelligence testing involves moving from "familiar to unfamiliar patterns in tasks requiring coordination between visual and motor abilities, such as when one must copy words but interchange capitals with lower-case letters" (Balties and Schaie 1974, p. 35). The other dimensions tested were "crystallized intelligence," which measures the skills gained through education and specific cultural experience; "cognitive flexibility," which gauges one's capacity to move from one way of thinking to another; and "visualization," which seeks to measure the ability to "organize and process visual materials." In these dimensions,

> There is no strong age-related change in cognitive flexibility. For the most important dimensions, crystallized intelligence, and for visualization as well, we see a systematic *increase* in scores for the various age groups, right into old age. Even people over 70 improved from the first testing to the second (Balties and Schaie 1974, p. 36).

The Asexual Elder

Another age-related stereotype involves the supposed decline in sexuality that comes with advancing years. In a society that transforms sexual relationships into a commodity, the Madison Avenue advertising symbols of sensuality are the young. Moreover, there is a fading but lingering belief that sex should be instrumental. In other words, sex is not an end in itself, but rather incidental to reproduction, or strengthening family ties. Thus, when one is no longer young, asexuality follows. The neutering of the aging is a social, psychological, and cultural process, not a biological one. In a hallmark study of human sexuality, Masters and Johnson (1966) found that age is not necessarily a barrier to sexual fulfillment. For the woman, there is some loss of responsiveness with advancing years. However,

> The aging human female is fully capable of sexual performance at orgasmic response levels, particularly if she is exposed to regularity of effective sexual stimulation. . . . There seem to be no physiologic reasons why the frequency of sexual expression found satisfactory for the younger woman should not be carried over into the postmenopausal years. . . . In short, there is no time limit drawn by the advancing years to female sexuality (Masters and Johnson 1966, p. 223).

Male sexual response tends to diminish after age sixty. The researchers declare however that

> There is every reason to believe that maintained regularity of sexual expression coupled with adequate physical well-being and healthy mental orientation to the aging process will combine to provide a sexually stimulative climate within a marriage. This climate will, in turn, improve sexual tension and provide a capacity for sexual performance that frequently may extend to and beyond the eighty-year age level (Masters and Johnson 1966, p. 270).

A Louis Harris poll was conducted in 1975 for the National Council on the Aging. As the following table demonstrates, the public view of "most people over 65" minimizes sexual activity. This view is held not merely by the young, but by the old as well.

TABLE 12–2
Total Public's View of "Most People Over 65"

	Total Public			
	Very	Somewhat	Hardly at all	Not sure
Friendly and warm	74%	24%	1%	1%
Wise from experience	64%	30%	3%	3%
Physically active	41%	46%	11%	2%
Good at getting things done	35%	53%	10%	2%
Bright and alert	29%	55%	14%	2%
Open-minded and adaptable	21%	49%	26%	4%
Sexually active	5%	28%	35%	32%

Source: Louis Harris 1975, p. 47.

Stereotypes of Aging

The development of aging stereotypes occurs in specific contexts. In one thirty-year study of the portrayal of older persons in realistic fiction books for children (1945 to 1975), the researcher found that the social construction of the elderly begins at an early age (Blue 1978). However, Blue reached the conclusion that the literature is neither stereotypic or negative. The composite picture presented is not "negative" in that older persons are presented neither as senile ogres or as modern-day trolls. Perhaps what Blue overlooks is that her findings clearly support the prevailing ideology that the elders become "super grandparents" dispensing sage advice to children. Thus, "the majority of older persons were family members, predominantly grandparents, although some characters (10 percent) were depicted as persons outside the family" (Blue 1978, p. 188). A further finding was that older persons are not typically depicted as workers.

Perhaps more revealing is another study of children's literature that found that only 108 of 656 books even had an elder included in the story (Ansello 1976, 1977). In sum, in children's literature the aging are largely missing. If they are featured, they are kindly grandparents functioning as friends of children. They are generally without visible occupation, and when they do work they represent the lower echelons of the labor force. Once must be careful in the interpretation of stereotypes. At first glance, lauding black people as "good athletes" and "musical" does not appear negative. Frequently, what a stereotype omits is more important than what it may include. Just as there are uncoordinated black people who sing off key, there are other black people who excel in many walks of life. In like fashion, "grandparenting" may not appear negative unless, of course, that's about all there is for the aged to do.

Other myths of the elders can be more briefly overviewed. One common assertion is that older people become rigid or "set in their ways." Maas and Kuypers (1974) in a longitudinal study of 142 Californians over a period of four decades found no "narrowing," but rather a continuation of basic personality traits. A study with similar focus found the aging willing to use a computer center placed in a retirement hotel. Some 70 percent of those involved in the project saw it to be a valuable device for solving relevant problems (Danowski and Sacks 1976).

Unemployment of the Elderly

A final commonplace stereotype clearly benefits the continuation of one major property of the corporate system: the devaluation of workers and potential workers. Unemployment has been a chronic and continuous problem in the corporate society since the Industrial Revolution. *Work in the existing order is not a human right;* rather labor becomes an element in the cost of production. Holding down the cost of production may be achieved through the substitution of machines for human labor. Beyond this, marked conditions that threaten profits frequently lead to layoffs. And finally, because the corporate system is based on private decisions directed toward narrow interests, the public planning and programs required to educate and train each invaluable human resource will be less than effective.

The problem of unemployment may be distorted, but it cannot be denied. Its dimensions threaten to bring the corporate system into question and thus demand an "explanation." One way of legitimating unemployment is to "blame the victim." Thus the unemployed person is portrayed as having one or more of the following deficiencies: lacking in ambition, untalented, unskilled, untrained, inexperienced, undereducated, over-educated. In the case of the aging, the precise form of victim-blaming is that of "decline in productivity." Thus the "old blood" exits through the back door to make room for the "new blood" demanding entrance. Like education, age functions as a "gatekeeper" for the labor force.

Ideologies change, however, with historical conditions. As noted in Chapter Eleven, the image of women as workers underwent radical alteration during the Second World War. During this same time frame, it also became necessary to employ retired workers in the aircraft industry in California. A study of such workers found them more stable, less prone to accidents, and less subject to absenteeism when compared with younger workers (McFarland 1973). Other research conducted by the National Council on Aging and the Department of Labor confirms that older workers are at least equal if not superior to their younger counterparts in both the quality and quantity of work (U.S. Congress, House Select Committee on Aging 1977).

The Best Years of Our Lives

An obsession with the measurement of happiness abounds in the gerontological literature. When those who formally study aging attempt to assess or measure the "happiness syndrome," they do so most frequently by means of a survey. A sample of a population of elders is requested to respond to questions bearing on "satisfaction" with life in general or specific dimensions of it such as work, health, community service. Attempting to assess intangibles like satisfaction and morale, euphoria and joy by asking people about them seems plausible enough. Such an approach forces us to accept whatever a research chooses to define as happiness or satisfaction, and to regard whatever answers are given by the aging as *reality*.

While we do not dismiss the importance of such inquiry, there are perhaps other measures of well-being that flow from different assumptions. Suppose one prefers to study the question of the well-being of the elders as a matter of *objective reality* rather than subjective responses. If we assume, for example, that well-being can be defined by health, economic security, access to medical care, availability of work, length of life, and so on, then we would study these areas and infer that the answers to these questions bear on the "happiness" syndrome. Unfortunately, in gerontology as in the broader society a major emphasis appears placed on belief systems and the power of positive thinking. Whether the topic is transcendental meditation, charismatic religion, or self-improvement seminars, each of these shares with much research in the social sciences the contention that "happiness is a state of mind." This bias when applied to the aging in North American society is perhaps best expressed in the cliché: "You're as young as you feel."

The obsession with "happiness" pervades corporate culture and emerges as a master perceptual symbol that shapes how we define the "problem" of aging. It is important to understand the implications of this symbol for the period known generally as "retirement." Despite what the objective indicators may show in the way of planned human obsolescence, the corporate message is clear: old age can be golden if you only believe. Thus Clairol argues "You're not getting older; you're getting better"; and books are written on how to *enjoy* retirement. The focus is on individual talents and resources. Such an emphasis on self-reliance as the source of "happiness" is a common ideological theme.

If the logic of the marketplace is to be believed, there must be an enormous demand for "how to be happy" answers. The simple prescription that one will find a golden age through perseverance, hard work, planning, and all that goes into "self-reliance" is an appealing one, especially if this provides a diversion from the not so pleasant.

> Escape into fantasy helps to make a dismal reality tolerable, especially as long as the prospect of hope is justified. The same holds true when a hard-working middle-aged man or woman dreams about early retirement. It is quite natural to hope for a better future when the present becomes too difficult to bear, and when the monotony of life takes away the joy of living. As the years go by, and the date set for the planned retirement comes closer, however, most of these dreamers begin to reconsider and postpone as long as they can the date that was supposed to bring them freedom (Knopf 1975, p. 54).

Retirement and Income The "self-reliance will make you happy after retirement" message makes what happens to the elders a personal trouble rather than a public issue. Such an individualistic message functions in the support of the corporate system by blaming the elderly for their problems. However, the objective reality of retirement suggests we look at other indicators. For example, one survey found that *the most important factor* related to whether or not the elderly person reported himself or herself as happy was *income* (U.S. Congress Select Committee on Aging 1977, p. 87). In 1977, 3.2 million persons, 14.1 percent of those age 65 and over, lived below the official government poverty line in the United States[1] (*Statistical Abstract of the United States* 1978, p. 472). It is little wonder that in a recent Harris poll (1975) 40 percent of the public 65 and over reported as a *very or somewhat serious problem* "not having enough money to live on."

In a nationwide study of retired people in Canada, only 25 percent of

---

[1] As demonstrated in Chapter Three, "Official" poverty lines represent meager income indeed.

the sample rated their income as adequate (Ciffir et al. 1976). In 1975 the average income of families with a head 65 or over was $10,171, about two-thirds of the national average ($16,613), while the unattached elderly made $4,138 compared with $6,595 for all unattached individuals) *Statistics Canada* 1979). If we go beyond the average Canadian income and look at the median by age group, we find an even worse situation. In 1975 average family income for the 65–69 group was $12,149 while the median was $9,421; for those over 70 years old the average was $9,384 while one-half of these families earned $6,550 or less (*Statistics Canada* 1978, p. 268). The longer one survives, the tougher it gets.

Postretirement Survival   Another objective measure of the "golden years" can be gleaned from the survival rates after retirement. In one study, the mortality rate of early retirees (age 62–64) among rubber tire workers in the United States was compared with that of late retirees from the same occupational category. The mortality rates were higher than would be expected in a working group apparently because many were forced to retire early due to poor health. For normal retirees (age 65), mortality rates for the first two years were lower than normal. However, during the third and fourth years of retirement, the mortality rate was greater than expected. Individuals not in good health as well as persons of *lower socioeconomic status* were more likely to die during their first three years of retirement (Haynes et al. 1978). Unsafe work takes its toll in occupational accidents and disease.

Another tragic finding is that work exclusion also appears to lower the survival rate. For example, the suicide rate in the United States was 12.5 per 100,000 population in 1976. For *males 65 years and older*, the suicide rate was 37.3 per 100,000, by far the highest for any group in the country (*Statistical Abstract of the United States* 1978, p. 76). In Canada, the aging population has one of the highest rates of suicide; however, the rates for young people are increasing more rapidly than for the elderly. This might be explained by the fact that more of the elderly are becoming institutionalized and, as one report notes,

> Those who work in these institutions are understandably shy about reporting self-inflicted deaths occurring under their care (Boldt 1976, p. 282).

Nonetheless, in 1974 the leading age group for suicides was 70–76 year-old males with a rate of 35 per 100,000, compared with the next highest at 31 per 100,000 for the 20–24 and 50–54 year-old groups (*Statistics Canada* 1977, p. 77). Retirement is seen as a major factor in the suicide scenario (Miller 1978).

Stereotypes that blame the victim and master ideological systems that direct attention toward individual and family while romanticizing the "golden years" deny or downplay aging as a social problem. The serious thinker who moves past such myths will encounter both formal academic evaluations (theory) and other informal conventional interpretations that distort the problem.

Disengagement

Scholarly recognition of the problem of aging includes several formal theories. According to Cumming and Henry (1961), "disengagement" theory accounts for the particular place the elders come to occupy in societies in general. Disengagement occurs on three dimensions: (1) In the physical sense, the process refers to the diminishing sphere of life activities. (2) Psychologically, such withdrawal means an acceleration of egocentrism, an emphasis on the subjective world of feeling and memories. (3) Finally, disengagement has a social dimension that describes a "mutual withdrawal" between the elders and others. Supposedly, such a process benefits both the elders and the society in which they live.

As a functionalist theory based on the order paradigm, disengagement finds the silver lining in social events that critics would urge be changed. Accordingly "slowing down" is necessary for those whose biological capabilities are in decline. This signifies acceptance of the realities of old age: diminished competence and declining energies. As "adaptation," such a process readies one for the inevitability of death and renders the old healthier and happier than they would be if they struggled to remain "active." The equilibrium of the social order is thus preserved as important social functions and responsibilities are passed on to the young.

The assumptions of necessity and reciprocal benefit can be challenged. Disengagement theory makes a case for the universal "putting out to pasture" of the aged. Cross-cultural evidence, however, paints quite a different portrait. Leo Simmons (1945) examined the place of the aged in seventy-one "primitive" societies and there is nothing in his data to support universal disengagement. In specific studies, Shelton (1965) found that among the West African Ibo, the aging did not withdraw from their culture, nor did their culture withdraw from them. Accordingly, there was a virtual absence of what is sometimes called senility in Western societies. Missing, too, were the feelings of uselessness, forced idleness, and estrangement admitted to by a substantial number of the American aged. Similar findings were noted by Palmore in a study of the aging in Japan (1975). In Japan, the elders are more integrated into their social order than is the case in Western industrial societies. Among the older Japanese, the more active are healthier and report greater life satisfaction. Such a finding is also counter to what the "withdrawal" proponents argue.

Modernization and the Aging

Cowgill and Holmes (1972) account for the condition of the aging in terms of the *modernization* of society. Just as technology in a general sense has been accused of stripping the worker of meaning, the same forces supposedly shatter the esteem accorded to experience.

> Modern society is compartmentalized. Whereas the family once encompassed practically all the institutionalized patterns people needed in order to achieve their goals, we now have a great many relatively autonomous institutions. One's positions in one institution are no longer necessarily related to one's positions in other institutions (although they still tend to be). This trend means that being the head of a large family no longer carries with it a large measure of economic power in the local community. Elders rarely have significant influence on economic decisions and policy (Atchley 1977, pp. 234–35).

The position is straightforward. With industrialization, the family is no longer the economic center of production and distribution. With modernization, the experience of age is replaced by the more specialized knowledge of the "expert." As nations "develop" into industrial centers, a fragmented division of labor emerges that subordinates the worker to the machine and disvalues craft experience and mastery. Taken together, such forces result in the forced exclusion of the aging from society's mainstream.

According to this particular evaluation, modernization produces another "problem" of the elders in the clear sense of increased longevity. Thus, industrialized societies can be expected to have a relatively high proportion of older members because of medical and nutritional advantages.

Recent estimates of the proportion of aged in the population show France and the United Kingdom with 14 percent, Sweden with 15 percent, the United States with 11 percent, and Canada having approximately 9 percent of its population 65 years or older (*Statistics Canada* 1979). Ironically, as the number and proportion of the aging population increases, the status of the elders decreases. The aging members of industrial society are both the beneficiaries and victims of social change. As the former, they enjoy increased life-span. As the latter, they have no productive place.

In agricultural "folk societies," older people often possess property rights in land. This endows them with a form of security and influence. Because such societies emphasize heritage and ceremony, the elders, who can be expected to know the rituals and lore, will be accorded prestige. Especially in preliterate societies, the older members are the cisterns of knowledge, the transmitters of the oral history that forms the social bond. "Folk societies" (Redfield 1941) also provide the aging with a continuous and productive economic role. *Retirement is a consequence of the modernization process.*

With the development of the industrial society, the elders most frequently reside in separate households and provision for the aging is transferred from the family to the State. Given the loss in both economic and familial status, the decline in leadership roles for the aging is predictable. Those whose past labor laid the foundation for the present order become expendable, acquiring the dubious status of a *minority group.*

Cowgill and Holmes conclude their cross-cultural argument with a statement on values

> It is inevitable also that position of the aged should be relative to the dominant values of the society. *A value system which emphasizes ego development and individualistic achievement places the older person at a disadvantage as compared with a value system which submerges the individual in the group which in turn provides security for dependent or incapacitated members.* In Western society, the Puritan Ethic has tended to stress the work role and to encourage individual striving within a competitive situation (1972, p. 12).

There remain two central criticisms of this account that require examination. The first has to do with the tendency of modernization theories to identify the problem of the aging as a consequence of *social change.* The second concerns the familiar tendency in sociology to find cultural explanations (such as the puritan or Protestant ethic) while ignoring the structural properties of a corporate social order.

Social Change and The Elderly   No one can deny the importance of change. It is certainly true that the elders have faced a redefinition of role with the coming of the industrial society. However, *technological growth does not in and of itself determine the expulsion of the aging from positions of economic and political importance.* The application of science to human tasks may indeed lighten the burden of human labor. One possibility most certainly is an increase in leisure time. However, leisure need not be reserved for the final chapter of life, when it may assume the nature of forced retirement. The leisure-time potential of technology has not been used to shorten the workday or workweek in the recent past. Tearing down the legal and psychological supports of retirement means doing away with not only the laws and policies, but also the definition of advancing age as "useless." Such an achievement bears the prospect of providing full- and part-time work options for the elders, depending only on such vital questions as health. The reentry of those excluded from the labor force might signal the increase of leisure time for younger workers.

We must examine certain constraining properties of the corporate economic order. First, an increase in the labor force and a subsequent reduction in the work week carries with it the specter of loss in pay. This constitutes a threat to workers whose wages are already eaten away by inflation. Further, any increase in the work force necessitates an increase in the cost of training workers. Perhaps these problems may be resolved within the context of a social order committed to human actualization for the many rather than profit maximization for the few. If we assume that work is basic to human beings, then its availability commands a greater share of our resources. If work is only an element in the cost of production, if it is bound up in a wage system that calls for reducing wage payments as a means of increasing profits, then wage labor will not be available for many (unemployment) and *meaningful* work typified by independent responsibility and control may be absent for all (alienation).

A Cultural Root to the Elderly's Plight? Attributing social problems to what might be termed loosely the "modernization/industrialization/ change" syndrome is paralleled by cultural forms of explanation. Cowgill and Holmes may well be correct in identifying individualistic values as central to the exclusion of the aging. However, to find the origin of such values in the puritan ethic represents a return to customs of the past and a corresponding deemphasis of the material conditions of the present. Individual achievement, privatization, and the fragmentation of social life are not related to Protestantism per se. The Massachusetts Bay Colony appears to have been a community with great solidarity. Its members undertook hard work not merely to demonstrate obedience to the will of God, but to survive. "Shove thy neighbor" is not to be found in the sermons of the noted Protestant John Calvin. This shibboleth along with the imperatives of growth, expansion, concentration, and elimination of the "unfit" seems to flow logically from the political-economy of advanced capitalism.

Palmore (1975) cites the case of Japan to support the argument that culture can override the material realities of economic and social structure. He notes that the condition of the elders in this highly industrialized nation is one of respect and esteem. Thus, the "Oriental tradition of respect for elders" has supposedly prevented "a major decline in the status and integration of the aged despite industrialization" (Palmore 1975, p. 4). While it is important not to understate the impact of culture, the Japanese experience with capitalism is as yet not long enough to furnish conclusive cross-cultural evidence on the question of aging and esteem. One must keep in mind that the political-economy of industrial capitalism originated only recently in Japan with its defeat in the Second World War. The United States brought the Japanese into its own increasingly global economic camp and, given the realities of postwar relations, assumed the enormous expense of military defense, thus freeing its former enemy of the waste associated with what Seymour Melman terms "Pentagon Capitalism" (1970). However, the impact of economic changes wrought by the Japanese version of the corporate social order suggests that the material conditions of the elders will be affected.

> In a recent white paper issued by the Ministry of Health and Welfare on "Social Security for a Society with a High Proportion of Senior Citizens," the Japanese government compares its performance to that of foreign countries. . . . When comparing total social security expenditures as a percentage of national income, Japan spends 20% compared to 30% in Sweden, 20% in the Federal Republic of Germany, and 15% in the United States and the United Kingdom.
> . . . With the percentage of persons over 65 expected to increase from the current 8% to 14% by the year 2000, Japan cannot much longer afford to start paying welfare pensions at age 60. The white paper proposed that eligibility be raised to age 65 and that more jobs be made available to older people (Nusberg 1978a, pp. 16–17).

Forced Retirement: Society's Burden As we shall see later, forced retirement in the United States as well as in Japan has come under increasing criticism. The reasons appear to have little to do with respect for the aging but rather concern for the increasing cost of support. This contradiction has produced the suggested resolution of delayed retirement. However, we propose that to the extent such a solution is implemented in the corporate type of social order, to that extent a new contradiction will emerge. The reentry of older workers may create greater unemployment for the younger marginal members of the work forces in both societies. Further, the paternal relationship between Japanese corporations and their employees may be shaken. If so, the assurance of virtual life-time employment would then begin to falter. Perhaps more important than the actual impact on unemployment rates for marginal workers will be the scapegoating potential of the graying of the work force. It is common today in North American society to find unemployed and unpromoted males attributing their plight to the increasing number of women in the work force, together with the mythological advantages of "affirmative action." Blaming older workers may join the blaming of women and other minorities as ideological diversion. Perhaps it is more to the point to question the nature of an economic order that does not make rational and planned use of the talents and potential of all the people.

Although industrialization constitutes a paramount problem for the elders, there are cross-cultural examples that show that industrialized societies are indeed capable of providing improved services for the aging. One precondition may well be a national health system that provides care on the basis of medical need rather than class standing. In Sweden all hospital patients receive their services with no "out-of-pocket" costs. Costs for consultation with dentists or physicians, as well as paramedical treatment and drugs, are low. For example, individuals pay $3.00 for appointments with physicians, 25 percent of the cost of preventive visits to dentists, up to one-half the cost of dental service for the first $400, and 25 percent of the amount above that level. Paramedical treatment prescribed by a physician costs $1.50. There is no cost for a prescription for life-saving drugs needed to control chronic disease. Other prescriptions cost $4. The Swedish health system is financed by contributions by the State (15 percent), employers (8 percent of payroll), and the self-employed (8 percent of earned income) (Nusberg 1978b, p. 3). One distinctive service for the old in Sweden is a highly organized home-care system featuring "home samaritans." The growth of this service has been phenomenal: "from 11,000 samaritans providing 8 million hours of service in 1960 to some 60,000 providing 45 million hours of service in 1972." Typically recruited from the ranks of middle-aged women, samaritans provide the services necessary to keep many of the Swedish aging from becoming long-term care patients. To remain at home means further improvement in the quality of life for older citizens (Bozzetti 1977).

By 1972, all provinces in Canada and the two territories (Northwest and Yukon) were participants in the federal cost-sharing medical plan. This essentially covers the entire population for all required medical services plus a limited range of oral surgery. Only service not medically required has a dollar limit or is excluded completely. While there are some problems with this system in utilization fees and coverage, such a national health plan covers 99 percent of the eligible population and provides the elderly with a minimum care level unavailable in the United States (*Statistics Canada* 1978–79, pp. 199–204).

Ideologies such as "ageism" do not simply float in limbo, creating false pictures and destroying accurate communication. There is rather a method in this madness. Ageism at one and the same time justifies the forced exclusion of the elders from meaningful political, economic, and familial roles while it restricts the expectations of those who enter later life. It appears to be less expensive and not so disturbing to challenge individual attitudes rather than institutional-based ideology.

In a social order where productive workers are disvalued, it is perhaps illogical to expect that retired workers will escape status loss. In the corporate society, the economic function of production is joined by another vital function, that of consumption.

> Most older people are living on inadequate incomes, and obviously they cannot buy things when they have no money. On the average, older people spend far less for goods and services than younger people do, and are less likely to spend beyond their incomes. . . .
>
> Very little attention has been paid to the older person as a consumer. Ad agencies have not yet come to view the older person as a significant market. Aside from aspirin, laxative, denture adhesive, and iron tonic commercials, few appeals are aimed directly at older people (Atchley 1977, p. 239).

Retired workers and their dependents received over $45 billion in social security payments in the United States in 1976. However, the average monthly benefit for retired workers was only $222.37. For those 65 and over, 8.0 percent of older families headed by a man were below the poverty level and 14.4 percent of such families headed by women were "offically" poor. For "unrelated individuals" (typically widowers and widows), 25.9 percent of the men and 31.5 percent of the women were living below the poverty line (*Statistical Abstract of the United States* 1978, pp. 340, 341). Though the sum total of money spent by the aging may appear large, it goes largely for basic necessities. The elderly spend a higher proportion of their income on food and shelter. For example, in 1974 unattached younger individuals in Canada spent 37 percent of their budget on food and shelter while the elderly spent 53 percent (*Statistics Canada* 1979). Those living on fixed income after retirement will not likely obtain installment loans, nor are they large purchasers of "durable goods" such as major appliances and automobiles. Rather, the elders spend for goods and services necessary to survival and thus become economic pariahs, nonconspicuous consumers, in a growth society.

The support of the corporate economy requires the artificial creation of needs (via advertising) and the adding of value to nonessential products. For example, the private automobile is fundamental to the North American economic order, given the power, wealth, and jobs associated with the petroleum-automotive alliance. As consumers, the aging do not constitute a significant market for the automobile. A recent survey conducted in Philadelphia on the transportation needs of older Americans found that only 11 percent drove their own cars, 12 percent used Senior Center transportation, 12 percent were dependent on someone's volunteering to drive them to their destination, 13 percent walked, 7 percent did not travel at all, and 39 percent made use of public transportation (Stirner 1978, p. 207). A shoddy system of public transportation may bring happiness to the stockholders and managers of the private transport industry, but it represents a form of age discrimination.

EMERGENCE

Phillippe Aries argued in *Centuries of Childhood* (1962) that the creation of the status and role of "child" awaited the coming of industrial capitalism and the privatization of the family. Prior to such historical development, children functioned as "little adults." We must also point out that when technological change made child-labor incompatible with productivity growth, child labor legislation followed. This confirmed in law a special status for children. Similarly, the coming of industrial society has brought the twentieth-century development of "retirement" and its official confirmation in law. Thus, the designation of youth and the aged as distinctive social categories is a product of historical changes in economic relationships.

The number of persons 65 and over in the United States has grown slowly but steadily over the past two decades. In 1960, the 16.6 million "official" elders constituted 9.2 percent of the total population. By 1970, some 20 million aging represented 9.9 percent of the total. For 1977, the corresponding figures were 23.5 million, making up 10.9 percent of the population. Using a base year of 1976, the United States Bureau of the Census projects that by 1985, those 65 and over will number 27.3 million; by 1990, 29.8 million; and by the year 2000, 31.8 million persons. The percentage of the total population represented by those 65 and over is of course dependent on fertility, mortality, and net immigration rates. Assuming a slight drop in mortality, an annual net immigration of some 400,000, and a fertility rate of 2,700 lifetime births per 1,000 women, the United States population would number 238.9 million in 1985, 254.7 million in 1990, and 282.8 million in the year 2000. Using these projections, persons 65 years and over will respectively constitute 11.4 percent, 11.7 percent, and 11.2 percent of the total population for those base years. Should the fertility rate drop to "replacement level," (2,100 lifetime births per 1,000 women), then the aging would comprise a larger percentage of the total population. (Compiled from data in the *Statistical Abstract of the United States* 1978, p. 8.) *Thus it is the reduction of the birthrate rather than simple longevity that is expected to account primarily for the "graying of America."* In Canada in 1976 the elderly constituted 8.7 percent of the population (*Statistics Canada* 1979). The official projected population statistics show this group increasing to 11.8 percent by 2001. (*Statistics Canada* 1978, p. 155). This is explained by declining birth rates, large immigration in this century, and increased life expectancy.

However, the "aging problem" at this historical moment *goes beyond simple increase in population.* The contention that the problems of the aging will dominate the national scene over the last two decades of the twentieth century is based by some on the assumption of increasing numbers, and, consistent with pluralist logic, increasing political influence. One recent Canadian study of the aged begins with this statement:

> Increasing proportions of the elderly will represent a larger fraction of the voting population. They will command more public attention and will exert a stronger influence on economic, political and social policies in the future (*Statistics Canada* 1979).

We believe that power bears no necessary relationship to numbers (witness the historical condition of women in the North American society). We shall have to look to other sources to understand the "coming of aging" in North America.

Aging: An Issue Without a Movement Unlike the other problems presented in this text, the aging question represents an issue without a movement. This is not to deny the existence of loosely knit organizations that attempt to lobby on behalf of the elders. In the United States the National Retired Teachers Association in concert with the American Association of Retired Persons represented a combined membership of some 11 million persons in 1978. However, these organizations together with earlier political action groups primarily concerned with the problems of the aging have been ineffective in influencing progressive legislation directly. Although attributing a "sensitizing" role to such organizations historically, Atchley (1977) and Carlie (1969) agree that the "banner" was held aloft by other groups, such as unions and political parties. Atchley subscribes to the popularly held *contractual solution* in accounting for this sensitizing influence. He asserts that it is possible to attribute the passage of social security and Medicare legislation if not to direct political action on the part of the aging, then to their increased power in the voting population.

The belief that the disadvantaged can rectify their political and economic liabilities through the vote is a common assumption of corporate ideology. The 1976 presidential campaign in the United States suggests that the Carter campaign demonstrated little in the way of systematic appeal to the "senior vote" (Riemer and Binstock 1978). As with all presidential campaigns since 1960, the Democratic Party established a Senior Citizens Desk charged with gaining support from older Americans. Since those 65 and over represented some 15 percent of the vote in the 1972 election, this age cohort was seen by those operating the desk as a possible kingmaker. However, while Carter accused the Republican party and its candidates of "callous" and "disgraceful" records on the needs of the elders, the evidence suggests that the concerns of the aging as well as the potential of their vote did not receive high priority with the Democrats either. To be specific, the Senior Desk received the lowest amount of funding ($6,500) of any of the eleven campaign desks, and was one of two without paid staff. Further, analysis of transcripts of the two nationally televised Carter–Ford debates, which were designed to give the candidates maximum opportunities to address national issues, reveal that any appeal to the specific issues of the aging was well-disguised.

Can You Spare a Dime?

Apart from the ideology of the vote are the issues of social insurance and Medicare. The Social Security Act of 1935 was passed during America's worst depression. The spectacle of steep economic downturn had occurred periodically prior to 1929 indicating that crisis is a continuing part of the structure of the corporate system. However, historical dramatists point with some sense of awe to the stock market crash of October 24, 1929. Unemployment began a terrifying upward spiral from that autumn to the spring of 1933. In March 1929, the estimates ranged from nearly 3.25 million to somewhat over 4 million workers without jobs. A year later, the figures had doubled. And by March 1932, some 11.25 million, to 12.5 million persons were unemployed. The height of unemployment was reached in March 1933, when more than 16 million workers were on the streets (Webbink 1941, pp. 250–251).

Those who were "lucky" enough to retain their jobs suffered hardships of another variety. In the last quarter of 1930, the first evidence that hourly wages were to drop appeared. Manufacturing wages slipped from the 59 cents per hour average in 1929 to approximately 58 cents. The trend continued through 1931, with the wage loss amounting to an average of 3 cents per hour. The average weekly wage declined from $28.50 in 1929 to $22.64 in 1931. The average work week dropped from 48 hours in 1929 to 38 in the last four months of 1931 (Commons 1935, p. 92).

Many who managed to find "employment" were selling apples and shining shoes. Shine "boys" ranged in age from sixteen to seventy, and the streets were filled with peddlars, hawking everything from rubber balls to neckties. Selling newspapers became a fiercely competitive business, and the number of vegetable hawkers in the first two years of the Thirties increased by 40 percent in New York City. The age-old custom of shirking jury duty disappeared. In 1932, the Hall of Jurors in the Criminal Courts Building was overflowing with prospects whenever court was in session. Jurors received $4 for every day they served.

One of the most striking indicators of change in the American society centered around a remarkable offer made by the Soviet Union in 1931. In need of skilled workers to accelerate industrial development, Russia offered 6,000 jobs to the unemployed of depression-ridden America. Even though the acceptance of such work meant going to Russia and being paid in rubles, over 100,000 applications for the 6,000 jobs were received. Some 85 percent of the applicants were citizens of the United States; some 60 percent were foreign born, most of them immigrants from Eastern Europe (Perdue 1975).

The Roosevelt years prior to America's entrance into World War II are of central importance to those seeking to grasp the social reality of the Great Depression. The commonplace view that FDR's "New Deal" terminated the economic ordeal of the Hoover years is without basis in fact.

The new leader and his advisors did initiate far-reaching "reforms" that were to leave a lasting imprint on American economic arrangements. These were successful inasmuch as they relieved somewhat the personal distress of the times and effected a partial recovery of the economy. However, some four years into the New Deal and early in Roosevelt's second term, the business cycle took another slide. This "depression within a depression" held sway until about the middle of 1938, when the general economy showed some further improvement. Even at that point, the Great Depression was still in evidence. The record of industrial production set in 1929 was not reached again until 1940, when the outbreak of

World War II in Europe provided some impetus for American factories. Still, it is critical to note, that even in 1940, over 7 million workers, approximately 14 percent of the work force, were unemployed (Shannon 1960, p. x). The dream of "full employment" and the end to the long night of depression were to await the coming of the Second World War.

Social Security   Social security was one of a number of federally sponsored programs intended to spur the recovery of an economic system in chaos. It was a single component of a larger program designed to conserve a threatened social order. Within this particular era, "old age insurance" was coupled with a host of other pension and work programs to provide a "structure of economic security" (Skidmore 1970). The issue was not one of responding to the potential voting power of the aging. Rather, the larger question concerned the political ability of the corporate system to spare large segments of the population the threat or reality of pauperism in later life.

The question of social security and Medicare legislation will be analyzed in detail in the next section of this chapter. However, it is vital to understand Medicare in the larger context of health insurance. Social security in any form was late in coming to the United States. What is striking, however, is that a severe depression proved to be the necessary catalyst for this program. Even when it was instituted, the program had a glaring hole. No provision was made for systematic, publicly supported health care (Feingold 1966). As early as 1939, Senator Robert Wagner of New York introduced a bill designed to establish a health program on a national basis. It was strongly opposed by the American Medical Association in the opening round of a protracted campaign by medical entrepreneurs and the private insurance industry of the United States to prevent the establishment of some form of national medical care (Skidmore 1970).

> The attitude of opposition by the American Medical Association had begun as far back as 1920, and with the renewal of the issue in the 1930s, the association's pronouncements came to be characterized by extreme language frequently linking any suggestion not to the liking of organized medicine to socialism and communism and even specifically to the Soviet Union. The continuous, unified, massive campaign, however, arose during the 1940s as did organized medicine's strategic pattern of opposition. Before this time, the opposition had taken varying forms, apparently as disconnected responses to events rather than as a concerted effort to halt a general tendency toward a governmental program (Skidmore 1970, p. 77).

As Skidmore details, a series of attempts at national health care were thwarted. In 1943, 1945, and 1947, a succession of bills were introduced, all with the same sponsors (Wagner-Murray-Dingell). All would have established a system of medical benefits and hospitals paid for by the same method used to finance the social security system: a tax on employers and employees. The surgeon general would have established a fee schedule and regulated patient caseload. The National Physicians Committee cast the issue as one of "human rights as opposed to slavery." In 1949, a similar program was backed by the Truman Administration. It was opposed by the AMA, which had collected a $3.5 million "war chest" to mount a public relations campaign directed by the firm of Whitaker and Baxter. As a consequence, some 55 million pieces of literature proclaiming the evils of "socialized medicine" reached 100 million Americans. In 1952, an AMA "front" organization called the "National Professional Committee for Eisenhower and Nixon" worked to elect an administration opposed to national health insurance. The record of opposition continued despite the escalating cost of medical care. Finally, in 1960 Congress adopted the Kerr-Mills Act as an amendment to the Social Security Act. This legislation was designed to provide grants to the states to provide some assistance for the indigent, *and the aged who were "medically indigent."* Kerr-Mills had AMA support.

> This support was the first sign of a crack in the solid front presented by organized medicine against any extension of governmental involvement in either health care or its economics. The crack was very small, but it ultimately widened to include an intensive AMA effort in support of its own "eldercare" program, which also called for federal support (Skidmore 1970, p. 82).

Also in the early 1960s, inflation in the cost of medical care and the fear of political action spurred the private health insurance industry to initiate drives to increase the enrollment of those *sixty-five and over.* In July 1963, however, the Senate Subcommittee on the Health of the Elderly issued a report demonstrating that 75 percent of the elders in America did not have the degree of insurance coverage termed adequate by the American Hospital Association (that which would pay 75 percent of hospital-stay costs). In 1964, President Lyndon Johnson committed the administration to a health insurance program for *older Americans.* "Medicare" for the aged was to be financed through the social security system. As the question of national health care for all had been drastically narrowed to include only some relief for the aging, the cause attracted broad-scale political support. Even the AMA was amenable to federal participation in the form of grants to pay the private insurance premiums of the older citizens whose incomes were insufficient to permit medical coverage. "Medicare" was passed and signed into law on July 30, 1965 (Skidmore 1970, pp. 75–95).

A careful reading of the historical record makes clear that Medicare legislation was in no sense a reflection of the voting power of older Americans. To the contrary, Medicare emerged as a vastly restricted alternative to much more comprehensive health insurance for the whole people. Given that this substitute required three decades of political deliberation and has forestalled further national health insurance in the United States over fifteen years at this writing, Medicare stands as a triumph for the private insurance industry and the medical entrepreneurs of the corporate society. In Canada, a comprehensive medical plan was first instituted in the progressive province of Saskatchewan, where the first socialist government in North America was elected in 1944 (Grescue 1980). As earlier noted, by 1972 all provinces had a form of socialized medicine.

With some sense of the historical forces that shaped social security and Medicare, we turn to a recent piece of legislation for the aging in the United States. When it passed the Older American Act of 1978, Congress addressed the issue of mandatory retirement for most workers. Accordingly, mandatory retirement is now absent in the federal Civil Service, while the age for "forced exclusion" in the private sector has been raised to seventy. The only exceptions are workers in occupations where age may be related to performance, such as police officers and fire fighters, high-ranking executives who retire with incomes of $27,000 or more, and tenured university professors. (The latter exemption will expire in 1982.)

One can identify a number of excellent arguments in opposition to mandatory retirement. It constitutes a devastating loss of income for lower echelon wage earners. It is also related to higher mortality rates. And as earlier noted, older workers are not affected by "production senescence" (Nusberg 1978c, pp. 14–15). However, political power is seldom forged from reasonable or philosophical positions. Despite the view in some quarters that mandatory retirement was softened due to the "senior" vote potential, we believe the true reasons involved an emerging contradiction.

The establishment of the social security system in 1935 was *followed* by the institution of a "retirement age," typically 65, for most public and private employees. This was done ostensibly to reduce the rate of unemployment among younger workers (Nusberg 1978c). Though this is an admitted *consequence* of mandatory retirement, it should not be overlooked that such a policy serves to *replace many highly paid older workers with entering wage younger workers.* With the expansion of the social security system over time, a real if inadequate promissory note was issued by the federal government to retiring workers. As Table 12–3 demonstrates, however, the participation of older workers in the labor force has declined dramatically. Whereas in 1960, only 67.3 percent of the male population 65 and over *was not* in the labor force, the corresponding percentage for 1977 was 80.6 percent.

In 1921, nearly two thirds of Canada's elderly *were not* in the labor force, while by 1976 almost 88 percent were so defined. However, the participation rate for elderly women has increased since 1951. This may be in part due to their being more likely single than elderly men (*Statistics Canada* 1979).

The trend toward early retirement with its mounting pressure on the federal social security system was not lost on those in power in the U.S.

In 1956, the Social Security Act was amended to allow wives and female workers to begin receiving actuarially-reduced benefits at 62 years of age. In 1961, the age for male retirees to receive similarly reduced benefits was lowered to 62 and was viewed at least in part as *an anti-recession measure to help contain unemployment among all age groups in the population.* Since that time, the trend in social security retirement has been for earlier retirement at reduced social security benefits. Since 1962, over half the men awarded initial retirement benefits have received reduced benefits. In 1974, 72% of all new awards made to retired workers were reduced benefits (67.3% male, 78.9% female) and age 62 was the overwhelming most common age (U.S. Congress, Select Committee on Aging 1977, p. 9; italics added).

In sum, social security retirement benefits were conceived during the Great Depression. They were amended in 1956 and 1961 to provide reduced benefits for those choosing early retirement. In each case, these benefits were designed partially to solve a *crisis of unemployment.* However, such a strategy of unemployment containment was to become increasingly expensive with early retirement. As long as unemployment continues as a chronic problem, the issue of forced exclusion will remain a no-win contradiction. If the relaxation of mandatory retirement does not succeed in drawing workers back into the labor force, the pressure on retirement systems will continue. "A few years ago, the ratio of workers to social security beneficiaries was 4 to 1; today, the ratio is 3.2 to 1" (U.S. Congress, Select Committee on Aging 1977, p. 46). To the extent that the relaxation of mandatory retirement is successful, the graying of the wage and salary schedules will be defined as a barrier to entry and advancement. Canada at this writing maintains a policy of mandatory retirement at sixty-five years of age.

TABLE 12-3
Persons 65 and Over—Labor Force Participation in the U.S.
(Percentage)

	1960		1970		1977	
	Male	Female	Male	Female	Male	Female
Employed	30.9%	9.9%	26.2%	10.0%	18.0%	8.1%
Unemployed	1.7	.4	1.0	.3	1.3	.4
Not in the labor force	67.3	89.7	72.8	89.7	80.6	91.6

Source: Compiled from the *Statistical Abstract of the United States* 1978, p. 31.

INSTITUTIONALIZATION

As Skidmore (1970) notes, the first modern social welfare system began under Bismarck in Germany in the year 1883. It required the hardships of the Great Depression to bring about the American Social Security Act of 1935. The historical background of this Act may well begin with the White House Conference on the Care of Dependent Children held in 1909. It contained the seeds of social insurance (at least for those widows with dependent children). Conferees suggested that these women's lack of means of support should qualify them for government pensions. Perhaps the most influential work on the topic was I.M. Rubinow's *Social Insurance*, published in 1913. Although this author asserted that the workers' wages were not usually sufficient to provide a savings surplus for old age, such humanistic arguments were largely ignored. The Social Security Act of 1935 was one element of a federal attempt to save a social order. It was not a simple political act of compassion.

When Franklin D. Roosevelt assumed the presidency in 1933, he appointed Frances Perkins as Secretary of Labor and Harry Hopkins as the Federal Emergency Relief Administrator. Both had backgrounds in social work and social reform movements. Perkins was to chair and Hopkins was to be a member of the Committee on Economic Security. This committee's report, released on January 15, 1935, outlined what was to become the "social security system" in the United States. One central ideological feature of the plan and the legislation that followed was its reliance on the private insurance model.

Social Security Modeled on Private Insurance

Those responsible for the execution of state power understood that the preservation of the corporate society required minimizing the extent to which social welfare becomes a truly public issue. Accordingly, old-age benefits did not begin until 1940, some five years after employers and employees began to pay taxes on that part of the social security program designed to be self-financing. (The payments to the blind and to families with dependent children were also elements of the social insurance system and obviously could not follow the private model.) The Administration and Congress agreed that there would be no financing of "retirement benefits" under social security from general tax revenues. Thus, the role of the State was simply one of impartial administrator in a compulsory and contributory retirement system (Skidmore 1970, pp 39–50).

The insurance nature of social security is reflected in its contemporary structure. The system has three trust funds. In addition to the old-age and survivors insurance trust fund, there is a disability insurance trust fund together with a hospital insurance fund. The latter was legislated into existence with Medicare coverage in 1965. In 1977, the combined employer-employee payroll tax rate was 11.7 percent. As a consequence of the 1977 amendments to the Social Security Act, the combined tax rate is to reach 15.3 percent by the year 1990. To keep each fund solvent, continual amendments of the Social Security Act of 1935 are necessary to alter the percentage of the total tax that goes into each of the three trust funds (Campbell 1978, p. 9). The major point, however, is that benefits for the elders remain largely tied to their individual contributions. Important inequities logically emerge. For example, single women experience both age and sex discrimination. First, women have been concentrated historically in low-paying jobs. Further, their work careers have often been interrupted by childbearing. And finally, the widows of deceased pensioners do not receive the full pension based on their husband's earnings.

A System of Inequalities

The individualistic nature of the social security system also had racist implications. Given the disproportionate concentration of minorities in poorer paying jobs, retirement benefits are lower for such disadvantaged groups. Ironically, a system designed to benefit the older person represents a form of institutionalized "ageism." As a general principle, *smaller social security pensions are paid to older retired workers.* The "old old" as a group paid less into the system and so receive less than the more-recent retirees. This is tragic, given the increased health and support needs of this group (Atchley 1977, pp. 128–129).

In 1974, Congress passed the Supplemental Security Income (SSI) program, which replaced a series of federal grants to the states to support services and payment to the poorest of the aged, blind, and disabled. SSI established a baseline for these groups (*Statistical Abstract of the United States* 1978, p. 325). In 1974, that baseline amounted to $146 monthly for older single persons and $239 for older couples, without regard to previous work history (Atchley 1977, p. 133). Federal support of public assistance for the aged, blind, and disabled was thus folded into the social security system.

Supplemental Security Income *adds* the amount necessary to social security benefits based on earned income (if any) to bring the total award to the baseline level. In 1977, some 2.05 million older Americans drew an average payment of $97 from SSI (*Statistical Abstract of the United States* 1978, p. 356). When the meager payment is contrasted with the 2 million eligible recipients, a portrait of economic destitution emerges. As a logical extension of the corporate ideology, the social security system was to modify only the most oppressive conditions of class society while leaving intact a system of structural inequality. Workers found themselves locked into a miserly program financed by a regressive form of taxation. Such inherent problems have not been eliminated.

Table 12–4 depicts the number of beneficiaries and the average benefit for recipients of OASDI (Old Age, Survivors, and Disability Insurance) in the United States in early 1978. The average benefit awarded a retired worker in February 1978 was $243.83 (excluding lump-sum and retro-active payments and adjustments). Further, the average monthly benefit for a retired worker and wife in 1977 was $404 (*Statistical Abstract of the United States* 1978, p. 336). Such figures must be measured against the fact that for eight of ten older Americans, social security is their only significant source of income (Atchley 1977, p. 128).

The historical emphasis on a contributory system reflects the institutionalization of the ideology of individualism. Thus, there are inequities

TABLE 12–4
OASDI Beneficiaries and Benefits: February 1978

	February 1978
Beneficiaries (in thousands)	
Monthly beneficiaries, total	34,137
Aged 65 and over, total	22,039
Retired workers	16,030
Survivors and dependents	5,854
Special-age 62 beneficiaries	154
Under age 65, total	12,098
Retired workers	1,899
Disabled workers	2,843
Survivors and dependents	7,356
Benefits	
Total monthly benefits (in millions)*	$7,217
Average benefit in current-payment status:	
Retired worker	$243.83
Disabled worker	265.91
Aged widows and widowers	222.35
Children of deceased workers	166.30
Average benefits awarded:	
Retired workers	$258.88
Currently payable awards	245.88
Disabled workers	297.87
Aged widows and widowers	228.04
Children of deceased workers	172.04

*In current-payment status; excludes lump-sum and retroactive payments and adjustments.

Source: *Social Security Bulletin*, June 1978, p. 1.

built into the social security system that reflect the inequalities of class society. In general, the more one contributes to the system, the more one receives. However, the percentage of covered income paid into the system remains the same despite vast income differences among workers. Further, workers in the upper-income bracket do not pay a social security payroll tax on their entire wage or salary.

As a consequence of the 1977 amendments to the Social Security Act, the maximum wage base on which social security is paid was raised to $22,900 for 1979, and will increase to $29,700 by 1981. After 1981, the maximum wage base will increase automatically as a function of the rise in average wages covered by social security. Although such an increase in the wage base will increase the percentage of workers whose entire wage is subject to the payroll tax, the regressive nature of the tax is clear. In 1937, the entire earnings of 96.9 percent of those workers covered by social security were taxed. In 1975, the corresponding percentage was 84.9 percent. It is safe to say that those in the highest earning brackets will find a large segment of their income shielded from this particular tax. Such a state of affairs is rationalized in the same way as the regressive income tax system. Shielding the income of the well-to-do and the wealthy is supposed to ensure the continuation of investment capital formation in the economy (Campbell 1978). Such capital fuels the fires of growth and of course produces a return on investment for the stockholder. Advocates of the trickle-down theory argue that such investment finds its way to the bottom of the economic order in the form of new jobs and increased tax revenues. The former consequence of capital formation is a far greater certainty than the latter. (See Chapter 3.)

Institutionalization: Medicare

With the passage of Medicare in 1965, a health component was added to the social insurance program in the United States after three decades of debate. The program administered by the Social Security Administration contains two parts. *Hospital insurance* (part A) is available to nearly all persons sixty-five and over, and is financed by means of payroll tax. Supplementary *medical insurance* (part B) is a voluntary program requiring a premium payment by the enrollee with a matching sum paid by the federal government. *Some 1.1 million older Americans have only hospital insurance* (U.S. Congress, Senate Select Committee on Aging 1978).

Earlier we made the point that one immediate consequence of Medicare insurance was the substitution of a limited target area (the elders) for a national program of health insurance. However, the "catch" did not stop here. When coinsurance and deductibles are excluded, *Medicare pays for only some 38 percent of the health-related expenses of older*

Americans. Eliminated are the largely preventive services such as regular checkups as well as prescription drugs, eyeglasses, and most dental services, including dentures (U.S. Congress, Senate Select Committee on Aging 1978, p. 275).

The loopholes in Medicare thus exceed its area of coverage. Such a state of affairs leaves the well-being of the aging poor to *Medicaid* programs administered by the various states, and of the more fortunate elders to the private insurance companies. This crazy quilt of conflicting programs will be examined in detail at a later point. However, when state governments face funding shortages, Medicaid becomes a popular target (U.S. Congress, Senate Select Committee on Aging 1978, p. 4).

Freedom from disease is not regarded as a fundamental human right in the United States. Therefore, those requiring public-supported treatment are fitted into the conflicting eligibility requirements of a myriad of inadequate and fragmented programs. The type of care extended is thus determined by bureaucratic criteria rather than need.

> Institutional care is often not the best mode of care, but because Federal policy has closed the door to other health care alternatives, it becomes necessary. A study contracted by the Department of Health, Education, and Welfare in 1975 cited figures which draw attention to this situation. The study indicated that between 14 and 25 percent of the 1.2 million institutionalized elderly may not need that form of care. On the other hand, the remaining institutionalized population, which HEW considers appropriately placed, represents only a portion of those in need of such care. A recent GAO report estimates that 17 percent of the non-institutionalized elderly could be appropriately cared for in institutions (U.S. Congress, Senate Select Committee on Aging 1978, p. 7).

Thus, the aging, and particularly the poor among them, are channeled into a system with objectives other than health care. In a statement prepared for the House Subcommittee on Fiscal and Government Affairs on the topic of "Health Services," Ms. Frances Klafter, Co-Chairperson, National Health Task Force of the Gray Panthers, offered the following insightful view:

> . . . we believe that the overriding reason [for inadequate health care for the aging] is that we have a health care system geared primarily to private profit rather than to the health needs of the people. Public health facilities and services are not profitable to the private entrepreneurs who control our health care delivery system—the hospitals, the doctors, the nursing homes, the drug and medical merchants. With the advent of Medicaid and Medicare, the private hospitals began to clamor for the poor whom they were formerly only too happy to leave to the care of public institutions but who had suddenly become profitable patients. Since Medicare does not pay all of either hospital or doctor bills, they clamored

less enthusiastically for the elderly, but government payments from this program also helped to bolster revenues of hospitals and doctors (U.S. Congress, House Subcommittee on Fiscal and Government Affairs 1977, p. 345).

MAINTENANCE

As always, the fundamental question relating to the maintenance of social problems is: Who benefits? In the case of the "aging problem," it is possible to identify a number of beneficiaries, given the particular definition of the aging problem generally accepted in the corporate society.

In a contractual system much emphasis is placed on the resolution of conflict through the rule of law. American gerontology has recently seen the development of a new concern: law and aging. The Office of Economic Opportunity has funded legal services for the aging. An initial grant went to Legal Services and Research for the Elderly of the National Council of Senior Citizens. Subsequently, financial support was directed to the National Senior Citizens Law Center. Further, a few law schools have developed course work and clinical programs in law and aging (Cohen 1978, p. 229).

The intersection of law and the aging has generated a number of related issues. Gerontologists have been asked to consider the implications of "informed consent" for research using the elders as subjects. English common law holds that individuals are to be spared bodily intrusions unless they provide free and knowledgeable agreement. Such a principle has been adopted by the judiciary in the United States, and is found in current regulations of the Department of Health, Education and Welfare (now the Department of Health and Human Services) (Berkowitz 1978). Those who study the aging are also informed of legislative trends in the protection of human research subjects and the consequences of guardianship appointment (Regan 1978). In the former area, law holds that there are special risk groups like children, prisoners, and the institutionalized who must be protected from harm, and an argument has been advanced that the aging should also be included. In the latter, Adult Protective Services programs, growing out of Title XX of the Social Security Act passed in 1974, are seen as possible infringements on civil liberties. Such programs allow for the establishment of a guardian in cases where the aged client is viewed as incapable of rational decision-making. Another related concern has to do with the civil rights of nursing home patients (1.2 million in the United States) found in Medicare and Medicaid regulations; however, such rights remain largely promissory (Wilson, 1978).

In a society of privatized families, existing in a social order of structured inequality, the law will be increasingly called upon to provide support where there is no community and justice where there is no equality.

703

The concern with personal liberties and civil rights is more than a matter of law. It has the standing of a prime ideological symbol in class society. Accordingly, personal liberties draw attention from the absence of material freedoms. While it is important that the elders be protected from unwarranted bodily intrusion, it is perhaps more vital that they be protected from disease by means of a comprehensive health care system. While one might applaud formal concern with potential research abuse, and the dangers of competency procedures, these should not detract from the realities of forced obsolescence and the often meager nature of retirement income. While nursing home patients should be free from violation of their civil rights, it is perhaps more central to question the forces of fragmentation and alienation that necessitate such human warehouses. Nursing homes can be faulted at one and the same time for being both pervasive and inadequate (U.S. Congress, House Subcommittee on Health and Long-Term Care 1975). If the resolution of the aging "problem" is through law, then those involved in policy making, program formulation, lawmaking, legal research, and practice will experience a continued demand for their services. It remains easier to fund programs and pass laws, thereby providing state capital for the stimulation of the aging "industry" than it does to break the dichotomy of the greedy and the needy.

Maggie Kuhn, National Convener of the Gray Panthers, delivers a suggestive critique of the theoretical and ideological bent of functionalist gerontology (1978). She identifies the "psychologized" thrust of the research and the simultaneous avoidance of the major issues of class and state power. Ms. Kuhn also mentions the emphasis on adjustment to the existing order that abounds in the literature, along with a professional ideology that inhibits criticism of established institutions. Studies on aging are seen as lacking a radical edge, while state funding for such research provides jobs for professionals and builds constantly expanding bureaucratic networks.

Aging Benefits the Bureaucracy

In 1978, the Senate Committee on Human Resources reported that since the 1973 amendments to the Older Americans Act of 1965, a total of 536 area agencies for the aging were established across the country. With the state development of age-specific programs, the new "problem" has simply been superimposed on existing programs. Age programs may be administered according to geography, such as general revenue sharing. Housing programs and others are organized according to the service being delivered. Also existing are special status programs such as those exclusively for veterans. Depending on definition, there are some 50 to 200 federal programs furnishing "major assistance" to the elderly. Each program operates on the basis of independent criteria such as age, health, or area of residence. Aging Americans thus find themselves playing bureaucratic shuffleboard, filling out forms, moving from office to office, often never locating services they need and to which they may be entitled.

Although largely dependent on social security, older Americans may receive income from five or six federal sources, including Social Security Supplemental Income (SSI), federal rent support payments, food stamps, and others. The Older American Act of 1965 *forbids* service providers to ask about participants' incomes. Title XX of the Social Security Act, which funds many of the same services, *requires* that income eligibility be determined in most cases. Home health services may be funded under any of a half-dozen programs and there were in 1976 over thirty-one federal funding sources for the transportation of the aging.

The recognition of such fragmented programs in the late Seventies generated a number of congressional hearings and proposed remedies. However, the "remedies" advanced most often were the establishment of new programs and services to coordinate the old programs and services. Such a "solution" is not novel. In 1965, the *Administration on Aging* was created to coordinate federal programs serving the elderly. The *Area Agency on Aging* was added in 1973 to facilitate coordination of services at the local level. The *Intergovernmental Cooperation Act* of 1963 called for state and local input on the issue of consistency between proposed federal projects and state and local policies. The *Joint Funding Simplification Act* of 1974 was designed to streamline procedures in gaining funding from two federal sources. The *Integrated Grants Administration (IGA) and the Consolidated Funding System* were meant to coordinate programs through joint funding of projects. The latter no longer exists, and the IGA was superseded by the Joint Funding Simplification Act. In addition, H.E.W. (now Human Resources with the establishment of a separate Department of Education), has funded Services Integration Targets of Opportunity, Partnership Demonstrations, Project Share, and has even called for the waiver of its own rules, all in the interest of coordination. These are but a few of the initiatives at the federal level to address the problem of "fragmentation" (U.S. Congress, House Select Committee on Aging 1977, pp. 139–142).

Given the nature of the political process, initiatives come and go, are modified and streamlined on a regularly recurring basis. Our intention is not to present information about services that is to be memorized. Rather, it is to demonstrate that a fragmentation of services serves as a stimulus to political debate and action, and to bureaucratic growth and survival. Even well-intentioned programs competently administered are forced to expend resources to justify their existence while providing services with inadequate funding. In such cases, the supposed beneficiaries of programs at all levels of government suffer.

We believe that the real issues of aging implicate a social order that subjugates human rights to property and transforms people into a commodity. Given this pricing of humans, the aging are of lesser value as producers and consumers, and so will suffer. In short, powerful economic interests will shape state policy for the aging (as they do for other groups). When such organized private interests have established a profitable industry with the elders as its consumers, it follows that state-supported programs will be designed to ensure the continued well-being of that industry. As a specific example, we shall examine the nature of health insurance in the United States.

Health Uninsurance: Schemes and Arrangements

Sociologists and others have grappled over the years with a distinction between those problems that reflect the inherent contradictions of a specific social order and those that simply involve the occasional and temporary exploitation of an isolated few by the "unscrupulous." In the field of criminology, it is important to make clear the difference between offenses perpetrated by those in a position of trust that are clearly *opposed* to organizational norms, and offenses clearly designed to further organizational objectives. Thus, one can distinguish conceptually between embezzlement and fraud on the one hand and on the other the compliance by executives with the profit imperative that may contribute to unsafe working conditions, ecologically damaging production processes, and the exploitation of consumers (Vold 1958, Schrager and Short 1978).

With this distinction in mind, we can analyze the nature of health insurance for the aging in the United States. We shall employ the terms "schemes" and "arrangements" to distinguish between two sets of outcomes that flow from the particular organization of medical care. "Schemes" shall refer to practices bordering on rackets. They do not always clearly involve the classic "con" or "sting" artist whose behaviors are in violation of the law. However, the forms of misrepresentation and deceit employed by some clearly result in victimization. "Arrangements" refer here to inherent, systemic properties of the organization of health insurance. Whereas schemes clearly are promoted by those of questionable repute working on the fringes of a legitimate industry, arrangements refer to the actions of respectables executing a structural role. Schemes occasionally draw fire because they damage the image of "legitimate" industry, but arrangements are largely ignored, defined as normal, or occasionally falsely defined as schemes involving a few disreputables or "conspirators."

In the late Seventies in the United States, public attention came to be focused on "medi-gap." This term refers to private health insurance supplements to Medicare. Because of the restrictions on Medicare coverage, older Americans live in fear of health-related expenses they cannot pay. In this context, fear becomes a commodity in the form of private insurance policy sales to the aging. According to the Social Security Administration, some 63 percent of those age sixty-five and over paid for private health insurance coverage for hospital care in 1976, while 55 percent had private insurance for physicians' services. However, only 5 percent of the cost of health care for the elders is paid for by "medi-gap" insurance. Further, most of the insurance sold to Medicare recipients leaves the largest gaps uncovered. This is to say that neither Medicare nor private supplemental insurance typically covers such things as prescription drugs, dental care, or custodial nursing home care. The Social Security Administration documents that less than 3 percent of older Americans have dental insurance, only 20 percent have nursing home insurance, and 22 percent have coverage for out-of-hospital prescription drugs (U.S. Congress, Senate Select Committee on Aging 1978, pp. 1–2).

Viewing "medi-gap" insurance as a frequent *scheme* is supported by a press release from the Pennsylvania State Insurance Department. In describing the characteristics of sales "exploitation," the release included the following:

> Recontacting longtime elderly insured of the companies, getting them to lapse their policies and buy new ones.

> Passing the names of elderly, sometimes senile consumers from agent to agent and thus causing multiple sales of insurance policies.

> Taking premiums for annual policies and having them issued on a quarterly basis to get a larger commission.

> Writing many policies under a variety of names to avoid detection of the multiple sales ("Mary Smith," "Mary A. Smith," "M. Ann Smith," etc.).

> The worst case to come to our attention is that of an 80-year old woman . . . who spent $50,574 in a recent 3-year period on 31 policies, all of which lapsed. . . .

> In still another case, an 87-year old . . . woman bought 22 policies in 28 months from six different agents . . . (U.S. Congress, Senate Select Committee on Aging 1978, p. 33).

The point to be made is that when a problem is defined as a scheme, the broader organizational and structural questions and connections are ignored. It follows that medi-gap abuse will not be seen as a logical organizational outgrowth of the private insurance industry to increase sales. Nor, in the broader sense, will the medi-gap issue be related to the absence of comprehensive health care at the national level. Rather, in the expected sense of a "racket," the "unscrupulous agent" in search of large first-year commissions (frequently in the neighborhood of 65 percent of premiums paid) is attacked. (For the construction of the medi-gap scheme, see Parts I and II of the Report of the Senate Select Committee on Aging, May 16, 1978, and June 29, 1978.)

The definition of health-care problems as an "arrangement" is exemplified in recent federal inquiry into the rampant increase in the cost of health care. Of specific concern here is the inflationary role of Blue Cross-Blue Shield health plans in the United States. The total bill, both public and private, for health care in the United States amounted to $42 billion in 1966, $69 billion in 1970, $118 billion in 1975, and $140 billion in 1976. The 1976 figure averaged out to a $2600 yearly expenditure for a family of four. It is within this context that the membership composition of Blue Shield boards came under scrutiny by the House Subcommittee on Oversight and Investigations in the spring of 1978.

Blue Shield plans came into existence during the Great Depression as a reaction to the desires of physicians for insured payment for their services. Blue Shield plans, together with Blue Cross, are the largest underwriters of health insurance in the United States. In 1976, these plans covered more than 80 million Americans. Blue Shield alone paid out $4 billion of the $9.5 billion total paid by private insurance to physicians in 1976. In addition to this enormous underwriting role, Blue Shield plans provide coverage under Medicare and Title XIX of the Social Security Act—Medicaid (House Subcommittee on Oversight and Investigations 1978, pp. 1–3).

Reimbursement by Blue Shield involves the UCR method (usual, customary, and reasonable). If the physician charges for service an amount equal to or less than 90 percent of the Community rate, he or she will be totally reimbursed. Charges above the ninetieth percentile go into the determination of the community rate at the time of the next UCR update (usually done quarterly). The UCR method is also the basis for Medicare reimbursement. *The payments to physicians are thus determined by what physicians charge. "Usual, customary, and reasonable" becomes a direct statistical function of the fee level.* Thus, an economic incentive for physicians to inflate their fees continually is built into the reimbursement system. As the reimbursement system is clearly designed in the interest of physicians, it should come as no surprise to find that physicians dominate Blue Shield boards. The nature of this health care connection is found in the following arrangement:

> . . . Many disturbing practices emerged from the testimony, including involvement or control of plans by medical societies, doctor domination of Blue Shield boards, and conflicts of interest of board members. In Indiana, we found that the State Medical Association must approve all physician board members, and that the treasurer of Indiana Blue Shield was also the president of the bank holding in excess of $100 million of Blue Shield funds. In Ohio, the Assistant Attorney General reported to us that Blue Shield—or Ohio Medical Indemnity, as it is called—is a wholly owned subsidiary of the Ohio State Medical Association.

We learned from the Federal Trade Commission that the majority of Blue Shield boards are doctor dominated and that even in those that are not, the majority of fee setting and adjudication committees are controlled by physicians (House Subcommittee on Oversight and Investigations 1978, p. 393).

Under this arrangement, the reimbursement policies of the major health insurer in the United States are controlled by the persons benefiting from them. "Usual, customary, and reasonable" for whom?

Whether schemes or arrangements, our two contrasting examples of the problems of health care in the United States reveal the same structural source. The private organization of medical care is made up of both the insurance industry and a professional society of medical entrepreneurs. It is in accordance with these specific interests and the basic imperatives of the corporate social order that health care in the United States has been organized. We would predict that national health insurance legislation pending in the United States will be shaped more by the requirements of the industry than of the people's health needs.

Meeting the needs of the elders requires structural change in the corporate order and its supporting ideology as the following alternative clearly demonstrates.

ALTERNATIVE

HOUSE SELECT COMMITTEE ON AGING PUBLIC HEARING ON FRAGMENTATION AND PROLIFERATION OF SERVICES

Testimony presented by Maggie Kuhn of the Gray Panthers on Monday, April 4, 1977

(Excerpts)

The Gray Panthers are a national coalition of old, young, and middle-aged activists and advocates working to eradicate ageism and all forms of age discrimination in our society. We define ageism as the arbitrary discrimination against persons and groups on the basis of chronological age. The majority of Gray Panthers are over sixty years of age. Our movement includes many young and middle-aged people; age is not a barrier in our movement! We are concerned with national issues pertaining to the status, health, and well-being of older and younger Americans. We are not providers of services, but we have observed and monitored many of the services under the various titles of the Older Americans Act and other acts providing services to older people.

This is the age of liberation and self-determination for all alienated groups that are struggling for freedom and social justice. Old people constitute America's largest untapped and undervalued human energy source, yet I have observed only token effort to give us a chance to be self-determining and substantively involved in planning and developing the programs that are designed to help us. Federal guidelines call for our representation in advisory bodies, but we are not encouraged or empowered to serve effectively on advisory boards with the resulting tragic loss of skill and experience, loss of human energy and a perpetuation of powerlessness and fragmentation of services. Indeed we see the lack of involvement of older Americans in planning and decision-making for the service delivery system as a major cause of the fragmentation and proliferation of service. Well-meaning staffs, who frequently act like bureaucrats, plan and administer programs *for* us, patterning their administration on the American management model. Old people are seen as clients for particular, specialized services, not as a whole person with insights and wisdom to share. We find the process demeaning and calculated to make us wrinkled babies rather than mature, responsible adults concerned about helping ourselves and healing the ills of our sick society.

There is further fragmentation and duplication of services because the State and Area Offices on Aging are placed without proper regard for the programs already in operation by established social agencies and denominational groups, coordinated planning and budgeting are not done with the traditional agencies for such services as: information and referral services, counselling services, Meals on Wheels, health screening, etc. Private agencies operate these programs with the help of many volunteers and private contributions. However, we have observed few efforts to bring nongovernmental, private agency services and governmental services together. In metropolitan areas like New York City and Chicago, we have seen that the area offices operate on a highly centralized basis and are administered by American management techniques. Departments of Aging are rapidly becoming bureaucracies, with their staffs hobnobbing with other staffs and further and further removed from daily contact with the people to be served—all this with limited input from the ideas and experiences of the older person.

Critique of Training

The providers of services have training in their specialized fields as doctors, nurses, social workers, gerontologists, administrators of hospitals and extended-care facilities, nutritionists, and administrators of area planning agencies. Schools of gerontology and courses in gerontology attempt to bring groups of service providers together but the basic training systems are largely specialized and fragmented. Furthermore, there is a dearth of training opportunities for the old people. These specialists need to recognize the interdependence of these "parts" of their professions which impact on the whole person. Participation of older people in contributing to the decision-making processes of professionals can often affect the success or failure of outcome.

Funds and staff time have been allocated for the training of staff members of state and area agencies. Such staff training is necessary and should be carried on jointly with the old people who should be preparing for service in advisory councils and boards. Indeed, training should be equally available to old people, with travel expenses to training events and per diem reimbursement. I have participated as a workshop leader and trainer in a number of area staff training events—usually as the token old person. Many more of us should be involved in the training of our peers, as well as staff for effective participation in decision-making, planning and coordinating groups. Retired professionals should be trained to be trainers and to serve as resource persons and counsellors to area agency staffs.

If there were more involvement of old people in the delivery of services, the professional staffs might be more sensitized to the effect of age discrimination in our lives. For example, when our involuntary poverty, created by arbitrary retirement, forces us to participate in the welfare system, we lose self-esteem and status. It involves being subjected to means tests, filling out of endless forms to validate our poverty, and standing in long lines to be hassled by competing systems. Many of my peers refuse the benefits to which we are entitled. We resent the fact that bureaucratic rules, forms, and paperwork take precedence over people and their needs.

I cite one instance as a case-in-point: A woman in her late eighties called our Philadelphia office and asked for assistance. It was her last resort. She suffers from Lupus, a painful, incurable disease which has affected her legs. She cannot travel by mass transportation and lives alone. The social worker told her that she could be reimbursed for taxi fares to doctors and hospital, but that she would have to come to the office to get the form required for taxi fare reimbursement. She asked us how to get out of that dilemma and our advice was to take the taxi and charge it to the agency.

My colleagues and I wish that some of the staff time and energy required to fill out forms could be allocated to the development of self-determining senior advocates who would be able to plan and coordinate our own services and "manage our own show." I have seen relatively few advisory committees that were more than paper tigers. In most communities there are established, experienced groups of old people who could be commissioned to plan and administer service programs. We reiterate—a great leap toward the elimination of fragmentation would be to strengthen and empower the people themselves, as the biggest cause of fragmentation is paternalism and the docile, passive recipients it creates.

Health services provided us through the US health care system is sickness care. It is crisis-oriented, highly specialized, and focused on disease and dysfunction, rather than on health maintenance and prevention. Furthermore, it is tied to complex hospital systems with their specializations, expensive machines, and technology. Nursing homes and neighborhood clinics are patterned after hospitals and the endemic specialization results inevitably in fragmentation of the person and the services. We believe that fragmentation can be eliminated only by a radical shift to primary and holistic health care, which will bring together mental, physical, and environmental health in an integrated and decentralized delivery system, and controlled by the people.

BIBLIOGRAPHY

Alexander, Shana
1976   Talking Woman. New York: Delacorte Press.

Ansello, E. F.
1976   "How Older People Are Stereotyped." Educational Gerontology: An International Quarterly 7:4–6.

1977   "Age and Ageism in Children's First Literature." Educational Gerontology: An International Quarterly 2:255–74.

Aries, Phillippe
1962   Centuries of Childhood. Translated by Robert Baldick. London: Jonathan Cape.

Atchley, Robert
1977   The Social Forces in Later Life. Belmont, Calif.: Wadsworth.

Balties, Paul B., and
Shaie, Warner
1974   "Aging and I.Q.: The Myth of the Twilight Years." Psychology Today March: 35–40.

Berkowitz, Sandra
1978   "Informed Consent, Research, and the Elderly." The Gerontologist 18(3):244–249.

Blue, Gladys F.
1978

"The Aging as Portrayed in Realistic Fiction for Children 1945–1975." The Gerontologist:April 187–192.

Boldt, Menno
1976

Report of the Task Force on Suicides. Edmonton, Alberta: Minister of Social Services and Community Health.

Bozzetti, Louis P. and Ingrid L.
1977

"The Home Samaritans and the Marginal Elderly." Psychiatric Annals, March.

Campbell, Colin D.
1978

The 1977 Amendments to the Social Security Act. Washington, D.C.: American Enterprise Institute for Public Policy Research.

Carlie, M.K.
1969

"The Politics of Age: Interest Group or Social Movement?" Gerontologist 9:259–263.

Carlson, Avis
1977

In the Fullness of Time. Chicago: Contemporary Books.

Ciffin, S.; Martin, J.; and Talbot C.
1976

Retirement in Canada: Summary Report. Ottawa: Department of National Health and Welfare.

Cohen, Elias S.
1978

"Editorial: Law and Aging, Lawyers and Gerontologists." The Gerontologist 18(3):229.

Commons, John R.
1935

History of Labor in the United States, 1896–1932. Volume III. New York: Macmillan.

Cowgill, Donald, and Holmes, Lowell
1972

Aging and Modernization. New York: Appleton Century Crofts.

Cumming, E., and Henry, W.
1961

Growing Old. New York: Basic Books.

Danowski, James, and
Sacks, William
1976

"Computer Communication and the Elderly."
Annenberg School of Communication and Andrus
Gerontology Center. Unpublished study, February,
University of Southern California.

de Beauvoir, Simone
1972

The Coming of Age. New York: Putnam.

Dowd, James J.
1980

Stratification among the Aged. Monterey, Calif.:
Brooks/Cole Publishing Company.

Feingold, Eugene
1966

Medicare: Policy and Politics. San Francisco:
Chandler.

Foner, A., and Kertzer, D.
1978

Transitions over the Life Course: Lessons from
Age-Set Societies. American Journal of Sociology
83:1081–1104.

George, Linda
1978

"The Happiness Syndrome: Methodological and
Substantive Issues in the Study of Social-Psychologi-
cal Well-being in Adulthood." The Gerontologist
April 210–216.

Grescoe, Paul
1980

"Socialism Pays Off." Canadian Weekend,
February 23:3 + .

Harris, Louis
1975

"The Myth and Reality of Aging in America."
Washington, D.C.: National Council on the Aging.

Haynes, Suzanne G.;
McMichael, Anthony J.;
and Tyroler, Herman A.
1978

"Survival after Early and Normal Retirement."
Journal of Gerontology March: 269–278.

Hunt, Bernice and Morton
1975

Prime Time. New York: Stein and Day.

Knopf, Olga
1975

Successful Aging: The Facts and Fallacies of Growing Old. New York: Viking Press.

Kuhn, Maggie
1978   "Open Letter." The Gerontologist 18(5):422–24.

Maas, H., and Kuypers, J.
1974   From Thirty to Seventy. San Francisco: Jossey-Bass.

Masters, W., and
Johnson, V.
1966   Human Sexual Response. Boston: Little, Brown.

McConnell, Adeline, and
Anderson, Beverly
1978   Single after Fifty: How to Have the Time of Your
                                 Life. New York: McGraw-Hill.

McFarland, Ross
1973   "The Need for Functional Age Measurements in
                                 Industrial Gerontology." Gerontology
                                 Fall:1.

Melman, Seymour
1970   Pentagon Capitalism: The Political Economy of
                                 War. New York: McGraw-Hill.

Miller, Marv
1978   "Geriatric Suicide: The Arizona Study." The
                                 Gerontologist October: 488–95.

Mitchell, Broadus
1947   The Economic History of the United States, Vol IX.
                                 New York: H. Wolff.

Mumford, Lewis
1961   The City in History: Its Origins, Its Transforma-
                                 tions, and Its Prospects. New York: Harcourt, Brace
                                 & Jovanovich.

Nusberg, Charlotte, ed.
1978a   "Japan." Aging International 5(3) Autumn.

1978b   "Sweden." Aging International 5(2) Summer.

1978c   "The Struggle against Mandatory Retirement: A
                                 Victory in the U.S." Aging International 5(2)
                                 Summer.

Palmore, Erdman
1975   The Honorable Elders. Durham, N.C.: Duke Uni-
                                 versity Press.

Perdue, William D.
1975

"The Ideology of Depression Sociology." Paper presented to the annual meeting of the Pacific Sociological Association. Victoria, B.C., March.

Puner, Morton
1974

To the Good Long Life. New York: Universe Books.

Redfield, Robert
1941

The Folk Culture of Yucatan. Chicago: University of Chicago Press.

Regan, John J.
1978

"Intervention through Adult Protective Services Programs." Gerontologist 18(3):250–54.

Riemer, Yosef, and Binstock, Robert
1978

"Campaigning for 'The Senior Vote': A Case Study of Carter's 1976 Campaign." Gerontologist 18(6): 517–24.

Ryan, William
1971

Blaming the Victim. New York: Pantheon Books.

Schrager, Laura, and Short, James F.
1978

"Toward a Sociology of Organizational Crime." Social Problems 26 (June):411–12.

Shanas, Ethel
1979a

"Social Myth as Hypothesis: The Case of the Family Relationship of Old People" Gerontologist 19 (1): 3–9.

1979b

"The Family as a Social Support System in Old Age." Gerontologist 19 (2):169–74.

Shanas, E., and Sussman, M.B., eds.
1977

Family Bureaucracy and the Elderly. Durham, N.C.: Duke University Press.

Shannon, David A.
1960

The Great Depression. Englewood Cliffs, N.J.: Prentice-Hall.

Shelton, Austin
1965

"Ibo Aging and Eldership: Notes for Gerontologists and Others." Gerontologist 5 March.

Simmons, Leo W.
1945   The Role of the Aged in Primitive Society.
                         London: Oxford University Press.

Skidmore, Max
1970   Medicare. Tuscaloosa, Ala.: University of Alabama
                         Press.

Statistics Canada
1977   Perspective Canada II. Ottawa: Minister of Supply
                         and Services Canada.

1978   Canada Yearbook, 1978–79. Ottawa: Minister of
                         Supply and Services Canada.

1979   Canada's Elderly. Ottawa: Minister of Supply and
                         Services Canada.

Stirner, Fritz
1978   "The Transportation Needs of the Elderly in a Large
                         Urban Environment." Gerontologist 18 (2):207–11.

Sugden, E.
1971   Enjoy Retirement: Stay Young Getting Older. New
                         York: Exposition Press.

Sussman, M., and
Burchinal, L.
1962   "Kin Family Network." Marriage and Family
                         Living August.

Toennies, Ferdinand
1957   Community and Society. Translated by C. P.
                         Loomis. East Lansing, Mich.: Michigan State Uni-
                         versity.

United States Bureau of
the Census
1978   Statistical Abstract of the United States. Washing-
1979   ton, D.C.: U.S. Government Printing Office.

United States Congress,
Committee on Human
Resources, U.S. Senate
1978   "Report on the Older Americans Act of 1978."
                         May 15. Washington, D.C.: U.S. Government
                         Printing Office.

United States Congress,
Select Committee on Aging,
House of Representatives
1977a
    "Mandatory Retirement: The Social and Human Cost of Enforced Idleness." August. Washington, D.C.: U.S. Government Printing Office.

1977b
    "Fragmentation of Services for the Elderly." April 4. Washington, D.C.: U.S. Government Printing Office.

1977c
    "Mandatory Retirement: The Social and Human Cost of Enforced Idleness" Washington, D.C.: U.S. Government Printing Office.

1978
    "Health Care Problems of the Elderly in New Jersey." February 13. Washington, D.C.: U.S. Government Printing Office.

United States Congress,
Select Committee on
Aging, U.S. Senate
1978
    "Medi-GAP: Private Health Insurance Supplements to Medicare." Part 1, May 16, Part 2, June 29. Washington, D.C.: U.S. Government Printing Office.

United States Congress,
Subcommittee on Fiscal
and Governmental Affairs,
House of Representatives
1977
    "Health Services." September 29, 30. October 3, 4, 5, 6, 12, 13, 19, 20. Washington, D.C.: U.S. Government Printing Office.

United States Congress,
Subcommittee on Health
and Long-Term Care,
Select Committee on
Aging, House of
Representatives
1975
    "Auditing of Nursing Homes and Alternatives to Institutionalization." Washington, D.C.: U.S. Government Printing Office.

United States Congress, Subcommittee on Oversight and Investigations, Committee on Interstate and Foreign Commerce, House of Representatives
1978   "Skyrocketing Health Care Costs: The Role of Blue Shield." March 21, 22; April 5, 6, 7. Washington, D.C.: U.S. Government Printing Office.

United States Department of Health, Education and Welfare
1978   "Social Security in Review." Social Security Bulletin 41(6):1–13.

Vold, George Bryan
1958   Theoretical Criminology. New York: Oxford University Press.

Webbink, Paul
1941   Unemployment in the United States, 1930–1940. Papers and Proceedings of the American Economic Association. 30 (February):250–51.

Wilson, Sally Hart
1978   "Nursing Home Patients' Rights." Gerontologist 18(3):255–61.

World Almanac and Book of Facts
1979   New York: Newspaper Enterprise Association, p. 956.

INDEX

ABC, 59–60, 63, 562
Abortion, 31, 646
Abramson, Joan, 632–633
Abstraction, levels of, 7–9, 11
Absentee corporations, 44
Accidents
automobile, 205, 297
environmental, 244–251
work-related, 56, 207, 209
Acid rain, 248
Act for the Better Establishment and Maintenance of Public Schools in Upper Canada, 550–551
Addict, drug
criminalization of, 513–515, 516
treatment of, 530–532
Administration of Aging, 705
Adult Basic Education Program, 132
Adversary system, 450
Advertising, 60–62
women and, 655–656
Advertising Council, 54–55, 56
Affirmative action, 346, 644–645, 648–650
Affluent worker, 176–182
AFL, 189, 190, 191–196, 198
"Age, Class, and Social Inequality" (Dowd), 672
Age Discrimination in Employment Act, 653
Ageism. See Aging.
Agent Orange, 246–247
Age stratification, 762
Aggregate concentration, 353–354
Aging
biological, vs. chronological, 677
emergence of, 690–697
ideologies of, 673–690
intelligence and, 677–678
institutionalization of, 698–703
maintenance of, 703–709
stereotypes of, 679–680

Aid to the Blind, 132
Aid to Families of Dependent Children (ADFC), 113, 132
Aid to the Permanently and Totally Disabled, 132
Air Force, 57
Airlines, 292
Alcatraz Island, 582
Alcohol, 490, 496, 498, 500, 503, 527–528
Alcohol industry, 527
Alcoholism, 8, 20, 31
Alfred A. Knopf, 57
Alienation, 163–167, 176, 687
Alienation and Freedom (Blauner), 165
Alien Contract Labor Law, 193
Allen, Michael, 40
Altes, Earl, 224–225
Amalgamated Association of Iron and Steel Workers, 191
Amendments, constitutional. *See* Bill of Rights; *see also names of individual amendments.*
American Association of Retired Persons, 692
American Bar Association, 517
American Conservation Association, 275
American Federation of State, County and Municipal Employees, 220
American Indian Movement (AIM), 342, 592–593
American Legion, 517
American Medical Association, 74, 694, 695
American Petroleum Institute, 257
American Society of Newspaper Editors, 631
American Telephone and Telegraph, 531
Ammon, Otta, 568
Amnesty International, 117

"Amos 'n' Andy," 561
Anaconda Copper, 240, 263
Anarchists, 342
Andelin, Helen B., 617–618
Anderson, Charles, 298
Anderson, Robert O., 275
Angiosarcoma, 213
Anslinger, Harry J., 73, 518, 519, 520, 521
Antidepressants, 526
Antiintellectualism, 46
Antinomian controversy, 327
Antinuclear organizations, 342
Anti-Saloon League, 516
Anti-Semitism, 577, 578
Antitrust legislation, 193, 201–202, 341–342
Antiwar demonstrators, 342
Appalachia, 258
Appellate courts, 457
Arabian American Oil Company (ARAMCO), 259
Area Agency on Aging, 705
Arden, Elizabeth, 640
Argan, Larry, 249, 250
Aries, Phillippe, 638, 690
Aristotle, 615
Army, 57
Army Corps of Engineers, 268–269
Arrests, 318, 406, 407
Arsenic pollution, 211, 359
Aryan race, 568–569
Asbestos workers, 211, 250–251, 349, 360
Asexual elder, 678–679
Ashland Oil, 315
Asian *Wall Street Journal*, 67
Assets, corporate, 139, 141, 648
Assimilation
racial, 570, 579
of women, 636
Asylums (Goffman), 34
Atlantic Richfield (ARCO), 240, 263, 275
Atlantic Underseas Test and Evaluation Center, 57   **721**

INDEX

Atomic Energy Commission, 275, 276
Auburn Penitentiary, 460
Audubon Society, 275
Auschwitz, 586, 587, 588
Authority, 162
Automobiles, 56, 205, 269, 296–299, 690

Badges of ability, 167
Bagdikian, Ben, Ben H., 54, 56
Bail, 478
Baldwin, James, 456
Ballantine Books, 57
Ballistic Missile Early Warning System, 57
Banfield, Edward, 9
Banishment, 453
Bank of England, 118
Banquet Corporation, 57
"Barbarous Rituals" (Morgan), 607–614
Barnum and Bailey circus, 240
Barron's National Business, 66
Batista, 116
Beard, Charles, 186–187
Beauvoir, Simone de, 622, 674
Beccaria Cesare, 395
Becker, Howard, 31–32, 33–34, 73
Behavior modification, 411
Behram v. *United States*, 514
Bell, Daniel, 394
Benito Juarez Mutual Aid Society, 509
Bend, E., 20
Bentham, Jeremy, 395
Benzene, 214
Beothuck Indians, 550, 557
Bernard, Jesse, 623
B.F. Goodrich, 213, 214, 218
Bible, 618
Big Brothers, 414
Big Foot, Chief, 585
Big Oil, 256–258. *See also* Oil companies; Petro-corporations.
Bill of Rights, 346, 456, 581
Biological determinism, 397–399, 410–411, 417–419
Bismark, 698
Black lung disease, 211
Black Panthers, 342, 408, 592
Black Power, 590–591

Blacks, 344–347, 583, 385, 386, 588
arrests of, 406, 407
income of, 544–545
legal protection of, 580–581
lynchings of, 585–586
media portrayal of, 560–563
perceptions of police, 440–443
police brutality and, 469–470
terrorism against, 594–595
transfers of, 583
well-being of, 547–549
Blackstone, Sir William, 395
Blaming the victim, 47, 205, 206, 677
Blauner, Robert, 165–166
Bloody Code, 452
Blue, Gladys F., 679–680
Blue collar workers, 37, 50, 102–103, 172, 173
diseases among, 207, 210, 213–214, 249–251
Blue Cross, 708–709
Blue Shield, 708–709
Bluestone, Irving, 182, 184
Blum, Richard, 489–490
Blumberg, Abraham S., 477
Blumer, Herbert, 4, 32, 49, 76
Boggs, Hale, 521
Boggs Amendment, 520
Boise-Cascade, 44
Branding, 452, 453
Braverman, Harry, 103–104, 172, 406
Breeder reactors, 236–239, 276–277, 282
Brent, Charles, 505
Bribery, 315–316
Bride, 66
Broadcast industry, 60–63. *See also* Mass media.
Broatch, A. G., 197–198
Brower, David, 275
Brown, Lee, 61, 62
Brown, Rap, 343
Brown, Rosemary, 659–660
Brown Berets, 593
Brown v. *Board of Education*, 346, 581, 642
Bryan, Rorke, 244
Buchenwald, 586

Bunting, David, 41
Bureaucratic power, 17
Bureau of Labor Statistics (BLS), 178, 179, 180, 214
Bureau of Indian Affairs, 79, 582, 589, 590
Bureau of Narcotics and Dangerous Drugs, 522
Bureau of Narcotics and Dangerous Drugs Bulletin, 523
Burgess, Anthony, 418
Burroughs, 315
Burt, Cyril, 169
Bus boycott, 641
Business elite, 40

Caffeine, 503
California, 44, 397
California State Law Enforcement League, 397
Calley, William L., Jr., Lt., 414
Calvin, John, 687
Canada, 36, 41, 43, 52, 77, 102, 136, 143, 172, 293, 341, 356, 455, 457, 466, 579, 623, 640
drug policy of, 506–507
ethnic groups in, 351, 397–398, 545–546
income in, 138–140, 683
labor law in, 203–204
media in, 68–69
medical care in, 689, 696
Natives of, attitude toward, 75–76, 79
racism in, 549–559, 581, 584, 589
trade union movement in, 72, 196–198, 201
unemployment in, 176–177, 180
work-related diseases in, 211, 215–217
Canada Labor Relations Board, 355
Canadian Broadcasting Corporation, 54, 58
Canadian Federal Criminal Code, 360
Canadian Immigration Act, 584

722

Canadian Imperial Bank, 355
Canadian Labor Congress (CLC), 198, 199
Canadian Pacific Railway, 455
Canadian Union of Public Employees (CUPE), 199
Cancer, work-related, 207, 210, 213–214, 249–251
Capitalism, 6, 17, 36, 333, 498
  and family, effect on, 638–639, 674–675
  ideology of, 18–19
Capital punishment, 459
Carcinogens, 210, 250–251, 526
Cardinal, Harold, 592
Careerism, 46
Carnegie, Andrew, 110, 112, 168
Carrier's Case, 336
Carroll, Diahann, 561
Carson, Rachael, 248, 266–267
Carter, Jimmy, 18–19, 141, 247, 692
Castration, 411
Castro, 116
Catholics, 121, 498
Caveat emptor, 471
Cavtat, 246
CBS, 58–59, 60, 63, 274
Census of Agriculture, 44
Central Republic Bank and Trust, 123
Centuries of Childhood (Aries), 638, 690
Cervinka, Claudette, 178
Chamber of Commerce, 205
Chamberlain, Houston Stewart, 568
Chambliss, William J., 329
Chauvin, Nicolas, 626
Chauvinism, male, 626–629
Chavez, Cesar, 593
Cherokee Nation, 583
Chicanos, 509, 589–590, 593–594, 595
Child labor, 690
Child-saving movement, 339–340, 413
Chile, 117
China, 131, 350

China (cont.)
  opium and, 504–505, 508–509
China syndrome, 277
Chinese, 345, 507, 509, 510–511
  Canadian attitude toward, 397–398, 552
  transfers of, 583–584
Chinese Exclusion Act, 193
Christianity, 270, 618
Chrysler Corporation, 297
Churchill Forest Industries, 324
CIA, 146, 324, 356
Cigarette smoking, 526–527
Cigarmakers' Union, 190
Cincinnati Enquirer, 65–66
CIO, 194–196
Cirrhosis, 527
Cities with Little Crime: The Case of Switzerland (Clenard), 422
Citizens' Advisory Committee on Recreation and National Beauty, 274
Civilian review board, 476
Civil laws, 334
Civil Rights Act of 1866, 647, 653
Civil Rights Act of 1964, 643–644
Civil rights movement, 342, 346, 468
  and women's movement, 642–645
Civil Service Commission, 647, 753
Civil Service Commission Fair Employment Board, 648
Civil Service Regulation, 647
Civil War, 188, 581
Clark, Ramsey, 404
Class action suits, environmental, 288
Classes, social, 14, 16–17, 33, 34, 101, 135, 161–162
  aging and, 672–673
  in U.S., 98–99
Classless society, 104
Class stratification, 672
Clayton Act, 193, 202, 470
Clean Air Act, 284

Clean Water Act, 284
Cleaver, Eldridge, 408
Clement, Wallace, 36, 41, 54, 68–69
Clerical workers, 103–104, 172, 633
Cleveland, Grover, 191
Clinard, Marshall B., 354–355, 389, 422, 473
Clitorus, 625
Clockwork Orange, 418
Coal, 258–259, 293, 294
Cobb, Jonathan, 162
Cocaine, 494, 500, 524
Coffee, 503
Cognitive flexibility, 678
Cohen, Albert, 9
Cold War ideology, 48
Cole, G.D.H., 577
Collective bargaining, 220
Collectivism, 6
College Work Study Program, 132
Colonialism, 571–573
Colonial model, 589–590
Colson, Charles, 408
Combination movement, 119–120
Combine Act, 341
Committee of the Anti-Opium Society, 505
Committee on Economic Security, 698
Commodity News Service, Inc., 66
Commoner, Barry, 236–242, 255, 296
Communism, 106, 300
Communist Party, 196
Communists, 48, 342, 343
Community Action Program, 132
Community-based corrections, 415
Comprehensive Drug Abuse Prevention and Control Act, 523–524
Comprehensive Employment and Training Act, 653
Concentration, corporate, 353–354
Concentration camps
  Japanese in, 584
  Nazi, 586–587

INDEX

Conde-Nast Publications, 66
Conflict paradigm, 1, 10–18, 135
  on crime, 404–406
Conglomerate, 120
Conscription Act, 188
Consent decree, 473
Conservation, 271–274
Conservation Foundation, 274, 275
Consolidated Coal, 259
Consolidated Edison, 237
Consolidated Funding System, 705
Conspicuous consumption, 45, 654
Constabulary, 450–451
Constitution, U.S., 186–187, 456, 574
  on race, 344, 346, 580
Consumer Price Index, 107
Consumers United Group, Inc., 219
Container Corporation, 240
Contractual relationships, 37
Contractual solution, 636–637, 660–661, 692
Cook County jail, 378
Cooley, Charles Horton, 33
Cooper, M.R., 175
Cooperative Central Ranch, 225
Cooperative Commonwealth Federation (CCF), 198
Core meltdown, 277
Corporal punishment, 452–453
Corporate assets, 139, 141, 648
Corporate crime, 314–316, 321–325, 352–356, 479–480
  ideology of, 471–474
  maintenance of, 349–350
  as rational response, 394
Corporate elite, 38–41
Corporate gigantism, 40–41
Corporate ideology, 44–46, 104–105, 147, 348
Corporate ownership, 37, 42–44
Corporate system, 35–38
  defense of, 116–117
  pollution control and, 290–295
  women in, 654–655

Corporations, 36, 39, 40. *See also* Corporate crime.
  consolidation of, 119–120
  dominance of, 113, 116
  largest, 143, 144
  regulations and, 472–474
Correctional institutions, 459–462, 479
Corrections, ideology of, 447–448
Council of Economic Priorities, 293
Court system, 456–457. *See also* Supreme Court, U.S.
Cowgill, Donald, 685–686, 687
Cox Broadcasting Corporation, 68
Credit, women and, 657–658
Crime. *See also* Corporate Crime.
  definitions of, 1–2
  explanations of, 385–386, 388–389
  political, 342–343
  problems and remedies, influence of tv on, 51, 52
  public image of, 316–319
  as rational response, 391–392
  statistics on, 319–320
  street, 312–314
  suite, 314–316
Crime control model, 466–470, 476
"Crimes and Criminals" (Darrow), 378–384
Criminal
  born, 397–400
  stereotype of, 386–387
Criminal behavior
  biological explanations of, 397–399, 410–411, 417, 419
  classical school on, 395–396
  Darrow on, 378–384
  ecological theories of, 402–403
  environmental explanation of, 400–404, 413–416
  ideologies of, 385–394
  institutionalization of, 407–416

Criminal Behavior (cont.)
  positivist school on, 396–397, 410
  power-conflict explanation, of, 404–406, 415–416
  psychological explanation of, 399–400, 411–413
  typology of, 389, 392–393
Criminal Code of Canada, 313
Ciminalization of addicts, 513–515, 516
Criminal justice industry, 436–439, 462
Criminal justice system, 435–436
  alternative to, 474–480
  emergence of, 450–453
  employment in, 465
  expenditures on, 462, 463, 464
  ideologies of, 439–450
  institutionalization of, 453–461
  maintenance of, 462–474
Critical Mass, 281
Crown-Zellerbach, 224
Crystallized intelligence, 678
Cuba, 116
Cumming, E., 684
Current Population Survey, 178
Currie, Elliot, 14, 337
Cycle World, 58

Dalmane, 501
Dangerous Drug Act, 532
Darrow, Clarence, 378–384
Darwin, Charles, 398, 568
Davis, Kingsley, 170
DDT, 267
Death penalty, 409, 447–448, 459
Death rate
  of early retirees, 583
  of infants, 112, 546
  of nonwhites, 544
Deaths, on-the-job, 56, 205–206, 208
Decent and Indecent (Spock), 629
Declaration of Independence, 344, 574
Declaration of the Rights of man, 408

Defense Department, 56–57
Defense spending, 141, 143, 145–146
Deloria, Vine, 592
Democracy, 35–36
Democratic Party, 692
Demologic (James I), 337
Demonology, 407–408
Deportation, 453
Depreciation, 129
Deterrence, 409, 447, 479
Deviants, stereotypes of, 49
DeWitt, J.L., 584
Diamond, Stanley, 336
Dickson, Donald T., 80
Dioxin, 246
Directors Guild, 631
Discrimination, 555–559, 564
Disease, work-related, 56, 207, 210–212, 360
Disengagement, 684
"Dismantling the System" (Jobson), 436–439
Displaced homemakers, 620
Disque, Brice P., 194
District courts, 457
Diversion, 420–421
Divsision of labor, 162–163
Domhoff, William, 38
Dominion Elections Act, 552
Dope fiend mythology, 489–500
Dachau, 586
Dougherty, Alfred F., Jr., 239
Douglas, Jack, 30
Douglas, William O., 268
Dow Chemical, 218
Dowd, James J., 672–673
Dow Jones, 66–67
Downs Syndrome, 567
"Dragnet," 441–442
Drucker, Peter, 97
Drug addiction, joint ABA-AMA report on, 521
Drug Addiction: Crime or Disease?, 521
Drug education, 531–532
Drug problem, 3, 20, 48–49, 73, 326–327, 489–492
alternative to, 532–534
emergence of, 502–519
ideologies of, 493–502
institutionalization of, 510–519
maintenance of, 519–532

Drugs
definition of, 493–495
prescription, 500–502
Drunkenness, 338
Dryden Chemical, 323
Dubois, W.E.B., 543–544, 591
DuBose, Hampden D., 504
Ducking stool, 452, 453
Due process model, 466–467, 476–477
Durkheim, Emile, 1, 2, 32, 632
Dye, Thomas R., 39–40
Dye workers, 250
Dying for a Living (Tataryn), 211–212, 360

Easley, Ralph, 194
East India Company, 508
East Indians, 552–553
Ecological theories of criminal behavior, 402–403
Economic Council of Canada, 355
Economic institution, 4, 14, 35, 36
Economic Opportunity Act, 132
Economic problems, 56. *See also* Great Depression; Inflation; Unemployment.
Economic Research Service, 44
Economies of scale, 46
Ecosystem, 242
Editor and Publisher, 66
Education, 15, 50, 645
discrimination and, 556–557
drug, 531–532
legal, 310–312
Education Amendments Act, 645
Edward I, 450
Edward IV, 336
Ehrlich, Anne, 267
Ehrlich, Paul, 267
Eighteenth Amendment, 516, 517
Eighth Amendment, 456
Eisenhower, Dwight David, 130
Elderfare, 671
Elderly. *See also* Aging.
in labor force, 697

Elderly (cont.)
modernization and, 685–686
number of, living alone, 676–677
population of, 691
sexuality of, 678–679
suicide rate of, 683
social change and, 686–687
unemployment of, 680–681
Elean Institute for Cancer Research, 213–214
Eliot, Charles W., 192
Elite, 17
corporate, 38–41
Emancipation Proclamation, 575
Emergence of social problems, 71–74
Emergency Relief Act, 123
Employment. *See also* Labor force; Unemployment.
definition of, 178–179
Employment and Earnings, 178
Energy, 236–242, 291
Energy crisis, 48, 55
Engels, Frederick, 69, 121, 189
English Code, 452
Enola Gray, 275
Environment, as explanation for criminal behavior, 400–404, 413–416
Environmental Handbook, 275
Environmental Protection Agency (EPA), 80, 247, 262, 263, 283, 284, 285, 292, 472
Environmental movement, 271–281
Environmental problem
ideology of, 242–271
institutionalization of, 281–288
maintenance of, 288–295
Environmental Quality Council, 283
Equal Credit Opportunity Act, 657
Equal Employment Opportunities Commission (EEOC), 644, 653
Equal opportunity, 46, 47, 104
Equal Pay Act, 648, 653

Equal Rights Amendment
ERA), 347, 635, 645–
646
Equity, 100
Erikson, Erik, 625
Erikson, Kai, 47–48
Eros, 8
Esso, 285
Ethnocentricism, 560
Eugenics, 567
Exclusionary rules, 476
Executives, 100, 111, 289–290
Exile, 453
Existentialism, 618
Expenditures for criminal
justice, 462, 463, 464,
466
Expertise, 46
Export-import policies, 128
Extended family, myth of,
674–675
Extermination, 585–586
Exxon Corporation, 45, 74,
240, 255, 272, 275,
285, 297, 314
Eyre v. *Shaftsbury*, 339

Familism, 414, 416
Family, 8, 15, 45, 620–621
aged and, 671, 673–675
changes in, 638–639
criminal behavior and,
385–386, 401–402
extended, myth of, 674–675
Fair Employment Practice
Committee, 648
Fanon, Frantz, 572–573
Farms, 42–43, 44
Fascinating Womanhood
(Andelin), 617–618
Fascism, 576–578
Fawcett Crest, 58
Fawcett Gold Medal, 58
FBI, 76, 317–319, 324, 356–
357, 406
public perception of, 444–
445
Featherbedding, 204
Federal Border Patrol, 593
Federal Bureau of Narcotics
(FBN), 73, 509, 518–
521
Federal Communications
Commission (FCC),
57, 62–63

Federal Drug Administration
(FDA), 525, 534
Federal Energy Administra-
tion, 275
Federal government, 43
expenditures of, for criminal
justice, 462, 463, 464
Federal Oil Conservation
Board, 257
Federal Reserve Board, 657
Federal Trade Commission
(FTC), 239, 472
Federal Water Pollution Con-
trol Act, 284
Federation of Francophones
Outside Quebec, 554
Federation for the Liberation
of Quebec (FLQ), 594
Federation of Organized Trade
and Labor Unions of
the United States and
Canada, 189–190
Feminine Mystique, The
(Friedan), 642
Feudalism, 332–333, 394–395
Field and Stream, 58
Fifteenth Amendment, 346,
381
Fifth Amendment, 456
Final solution, 587–588
Financial Weekly, 66
Finestone, Harold, 9
Finley, James B., 460
Firestone, 218
Flogging, 453
Folk societies, 685, 686
Food stamp program, 128, 656
Forbes, 139
Ford, Henry, 184–185
Ford Foundation, 273, 275
Ford Motor Company, 297,
358
Foreign policy, U.S., 116–117
Fort, Joel, 490, 496
Fortune, 40, 55
*Foundations of the Nineteenth
Century* (Chamber-
lain), 568
Fourteenth Amendment, 346,
581
France, Anatole, 310
Frankfurter, Felix, 194
Fraud, commercial, 358–359
Frederick, Calvin J., 401
Freedom, 36

Freedom of Information Act,
349, 356
Free enterprise, 36. *See also*
Capitalism.
Free-market economy, 118–
119. *See also* Capi-
talism.
Friedan, Betty, 642
Frietag, Peter, 39
French-Canadians, 546, 579,
590, 594
French Penal Code, 396, 409
Freud, Sigmund, 8, 625
Friends of the Earth, 275
Fuller, Richard C., 31
Functionalist paradigm. *See*
Order paradigm.
Future Shock (Toffler), 97

Gannett, 65–66, 67
G.D. Searle, 316
Geiger, Zachary U., 184
Gellin, Martin, 290
*Gemrenschaft und Gesell-
schaft* (Toennies), 675
General Electric Co., 56, 473
General Foods, 221
General Motors, 45, 270, 272,
297
Genesis, Book of, 270
George, Vic, 95–96
Gerentology, 670–671, 675,
681, 703, 710–711
German Ideology, 69
German immigrants, 516
Germany, 576–577, 698
Gerstenberg, Richard, 185
"Get Christie Love," 562
Giordano, Henry L., 521
Glamour, 66
Glasleek, H. J., 360
Gleason, Jackie, 61
Gobineau, Arthur de, 568
God, 270, 618
Goering, 587
Goffman, Erving, 34
Gompers, Samuel, 191–194,
196
"Good Times," 562
Goode, Erich, 524
Gordon, David M., 393–394,
395
Governmental elite, 40–41
Government crime, 348–350,
356–358

Goyer, Jean-Pierre, 356
Graham, Robert K., 567
Gramsci, Antonio, 69, 162
Gray Panthers, 702, 704, 709
Great Britain, 118, 256, 456,
    508, 532, 572
Great Depression, 122–125,
    131–132, 517, 576,
    640–641, 692–693,
    697, 698, 708
Greensborough State, 468
Growth, economic, 37, 45
Guest, Robert A., 175
Gulf Oil, 240, 259, 297, 314
Gusfield, Joseph, 33

Hacker, Helen, 632
Hague International Opium
    Convention, 505
Hale, Sir Matthew, 337–338
Haldol, 502
Haley, Alex, 562
Hall, Wesley, 495
Hallucinogens, 500
Hanford nuclear reservation,
    276
Happiness syndrome, 681–682
Harrington, Michael, 128
Harrison Narcotics Act, 511–
    513, 514, 523, 532
Harvard Business Review, 175
Headstart, 132
Health, Education and Wel-
    fare, Department of
    (HEW), 703
Health insurance, 706–709
Health services, 712
Hearst, Patty, 414
Hearst, William Randolph,
    63, 65, 67
Hearst Corporation, 67–68
Hegemony, ideological, 69–70
Henry, W., 684
Henshel, Anne-Marie, 21
Henschel, Richard L., 21
Herbicides, 248
Heroin, 444, 498, 524
Heroin maintenance program,
    533
Herrnstein, Richard 8, 169
Hertz, 57
Hidden Injuries of Class, The.
    (Stennett and Cobb),
    162

High Fidelity, 59
Hill, Daniel, 553–559
Himmler, 587
Hirsch, Glenn, 54, 55
Hitler, Adolph, 576, 587
Hobbes, Thomas, 161
Holt, Rinehart and Winston,
    58
Holmes, Lowell, 685–686, 687
Holocaust, 586–588
Home ownership, 100
Hooker Chemical Co., 247
Hoover, Herbert, 123
Hoover, J. Edgar, 444
Hope, Bob, 97
Hopkins, Harry, 698
Horizontal merger, 120
Horkheimer, Max, 615
Horton, John, 2, 5
House and Garden, 66
Hughes, Harold, 523
Human Betterment Founda-
    tion, 410
Human nature, contrasting
    views of, 1, 6, 10
Human Sexual Responses
    (Masters and Johnson),
    625
Hunter, Lawson, A. W., 254
Hygeia, 519
Hyperkinesis, 417–418
Hypoglycemia, 418

Ibo, 648
Ideological approach to social
    problems, 3
Ideological hegemony, 69–70
Ideology, 18, 34–35
    of aging, 673–690
    of capitalism, 18–19
    corporate, 44–46, 104–106
    of corrections, 447–448
    of criminal behavior, 385–
        394
    of drugs, 493–502
    of ecology, 242–271
    of law, 312–331
    "piece-of-the-action," 632–
        635
    of racism, 559–570
    of sexism, 613–635
    of social problems, 35–38,
        46–49
    of sociologists, 19–21

Ideology (cont.)
    transmission of, 50–53
    of work, 167–201
Ideology and Utopia (Mann-
    heim), 19
Immigrants, antidrug laws
    and, 507–509, 510–
    511, 516
Immigration laws, 410–411,
    557–558
Imperial Oil, 255
Imprisonment, 458–459
Income, 100, 106–109
    distribution of, 135, 138–
        140, 650
    family, 649
    of retired people, 682–683
    white and black, 544–545
Income tax, 135–136, 143
Index crimes, 317–319, 406
Indentured servants, 453
Indian Acts, 79, 551
Indians, 561, 588. *See also*
    Native Americans.
    extermination of, 585–586
    transfer of, 582–583
Indian Removal Act, 583
Indian trust lands, 44
Individualism, 6, 170, 332
Industrial concentration, 354
Industrial Disputes Investiga-
    tion, Act, 204–205
Industrial Revolution, 36,
    338–339, 131
    impact of, on family, 674–
        675
Industrial Workers of the
    World (IWW), 189,
    192–194
Inequality, social, 13, 52–53,
    96–116, 170–171
    alternatives to, 147
    emergence of, 117–126
    institutionalization of, 126–
        135
    maintenance of, 135–147
    sources of, 16–17
Infanticide, 411
Infant mortality, 112, 546
Inflation, 74, 649–650
Information Machines, The,
    56
Ingersoll, John E. 523, 524
Injunctions, 288
Insanity, defense of, 412

Insecticides, 248, 267
Instincts, 8
Institutional discrimination in Canada, 556–557
Institutionalization, 74–78
of aging, 698–703
of criminal behavior, 407–416
of criminal justice system, 453–461
of environmental problem, 281–288
of inequality, 126–135
of law, 331–343
of racism, 406–407, 478
of sexism, 643–650
of work, 201–219
Institutions, social, 15–16
Insurance, health, 706–709
Insurance industry, women and, 658
Insurgency, legal, 350–352
Integrated Grants Administration (IGA), 705
Intelligence tests, 8, 168
Interest groups, organized, 74
Intergovernmental Cooperation Act, 705
Intergovernmental Personnel Act, 653
Interlocking directorates, 37, 40, 41, 54–55, 63
International Group Plans (IGP), 219, 223–224
International Workingmen's Association, 189
Interstate Commerce Commission (ICC),120, 472
Investment, 45
Investment credits, 129–130
Invisible Woman (Abramson), 632–633
IQ, 169, 567, 678
Iran, 116, 145
Ireland, 121
IRA, 98, 136, 357
Irwin, John, 420
Island Creek Coal, 259
Isolation, 165–166

Jackson, Andrew, 583
Jaffee, Jerome, 530
James I, 337
Japan, 684, 687–688
Japanese, 552, 557
transfers of, 583–584

"Jeffersons, The," 562
Jeffery, C.R., 417, 418
Jensen, Arthur, 8, 169, 568
Jews, 498
extermination of, 586–588
"Jim Crow" statutes, 346, 581
Jin Fuey Moy v. *United States*, 514
Job Corps, 132
Jobson, Keith B., 436
John Birch Society, 445
Johnson, Lyndon, 695
Johnson, Virginia E., 625, 678
Joint Committee on Taxation, 129
Joint Funding Simplification Act, 705
Journal of Drug Education, 531
Judaism, 270
"Julia," 561
Justice, 456. See also Criminal justice system.
class-based, 462, 463
public perception of, 446–447
Justice Department, 473–474, 522–523
Justice model, 419–420
Juvenile court, 33, 340
Juvenile delinquency, 8, 9, 339–340, 461
Kaplan, John, 500
Kefauver Committee, 520
Kendall, Henry, 278
Kennedy, John F., 648
Kent State, 468
Kerr-Mills Act, 695
Killian, Lewis M., 72–73
King, Mackenzie, 507
King, Martin Luther, Jr., 346, 356, 561, 591–592, 641
Kingston Penitentiary, 460–461
Kinship, 334
Kinte, Kunta, 562–563
Klafter, Frances, 702–703
Klu Klux Klan, 347, 445, 553, 595
Knight-Ridder, 66
Knights of Labor, 190, 191
Knowledge, sociology of, 50
Know-Nothings, 345
Kosser, Dr., 324–325
Kuhn, Thomas, 4
Kuhn, Maggie, 704, 709–711

Labor
discrimination and, 558–559
prison, 458–459
vs. work, 162–163
Labor Department, 188
Labor force, 45, 102–103
women in, 623–624, 648–650
Labor-Management and Disclosure Act, 203
Labor movement, 342, 567. See also Trade union movement.
Labor policy, U.S., 201–204
Laissez-faire, 18, 118, 124
Land, ownership of, 42–44, 293, 295
Landrum-Griffin Act, 203
Lanpher, Merle, 222
Lapouge, G. V. de, 508
La Raza, 593
Lasser, David, 123–124
Laws, criminal
alternate view of, 350–360
ideology of, 312–331
institutionalization of, 331–343
maintenance of, 343–350
social problems and, 76–77
Law Reform Commission of Canada, 403–404, 405
"Law School, The," 310
Lawyers, attitudes toward, 449–450
Lead poisons, 248
Learning disabilities, 418
LeDain Commission, 529
Legal education, 310–312
Leggett, John, 178
Legislative discrimination, 557–558
Leisure time, 686
Le Monde, 147
Lennet, Edwin, 34
Leslie, Gerald R., 2
"Letter from Birmingham Jail" (King), 346
Lévèsque, René, 594
Lewis, John L., 194
Librium, 501
Licit and Illicit Drugs, 532–533
Lieberman, Jethro K., 348–349
Lincoln, Abraham, 189, 575
Linder v. *United States*, 515

Lindesmith, Alfred, 48, 499
Lobotomy, 411
Local government, 44
Lockheed Aircraft, 316, 531
Lombrosco, Cesare, 8
London *Observor*, 240
Lost work time, 206–207
Love Canal, 247
LSD, 494, 498, 500
Lung cancer, 526
Lynchings, 585–586

McCarran Act, 343
McCarthy, Joseph, 48, 196
McCloskey, Pete, 275
McClung, Nellie L., 640
McConnell, Douglas, 316
McCormick, Anne O'Hare, 640–641
McDonald, Lynn, 52, 320–321
McDuffie, Arthur, 469
McGrath, W. T., 403
Machinists Union, 191
McKinley, William, 193
McNaughton, Daniel, 412
McNaughton, Donald S., 98
McNeil Laboratories, 502
MacPherson, G. B., 36, 164
Mademoiselle, 66
Magna Carta for labor. *See* Clayton Act.
Maine, 44
Maintenance, 79–80
  of aging, 703–709
  of criminal justice system, 462–474
  of drug problem, 519–532
  of environmental problem, 288–295
  of inequality, 135–147
  of law, 343–350
  of poverty, 347–348
  of racism, 344–347, 588–590
  of sexism, 347, 650–658
  of work, 212–219
Male chauvinism, 626–629
Malinowski, 623, 624
Malthus, Thomas, 267
Managerial model, 38
Manganese toxicity, 248
Manifest destiny, 589–590
Mannheim, Karl, 19, 44
Manufacturing Chemists Association (MCA), 213, 214
Marijuana, 34, 496, 498, 500,

Marijuana (cont.)
  509, 518–520, 522, 524, 525, 528, 529, 532
Marijuana Task Force, 522
Marijuana Tax Act, 34, 73, 80, 509, 519, 523, 524
Marriage, 619–620
Marshall, Chief Justice, 345, 583
Marthausen, 586
Marx, Karl, 16–17, 32, 69, 70, 79–80, 161, 163–164, 121, 219
Massachusetts Bay Colony, 48, 327, 687
Mass media, 51–56. *See also* Networks; Television.
Mass transit, 299
Masters, William H., 625, 678
Materials Policy Commission, 273, 274
Matza, David, 122
Mead, George Herbert, 33
Meals on Wheels, 710
Meaninglessness, 165–166
Mechanics Union of Trade Associations of Philadelphia, 187
Mechanix Illustrated, 58
Media, mass. *See* Mass media.
Medicaid, 112, 646, 702, 703, 708
Medical Assistance to the Aged, 132
Medical model of criminal behavior, 417–419
Medicare, 112–113, 692, 694, 695–696, 699, 701–703, 706–707, 708
Medi-gap insurance, 707
Melman, Seymour, 687
Men, as victims of sexism, 627–629
Mens rea, 408
Mental illness, 8, 20, 34
Mercantilism, 117–118
Merck, 316
Merger, 119–120
Merton, Robert K., 564
Methadone, 531
Methylmercury, 247
Metis, 551, 557
Metropolitan Energy, 278
Mexican War, 589
Meyer, Roger, 523
Mid-Century Conference, 273

Middle Class
  crime control and, 468–469
  myth of, 102–106, 172
Military elite, 131
Military expenditures. *See* Defense spending.
Military-industrial complex, 130–131
Miller, Walter B., 9, 402–403
Mills, C. Wright, 10, 12, 17, 20, 38, 50–51, 55, 103, 131, 167, 266
Minneconjou Sioux, 585
Minorities. *See also* Blacks; Chinese; Indians; Japanese; Native Americans
  crimes against, 357–358
  legal protection of, 580–582
Minority
  aged as, 670
  women as, 632–635
Mintz, Betty, 39
Missile Tracking System, 57
Missionaries, 504–505
Mitchell, John, 191
Mobil Corporation, 46, 240, 257
Modernization, aging and, 685–686
Modern Library, 57
Modern Photography, 59
"Mod Squad," 562
Mohawk Valley Community Corporation, 22
Monopolies, 353
Montague, Ashley, 559
Montgomery Ward, 46, 240
Monthly Labor Review, 178
Moody's Industrial Manual, 56
Moore, Willard, 170
Moral entrepreneurs, 73
Morgan, J. Pierpont, 168, 193
Morgan, Marabel, 618–619
Morgan, Robin, 607–614
Morgan, Thomas J., 191
Norris and David Jones, Ltd., 57
Mosca, Gaetano, 38
Motherhood, 620–622
Motorola, 220
Mott, Lucretia, 639
"Mr. Novak," 562
MS, 642
Much is Taken, Much Remains (Bryan), 244

INDEX

Muir, John, 271
Multiple and Use-Sustained Yield Act, 205
Mumford, Lewis, 269, 674
Murad IV, 502
Murphy, Emily, 507
Murphy, Justice, 584
Mutilation, 452–453
Myers, Richard P., 30
My Lai, 414

NAACP, 561, 591
Nabisco, 222
NBC, 56–57, 60, 63
Nader, Ralph, 44, 359
Napolean, 626, 627
Narcotics, 490. See also Drugs.
Narcotics Control Act, 520–521, 525
Narcotics Division, 513, 515, 516, 517
Narcotic Drugs Act, 518
National Advisory Commission on Criminal Justice Standards and Goals, 435–436
National Advisory Committee on Occupational Safety and Health, 212
National Aeronautics and Space Administration, 57
National Association of Manufacturers (NAM), 205
National Association of Women Business Owners, 652
National Bureau of Labor Statistics, 188, 193, See also Bureau of Labor Statistics.
National Cancer Institute, 251
National Civic Federation, 191
National Commission on Marijuana and Drug Abuse, 496, 500, 530, 533
National Commission on the Observance of International Women's Year, 658
National Council of Senior Citizens, 703
National Drug Trade Conference, 511
National Environmental Policy Act, 283

National Farm Holiday Association, 123
National health program, 688–689, 694
National Institute for Occupational Safety and Health (NIOSH), 212, 213
Nationalism, 573
Nationalization, 147–148
National Labor Relations Act. See Wagner Act.
National Labor Relations Board, 195, 196
National Labor Union (NLU), 188–189
National Lung and Heart Institute Task Force, 211
National Organization for Women (NOW), 642
National Petroleum Council, 241
National Physicians Committee, 695
National Professional Committee for Eisenhower and Nixon, 695
National Retired Teachers Association, 692
National Safety Council, 205
National Security Agency, 356
National Senior Citizens Law Center, 703
National Socialist Party. See Nazi party.
National Teach-In, 275
National Welfare Rights Organization (NWRO), 125–126
Nation-state, 533–534
Native Americans, 14, 74–75, 79, 358, 592–593. See also Indians.
Nativism, 516
Natural gas, 237, 238, 239, 240, 241
Navy, 57
Nazi party, 576–578
Neglect syndrome, 621
Neighborhood Youth Corps, 132
Nelson, Gaylord, 275
Neocolonialism, 576
Networks, 56–63. See also Television.

New Deal, 194, 517, 641, 693
New Democratic Party, 198
Newhouse, 66
Niagara Movement, 591
Nicaragua, 117
Nicotine, 990, 496, 498, 500, 502–503
Nielsen ratings, 62
1984, 418
1968 National Democratic Convention, 468–469
Nineteenth Amendment, 640
Nisbett, Robert, 162
Nixon, Richard, 9, 272, 281–282, 324, 343, 357, 390, 399, 523
N.L. Industries, 360
Noise Control Act, 285
Noise pollution, 259–262, 292, 298
Nonwhites, 389, 544. See also Blacks; Chinese; Japanese; Indians; Native Americans.
  justice for, 478–479
  occupations of, 546–547
  and police, perceptions of, 440–443
Nonviolence, 592
Norris-LaGuardia Act, 202–203
Northern Ireland, 121
Northrup, 316
Nuclear familism, 45
Nuclear family, 620–621, 674–675
Nuclear energy, 275–281
Nuclear Regulatory Commission (NRC), 277, 278–281
Nursing home, 704

Oakland Tribune, 66
OASDI (Old Age, Survivors, and Disability Insurance), 143, 700
Oberschall, Anthony, 71–72
Objective approach to social problems, 3
Occidental Petroleum, 259
Occupational Safety and Health Act, 212, 213, 214, 215, 349–350
Occupational Safety and Health Administration (OSHA), 212–218, 300

Occupations
    female, 633–634, 651–652
    nonwhite, 546–547
Office of Economic Opportunity, 703
Office of Noise Abatement and Control, 262, 285
Office of Occupational Safety and Health Statistics, 214
Official Languages Act, 351, 579
Oil and Gas Journal, 239, 240
Oil companies, 238–240, 297–299. See also Big Oil; Petrocorporations.
Oil spills, 285
Oil tankers, 285, 286
Old Age Assistance, 132
"Older Americans," 670, 671
Older Americans Act, 696, 704, 705, 709
Ombudsman, 476
Omnibus Bill, 343
One Big Union, 196–198
OPEC, 254, 255–258
Opium, 503–509, 510, 511
Opium and Drug Act, 510
Order paradigm, 1, 6–9, 15, 170
    view of law, 329–330, 331–332
Organism, society as, 6
Organizational crime, 352–356
Orgasm, female, 625
Oriel Foods, Ltd., 57
Origin of the Species, The (Darwin), 398, 568
Orwell, George, 418
Overlords, 332
Ownership
    of corporate assets, 139, 141, 648
    of land, 42–44, 293, 295
    press, 65–69
    public, 147–148

Pacific Stereo stores, 58
Pakistan, 117
Paley, William S., 274
Palme, Olaf, 624
Palmore, Erdman, 684, 687
Pantheon, 57
Paradigms, sociological, 1, 4–14
Parens patriae, 339

Pareto, Vilfredo, 38
Parker, Richard, 649–650
Parsons, Talcott, 98, 626
Parties, political, 17, 33. *See also* Communist Party; Democratic Party; Nazi party; Parti Quebecois; Republican Party; Socialist parties.
Parti Quebecois, 342, 594
Partnership Demonstrations, 705
Pearl Harbor, 195, 584
Pearson, Karl, 568–569
Pendleton Act, 647
Penn Central, 44
People's party, 191
Pension funds, 137
Pentagon capitalism, 130, 687
Penitentiary, 460
Pennsylvania system, 460
Perkins, Frances, 698
Pesticides, 248, 267
Peterson, Russell, 290
Petrocorporations, 48, 254, 256–258. *See also* Big Oil; Oil companies.
Petroleum, 253
Pfizer Laboratories, 501, 502
Pharmaceutical industry, 525–526
Pharmakos, 491
Physicians' Radio Network, 502
"Piece-of-the-action" ideology, 632–635
Pillory, 452, 453
Pinchot, Gifford, 293
Pinckney, Charles, 574–575
Pinto gas tank, 358, 359
Pittsburgh and Midway Coal, 259
Plantation system, 573–576
Platt, Anthony, 33
Pluralism, 579–580
Pluralist model, 12–13
Plutonium, 276
Police, 454–456
    public confidence in, 442–445
    public perception of, 440–442
Police abuse, combating, 475–476
Police violence, 467–470
Political crime, 342–343

Political-economy, 16, 30
Political institutions, 15, 35–36
Politics of Energy, The (Commoner), 236–242
Pollution, 55–56, 299
    Canadian perceptions of, 244, 245
    control of, 290–295
Pollution industrial complex, 290–291
Poor Laws, 131
Poor people's movement, 121–126
Poor's Register of Corporations and Executives, 55
Popular Library, 58
Population transfers, 582–585
Populist movement, 121
Positive Peer groups, 414
Positivism, 396–397, 400, 410
Possessive marketplace, 167
Poverty, 8, 9, 52, 106–109
    advantages of, 110, 112–113, 146–147
    crime and, 403–404
    maintenance of, 347–348
    women and, 620
Power, 33, 34–35, 37
Power Elite, The (Mills), 17
Powerlessness, 165–166
Prejudice, racial, 564
Presidential cabinets, 39
Presidential commissions, 77–78
President's Commission on Law Enforcement, 474
President's Report on Occupational Safety and Health, 207
Press ownership, 65–69
Price-Anderson Act, 277
Price supports, 128
Prisoner rights movement, 416
Prisoners, justice model and, 420
Prison labor, 458–459
Privatism, 44, 563
Producers Guild, 631
"Professional Ideology of Social Pathologists, The" (Mills), 20
Profit, 37, 139, 355
Progress, 45
Prohibition, 31, 33, 338, 503, 516–518

INDEX

Prohibition (cont.)
    Bureau of, 517–518
Project Share, 705
Property, 96, 100
Proposition 13, 659
Prostitution, 411
Protection of Privacy Act, 357
Protestant Christianity, 618
Protestants, 121, 498, 503
*Protestant Ethic and the Spirit
    of Capitalism* (Weber),
    498
Proudhon, 161
Prudential Life, 98
Psychoactive drugs, 500–502,
    526
Psychoanalytic theory, 8
Psychodiagnosis, 412–413
Psychological determinism,
    394–400, 411–413
Psychology of Women (Freud),
    625
Psychopaths, 412
Public defender system, 478
Public ownershp, 147–148
Puget Sound Plywood, Inc.,
    224–225
Pullman, George, 191
Pullman Co., 191
Punishment, early forms of,
    452–453
Puritans, 48
  on crime, 390
  drugs and, 497–498, 503

Quakers, 327, 460
Quartering, 407–408, 452
Quebec, 553–554, 579, 594
Quinn, Robert P., 175
Quinney, Richard, 330, 332,
    389

Race, ideologies of, 559–570
Race riots, 594
Racism
  alternatives to, 590–595
  emergence of, 570–588
  ideology of, 559–570
  institutionalized, 406–407,
    478
  maintenance of, 344–347,
    588–590
Radical Nonintervention
    (Schur), 416
Radinowicz, Leon, 400
Rail Reform acts, 478

Railroads, regulation of, 120
Railway Labor Act, 202–203
Random House, 57
Rape, 411
Rape laws, 336–338, 437,
    646–647
Raytheon, 531
RCA Corporation, 56–57, 60,
    63
Reagan, Ronald, 18
Reasons, Charles E., 353
Reconstruction Finance Corp-
    oration, 123
Reflection hypothesis, 53, 55
Reformatories, 461
Regina Manifesto, 198
Rehabilitation, 408, 411–413,
    419, 447, 449, 479
Rehabilitation Act, 653
Reiman, Jeffry, 1–2, 423–424
Reith, Charles, 451
Religion, 15, 270–271
  and criminal behavior,
    394–395
Regulatory agencies, 472–474.
    *See also names of indi-
    vidual agencies.*
Reorganization, 14
Report on Corporate Crime,
    247
*Report on Narcotics and Drug
    Abuse*, 76
*Report on Respiratory Dis-
    eases*, 211
Republican Party, 124, 692
Resources for the Future
    (RFF), 273–275
Retirement, 682
  forced, 688–690, 696–697
Reuther, Walter, 196
Rideout, Greta, 647
Riel, Louis, 551
Riesman, David, 74
Rist, Ray C., 78
Roach, Jack, 126
Roach, Janet K., 126
Road and Track, 58
Robber barons, 119, 120
Roche Laboratories, 501, 502
Rockefeller, Laurance, 274
Rockefeller Foundation, 275
Rockefeller oil trust, 119
Rockwell, David N., 310
"Room 222," 562
Roosevelt, Franklin D., 124–
    125, 194, 195, 517,

Roosevelt, Franklin D. (cont.)
    519, 584, 641, 647,
    648, 693, 698
Roosevelt, Theodore, 273,
    293, 505
Roots (Haley), 562–563
Rose, Arnold, 76–77
Rosenfelt, Frank, 110
Ross, Robert, 32, 51, 79
Rossi survey, 320–321
Rowland, S., 360
Royal Canadian Mounted
    Police (RCMP), 76,
    197, 324, 356, 444,
    455, 469, 528
Royal Commission on Bilin-
    gualism and Bicultur-
    alism, 579
Rubber workers, 250
Rubenstein, Helena, 640
Rubinow, I. M., 698
Ruiz, Javier, 225
Ruling class, 69
Rural Loan Program, 132
Ryan, William, 417

Sachsenhausen, 586
Saint Francis of Assisi, 271
Saint-Simon, 161
Salaries, 182, 183. *See also*
    Wages.
Sallach, David, 69–70
Samoza family, 117
Sandanista movement, 117
Santayana, George, 168
Saratoga Knitting Mill, 222–
    223
Saref, Michael, 41
Sarge, Friedrich, 189
Scab, 192
Schafly, Phyllis, 645
Scheff, Thomas, 34
Schrager, Laura Shill, 353
Schur, Edwin, 416
Second World War. *See* World
    War II.
Securities and Exchange Com-
    mission (SEC), 472
Sedition Act, 342
Segregation, 581
  in Canada, 550–551
Seidman, Robert B., 329
Self-estrangement, 165–166
Sellin, Thorsten, 403
Senators, wealth of, 112

Seneca Falls Declaration of Rights and Sentiments, 639–640
Senequan, 502
Senescence, 677
Senility, stereotype of, 677
"Senior citizen," 670, 671
Senior Citizens Desk, 692
Sennett, Richard, 162, 167
Services Integration, 705
Separate-but-equal doctrine, 346, 581, 642
Separatist movement, 553–554, 579, 594
Serfs, 332
Sexism, 3–4
    alternatives to, 658–661
    defined, 616–617
    emergence of, 636, 643
        ideologies of, 615–635
    institutionalization of, 643–650
        maintenance of, 347, 650–658
    science and, 624–626
Sexist socialization, 629–632
Sexual assault laws, 646–647
Sexual conflicts, 8
Sexuality
    aging and, 678–679
    female, 624–626
Shaft," 562
Shah Mohammed Pahlavi, 116, 145
Shanghai Opium Convention, 505–506
Shareholders, 36
Shepard, Linda J., 175
Sherman Antitrust Act, 201–202, 325, 341, 470
Shifting orgasm, 625
Shirereeve, 450
Shires, 450
Shock aversion therapy, 411
Shockley, William, 567
Short, James F., Jr., 353
Sierra Club, 268, 271–273, 275
Silent Spring (Carson), 248, 266
Silicosis, 211
Simmons, Leo, 684
Sisterhood, mystique of, 661
Sitting Bull, 585
Sixth Amendment, 456
Skelton, Red, 61
Skolnich, Jerome, 14

Slavery, 344, 566–567, 580
    in Canada, 550
Slave trade, 573–575
Sleep disturbances, noise and, 261
Small Business Loan Program, 132
Smith, Adam, 118
Smith, Derek G., 75
Smith, James D., 99
Smith Act, 343
Social being, 32
Social change, elderly and, 686–687
Social consciousness, 32
Social Darwinism, 168, 391, 567
Socialism, 6, 106
Socialist parties, 148–149, 567
Socialization, sexist, 629–632
Socialized medicine, 697
Social movement, 71–73
Social problems. *See also*
        Aging; Criminal behavior; Criminal justice system; Drug problem; Environmental problem; Laws, Poverty; Racism; Sexism
    approaches to, 3–4
    creation of, 30–32
    definition of, 2–3, 12, 20–21
    emergence of, 71–74
    ideology of, 35–38, 46–49
    institutionalization of, 74–78
    maintenance of, 79–80
    paradigms of, 4–15
Social Reality of Crime, The (Quinney), 330
Social relationships, 46
Social Security Act, 132, 692, 695, 699, 701, 703, 705, 708
Social security, 143, 689–690, 694–701
Social Security Administration, 107, 701, 707
Social Insurance (Rubinow), 698
Society
    as conflict, 10–14
    as order, 6–9
Society for the Suppression of the Opium Trade, 505
Sociobiology, 8
Sociological Tradition (Nisbet), 162

Sociologists, ideology of, 19–21
Sociology of knowledge, 50
Solar energy, 237–239
SONY Corporation, 58
South Bend Lathe, 223
Southern Pacific, 44
Southern University, 468
Soviet Union, 16, 352, 693
Spencer, Herbert, 168
Sperry Rand, 220, 222
Spock, Benjamin, 629–630
Spray, S. Lee, 175
Staines, Graham L., 32, 51, 79
Standard Oil Co., 44, 240, 257
Stanton, Elizabeth Cady, 639
Star Chamber, 452
State
    as corporate ally, 120
    rise of, 333–335
State and Local Fiscal Assistance Act, 645, 653
State government, 43–44
State intervention, student attitudes toward, 106
Status groups, 17, 33
Status offenses, 340
Steinem, Gloria, 642
Steinhauer, Ralph, 551–552
Steelworkers, 250
Sterilization laws, 410
Stern, Philip, 128
Stocks, 452, 453
"Storefront Lawyers," 562
Stratification, 96
    functionalist theory of, 109–110
Street crime, 312–314, 322–323, 405
Stress, noise and, 261
Strike, 196–197
    right to, 204
Strip mining, 259
Strontium, 90, 267
Structural imperatives, 29–30, 35, 44, 46, 126
Structural sociology, 15–18
Structure of Scientific Revolutions, The (Kuhn), 4
Students for a Democratic Society (SDS), 342
Subcultures, 8–9
Suicide, 20, 683
Suite crime, 314–316, 322–323
Sun Oil, 240
Supplementary Data System, 214

Supplemental Security Income (SSI), 113, 699–700
Supreme Court, California, 345
Supreme Court, U.S., 344–345, 346, 457, 646
Surface Mining Control and Reclamation Act, 285–287
Survival of the fittest, 168
Sutherland, Edward, 321, 401
Swados, Harvey, 171
Swartz, Joel, 323
Sweden, health service in, 688–689
Sweringen, John E., 240–241
Symbionese Liberation Army, 414
Symbolic interactionists, 33–34
Synanon, 530
Szasz, Thomas, 490–492, 496, 531

Taft-Hartley Act, 195–196, 203
Taney, Chief Justice, 344–345
Targets of Opportunity, 705
Task Force on Resources and Environment, 274
Tataryn, Lloyd, 211–212, 360
Taxation, 128–130, 134, 135–138, 143
social security and, 698–699, 701
Taylor, Frederick W., 171, 184
Teaching Prejudice, 556–557
Technocracy, 37
Technology, 45, 165–166, 686
environment and, 266, 269–270
Television, 51, 54, 63
and ethnic groups, portrayal of, 560–563
and police, portrayal of, 441–442
and women, portrayal of, 630–631
Television Establishment, The (Tuchman), 56
"Tenafly," 562
Tenneco, 218
Texaco, 257, 297
Texas Rangers, 455, 593
Thalidomade, 349

Thanatos, 8
Theft laws, 336
Theory, vs. paradigm, 5
Theory of the Leisure Class, The (Veblen), 654
Three Essays on the Theory of Sexuality (Freud), 625
3M Company, 531
Three Mile Island, 205, 277–281
commission report on, 77, 78
Times Mirror Corporation, 44, 66
Timber industry, 55
Title VII (Civil Rights Act), 643–644, 653
Title IX, 645
Tobacco, 502, 527
Toennies, Ferdinand, 675
Toffler, Alvin, 269
Total Joy (Morgan), 618
Total Women (Morgan), 618
Towns, Charles B., 73
Toys, 58
Trade Agreement Act, 257
Trade-offs, energy, 251–263
Trades and Labour Congress of Canada, 198
Trade union movement, 13, 342, 567. *See also* Unions.
in Canada, 72, 196–198, 201
in U.S., 72, 186–196, 199–200
Traffic in Opium and Other Dangerous Drugs, 522–523
Trail of Tears, 583
Train, Russell, 274
Tranquilizers, 500–502, 526
Transfers, population, 582–585
Translocation of elites, 37, 39–40
Transportation, 296–299
of criminals, 453
Treasury Department, 514–515, 516
Treblinka, 586
Trial by combat, 451–452
Trial by ordeal, 394–395, 452
Truman, Harry, 195
Trust funds, federal, 143, 145
TVA, 124

Tuchman, Gaye, 56, 630–631
Turk, Austin, 330
Turner, Jonathan, 127
Turner, Ralph H., 72

UCR method, 708
UHF, 62
Unconscious motivation, 8
Unemployment, 176–181, 566, 687, 693, 697
crime and, 406, 407
of the elderly, 680–681
Unemployment Relief Act, 647–648
Uniform Crime Reports, 316
Unions, 105–106, 217. *See also* Trade union movement.
discrimination and, 558–559
Unionism, white collar, 198–199
Union Temperance Society, 516
United Auto Workers, 196
United Brands, 316
United Farm Workers, 225, 593
United Independent Broadcasters. *See* CBS.
United Mine Workers, 194, 206
United Paramount Theatres, 59
United States, 36, 294
corporations in, 42, 144
drug policy of, 505–506, 511–513
economic development in, 118–120
income distribution in, 107–109, 135, 138–140
labor law in, 201–203, 204
Natives of, policy toward, 75–76, 79
trade union movement in, 72, 186–196, 199–200
unemployment in, 176–181
wealth in, ownership of, 42–44, 98–99, 142
University of California at Berkeley, 54
Upward Bound, 132
Upward mobility, 172, 174
Uranium, 276
Urbanization, crime and, 327–328, 422–423

Unseem, Michael, 40
U.S. Court of Appeals, Fifth
    Circuit, 214–215
Utilities, 236–238

Vaginal organism, 625
Vagrancy laws, 338
Valium, 501, 502
Varni, Charles, 441–442
Vassals, 332
Veblen, Thorstein, 654
Vermont Asbestos Group, 222,
    223
Vertical merger, 120
VHF, 62
Victimless crime, 325–327,
    338
Vietnam, 116
Vietnam Era Veteran's Re-
    adjustment Assistance
    Act, 653
*Vindication of the Rights of
    Women, The* (Woll-
    stonecraft), 638
Vintage, 57
Vinyl chloride, 213–214, 218
VISTA, 132
Visualization, 678
Visuomotor flexibility, 678
Vocationalism, 50
Vogel, Gerald, 223
Vogelfanger, M., 20
Vogue, 66
Volstead Act, 516–517
Voting
    elderly and, 692
    women and, 634–635, 640

Wages, 182, 183
    of women, 649, 650
Wagner, Robert, 694
Wagner, Act, 195, 203, 204,
    217
Walker, Charles R., 175
Walker, Madame C. J., 640
Wallace, George, 557
Wall Street Journal, 66
Walnut Street Jail, 459–460
War crimes, 359–360
Warfare state, 130–131, 141,
    143, 145–146
War Measures Act, 343
War on Poverty, 132–133
Washington, Booker T., 591
Washington Post, 54
Watergate, 390

W.B. Saunders, 58
Wealth, 35, 42–44
    distribution of, 139, 141,
        143, 648
    of senators, 112
Wealthfare state, 127–130,
    135, 650
Wealth of Nations, The
    (Smith), 118
Webb v. *United States*, 514
Weber, Max, 16–17, 32, 33,
    162, 498
Weisberg, Barry, 272, 273
Welfare programs, 112–113,
    114–115, 134
Welfare recipients, 108, 112–
    113
Welfare system, 126–130
Welk, Lawrence, 61–62
Western Federation of Miners,
    189, 192
Westinghouse Corporation,
    237
Weyerhauser, 224
White Citizens Councils, 595
White collar crime, 352–353
White collar unionism, 198–
    199
White collar workers, 37, 50,
    102–104, 172, 173
Whitehead, Alfred North, 51
White House Conference on
    the Care of Dependent
    Children, 698
White House Conference on
    Natural Beauty, 274
White House Plumbers, 324
Whitehurst, Carol A., 625–
    626, 630, 635
White man's burden, 345, 572
Whites
    and criminal behavior,
        views of, 384, 385
    income of, vs. blacks, 544–
        545
    and perception of police,
        440–443
White Sands Missile Range, 57
Who's Who, 55
Wilding, Paul, 95–96
Wiley, Harvey, 512
Wilkie, Wendell, 124
Will, triumph of, 45, 47
William the Conqueror, 334,
    451
Wilson, Charles, 125, 131

Wilson, James Q., 469
Winnepeg General Strike,
    196–197
Wiretaps, 357
Witchcraft, 327, 337–338
Witches, 48, 408
Wobblies, 189, 192–194
Wolfe, Alan, 9, 16, 35–36, 202
Wollstonecraft, Mary, 638
Woman's Day, 58
Women. *See also* Sexism.
    assimilation of, 636
    in labor force, 623–624,
        648–650
    television portrayal of, 630–
        631
Women's Insurance Bill of
    Rights, 658
Women's movement, 636–645
Women's Organization for
    National Prohibition,
    517
Women's Christiain Temper-
    ance Union (WCTU),
    516
Women's Trade Union League,
    661
Woodward, C. Van, 345–346
Word Inc., 59
Work. *See also* Labor.
    alternatives to, 219–226
    alienation and, 163–167
    differences in worth of,
        170–171
    ideologies, of 167–201
    importance of, 160–161
    institutionalization of,
        201–212
    maintenance of, 212–219
    right to, 680
Worker, myth of happy, 171–
    182
Workers. *See* Blue collar
    workers; White collar
    workers.
Worker's Alliance of America,
    124, 125
Worker satisfaction, 174–176
Workers' control, 219–226
Work Experience Program,
    132
Workplace
    accidents, disease, death
        arising from, 56, 205–
        212
    humanizing, 182–185

"Workplace Democracy,"
219–226
Workshop on Alternative
Energy Strategies
(WAES), 292
World Health Organization
(WHO), 250, 261
World War II, 195, 203, 584,
641, 693–694
Wounded Knee Creek, 585

Wright, Hamilton, 505–506,
511. 512–513
Wurf, Jerry, 220

XYZ chromosome anomaly,
398–399, 417

Yellowknife, 211, 359
"Yellow peril." *See* Opium.
Yannacone, Victor, Jr., 246

"Young Interns, The," 562
"Young Lawyers, The," 562
Youth, 423
drugs and, 524–525
and perceptions of police,
440–443

Zeitlin, Maurice, 97–99
Zwerdling, Daniel, 219–226
Zyklon B, 587

HIEBERT LIBRARY

3 6877 00048 8956

DATE DUE

MAY 25 '8			
MAR 3 '89			
DE 11 '96			
OC 28 04			

HN
16
.R4

111309

Reasons, Charles E.
    The ideology of
    social problems

HIEBERT LIBRARY
Fresno Pacific College - M. B. Seminary
Fresno, Calif. 93702   DEMCO